D0560431

Major General George H. Sharpe and the Creation of American Military Intelligence in the Civil War

Peter G. Tsouras

CASEMATE

Philadelphia & Oxford

Published in the United States of America and Great Britain in 2018 by
CASEMATE PUBLISHERS
1950 Lawrence Road, Havertown, PA 19083, USA
and
The Old Music Hall, 106–108 Cowley Road, Oxford OX4 1JE, UK

Hardcover Edition: ISBN 978-1-61200-647-5
Digital Edition: ISBN 978-1-61200-648-2 (epub)

A CIP record for this book is available from the British Library

Printed and bound in the United States of America

Typeset in India by Versatile PreMedia Services (www.versatilepremedia.com)

For a complete list of Casemate titles, please contact:

CASEMATE PUBLISHERS (US)
Telephone (610) 853-9131
Fax (610) 853-9146
Email: casemate@casematepublishers.com
www.casematepublishers.com

CASEMATE PUBLISHERS (UK)
Telephone (01865) 241249
Email: casemate-uk@casematepublishers.co.uk
www.casematepublishers.co.uk

Contents

This book is gratefully dedicated to Col. Stuart A. Herrington, US Army (ret), a master of the art of military intelligence, a paragon of charismatic and moral leadership, and my friend. If any man resembles Sharpe, it is Stu Herrington.

Foreword

In war, wrote Union general Phillip H. Sheridan, information on the enemy figured so prominently in victorious battles and campaigns that it was truly the "great essential of success."[1] During the early days of the Civil War, however, Sheridan's observation was not self-evident to predominantly civilian-turned-volunteer officers in the Union army whose knowledge of war extended little beyond what they gleaned from reading Sir Edward Creasy's *Fifteen Decisive Battles of the World* (1851) or from a quick spin through a borrowed tactical manual. In fact, teaching military neophytes how to go from the march into battle line or how to fire by file took precedence over pursuing that "great essential." Many soon discovered through experience, however, that tactical proficiency alone could not win battles and campaigns and that efficient intelligence-gathering and skilled analysis could be the difference between victory or defeat. But achieving this proved a tall order unless, of course, one could find a talented officer with the necessary skills and judgment to tackle the challenges of information collection and assessment under fire. For Union generals Joseph Hooker, George G. Meade, and U. S. Grant, however, a 34-year-old balding lawyer from New York was that man.

George Henry Sharpe came from the Hudson Valley in New York and, like many in the North, answered his nation's call after Confederate forces fired on Fort Sumter on April 12, 1861. He quickly raised a regiment, the 120th New York Volunteer Infantry, and commanded it during the early days of the war. In 1862, Gen. Joseph Hooker, then head of the Army of the Potomac in Virginia, needed an officer with a keen and discerning mind to create and head his intelligence apparatus later known as the Bureau of Military Information (BMI). He chose Colonel (later General) Sharpe, who remained the BMI chief under Hooker, Meade, and Grant during many of the most important battles and campaigns of the conflict. But in this role Sharpe did far more than merely collect random bits of information and forward them to his bosses. He realized that information was only as reliable as its source and useful only if a commander could quickly make sense of it and use it. With this in mind, Sharpe created a tightly-knit unit staffed with smart and skilled intelligence professionals who collected raw information and then, through careful assessment and analysis, produced camera-ready *military intelligence* for use in the field.

Under Sharpe's leadership, the BMI set the standard for efficient and effective intelligence work in the Civil War, becoming an "all source intelligence" unit that systematically gathered raw information from a multitude of sources (spies, scouts, cavalry reconnaissance, balloon ascensions, captured enemy correspondence, signal intercepts, enemy newspapers, and the results of interrogations of local civilians and prisoners of war), subjected it to rigorous corroboration and analysis, and then packaged it in a concise intelligence brief for the Army of the Potomac commander. Of all these sources, however, one of the most valuable was information derived from the interrogation of Confederate prisoners and deserters. Though far less exciting than the daring exploits of spies, the BMI extracted valuable information on the organization—or "order of battle"—of Robert E. Lee's Army of Northern Virginia. Determining the identity of a prisoner's regiment, brigade, and corps—something a captured soldier would certainly know and easily divulge—allowed Sharpe's principal subordinate and former architect, John C. Babcock, to create an organizational flow chart of Lee's army that was then used to track its dispositions and movements. The BMI became so proficient at collecting order of battle intelligence that Sharpe once bragged that he had identified "each regiment, brigade, and division" in Lee's army and, as a result, knew their exact positions and any movements they made. In the midst of the campaign against Richmond in 1864, U. S. Grant confirmed Sharpe's boast. "Deserters come in every day," he told the War Department, "enabling us to keep track of every change the enemy makes."[2]

During the siege of Richmond and Petersburg from June 1864 to April 1865, the BMI reached peak efficiency. The unit employed numerous spies behind Confederate lines, posted scouts along Lee's logistical connections, established covert lines of communication with Union spy Elizabeth Van Lew and her so-called "Union Underground" in the Confederate capital, and placed BMI branch offices with other commands in Virginia and North Carolina to transmit *strategic* intelligence to Grant's City Point headquarters. In addition, after Lee's surrender at Appomattox, Sharpe was charged with issuing paroles to the men of the Army of Northern Virginia, which proved challenging because Lee's army had become quite disorganized during the final months of the siege as ever-shrinking numbers led to numerous unit consolidations and reorganizations that, in turn, muddied their order of battle. As a result, many Confederates lining up for their paroles were confused about the new identities of their regiments and brigades and where they fit in the organizational chart. But the BMI had done its job well. Much to the surprise of puzzled Confederates, Sharpe was able to tell them where they belonged using Babcock's up-to-date order of battle for the Army of Northern Virginia.

In the final analysis, Sharpe's BMI was the most sophisticated and efficient intelligence organization during the war but also the first systematic "all source" intelligence organization in U.S. military history to that time. And it all emanated from the lawyerly mind of George H. Sharpe who, despite his incredibly important contributions to Union victory, remains virtually unknown in Civil War history.

After the war, which included Sharpe's unsuccessful trip to Europe in search of evidence of the Confederate government's complicity in the assassination of President Abraham Lincoln, the BMI and its chief faded from view even as reminiscences written by other officers and common soldiers poured from the presses detailing their experiences during the "late unpleasantness." Former scouts and spies like Allan Pinkerton, Lafayette Baker, Belle Boyd, and others also jumped in to this literary war, writing memoirs laced with embellished tall tales that would have made a dime novelist blush. Written more for profit and fame than to render an accurate depiction of intelligence work during the war, these offerings unfortunately obscured more than they revealed. Sharpe and his principal subordinates, however, contributed little to this literary outpouring, which meant that the thrilling adventures stories that so transfixed the public—many with only a nodding acquaintance with the truth—soon became authoritative representations of the intelligence war.

When it came to the activities of the BMI and its operatives, Sharpe maintained a sphynx-like silence after the war, understanding that discretion was not only the better part of valor but also essential for maintaining the anonymity of former scouts and spies still living in the South to protect them from vengeful ex-Confederates. Although Sharpe's chief scout Judson Knight wrote about his exploits in the pages of the *National Tribune*, his boss remained quiet, turning down even those who urged him to preserve those hard-won intelligence lessons for future generations. Finally, in 1898, the 70-year-old former spymaster agreed to put pen to paper but his death shortly thereafter settled the issue once and for all. With his passing, the most important figure in the Civil War's intelligence duel took his secrets to the grave and proved beyond doubt that, as historian Peter Maslowski observed, "spies who wrote memoirs are invariably more famous but were often less important than those who did not."[3]

Though Sharpe's insider's view was forever lost, the story of the BMI was not. The unit's history could still be found in dozens of reports and other correspondence found in the volumes of the *Official Records of the War of the Rebellion,* in Record Groups 108, 110, and 393 at the National Archives and Records Administration and in the wartime papers of Hooker, Grant, John C. Babcock, and others. Edwin C. Fishel, the dean of Civil War military intelligence studies, brought Sharpe to the forefront in his magisterial *The Secret War for the Union: The Untold Story of Military Intelligence in the Civil War* (1996) but even after this big debut, no historian accepted the challenge of writing a full biography of the spymaster from New York.

Until now, that is. Peter Tsouras, author of over thirty books on military history, has grasped the many threads of Sharpe's life and spun them together in an exciting and informative biography grounded in primary research at the National Archives, the Library of Congress, the Huntington Library, and in countless contemporary newspapers now available online for the first time. Having already peeked behind the curtain of the BMI's operations in his edited work entitled *Scouting for Grant and Meade: The Reminiscences of Judson Knight, Chief of Scouts, Army of the Potomac* (2013), Tsouras has built upon this strong foundation to produce a first-rate biography of the pre-war life, Civil War career, and postwar activities of a remarkable man and the true father of modern American military intelligence. This is a tale Sharpe never told himself but, thanks to Tsouras' solid research and gifted prose, we have the next best thing. At long last, Gen. Sharpe has found his biographer, and one truly worthy of his subject.

William B. Feis, Ph.D.
Buena Vista University, Storm Lake, Iowa
May 2018

Acknowledgments

This book owes an immense debt to the support, advice, and insightful review of my friend, William B. Feis, professor of history at Buena Vista University in Storm Lake, Iowa, the acknowledged expert on Civil War military intelligence. Bill was a protégé of Edwin Fishel, author of the magisterial and ground-breaking *The Secret War for the Union: The Untold Story of Military Intelligence in the Civil War* (1996), and his own book, *Grant's Secret Service: The Intelligence War from Belmont to Appomattox* (2002), was a worthy continuation of his mentor's work. In the finest tradition of scholarship, Professor Feis has been as generous with me as Fishel was with him. I cannot thank him too much.

My search for George Sharpe began in his hometown of Kingston, NY, when I contacted Deana L. Preston, the Interpretive Program Assistant at the Senate House State Historical Site, in search of Sharpe's remaining collection of letters. No researcher could find a more helpful and enthusiastic guide, and I thank her for her cooperation and assistance in providing all the resources of the Senate House—not only Sharpe's letters, but a number of newspaper articles and vital biographical information. Two Ulstermen, Seward Osborne and Walter Witkowski, were of the greatest help in bringing their county's most famous son back to life in the pages of this book. I am especially grateful for all the photos they provided. Seward Osborne is an acknowledged expert on Ulster County in the Civil War and author of *The Civil War Diaries of Col. Theodore B. Gates, 20th New York State Militia* (1991), with its many references to Sharpe, a copy of which he graciously gave me.

To the dedicated researchers at the National Archive, I can only offer my deepest appreciation for their positive assistance in searching the military service records, pension files, payrolls, and other resources, without which the history of George H. Sharpe and the Bureau of Military Information (BMI) and so much of the context of this book could not have been written. I particularly want to thank Archivist DeAnne Blanton; Archives Specialists Jill D'Andra and Rebecca Crawford; and Archives Technicians Dorothy Simmons, Andrew Brethauer, Ray Bottorff, and Alison Gavin.

At the Library of Congress, the help of American History Specialist and Curator of Rare Americana, Rosemary Plakas, and Reference Librarian Meagan Halsband was of inestimable value in completing this book. The Prints and Photographs Division was a treasure house of Civil War art and photographs that grace this book and breathe a little life back into a bygone era. The Library's collection of the drawings of Edwin Forbes are especially evocative and a favorite of mine.

I wish also to thank for all their assistance Alisa M. Monheim and Jaeda Snow at the Huntington Library in Pasadena in the midst of its beautiful gardens. These researchers and librarians at these great institutions are the quiet guardians and stewards of our civilization, and the vital allies of the historian.

My thanks also go to James A. Goecker, who freely provided essential details from his own extensive research on BMI scouts from Indian regiments. Finally, to my friend, Paul H. Vivian, whose encouragement in the writing of this book over the last decade has been so much appreciated.

As always it has been my wife, Patty, who has been a font of loving support and encouragement, without which I could never have stepped out onto the writer's path.

Introduction

Few men have done as much for their country and been as quickly forgotten as George Henry Sharpe. As the creator of all-source military intelligence, he and the organization he created were the critical combat multiplier without which, it can be seriously argued, the victory of the Union in the Civil War would not have been achieved. It was a closer run thing than is generally supposed.

Who then was this most interesting of men in age filled with interesting men? Of German and Huguenot stock, the Sharpes had become Hudson Valley gentry by the time of George's birth in 1828. He was surrounded from childhood by men and women of education and intellect who encouraged this precocious boy. He graduated with honors from Rutgers and later married the university president's daughter, then sailed through Yale Law School in a year. Before marrying he went to Europe for three years, learning fluent French in Paris and serving in the U.S. legations in Vienna and Rome. Europe gave him an intellectual and cosmopolitan high polish and a wider sense of the world, which he was shrewd enough to appreciate. Returning home, he married, set out his shingle, and joined the militia. Such was the young man when President Davis of the new Confederacy gave the order to fire on Fort Sumter in Charleston Harbor. From that point Sharpe's life was forever changed.

He did 90 days' service with the militia in the protection of Washington. In the summer of 1862, when President Lincoln called for 300,000 more men, he rose from a sick bed and raised his own regiment, the 120th New York Volunteer Infantry, in three weeks. The next five months were an intensive course in command and leadership. No man loved his regiment more and cared for his men more than Sharpe. Yet when Maj. Gen. Joseph Hooker decided he needed a special man to professionalize the production of military intelligence, Sharpe did not hesitate to accept the opportunity. Sharpe's initiative at the battle of Fredericksburg, as well as his interview, impressed Hooker. It was an inspired choice, which would eventually be of as great a service to the Army of the Potomac as his other organizational improvements. Sharpe took the job on February 12, 1863.

Colonel Horace Porter, one of General Ulysses S. Grant's chief aides, made it clear that Sharpe "rendered invaluable service in obtaining information regarding the enemy by his employment of scouts and his skill in examining prisoners and refugees."[1] This was an understatement. Sharpe made it possible for his commanders, beginning with Major Generals Joseph Hooker and George G. Meade and ending with Grant, to know the enemy so well that their blows could be intelligently guided for maximum effect. Sharpe's unique contribution was the creation of what is today called "all-source military intelligence." The U.S. Army defines it as "the intelligence products, organizations, and activities that incorporates all sources of information, in the production of intelligence."[2] The magic element that turns all the sources of information into intelligence is analysis. In the past commanding generals were their own intelligence chiefs who put all the pieces together. By the time of the Civil War, that function had become far too complex for commanders to perform by themselves. Hooker was the visionary who recognized this and chose Sharpe to professionalize that effort. In the 10 weeks between his appointment and the beginning of the Chancellorsville Campaign, Sharpe created—almost from a standing start—a completely integrated and efficiently operating all-source intelligence organization, The Bureau of Military Information (BMI). Sharpe brought all the right personal elements to this creation—the organized mind, a lawyer skilled at questioning, a shrewd ability to judge men, the creativity to forge a new entity without precedent, the good nature to get along with others smoothed out with almost legendary skill as a story-teller, personal leadership of a high order, and a sense of humanity in his dealings with prisoners, deserters, refugees, and contraband slaves.

Sharpe had control of the areas of document exploitation, interrogations, army-level scouts, and networks of agents behind the enemy lines. Hooker encouraged him to coordinate with the cavalry, the Signal Corps and the Balloon Corps, the other intelligence collectors, and any other entity outside the Army of the Potomac. Sharpe took full advantage of this latitude and established fruitful allies in Washington and Baltimore, which gave him access to spies placed in Richmond.

By any standard, it was a brilliant achievement and one which provided Hooker with the intelligence that put Gen. Robert E. Lee's head on a silver platter. The plan, based on that intelligence, was to be considered one of the boldest and best thought-out in the war, even by Confederate observers. Unfortunately, as the Prussian Field Marshal Helmuth von Moltke observed, "No plan survives first contact with the enemy," and so with Chancellorsville, though through no fault of Sharpe's.[3]

It was Sharpe's analysis that gave Hooker a head-start on moving to intercept Lee's invasion of the North that led to the titanic collision at Gettysburg. During the battle his staff worked continuously to present the army's new commander, Meade, with three golden gifts at the tactical, operational, and strategic levels of war that in their total effect were probably the most thorough, accurate, and decisive intelligence reporting ever supplied to an American commander before the Gulf War of 1991.

Sharpe and his staff would continue to keep a precise order-of-battle and ration strength of Lee's army of almost uncanny accuracy. To this author, a former order-of-battle analyst for the U.S. National Ground Intelligence Center, that achievement, separated by 150 years, is awe-inspiring. But Sharpe did more than count the enemy. He added new realms to the traditional reporting that concentrated on the immediate enemy. He brought into his reports a larger picture of the enemy, one that explored Confederate subsistence, morale (both of the troops and the home front), logistics, communications, and war production. He was educating his commanders to look beyond the enemy's numbers and tactical intentions. In effect, he fulfilled not only the functions of today's army G2 but of the Defense Intelligence Agency (DIA). This was especially important since the government had no national-level or War Department intelligence agencies.

The arrival of Grant as general-in-chief of the Armies of the United States in March 1864 would come to give a greater scope to Sharpe's special talents. Grant would say during the Overland Campaign that he had never before been provided with such a knowledge of the enemy as that by Sharpe and his BMI. Later, during the siege of Petersburg, he stated flatly that Lee could not make a move without his knowing it. This was all due to Sharpe, but hard-learned by Grant. At the beginning of the siege of Petersburg, Grant had taken the notion that Early's II Corps was there, despite Sharpe's insistence that he could not confirm that. For Grant it was a case of the wish being father to the thought. This led to Maj. Gen. Jubal Early coming within a hair of capturing Washington in July 1864. Lesson learned, he immediately transferred Sharpe to his own staff from Meade's. This would give rise to one of the great command-staff relationships in military history. Grant would promote Sharpe from colonel to major general because of it. That relationship was the margin of victory. By the time Lee surrendered, the patience of the Northern people had reached near exhaustion. Had not Sharpe helped to guide Grant's blows, it is probable that Lee would have fought Grant to a standstill until the North said, "Enough. Let them go." One of his greatest accomplishments after the armies besieged Richmond and Petersburg was to make contact with Elizabeth Van Lew, the gallant Unionist lady who had held the loyal community together for three years and was eager to provide information to Grant. She became one of the great spymasters in history, providing a flood of largely accurate information within 24 hours to Sharpe. She was the ULTRA system of the Civil War.

Sharpe knew how to pick good people and allow full scope for their talents and initiative, and that paid high dividends. Finding no previous organizational model, Sharpe was free to create his own. Realizing that military intelligence is an intuitive art rather than the rigid template sought by little minds, he fostered an unconventional and informal approach to his mission. Certainly, had the modern Director of National Intelligence (DNI) guidelines—that lawyer-driven template for timidity—been in effect, it would have crushed the creative spirit of his team and driven a stake through the heart of timely intelligence. The result would have been a victorious Confederate States of America.

Sharpe was certainly ambitious and not hesitant to put himself forward, but there was no meanness to it. Blessed with a healthy and self-confident ego, for Sharpe it was never about himself. In none of his many reports did he ever use the personal pronoun "I"—only "we"—and so trusted his deputies that were freely able to sign for him. He was respected and admired by his staff and scouts. He had been seconded to Hooker's staff while commanding the regiment he raised, the 120th New York Volunteer Infantry. He never formally gave up command of the regiment because his rank was tied to it but stayed in close touch, doing everything he could for the welfare of his men. He was the only commander in the Civil War to set up an allotment system so his men could send their pay home to their families. After the war he remained devoted to the men of the regiment. He commissioned a statue to his regiment, the only commander to do so, rather than having his men dedicate one to him. He also stayed in close touch with the men of the BMI and did everything he could to secure pensions for the scouts whose health was ruined by constant exposure in the worst weather. For Elizabeth Van Lew, the brilliant spymistress of Richmond, he worked hard to secure her compensation for the expenditure of her fortune in support of the government.

When Grant planted his flag as general-in-chief of the Armies of the United States near that of Major General Meade, Sharpe became a frequent visitor to his headquarters. More and more Grant found himself listening to Sharpe's evaluation of the enemy, enlivened by a good story here and there. During the Overland Campaign he would exclaim that "he never had any information while he was in the West that would compare" with what he had been receiving on this campaign from Sharpe's organization.[4] It was, however, Grant's failure to heed Sharpe that cemented the general's estimation of this staff officer. As Grant settled into the siege of Petersburg, he fixed on the belief that General Early's II Corps of the Army of Northern Virginia was with Lee there. This was despite Sharpe's lack of certainty and finally his growing realization the he was in the Valley heading for Washington. At the proverbial last minute, Grant realized he had been wrong and rushed reinforcements to Washington just in time to warn off Early. That sobering experience confirmed his opinion of Sharpe's value. He immediately transferred him to his own staff, much to Meade's displeasure. There Sharpe became one of Grant's military family and a close advisor, not just in a military sense, but also in gathering political intelligence in Washington and acting as Grant's agent there. Sharpe became the only one of Grant's staff to be personally known by Edwin Stanton, the Secretary of War. At the end of 1864, Grant rewarded Sharpe by promoting him to brevet brigadier general. The end of the war would see a promotion to brevet major general. Grant would not forget the skills and loyalty of George Sharpe.[5]

Sharpe was a man defined by loyalty—to his country, to his regiment, to the BMI, to the Republican Party, and ultimately to Grant himself. Even before the war, Sharpe had found the Republican Party to be a perfect fit, and nothing would shake his political loyalty for the rest of his life. That loyalty was based on what the party represented then and later—adherence to national unity and the constitutional order, economic expansion, equality of opportunity, emancipation, and African-American civil rights.

He was adamant that the terms of national reconciliation were that the South recognize the decision of the sword as regards secession and slavery. As he had been determined to defend the Constitution, so was he equally a supporter of African-American civil rights in New York. His wartime reports reflect none of the prejudices of the time but are objective in their description of prisoners of war, deserters, civilians, and contrabands (runaway slaves). An expert on the history of his hometown of Kingston, he wrote its history in the War of Independence and gave full credit to its black population's resistance to the British when all the whites had fled.

Sharpe could have dined out on his experiences of the war if he had done nothing else for the rest of his life. Yet, his postwar life was rich in accomplishment. Secretary of State William H. Seward sent him on a secret mission to Europe in 1866 to ferret out any Confederates there who had a hand in Lincoln's assassination. When Grant was nominated for president in 1868, Sharpe leapt to the support of his old chief, lending his powerful oratorical skill to the campaign. In 1870 Grant turned to his old intelligence chief and appointed Sharpe to be the U.S. Marshal of the Southern District of New York to break the Tweed Ring's corruption of elections to the House of Representatives. Three years later, Grant appointed him to be the Surveyor of the Port of New York, probably the most important appointive position in the U.S. Government. The friendship between Grant and Sharpe only deepened over the years, and the press referred to them as bosom friends. Sharpe would be a lifelong supporter and a "Stalwart" in the determination to nominate Grant for a third term in 1880. Though that failed, it was Sharpe who was a kingmaker for another president. Sharpe pushed through the nomination of his friend, Chester A. Arthur, as Garfield's vice-presidential running mate. Within a year, Arthur was president upon Garfield's death to an assassin's bullet. Sharpe would be a close and valued advisor for the remainder of Arthur's term.

Sharpe still had time to become a prominent member of the New York state assembly (1868–82) and a very well thought of speaker for two terms, praised even by the Democrat opposition for his fairness and willingness to listen. President Harrison, in appreciation for Sharpe's help in securing his nomination, appointed him to the United States Board of General Appraisers, a semi-judicial position for pay, which was only second to that of a Supreme Court justice.

All this time, Sharpe remained the political power in Ulster County, and the machine he created survived his death. He remained a respected and well-liked citizen of Kingston. On any special occasion, it was Sharpe who was asked to lead or to speak. Again and again he was referred to as a man of personal integrity and generous spirit, a man of many warm friends and few personal enemies. He was a man of wide acquaintance. One writer of the period, Edward P. Kohn, noted, "Sharpe's career seemed to cross paths with every prominent American since the Civil War."[6]

Sadly, we have no direct accounts of Sharpe's personality or a physical description other than photographs. From these he appeared to be of medium height, with short, neatly trimmed (a rarity in this period) dark brown hair. In a very bearded age, he was clean-shaven except for a drooping mustache.

We can infer from indirect references that he was a most interesting dinner companion and good company. His gifts as a storyteller were legendary and would have given Lincoln a run for his money. It was this gift that Grant found so engaging. Sharpe was also a man who liked to have a good time. Brig. Gen. Marsena R. Patrick, his nominal boss during the war, noted with puritanical disapproval that Sharpe had come back from the Irish Brigade's St. Patrick's Day party in 1863 "tight as a brick." Patrick's comment aside, he was not averse to enjoying a drink and being sociable. By all accounts he was a hail-fellow-well-met. His success in the law, politics, and the army suggests that he had an engaging and compelling personality. He genuinely cared about the welfare of others as shown by his efforts to ensure the welfare of the regiment's families. He must have come across as an honest and earnest man, for he would be four times elected to the New York State Assembly after the war. His performance as speaker was followed by effusive praise by the Democrat minority for his fairness and open-mindedness. He was considered a powerful and effective public speaker, and his numerous speeches, historical papers presented, and lectures on subjects as far afield from Kingston as the Nile River or as close as the local history of the Revolution indicate a confident man at ease with himself.

At the annual reunions of the Society of the Army of the Potomac, Sharpe led the post-meeting fun and games in the Society of Bummers. A former congressman from Ulster remembered of Sharpe:

> In one way or another I have been in touch with all the leading Ulster politicians of the time. If I were to name the best one of each of the great parties I would name General George H. Sharpe from the Republican ... Sharpe was a college graduate, a scholar, widely read, a good talker, had travelled abroad, was in touch with all the prominent men of his day. Sharpe could go to East Kingston when the brick yards were in full blast, enter the dance hall, grab the first pretty girl he saw, swing her in the waltz, take the whole crowd up to Garry's and buy the drinks, then call upon and smoke a cigar and drink a glass of wine with the priest, start for home and if it wasn't too late stop and express his absolute belief in the doctrines of election and predestination to the Dutch Domnie.[7]

DeAlva Stanwood Alexander, author of *A Political History of the State of New York*, summarized the general opinion of Sharpe:

> Sharpe's credible service on Grant's staff, his cleverness as a Stalwart manager, and his acceptability as a speaker of the preceding assembly, brought him troops of friends. Although making no

pretensions to the gift of oratory, he possessed qualities needed for oratorical success. He was forceful, remarkably clear, with impressive manners and a winning voice. As a campaign speaker few persons in the state excelled him. Men, too, generally found him easy of approach and ready to listen.[8]

Despite the successes of his postwar life, Sharpe's defining experience had been the war fought in the defense of the Union. For him, it was a sacred and ennobling experience, redolent of drama, sacrifice, shared brotherhood, and heady deeds. For all his postwar titles—Marshal Sharpe, Surveyor Sharpe, Speaker Sharpe, Appraiser Sharpe—it was General Sharpe that he most treasured and by which he was best known. He was in great demand as a speaker at veterans' events sure to inspire his audience with artful and stirring words. To the veterans of the Army of Northern Virginia, he extended the hand of reconciliation and respect for a gallant foe. He was instrumental in organizing the first reunion at Gettysburg and personally traveled to Richmond to invite the former men in gray. From that would come a friendship with the Georgian Gen. John B. Gordon. It was fitting that his last military speech was to welcome home veterans of the Spanish-American War.

Why then did a man who made such a significant contribution to winning the war largely disappear from the study of that conflict? The very nature of military intelligence is to be in the shadows. At his death, his comrades in the veterans' organization, The Military Order of the Loyal Legion of the United States (MOLLUS), wrote of Sharpe's BMI and its efforts:

> The system was an admirable one, and the service was full of fine achievements and romantic adventure. The very fact, however, that it was a secret service made it necessary, as a matter of course, to conceal in a great measure both from the Army and the public the admirable work of the men who directed it and those who carried out their orders.[9]

Although proud of his service and devoted to the veterans of his regiment, Sharpe left a very light footprint as to his duties as chief intelligence officer for the Army of the Potomac and then the Armies Operating Against Richmond (AOAR), essentially the army group consisting of the Army of the Potomac and the Army of the James. He wrote no memoirs and gave only one lecture on the subject. Neither of his two deputies, Capt. John W. McEntee and John C. Babcock, wrote memoirs or accounts. Only Sharpe's second chief-of-scouts, Judson Knight, would write of his scouting adventures in a series of articles in the 1890s wherein Knight brings Sharpe to life here and there as an admirable and humane man. Grant, for whom he had done so much, never mentioned him in his memoirs. There was a general agreement, it seems, to draw a veil over Sharpe's efforts. By von Moltke's standards, he met the primary duty of a staff officer to be more than he seemed. He declined to write his own memoirs, though he was a skilled writer who would later write valuable histories of Kingston. It was an age when every distinguished general was writing a memoir. Winston Churchill would observe the same phenomenon after World War II, when he observed, "I hear my generals are selling themselves dearly." There was no resentment on Sharpe's part, and his friendship with Grant would only grow. If anything, he was loath to write anything that would tend to lesson Grant's contributions.[10]

Only after his wife's death in 1898, with Grant in his grave 13 years, did he agree at his son's urging to write his memoirs, but death drew the curtain on his life before he could start. Slowly, his name sank into obscurity. He had been a prolific correspondent, but only 20 of his letters have survived. There was no body of work that would keep him as a key participant in the war. Many of his reports survived to be included in the War Department's masterpiece, the 78 volumes (128 books) of *The War of the Rebellions: A Compilation of the Official Records Union and Confederate Armies* (1881–1901), commonly referred to as the *Official Records* (OR). Yet, there was no story to tie them all together. They were comprised of just the reporting that ended up in the files of the commanders of the Army of the Potomac. All the great military histories of the Civil War pass over Sharpe's decisive contributions.

It was left to an intelligence analyst and the National Security Agency (NSA), Edwin Fishel, to play Odysseus and summon Sharpe's ghost. This extraordinary man spent a lifetime researching the history of military intelligence in the Eastern Theater during the Civil War. His papers are now at the Georgetown University Library. His search took him to an obscure collection filed under an innocuous title in the National Archives. There he found the files of the Bureau of Military Information (BMI). Here were hundreds of interrogations, scout and agent reports, analyses, and the finished intelligence of this remarkable little band of intelligence professionals that did not find their way into the OR. Fishel's monumental *The Secret War for the Union: The Untold Story of Military Intelligence in the Civil War* (Houghton Mifflin, 1996) was the first book to assign Sharpe his proper place in the context of the Civil War. Fishel's book told the story from the beginning of the war through Gettysburg. It was left to Fishel's protégé, Dr. William Feis, to carry the story from Grant's arrival as general-in-chief to the end of the war in his *Grant's Secret Serve: The Intelligence War from Belmont to Appomattox* (University of Nebraska Press, 2002).

These seminal works in the study of Civil War military intelligence concentrate on military operations but not so much as address Sharpe the man. This present work draws Sharpe's entire life together and attempts to bring the man into the light of history, not only in the context of the war but also in a long and distinguished public life. Sharpe's history then becomes the history of his BMI, that band of talented men and their adventures. We learn how Sharpe organized the BMI and how it functioned. It is also a story of relationships—within the BMI and between Sharpe and his commanders, the wide latitude given him by Hooker, the constraints imposed by a bad-tempered Meade, and finally the blossoming of one of the great commander–staff relationships in military history with Grant.

More than the OR and the BMI files were necessary to complete this story. I was fortunate to live in Alexandria, VA, just across the Potomac River from Washington,

DC, and the historical riches of the National Archives and Records Administration (NARA) and the Library of Congress, where I spent countless hours sifting their holdings. The military service records (MSR) and pension files of the participants located at NARA yielded a treasure trove of biographical information. Another treasure was found in the Library of Congress's John C. Babcock Collection, as well as the collections of papers of Presidents Grant, Garfield, Arthur, and Hayes, and also Grant's Secretary of State, Hamilton Fish. NARA was further scoured for more reports, to include telegrams sent and received. The Huntington Library in Pasadena contained the Hooker Papers, most of which were official documents he took with him when relieved of command of the Army of the Potomac, many of which are not found at NARA. They include the detailed tables of railroads, fords, and road march distances that Sharpe and the BMI created in their intelligence preparation of the battlefield (IPB) for the Chancellorsville Campaign. Their precision and comprehensiveness make them models of such reporting.

The articles written by Judson Knight, Sharpe's second chief-of-scouts, in the *National Tribune* in the early 1890s are the only extensive account written by a member of the BMI. I was privileged to edit the collection in *Scouting for Grant and Meade: The Reminiscences of Judson Knight, Chief of Scouts, Army of the Potomac* (Skyhorse, 2013), which yielded engaging and well-written details of scouting techniques as well as insights into Sharpe, not published before. Vital to the story of Sharpe's postwar life was the record of the times found in newspapers.com. Searches showed thousands of references to Sharpe.

In order to make all of this efficiently useful, they were combined into a chronological database of 4,000 documents by and to Sharpe and the members of the BMI and the various commanders. Studying this comprehensive collection in chronological order offers insights and relationships not readily apparent in traditional research. The organization of the material, the metadata in modern terms, has been a priceless lens that brings history into focus. Templated onto the record of military operations, both the interaction and influence of military intelligence becomes clear to a degree not seen before. Through the review of Sharpe's reporting and other documents in chronological order, we see what the commanders themselves saw and when they saw it, the analyses upon which they based their actions. This is an invaluable vantage point from which to understand what drove so many military operations.

With the passing of Sharpe, Babcock, and McEntee, the thread of all-source intelligence for the army was lost for generations. The country was so anxious to put the Civil War behind it that all thought of incorporating lessons learned fell before the budget ax. The Army was shrunk back to a small force and dispersed in company-sized detachments across the continent; with it, the war's experiment in all-source, professionalized intelligence was forgotten.[11]

Although the U.S. Army established the first permanent intelligence organization in 1889, it was at the national level. The rebirth of all-source intelligence at the operational and tactical levels had to wait until World War I, when organic intelligence elements were introduced from regiment to army level by copying the French system. At the army and corps level in 1918, intelligence had once again become all-source—55 years after Hooker and Sharpe had created the same system. For the first time since Sergeant Cline and Hooker's Horse Marines, NCOs would be incorporated again into the tactical intelligence system. It would take World War II, however, for the army to develop a standard S2/G2 structure.

The professionalization of intelligence personnel would have to wait almost another 20 years. The Army finally recognized military intelligence as a distinct profession in 1962 when it created the Military Intelligence and Security Branch which subsequently was converted into the Military Intelligence Branch. In 1987 the Army created the Military Intelligence Corps to consolidate all military personnel and units into one large regiment. Military Intelligence prospered in the 1980s as it had never done before, as it created TOE units for the first time—five MI brigades and 30 MI battalions to support tactical units in the field and another five brigades and 10 battalions to carry out theater and national-level missions. The Army had 25,000 intelligence specialists, 15 percent of them women, the total equal in strength to the entire Army in 1885 shortly before the first post-Civil War intelligence function was established. The army had, in the words of retired Lt. Gen. James A. Williams, a former director of the Defense Intelligence Agency, "the equivalent of two combat divisions in collection and analysis."[12]

Sharpe would certainly have been impressed but may also have wondered how so many people could help but get in each other's way. Having run a brilliant intelligence operation with never more than 70 men and women carefully selected for their talents, he may have wondered whether the army had not gone to the opposite extreme and achieved only the rigidity and bureaucracy of the army staff bureaus of his day.

And well he might. During the Gulf War of 1991, despite its massive intelligence infrastructure, the army had to put its entire interrogation effort into the hands of one exceptional man, a man on the Sharpe model—Col. Stuart A. Herrington, to whom this book is gratefully dedicated. It was perfect proof that the art of intelligence flourishes in the hands of talented and exceptional minds, not bureaucracies. It was also perfect proof that such minds are driven out by a bureaucratic structure that is both perplexed and fearful of such one-of-a-kind creatures.

He would have been far more pleased with the performance of military intelligence after 9/11, when the forge of war and myriad new technologies drove the art of intelligence into unprecedented realms. Certainly, he would have been amazed at the magnitudes of complexity the art of intelligence must work within—the volume of data that is overwhelming. Without taking anything away from his ground-breaking efforts, he was dealing with a far more simple problem set. He was operating in an environment where the combatants shared the same language and culture and where the theater of war was geographically limited to his own country.

The army's MI Corps today comprises thousands of professional military intelligence personnel, a far cry from the modest numbers of officers, civilians, and enlisted men in the BMI in 1863. Its resources are complex, deep, and almost of magical power. Yet, it would behoove this mighty structure an occasional look backward, to consider those who came before and put that sharp sword of effective military intelligence into Meade's hand at Gettysburg and into Grant's thereafter. It is a standard of intelligence excellence that may be equaled but never surpassed.

After immersing myself in the life of George H. Sharpe for 10 years, I freely admit that it become impossible not to like and admire this most interesting and big-hearted man who did so much for his country. Further cause for admiration and respect was that he embodied the ideal military intelligence professional, my profession for many years. He recognized intelligence as an intuitive and creative art, something we today are in danger of forgetting with all our technological toys and politically correct induced distortions of reality. I have endeavored to do his memory justice, not only as a recognition of his deeds but as an example to those who follow in the honorable profession of intelligence.

On a personal note, I was struck as I neared completion of this book that Sharpe and I share something in common. Both our mothers were named Helen, and we both had three children with two boys followed by a doted-upon daughter named Katherine/Kathryn.

I have on occasion thought that if I could go back in time, I would knock on his door and say, "For the love of heaven, General, write your memoirs!"

CHAPTER ONE

Enter Sharpe

Colonel George Henry Sharpe, commander of the 120th New York Volunteers, was probably not a very happy man in early February 1863. His regiment had not seen much combat since it was formed the previous August when it had marched off to war from Kingston, New York. Instead, it was wasting away from sickness in the despondent camp at Falmouth, Virginia, after the disastrous defeat of the Army of the Potomac in December at Fredericksburg and the demoralizing "Mud March" of mid-January. Sharpe was a talented man with an active intelligence, and in the cold and mud of the camp near Falmouth he was intensely frustrated. But he cared for his men as intently as a mother hen, and they returned the affection, asking him sometimes to lead them, in his fine voice, in a variation on "Benny Haven's Oh," whose last verse was touched with the sadness all now felt.

> From the courts of death and danger, from Tampa's deadly shore,
> A wail of manly grief comes up, O'Brien is no More.
> In the land of sun and flowers, his head lies pil-lowed low,
> No more he'll sing Petite Coqulle, at Benny Haven's O.[1]

A Scion of the Hudson Valley—Thanks to Louis XIV

The 35-year-old George Henry Sharpe was a native of Kingston, Ulster County, New York, well-connected, well-educated, and well-moneyed—what passed for an aristocrat in the Empire State. His ancestors, great-great-grandfather Jacob Scherpe and his wife, Anna Marie, emigrated from the Palatinate in Germany in 1711 as refugees from its devastation by Louis XIV. They settled in nearby Columbia County with many other Palatinate Germans. Sharpe's great-grandfather was Peter Scherpe, a prosperous farmer who married Eva Schneider and settled in Duchess County, where their son George was baptized in the German Reformed Church on April 24, 1748. By that same year, the name had been anglicized to "Sharp" (without a final "e"). George, in turn, married Rebecca Teator of Rhinebeck. They had eight children.

Their son, Heinrich, was born on September 22, 1782. He anglicized the name to "Henry," settled in Kingston, and became a wealthy merchant. This generation of Sharpes was on the rise. Henry's older brother, Peter (b. 1775), also settled in Kingston and became an equally successful merchant. Younger brother George (b. 1784) became a member of the successful legal firm of Sharpe and Tuttle in Kingston and a member of the state legislature. Henry Sharpe married Helen Hasbrouck (1797–1886), of that prominent Ulster County clan. She was descended from Abraham Hasbrouck, a Walloon noble from northern France and a Protestant or Huguenot. The revocation of the Edict of Nantes in 1685, which ended tolerance of the Huguenots, again by Louis XIV, forced the family to flee to the unfortunate Palatinate and from there briefly to Holland and England before emigrating to New York. Many of his descendants married women of Dutch heritage, and a strain of Norwegian blood also found its way into the family tree. By this time the Sharpe family name had acquired its final "e."[2]

George Henry Sharpe was born to Henry and Helen Sharpe on February 26, 1828, in Kingston, New York, a pleasant town on the Hudson about 50 miles south of Albany. The town was founded by the original Dutch settlers and named Esopus after a local Indian tribe. Later it was renamed Wiltwyck, Dutch for "wild neighborhood." It was one of the three large settlements in the Dutch colony of the New Netherlands. After the British seized the colony in 1664, the town was renamed Kingston. The Sharpes owned slaves as was all too common even in New York at the time. The last slaves in New York were freed on July 4, 1827, the year before George was born. The last of the family slaves, Sarah Eladorf, was born in 1787 and died 110 years later, having lived the first 40 years of her life in bondage. The family history may have been a major impetus to George's future profound support of emancipation and black civil rights.[3]

In 1875 Sharpe would write a charming history of the town. Sharpe was proud that his hometown had been New York State's first capital during the Revolution and was the birthplace of Governor DeWitt Clinton. He wrote of the original inhabitants, stolidly Dutch and French Huguenots, as a "prudent, economical and frugal people of a strong religious character and simple unostentatious in their lives." That does not mean the history of the town lacked color and drama. Kingston had served as a rallying point for Patriot forces of New York during the Saratoga Campaign, for which it was burned, though a few buildings escaped the wrath of the Crown. Sharpe would tell his tale of the town through the histories of its stone buildings, especially those that had been burned by the British and rebuilt. One was "the old beer house, whose production was famous all over the State—frame building, not burned by the British, because, it is said, a negro servant of the owner remained at his post and rolling out beer barrels defeated their purpose to fire the building." Unusual for the time, Sharpe gave full mention to the considerable black population of Kingston, remarking that they were "so numerous that there was a colloquial saying abroad … that every other house was a barn and every other white man a negro!"[4]

In 1828 Henry Sharpe built the stately family home on a piece of land owned by Helen's family for 200 years. The home and estate was named "The Orchard" for the grove of fine trees that graced it.

Sharpe's father died at the age of 42, when young George himself was not yet two, and his mother took the boy, her only child, and traveled abroad for three years, returning in 1833. From the start the boy lived in a well-traveled and sophisticated world that offered every encouragement to the growth of an active mind. As a little boy George would be remembered in Kingston as a wiry, blond youth with a gray-blue eyes, in love with books and "passionately fond of study, and all thro' his schools and college life he excelled in whatever he took up." He received a first-rate education in Kingston schools, especially the Kingston Academy, at the time a combination high school and college preparatory school.[5]

Although his mother was an intelligent and educated woman, the law required a male guardian, a role filled by one of his uncles until he was nine years of age. Sharpe would later write that "throughout the whole of the management my interests and happiness received the highest care of his skill and precision. I can recollect very little of his intercourse at that time except this uniform kindness." His uncle was succeeded by a new guardian, a friend of the family, Judge Severyn TenHout Bruyn (1817–56), a distant relative by marriage of Sharpe's mother, for whom he was to retain a lifelong respect and affection. The man who was to have such influence over young Sharpe was described as:

> A true patriot, a fine classical scholar, was possessed of a keen sense of humor and an unusually lovable disposition, and was, in the estimation of all who knew him, above and beyond all else a Christian gentlemen, "an Israelite in whom there was no guile." Tender and thoughtful in a rare degree of the needs of others, he never left home for any prolonged absence without placing in the hands of his minister a sum of money for the use of the poor of the church. This, with many other benefactions, was done so quietly as to be unknown until after his death.

Bruyn provided the male role model in Sharpe's life through university. Sharpe's letters to Bruyn in this period showed a close relationship that was in effect that of father and son, which Sharpe explicitly recognized and happily acknowledged.[6]

At an early age Sharpe demonstrated a good-natured and generous personality that won him friends and goodwill everywhere. His high intelligence, which is often seen as a threat by many, in his case simply made him more attractive, especially since he had the talent of never making himself the center of attention or praise but giving that freely to others. His sense of humor comes through in a letter to Bruyn, in which he notes with evident delight, "An Irish sign board standing at a fork in the road, after directing the traveler [sic] to the places, wound up by saying, 'If you can't read, please axe [sic] at the blacksmith shop."[7]

As a boy Sharpe attended the Kingston Academy, at 35 Crown Street, one of the earliest institutions of learning in New York, or the young nation for that matter, which had educated some of the most distinguished men of New York to include De Witt Clinton, Stephen van Rensselaer, and Edward Livingston. Sharpe showed an early gift for scholarship and a facility with the English language in both speaking and writing, as well as with foreign languages, including Latin and French. He attended Rutgers University in New Brunswick in 1843 at the age of 15. The choice of Rutgers was surely influenced by the fact that the president of the university was his second cousin on his mother's side, Abraham Bruyn Hasbrouck (1791–1879). Abraham was also the brother-in-law of Sharpe's guardian. Family ties were close, and young Sharpe was a frequent guest in the Hasbrouck home, where he came to know his third cousin, Caroline, two years his junior, born on July 3, 1830. Sharpe's passion for learning found rich opportunities at Rutgers. He was an honors graduate in 1847 and delivered the salutary address in "polished and graceful" Latin. He was considered the best educated man in Ulster County. Interestingly, although university records showed his name spelled with a final "e," he signed his letters without it.[8]

From Rutgers he went directly to Yale Law School and graduated in 1849 at the age of 21. While at Yale, Sharpe applied in early October 1848 to several prominent lawyers in New York City for the opportunity to study law, a practice of the early 19th century in which a young man put himself under the tutelage of an experienced lawyer. He was accepted by George W. Strong, "A corpulent old gentleman with his spectacles shoved upon his forehead—asks very direct and pertinent questions and appears to be pleased with direct and pertinent answers." Sharpe was clearly impressed with the old man. "It needed but a glance to see that [he was] was a gentleman." Strong was equally impressed with the name Sharpe dropped, a Mr. Lord, as recommending he apply to Strong. The old lawyer focused intently on the young man and asked for his full name and residence, if and from where he had graduated, and "where-what I had been doing since." He was surprised that Sharpe "was not age"—had not reached his majority. He also commented that he knew Severyn Bruyn by reputation.

Strong had come to a decision to take him on but wanted him to know the conditions of his tutelage. He told Sharpe that it was a bad time to study law; he himself was actively studying because of changes in the law code. He also made it clear that he expected his students (he already had three) would be expected to work six hours a day in his office and that he would examine them twice a week in the evening at his own home, "when they had talks." Strong's fee was $100, which he generously said could be paid anytime within the year. He concluded by saying that if with Bruyn's "advice I concluded to come with him, he would receive me." Sharpe's enthusiasm was whetted when one of Strong's former students gave his lectures high praise. In a few days, Sharpe accepted Strong's offer, and a week later was writing to Bruyn, "I should say without hesitation that he is far superior to either or both of our Professors at Yale."[9]

By January Strong had trusted his abilities enough to let him represent minor cases in the courts. He was an aggressive advocate for his clients, not hesitant to wield a suit like a sword. He regaled Bruyn on February 3 with an account of his current cases:

> I commenced suit in the Marine court for a seaman's wages as intended, but the defendant was frightened at the summons, and paid up the full amount of sixty dollars, before I could get to trial. My second suit (for $32) was commenced last week in the War court, and was to have been tried this morning. The defendant showed fight with a very large lawyer, and made out to get an adjournment until next Thursday, when I shall insist upon a trial. I think we shall get the money if the defendant does not beat us on execution, as Mr. Strong regularly says.[10]

Sharpe had other matters on his mind at this time as well. His birthday was only a few weeks away. He would turn 21 and his legal majority. For the last six years, as he grew from a boy to man, Bruyn had been there as a beloved father-figure, attending with great skill and solicitude to young Sharpe's affairs. On his birthday, those weighty affairs, which involved much property, would suddenly fall on his own shoulders. It was a sobering realization. Sharpe poured out his heart to Bruyn in a letter of February 20. The importance of that letter is evident in the care he took to write in the most beautiful script, when compared with the normally swift and not always legible course of his pen across the paper.

> ... it has been under your guidance in mature years that my character has been in a great degree formed, and my mind has received those indelible impressions that time can never efface. It has been my lot to know of you all that I have ever known of a father, and this is enough to set the connections which have existed between us ever sacred to me.
>
> It was natural in such a case that I should look for something more in my guardian than a mere trustee of the property which had been left me, and I was so fortunate to enjoy the superintendance [sic] of one whose example was one of imitation, and whose counsel if they have been obeyed have always led me in the path of duty.

Sharpe went on to say that he hoped that Bruyn, after Sharpe had reached his majority and took his affairs in hand, would extend the same counsel to a friend that he had given as guardian. He ended this letter by thanking Bruyn for the "manner in which you have discharged those other duties as a guardian which no law but that of affection could impose." Sharpe's sentiments were as generous and gracious as they were heartfelt, characteristics that over the years would win him the affection and devotion of others. In later years, Sharpe would show the ultimate proof of his respect and affection by naming his first son after Severyn Bruyn and his second son after his late father.[11]

By October 1849, Helen Sharpe had become convinced enough of her 21-year-old son's abilities that she designated him as her lawyer and gave him complete power of attorney. She had inherited a considerable part of the estate of her father, Abraham

Hasbrouck, and freely placed that in Sharpe's hands. He would justify her trust, and throughout his life he proved to be both a shrewd investor and a careful manager of his assets.[12]

He was described in the early 1960s by those residents of Kingston who had known him in their youths and from the stories of their elders, as not a handsome man but "possessed of a high quality of personal magnetism." He was on the short side of medium height, and the blond hair of childhood had turned a nondescript brown. Although unprepossessing in appearance, he won friends easily by his charm and good nature. His round shoulders and lack of stature belied the fact that he had become an outstanding horseman, a skill afforded by his family's money and once more in keeping with the expected accomplishments of a Southern gentleman.[13]

Despite his good nature, Sharpe had come by a certain sense of noblesse oblige. He was the scion of an old and prominent clan on his mother's side, the Hasbroucks. Old residents of Kingston would still remember in the early 1860s that the Sharpes thought they were a cut above anyone else in Kingston society. While studying under George Strong in early 1849, he wrote Judge Bruyn frequently about acquiring a copy of the Hasbrouck coat of arms, displaying on its shield an arm and a dagger, to which he "had as good a right as any one else." Despite his attachment for his mother's family coat of arms and noble lineage, he was proud of his own family, and remained close to them, particularly to his Uncle Peter and a cousin, Jacob Sharpe.[14]

Sharpe's father had laid down the basis of the family's wealth, augmented no doubt by wealth from his mother's Hasbrouck family. Judge Bruyn had increased that wealth by careful and shrewd management and investment. Much of that had been in real estate. Now that he was handling his own affairs, Sharpe was looking into the even greater income-producing opportunities offered by the country's rapid technological growth. He had invested in the Hudson River Railroad and found its potential even more impressive than the not inconsiderable rise in its stock. He noted that the "travel is almost entirely diverted from the [Hudson] River to the [rail] road. The time of the cars from Peekskill to the city is one hour; that of the boat three." He also noted that the passenger traffic on the river was almost completely drying up in favor of the railroad. The future was obvious, and he would maintain a lifelong and profitable interest in railroads. But, being 21, there were more things than railroads to keep his attention. His cousin Caroline was entering into womanhood and already had the blush of a great beauty. On a visit to New Brunswick, her mother insisted that Sharpe stay with the Hasbroucks, a few days which he described as passing "very pleasantly." Mrs. Hasbrouck would not be the first mother to see what a future great catch such a young man was.[15]

Before entering the bar, he decided to travel for several years. His first journey took him through the South to Cuba in early 1850. In a letter to Bruyn, he related with no little amusement what would be his first encounter with military interrogation:

My only <u>adventure</u>, which can really be called so, on the Island, (and which I haven't yet communicated to the Mother of an only son) was a short imprisonment in the Moro [sic Morro] Castle. Bradish [his traveling companion] and I having sought for admission and been refused were leisurely walking beyond the circumvallation towards the sea-shore when some vessels coming into sight, I pulled out a sort of pocket guide (*La Isla de Cuba en la mano*) to see of what country were their colors. We were soon joined by an ugly looking soldier from the Moro who by his gestures & jabbering seemed to want to take us back with him, but we as <u>significantly</u> declined. Thereupon six men were sent after us and we had the honor of marching into the castle with three of H. C. [His Catholic] Majesty's defenders in front and rear. The officer of the guard after in vain endeavoring to make us understand one word of his examination dictated a very lengthy and sonorous commitment to his secretary, and then offered us his lunch of cigarettes as a solace in adversity. The document was sent off somewhere, and in the course of another half hour, an epaullatted & decorated sinner with one eye, made his appearance with a French Interpreter for whom we had asked. My book & our persons were then closely inspected and after a long examination in which the same questions were often repeated, we were suffered to go.[16]

That he carried off the engagement with a cool charm and self-possession would be echoed years later when he would call on those qualities to rescue thousands of wounded men.

Upon his return to New York, he embarked for Europe for three years, studying to perfect his French in Paris until he had achieved an elegant fluency. Sharpe also served in 1850–51 as an attaché at the U.S. embassy in Vienna under chargé d'affairs Judge Charles Johnson McCurdy. Before returning to the U.S., he also served briefly at the U.S. embassy in Rome where he learned some Italian. He returned to the United States an accomplished linguist, a connoisseur of art, literature, and fine food—and an experienced diplomat.

In 1854 he passed the bar and went into partnership with the firm of Hasbrouck, Sharpe, and Linderman and with John B. Steele, who would be elected to Congress in 1860 and 1862. Steele would remain an important contact for Sharpe throughout the war.

That same year his relationship with cousin Caroline became serious. In August he would write Judge Bruyn and say impishly that "the little finger of my left hand now sports a small hoop ring ... which a fortnight ago could not have been wrung from the hand of a fair young lady."[17] The next year he married Caroline Hasbrouck, always "Carry" to him. It was obviously a love match, but like most Victorian wives, even those of great accomplishment, Carry would remain largely silent in the record of Sharpe's life. It was clear, from various references, that she had a mind of her own but that she and George would be a devoted couple for the next 43 years. So intertwined were their lives that her death in 1898 would be a devastating blow from which he would not long survive. They would have three children—Severyn Bruyn (June 1, 1857), Henry Grenville (April 3, 1858), and Katherine Lawrence (April 26, 1860) in a loving family. His children were to remember their father with deep pride and affection.[18]

A Political Man

The year 1854 marked an important step in Sharpe's life—it was the year he fell in love and started his law career. With those preoccupations, he may not have noticed the founding of the Republican Party in Wisconsin that same year. This new party was established by a coalition of former Whigs, Northern Democrats, and Free-Soilers, all united in their opposition to the extension of slavery, determination to encourage opportunity, and a vision for the modernization of the United States. By 1856 the party's rise had been so rapid that it had replaced the collapsed Whigs as the second national party ran its first candidate for president.

The next four years would see the country spiral toward civil war under the ineffectual presidency of Buchanan. The Republicans had drawn a line in the sand in their opposition to what they called the "Slave Power" of the South, which was attempting to achieve permanent control of the Federal Government to secure its "peculiar institution" in its own states, and its spread to new states and territories.

The party grew quickly in New York State. New York's former governor and United States senator, William H. Seward, one of the most distinguished men in American public life, abandoned the Whigs for the new party in 1856. There was some positive but shadowy connection between Sharpe and Seward, and the older man may have been a profound influence on the young lawyer's politics. The Republicans were the rising tide in New York politics as the decade drew to its contentious end, and it was a party that Sharpe found both politically congenial to his own beliefs and one able to meet his own ambitions.[19]

There is little evidence of Sharpe's political opinions at this time, but an examination of his later positions gives some indication of how they evolved. The modernization of the country and its institutions would be a life-long enthusiasm for Sharpe. In particular, he was an advocate of the rapid integration of immigrants into American life. Sharpe could see how powerful and vital was the dynamism of Americanization. At the funeral of an uncle in 1854, he had noted that the old gray-haired farmers "talked Dutch in groups together," but that if he lived to the age of his uncle, it was unlikely that Dutch would be spoken at his own funeral.[20]

Overshadowing this, however, was his active support for the political rights of black Americans. There was plenty to do in New York without having to address the South's peculiar institution. As the election of 1860 loomed, the issue of complete black suffrage in New York was on the ballot in the form of a referendum. Free Northern blacks had voting rights on the basis of equality in only the five New England States. New York had onerous property qualifications on black suffrage. A similar referendum had been soundly defeated in 1846. But the issue had been given new power with the rise of the Republican Party. In 1857 the New York Assembly passed an equal suffrage resolution fueled by Republican anger over the Dred Scott decision. In every vote on black suffrage in the Assembly from 1856, 90 percent of the Republican members supported it just as consistently as 90 percent of the Democrats opposed it. Yet the party never made it a part of its state platform; its new coalition was too fragile to push the issue strongly, so that though Lincoln carried the state in the 1860 election, black suffrage went down to defeat, with only 37 percent of the vote in favor, which was only 10 percent higher than in 1846.

Opposition had been heavy in the older, southeastern section of the state where the influence of the old Dutch stock was strongest, where slavery had once flourished, and where the largest number of blacks lived. Kingston was just such a place, with a strong Dutch flavor and a substantial black population that was still there in the 1890s. It is not known how Sharpe voted on the issue nor have any statements or opinions survived in the written record. The historian can only go by the subsequent actions of the man later in life.[21]

There is nothing in Sharpe's history that suggests any overt racial animosity. In his writings, including hundreds of military reports, he never uses any derogatory terms for black Americans. When evaluating the native intelligence of Confederate prisoners and deserters and that of free blacks and contrabands (runaway slaves), he uses the same descriptors for all groups and does not weight one group above the other but identifies brains or lack of them equally as he found them. Where the objectivity of his reporting allowed, he expressed a sympathy for the plight of the slave. After the war he was a die-hard proponent of full black rights in New York State and an equally die-hard supporter of the Fourteenth Amendment. He was a frequent and much appreciated speaker at black community political rallies in New York City. Using this information to extrapolate a man's stand on issues backwards in time is difficult at best. It does not allow for the evolution of opinion, especially in the forge of the revolutionary experience of the Civil War.

Marching to the Sound of the Drums

Upon his return to the United States, Sharpe also joined the 20th New York State Militia (NYSM) Regiment, later known as the Ulster Guard, based in his hometown. Whether he was genuinely interested in military service, saw it as merely a civic duty of a man of his station and background, or, like many a budding politician then and now, saw token military service as a good career move, is unknown. It may well have been for all of these reasons, as it often is. But if his later life is any proof, he had a genuine interest and pride in soldiering. The militia offered the only outlet for such men who found the small regular army with its poor pay and low esteem unattractive.

In 1861 he was a man on the rise, with a successful law practice and growing reputation. He had also been directly commissioned to the rank of captain and had been elected to the command of Company in the 20th NYSM, but his law practice left too little time for the military duties, and he resigned in spring 1861.

He was far away from home on business in Delaware County drawing a will for a prominent personage, Colonel Dimmick, who lay near death, when the news of the Confederate attack on Fort Sumter on April 12 reached him. A New York paper was thrown out of a stage at the colonel's door. Sharpe read the news to the colonel, whose patriotism was so outraged that he rose from his sickbed spewing invective at traitors to throw himself into work. With this model before him, Sharpe informed Dimmick that he was returning to Kingston the next morning by the first stage. "The old Colonel wished him well, with renewed vigor and light in his eyes."[22]

Sharpe almost flew back to Kingston, and at dawn with Capt. J. Rudolph Tappen, hung out the Stars and Stripes, and began enrolling additional soldiers without waiting for orders or permission from his colonel. Apparently, the inconvenience of his resignation was simply overlooked by everyone. There is little wonder; both Tappen and Sharpe were well liked and well respected as leaders. Their goal was to enlist 100 men to form a single company. Sharpe remembered, "from the time we hung a flag out of the old Brick Church,[23] between the morning of one day and the evening of another we enlisted two hundred and forty-eight men. Obliged to reject some on account of disqualifications, we divided the remainder into two companies, each being beyond the number allowed by law." This was the first time that Sharpe's gifts of personal magnetism and oratory had had such a positive public effect. On the 18th the governor of New York called for a muster of the state's militia and for Ulster County to furnish its quota.

The 20th NYSM, however, was already ahead of the game. Since 1857 it had been commanded by the able Col. George Watson Pratt, who was largely responsible for pulling the regiment together for active duty, aided by Sharpe's bold alacrity in opening recruiting as well as other officers recruiting outside of Kingston.[24] On the 19th Sharpe was appointed to a committee to report on the regiment's readiness; he was also chosen to "receive subscriptions to maintain the families of the soldiers," a mark of extreme trust and a sign that he was noted for his care of the welfare of the men.[25]

As the companies swelled with new recruits, they were sent to the Academy Green, where they received instruction in the manual of arms and the school of the soldier. The regiment's "two principal drill instructors" were Sharpe and Tappen.[26]

He abandoned his lucrative practice and left with the regiment two weeks later, captain of Company B's 113 men for 90 days' service. One of the officers in his company was a second cousin, Jacob Sharpe, who had spent two years at West Point. On June 2, the regimental lieutenant colonel resigned, and the officers gathered to elect his replacement. The 26 voting officers chose Maj. Theodore B. Gates, with 23 votes, against one for Captain Sharpe, one for the adjutant, and one abstention, according to Gates. Gates would eventually become colonel of the regiment and command it until late in 1864 when he resigned to run for Congress. Hasbrouck's account makes the election more of a contest, with 36 voting officers, of whom

24 voted for Gates and 12 for Sharpe. In either case, the election shows that Sharpe had achieved a certain prominence in the regiment.

The men were still learning how dangerous firearms could be and had not obtained the veterans' easy but respectful handling of them. The first man to die on active duty was a member of Sharpe's Company B. On June 20, Lance-Corporal Dunbar Schoonmaker had put a pistol in his shirt pocket and leaned over. The pistol fell out, struck the butt of his Springfield Rifle, and discharged. The bullet struck near his heart. He staggered toward the first lieutenant's tent and fell dead. Sharpe and several of his enlisted men accompanied the body back to Kingston.

The 20th saw mostly guard duty at Annapolis and Baltimore despite its colonel's repeated requests for a Virginia assignment. Sharpe enjoyed retelling the story of the desperate days in late July when the crisis of the battle of First Bull Run caused the government to ask the 20th to stay on active service beyond its 90 days' enlistment.

> There was dissatisfaction with this arrangement. Colonel Pratt had the men paraded and addressed them in an earnest and impressive speech. Then had the line officers in consultation when Captain Patrick Flynn suggested that the different companies decide the matter. When he [Sharpe] met his company he opened the ranks and addressed them by saying that it would be disgraceful for the men to return home just when they were needed so badly. He added: "If there are any here in favor of going right home step three paces to the front, but be careful that no one shoots you in the back. Any one going home shot in the back will be justly considered a traitor." Not a man stepped forward and the regiment stayed until the crisis had passed.[27]

Sharpe undoubtedly did not enjoy retelling another story concerning the flinty Captain Flynn and his "Irish Company F." On June 26, after a long and tiring march which had sharpened everyone's temper, the regiment camped after dark on a moonless night. Colonel Pratt ordered rations issued in the normal sequence of companies by the commissary. His attention was soon drawn to shouting at the commissary wagon, where he found that Sharpe and his officers were demanding that Company B be fed immediately and out of turn. Sharpe's normally paternal and aggressive concern for the welfare of his men had apparently trumped his good judgment, egged on by the short tempers magnified by the darkness. Pratt ordered Sharpe to desist and resume his normal place in the order of rations issue. Sharpe refused point blank. Pratt did not flinch at the challenge and ordered up Captain Flynn and his company fully armed. With Flynn's Irish behind him, Pratt again ordered Sharpe to return his men to their bivouac area. He added that if he did not do so, he would order Flynn to fire. Sharpe's good judgment returned with a flash as he declined to call the colonel's bluff. He immediately marched his men back to their bivouac. Sharpe's confrontation with Pratt was a rare act of bad judgment that he would not often repeat.[28]

Sharpe served through the end of July, when the regiment's extended 90 days' service expired. Keeping the regiment up to strength became problematical after it returned home. Gates reported on the tart comment from higher headquarters on

Sharpe's inability to keep his company recruited to strength. "On the 31st day of August, B Company, Captain Sharpe, and E Company, Lent, which companies had not participated in the reorganization of the regiment, were disbanded by orders from Brigade Headquarters for 'not having the required number of men to be effective at this critical period of our national history.'" Sharpe's membership in the regiment was due to his position as a company commander. When that company was disbanded, he was left without a position and returned to civilian life.[29]

The 20th was reorganized and left for service again in October but without Sharpe. Recruiting the regiment back to strength was in doubt until the popular and able Captain Tappen rejoined. Following his example, the regiment was quickly back up to strength. The men of the 20th felt strongly about their unit designation, and despite being given a new state designation as the 80th New York, always insisted on using their old name. They argued that it predated all the war-raised regiments and had precedence over them. That argument was insistent enough that in all official order-of-battle listings of the Army of the Potomac, 80th New York is always followed by 20th Militia in parentheses.[30]

A civilian again, Sharpe resumed his interest in politics and ran for supervisor in Kingston in March 1862 but lost. Undeterred, he involved himself enthusiastically in public life. He was the perfect example of the old saying that if you want something done, ask a busy man. In addition to a growing and rewarding law practice, he found time to be the secretary of the board of trustees of the Kingston Academy. In the fall he was elected a delegate to the Republican state convention and was chosen to be a member of the state committee. He also attempted to build bridges with the emerging so-called War Democrats, the members of that party who supported the war for the Union. They called themselves the People's Party and locally elected Sharpe as a delegate to their county convention in late September. There he strongly urged cooperation between the Republican and People's Parties, which led to the latter joining a bi-partisan county ticket and supporting the Republican state ticket.[31]

"We Are Coming, Father Abraham!"

In the summer of 1862 Lincoln called for 300,000 more volunteers as the war deepened. The North responded with a flood of new regiments as the song "We Are Coming, Father Abraham, 300,000 More!" swept the North. Sharpe had been suffering from bronchial illness since the spring. Secretary of State William suggested to New York's governor, Edwin Morgan, that he encourage Sharpe to raise a regiment. Seward was aware of the Sharpe family's influence in Ulster County. Sharpe was also recommended for this position on July 12 by a committee formed to organize recruiting for the 10th Senatorial District of Ulster and Greene Counties. Upon receipt of the governor's request, Sharpe rose from his sick bed and set about the task. On July 21 he wrote J. H. Tuthill of the Military Executive Committee of the 10th Senatorial District, authorizing his representative to begin enrolling volunteers. He forwarded a package of blank applications with the note that they had to be signed in triplicate. For three weeks, he traveled and spoke each day,[32] as the regimental history describes:

> ... [Sharpe] entered actively and earnestly upon the task of recruiting, holding meetings almost daily in the several sections of the county and addressing large audiences drawn together by interest in the country's cause. These meetings, were at times addressed by other influential citizens of the country, who placed country before party, and by the fervor of their appeals, swelled rapidly the number of recruits and raised to a higher pitch the loyal zeal and ardor of the people.

One well-known village in the county, however, did not produce a single recruit, though the people were known to be loyal and enthusiastic in the cause of the Union. Sharpe traveled there and called a town meeting, though the local notables said it would be well attended but would not produce a single recruit and would be a waste of time. Sharpe was not deterred. In addressing the large crowd:

> He said that he had been given to understand that in the regiment to be raised that locality would be unrepresented. He had always had a high opinion of the courage and enthusiasm of its citizens, and rather than leave the town without representation in the regiment, he proposed to return to Governor Morgan his commission as Colonel, and to enlist as a private for that locality in order the whole county be represented.

At the close of the meeting enough young men came forward to enlist to form a platoon, requiring the issuing of a commission to one of them. With such energy and pluck, Sharpe was able to recruit the regiment to a strength of 1,041 men in a record 22 days—seven companies from Ulster and three from Green Counties. In addition to Sharpe's considerable gifts as a public speaker, several thousand dollars of Sharpe family money had lubricated the recruiting effort as well.[33]

Sharpe was also drawing heavily on his fragile health. He had not recovered from his bronchial illness but had suppressed it with a burst of adrenalin and energy that pushed the illness into recession. He would write:

> I had not entirely recovered from the last spring's attack which [had] a disposition to settle in my lungs, when we were called on to raise this regt. I then talked and walked hard every day—rode every evening and spoke in the open air every night—often riding home after so doing. The excitement must have kept me up, for I did not notice any harm to myself ...[34]

As he threw himself into recruiting, another officer was also in the middle of a frenzied recruiting campaign in New York City. Brigadier General Daniel Sickles was recruiting his Excelsior Brigade back to full strength after strenuous fighting in the Peninsula and at Second Bull Run had depleted its strength. Sickles was notorious as a rough and tumble Tammany Hall lawyer whose ambitions had taken him to Congress; he was infamous for having shot his wife's lover, the U.S. Attorney for the District of Columbia, Barton Key, in front of the White House. The 19th-century

"Dream Team" he assembled in his defense included the future formidable Secretary of War, Edwin McMasters Stanton, and marked the first successful uses of the insanity defense in the United States. Before the year was out, Sharpe and Sickles would cross paths to create a life-long friendship between the Hudson Valley Patrician Republican and the Tammany Hall Democrat.[35]

While Sharpe spoke in town after town, canvassing for recruits, he had left the growing mountain of paperwork in the capable hands of his adjutant, Major C. D. Westbrook, who patiently brought order out of chaos. Westbrook had also served in the 20th NYSM as a captain with Sharpe. Sharpe also put him command of Camp Samson, where the regiment was assembling as volunteers trickled in.[36] Sharpe soon designated Westbrook as the regimental lieutenant colonel. Westbrook had proven to Sharpe that he had the ability to take charge of the regiment in the commander's absence. Sharpe's choice of his company commanders was equally shrewd, particularly that of a young man of promise, Capt. Abram L. Lockwood, commanding Company A. At that time, Sharpe made another inspired choice for the position of regimental major. "My own, and the thoughts of others, naturally turned to Tappen, and he was commissioned a Major, joining us at Fairfax Seminary, where we can well recall his cheerful voice and gay manner as he came riding into camp with head still bound up with bandages." Tappen had been wounded at the battle of Second Bull Run in the 20th NYSM's bayonet charge on Jackson's men defending the blood-soaked railway embankment, referring to it in his good-natured manner. "A bullet struck me just above the forehead, passed under the skin, and came out the corner of my forehead … There, you can see the benefit of being thick-headed."[37]

The regiment was representative of New York and the United States at that time, with a large foreign-born element of 177 men, fully 19.5 percent. Of that number the two largest groups were the Irish (73) and the Germans (62), of whom six proudly identified themselves as Prussians. There were 15 English, eight Canadians, and five Scots. The rest were a smattering from all over Europe—France, Sweden, Holland, Switzerland, Hungary, and Portugal. There were also 31 men from other states, mostly neighboring New Jersey, Pennsylvania, and Connecticut. The rest of the men were New York-born, mostly from Ulster and Greene Counties.[38]

The new regiment organized at Camp Samson, the same site where the 20th New York State Militia had assembled the year before, and was mustered into service on August 22. On August 23 the regimental colors, purchased by the ladies of Ellenville and Kingston, were presented at the camp with great ceremony in front of the largest crowd that Kingston had ever seen, come in from all over Ulster and Greene Counties. The spokesman for the women said, in words replicated in countless such villages, towns, and cities in both North and South, "Colonel Sharpe …. You, and the brave men with you, will regard these flags, not only as an evidence of your country's greatness and glory, but also as having clustered about them all the hallowed influence of home. Let these flags speak to you with the voice of wife, mother and sister, bidding you to deeds of noble daring."

Sharpe replied that he would not boast of the deeds to be done under these flags, or the condition in which they would be brought home, or even that they would even be returned to Kingston, but he did pledge that the men who carried them would do their utmost to preserve them from any dishonor, "even though they had to struggle until the last man should have the last shred to bear back to the place from whence they had been received." There would be a certain prophecy in his words. That same day orders were received to depart the following morning.[39]

Breaking in a New Regiment

So great was the need in Washington for fresh troops that the 120th marched away from Camp Samson on August 24 without any drill or training. It was a Sunday, bright and clear, and even greater crowds than the day before assembled to see the regiment off. Sharpe rode at their head on a bay gelding named Dandy, which he had just purchased. Sharpe took with him 900 men, leaving behind one company and skeletons of others to be incorporated by the 156th NY, which was also raised in the same region. It was at the very last minute that the regimental number was decided. Sharpe would recall:

> As the regiment was about to leave, Governor Morgan sent an aide-de-camp with a list of the numerical designations to which we would be entitled. Passing over a number which would have placed us numerically far higher in the roster of the state, I selected that of the One Hundred and Twentieth, in order that in name, as well as in feeling, we might be associated with that other regiment, the Old Twentieth, raised and commanded by Col. George W. Pratt, which so long represented the county of Ulster upon the fields of Virginia. Col. Westbrook, Major Tappen, and myself had been captains of the Twentieth. Following the thought thus expressed by myself, Col. Erastus Cooke, in choosing the numerical designation of the regiment which succeeded us, took the number One Hundred and Fifty-Sixth, in order also to ally it to the Fifty-Sixth New York, to which this county had furnished three companies.[40]

After the 20th NYSM and the 120th NY Volunteers, the 156th NY Volunteers was the third regiment raised from the same general area of Ulster, Greene, and Richmond. This regiment, known as the "Mountain Legion," was organized at Kingston, where it was mustered into U.S. service for three years on November 17, 1862 from the elements left behind by the 120th NY. The regiment's lieutenant colonel was Sharpe's second cousin, Jacob Sharpe. After serving with the 20th NYSM, Jacob had been a major in the 56th NYSM and certainly would have approved his cousin's idea of honoring the original regiment. He would eventually succeed to command of the regiment and ultimately to its brigade and be brevetted brigadier general for "gallantry and meritorious service at the battle of Winchester" in 1864.[41]

The120th marched to nearby Rondout on the Hudson, where they took a steamer for New York City. Down the river every passing boat and ship offered them cheers and honors. The next morning they landed and marched to city hall, where they were issued their muskets from the state arsenal. All the other equipment required by the regiment to include ammunition was in short supply and would only be provided when the regiment reached Washington. That same day, Sharpe marched his men through the city to the Jersey Ferry, and, after crossing, the regiment boarded trains for Philadelphia which it reached on August 26. Climbing off the none too comfortable cars, they were met with a great surprise. The citizens of Philadelphia had built a huge welcoming hall for incoming troops, to provide meals and other comforts. The regiment remembered their breakfast as "sumptuous." This establishment functioned through the end of the war, with the express mission of providing a meal to every regiment or soldier that passed through the City of Brotherly Love. Medical care for the sick was also provided until recovery when they were sent on to their regiments, or, if the man had to be sent home, the establishment covered the complete cost. Writing materials were provided, and no soldier was allowed to buy a stamp. For the men of the 120th, it would be a lasting golden memory of good will and charity.[42]

The next morning the regiment left the benevolent arms of Philadelphia by train to arrive in Baltimore in the afternoon and started for Washington, reaching the capital at midnight on August 27, only three days after leaving Kingston, and bivouacked on the streets amid countless other soldiers, wagons, cavalry, and artillery. The next morning Sharpe marched his men across Long Bridge to Arlington Heights. The regimental biographer would write of the effect the site had on the men. It had been confiscated by the U.S. Government and turned into a cemetery for the war dead. "Those who knew the history of Arlington, long the home of General Robert E. Lee, then in command of the rebel armies, and saw how the iron heel of war had stamped out its beauty, and spread desolation around, would find a fruitful lesson inspired by the spot where their first night in Virginia was spent."[43]

That day and the next the battle of Second Bull Run was raging to the south. As the 120th set up its camp they could hear the ominous rumbling of the battle, every man knowing that their kin and friends of the 20th NYSM were in the thick of it. The next morning they were hastily issued rations and ammunition and marched 10 miles to Fort Allen to guard against any attempt of the victorious Confederates to bounce into Washington. Major General McClellan was recalled to duty to gather up and restore the fighting strength of the shattered Union troops, which he did with great skill, leading them to successfully fight Lee at South Mountain and Antietam in a matter of weeks. The 120th, however, took no part in these battles, but moved out of the defenses of Washington, finally settling into the Fairfax Seminary near Alexandria, where they found many wounded friends from the old 20th NYSM in the numerous hospitals there. Sharpe must have chafed at this seeming relegation to garrison duty, but he put the time to good use in drilling his men. It was a respite that would serve them in good stead in future battles.[44]

The regiment had not seen a month's service when they suffered their first loss when John K. Brown of Company E died near Mount Vernon, Virginia. Sharpe ordered the company commander, Capt. Daniel Gillette, to turn over the man's effects to his brother's representative.[45]

The first few months of service had required an intensive shake down and introduction into military life for almost all the men except Sharpe and the handful of officers and men who had served in the 20th NYSM. As early as August 27 he had to deal with the bane of Civil War soldiering—desertion—when he sent two lieutenants back to Kingston to round up 32 deserters. His legal and military experience was evident in the instructions he gave them to call upon the local county sheriffs for assistance in apprehending the deserters. On September 24 he dealt with another bane of Civil War soldiering—drinking—by putting the sutler's tent off limits after tattoo under threat of the guardhouse. To provide a salutary example that his orders applied to everyone, he arrested Capt. James M. Pierson, the K Company commander, who was caught slipping into the sutler's tent for a nightcap, releasing him after a week's embarrassment had done its work.[46]

He was quick to punish those taking advantage of privileged positions to goof off, as in the case of sending Drummer Leartus Many back to the ranks with the admonition that he would be held "strictly accountable" for his conduct, a believable threat by now. He was hard on crime of any sort. On October 15 he broke Sergeant S. Quick to the ranks for stealing. "The colonel commanding pledges himself to the Regiment to do all in his power to repress the state's prison vice of thieving, and asks his fellow soldiers to assist him in the attempt." Hygiene did not escape his attention either. He had to admonish his company commanders to stop the men from washing in or otherwise polluting the mill stream near the Fairfax Seminary where they were stationed. The mill stream fed into the reservoir of Alexandria, where there were many military hospitals that relied on it for drinking water. Sharpe made it clear that pollution of the reservoir was delaying the recovery of the wounded, their brother soldiers.[47]

Sharpe's order book clearly showed that he was dealing with every conceivable problem that affects soldiers, no matter the war. Although he was a devoted and even affectionate commander, he was also a no-nonsense commander, especially where discipline was concerned. He broke a corporal on October 30 for a very public and noisy display of disrespect and insubordination, which persisted even after the man was promptly arrested. Sharpe announced in his special order reducing the man to the ranks that he "was unfit to command men of this regiment."[48]

Sharpe also discovered army paperwork at this time. He was shocked by the extent of the official correspondence that fell upon his writing table. The endless official paperwork was bad enough, but he received from five to seven letters each day inquiring about men in his regiment. A number of letters were from officers' parents asking how their sons were doing. Sharpe felt duty bound to answer every letter promptly and fully. He recognized that maintaining the morale of the families at home was an important element in maintaining the morale of his men.[49]

In September Sharpe was felled by another bronchial attack. The illness had only been suppressed, not cured, by the excitement of raising the regiment. Now it came back powerfully to feed on the "fatigue and anxiety" that fell upon him while the regiment was on the road from New York to Washington. He wrote his uncle, "So I arrived in Virginia in the worst of the fever weather of the year, with every predisposition toward any epidemic that might be going where we were then ..." But the charge of responsibility lay heavily upon him. He felt a fever coming on but struggled against its onset for a week because a Confederate attack was expected at Chain Bridge, which crossed the Potomac into Washington from Virginia, and he said, "I would not claim to be ill then." The first two weeks of September carried that last wave of summer heat that bakes Virginia and Washington. His duties often sent him "furiously" galloping in the oppressive heat so much that "During two weeks, I could not get a particle of moisture from any part of my body." Dehydration was reinforcing the resurgent fever and bronchial illness. When the regiment was transferred to Mount Vernon, he was sent to Washington, where he was treated by an assistant surgeon general who "seemed to know exactly what was the matter—broke the fever in two days."

His health returned deeper and sounder now, reinforced by exercise and outdoor living, giving him the exuberance of good health. "From that time to this I have been steadily gaining, and without being boastful, or claiming to be the heartiest man in the regiment (and I am very near it) if you remember my splendid physical condition during the 3 mos service, I can only say that I am rapidly approaching it."

Sharpe had need of his newly restored vigor. In October he was doing a lot of active soldiering since he had been given command of the forward post at Upton Hill, in command of an artillery battery and a second infantry regiment in addition to his own.

> I stood the fatigue at Upton's Hill where I was constantly on duty (from choice) during the several days an attack was expected there, <u>day and night</u>, and where I was commanding two regiments and a battery. It was the key to the whole front of Washington, and had, as I think, been most insanely abandoned by a whole brigade of infantry, and several regiments of cavalry <u>at once</u>—and the rebels knew it as soon as we did. I had four field officers under me, but did not care to figure as a paroled prisoner at this early state of service, and kept at work all the time. When I visit the picket lines, which is now nearly every day as [Major] Tappen & I are alone on duty—the Lt. Col. being detached on Court Martial, I ride some 10 miles between breakfast & dinner—and I assure you there is no officer in the hqs whose claim to indulgences on account of health would be considered more preposterous than mine.[50]

He consistently exercised a sense of responsibility beyond the narrow limits of his own authority. When unexpectedly another force was designated to take over the post, Sharpe ensured that his superiors understood that the artillery battery that had been stationed with him would have to be replaced.[51]

Sharpe's bay gelding, Dandy, had proven not to be a good animal under the saddle. He was able to buy another from a friend, a sorrel gelding with a white face and white hind feet named Babe. One can imagine the effect the animal had on Sharpe; it was intelligent, spirited, and brave. For Sharpe it became the perfect horse, and more—a friend. He would keep him throughout the war and ride him back into Kingston almost three years later. The regiment finally received its orders to join the army in the field on October 26; McClellan had received peremptory orders from Lincoln to attack the enemy.[52]

When Burnside succeeded McClellan in early November, the 120th found itself with the rest of the army at Warrenton in Virginia. Burnside's reorganization of the army incorporated the regiment into the 2nd Excelsior Brigade, commanded by George B. Hall, in Maj. Gen. Daniel Sickles's 2nd Division of III Corps of the Army of the Potomac. III Corps was commanded by Maj. Gen. Daniel Hooker. Sharpe's old 20th NYSM was also part of this division. Sharpe, who had just been temporarily detailed to command the post at Centreville, had fallen under the command of one of the great politicians of the era, a Union Democrat, who undoubtedly sensed in Sharpe another member of the political species, though a Republican. Sickles had a reputation for dirty politics as a member of the notorious Tammany Hall Ring that ran New York City and an equal reputation for high living, but whatever else he was, he was a hard fighting man who could throw a nasty punch on the battlefield as well as in New York politics.[53]

While in command of the post at Centreville, Sharpe experienced the inefficiency of the cavalry organization of the army in which so many mounted men were split into small groups to act as couriers and escorts. He obviously did not think highly of the 20 men of the 1st Virginia Cavalry at his post, sent Major Tappen to report on their inefficiency, and asked for another 30 in a letter to the III Corps chief of staff.[54]

Fredericksburg and the Mud March

Sharpe developed into a fine leader, earning the respect and devotion of his men by his care for their welfare. He needed every bit of that good will in the months to come. During his detail to command the post at Centreville, he had left Lieutenant Colonel Westbrook as acting commander, which would be good practice for this very able officer. Late November found the regiment at camp at Falmouth on the north side of the Rappahannock, as Burnside prepared his attempt to cross the river and strike at Lee near Fredericksburg.

The 120th was set to work with the smaller 4th Maine, cutting wood and building corduroy roads for the army in the increasingly cold and wet early winter. The two regiments cut 300 wagon teams' worth of wood. Often their axes could be heard across the river by the Confederates as they worked through the night. The only ones excused from this arduous work did picket duty along the river.

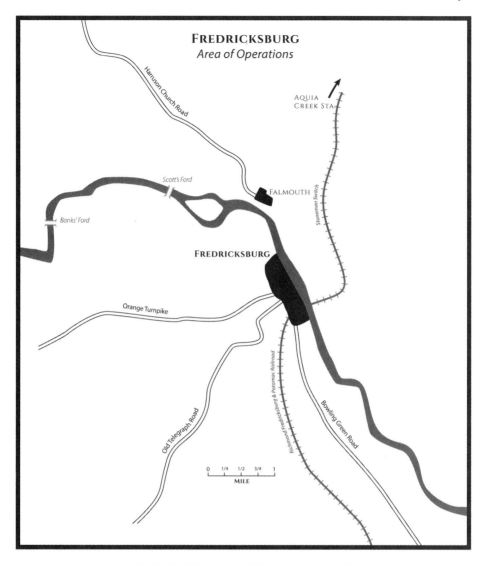

The Fredericksburg Area of Operations, 1862–63.

On the night of December 12 the brigade to which the regiment belonged was moved 5 miles downriver to bivouac in the woods, "for the purpose of deceiving the enemy, only a small portion being left in camp, which, however marched with the colors, under Colonel Westbrook, across the river." The next day, December 13, as the battle began, the brigade was posted with the rest of Sickles's Division in reserve on the heights overlooking Fredericksburg from the north side of the river. Sharpe and his men had a clear view of the battle and were horrified to watch Burnside throw the relentless, bloody assaults against Marye's Heights.

Sickles's Division began crossing the river about 3:00 p.m. Sharpe and Tappen brought over the "the full body of the regiment, which, although not exposed to rifle fire, behaved extremely well under the long range artillery fire to which it was exposed—the only casualty being in the detachment which had been taken over by Colonel Westbrook." Sharpe brought the regiment into the brigade in line of battle about 4:00 p.m., when a shell sailed over their heads to land directly behind them. Some began to cheer their first shot directed against them, but their cheers died suddenly as men realized that it was not wise to call attention to themselves. They were quickly acquiring field craft.

Shortly after dark, Sharpe was ordered to send skirmishers forward. He sent a company of 80 men, which reached a ditch parallel with the front, the dead and dying of that day's fighting strewn across the ground they passed over. Shape dispatched from there a lieutenant and 10 men to creep as close to the enemy as possible. They inched their way forward over the carnage to a position so close they could overhear the enemy's conversations. After midnight they crept back with only one wounded man.[55]

The next day the regiment stood under arms, though the firing was brisk between the lines of skirmishers. In his official report, Sharpe wrote, "On the night of the 14th, toward morning, the skirmishers were driven in by an advance, accompanied with rapid firing on the part of the enemy." Now was the supreme moment when the men of Kingston would feel the full shock of the onset of screeching Rebel fury. "The regiment immediately arose from where it was lying in line, and without noise or confusion prepared to receive any proposed attack." The moment had come, but it went as suddenly, as "our skirmisher soon, in their turn, drove back the enemy's skirmishers." A prudent man, Sharpe was taking no chances that another determined advance would strike his front, and "I directed a small squad from each company to remain on the alert during the night, and ordered the men again to lie down on their arms."[56]

The next day, the 15th, Sharpe's pickets mingled with their Confederate counterparts to exchange news and Yankee sugar and coffee for Johnnie hoecake and tobacco, the staple barter items of both armies. On the 16th the army trudged back across its pontoons and to its camps at Falmouth, where the men of the 120th began to shiver in their flimsy shelter-half tents in the increasingly bitter cold of December.[57]

Eager that his men be recognized for their role at Fredericksburg in December, even though it did not include severe combat, Sharpe stated in his after-action report:

> To most of the men of this regiment this was the first opportunity they had had of finding themselves in the presence of the enemy and under fire both of musketry and artillery, and I take the liberty of respectfully adding, for the approval of the colonel commanding, under whose eye we were during the whole time, that, although the operations of this command were

not of the most serious nature, the conduct of the officers and men under my command was marked with coolness and propriety in the discharge of their duties.[58]

Sickles added his praise: "This regiment … had not before been under fire, and I had great pleasure in observing the steadiness and spirit which characterized all movements." (For the full report see Appendix A.) Despite this lack of a heroic combat record, Sharpe's conduct as a commander had been such that he was offered the command of a brigade. Yet he was so attached to his men that he refused the command when he found out that the brigade would not include the 120th New York.[59]

Morale utterly collapsed in the army after Burnside had put the army on the road on January 20 for his move against Lee in a downpour, only to find the rains were turning the roads into mud soup in which the army stuck fast, advancing barely a mile and a half in one day in the sorry spectacle named "The Mud March" by the troops. A very soggy and unhappy army sloshed back into camp. Sharpe wrote his uncle:

> As you have no doubt heard ere this from the papers the army moved last Tuesday (after two postponements) to attack the enemy and cross the river. On Wednesday & Thursday the rain came down in torrents. Friday was spent in the attempts to get our artillery back. I saw often 16 horses endeavoring to move a single caisson without success. We built corduroy roads, and finally succeeded in withdrawing the trains out of danger."[60]

Major General Franklin expressed everyone's relief that the march had gone no further. "So I looked upon the rain which stopped his second attempt to cross the river as a Providential interference in our behalf." It was an observation also made by Sharpe, who wrote, "Had we crossed the river, and then had the storm come on, we must have been destitute of supplies, and perhaps would have sacrificed the greater part of the army in the retreat."[61] Even the self-sustained provost marshal of the Army of the Potomac, Brig. Gen. Marsena Patrick, was feeling the effects. He wrote in his diary:

> Have not been very busy today, excepting to give, or sign furloughs—The whole Army seems to be asking for them—I believe that, at last, a dozen officers, perhaps more, left here (Head Quarters) this morning—I have been trying to work, but there is a very oppressive feeling in Camp, among both Officers & men, which prevents work from being done.

Sharpe expressed the sentiment of the whole army once it had struggled back into camp. "I think we are now stationary—nothing but balloons can move us."[62]

The straggling during the "Mud March" had been severe, and Sharpe felt compelled to convene a regimental court-martial to deal with those who had flagrantly abused the opportunity to absent themselves. Despite the dreadful conditions, Sharpe believed that to overlook the straggling would set a bad example that would surely be abused on even a greater scale in the future under less provocation. Yet, he cautioned his company commanders not to go too far in pressing charges, directing them "to use care that no unnecessary or trivial charges be preferred, and for their purpose they are vested with discretion." It was a tactful way to make his point without laying an overly heavy hand on the regiment that would have been sure to be resented. By handling the problem in this way, he maintained both discipline and harmony.[63]

Sharpe found that the weather was putting many of his men in the hospital or the grave. The first three men died in the regimental hospital on December 21, including the commander of Company H, Captain Charles M. McEntee. The young officer had been highly thought of, and his death was directly attributable to his exemplary conduct on the field at Fredericksburg, as a committee of the regiment's officers affirmed:

> ... the late comrade met his death from exposure and fatigue, having lain upon the field, in the front rank of battle for forty hours, half of which time he was directing a line of skirmishers and repelling an advance of the enemy. And that when carried from the field, though evidently stricken with death, he was in full possession of his mental faculties. That throughout his term of service he had maintained the reputation of an ambitious, brave and efficient soldier, and of an honorable man.[64]

McEntee's death would have a deep impact upon Sharpe. He was the first man and first officer lost by the regiment due to battle, though two enlisted men would die later that day. Sharpe in his own way memorialized him long after the war by never failing to mention his loss, among others, at those veteran gatherings of the regiment where he was asked to speak. Acting for Sharpe, Lieutenant Colonel Westbrook requested permission for the dead officer's brother, Capt. John M. McEntee of the 20th NYSM, to take the body home to Rondout, near Kingston. The late captain's company formed an honor guard to escort his body to the railhead.[65]

Charles McEntee would not be the last to die in camp. One man wrote, "Much sickness prevails. Almost every day we heard the muffled drum, as one of our comrades was carried to the grave." Of the 900 men that left Kingston in August, only 400 were fit for duty on January 16. Westbrook wrote to the division commander on December 28 that the regimental surgeon had resigned eight days before; the previous week they had three men down with typhoid fever, and since they had had an average of 100 sick each day in a regimental hospital that could accommodate 22 at most. Most of the sick were suffering from bronchial infections, with some cases of dysentery and diarrhea. The surgeons ascribed the sick rate to the exposure of the battlefield at Fredericksburg followed by constant exposure thereafter with inadequate clothing and shelter. Sharpe ordered the building of log cabins, "made tight and comfortable by the craft of the soldier workmen," as early as January 9 to get his men out of the cold. But such a project required the army to stay in winter quarters. Burnside's plans for another grand maneuver against Lee pulled the army out of its semi-finished new quarters and sent them into the cold and mud.[66]

It was no wonder then that Sharpe tried to have his regiment transferred to the provost guard. The 20th NYSM already had been transferred on January 7. Patrick had explained that "he wants troops he can depend on." And he had the most confidence in New York troops. On February 6, Gates of the 20th NYSM visited Sharpe at the house he had rented in Washington at the corner of Pennsylvania Avenue and 20th Street. Sharpe had brought his wife and children to Washington to be closer to him. At the meeting Sharpe proposed to Colonel Gates that their regiments, now depleted, be consolidated, something Gates was clearly not going to endorse. Obviously, Sharpe's frustration was intense. Between Burnside and the mud and sickness of Falmouth, the future looked bleak.[67]

CHAPTER TWO

Joe Hooker: The Transformational Man

Burnside's manifest ineptitude for army command deepened, if possible, after his stinging defeat at Fredericksburg. He had long since lost the confidence of his generals, and one in particular, Maj. Gen. Joseph Hooker, was shamelessly out for his job. On January 26, 1863, a desperate Lincoln gave it to him. Lincoln had some hope amid many reservations in this appointment. Hooker had fought with distinction in every battle, earning command of a corps, which if it had been supported properly by McClellan at Antietam, may have turned the drawn battle of Antietam into a crushing defeat for Lee.

If Burnside had been scorned for his lack of ability, Hooker would earn as much scorn for another reason. History would be unkind to him. Even his epithet, "Fighting Joe," has become an object of derision for his coming defeat at Chancellorsville. He is remembered as the bombastic conspirator, the profoundly "unsubordinate" (in Grant's wording) man, the dictator in waiting, the womanizer whose tent "was a place to which no self-respecting man liked to go, and no decent woman could go. It was a combination of bar room and brothel."[1] The army headquarters became so notorious for its feminine company that the red light district in Washington became known as "Hooker's Division." But, for all that, he knew how to rouse and organize an army for battle.

He immediately granted large numbers of morale-building furloughs and initiated a series of organizational reforms that would carry the army through to the end of the war. One of the more colorful and morale-boosting was the introduction of unit cap patches for the first time at army level. Major General Phillip Kearny, killed at Second Bull Run, had originated the concept in his own command. Major General Darius Couch, designated his second-in-command, exclaimed, "I have never known men to change from a condition of lowest depression to that of a healthy fighting state in so short a time."[2]

Hooker's greatest triumph was to institutionalize and professionalize the intelligence operation of the army. Joe Hooker was the godfather of modern American military intelligence. Although he faded from center stage after Chancellorsville, the military intelligence structure he created soldiered on to tip the scales of victory in the Union's favor at the decisive battle of Gettysburg that followed days after his relief. That structure went on to play a vital role in the subsequent victory of the Army of the Potomac.

The year 1862 found him commanding a division under George B. McClellan but operating in Maryland in what was almost an independent command. He quickly found himself frustrated and wrote, "[I]t has been necessary to form an opinion [of enemy positions and strength] almost wholly from their camp fires, for, strange to say, I have not … fallen in with any one able or willing to enlighten me on this subject."[3] This was the normal state of affairs. Each war was the occasion to recreate the function anew—at great cost. The U.S. Army would not create a standardized S2/G2 structure until World War II and a permanent military intelligence corps until 1962.[4]

Hooker Finds his Horse Marines

Hooker quickly set about to fill that void. Initially, he had relied solely on his pickets to count the number of camps from which bugles could be heard, on the basis that each bugle that sounded reveille or tattoo indicated a regiment. Unfortunately, that put him at the mercy of the shifting wind.[5] The air, however, offered him another source in the form of Professor Thaddeus Lowe's controversial observation balloons of the Balloon Corps. Despite initial misgivings, he began making ascents himself and became an enthusiastic supporter.[6]

Hooker also eagerly availed himself of the services of the special provost marshal of the War Department, Lafayette Baker, who took a detachment from the 3rd Indiana Cavalry and rounded up a spy ring. The 3rd Indiana had been good students and took to the counterintelligence and scouting roles naturally. They were soon known as "Hooker's Horse Marines" after their capture of a Rebel trading sloop.

Hooker also saw that Confederate deserters and officers' black servants were carefully questioned and that spies in Confederate territory opposite his command were recruited and exploited. His reporting was restrained and even conservative and his reports showed a strong confidence in his conclusions. It should have. Hooker was operating a budding all-source intelligence operation where all the information gathered by scouts, spies, Balloon Corps, Signal Corps, and pickets was all coming to one place to be evaluated, checked, and corroborated.[7]

McClellan's Multiplication Problem

This was a remarkable development given that the intelligence operation (referred to as the Secret Service) of his commander, Major General George B. McClellan, was not up to the same standard. McClellan had placed his intelligence requirements in the hands of Alan Pinkerton, the famous detective. Pinkerton excelled in counterintelligence but was weak in "positive intelligence" or that which is actively acquired, the very means that Hooker was developing. He also passed on raw or unevaluated intelligence.

Pinkerton has received most of the blame for the scandalous failure of McClellan's intelligence operation—the consistent compulsion to see the enemy as outnumbering his own forces by a factor of at least three or four to one. But the fault was profoundly McClellan's.[8] "Little Mac," as he was called, was a walking contradiction. On the one hand he acted and talked like a great commander and was indeed a great organizer. On the other hand, he had deep-seated fears of actually risking combat. He would invariably flinch in a crisis. Overestimating enemy strength was his unconscious mechanism for always putting off battle. He was never strong enough, so he would argue, to meet the enemy on reasonable terms.[9]

Modern analysis indicates that he was suffering from severe paranoid personality disorder with narcissistic tendencies, in which he "formed initial or preconceived expectations and clung to them rigidly, obscuring all information that contradicted the original assessments. He grossly exaggerated the strength of obstacles, took extreme precautions, and in failure blamed everyone except himself."[10]

Pinkerton himself consistently overestimated Confederate strength in Virginia by a factor of two to one. But McClellan would never show even these figures to his superiors and substituted his own, for which no source is known. McClellan's figures, which he did not share with Pinkerton, doubled the detective's already inflated numbers. The fighting men under McClellan's command would be supported, not by solid intelligence of the enemy, but by multiplied fantasy.

The ambiguity surrounding the meaning of the word "intelligence" during the Civil War era perhaps added to the confusion:

> Like the name "secret service," in the mid-19th century the terms information and intelligence were also imprecise. In the modern definition, *information* is defined as raw, undigested bits of news not yet analyzed, which is compared with other evidence, and evaluated for its importance. *Intelligence* is the end product of the evaluation, corroboration, and interpretation of information. In the Civil War, however, military and political leaders used both terms synonymously. When someone claimed to have received *intelligence*, they most likely referred to unprocessed *information* that had yet to be examined.[11]

George Washington had been the first to consciously make the distinction between information and intelligence in the modern sense, but after the Revolution his innovation died out of American English usage. Washington had been his own chief intelligence officer and was the last great general to be able to master the creation of all-source intelligence by himself, with the possible exception of Robert E. Lee; undoubtedly, Washington's intense and successful management of intelligence had focused his thoughts on the necessity of using the two distinct words with the precision of professional terms of art, rather than the generally synonymous terms in use.[12]

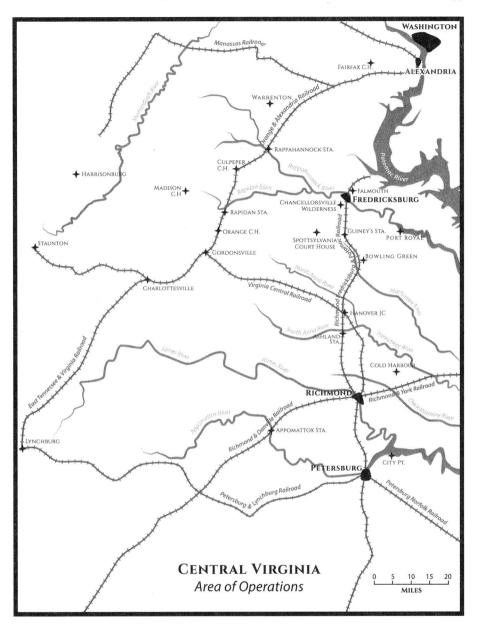

CENTRAL VIRGINIA
Area of Operations

0   5   10   15   20
MILES

The Central Virginia Area of Operations, 1862–65.

Starting from Scratch

Hooker had to start almost from scratch. McClellan and Pinkerton had made off with all the files of the Secret Service to write their final reports. Hooker's new chief of staff, Major General Daniel Butterfield, would later testify that "When General Hooker took command of the army there was not a record or document of any kind... that gave any information at all in regard to the enemy. There was no means, no organization, and no apparent effort to obtain such information. And we were almost as ignorant of the enemy in our immediate front as if they had been in China."[13]

Hooker realized that the Union forces operating in Virginia were at the disadvantage of operating amidst a hostile population, one that gave its full support to the enemy. He was determined to right that imbalance by applying energy, system, and talent to the production of intelligence. Three men at the headquarters would help Hooker get started.

Three Helpful Men

Butterfield

The first was Hooker's new 31-year-old chief of staff, Maj. Gen. Daniel Butterfield, a graduate of Union College and a scion of the American Express fortune. He commanded a New York militia regiment when the war started. Because the regiment could not be mustered fast enough, he asked the War Department for any position available and was made drill sergeant. His regiment arrived soon thereafter, allowing him to resume command. He did not hold it long before he was promoted to command a brigade and then to brigadier general. He was a talented, energetic, and brave man and won the Medal of Honor for action at Gaine's Mill during the 1862 Peninsular Campaign and also wrote the army manual "Camp and Outpost Duty for Infantry." While there he was credited with composing the bugle call "Taps," which was quickly adopted by both Union and Confederate armies. At Antietam he commanded a division and V Corps at Fredericksburg.

He was Hooker's second choice for chief of staff but a fortuitous one. They made an odd pair, with the slight Butterfield barely coming up to the stocky Hooker's shoulder. But the two developed a close personal and political relationship no doubt made more congenial by the fact that Butterfield shared Hooker's other tastes that made the army headquarters a scandal.

Nevertheless, the two worked well in successfully reorganizing the Army of the Potomac, and the concept of unit patches was Butterfield's. "The badge Idea was an old favorite of Butterfield's. He had urged it on McClellan without success," though the late Maj. Gen. Phillip Kearny had on his own designed and issued such patches to his division. Butterfield regularized them for the entire army and designed them himself. Butterfield proved to be a near genius as an administrator and a highly effective chief of staff, fully attuned to Hooker's interest in military intelligence.[14]

Marsena Rudolf Patrick

The next was provost marshal, Brig. Gen. Marsena R. Patrick, who "combined the qualities of a regular army disciplinarian with those of an Old Testament Prophet." His men agreed that he looked as if "He could bite the head off a ten-penny nail." Patrick was West Point, class of 1835, had seen service in the Mexican War, and had served for 15 years before resigning and becoming a college president. He also had a great interest in scientific farming. He was appointed Inspector General of the State of New York in May 1861, and in March 1862 was commissioned brigadier general of volunteers. He commanded brigades at Second Bull Run, Chantilly, and Antietam. In October Burnside appointed him provost marshal general of the Army of the Potomac. Under his command was the provost marshal guard, a brigade-sized unit of several regiments. Few jobs in the army gave such an opportunity for corruption as that of the provost marshal, yet he was a man of unimpeachable integrity. Memories of him by those who knew him reflected "industry, honesty, courage, and piety," yet there was not a hint of "cordiality or affability" that brings to life other personalities of the time. He was a difficult man to work with. Yet, "[h]is sympathy for the innocent victims of the war was proverbial."

> He was convinced that good order in the Army would go far toward returning Virginia to its former loyalty. In his frequent sermons to his assembled troops, as well as to the endless line of terrified soldiers who were hauled before him for individual offenses, Patrick sought to impress upon them that, but for the grace of God, the people they were robbing and plundering might be their own fathers, mothers, or sisters. This conservative and more civilized view of a proper occupation policy became a casualty of the Civil War but there were many, like General Patrick, who sought to maintain it as long as possible.[15]

In April 1862 the men of Sharpe's old 20th NYSM were amused to notice a slender, bald-headed, full-whiskered man sporting a Mexican poncho strolling through their camp on foot. The next day they were much surprised to see that same man arrive in the uniform of a brigadier general mounted on a magnificent horse, trailing his staff officers to take command of their brigade. They soon discovered that he was not out to make friends; he was out to make soldiers. Colonel Gates, commanding the 20th NYSM, penned the following character sketch:[16]

> He was a thorough soldier, and he exercised the authority of his grade with the inflexible severity of an old army officer, whose education and habits of life, for fifty years, had made him a thorough disciplinarian and a stickler for every point of military etiquette and army regulations, in so far as they were deemed conducive to the well-being and efficiency of the troops under his command. He was by no means a martinet, but he believed the regulations of the army were wise rules for the government of troops, and that their enforcement was necessary for the preservation of that gradation of authority and that maintenance of discipline, without which an army becomes a mob. He was quick to detect, and stern in the punishment of any willful [sic]

breach of these regulations, and officers and men were not affectionately disposed toward him. He did not care—or, at least, did not appear to care. Yet, when I came to know the General better, I believed that during all the weeks of his early command of the brigade, when his hand seemed to be really against us all, he was longing in his heart for the sympathy, respect and love of his officers and men. Well, if he was, he consoled himself with the well-grounded faith that these sentiments would grow up in the course of time, and he did not have long to wait.

The benefit of General Patrick's thorough system with his command was appreciated by all, when the real business of war came to demand the exercise of those qualities which make men soldiers, and inspire them with a consciousness of the strength the organization gives them., either for offense or defense ... As we more and more appreciated these facts, we more and more appreciated our Brigade-commander, and at length, there was probably no general officer in the army who was held in higher esteem by the officers and men under his command than General Patrick was by his brigade—and as for the Twentieth, it idolized the General, and I believe he had a very good opinion of it.[17]

For his part, Patrick fully reciprocated that affection and trust, as the 20th came to hold a special place in his estimation. After the war he would write, "As Provost-Marshal-General of the Army of the Potomac, from the battle of Antietam, it was absolutely indispensable that I should have troops around me on whom I could rely." On January 7, 1863, at his request his old brigade was assigned as provost guard. Less than six months later, only the 20th remained; the enlistments of the other regiments had expired, and they had been mustered out. The 20th would remain with him for the rest of the war, and its conduct filled him with pride. "Although the Provost troops were not, on ordinary occasions, in line of battle, yet, in every time of peril, from Gettysburg to Petersburg, the hasty call on me was, "'Put in your Twentieth ...'" Despite all the other regiments that passed through the provost guard, "the rank and file of the Twentieth seemed to share with their officers the feeling, that somehow, they were the legitimate and special custodian of the reputation of the Provost-Marshal-General's Department, and the honor of its chief." For Patrick this regiment became "almost a member of my military family, and the welfare of its members became a matter of deep personal interest."[18]

The two wet, cold, and dreary winter months after Fredericksburg were difficult for everyone, especially the provost marshal general, who had by this time lost all confidence in the army commander, a feeling shared by the entire army. Patrick was doing his best to fill the intelligence role the army so desperately needed, but it was almost impossible to work with Burnside. "Was with Burnside some hours about Guides & that class of men, looking over the maps & giving that kind of information... Burnside is rather obtuse in his conceptions & very forgetful."

Patrick was trying to provide intelligence to support Burnside's plans for a move against Lee, by gathering information about the country to be crossed. He was using guides attached to the army, but wrote in his diary, "Have had more work on hand ... than I could carry." He was clearly being overwhelmed by the effort to collect intelligence to support an operation on top of his normal already onerous provost marshal duties. To ruin his whole frame of mind, deserters were telling him that Burnside's plan was well known to their side and that they had made full preparations.[19]

John C. Babcock

The third man to help Hooker was the only remaining civilian employee of Pinkerton's operation, the 27-year-old civilian John C. Babcock. Born in Rhode Island in 1836, life had taken him to Chicago, where he had started a successful career as an architect and draughtsman. The handsome and trim, 5-foot 10-inch, brown-haired and brown-eyed Babcock cut a dapper and well-dressed figure. As a civilian employee or contractor with the army, he was not limited to uniforms. Unusually for that age he had tattooed on his right arm his initials "JB" and on his left arm a five-pointed star. Happily, this idiosyncratic young man was a round peg in a round hole. He possessed a precise and organized mind and the experience that would make him as perfect an intelligence analyst as ever served the United States Army.[20]

He had joined the army as a private in the Sturgis Rifle Corps in 1861, and like so many other young men off to war, married his sweetheart, Mary Ann McCabe, a few days after enlisting. The Sturgis Rifles were attached to McClellan's headquarters for "special service" with the commander-in-chief. Babcock quickly realized it was not all glamour, as the company was in charge of the Central Guard House, a useful but unedifying experience. "No one can describe such scenes of misery cruelty and degradation that it has been my lot to witness." Far more edifying was the guard duty at "Prison Greenhough," the name of the facility in which the famous Confederate spy, Rose Greenhough, and about 30 other ladies from Virginia were held for "possessing secession proclivities of too strong a nature, for the welfare or interest of our government."[21]

Before long he found the proverbial soft billet for a soldier, one that an alert and well-educated man with his wits about him can land. He was made assistant to the officer in charge of the "Pass Department" at the headquarters of the provost marshal general of the army (Maj. Gen. John Porter), describing it as "secret and detached service. We are relieved from ordinary military duties having all the liberties and privileges of a civilian with an extra salary enabling us to live independent of our company." At that time, Brigadier General Burnside was helping him with his application for a commission in the Army Corp of Engineers, though West Point's legal stranglehold on commissions in that branch eventually defeated the effort. He had worked for Burnside before the war as an architect, and the two remained on friendly terms. Even the cushiest billets come to an end, as his did on 1 March 1862, when he was transferred to, as he recorded in a summary of his wartime service, "special duty with Maj. E. J. Allen (Allen Pinkerton), taking the field with the Secret Service Dept. at the Genl Hd Qrs of the Army of the Potomac under Maj. Gen. Geo. B. McClellan." His assignment with the famous Allen Pinkerton was to be the critical experience of his life.[22]

Babcock's brains and diligence in the pass office and the fact that he was a highly skilled architect and draughtsman had come to the attention of Pinkerton, who was on the prowl for military talent. He was detailed by Porter as the lone soldier in the role of "topographical engineer," to Pinkerton's otherwise all civilian organization at McClellan's headquarters just in time for the Peninsular Campaign of 1862. His precision skills as architect and draughtsman must have recommended him, because McClellan's topographical engineers were short-handed. Just before he left for Fortress Monroe, he had been offered a lieutenant's commission in Berdan's Regiment of sharpshooters but had declined, thinking that this would not lead to a career in the regular army. His duties in the field consisted of "sketching and delineations of maps and fortifications belonging to the enemy to be obtained from descriptions of returned spies—prisoners—or any other source of information, perhaps for ought I know." His innovative methods produced maps of such quality that they were clearly superior to those of the army's topographical engineers or anything produced by Pinkerton's staff. Refusing to rely on secondhand information, he personally scouted out the terrain to be mapped on his horse Gimlet or ascending in one of Professor Lowe's balloons, often coming under fire. He became close friends with Pinkerton's son, William, an association that would remain until his death. Another friend of his at this time was a Mathew Brady employee, Alexander Gardner, hired to take photographs for Pinkerton. Gardner's photographs and publication of Babcock's exploits in the well-known *Photographic History* made him the most famous Union scout in the Civil War. It was clearly worth the effort. It was an exhilarating time for Babcock. He wrote his aunt:

> There is probably nothing for which I am in every way so well qualified to perform, as the duties that have devolved upon me during my connection with the Secret Service. I have not only found ample chances to display my qualifications as an engineer and draughtsman, but on more than one occasion my gymnastic education had also been displayed. I knew as little as you did at the time I entered the S. S. the nature of the duties I should be called upon to perform only that they were dangerous and trustworthy. It was like taking a "leap in the dark" and knowing I had oft times to run the gauntlet between a bullet and a halter, I had more fear of my incompetency in the trust, than I entertained for the rebellious sons of the South.[23]

Babcock's reputation in the press was mirrored in the army as well by the numerous senior officers who found his work to be outstanding, in sharp contrast to the expensive and inferior work of the regular army's topographical engineers, who relied on too many secondary sources. Babcock's firsthand and up-front collection methods gave an accuracy and detail that were much in demand. His method was to conduct a detailed reconnaissance of small parts of the front one at time and piece the drawings into larger sections of the front or of the whole front. He also incorporated into his work a published map of Richmond and its environs. His maps were copied photographically at great expense and distributed down at least as far as brigade commanders. McClellan did not, as Babcock related, stint his praise and "pronounced it as the finest piece of topographical work he has ever seen, and a remarkable work in consideration of the time and place in which it was made. He gave me his special regards for it and says it is invaluable to him, as his engineers have proved to be very unsatisfactory in their profession."

It is no wonder that he was to add, "I have made many friends among the officers in the Army here, and some enemies." In his enthusiasm he no doubt did little to avoid stepping on toes. Those enemies, as to be expected, were among the topographical engineers, to include their chief, Col. Andrew A. Humphreys. It was no little professional affront to be shown up by a 26-year-old enlisted man working on his own, especially when their efforts cost the government $3,000 a day and whose maps' valued cost of $30,000 proved worthless in comparison. It was an animosity that would come back to haunt Babcock.[24]

Apparently, both McClellan and Pinkerton sent Lincoln copies of Babcock's overall map. Pinkerton took credit for the map, showing Babcock as an assistant on the project. This did not affect Babcock's respect for Pinkerton which endured until he died. He understood that the boss gets the credit, but he also understood that "nothing of this kind has ever before appeared, the production was so unexpected for the author to be mistaken."[25]

Babcock had been one of many to fall upon the spell of McClellan's charismatic leadership, especially as McClellan appeared to take a personal interest in his prize mapmaker and did not stint the praise. McClellan's relief after the failure of the Peninsular Campaign would not have pleased him, but the general's return to command in time to counter Lee's invasion of Maryland put Babcock back in the saddle, as he recounted years later to William Pinkerton: "my South Mountain night ride before Antieman with dispatches to Franklin was extra dangerous, and was highly commended by McClellan and your father."[26] On November 5 a fully exasperated Lincoln relieved McClellan for the failure to exploit his victory at Antietam in the succeeding seven weeks. Babcock had spent his time since Antietam preparing a map of the battle for McClellan's formal report. With his relief, the project was indefinitely postponed. Babcock thought highly of McClellan and took his relief badly, to the point of defiantly accompanying "the general to Washington without permission for which I was ordered back to the ranks. Not long did I have to bear this galling treatment, for thanks to Gen McClellan, who soon put me beyond the power of military law, by discharging the whole company from the service, to which I was attached to the service, so the Sturgis Rifles, 'McClellans [sic] Body Guard,' are no more."

Pinkerton, who was McClellan's employee, also resigned. Two other officers who had worked in the Secret Service were arrested in Washington but were released and reassigned. There was almost a clean sweep of anyone with experience in intelligence on the staff of the Army of the Potomac. With the Secret Service in ruins, Babcock was preparing to return to Chicago, when he received a request from Burnside to prepare a report on the condition of the Secret Service Department. Because of his past friendly relations with Burnside, he furnished the report "per gratis" and was surprised by an offer from Burnside, "to take the place of Maj Allen, as Chief of S. S. Army of the Potomac." He accepted conditionally, knowing that Burnside was anxious to reconstitute the Secret Service. He asked to be hired as a civilian employee of the Army of the Potomac, with a monthly salary of $250 and official expenses. Burnside accepted eagerly. Babcock may not have been so eager to clean up the mess. "I am now a free man, though of as much importance in this bailiwick as though I had all the birds and stars in the heavens on my shoulders. My military ambition has settled into my pocket, for the present at least, until a new order of things is brought about."[27]

Babcock was retained at the army headquarters as a "confidential agent" reporting directly to Burnside. He found that, in addition to the departure of almost everyone with intelligence experience, there were no records to be found. McClellan and Pinkerton had cleaned out the files; Pinkerton was to write his final report to McClellan, and McClellan to write his final report to the chief of staff of the army. Babcock was quickly disappointed:

> I thought he [Burnside] would have made it very pleasant for me, for … I was his architect in Chicago, and all was going well when one day the chief of staff made some remarks concerning your father, which I foolishly resented, to my regret, for I could not afford to speak my mind from my humble position, so I had to suffer for it …[28]

Babcock could do little, and Burnside was not the man to sort out problems. He did place him under the supervision of Provost Marshal Patrick, but no use was made of him, as Patrick and even Burnside himself continued to interrogate prisoners. Babcock prepared a memorandum for Burnside on what the intelligence operation of the army should be, but it made no impression.

Babcock's greatest contribution in this fallow period of Burnside's command was to attempt to recreate Pinkerton's missing order-of-battle records by finding the copies of reports sent to Washington. He was not encouraged by either the new commander or his staff. "I have nothing to say disparaging Gen Burnside for I like him as a friend and a gentleman, too well. But I do say, and he will say so himself, that Gen. Geo B. McClellan is his superior in military ability. As to Genl Burnsides [sic] staff, with a few exceptions, they are worthless and inefficient for their positions."[29]

One of the projects he undertook at this time was to recreate the order-of-battle of Lee's army previous to the battle of Antietam, using, no doubt, the intelligence reports he had collected from the War Department. Unfortunately, there had been none of the rigorous analysis that transforms raw information into military intelligence, much of which would have come from direct interrogation of prisoners of war and deserters, which was no longer available. From that raw information he concluded that Lee's army had numbered over 97,175 men at the battle.[30] The missing analysis would have told him that Lee's strength was closer to the 51,844 he had actually engaged. Given this gross error of over 40 percent, one can understand how it and similar reporting so encouraged McClellan to take counsel of his fears.

It All Comes Together

After Hooker assumed command on January 25, 1863, his new chief of staff, Dan Butterfield, "requested a report from Babcock on the methods and activity" of the Secret Service and any recommendations he might have "for its continuance." On February 4 Babcock wrote Hooker, describing the duties of the Secret Service Department. They were approved, especially his recommendation that "the service should be conducted by commissioned officers, of fitness … particularly in the examination of prisoners of war, deserters, etc."[31] At the time, no one appreciated that history would pivot on this report.

Hooker's choice of officers was a delicate one. In the words of a backward-looking eulogy to Sharpe, he already appreciated what was required:

> to get information it was necessary to get all kinds of men: smart men, men who could act their parts, men of constant resource and fidelity. The first requirement of the work was to be a good judge of men, a man who knew human nature, and knowing it, had the capacity to sympathize with all its faults, ambitions, desires, and excellences. He had to have a man of the most approved fidelity—proof against the allurements of power and money. He needed a man who could take up the fag ends of the Pinkerton outfit and with additions create an organization.[32]

Babcock's report was just what Hooker was looking for, and he acted quickly. The next day he ordered Patrick to "organize and perfect a system for collecting information as speedily as possible… All deserters, contraband, prisoners &c" would be sent to this new department. It was a job easier said than done. Patrick was not happy about the assignment based on his experience with Pinkerton and wrote, "I am trying to make up a system of Secret Service, but find it hard to organize where there is so little good material—It seems probable that I shall take a few men into my employ at once—Several have offered, but as yet none have been employed—I do not fancy the class of men & think they do not fancy me."[33] He would come to change his mind.

Five days after he had penned these depressing lines, he had found the right man when he interviewed Sharpe for the job. Certainly, Patrick already knew Sharpe from a web of connections in what was a comparatively very small group of senior New York officers in the army. Sharpe's attempt to get his regiment assigned to the provost guard certainly would have brought him to the attention of Patrick. He probably already knew Patrick from their service in the same division, when the latter had commanded a brigade there. Further tying Sharpe to Patrick was the bond of respect and affection that had developed between the 20th NYSM and Patrick. Sharpe and Patrick may well have met through the regiment's commander, Col. Theodore B.

Gates. In any case, it was highly likely that Patrick already knew Sharpe. Patrick, Gates, and Sharpe were all New York men as well, a cliquish bond in an era when state allegiance was so important.[34] Sharpe and Gates remained close, frequently dining with each other or seeking each other's hospitality. Sharpe would be important enough to Gates to record every meeting with him for the next two years.[35]

Sharpe's service at Fredericksburg also brought him to the attention of his corps commander—Hooker. Sickles was a close friend of Hooker as well. Sickles had not stinted his praise of Sharpe.

A biographer of Sharpe and a family relation, G. B. D. Hasbrouck, had another account of how Sharpe came to Hooker's attention. Hooker was impressed with Sharpe's timely and useful command of French on the battlefield. A New York regiment of French immigrants, whose knowledge of English in an emergency left something to be desired, was being mishandled by its English-only-speaking commander, and milled in confusion, threatening to make a break in the line of battle. Sharpe intervened to issue the commands in fluent parade-ground French, which sent the regiment promptly into the line.

When Hooker took command, he asked to learn the name of the officer that had put the French-speaking regiment into its proper place in the line. Finding it was Sharpe, he ordered the colonel to his headquarters for an interview. He asked Sharpe if he had indeed been the officer who helped the regiment; when he replied that he was, Hooker further asked how rapidly he could translate French. Sharpe told him he could translate it as fast as he could read it. Hooker had been interested in translating a French book on the organization of a secret service and asked Sharpe to do it as soon as possible. Sharpe quickly delivered the translation and requested to return to his own regiment. Instead, Hooker asked him to prepare a plan for the organization and operation of a secret service to obtain information from the enemy. Hooker was evidently impressed enough to send him to Patrick and Butterfield for further interviews.[36]

Hooker, Sickles (who succeeded to command of Hooker's III Corps), and Butterfield, all of whom were the epitome of what was known as the "political general," were probably well aware of Sharpe's political connections in New York. Networking was as powerful a factor then as today. Although Patrick and Butterfield had interviewed Sharpe on February 10, Hooker had probably already selected him and wanted his senior staff to vet him and be comfortable with his unspoken choice. It showed the deft hand Hooker was playing in restoring the morale and confidence of the army. A week earlier, on February 3, Sharpe had written his uncle, "I am very much hurried & have only time to say confidentially that you may not be surprised to see me announced on Genl Hooker's Staff. I have the offer, if I choose to accept it."[37]

The gruff old provost marshal, who was anything but a political general, saw his apprehension melt away in the interview. "I have made some arrangements about secret service Department—Have had a long conversation with Col. Sharp[e] of the

120' N. Y. as to the organization of the Dept. with him, a Lawyer, for its chief—He appears well, & I think he would be a pleasant man to be Associated with..."[38]

Butterfield also interviewed him, and both Patrick and he claimed credit for his appointment. But it was, after all, Hooker's doing, for he was to put it plainly when later testifying to Congress, "I called Colonel Sharpe, commanding a regiment of New York troops, to headquarters, and put him in charge of that bureau as a separate and special bureau."[39]

Despite reservations about leaving his regiment, Sharpe, who was evidently intrigued by the possibilities, accepted the appointment the next day, on February 11. He spent his last day in command of the 120th in a flurry of paperwork, taking care of the men with promotions and transfers within the regiment. His last order promoted Pvt. Eugene F. Hayes "to Commissary Sergeant to fill the vacancy occasioned by the promotion of Wm. J. Cockburn to 2nd Lieutenant."[40]

At this point there is a question begging to be asked, as the author of the "Eloquent Tribute to General Sharpe" penned over a hundred years ago. He said that it was "no wonder" that Hooker picked Sharpe for the job. "The wonder is that Sharpe accepted it. For he knew when he undertook the hidden, secret dangerous work required that he was forsaking the paths of glory. He knew no opportunity would come to him to lead his regiment in the field and to place his humble name conspicuously upon Fame's Military roster."[41]

The why remains speculative. Sharpe left us no reasons, but he was a very ambitious man in an age defined by personal ambition. Yet, most men would have sought, "the bubble of reputation in the cannon's mouth." Sharpe commanded as fine a regiment as any in the armies of the United States. They would have carried his name far. He had seen action at Fredericksburg, though he was not in the thick of the fighting against Jackson but behaved coolly and with presence, vital attributes in a combat commander. No one was ever to accuse him of cowardice and some were to praise his gallantry in other battles, especially in the catastrophe of Chancellorsville.

The work Hooker proposed surely would have fascinated a man of his keen, cosmopolitan intellect and experience. Perhaps reading the book on secret service had intrigued his Francophile nature and triggered the instinctive realization that he was meant to play this role. He could only have reached this conclusion because he knew himself. Yet, there had to be more than confidence in himself. Sharpe knew people referred to previously, and he knew he had talent to instill confidence, to ingratiate himself, to set others at ease, and to establish empathy. These were all the qualities of a master interrogator. They were also highly useful qualities in establishing his working relationship with his superiors.

Ambition, in another form, may well have played a role in his decision. As commander of a regiment, he was competing against more than a hundred other such men in the Army of the Potomac for that "bubble of reputation." On the staff, he would constantly be at the elbow of the army commander in the center of things, playing a unique and dramatic role. He would stand next to Hooker on his warlord's hill (*Feldhernnhügel*), surveying great events. To be at the right hand of the man who crushed the rebellion would surely open the doors of political ambition.

He and his horse Babe—inseparable by now—moved immediately to the provost marshal general's staff at army headquarters. His orders followed on February 19, stating that he was "temporarily attached to these Head Quarters in The Department of the Provost Marshal General." The orders gave the usual boiler plate regarding an officer assigned to that department. "Commanding officers in the Army, and officers of Pickets and Outposts attached thereto are directed and Officials in the Civil Departments of the Government are requested to furnish Colonel Sharpe with proper aid and facilities in the performance of his duties." On March 30 he received further orders appointing him as deputy provost marshal general. Interestingly, the next appointment listed was that of Capt. Ulric Dahlgren as aide-de-camp to the commanding general, an association with Sharpe that would later bear much fruit and ultimate tragedy. It would be an important day for the future of the Army of the Potomac and a milestone in the history of the U.S. Army itself.[42]

Whoever was responsible had made an inspired choice. Sharpe brought an active and sophisticated intellect and an excellent lawyer's analytical mind to the job, as well as strong executive ability, strength of character, and a good knowledge of human nature and soldiering. His designation as deputy provost marshal general to Patrick was an administrative convenience to cover the U.S. Army's lack of a formal intelligence organization. It was also the most logical place on the staff, since it would give him access to the prisoners under the control of the provost guard as well the army's security force. Today Sharpe would be designated an army G2, the senior military intelligence staff officer, but that designation would have to wait for reforms of Secretary of War Elihu Root almost 40 years later. Although he would fill in for Patrick in his absence, as the head of the intelligence effort, he reported directly to Hooker. He was supervised on a daily basis by Butterfield, the proper role of a chief of staff. Butterfield realized the importance to Hooker of Sharpe's new mission and positively integrated its efforts into the overall functioning of the army's staff.

Sharpe's position on the staff was an anomaly. He held his rank solely as commander of the 120th New York. There was no question of his resigning his commission to accept a civilian appointment as had Pinkerton or Babcock. Therefore, he remained the official commander of the regiment while the lieutenant colonel actually commanded it for the rest of the war. Although his command remained official only, he never lost interest in the welfare of its men, and, in fact, watched over them like a mother hen from his position on the staff. His concern was extraordinary by any measure.

He never relinquished his fatherly interest in it, he continued to be consulted often about its problems, and he even operated an unofficial system of pay allotment for it. After each payday the men brought him much or all of their money; Sharpe deposited it in the Riggs Bank in Washington and then wrote a check on his account there and sent it to his uncle Jansen [Hasbrouck], president of one of the Ulster County banks. The soldiers' families then drew on these credits. A single check amounted to $5,000 or $6,000…[43]

For example, on January 27th, two weeks before transferring to Hooker's staff, he requested a leave of 48 hours. "The men have deposited in my hands a fraction of their pay amounting in the aggregate to ten thousand Dollars for which I have given my check on the Bank of Rondout. I desire to visit Washington to forward the same to my credit at said bank. A field officer would be left with my regiment." Sharpe's fatherly attention extended to giving loans out of his own pockets to men who had been absent on payday. Sharpe's Uncle Jansen was equally generous, giving the families free credit when his nephew did not have enough funds in the bank to immediately cover their payments. Sharpe's transfer to the staff was "much to the regret of the regiment," according to the 120th's regimental historian, Cornelius Van Santvoord, the regimental chaplain. He continued running an allotment system even after being transferred to the army staff and kept a keen eye on the 120th NY, of which he was still the official commander.[44]

After his own detail to Hooker's staff, Lieutenant Colonel Westbrook had been in turn detailed to lengthy engineering duties. That left Major Tappen in acting command. Sharpe could not have been more pleased with the result. In 1875 Sharpe would address this period in the regiment's history in a memoriam to Tappen:

> Major Tappen, while in command, rendered most effective service in the drill of the regiment. In fact it received very much at this time the impress of his character, as Colonel Westbrook, himself an admirable tactical officer, would readily admit. Throughout the winter he also acquired the esteem and attachment of the men by the particular care he exercised to see that their rations were fully secured and properly treated by the company messes.[45]

Patrick, for his part, fully supported Sharpe in any way that he could. He would come to have mixed feelings about Sharpe because he did not fit into his own strait-laced ideas of rectitude. Brigadier General Thomas Francis Meagher of the Irish Brigade invited the staff to a St. Patrick's Day celebration at his headquarters, which naturally turned into a party where the punch flowed with Gaelic enthusiasm. Patrick found it "no place for me—so I came home" and noted later that Sharpe and another officer "remained & came home at dusk, tight as bricks."[46]

A devoted family man, Sharpe moved his wife and children to Washington during the war to be near them. We see Mrs. Sharpe as a frequent visitor to the army headquarters, much to Patrick's annoyance, for Sharpe freely flouted the prohibition against wives visiting the camp.

CHAPTER THREE

The Bureau of Military Information: Stands Up

Assembling a Staff

Sharpe wasted little time in assembling a talented staff and threw himself into his new challenge. Colonel Gates visited him shortly after his appointment and commented in his diary, "He does not seem so anxious to consolidate as he was…"

He obviously was impressing those around him. On March 14 his brigade commander, Col. Paul Revere, requested his return to the command of his regiment. "This regiment having been recently organized and needing all the attention of its field officers for drilling and disciplining it, in order that it may keep pace with the other regiments of the Brigade, and be effective for the field, is my reason for making this request." Hooker turned him down flat. Sharpe was staying where he was.[1]

Indicative of the novel nature of Sharpe's new duties was that there was no standard army term for the organization he was to set up. His office was initially called the Secret Service, a name already used and discredited by Pinkerton and McClellan. That was quickly dropped as several other titles were tried:

5 March	S. S. Department
11 March	Bureau of Scout Information
15 March	Bureau of Secesh [Secessionist] Information
15 March	Bureau of Information

Each was quickly discarded until the Bureau of Information was adopted on March 22 and used through May. Eventually, several months later, the term Bureau of Military Information (BMI) would become fixed with a letterhead and all. That title was certainly less of a giveaway to inquisitive Confederates than the Secret Service. Yet most of Sharpe's official correspondence simply states it is from the Office of the Provost Marshal General, another form of cover.

Sharpe quickly appreciated Babcock's talents and experience. Finding such a man at hand must have been an immense relief, and Sharpe made him his chief assistant despite his civilian status. Later Babcock would be referred to with the honorary rank of captain. Sharpe was fortunate to have Babcock conduct the order-of-battle analysis. He was a man of precision and order, as indicated by his dapper attire as well as the beauty and clarity of his handwriting. His surviving order-of-battle charts and maps were drawn with a fine pen with such exactness as to be almost confused with the printed word. The man simply exuded ability, and for Sharpe, he had the added quality of manifestly being a gentleman.

In addition to Babcock, there remained only two scouts from McClellan's and Burnside's commands. Both Patrick and Sharpe were distrustful of professional detectives and preferred men that had actually been proven in the field. Although Babcock was priceless, it was clear to Sharpe that he needed more analytical and administrative support.

In his travel to Fortress Monroe, the headquarters of Maj. Gen. John A. Dix, commanding the Department of Virginia, he had met 1st Lieut. Frederick L Manning. He was a company officer with the 148th New York and had joined up in Geneva, also in response to Lincoln's call for 300,000 more men that had given birth to Sharpe's own 120th New York. Sharpe had been impressed with the young man. Sharpe wrote a draft letter to Dix which Hooker signed on March 17:

> You will oblige me if you will allow 1st Lieut. Fred. L. Manning, 148th N. Y. Vols, to report to me for temporary duty as a Short hand writer. His service in that capacity will be of great value to me for a few weeks. He shall be returned to your command as soon as possible—If you can spare this Officer, I will make an application to the Adjutant General for his temporary detail to my Head Quarters.

Dix approved, and the wheels of administration delivered Manning to Sharpe three weeks later on orders dated April 8. His stay would be anything but temporary, and it would be the road to success for the able young lieutenant.[2]

As his team and its workload grew, Sharpe realized the need for another senior assistant in addition to Babcock, and he needed a more experienced officer than Manning. On April 22 he requested the detail to his bureau of 27-year-old Captain John McEntee. In his requested he stated, "... as the reason for preferring this request, that the interests of the service demand the labors of an additional officer in this department, and that from my long acquaintance with Captain McEntee I believe him to be well fitted therefore." McEntee was a neighbor from Kingston and was serving in that repository of old friends, the 20th NYSM, where he was commanding Company A. His brother, 20-year-old Captain Charles H. McEntee, had commanded H Company in Sharpe's own 120th New York but had died of "brain fever" on December 21, 1862, one of the many sickness had carried away in the winter after Fredericksburg. Sharpe saw something more than the reliable hometown friend. Although good-natured and punctilious where honor was concerned, McEntee was no stranger to danger. Even before the war, he bore the scar on his left breast of a gunshot wound. Sharpe came to trust him to work independently in the field to organize and monitor the work of scouts, write reports, and, when necessary, to establish what were essentially "branch offices" in other commands.

McEntee was a tall, gaunt, dark-complexioned man who in later years would remind his neighbors of Lincoln. By all accounts, "he was not an outstanding personality, but rather a reserved type; industrious, extremely patriotic and scrupulously mindful of carrying out his duties to his country, or as a private citizen, giving his services unstintingly for the betterment of life in his community."[3] Sharpe made McEntee his second deputy after Babcock, and these three men and Manning would be the brains at the center of the BMI.

Hooker's new broom also brought in talent on the army staff that would later be of much assistance to the BMI. One such officer was Lieut. Paul A. Oliver, whom Butterfield pulled out of the 12th New York Infantry to be an aide. Butterfield had been impressed with his performance in battle during the Peninsular Campaign and had written glowingly of his conduct in the Seven Days battles. Oliver had been born at sea in 1831, the son of a sea captain, and educated in Altoona, Germany. He settled in Fort Hamilton, New York, and went in the shipping business, then later in the cotton trade with his brother in New York and New Orleans. During the 1856 yellow fever epidemic, he organized and led the relief society, cared for the sick, and prevented the disease from spreading to Brooklyn. Much more would be heard of him in the future.[4]

The Scouts

Sharpe's pressing need was for scouts, and he immediately began a search for experienced and willing men. The army already used a significant number of scouts attached to most commands at brigade, division, and corps. The Grand Reserve Division reported on February 2 that it maintained 10–30 scouts at any one time.[5] Over the next several months Sharpe assembled a group of very able men. It did not take him long to tap "Hooker's Horse Marines" for talent. On February 25 he arranged for the transfer of three of the cavalrymen from 3rd Indiana Cavalry, including Sergeant Milton W. Cline, Daniel Cole, and Daniel Plew.

At the same time, Butterfield canvassed the corps commanders and army headquarters in Washington for qualified recruits for the scouts. Major General John Sedgwick nominated a cavalryman from New York, D. G. Otto. He had done well as a scout for Brigadier General Pleasonton and had the value of having taught school in the South for a number of years. Two Ohioans, Sgt. Mordecai P. Hunnicutt, of the 73rd Ohio Infantry, who had been a detective, and Pvt. Henry Dodd, 1st Regiment, Ohio Light Artillery, who had been a scout, were recruited by Sharpe in March and April. Major General Heintzelman, who commanded the defenses of Washington, turned over his best scout, a German immigrant with the anglicized name of Ernest Yager [Ernst Jaeger]. Yager had been scouting since March of the previous year and was very familiar with the area west of Manassas.[6]

Three more New York cavalrymen, the brothers Edward A. (Augustus) Carney and Philip Carney, and a cousin, Anson B. Carney, were added. The latter was a 21-year-old, bold fighting man with a ruthless streak. Anson and Edward had served in Sharpe's Company B in the old 20th NYSM back during their three months' service in 1861, then reenlisted with the regiment in September when it was reorganized for three years' service. In October they transferred to the 5th U.S. Cavalry, in which Phil Carney was already serving. On April 19, Edward and Anson Carney were detailed to work for Sharpe, who undoubtedly remembered their abilities from their association with the 20th NYSM—hometown men he knew and could rely on. There was something about Anson especially, with his dark complexion, black hair, and gray eyes, that marked him as one of the "Black Irish," and a dangerous man. Perhaps that is what Sharpe wanted because that is what he would get.[7] Phil Carney would be detailed to work for Sharpe in July, shortly after Gettysburg.

The canvas of the army for experienced scouts also brought in Martin E. Hogan of H Company, 1st Indiana Cavalry, in June. He was one of those rare Union cavalrymen, like Cline, who supplied his own horse and equipment. A young Irish immigrant, Hogan had joined in the first rush of patriotic recruiting in July 1861 and spent most of 1862 as a scout for Maj. Gen. Franz Siegel, and was on one occasion captured and luckily paroled and exchanged. Hogan was another unconventionally bold personality, the bane of the regular army mind. In December 1862 the provost marshal office in Washington ordered his arrest for passing himself off as a commissary officer in Baltimore. He wiggled out of that and landed in Sharpe's lap. Hogan found a friend in Anson Carney, and the two of them would often pair up on scouting expeditions.[8]

Late in 1863 Sharpe would acquire the services of another talented scout, William J. Lee, a 26-year-old, black-haired, hazel-eyed cabinet maker from Orange County, Virginia. Sharpe would later attest that Lee "reckoned among the most effective and faithful men." Before joining the BMI Lee had worked for Burnside as a scout and later for the provost marshal general of the army. In that capacity, as a native Virginian, he had operated undercover in the headquarters of the Confederate provost marshal general, Maj. Gen. John H. Winder, as well as posing as a sutler at the headquarters of Robert E. Lee himself. He was arrested and tried as a spy but acquitted in the spring of 1862.[9]

Milton Cline was the real treasure among this very talented group, and Sharpe would eventually make him his chief of scouts. His German-born parents had anglicized the name from Klein to Cline. They settled in upstate New York in the Lake Champlain region where he was born. He had already been toughened by the life of a sailor aboard the whaler S.S. *South Carolina*, during which Brig. Gen. Alfred Pleasonton had acquired on his left arm a tattoo of a wild pirate woman and, on his right, a crucifix. After that he had moved to Indiana and settled down to the life of a farmer when the war called him.[10]

Like most of the rest of Company G, 3rd Indiana Cavalry, Cline had enlisted from Switzerland County, Indiana, on August 22, 1861. Uniquely among Union cavalrymen, the men of the 3rd Indiana, including Cline, owned their own horses. He would ride one to death for Hooker and see another killed in action at Gettysburg. This short, blond, gray-eyed man was 38, three years older than Sharpe himself, but he had the everyman quality that would allow him to blend in unobtrusively anywhere, so much so that this son of New York would be able repeatedly to pass himself off as a soldier of Dixie. As the old expression went, butter wouldn't melt in his mouth, so utterly calm was he in the midst of the enemy pulling off one masterpiece impersonation after another. Calm stealth was not all of Cline's talents. When called for, he was the bold fighting man who was always able to get the drop on an opponent. By all rights, he should be considered one of the patron saints of U.S. Army reconnaissance and special operations.[11]

Not far behind him in ability was the 32-year-old New Yorker, Judson Knight, a veteran of the Mexican War, though his only duty had been with the garrison of Ft. Columbia on Governor's Island in New York Harbor. When the Civil War started he enlisted in the 2nd New Jersey Infantry. Sandy-haired, with hazel eyes and a fair complexion badly marked from smallpox caught on Governor's Island, Knight was a powerful man at 6 feet and a quarter inch and 200 pounds. From July to December, 1861, he had been detailed for "special service" as a scout for Brig. Gen. Phillip Kearny. For months he worked on filling in the details for the maps made for Maj. Gen. Irving McDowell, the commander of the army that would be beaten at Bull Run. He served ably under Kearny in the Peninsular Campaign and the Second Battle of Bull Run, where the gallant general was killed. Year's end saw him in a prolonged illness at the end of which some incident in December resulted in his being reduced from sergeant to private. On December 31, 1862, he was given a medical discharge. Shortly thereafter he was working for Lafayette Baker's Secret Service in Fairfax County, Virginia. Baker did a background check on him that reported he was of "excellent character" and was highly recommended.

His service with Baker would be brief, because as soon as he heard that Sharpe was recruiting for scouts, he applied. Sharpe would later write of him, "When he came to headquarters he brought high testimonials of his services with the late General Phil. Kearny. He was immediately engaged by me to serve with us." He would come to enjoy, according to Sharpe, an "enviable reputation as a man to whom a bold enterprise could be entrusted without endangering the confidence of his superior officers." Unlike most of the rest of the scouts, Knight was a civilian employee. Today, he would be called a contractor. Yet he would eventually succeed Cline as Chief of Scouts.[12,13]

The scouts were as diverse a group as ever, assembled by physical type, age, and occupation. Most were very young—in their early 20s; however, the two men who would become chiefs of scouts, Cline and Knight, were in their 30s, more mature and experienced, as was Hunnicutt. Their occupations ranged from clerk to boatman to plasterer. What unified them was an independence of character, a cool boldness, a taste for danger, and a good dash of the actor, for they spent much time passing themselves off as Confederates or Southern civilians, with remarkable success. Sharpe was to prove a shrewd judge of these qualities, and his careful selection of just the right men would be vital to the success of his mission. (See Appendix B for a list of members of the BMI.)

Chaplain L. P. Roe of the Harris Light (20th NY) Cavalry, from which some of the scouts came, described how Sharpe handled them. "Scouts taken from the Union army were generally reliable men, and they were tried before they were admitted into the secret service. If they proved good scouts they were promoted and paid from two dollars to five dollars per day, and sometimes $500 for an excursion." The men Sharpe assembled for his scouts were a bold band. "These men differed in character, some being remarkable for locality and others for unlimited brass. Their plan was generally to cheat and deceive as long as they could, and when discovered they would endeavor to fight their way out of their difficulties."[14]

An Excelsior Flavor to the BMI

More than a month and a half after accepting his position, Sharpe finally received his orders on March 30, appointing him as deputy provost marshal. Very much a constant in the army across the centuries is that one must wait for orders to catch up with them. With unintended prescience, the clerk who prepared the order followed Sharpe's name with that of Capt. Ulric Dahlgren's appointment as an aide-de-camp to Hooker. They would be linked not by an administrative accident but by great events in the not too distant future.[15]

It is interesting to note that with the exception of Babcock, the BMI and the provost marshal general's organization was made up almost entirely of New York men to include Patrick, Sharpe, McEntee, Manning, Davenport, and the chiefs of scouts, Cline and Knight. Much of this was based on the web of prewar associations and the comfort level of dealing with others from the Empire State. Patrick, for instance, always preferred New York regiments for the provost guard when he could get them, which accounted for his affection for the 20th NYSM.

Remarkably, the BMI permanent staff was to remain modest in size. Sharpe would never have more than 70 men on his full-time payroll at any one time. The total number of men who served in the BMI was only slightly more than 200. The BMI staff even had its own mess, with three employees designated as "colored." (See Appendix C: Strength of the BMI 1863–65.) Two of them appear in a photograph of the scouts at Brandy Station in 1864. The BMI had its own encampment as well within the area of the headquarters of the Army of the Potomac.

Sharpe's first priority was to make sure his staff would be paid. The commissioned officers were being paid by the army paymaster. Babcock was already paid by the

War Department's Secret Service Fund. For a while the same fund was used to pay everyone else in the BMI. Eventually a separate army payroll was set up by Patrick's quartermaster that would pay all subsequent civilian and enlisted military members of the BMI through the normal paymaster.

With a few exceptions, such as Babcock's princely $7.50 a day, the standard rate was $.50 to $2.00 a day, a rate that would hold through the Gettysburg Campaign. Thereafter, the most effective scouts could be paid as much as $4.00 a day. Many of the men hired were civilians who would be considered contractors today. The soldiers among the scouts apparently continued to receive their normal soldier's pay in addition to the special pay. The specific rate for each man depended upon both experience and proven ability. The upper and lower rates worked out to monthly totals of $15.00 to $120.00 a month, a considerable improvement over the private's $8.00 and later $13.00 a month. The rate of $4.00 a day was roughly equivalent to the pay of a first lieutenant ($115.50 a month) and was awarded to very few men. Most of the scouts were paid at $2.00 to $3.00 a day. Other support personnel such as teamsters and cooks were paid at the rate of $.50 to $1.00 a day.[16]

In a letter to the Inspector General a few months after the end of the war, Sharpe wrote:

> Scouts in the army, employed by me, were paid according to the services they rendered. No contract was made with them, but their names were placed on a roll, with a remuneration attached, for which it was intended to recommend them at the end of each month; and this was known to themselves and to each other. The right was at all times claimed and used to drop names from the roll & to advance or lessen the compensation for general services, while for special and striking services, special remunerations were made, on recommendations, by order of the Commanding General.
>
> No contract was ever made with a scout. A soldier employed as such [if dismissed] was ordered to H. Q. and a civilian could leave whenever dissatisfied. No agreement was ever made to furnish scouts with rations or commutation herefor, but rations were furnished scouts while actually with the army ... Leaders of parties of scouts were always paid more than others.[17]

In addition, bonuses for particularly difficult missions were offered, as in the instance in May 1864 when Ulysses S. Grant offered Judson Knight $300 for a special mission. Sharpe ensured that new scouts, civilian and military, would not be paid until they had successfully completed a first mission. By May the BMI monthly salary payroll had reached $1,697.00, an indication of the relatively few scouts and agents Sharpe was using. When he made his first monthly report in March, he was sure to remind Hooker that, "the number of persons employed and the expenditures are very inconsiderable."[18] (See Appendix D: Expenditures of the BMI.)

All-Source Intelligence Takes Shape

Probably second only to creating the BMI was Hooker's gift of an almost complete free hand to Sharpe. He did not hesitate to use the broadest initiative to organize and run the BMI and coordinate with other sources and organizations, even those outside the Army of the Potomac. He freely used Hooker's authority to deal with the officials in Washington and with other army commands on his own initiative. His actions were invariably well judged and successful, and, amazingly, he seemed to have made few if any enemies in a very touchy age.[19]

Sharpe had four intelligence collection means under his direct control: scouts; agents; interrogation of prisoners, deserters, and refugees; and document exploitation. He quickly established a division of labor among himself and his two deputies. Babcock concentrated on interrogations and working out Lee's order-of-battle. In fact, both McEntee and Manning became adept at this skill which proved a crucial capability when Sharpe had to send his deputies off on detached duty or special missions. McEntee's other duties included organizing and directing scouting missions at the front. He did not accompany the scouts as it was not considered appropriate duty for an officer in either army. Both Babcock and he also became trusted report writers. Almost all of the BMI's reports were written in the hands of Sharpe, Babcock, McEntee, and Manning. If there were any enlisted clerks, it is not apparent from the writing of reports, at least until the last year of the war, when a few unidentifiable hands become evident.

Sharpe himself supervised the collection of documents, which included primarily letters and Southern newspapers. The importance of newspapers as conveyers of important information for both armies should not be underestimated. Both armies eagerly sought each other's publications. Then as now, much of the press assumed national security should take care of itself. One of Hooker's first acts, probably on Sharpe's advice, was to cut off the regular exchange of newspapers on the picket lines and during the meetings of flag-of-truce parties. Hooker rightly concluded that there was more useful military information in Northern than Southern newspapers. It was not a fair trade as had been assumed. Hooker was not interested in a fair trade anyway; he sought clear advantage. He concluded that his new intelligence organization would more than compensate for the cut-off of Southern newspapers. He also had another source for Southern newspapers; his scouts and agents frequently acquired copies.[20]

Sharpe also personally supervised the overall operations of his scouts and the running of agents in Confederate territory within the Army of the Potomac's area of responsibility. That territory was likened to the "Debatable Land" of constant strife on the old borders of England and Scotland, in which bands of soldiers fought, plundered, and harried their enemies, a land under no one's complete control. As one Southern writer noted, "Our 'Debatable land' was, in fact, all that fine and beautiful country between the Potomac and the [Rappahannock] river, over which the opposing armies of the North and South alternately advanced and retired."[21] Sharpe's scouts were the chief means by which information obtained by agents was transmitted back to the BMI.

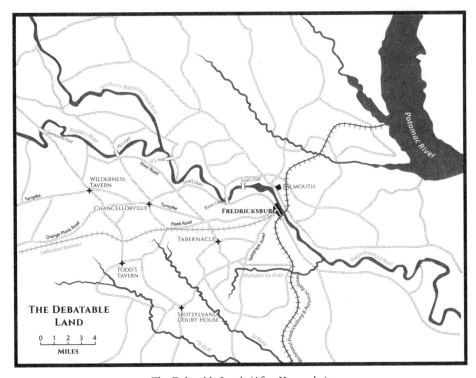

The Debatable Land. (After Karamales)

The scouts were the most active part of Sharpe's collection effort. This account by a Southern veteran of the Confederate scout applied equally to his Northern counterpart:

> The scout proper is "commanding in the field," with no one near to give him orders. He goes and comes at will, having that about him which all pickets obey. He is "on detached service"; and having procured certain information, reports to the officer who has sent him, without intermediate ceremony. Operating within the enemy's lines at all times, he depends for success and safety on the quickness of his eye and hand—and his reliance on these is great. He is silent in his movements, low-toned in his speech, abstemious in his habits, and as untiring on the track of the enemy as the Cuban blood-hound on the trail of the fugitive. He rarely sleeps in houses, preferring the woods; and always slumbers with "one eye open," on the look out for the enemy.[22]

These daring men, both military and civilian, would penetrate into Confederate territory in a variety of disguises, depending on the mission, to include Confederate uniforms, civilian clothes, and even their own blue uniforms. Invariably Confederate uniforms proved the most useful, as a number of the scouts were able to penetrate the enemy army and linger within it long enough to bring back detailed reports. The danger involved in scouting, especially in Confederate uniform or civilian clothes, was very real. Scout James Hensal, a veteran of at least seven missions behind the

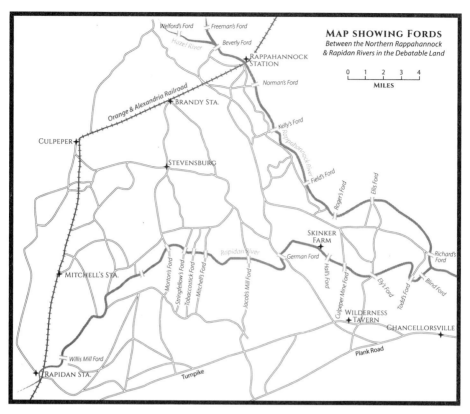

Fords Between the Northern Rappahannock & Rapidan Rivers in the Debatable Land.

lines, worked on the principle that "if I got through it would bee [sic] a merical [sic]." Another scout recounted that "the army scout, occupying as he does a position outside of the general military system, literally takes his life into his own hands [because] he may expect no quarter."[23]

An example of the daring-do of scouting was the case of Private D. G. Otto, Sharpe's first casualty. On March 10 another scout reported his capture. Otto had come upon two of the enemy's Black Horse Cavalry and captured them. He paroled them, but as he was mounting one of their superior horses, two others arrived and captured him. He was carried off across the Rappahannock to be questioned by Maj. Gen. J.E.B. (Jeb) Stuart and Lee themselves, where a tight lip apparently saved him. They wanted "to know if we were sending off troops from here," Otto related, but then added that he "gave them no satisfaction." Sent off to the Castle Thunder prisoner-of-war camp in Richmond, he was exchanged. The officer whose unit had captured him, despite having signed his parole, had recommended he not be released, but the Confederate general who administered the Richmond prisons ruled that no evidence could be found that he was a spy.[24]

However much the 20th NYSM came to revere Brigadier General Patrick, he was actively disliked by the scouts. Patrick's strictness worked well with line troops but was counterproductive among the type of men Sharpe had selected for just those qualities that would drive a disciplinarian to distraction. Sharpe consciously picked men that were quick-witted, independent-minded loners and individualists who boldly acted on their own initiative. Attendant with these qualities came a certain amount of affection for strong drink and the talent to forage well on the enemy's property, both pet peeves of Patrick.[25]

Despite the high quality and the often superb accomplishments of his scouts, Sharpe would come to feel that only in the last year of the war were they able to operate on "an equal footing" with their Confederate counterparts. In particular, he would identify the Black Horse Cavalry and the Prince William Cavalry (Companies H and A, 4th Virginia Cavalry) among other scouting commands as the most formidable scouts in the Army of Northern Virginia.[26]

Scouts were Sharpe's direct links with his agents, the other primary HUMINT or human intelligence source in the "Debatable Land." Agents included a surprising number of locally recruited loyal Virginians, and the scouts that were their contacts who conveyed the information they had acquired to the BMI. The locally recruited civilians were often transplanted Northerners, British immigrants, former noncommissioned officers of the old regular army, and a strong native Unionist element which had profoundly disagreed with Virginia's secession. These agents were resident in the areas occupied by Lee's army. Judson Knight offered a glimpse into the ability of the scouts to operate successfully in hostile territory:

> First, it will be understood that in no part of Virginia where the scouts of the Army of the Potomac principally were employed could you travel many miles without finding Union men and women. Sometimes they were natives of the State; not infrequently they were born in some of the Northern States, while quite a number of foreign birth, principally Englishmen, were found who rendered faithful and efficient service. Where we found one of these Union people, if there was another within 30 miles, he or she, as the case might be, were sure to know them; and it made no differences as regarded their social positions, they fully trusted each other. Such being the case, it will readily be seen that if the scouts could reach a Union family living within the enemy's lines, their danger of captivity or death was reduced to a minimum.[27]

In later years Sharpe would comment that the types of men and women who served as agents came from a variety of backgrounds. "Many of them had been non-commissioned officers of the Army before the war, and it was curious that while hundreds of Army officers had turned traitors, not a single non-commissioned officer or private could be found who would desert the old flag."[28]

It was through this Unionist network that Sharpe recruited his most important agents, as one contact led to another and then an entire network. The beginnings were already at hand when Sharpe took over. They came as undeserved gifts to Burnside as he was planning his attack at Fredericksburg. Both were

Virginians—Ebenezer McGee was working for the army on the railroad, and Jackson Harding came from the area just west of Fredericksburg. Harding lived on the north side of the Rappahannock between two of the up-river fords. McGee lived about 5 miles south of the Rapidan in the area known as the Wilderness and had found work with the army to avoid Confederate military service but would return home surreptitiously to visit his family. In early December 1862 he returned from a visit with information on the Confederate forces guarding U.S. Ford obtained by a Unionist, Isaac Silver. McGee returned through the pickets and passed on to army headquarters where he offered to show scouts back over the river and introduce them to Silver as well as other Unionists willing to help the army. "When he offered to go back and take some of the Headquarters scouts with him and teach them the route, and introduce them to his own people and Mr. Sylvia [sic—Silver], it is needless to say his offer was joyfully accepted, and a party was sent out with him."[29]

The route he showed them was arduous, as Knight's description graphically shows, but would prove a perfect conduit into the "Debatable Land" for the next two years.

> The place where he [McGee] had crossed the river was below the United States Dam and Ford. The two families [McGee and Sylvia—sic Silver] lived about four or five miles south of the Rapidan, in that portion of the State known as the Wilderness. Coming down to the edge of the river from the south was ravine, which commenced about half a mile from the river, and gradually grew steeper and narrower as it approached the river, until at the river's edge the sides of the ravine were very precipitous and at least 100 feet high. At some time in the past, not many years previous to the war, a wind-storm had thrown nearly all the trees down, and they now lay across the ravine, some broken in two, so that one had to crawl under them; in a few places you stand upright. The place was considered utterly impassable, and no attempt was made to have any pickets in the ravine, they always being stationed on the top of each side. The boys went through and came out a half mile inside the lines of the enemy.
>
> A small run emptying into the river on the north side through a thick fringe of bushes made a capital hiding-place for a boat, which was filled with stones and then sunk until again wanted. A small party of scouts were always left hid in the woods to take care of the horses and bring the men back across the river when they returned. This crossing was used for two years.[30]

Sharpe found McGee and quickly employed him to reactivate this route and put it into regular and productive use, especially to establish contact with Isaac Silver. This 52-year-old farmer was a native of New Jersey, and his wife was a Scottish immigrant, 27 years younger than he. His farm, 3 miles east of the crossroads of Chancellorsville and 7 miles west of Fredericksburg, was ideally located on the left wing of Lee's army. Sharpe would give him the cover name "The Old Man" in all his correspondence. McGee would be his primary contact. Silver had the added utility of having business interests in Orange County which would justify frequent travel there, where Lee would keep his headquarters for a year covering 1863–64. Silver would remain an important asset for the rest of the war. His first report was brought in on March 13 and immediately established his value.[31]

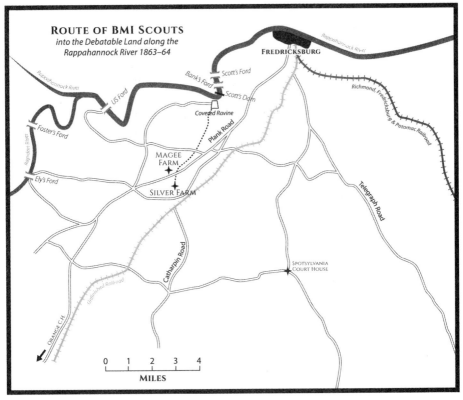

Route of BMI Scouts into the Debatable Land Along the Rappahannock River, 1863–64. (After Jespersen)

At this time Sharpe was unable to enlist agents in Richmond itself and had to depend on a careful analysis of Southern newspapers, obtained through the lines, for reporting from the Confederate capital. He also found it necessary before the upcoming campaign to request tens of thousands of dollars in Confederate currency to disperse to both scouts and agents to support operations.

Enemy personnel became another vital source of information. Sharpe established a systematic interrogation protocol to be used with refugees, escaped slaves, and especially from enemy deserters and prisoners. Each man from the latter groups was asked at a minimum to identify his regiment, brigade, division, and corps; when and where he entered the lines; location of his corps and when it arrived on the front; how he was captured or why he deserted; and other questions depending upon the kind of information needed.[32]

The BMI quickly devised protocols for determining the trustworthiness of informants using the following assessments: "The truth of the general story told by the prisoners and deserters; the circumstances of their capture; the location in which their commands were raised; the corroborative statement of other prisoners from the same commands ... [and] their conduct and declarations at the time of coming in or capture compared with their present state of mind."[33]

Sharpe also actively encouraged desertion as a prime source of intelligence by the promise of integration into the civilian life of the North in exchange for full and accurate cooperation. The act of desertion had already severed basic loyalties, making cooperation far easier than for a prisoner taken in battle. Sharpe explained to Maj. Gen. John H. Martindale, the commander of the military garrison of Washington, that this method was very efficient in obtaining the truth from deserters, "the state of our information [being] such as to form a standard of credibility by which these men were gauged, while each was adding to the general sum."[34]

Sharpe's innovation led to a wider Union program to encourage desertion with the rewards of travel, settlement, and employment in the North. It was eventually to lead to the War Department policy of February 18, 1864:

> Whenever refugees from within the rebel lines, or deserters from the rebel armies present themselves at U.S. camps or military posts they will be immediately examined by the provost-marshal with a view to determine their character and their motive in giving themselves up. If it appears that they are honest in their intention of forever deserting the rebel cause, care will be taken to explain to them that they will not be forced to serve in the U.S. Army against the rebels, nor be kept in confinement. The President's proclamation of December 8, 1863, will be read to them, and if they so desire the oath therein prescribed will be administered to them. They will then be questioned as to whether they desire employment from the United States; and if so, such arrangements as may be expedient will be made by the several army commanders of employing them on Government works within their commands. Those who come to the Army of the Potomac will be forwarded to the Military Governor of the District of Columbia, at Washington, with reports in their cases, that employment may be given them if desired; or, if not, they may be sent as far north as Philadelphia.[35]

By April of the following year, Sharpe's interrogation program was so effective, among both prisoners and deserters, that Lee issued a concerned circular reminding his troops that should they be taken prisoner, they should not divulge useful information to the enemy:

> I hope that few of the soldiers of this army will find it necessary at any time in the coming campaign to surrender themselves prisoners of war. We cannot spare brave men to fill Federal prisons. Should, however, any be so unfortunate as to fall through unavoidable necessity into the hands of the enemy, it is important they should preserve entire silence with regard to everything connected with the army, the positions, movements, organizations, or probable strength of any portion of it. I wish the commanding officers of regiments and companies to instruct their men, should they be captured, under any circumstances not to disclose the brigade, division, or corps to which they belong, but to give simply, their names, company, and regiment, and not to speak of military matters even among their associates in misfortune. Proper prudence on the part of all will be of great assistance in preserving that secrecy so essential to success.[36]

Another source of information that alarmed Lee was the steady flow of contrabands or escaped slaves that filtered through the lines. Frederick Douglass, the great champion of black emancipation, had identified in 1862 the contribution black Americans were already making to their country: "The true history of this war will show that the loyal army found no friends at the South so faithful, active, and daring in their efforts to sustain the government as the Negroes. Negroes have repeatedly threaded their way through the lines of the rebels exposing themselves to bullets to convey important information to the loyal army of the Potomac."[37]

Lee was just as aware of the problem and wrote in late May, 1863, "The chief source of information to the enemy is through our Negroes." Colonel Sharpe would have certainly agreed. Contrabands were uniquely placed to provide vital information to the Union. The Army of Northern Virginia could not have peeled a potato without its black slave contingent, which formed a vital part of its combat service support. A British Army visitor in 1863 would observe that each Confederate regiment was trailed by 20–30 black body servants.

Lee went on to say, "They are easily deceived by proper caution."[38] Here Sharpe would have vehemently disagreed with Lee. Contrabands were not only one of his most important sources of information but of *reliable* information. Blacks were a ubiquitous fact of life in Lee's army and an observant one. Confederate officers tended to discuss the most vital details of operations around their black body servants as if they were not there, so much were they a fixture of their lives. Not even a month after Lee made his statement, a contraband would provide Colonel Sharpe with the vital information that would put the Army of the Potomac in motion to a place called Gettysburg.

Coordination of Other Sources of Intelligence

In addition to the four collection methods directly under his control (interrogation, agents, scouting, and document exploitation), Sharpe eagerly integrated results of other means of collection within the Army of the Potomac to include reports from cavalry reconnaissance, Balloon Corps aerial observation, Signal Corps observation stations and flag-signal interception. Sharpe was fast off the mark. For example, within two weeks he was already receiving the reports of the Balloon Corps.[39] The mass of raw intelligence had reached such a volume that a commander could no longer successfully deal with it personally as had George Washington and his successors. Hooker's great contribution was to realize that he needed a professional staff to integrate the growing number of collection means, to diligently work through this mass of detail, and finally to analyze what it all meant. The mix of correct principles of source integration and analysis, organization, and talented personnel created what we now call all-source intelligence. What Sharpe created fits exactly the U.S. Army's current definition of all-source intelligence: "the intelligence products, organizations, and activities that incorporates all sources of information, in the production of intelligence." It also required a commander who believed in intelligence and would do everything in his power to make it work. Hooker had made intelligence history. His all-source intelligence operation was decades ahead of its time.[40]

The Signal Corps' contribution to this newly integrated whole is a good example of the possibilities for intelligence gathering by integrating the rich harvest of signal intercepts. Sharpe also made good use of the U.S. Military Telegraph (USMT) to speed the dissemination of intelligence within the various commands of the Army of the Potomac and army as a whole. Military telegraphs became collection sources as both sides tapped into each other's lines. Both sides responded with ciphers. Ultimately, the Union won the cipher war by breaking Confederate systems and maintaining the security of their own. "By 1864 the task of enciphering and deciphering dispatches became so crucial that Ulysses S. Grant never traveled without his cipher clerk."[41]

Early in April a captured Confederate signal officer revealed that the Union's signal code, its flag alphabet, had been broken. The Rebels were reading the army's signals. The army's chief of signals, Colonel Albert Myers, promptly issued the army's first signal cipher that the Confederates were never to break. However, the opportunity to deceive the enemy through the transmission of false information would be lost with the new cipher. It was Sharpe, now coordinating all sources of information, who informed the chief of staff of this problem. Butterfield came up with the solution so that the army could have its cake and eat it too. He suggested that messages be sent in the clear but without the formality of an official message, to simulate the common unofficial chatter among signalmen. The watching Confederates then would not suspect the clear messages among the new unreadable ciphered messages. Lee took the bait almost immediately. Union signalmen were able to read the deception message being retransmitted by Confederate signalmen under Lee's signature.[42]

If there was an area where integration of these collection means did not function as well as it could it was with cavalry reconnaissance. The cavalry looked upon its traditional intelligence collection as a jealous prerogative and all too often saw the BMI not as a partner but as a competitor.

Lee and Intelligence: A Classic

Up to this point, Lee's intelligence operation had been clearly superior in the efficiency of its elements and the talents of its personnel. During the Mexican War he had gained, through personnel experience, a keen appreciation for the intelligence value of reconnaissance. However effective, Lee's effort was that of the old style, in which the commanding general himself was the coordinator and ultimate analyst of intelligence, although he detailed some duties to key staff officers. Lee's staff was so small that these officers usually were overworked so that their contribution to intelligence operations can only have been peripheral. Lee himself, it seems, personally conducted many interrogations, as shown in the case of the lucky Private Otto. He took a great interest in Stuart's scouts who reported often directly to him. Most of their reporting correspondence is in fact addressed to him.

A factor that may have prevented Lee from developing a dedicated all-source organization was his strong desire to limit the size of his staff as an example to the rest of the army. Instead, his already existing staff appears to have handled much of what the BMI staff was doing but of necessity only on a part-time and far less detailed basis. Aides-de-camp Majors Charles Marshall and Charles S. Venable appear to have handled intelligence matters, the latter particularly engaged in handling "correspondence with scouts and agents behind enemy lines." Then as now, staffs have a way of growing if not ruthlessly pruned back, but Lee appears to have actually harmed the ability of his army to function in a number of ways—not only intelligence, but in logistics and administration—by his extreme reluctance to increase his staff. He would frequently burden himself with minutia handled by staff officers in the Union armies.[43]

Although Lee had no dedicated all-source staff like the BMI, what he did have was the brilliant reconnaissance efforts of Jeb Stuart's Cavalry Division, to whom he assigned the collection of tactical intelligence. In the words of one of the most daring scouts, Thomas Nelson Conrad, "Stuart's scouts performed duties of three kinds: observing the Federal Army in camp, so as to be able to anticipate a movement; hanging upon the flank of the army when in motion, reporting line of march and numbers of corps, et., and crossing the lines into Washington and beyond, bearing dispatches, interviewing certain parties and securing information."[44]

The Confederate scout had an unnerving ability to infiltrate Union camps even to general headquarters, as Conrad describes:

> [The scout] was generally in position to observe what was going on at all hours of the day and night, and I have known some of our scouts to hang for several days around the headquarters of a Federal general to ascertain their next movement on that military chess board… No detective ever shadowed a supposed criminal with greater vigilance than scouts did the Federal officers, and in but few instances were they deceived or misled.[45]

These men of keen observation and cool daring who served as scouts and agents included, in addition to Conrad, the famous John Singleton Mosby and his partisan rangers, and Lieutenants Channing Smith and Benjamin Franklin Stringfellow. Mosby was the ultimate scout who traced the enemy lines and guided Stuart's cavalry in its famous ride around McClellan's army in the Peninsular Campaign of 1862. He was later to raise the 43rd Virginia Cavalry Battalion, which would become the most famous partisan ranger organization of the Civil War and a bleeding wound in the side of Union logistics in Northern Virginia. Conrad, a lay preacher in civilian life, was so familiar with Washington that he was able to set up a spy ring that included War Department clerks, one of whom provided Lee with the Union order-of-battle, key to victory in the Peninsula.[46] "All through the Peninsula campaign our officers knew just what forces McClellan had, down to the exact number of pieces of artillery, and the pirated tabular statement was a factor at last in the bloody contests, which ended with Gaine's Mill and Malvern Hill."[47]

The daring Lieutenant Benjamin Stringfellow slipped into Washington in early 1863 as a result of Lee's instructions to Stuart to strengthen his sources of information in anticipation of another invasion of the North. Stringfellow was also able to recruit a ring within the clerks of the War Department, an organization badly in need of operations security (OPSEC). These agents reportedly were in close proximity to the chief of staff of the U.S. Army himself, Major-General Halleck. Conrad also had his sources in the War Department, as well as in Baker's Secret Service. It is no wonder that, to Lee, Stuart was to embody the intelligence operation of the Army of Northern Virginia. Stuart's absence, therefore, on the first two days at Gettysburg was to prove devastating.

Lee also had as a source a spy network, called the Secret Line. It was controlled by the Confederate Signal and Secret Service Bureau in Richmond. In this office, the Confederacy had a national-level intelligence operation, something the Union would never have. There were enough complaints about the Secret Line, however, that by late 1862 Conrad was given the mission of setting up another, independent operation which would report to Lee. The commander of the Army of Northern Virginia was often involved directly with such covert operations and wanted no amateurs in these matters. "[R]eports from citizens however intelligent and honest cannot be relied on" because of the tendency to inflate enemy strength and misinterpret facts. He wanted men experienced in scouting and espionage, "men accustomed to see things as they are, & not liable to excitement or exaggeration."[48]

It being a civil war, there was not unanimity of loyalty on either side. Both sides actively recruited willing agents in each other's territory. There was one major difference. Southerners working for the North were Unionists, still loyal to the old flag. They were—with a few exceptions during the siege of Petersburg, when Elizabeth Van Lew recruited a few Confederate War Department clerks—private citizens. The slave population was uniformly helpful in the South as the free black population was loyal in the North. Northerners working for the Confederacy were Southern sympathizers, vehemently anti-black and anti-abolition, or antiwar such as the Copperheads. They also included a number of government officials with access to important official information on the conduct of the war. This explains the often high degree of accuracy of the intelligence Lee was receiving at the strategic and operational levels of war.

At Lee's headquarters he was assisted in intelligence collection by his provost guard which, in addition to its military police duties and guarding his camp, processed prisoners and deserters and maintained contact with prisoner facilities in Richmond. It would also conduct interrogations and prepare reports. Although Lee's scouts and spy network were superb, all-source analysis of the painstaking type of order-of-battle preparation that Sharpe would initiate does not seem to have been done.

The Confederate Signal Corps was another intelligence source for Lee. Southern officers, such as Edward Porter Alexander, Lt. Gen. James Longstreet chief of artillery, had been participants in field tests before the war and helped set up the

Confederate Signal Corps in the fall and winter of 1861–62 with far more alacrity and aggressiveness than their Union counterparts. A general order in May 1862 formally established the corps. Confederate signal parties had shown themselves to be fearless and aggressive. They demonstrated considerable initiative and had done well at Second Manassas (Bull Run) and in the Antietam Campaign.

> Like their Union counterparts, signalmen in gray did not await the assignment of duties, they sought out opportunities for service. Mounted like cavalry, they headed for the best elevations to support communications and afford observation. Field glasses and telescopes (usually 30-power) extended their range. Lightly armed, they tended to depend on guard details to protect their stations, or simply took their chances and risked capture ... If their signal capability (a flag by day, torches by night) was not needed, they were available as couriers or messengers.[49]

By early 1863 the Confederates were losing their edge as the Union devoted more resources to systematize and professionalize the service. Lee's subordinate corps and many division commanders had signal officers attached to their headquarters, but Lee himself had no chief signal officer on his staff to control and organize signal assets to support his decision-making. It was not Confederate army policy to deny Lee such an asset, for the Army of Tennessee had a signal officer on its staff. It was an example of young, innovative officers introducing new means of war that an older Lee, a product of a different age, could not fully exploit. Nevertheless, as traditional as Lee's concepts were, they were employed by men of great talent not working at cross-purposes.[50]

Getting Started

Even before Sharpe took the job, Hooker had made it clear to Patrick that he considered intelligence a priority, and the provost started to take more interest in the opportunities that naturally came his way. Within less than a week of Hooker's assumption of command, Babcock suddenly found himself with work to do as an interrogator; prisoners from eight different Confederate regiments and batteries began to line up in front of his tent. A few days later, Patrick himself made a discovery on a Confederate pass issued to local Southern women whom he gallantly let through the lines. It carried the names of Lee, Longstreet, and McLaws, the signatures of the chain of command—army, corps, and division commanders. The whereabouts of Longstreet had been in doubt, and Patrick would write in his diary on February 8, "So Longstreet is here."[51]

In the meantime, Hooker gave Sharpe a coordination assignment to the headquarters of Maj. Gen. John A. Dix at Fort Monroe, while he was still considering the job offer. Sharpe was actively thinking beyond the acceptance of the mission on this trip. While at Fort Monroe, he talked over an idea with a friend and fellow-lawyer from Kingston, Col. Daniel T. Van Buren. Sharpe proposed sending over scouts in the guise of deserters engaged in smuggling to the South.

It was Sharpe's acceptance of the position that provided the critical mass to the uncoordinated attempts by Babcock and Patrick to give Hooker the intelligence he wanted. Patrick was far too busy with his provost marshal duties to devote the time that it required. Babcock was a civilian and too young to be taken seriously throughout the army. Sharpe brought authority and a powerful directing energy to the position that he had now come to see as rich in opportunity. It is no wonder that he would write his uncle that he was "one of the hardest working men in the army." Sharpe was a firm leader, but he had the great talent of identifying other talented men and letting them do their job with minimum guidance. As highly intelligent as he was, he never feared the intelligence of others as a threat but only as a resource to be given full rein. In Babcock he found the ideal subordinate, and they developed a warm professional and personal relationship that would be remembered until their deaths at the dawn of the next century. Sharpe made full use of the younger man's experience in Confederate order-of-battle and interrogation.

Sharpe would join Babcock in interrogation; there were enough subjects to go around at times, and he found that a lawyer's training in cross-examination made him an exceptional interrogator himself. But he left Babcock in overall charge of the order-of-battle and interrogation effort. Sharpe did not simply manage the work of subordinates; his staff was small, and he could not afford merely to guide and receive their work. He was, in effect, the BMI's senior analyst as well. He drew all the evidence presented by his staff and synthesized it to answer the great question of intelligence that every commander needs answered: "What does this mean?"

Sharpe was so fast off the block in putting the BMI together that he must have been the delighted recipient of the accumulated experience and ideas Babcock had been desperately trying to implement, without which, it is safe to say, Sharpe would never have succeeded; it would have taken much longer to produce the superlative intelligence operation that he did. And Sharpe would have been the first to say so. Along with Babcock's positive experience under Pinkerton, there was the equally useful negative experience under Burnside. Like the Duke of Wellington, who spoke of the disastrous British campaign in Holland in 1794–95, he could have said, "I learnt what one ought not to do, and that is always something."[52]

But it was just not Babcock that provided the vital support to Sharpe's eventual success. It was the coming together in time and harmony of a number of men, in the rare synergy of the creative moment upon which history pivots. Hooker, the transformational man, recognized that the time for change had come. Babcock provided the know-how and hard skills as a foundation for the structure. Patrick was the gruff old mother hen and backstop for the operation, ready to step in and shield it through its growing pains. And Sharpe was his renaissance man, able to combine all the techniques of this new art into something different and fitting for the organizational wars of the burgeoning industrial age. He was the keystone without which Hooker's support and Babcock's experience would not have held together any coherent or effective effort.

But we should not forget another unsung agent of Sharpe's success, the much-abused master of coordination, Hooker's chief of staff, Maj. Gen. Daniel Butterfield. No matter where the reports originated—whether from the uncooperative cavalry jealously guarding their ancient role, the eager to cooperate balloonists, or the team players in the Signal Corps, Butterfield made sure they circulated among all the players.

Hard Work and No Nonsense

Examination of the BMI's correspondence gives an insight into how Sharpe ran his department. First, Sharpe clearly was not a stickler for form or elegance of correspondence. The reports he wrote himself and those written by subordinates, either dictated by him or written on their own, show a wide variation in form—headings, abbreviations, salutations, punctuation, capitalization, and signature blocks. Sometimes they used a provost marshal general letterhead paper, and as often they did not. It would have driven a Colonel Blimp crazy, but Sharpe obviously did not care as long as the information was well written in a clear and logical form, and quickly forwarded up the chain of command. Second, Sharpe was not afraid to trust his subordinates, delegate authority, and encourage initiative. He allowed both Babcock and McEntee, and Manning on occasion, to sign his name when necessary—no more sure sign of a secure personality and an enormous statement of trust in a military context.

Perhaps the most striking feature of the BMI under Sharpe was its vigorous ability to learn and to learn as a team. James Morice, in his highly insightful article, concludes that the men of the BMI "had a sense of 'shared vision' built around 'a set of principles and guiding practices' that enabled them to demonstrate remarkable individual initiative; and the relatively relaxed and non-hierarchical environment Sharpe fostered allowed for a productive if unself-conscious form of 'team learning'." Sharpe was also lucky in not having a traditional model to follow. He was free to adapt his organization to the realities of the war as he saw it. He was fortunate to be able to attract unconventional subordinates who could not only function in an environment of ambiguity but function brilliantly and with intelligent initiative. He was triply lucky in that Hooker allowed him the widest latitude in doing his job.[53]

Sharpe's department was a very hard-working one. In World War II General MacArthur was told by a visiting dignitary that he was working his staff to death. He responded, "Well, could they die a nobler death?"[54] Whereas most of the rest of the army experienced war as long periods of boredom punctuated by a few savage battles leavened with picket duty, Sharpe's men were almost continuously busy, even when the armies went into winter quarters. BMI reports show that there were scouts out on almost a continuous basis, though not all of them all the time. Nevertheless, their exposure to the risk of capture, wounds or death was much greater. On many occasions scouts engaged in shoot-outs with enemy scouts and suffered wounds and captures in return. Cline and Anson Carney were particularly noted for their willingness to get the drop on enemy scouts or fight it out when necessary. Sharpe's scouts brought in not only information but prisoners and their horses and equipment as well. They were a bold and intelligent bunch. The less glamorous work in the BMI headquarters went on day-in and day-out, and dates on the reports show that they worked early and late. Boredom was rarely a problem. Although Sharpe wrote many of his reports himself, he found the need of assistance, other than Babcock and McEntee, in the actual preparation of the summary reports. A number of different hands are evident in the writing of these reports, each of which showed an idiosyncrasy in report format that Sharpe did not mind. The most prolific assistant was Manning, whose neat but leftward leaning letters must have been as irritating then as now, but whose analytical writing style was clear and concise. Another insight into Sharpe's leadership of his department is found in the very rare use of the first person singular. He consistently wrote "we" and "our" when referring to the efforts of his department. Wherever possible he gave full credit to his subordinates and never seemed to blow his own horn, at least not in his official correspondence. While being a hard opponent of secession, he never used vituperative terms to describe the enemy, limiting his words to "Confederates," "rebels," or simply, "the enemy." He never referred to Robert E. Lee without placing the honorific "General" before his name.

The analytical arm of the BMI was as busy keeping track and making sense of what the scouts discovered as interpreting the other types of information that Sharpe funneled into their arms. Sharpe ensured that a summary report of daily findings was provided to the army commander. Included in such reports were deeper analyses of issues of long-term interest, such as the state of morale, subsistence, and reinforcement in the Army of Northern Virginia. As the war dragged on, Sharpe developed a talent for what is today called Pol-Mil (Political-Military Intelligence) as well as strategic intelligence. Some of these reports are models of rigorous intellectual effort that would stand up in any age. They certainly do not betray the lowest common denominator of analysis found today in the U.S. Intelligence Community's committee-produced National Intelligence Estimates (NIEs).[55] None of the reports that Sharpe would write or those written by his subordinates were anything but frank in their assessments.

CHAPTER FOUR

First Test: The Chancellorsville Campaign
"Sharpe you are the best man I know"

By mid-April, Hooker's intelligence operation was working at a level of efficiency unprecedented in American military history. Hooker's confidence grew in parallel with the revelations of Lee's army set out by Sharpe and his men. One of Hooker's staff officers, J. E. Hammond, wrote that not only was Hooker confident but "so are all who know anything of the situation here. We have a moral authority of all that it is necessary to know in regard the enemy, every regiment and brigade, division, etc., all their latest arrivals and departures, etc., all collated, compared from many sources and fully confirmed. The secret service of Gen. Hooker is far superior to anything that has ever been here before."[1]

That so-called "Secret Service" (the name was still not fixed) had laid golden gifts before the commander of the Army of the Potomac in the seven weeks since its founding

Intelligence Preparation of the Battlefield—Sharpe Initiates Modern Methods

Sharpe's efforts quickly evolved into what would be called, by the modern term, the intelligence preparation of the battlefield (IPB), which is defined as "a systematic, continuous process of analyzing the threat and environment in a specific geographic area. It is designed to support staff estimates and military decision making. Applying the IPB process helps the commander selectively apply and maximize his combat power at critical points in time and space on the battlefield…"[2]

Sharpe understood clearly that this was a continuous process; the work of his organization would be unremitting. Even when the army rested between campaigns, they worked. He maneuvered constantly on the intelligence battlefield, which was one seamless, ongoing campaign. (See Appendices E and F.)

He quickly set himself to identify the enemy's location, strength, and condition. Almost the first problem he encountered was to sort out the status and location of Lt. Gen. James Longstreet's I Corps of the Army of Northern Virginia. There were

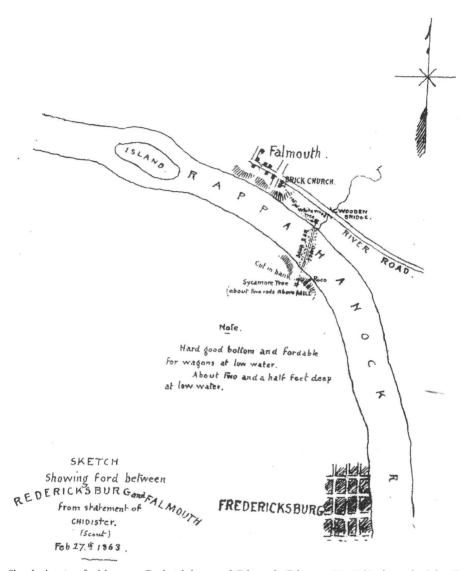

Sketch showing ford between Fredericksburg and Falmouth, February 27, 1863, drawn by John C. Babcock. Courtesy Huntington Library.

all sorts of rumors circulating that he was going to Tennessee, South Carolina, or Georgia. Prisoners and deserters from Longstreet's divisions seemed to dry up after February 25. Then he had a break in the contents of a captured mail bag. Letters revealed that a large part of Longstreet's command had departed, beginning February 20, and passed through Richmond four days later. By the beginning of March, Major General Dix at Fort Monroe reported that at least two of Longstreet's divisions,

Pickett's and Hood's, had arrived. Major General John J. Peck commanding nearby at Suffolk operated a very aggressive intelligence collection effort that confirmed Longstreet's presence. Longstreet had a third division, that of Ransom, as well, and settled into the siege of Suffolk.[3]

On the night of February 27, Sharpe unleashed the wily Sergeant Cline on the unsuspecting Confederates. Passing himself off as a Confederate soldier, Cline slipped across the Rappahannock at Port Royal, 5 miles below Fredericksburg. Presently, he encountered a Confederate captain, John W. Hungerford. The captain by strange coincidence commanded a company of the 9th Virginia Cavalry, the best scouts in the Army of Northern Virginia. They would be the counterparts of Sharpe's scouts for the next two years. Cline appears to have concocted a story which allowed him to accompany Hungerford on his ride, the purpose of which was not identified, from the Confederate right to its left across the rear of the Army of Northern Virginia for a distance of 50 miles to Orange County Courthouse, identifying encampments and units along the way. At the courthouse, Cline spoke with several Georgians who told him of the large fictitious force at Gordonsville. Hungerford took his party back to the right by a different route, this time through the Wilderness to the Confederate center at Fredericksburg and then back to his headquarters on the right, passing through all of Jackson's II Corps. On the night of March 4, Cline slipped away from Hungerford's camp, his departure unnoticed by those engaged in a well-lubricated card game.[4]

Upon his return to Sharpe's headquarters on the night of the 5th, he wrote a lengthy report from which Sharpe debriefed him in detail, as indicated by the margin notes in the colonel's hand. Through the use of information obtained from prisoner/deserter interrogations, Sharpe was able to identify the units of which Cline had only seen their camps. Fishel points out, "Altogether, Cline's written report and Sharpe's notes mentioned, in terms definite enough for the locations to have been determined on a map a total of sixty-four major installations, twenty-four camps, twelve locations of batteries or heavy artillery, twenty-three fortifications, and five wagon and ambulance parks."[5]

Of equal importance were Cline's observations of the state of the enemy. He noted that their rations, when they could be had, were a pint of flour and a pound of bacon a day. Frequently even this was not to be had, and the men were told to obtain food on their own locally. Even officers needed new shoes. It was clear that Lee's logistics were fragile and that few stocks were on hand. What little he obtained came up the railroad from Richmond. Sharpe did not know, but a reason for detaching Longstreet's three divisions was to relieve some pressure on Lee's starved commissary. Right after Cline's debriefing, Sharpe sent out more scouts, who were unaccountably stopped by their own cavalry. Brigadier General Patrick was incensed: "The scouts sent out by Col. Sharpe were arrested & sent back by Averill [sic], notwithstanding they had my pass—It was a great piece of arrogance & stupidity combined, which caused 'Fighting Joe Hooker' to swear very wickedly

& send for Averill [sic Averell] in a great hurry—What the said Averill [sic] caught is a question yet undecided…"[6]

Given Hooker's unstinted support for Sharpe and his mission, Averell most likely left with a stern admonition to cooperate fully with the BMI. That same day the cavalry passed another one of Sharpe's scouts, Dan Cole. This time the pass worked.

HEADQUARTERS, PROVOST MASHAL GENERAL
S. S. Department   March 5, 1863

Colonel TAYLOR,
Commanding Cavalry Brigade, Northern Neck:

COLONEL: The bearer Dan. R. Cole, 3rd Indiana Cavalry, is on peculiar duty, by proper authority.

In order that he may meet with no unnecessary detention, please furnish him with pass to outposts and return to this department, the pass he comes with, at earliest convenience.

Very respectfully, your obedient,
GEORGE H. SHARPE
Colonel &c.[7]

Cole chose not to rely on disguise but tried another method that involved just as much cool effrontery. He gave himself up to the pickets of the 9th Virginia Cavalry as a deserter. He was shunted from the headquarters of Fitzhugh Lee, Stuart, and Lee himself before being sent to Richmond where he was confined to Libby Prison. There he cleverly slipped in among the prisoners of war and got himself exchanged.[8]

Despite having a comprehensive understanding of the deployment of almost all of Lee's forces, Sharpe was not confident yet in the numbers. He was loathe to report information in which he did not have confidence and said so. His scouts were careful to rate their confidence in their information, such as when Skinker reported on March 13 that "I am sorry to inform you that I have been unable to obtain any additional information in regard to the strength of the Rebel Army near Fredericksburg but have again to report it, indefinitely, from 28 to 35 thousand."[9]

Everything now seemed to click into place, and on the 15th Sharpe delivered a summary report on the enemy's strength and dispositions that for detail, accuracy, and timeliness it would not be amiss to compare it with a modern report produced with a vast array of technological tools. It is worth quoting in its entirety.

HEAD QUARTERS, ARMY OF THE POTOMAC BUREAU OF SECESH INFORMATION

Major General DANIEL BUTTERFIELD,   March 15 1863
Chief of Staff:

GENERAL: Having reported thirty days since for duty at these Head Quarters, I beg leave respectfully to submit the following brief summary as the monthly report of what has been done in this department.

Rebel Army of the Potomac

Prior to the middle of January the Rebel Army of the Potomac consisted of two Corps of Lieutenant Generals Longstreet and Jackson, the Cavalry Division of General Stuart, (a summary of which is herewith annexed) and the artillery, of which the most diligent labor has only enabled us to form the barest skeletons, on which no reliance can be placed.

Longstreets command before the middle of January

Lieut Genl. Longstreet had five divisions – Viz:

Anderson's.	Pickett's.
McLaws's.	Ransom's.
	Hood's.

Jacksons command before and since.

Lieut Genl Jackson had four divisions – Viz:

A. P. Hill's.	D. H. Hill's.
Early's.	Trimble's.

And thus with their Cavalry their army consisted of ten divisions, which at their maximum ought to consist of five brigades each. This was not and is not now the case, as remarked below under the head of "Estimation."

Divisions gone South.

About the middle of January the enemy began moving forces south, and we now know that General Longstreet has gone south, and has taken with him (or there had been sent south from his Corps d' armée,) the divisions of Ransom, Pickett, and Hood.

It is also known that Gen. D. H. Hill has gone south, but it is not thought that any of his divisions has accompanied him.

Rebel Commanders.

Generals Lee, Stuart, and Jackson are now opposite us: Their Hd Qrs being located in the annexed "Extracts," together with the following divisions of the rebel army.

Of Jackson's Corps	Of Longstreet's Corps
A. P. Hill's	Anderson's.
D. H. Hill's	McLaws's.
Early's.	
Trimble's.	

This is all that is believed to be opposite to us. (Infantry)

Artillery.

From the fact that most of our informants have seen little Artillery, we believe that a fair proportion of that arm has gone south with the divisions of Longstreet—but it should be remembered that the greater part of it was sent back some time ago to Hanover Junction, or near it, to obtain forage along Pole Cat Creek, and from Louisa C. H.

Location

It is believed that the location of each of the divisions of infantry, before mentioned, is fixed with very considerable exactness, and reference is made to exact language used by the latest informant, (for the personal judgment of the general commanding) selected on account of their strong corroboration by all previous information.

Estimations

Each division should consist of five brigades of five regiments each. There are however some divisions which have only four brigades, and there are many brigades that have much less than five regiments. Some have four regiments, and others have two regiments and two battalions, or three regiments and one battalion.

These battalions were originally independent organizations, and are composed of four, five, and six, and sometimes (though rarely) eight companies. Thus, though representing a regiment in a brigade, they detract materially from the brigade strength.

Strength of A. P. Hill's Division

A. P. Hill's Division, seems to be the favorite one, and is an exception, in the whole rebel army. Whenever we get information from a regiment in his division we find it strong, and we are continually told that all the conscripts go to him. It is estimated by themselves as from 1100 to 1300. This would show that his brigades run over 2000 each; and all admit that this is the strongest division in their service.

Estimate

We think the six divisions before mentioned, (as comprising the entire infantry force opposite us) have doubtless twenty five brigades in all. And we have many evidences to show that 1700 men (for duty) is a liberal estimate of the average of their brigades—By this we should have

$$15 \times 1700 = 42,500 \text{ men.}$$

Estimate by regiment.

Again, we have many evidences that 350 men is a liberal average of their regiments—and four and one half regiments to a brigade is rather over than under the proportion.

By this we have

$$4 \tfrac{1}{2} \times 350 = 1575 \times 25 = 39,375 \text{ men.}$$

Lowest estimate.

On account of the numerous battalions which represent regiments in a brigade without their compounding strength, we think these figures are too large, and believe that a calculation of our own, from several scattering regiment is near the truth, viz—that the brigades will average about 1300 men for duty.

Mr Skinkers statement

Mr Jno. H. Skinker states that he understands from his relatives outside the lines (who sympathize entirely with the other side) that the rebel army is from 28000 to 35000 strong.

General Remarks

With the multiplied and laborious examinations which have led to the information contained herein, and in the exhibits forwarded herewith, an attempt has been made to establish communication with the other side of the river, which has been successful, and of which the General has been informed. Another has also been attempted which has not yet been fruitful, but from the short time which has elapsed since the departure of the agent it is hoped it may be—and if successful it will probably be productive of the highest results.

The enemy's lines have been penetrated a number of times, notice given of the Cavalry raid of February 26th and of other movements of the enemy—the number of persons employed and the expenditures very inconsiderable.

It is considered fair to add that, from the best information, we learn that the rebel organization has never before been obtained in this army, until it was too late to use it; and that no previous time has any attempt been made to locate the enemy's forces, that has proved anyway successful, or to estimate them within any reasonable number of men.

All of which is respectfully submitted in behalf of Mr. Babcock and myself –

Very respectfully your obedient servant
GEORGE H. SHARPE
Col & in charge[10]

This is an extraordinary document. From its submission can be marked the creation of professional U.S. all-source military intelligence. Sharpe makes it clear that all this has been done in the month since he was given the mission to set up his organization. He first lays down the organization of the Army of Northern Virginia from the corps to division levels and establishes the location of each division. Of vital importance is his statement that Lt. Gen. James Longstreet has taken three of the five divisions in his I Corps south of Richmond to the Petersburg area. That is fully one-third of Lee's nine infantry divisions. Then he identifies the division of Major General A. P. Hill to be the strongest of the nine, the one to which replacements are sent first.

Next the report dissects the organization of the divisions and brigades, showing that there is a generally uniform number of brigades and within the brigades a uniform number (five) of regiments. However, he points out that there are exceptions to this rule, with some brigades having only four regiments or a mix of regiments and battalions.

From this base, he then shows the analytical process and formulas by which the strength of each unit was calculated and provides high, medium, and low estimates of Lee's infantry strength. He appears to give greater confidence to the lower estimate but does not clearly commit himself.

This was the fruit of a body of cross-checked and cross-indexed information that had been accumulated over the preceding month and may have included information that Babcock had retrieved from the War Department files after he was hired by Burnside. It is a tutorial for the commander which Hooker no doubt appreciated, for it gave him confidence in Sharpe's ability.

While the analytical formulas and techniques would later be refined to produce highly accurate numbers, Sharpe's figures at even the upper levels (42,500) were wrong by only 15 percent. As his confidence grew so did the errors. The Army of Northern Virginia reported a "present for duty" strength as of the end of March of 60,298, with the six infantry divisions at the strength of 48,982 men. The medium estimate (39,275) is off by 20 percent. The lowest estimate (32,500) is off by 34 percent.[11] Nevertheless, for an effort that began from a standing start, a fact Sharpe was at pains to remind Hooker of at the beginning of the report, it was a vast improvement over anything that had been done in the past. Its importance was in the establishment of a systemized collection and analytical process—a historical first. It was a system that would only improve with practice and experience. (See Appendix G: Abstracts from Field Returns of the Army of Northern Virginia.)

Sharpe ended his report with the phrase "submitted in behalf of Mr. Babcock and myself" to ensure proper credit to his invaluable deputy. Nothing will poison the harmony of a staff more than the chief taking all the credit. In another such gesture of good will, Babcock noted in an added memorandum to another report of the same day:

> If not otherwise reported to the General it should also be stated, although the credit thereof is not due to this department, that Capt. Fisher (Chief Signal officer) is in possession of the full code of signals used by the enemy's Signal Corps, with the exception of the numbers, and that their messages are read, daily, by his officers, whenever they can be observed from our stations.[12]

This report consisted of a breakdown of all of Lee's infantry divisions by brigade and location. Importantly, Babcock made it clear that he was not sure of the full complement of each brigade. In still another memorandum of March 15, Sharpe provided an order-of-battle of Stuart's Cavalry Division down to brigade and regiment. His only significant error was to identify Col. Thomas A. Munford as commanding a separate brigade, when he only commanded the 2nd Virginia Cavalry in Brig. Gen. Fitzhugh Lee's Brigade, and to confuse that regiment with the 12th Virginia Cavalry.[13]

It did not take long for Sharpe to conclude that there is more to an enemy's strength than is found in his order-of-battle. Hooker had been interested in the Confederate intelligence collection and raiding activities based in the Northern Neck and had directed Sharpe to send an agent to investigate. To Sharpe there were larger implications in these activities than Hooker had anticipated. In a report (through Butterfield) to Hooker on March 21, he gave the following reply:

> In examination of prisoners and other agents furnishing information my attention has lately been drawn most strongly to the question of the subsistence of the Southern army, which seems to be nearing the point of total failure. From a mass of testimony, that in a court of record, would authorize the judge to rule, that no further evidence on that point would be received, we know that the ration of the army opposite us is as follows:
> 1 pint flour & ¼ lb bacon or pork per diem.

A month later he could report there was no improvement in the subsistence of the Army of Northern Virginia, as he describes in a letter to his uncle:

> I have sent you two or three times Richmond papers and hope you will not think that I tear them in two. All southern papers are only published on a half sheet. By remarking the advertisements as well as the editorials you will notice what a state of destitution they are approaching $3000 are paid for substitutes and none are to be had at that price. $160 a pair for ordinary boots $150 a lb for pork and $15. a bushel for potatoes.
> I have many prisoners brought out to me who have wretched shoes on for which they paid $20.
> I had a man from Richmond yesterday & he paid $8. per day at the hotel. Desertion is now taking place from Geo & Miss Regts which have heretofore stood firm. All this of course is intended to be private.[14]

A few well-clad boastful exceptions proved the rule, "but the ragged and beggarly fellows who formed their rank and file on the other side did not so understand the 'tea cup of flour and patch of bacon' which was daily issued them by those who are interested in the success of the rebellion." All other commissary stores, including candles, had simply been exhausted. The Confederate Government was forcing farmers to stop growing tobacco and cotton and grow wheat and corn instead. Government agents were essentially forcing the sale of meat and grain at below market prices. Sharpe described the sorry state of affairs:

> The spring wheat crop in the south is not a regular one—their corn always comes in more or less abundance but their wheat is only an occasional success—and it is now known that this year it will fail. There is therefore nothing to carry the southern army through to the next crop, if we exercise the greatest vigilance in closing against them their outside granaries. And I am convinced that one of the greatest of these I am satisfied is the Northern Neck.

Sharpe then described from a number of sources the immense amounts of foodstuffs and stock that the Confederates were obtaining from the Northern Neck and that "Southern agents are now employed in buying it up and crossing it over the Rappahannock." So robust was this traffic that Sharpe stated that even should all their boats be seized, it would hardly close down the operation since it was so lucrative. To emphasize its importance once again he stated clearly that four of the six Confederate divisions facing them had moved closer to the Northern Neck to be closer to their main source of supply. Finally, Sharpe concluded his report with the pointed hint, "Believing, General, that these facts are worthy [of] attention, they are respectfully submitted for such action as the judgment of the Commanding General may dictate."[15]

Sharpe's encouragement did prompt some attempts to stop the traffic, but lack of a sustained effort with anything more than small parties proved a failure. Sharpe, however, would continue to worry this bone of the Northern Neck even into 1865, when he finally convinced Grant to put a stop to it. Sharpe was clearly thinking beyond his normal tactical and operational purview. He had grasped how the enemy's national logistics difficulties would affect the ability of his army to fight and that this analysis was appropriate for the army commander to take into serious consideration. Ironically, no one on the Union side was able to conceive how long and hard Johnny Reb could fight on a "tea cup of flour and patch of bacon."

The next day Sharpe provided the report that Hooker had requested, showing that the Black Horse Cavalry was working closely with civilians in the Northern Neck. One of the civilians, already well known as a shady character by Brigadier General Patrick, was suborning desertions from the Union army, forcing his slaves to exchange clothes with them and then sending them back across the Potomac to head north ostensibly now civilians.[16]

That same day Sharpe reported on scout Dan Cole's return and his observations. They confirmed his own analysis of the subsistence crisis in the Army of Northern Virginia. In particular, he had spoken to a quartermaster in Richmond who told him there were 90 days' supplies stored there, but added, "God knows when we shall get any more."[17]

Sharpe had thrown a wide net after his appointment. Not only was he concentrating on the enemy's order-of-battle but also actively engaging in counterintelligence operations to disrupt the enemy's intelligence collection against the Army of the Potomac. The army, in fact, lived in a security sieve created by its location amid a hostile population that actively sought and transmitted information to the Confederates. Sharpe's reports led to the severe restriction on movement that would amount to house arrest for the local civilian population the closer the army got to striking.

In an effort to plug another source of leaks of information, and possibly at Sharpe's recommendation, Hooker issued General Orders No. 48, on April 30: "The frequent transmission of false intelligence and the betrayal of the movements of the army to the enemy, by the publication of injudicious correspondence of an anonymous character, makes it necessary to require all newspaper correspondents to publish their communications over their own signatures." Journalists who disregarded this requirement would be barred from the army and their publications banned from distribution. This had the unexpected effect of creating the byline in American newspaper journalism. Hooker went further to prevent information in the Northern press from being acquired by the Confederates by forbidding the exchange of newspapers. The stoppage of newspapers was quickly noted with annoyance by the *Richmond Whig* as one of the "new leaves turned over by Gen. Hooker."[18]

The BMI was able to identify other operational security gaps, such as when scout John Skinker, also on March 11, reported that the scouts from Averell's command completely neglected to cover an important area. Babcock immediately forwarded this report to Butterfield. This, however, could not have been popular with the cavalry, which resented the BMI's trespassing on its traditional intelligence collection role.[19]

Skinker, at Babcock's direction, established the BMI's signal station, employing a "clothesline code" on the Confederate side of the river in Fredericksburg itself. On March 11, Babcock reported to Butterfield that "A clothesline with one piece denotes that the forces in the vicinity of Fredericksburg are on the move. An empty line denotes that they have all gone away. Two pieces shows that they are in force as they have been since the fight, three pieces that they are being reinforced." Babcock's obituary in 1908 mentioned a clothesline code being operated by a Negro woman. Butterfield, in his communications with Hooker, referred to this as "Sharpe's signals."[20]

Sharpe's intelligence preparation of the battlefield included more than the enemy's order-of-battle and poor logistics. A thorough knowledge of the enemy's communications by road and rail would be vital in order to calculate the time required for enemy forces to move from one point to another and to sustain logistics support of those forces. That same information was equally vital for calculations necessary for planning friendly movement along these same routes. Without such knowledge, offensive operational planning was impossible.

Early in March Sharpe had written to the assistant adjutant general at Fort Monroe, trying to find a former employee of the Richmond, Fredericksburg & Potomac Railroad (the RF&P), Alexander L. Worrell, who had surveyed the line. Sharpe wanted either Worrell or the survey.[21] The fruit of this survey in the form of numerous tables is found in the Hooker Papers at the Huntington Library. This collection contains the official documents Hooker took with him after his relief from command of the Army of the Potomac in June 1863. These are original documents and in many cases may well be the only copies to have survived. Worrell's survey appears to have been the basis of a seriously expanded project. The various elements of this collection of tables shown below are a comprehensive analysis of the Confederate rail and road routes in Hooker's intended area of operations.

Lee's main supply route (MSR) ran along two railroads. The Richmond, Fredericksburg & Potomac Railroad (RF&P) and the Virginia Central Railroad. The RF&P ran 61 ½ miles from Richmond to Fredericksburg around which the Army of Northern Virginia was deployed. The Virginia Central ran roughly parallel to the RF&P until they both met at Hanover Junction, 24 miles from Richmond on the RF&P and 28 miles from Richmond on the Virginia Central. Hanover Junction lay 40 miles south of Fredericksburg. The Virginia Central then turned west through Gordonsville, Charlottesville, and into the Shenandoah Valley. Hanover Junction was identified as an especially critical target. Military supplies came up the RF&P to Lee from Richmond, while food supplies came through the Virginia Central largely from the granary of the Valley. Those supplies were stockpiled in warehouses at Hanover Junction for transfer to the RF&P. If there ever existed a vital communications/logistics node it was Hanover Junction. It was manifestly necessary to the survival of the Army of Northern Virginia.

These tables essentially were lists of the points of vulnerability of Lee's logistics windpipe—bridges. For example, there is a description of the major bridge over the South Anna River just south of Hanover Junction: "600 ft long 73 ft high, stone piers and abutments same character of construction as the bridge over the Rappahannock at Fredericksburg & 3 or 5 ft shorter."[22]

In addition to the railroad and road surveys, the Hooker Papers also yielded equally detailed analyses of the 19 Rappahannock and 14 Rapidan River fords. None of them show any evidence that Sharpe was involved in the creation or at least transmittal of these analyses other than the endorsement notation in his hand, "Memoir on the crossing places of the Rappahannock from Bealton to Kelly's [Ford]" found among these reports. However, another analysis, identical in form, of the Rappahannock and Rapidan fords, found at the National Archives, was completed by the BMI and dated May 13.[23] Sharpe's scouts were constantly crossing the fords of both rivers to conduct operations behind Confederate lines and would have been ideal observers.

These reports are typical of the detailed and patient work the BMI was doing. That contention is supported by Stephen Sears in his superb account of the battle.[24]

Table 4.1. Distances on the Richmond, Fredericksburg & Potomac and The Virginia Central Railroads

As Compiled by the BMI			
RF&P (from Fredericksburg)		Virginia Central R.R. (from Richmond)	
Station	Miles	Station	Miles
Fredericksburg	0	Richmond	0
Hazel Run	.5	Atlus	9
Massaponax Creek	6	Hanover Courthouse	18
Summit	8	Hanover Junction	28
Guineas Station	12	North Tavern/Noel's Turn	33
Milford Station	21	Beaver Dam	40
Mattapony River	22.5	Bumpas Turnout	[no miles shown]
Pole Cat River & Station	25	Frederick Hall	50
Reedy Swamp	26	Tallersville (Tollers)	56
Chesterfield	30	Louisa Courthouse	62
North Anna River	36	Travillian St. (Trevillians)	67
Hanover Junction	38	Wilton Station	73
Taylorsville	40	Gordonsville	76
Little River	41		
South Anna River	43		
Ashland	45		
Hungary Station	53		
Chickahominy Swamp	55		
Richmond	61.5		

The information in the ford analyses includes road access; condition of banks on both sides; ability of cavalry, artillery, and infantry to cross; and obstructions and water depth. Among all these tables there is only one date—April 22—an indication of how long it took to compile this information.

By the last week of March, Sharpe's operation was working smoothly. The scouts continued to bring a constant stream of information that fitted more pieces into the mosaic of the enemy's order-of-battle and dispositions as well as providing vital information on the enemy's own scouting and clandestine activities that helped maintain a higher level of operational security. Deserters and the occasional prisoner continued to yield order-of-battle information to Sharpe and Babcock's gentle guile. The number of subjects for interrogation had not been large. February yielded deserters and prisoners from only 20 regiments and four batteries; March provided only 12 regiments and April just 13.[25]

Unlike the large numbers of men captured during the heavy fighting of the Peninsula Campaign and Antietam, there had been little combat since the battle of Fredericksburg with resulting few prisoners. Most of the men interrogated had arrived by way of desertion, an overt act that severed loyalties and encouraged a desire to please and a willingness to be forthcoming. There may have been fewer deserters than prisoners, but the deserters more than made up the numbers by the quality of information they yielded, as Sharpe underlined when he wrote, "frequently deserters have been able to furnish us with complete organizations of their Brigades, Divisions &c."[26] The only problem with deserters was that they tended to come from the enemy units closest to Union lines. The further away a unit was, the less likely it was a man would risk such a long journey through an area thick with other units and suspicious provost guards. This was particularly true of the cavalry. (See Appendix H: Regiments/Battalions from which Deserters and Prisoners Were Interrogated.)

It was time, Sharpe decided, to fill a major remaining intelligence gap—lack of direct access to information from Richmond itself. Patrick knew the man who could help him.

James L. McPhail was the civilian provost marshal of Maryland. Formally that position entailed conducting conscription and apprehending deserters. Like Sharpe, McPhail saw that his duty lay beyond the official narrow confines of his job description. He had a nose for disloyalty and spies. He was a hard-headed Unionist who had achieved notoriety for his "sensational arrest of a pro-Southern country judge by force while court was in session." He had been praised for arresting a number of Southern agents in the secessionist-minded city of Baltimore. That city was the natural focal point for agents and contraband smugglers traveling up and down the river to the Chesapeake and Virginia. Patrick's and McPhail's police duties overlapped enough for Patrick to recommend to Sharpe the provost marshal, whose knowledge of the contraband situation would be a good man to help him fill his intelligence gap.

By the last week in March Sharpe was in Baltimore conferring with McPhail, who, by happy coincidence, had been grooming an agent to be placed in the Rebel capital. Both men would refer to this agent—subsequently identified as Joseph H. Maddox, a Southern gentleman and slaveholder—as "our friend" in all their correspondence. His cover was as a purveyor of Northern goods in desperately short supply in Richmond. A sloop dropped him off quietly onto Virginia's shore on April 11. Time would tell if McPhail's investment would pay off. Hooker would have great need of it.[27]

His relationship with McPhail was not a one-way street. As deputy provost marshal, Sharpe was also aware of criminal activities in the smuggling of contraband supplies to the Confederacy which he provided to McPhail. In May he notified McPhail of the contraband business conducted on St. George Island in the Potomac River to the Virginia shore by Samuel G. Miles. That was a valuable piece of information to

McPhail, who knew Miles as "an active Rebel" in Baltimore. Working together they ensured that Miles was unable to get his goods to Richmond. Eventually, this case would be linked to Maj. Gen. Benjamin Butler's murky cooperation with smuggling contraband supplies in the following year.[28]

In early April a unique informant presented himself to Sharpe. James Craig, a Scot immigrant and Unionist, had fled Richmond with a wealth of detailed information on the transfer of Longstreet's Corps from Fredericksburg through Richmond. That and other sources on Longstreet's absence would be critical to the development of Hooker's plan of campaign. Craig was also an eyewitness to the "bread riots" of starving women driven to desperation by unaffordable prices for food that had convulsed Richmond and had been reported in the *National Republican* on April 9. The report was a window into the social and economic tensions within Southern society that could have an eventual effect on military operations. For Sharpe, it was an eye-opener to the possibilities that lay with casting his intelligence net beyond the immediate military situation. There is nothing like the news of a starving family at home to destroy a soldier's morale. He also saw the propaganda value of the eye-witness account and leaked it to the *National Republican*. Four days later the paper ran an initial story about the riot:

> [The riot] caused the greatest consternation among the authorities. The women were the heads of families of the working classes, and were actually starving, many having been compelled to be on the street. A repetition of the demonstration is feared, and every precaution is being taken to avert it. The effect upon the troops was very demoralizing, the men being very clamorous, and demanding that their families be fed.

On April 25, the paper ran a fuller article, dated the day after Craig gave his statement and using some of the same phrasing such that the Richmond authorities had blamed the riots on "Irish and Yankee hags."[29]

In quick succession, the BMI began receiving from its various sources the signs of a splendid opportunity to take Lee unawares. Lee's army remained concentrated around Fredericksburg on the southern side of the Rappahannock River, and a wide gap in the forces guarding the upriver fords had opened up.

The intercepted deceptive flag signal that Lee had credited detailed an attack by the Union Cavalry Corps on the move up the river against the Confederates in the Shenandoah Valley. In response, Lee deployed Stuart's cavalry opposite the Union cavalry, leaving a 20-mile gap in the Confederate defenses northwest from Fredericksburg along the river and leaving the vital Kelly's Ford unguarded. Isaac Silver, living near Fredericksburg, reported that Lee's army continued to be concentrated in that area. He also reported that although the U.S. Ford 10 miles up the Rappahannock from Fredericksburg was guarded, there were no other Confederate forces within 5 miles. A Confederate deserter, another Virginian, provided detailed information that confirmed Silver's report. Sharpe's scouts confirmed it a third time in this summary on April 28, forwarded by Butterfield to the commander of the Cavalry Corps:

One of Colonel Sharpe's men just in from Kelly's Ford says in his opinion no large body of infantry there. Held mostly by cavalry and artillery. Rebel sympathizers on this side believe enemy have fallen back beyond Rapidan, meaning to make that their line of defense. Says also that Fitzhugh [W. H. F.] Lee has taken place of Fitz. Lee, between Kelly's and Culpeper. Latter gone to Valley, to join Hampton and Jones. Enemy's artillery horses said not to be able to move their guns. They think our cavalry move a feint, and that the crossing will be made at United States Ford, where they are still at work.[30]

The BMI analysis of Kelly's Ford called attention to it at this time as an excellent crossing point over the Rappahannock. It read:

> Good road and easy of access
> The banks are low on both sides
> Cavalry, Artillery and Infantry can cross
> The ford may be made less practicable by obstructions and an abattis, and defended by rifle pits.
> The water is about two feet deep known from personal observation
> Between Wheatly's ford on the left, there are two places may be crossed by infantry only.[31]

Hooker determined to seize this priceless opportunity. His plan of operations would be judged the best devised in the entire war. It essentially had three parts. The first element would be the departure of the entire Cavalry Corps under Brigadier General Stoneman, to sever the RF&P, Lee's main supply route to his logistics base at Richmond and beyond. Sharpe had identified the only two Confederate forces he was likely to encounter—Fitzhugh Lee's cavalry brigade at Culpeper and a small provost guard at Gordonsville. "It is not in the power of the rebels to oppose you with more than 5,000 sabers, and those badly mounted…" These figures were close to the mark. Sharpe also supplied the BMI analyses of the railroad to assist him in the destruction of key elements:

> Stoneman's orders were clear. From Gordonsville it is expected that you will be able to push forward to the Aquia and Richmond Railroad [RF&P], somewhere in the vicinity of Saxton's [Hanover] Junction, destroying along your whole route the railroad bridges, trains, cars, depots of provisions, lines of telegraphic communications, &c. The general directs that you go prepared with all the means necessary to accomplish this work effectually. As the line of the railroad from Aquia to Richmond presents the shortest one for the enemy to retire on, it is more than probable that the enemy may avail himself of it and the usually traveled highways on each side of it for this purpose…[32]

If this were the case, then Stoneman was to block or delay their retreat, and if that were not possible, to harry it aggressively.

Hanover Junction, with its surrounding bridges, was the primary target. As Sears observed, "Within a few miles of Hanover Junction were three good-sized wooden RF&P bridges … over the North Anna River, Reedy Swamp, and Pole Cat Creek, Burning any one of them would shut down the railroad instantly and for a substantial period." These great, high, wooden structures were begging for the torch. He certainly had the force to do it, with 9,895 cavalrymen and 22 guns manned by 427 gunners. Even if he unexpectedly ran into Stuart's entire command, he would outnumber it

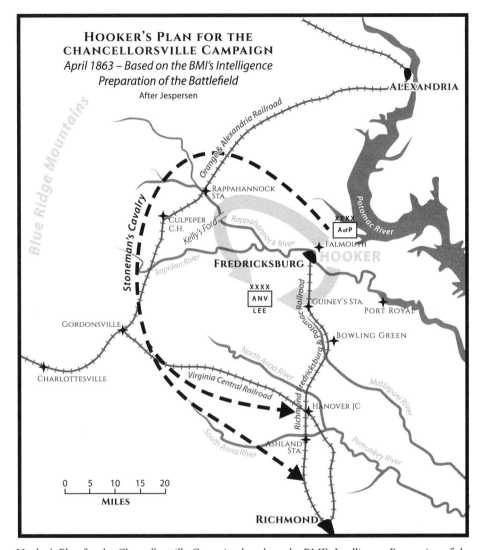

Hooker's Plan for the Chancellorsville Campaign based on the BMI's Intelligence Preparation of the Battlefield (IPB), April 1863. (After Jespersen)

by two and a half times. Certainly, Sharpe had done everything within his grasp to make this a successful mission.[33]

Second, Hooker would fix Lee's attention on Fredericksburg, with three corps (58,000 men of I, III, VI Corps) under Maj. Gen. John Sedgwick, commander of VI Corps. Then, third, he would take three corps (41,000 men of V, XI, XII Corps) and cross the Rappahannock upstream of Fredericksburg at Kelly's Ford and others, then march south quickly through the Wilderness to catch Lee between himself and Sedgwick. The choice of the three corps he would take on his encirclement was dictated not by their combat effectiveness but by the placement of their camps; they were nearer the fords, and their movement would be the most direct and shortest. Unfortunately, that meant that for this most critical maneuver, Hooker would be taking the newer, weaker, and less experienced XI and XII Corps. II Corps was left as a diversion east of Fredericksburg. As needed, Hooker would transfer Sedgwick's I and III Corps to join his three. Either group of corps was equal in strength to Lee's entire infantry force.[34] It was a magnificent trap.

Consider how all the parts of that plan depended upon information provided by Sharpe's BMI. His scouts had accurately identified the dispositions and encampments of all of Lee's divisions and most of his brigades, allowing Hooker to pick the most unguarded and thus advantageous route to strike them. That route revealed itself as Kelly's Ford by the combined work of the agent Silver, scouting, and the analysis of the suitability of the ford. The information that Longstreet had taken one-third of Lee's divisions to the siege of Suffolk told him that he would be facing a weakened enemy. It also made it clear that they were out of range of intervention in the coming battle, for several days at least. Thus, Hooker would be facing only two-thirds of Lee's force, which, combined with Babcock's strength estimates, established that Hooker would have an advantage of more than two to one in manpower. Finally, the analysis of the railroads revealed vulnerabilities and established that the destruction of Hanover Junction and bridges would effectively cut Lee off from his supplies and block his retreat.

Sharpe had handed Hooker General Lee's head on a silver platter. In a letter home on the 22nd, he expressed the optimism that had suffused not only the staff but the entire army. "I am not at liberty to say anything about our movements, but I beg you to rest strong in the faith that we are now commanded by a man who means to fight to win—and that when the blow is struck, it will be one of the heaviest ever felt on this continent—& with more than the results of a battle."[35]

Plugging Holes

In the week before the army would begin moving, Hooker's distrust of journalists appeared more than justified. In a letter of April 21 to Secretary of War Stanton, he described how the *Morning Chronicle* had published a letter by Dr. Jonathan Letterman, Medical Director of the Army of the Potomac, that revealed important information on the strength of the army. Hooker wrote, "The chief of my secret service department [Sharpe] would have willingly paid $1000 for such information in regard to the enemy at the commencement of his operations, and even now would give that sum for it to verify the statements which he has been at great labor and trouble to collect and systemize." The letter strongly suggests that Hooker by this point was well pleased with Sharpe's efforts.[36]

He was pleased enough to make Sharpe the president of a commission for the trial of a reporter who was charged with revealing vital information on the army in an article. An example needed to be made. E. F. Denyse had written an article for the *New York Herald*, published on March 14, that related all sorts of preparations for an advance of the army. Hooker had wanted a good example made, as Sharpe would write in the record of the proceedings:

> While none is more desirous than the Major General Commanding, to extend all proper facilities to the press in its efforts to supply the public with reliable intelligence, it cannot be tolerated that newspaper correspondents should abuse the privilege of remaining with the army by the publication of intelligence certain to be of use to the Enemy and most likely soon to reach him.

Denyse pleaded guilty and was sentenced to six months' hard labor, followed by permanent expulsion from the army. With a deft touch, Hooker commuted the sentence to expulsion, and Denyse was marched under guard and put on board a ship departing Acquia Creek for Washington. Sharpe and his staff would despise the *New York Herald* through the rest of the war for the way it fecklessly printed sensitive material.[37]

It was a responsible officer, Maj. Henry C. Jenckes, 2nd Rhode Island Regiment, who sat down after coming back from three days of picket duty and took pen in hand to alert his chain of command about the lax security he had become aware of. He wrote of his concerns on April 16 about how information was leaking across the river to the enemy despite orders forbidding any communication with the enemy by pickets. He wrote that a local civilian informed him of the move of the Union cavalry on the left on the 13th, the same day the Confederates called across the river that the cavalry had moved. On the 14th Confederate pickets announced that the paymasters had arrived in the Union camps only 15 minutes after Jenckes himself was officially informed. The Confederates also yelled across the river, "You need not be so still; we know all about it; you have got orders to move." His report triggered an examination by Patrick on the 21st.

He already had a poor opinion of the pickets' conduct, which he made a point to say he had complained of before. He found a lieutenant in command of the pickets actually engaged in sending little boats across the river with coffee, sugar, and newspapers. The young man was put out when Patrick smashed his boat. He then related a conversation between the pickets on the 15th.[38]

> The part of the conversation was about rations. Secesh [the secessionist] then asked, "Any signs of a move?" Reply, "Yes, we have got eight days' rations, and expect to move in a few days. We have three days' rations in our haversacks and five in our knapsacks." Secesh then asked, "Where is the move to be?" Reply, "Up to the right." Secesh then asked how we were going to get transportation, or whether we would use the railroads. Our picket replied that he thought the trains would be kept up by pack-mules.[39]

It was enough to give Hooker, who had thrown up such strict operational security measures, an aneurism. Luckily the Confederates did not seem to make any use of the intelligence gems the careless pickets were throwing across the river. The picket had said the army was going to move in a few days and it did not. That may have convinced whoever was receiving the information that it was a false alarm and made no more of it.

About the same time a rumor began spreading through the army camps that the Confederates had run a telegraph wire under the Rappahannock to supply intelligence to Lee. On the 25th The *Philadelphia Enquirer* ran the story. It related how a guard stationed outside a house on the Rappahannock at Falmouth heard a clicking sound resembling a telegraph coming from within and reported it. He was told to investigate, and "on opening the door, he discovered a party of four or five persons, one of whom was seated at a telegraph instrument, sending messages by a submarine telegraph wire across the Rappahannock."[40]

The *New York Times* published a similar story on April 28, with a header of "Headquarters Army of the Potomac, April 26, 1863." Edwin Fishel states that it was an official dispatch from the army that the censor in Washington stopped but that the correspondent mailed to his editor. Apparently smarting from the *Enquirer* story, Major General Stoneman ordered the newspaper's correspondent "immediately sent out of the lines of the army, never to return." Sharpe's hand can be seen in this since he perused not only Southern but Northern newspapers.[41]

The question remained whether there was any truth to the underwater telegraph story. The Confederates clearly had a rapid transmission system for intelligence from Falmouth to reach Lee's headquarters at Culpeper. The Confederates had advance knowledge of the attack by Brigadier General Averell's cavalry division across Kelly's Ford on March 17. Brigadier General Fitzhugh Lee received a telegram from Culpeper the day before as the Union cavalry concentrated and prepared for the next day's attack. The distance between Falmouth and Culpeper is over 30 miles. Averell's regiments received their orders from the Headquarters, Cavalry Corps, on the 15th, and his entire command departed the camps of the army on the 16th. It appears that Fitzhugh Lee received a warning in record time, the very day Averell's division departed its camps. That argues for some plausibility to the underwater telegraph story. On the other hand, there is no reference to this story in official records or in Patrick's diary.[42]

Further evidence for a Confederate spy in Falmouth is a letter that Lee sent to Stuart on March 12. He wrote, "The information from Falmouth is that the enemy will, as soon as roads permit, cross at United States Ford, Falmouth, and some point below, the attempt at Falmouth to be a feint." This is an astounding statement. Lee had summarized in broad strokes most of Hooker's operational plan for the coming campaign. Then he stated, "This information comes from citizens, and especially from a lady, wife of one of our officers, and I do not know how true."

Patrick frequently visited a Mrs. John Seddon, whom he thought of as friend, at her home in Falmouth. She was the wife of a Confederate officer and had been the specific object of an order "prohibiting against manipulation of window blinds or windows proper in a manner that could convey information." Whether Lee was referring to Mrs. Seddon in his letter to Stuart as his source is unknown. Whether the source of information was Mrs. Seddon, another woman, or an underwater telegraph or a combination, it went dead just before the Army of the Potomac marched out of its camps for the collision at Chancellorsville. The posting of guards at every private home on the route of the army may have done as intended to prevent civilians from sending information. The proof would be found in the complete surprise of Lee. He may have learned of the outline of Hooker's plan in March, but apparently never learned the vital "when." His letter also indicated that he was not sure of the information. There was nothing subsequent that confirmed the information and no trigger that warned him of the sudden movement of the Army of the Potomac.[43]

The Campaign Begins

Hooker put the army into motion on April 27. He had preceded the march with a ruthless exercise of local security to prevent the local population from sending news of the army's movement immediately to Lee. The entire population along the army's march was put under virtual house arrest. He also kept the full plan from his subordinates except for his second in command, Maj. Gen. Darius Couch, and Butterfield, his chief of staff. All this worked; not a word leaked to Lee that a giant trap had been sprung on him and the Army of Northern Virginia. The measure, however, by denying his corps commanders a thorough understanding of the commander's intent, would have unforeseen consequences. Sharpe would accompany Hooker on the enveloping movement, while Babcock and McEntee would remain with Butterfield at Falmouth.

Command emphasis on intelligence collection at this crucial time was intense, as Butterfield on April 28 "Cautioned Sharpe, signal officers, and Lowe [Balloon Corps] to be vigilant and watchful; to get all information possible." Sharpe also was able to report that deserters had revealed that as of April 26, three of the four divisions in Jackson's II Corps had not moved and showed no signs of moving. Unfortunately, strong winds kept Lowe from ascending with his balloons Washington and Eagle. Hooker was not ready to write off the balloons and ordered Lowe to ascend at night "to find the enemy's camp fires." He specifically wanted "Some one acquainted with the position and location of the ground and of the enemy's forces" to go up. He recognized that as intrepid as Lowe was, his reporting suffered from a lack of military training and experience. The winds abated, allowing the balloons to ascend in the day, but they were unable to see much due to dense ground fog. "What few camps that were visible, however, appeared to be occupied as usual." Both Sharpe's interrogations and Lowe's balloons were confirming that Lee had not stirred.[44]

Table 4.2. Strength of the Army of Northern Virginia in the Chancellorsville Campaign

	ANV Return 31 March	As computed by Bigelow	As computed by Babcock
Longstreet's I Corps			
Anderson's Division	8,132	8,050	8,200
McLaws's Division	8,567	8,345	6,500
Subtotal	16,699	16,395	14,700
Jackson's II Corps			
A.P. Hill's Division	11,400	11,351	11,600
D.H. Hill/Rodes's Division	8,732	9,663	8,300
Early's Division	8,234	9,276	8,400
Trimble's Division	6,530	6,669	6,800
Subtotal	34,896	36,959	35,100
Subtotal Infantry Divisions	51,595	52,354	49,800
Stuart's Cavalry Division	6,967	4,138	5,500
Artillery	1,699	no data	no data
Total	60,261	56,429	55,300
Total w/o artillery	58,562	56,429	55,300

The BMI now presented Hooker with a further gift, the refinement of the already reported enemy order-of-battle. On the 28th, Sharpe showed Hooker the fruit of Babcock's diligence—a complete order-of-battle of the Army of Northern Virginia. It included an estimate of its strength (55,300), down to the division, which would prove within 2 percent of the actual returns for April (56,492), compiled after the war by John Bigelow to reconstruct the missing returns for that month. To the March returns he added the 1,500 replacements received in April to Lee's divisions. Babcock also produced a detailed order-of-battle of Jackson's Corp on May 1, in which the only change was a 1,600-man reduction in the strength of Rodes's (formerly D. H. Hill's) Division, from 8,300 to 6,700. That dropped Jackson's estimated infantry strength to 33,500 without any explanation.[45]

The BMI's estimate of the artillery of the Army of Northern Virginia was similarly accurate at 240 guns, an overcount of only 20 guns or only 8.3 percent. Of the 240 guns, 166 were identified as held by the batteries attached to brigades and the remaining 74 in the batteries of the artillery reserve.[46]

General confirmation of these figures arrived on May 1 from McPhail. As soon as the information arrived, Butterfield telegraphed Hooker: "Sharpe's man from Richmond has returned. Reports 59,000 rations issued to Lee's army."[47] Apparently Maddox had learned this information from a commissary officer. It included Lee's

Table 4.3. Accuracy of Babcock's Order-of-Battle Compared to ANV Mar Return & Bigelow's Estimated April Return

	% Compared to ANV March Return	% Compared to Bigelow's est. April Return
Longstreet's I Corps		
Anderson's Division	100.8	101.9
McLaws's Division	75.0	77.8
Subtotal	88.0	89.7
Jackson's II Corps		
A.P. Hill's Division	101.8	102.2
D.H. Hill, Rodes's Division	95.1	85.9
Early's Division	102.0	101.5
Trimble's Division	104.1	102.0
Subtotal	100.6	95.0
Total of Infantry Divisions	94.0	96.1
Stuart's Cavalry Division	78.9	133.0
Artillery	no data	no data
Total w/o artillery	94.5	98.0

infantry and artillery but not his cavalry. Adding the figure for the artillery in the March returns of the ANV and Babcock's 55,300 estimate gives a figure of just about 58,000, within 1.7 percent of the Maddox figure. Maddox also identified the remaining forces in Virginia—10,000 men in the defenses of Richmond and Hampton's and Jones's cavalry brigades—all either too far away to intervene in the battle in time such as the cavalry or too vital to the defense of the capital to be detached. The identification of possible theater-level reserves operates at the operational level of war, rather than the tactical, which concentrates on only those forces likely to be immediately engaged.

A comparison of Babcock's two reports of April 28 and May 1 shows a significant fine tuning of the understanding of the order-of-battle of Lee's infantry brigades and regiments/battalions. They will be compared with the currently accepted Confederate order-of-battle shown in Stephen Sears's *Chancellorsville* (1996). The report of the 28th covers Longstreet's two divisions, Jackson's entire corps, and Stuart's cavalry. The report of the 1st covers only Jackson's Corps. By April 28th, Babcock had identified 114 of 129 regiments and separate battalions (31 of 39 in Longstreet's two divisions and 83 of 90 in Jackson's Corps) and 25 of 28 infantry brigades in Lee's six infantry divisions. The three missing brigades were O'Neal's Brigade in Rodes's Division (Longstreet), Perry's Brigade in Anderson's Division, and Kershaw's Brigade in McLaws's Division, both in Longstreet's Corps. By the

1st, Babcock had refined his order-of-battle of Jackson's Corps to count 89 of 90 regiments and separate battalions. Of course, not all the units on both lists were the same, but he had arrived at the exact overall number. As an example of Babcock's accuracy, Appendix I shows his estimates of the order-of-battle for Jackson's Corps. The list below, in Babcock's handwriting, contains his estimates of the strength of the Army of Northern Virginia in the opening stage of the battle of Chancellorsville. It was found as a treasured souvenir of his war service in surviving papers which now rest in the Library of Congress. For a small organization that had only been created and had to start from scratch less than three months earlier, the results were nothing short of miraculous.

That could not quite be said of the BMI's grasp of the enemy's cavalry. Babcock, in his April 28 order-of-battle, had listed under Stuart's Cavalry Division the brigades of Fitzhugh Lee, W. H. F. Lee, Wade Hampton, Mumford, and Jones. He had only a good understanding of the first two brigades, which had remained opposite the Army of the Potomac. However, the BMI analysts had missed the fact that Wade Hampton's Brigade had moved far south early in the month to recuperate their spent horses.[48] Mumford was John Mumford, colonel of the 2nd North Carolina Cavalry, in W. H. F. Lee's Brigade. He had had an independent command in the Antietam Campaign, but by this time that brigade was commanded by Col. William E. "Grumble" Jones. "Cobb's Legion and others" was the only information on the brigade's composition, and that was wrong. Cobb's Georgia Legion was in Wade Hampton's Brigade. The entry for Jones's Brigade refers to "Grumble" Jones and only identified the "6th Va [Cavalry] and others" for its complement. The 6th Virginia was indeed in the brigade which itself was in the Shenandoah Valley, with no opportunity to reinforce Stuart before the issue would be decided. Babcock's report showed a total strength for Stuart's Cavalry Division of 12,000, probably the BMI's most inaccurate estimate made during the war. Only Fitzhugh Lee's and W. H. F. Lee's brigades were available to take part in the battle and their actual strength was only 4,291 troopers, though they were credited with 5,500, an overestimation of 28 percent.

The Test of Battle

Hooker's optimism soared. Intelligence had allowed him to steal a march on Lee "the Incomparable"—the Confederate general's popular epithet—and begin to close a trap that was classic in its conception and initial execution. Taking Stuart completely by surprise, Hooker pushed V, XI, and XII Corps across Kelly's Ford on the evening of the 28th and morning of the 29th. He boasted on May 1, "The rebel army is now the legitimate property of the Army of the Potomac ... the enemy is now in my power, and God Almighty cannot deprive me of them."[49] But this wild mood swing was indicative of a greater problem. A mind that could soar could also crash. Lincoln had noted this in his late April official visit to the army. Lincoln was impressed with the improved condition of the army but remarked that Hooker's overconfidence was "about the worst thing I have seen since have been down there."[50]

To Hooker his confidence seemed justified. He had indeed completely taken Lee unawares. It was hours before Lee heard of the crossing and another 12 before he realized its extent. That allowed Hooker's three corps to deploy around the Chancellor House. By then, Lee was reacting with dispatch, moving McLaws to the north with Anderson to follow.

At this moment of excitement when the Army of the Potomac had been set in motion, Sharpe took the time to write a revealing letter to his uncle on April 28. Any dreams of martial glory seem to have receded as he realized what a sure fit he had found as chief of the BMI and what gift had so unexpectedly fallen into his lap.

> I have not sought the position—but I did not feel like running away from it. A short time since I was offered a higher position—with the command of a Brigade which I declined, because it would take me permanently from my regiment—and there upon I was announced in orders as Dep PMar Genl of the Army.
>
> I can still return at any time to my regiment—that is I suppose a request on my part to that effect would be complied with—after spending a few days in fitting another to take my place. A formal demand for my return, made by General Revere cmdg our brigade, was refused by General Hooker—but I presume I could effect it. It is not my intention to remain permanently away from the regiment unless I can do something for it; although I have reason to believe that nothing but my own action can take me from my present position or prevent my proper advancement from it. I have always believed that those positions which come and are not sought, are apt to be of the most permanent benefit—and I have not sought this chance.[51]

It took a steady hand on the BMI for it to function so well given the dramatics and tensions in the very small and often riotous army headquarters. Hooker's flamboyant personality has already been alluded to. So notorious was his weakness for the ladies and the bottle that his headquarters was called a cross between a bar-room and a bordello. He freely surrounded himself with political generals and cronies such as Butterfield and Sickles. He was abnormally indiscrete, but his indiscretion had a more political edge. He so frequently stated that the country needed a dictator, with little doubt as to the proper candidate, that it earned Lincoln's famous rebuke that only successful generals could become dictators and that he would risk the dictatorship if Hooker would only bring him a victory. It is a testament to Sharpe's good sense that, despite his daily proximity, he avoided being dragged into this toxic atmosphere or tainted by an association that would ruin other officers identified as Hooker's cronies. At the same time he was able to maintain a professional relationship with Hooker such that they would remain cordial after the war.

Even as the march began, Hooker's intelligence elements continued to serve him well. The balloonists and signalmen strung out along the river were actively reporting the movement of Lee's forces to contact. At Fredericksburg, in particular, the Balloon Corps was providing real-time tactical reporting of the fighting, communicated to

Hooker's headquarters by the telegraph line that the general had specifically ordered strung for that purpose with the telegrapher in the balloon itself. One observer noted that the balloons "were up and down like jumping jacks." Sharpe was also supporting Sedgwick by sending several "colored" men, residents of the Chancellorsville area, to serve as guides for the general's pincer movement on that place from the west.[52]

Yet Babcock was able to answer a vital question about Longstreet's whereabouts. He personally directed the interrogation of prisoners taken at Fredericksburg by Sedgwick, which revealed that neither of Longstreet's divisions had arrived from Richmond. But that issue was not entirely closed. Late at night on May 1 Butterfield passed on to Hooker, "Colonel Sharpe ... advises me that deserters from Early's division had heard their captain say on Wednesday that Hood and Pickett would be here in time for the fight."[53]

Intelligence collection by technical means was having its own problems. Night effectively put a stop to the work of the signalmen and balloonists, and the new and insufficiently tested short-range military telegraph system chose that time to begin breaking down. Hooker's refusal to properly prepare his staff for the operation due to excessive security had prevented the Signal Corps officers from ordering enough wire to support the attack.

At this point, when everything seemed to be going according to plan, Hooker uncharacteristically began to take counsel of his fears. Unfortunately, as he himself was to say later, "For once I lost confidence in Hooker, and that is all there is to it," just when he needed to close the trap with swift and decisive action. After successfully surprising Lee by deftly crossing the Rappahannock with four corps, Hooker's boldness evaporated. He hesitated with his army caught in the tangles of the Wilderness. He seemed to shrink from the last step that would take his army into the open ground where his numbers would have overwhelmed the Army of Northern Virginia, seemingly intimidated by the reputation of one man. Unbeknownst to Hooker, another part of his plan was falling far behind schedule. The Cavalry Corps, due to Stoneman's seemingly bewildered leadership, which does not seem to have been much informed by his orders, was nowhere near the RF&P. Lee had received no reason to worry about his communications being cut with his base of supply.[54]

That freed him to strike, and he suffered no such indecision as Hooker. As soon as the extent of Hooker's surprise dawned, he reacted with his typical speed and daring. McLaws's and Anderson's Divisions were already in contact with Hooker and had fixed his attention. He left only Early's division and one additional brigade to delay the Union corps facing him at Fredericksburg and sent Jackson's II Corps on its immortal flank march that would end in a crushing blow on Hooker's own hanging right flank. The absence of his cavalry deprived Hooker of his deep field reconnaissance and security arm, which allowed Jackson's maneuver to succeed. As Jackson was moving, Hooker inexplicably ordered his corps, which had been roughly handling McLaws and Anderson, to return to their positions of the previous day and fortify them. He had clearly thrown away the initiative which Lee had deftly caught.

The telegraph burnt up on the 1st, between Hooker and Butterfield, with information on the enemy as it was gained. There is no better illustration of the seeming chaos of intelligence reporting that this, trying to sort out the grain from the chaff, identifying the errors, misinformation, and deceptions. Making it difficult was the voluble penchant for Southern prisoners to pass on any rumors they had heard as well as engaging in outright deception measures. A perfect example is the report wired from Butterfield to Hooker at 2:05 p.m.:

> I have two deserters just from Hays' brigade of Early's division. They report A. P. Hill left here this morning to move up to our right. Hood's division arrived yesterday from Richmond. The deserter was from New York State originally; an intelligent man. He said he knew it was Hood's division, for he asked the troops as they passed along. He reports D. H. Hill, Early, and Trimble in front of Sedgwick. Anderson, McLaws, A. P. Hill, and Hood would therefore be on your front.[55]

The first deserter accurately reported the departure of A. P. Hill's Division and its intended destination. The second deserter, whose reliability was probably considered enhanced since he was a native New Yorker, was dead wrong in reporting the arrival of Hood's Division. That he said he had actually spoken to them when they were, in fact, hundreds of miles to the south at Suffolk, indicates at best a tall tale and at worst outright deception. Lee was known to send deserters over to the enemy primed with disinformation. A probable example of the latter, according to Bigelow, was found in the report sent by courier from Butterfield to Hooker of 5:30 that morning:

> From a deserter just in learn that Jackson's whole corps is opposite Franklin's Crossing. Camp rumor that Longstreet had gone to Culpeper; that Lee has said it was the only time he should fight equal numbers; that we had about 80,000. Some of Trimbles' division told him they had to march to Culpeper to-morrow. They all knew that we had crossed 40,000 men above.[56]

Everything the deserter said was not only wrong but misleading, except the last statement which may well have been designed to let Hooker know that Lee knew what he was doing. Jackson was no longer above Fredericksburg; his command had departed at 3:00 a.m. Putting him still at Franklin's Crossing was a perfect cover for his departure. It would be in Lee's interest for Hooker to believe they were still there. Placing Longstreet at Culpeper to the west of the growing Union salient and Lee's statements that he had equal numbers would have been designed to make him appear stronger than he was. Identifying Culpeper on Hooker's opposite flank as the concentration of Longstreet's and Trimble's divisions would have had the Union commander looking over his shoulder to the west while Lee was concentrating to the east. Of course, there is nothing more than the internal logic of the statement to support the speculation that it was a deception, but it could not have been better designed if it were a deception.

This sort of ambiguity fed right into Hooker's nervousness about his chief intelligence gap—what was happening with Longstreet's divisions based at Suffolk. Now, report after report passed on the news of the imminent arrival of Hood's and Pickett's divisions. Sharpe and Butterfield remained in almost constant communication with Maj. Gen. John J. Peck, commanding Union forces besieged at Suffolk by Longstreet. By 7:30 that night Peck was able to assure them, "Hood's and Pickett's divisions, of Longstreet's corps, are in our front, so reported by deserters and prisoners captured to-day. This will leave nothing of Longstreet's command in your front but Ransom, if he is there."[57]

Perhaps Hooker and Sharpe would not have been surprised to know that, on the 29th, Lee had already wired Richmond, "All available troops had better be sent forward as rapidly as possible by rail and otherwise." That request had been immediately forwarded to Longstreet as an alert. The next day Longstreet received the order, "Move without delay with your command to this place to effect a junction with General Lee." It was the logical decision Lee would have been expected to make. However, he fully expected Stoneman to be so effective in destroying the RF&P that it would make Longstreet's arrival in time to affect the battle impossible. In fact, Longstreet would be delayed even more by collecting his trains, which were dispersed over three counties collecting provisions, and would not break the siege of Suffolk until late in the evening of May 3.[58]

Yet, bit by bit an accurate picture of the enemy was emerging. Butterfield wired Sedgwick that "Deserters just received from Early's division, Hays' brigade, Jackson's corps. Their division relieved A. P. Hill, who marched up to our right. You have, I should judge from their statements, one less division to-day than yesterday in your front when they left." The next sentence was an enormous compliment to Sharpe and Babcock, underscoring how reliable their order-of-battle estimates were considered. "The table of regiments, &c, given you is confirmed by all statements yet received." It also indicates that such order-of-battle tables were routinely distributed to corps commanders.[59]

Hooker's Corps had initially moved aggressively east to drive back the Confederates that had rushed to stop him. Then, inexplicably, he ordered them back to occupy their original positions, to the consternation not only of his corps commanders but of the troops who had been successfully driving the enemy. Also on the 30th, Hooker ordered III Corps to march to join the others in the Wilderness.

Sharpe spent the day and night of May 1 interrogating prisoners. The next day he was able to wire Babcock, "we have evidence that Anderson, McLaws, Rodes & Trimble [Colston] are in front of us… I think only Early and A. P. Hill are left down there." He had accurately captured the enemy's dispositions, missing only the fact that A. P. Hill was on the move to Hooker's front. What led him to make that mistake is unknown, since several prisoners taken the day before had stated that Hill's Division was on the move to Hooker's front as shown in the report above.

Fishel points out that Hill's position in the rear of Jackson's Corps ensured that none of his men would be captured. Also, the new and largely untested short-range field telegraph system introduced for this campaign was malfunctioning. Messages never arrived or arrived garbled or late, contributing significantly to the failure to keep Hooker in the west and Sedgwick in the east fully informed of each other's actions, as Butterfield admitted when he wrote to Hooker by courier, "the telegraph had been interfered with and has not been in working order." The result was the breakdown in the passing of intelligence information between Babcock and Sharpe.[60]

Still, the worry on the whereabouts of Longstreet's divisions hung over everything. Butterfield added that "it was reported by officers at Hamilton's Crossing that Pickett & Hood were coming by way of Gordonsville." Purportedly a prisoner from Pickett's 30th Virginia had been forwarded to Babcock. Sharpe wanted him interrogated again.[61] That day he wired Babcock, "Send me by orderly all you know of the organization of Pickett & Hood..."[62] Against this was the back and forth communications between Butterfield and Peck at Suffolk. Peck wired Butterfield that he had prisoners taken the day before, who insisted they had seen Pickett and Hood that day and that no brigades had been sent from the command.[63] Butterfield wired back his account of two enterprising deserters from Pickett's Division who claimed to have left him on the Blackwater in the siege of Suffolk only on April 30. Apparently this pair had taken the train to get there in only two days, a reproach for the Confederate provost martial authorities.[64]

The absence of cavalry to warn of Jackson's concentration against Hooker's right wing was compounded by the failure of XI Corps commander, Major General O. O. Howard, to credit the reports flooding in on the morning of May 2 from pickets and experienced officers of the evidence of their own eyes. Hooker had even given Howard a direct order to refuse his flank, which he ignored.

Early on the morning of May 2, Lee wired Jefferson Davis a remarkably well-informed estimate of the situation:

> I find the enemy in a strong position at Chancellorsville and in large force; his communications extend to the Rapidan, at Germanna and Ely's Fords, and to the Rappahannock, at United States Mine Ford. He seems determined to make the fight here, and, from what I learn from General Early, has sent up troops from his position opposite Fredericksburg....

Lee had accurately described Hooker's strategy and his grouping of forces. His own intelligence collection means had served him well. Then he reviewed his options. He was clearly worrying about his communications. If successful, he wrote that Fredericksburg would "be saved and our communications retained." If he determined the enemy too strong, he would have to abandon Fredericksburg and fall back. Interestingly, he stated that he would have to fall back, not by the RF&P, but back to the Orange and Alexandria Railroad or the Virginia Central Railroad and would thus be able to "contest the enemy's advance upon Richmond." Falling back to those railroads would take him in a southwest direction away from Richmond, whereas the RF&P was the direct route to the Confederate capital. It was too early for him to have heard of Stoneman's ambling in the direction of the RF&P. What he feared was that the Union forces, in facing Fredericksburg, would cross the river, drive off Early, and then sit upon his communications along the railroad and attack west to trap him against Hooker. Had that happened his stated line of retreat would have made perfect sense.

He also stated, "I have no expectations that any re-enforcements from Longstreet or North Carolina will join me in time to aid in the contest at this point..." He then states that his forces had driven Hooker's men back, "on all the roads back to Chancellorsville, where he concentrated in a position remarkably favorable for him. We were unable last evening to dislodge him. I am now swinging around to my left to come up in his rear." Jackson was on his immortal march.[65]

No better example can be given that emphasizes the role of the commander as the final consumer of intelligence. Sharpe had provided Hooker with more and better intelligence than any American commander had ever received. Hooker's initial use of it to plan and move his army was flawless. Then, when everything was falling into place, he counseled his fears and froze. Lee, on the other hand, after being taken by one of the most complete surprises in military history, quickly gathered and processed his rapidly accumulating tactical intelligence into a clear and insightful understanding of the enemy's situation. He then used it to order one of the boldest maneuvers in military history, in sending Jackson around Hooker's right flank.

Fishel observed tartly that Hooker "had created a competent intelligence service, but evidently failed to impress on his subordinate commanders the basic point that they were all part of an intelligence *system*. This would be the beginning of disgrace for the "Half-Moon" (their corps badge was a half-moon) men of XI Corps. Recruited largely from German immigrants under Maj. Gen. Franz Sigel, they had boasted in fractured English, "I fights mit Sigel."[66] Patrick and Sharpe were with Hooker when the blow fell. Patrick believed that "All was working admirably and I believed the game was all in our hands ... when the whole mass opened and the 11 Corps ran away to 'fight mit Sigel' in the rear."[67] Jackson rolled up XII Corps as well. From that point on Lee held both the initiative and the moral ascendancy over his opponent.

Early on the morning of the 3rd, Hooker withdrew Sickles's III Corps from its central high position of Hazel Grove, which played right into Lee's plans to unite the two separated wings of his forces. His attacks were savage as they hammered the Union salient from both sides, magnificently supported by his massed guns on Hazel Hill. It was the most costly day of the battle, but finally the Union position collapsed, and the Confederates surged forward.

The crash of battle shook Hooker out of his funk. He was always a physically brave man and rallied his shaken corps, riding up and down the firing line on his white horse. Upon returning to his headquarters at the Chancellor House, at 9:15 a.m., a cannon ball struck a column against which he was leaning. The column split lengthwise in two with one piece striking Hooker along the length of his body. He was unconscious for an hour and was clearly badly concussed when he finally came to. Despite this manifest state, no subordinate moved to relieve him, nor would he turn his command over to another officer. From this incident arose the rumors that Hooker had been drunk. It was an easy rumor to spread, considering Hooker's reputation for drink in camp. On campaign, however, Hooker was as temperate as Carrie Nation. Sharpe, who had accompanied Hooker and was in his presence during the entire battle, was vehement in denying allegations of drunkenness, saying, "Whoever says that General Hooker was drunk at the battle of Chancellorsville lies in his throat."[68]

At the same time, Stoneman had finally debouched upon the RF&P and accomplished next to nothing. He had delayed so long that the authorities in Richmond had time to send forces to defend key elements of the railroad. Regiments were sent to Hanover Junction and to the bridges over the North and South Anna Rivers.[69]

Stoneman tried to destroy the masonry of the James River Canal, which was not on his target list but could not figure out how to attack such a structure. A regiment under Col. Judson Kilpatrick fell upon the Hungary Station, burned the depot, and tore up 2 miles of track. Their technique was simply to pull the spikes and throw the rails aside; a track crew could put the line in order in about the same time it took the raiders to dismantle it. A group from the 12th Illinois reached Ashland Station, "cut the telegraph line and 'tore up half a dozen rails' and burned a trestle so small that it was not on the BMI's list [of] RF&P's bridges." After this group had left, Brigadier General Gregg arrived at Ashland Station and detailed 200 to burn the 600-foot South Anna Bridge. The bridge guards, reinforced with the troops and guns from Richmond, easily drove them off. Not a single trooper got near Hanover Junction itself. In two days the damage to the RF&P was repaired by Confederate track crews. Stoneman then took his command across the RF&P to the safety of the Peninsula, also forgetting his primary orders to block or harry any attempt by Lee to retreat down the railroad to Richmond.[70]

All of the BMI's painstaking efforts to lay out the vulnerabilities of the two railroads had been wasted. Stoneman behaved as if he had not even read his own orders. Those orders gave him specific types of targets to be destroyed and instructed him to obtain the materials and expertise necessary for his work of destruction. The amateurish behavior of his subordinates showed that they approached their work in complete ignorance. Neither had Stoneman kept Hooker informed of his activities or whereabouts. The army commander was so sure that Stoneman was having a field day of destruction that he worked on that assumption.

Pursuant to Hooker's order of the evening of the 2nd, Sedgwick crossed the Rappahannock that night, took Fredericksburg, and the next morning drove Barksdale's Brigade from Marye's Heights, above the town. Now, if he moved fast enough, as Hooker desperately hoped, he could strike Lee in the rear. Hooker had not reckoned with "Uncle John" Sedgwick's caution, much increased by Hooker's failure to communicate his commander's intent for the battle. Deprived of that, Sedgwick was not able to exercise informed initiative.

Already at that morning, Butterfield was chiding Sedgwick for allowing an enemy deception to slow him down. Citing information from a deserter, he wrote, "the enemy formed column yesterday to frighten us. No great force there. Jackson's corps went above on Plank road. If an attempt had been made last night, we could have carried the heights."[71] Babcock had crossed to the southern bank as soon as the pontoon bridge was built. He immediately reported that a contraband servant of a Confederate officer had said the unit on Marye's Heights was in great fear of being cut off from Richmond. That might have given a false hope that Stoneman had cut the railroad to Richmond.[72] By 3 p.m. he was reporting the first interrogations from the prisoners taken on the Heights and able to identify the force as comprising only Barksdale's Mississippi Brigade from McLaws's Division, the rest of which had already departed to join Lee. The rumor was rife among them that Longstreet was momentarily about to reinforce them. They were also anxious about rumors that Vicksburg had fallen. Prisoners from the Washington Artillery from Louisiana were also much put out that their battery commander had been captured, a mortification the unit had never endured before.[73]

By 5:30 Butterfield was wiring Hooker a summary of what Babcock had found out from his interrogations:

> Captain of the Washington Artillery, captured, reports Hood's and Pickett's divisions as expected to-night. Another (North Carolina officer) prisoner says General Lee telegraphed last night to their right down here that he was driving us on our right, and if they would hold the place down here he would have reinforcements to-night. The general impression of the prisoners seems to be that we shall hear from Hood before long.[74]

Again the specter of Longstreet's imminent arrival on the battlefield hovers over the reporting. What emerges is a fog of rumor unsupported by any identifiable fact of the presence of any of Longstreet's men. That was understandable, because at this time Hood's and Pickett's Divisions were marching through a driving rain in southern Virginia toward a railroad that would take them north. They would not climb onto those cars until May 6.[75] Amid this rumor clutter, however, was the gem reported by a North Carolinian officer that Lee was hammering Hooker and would detach reinforcements to strike Sedgwick's Corps before long. In either case, the report, if shared with Sedgwick, would only serve to heighten his caution. Rather than catching Lee in a vice, a Confederate vice would seem to be pressing on him.

Later in the day, however, Babcock cut through this Gordian knot of confusion. Clearly the reoccurring stories of Longstreet's approach were a case of the wish being father to the thought by desperate men: "Nothing definite can be ascertained from the prisoners brought in to day in reference to reinforcements from Richmond or elsewhere. Some of them report Longstreet has arrived with 20,000 men, that he arrived at Hamilton's crossing night before last… I can find none of them who have seen any of the reinforcements spoken of."[76]

May 4 saw Lee take advantage of the moral ascendency he had over Hooker. He detached the divisions of Anderson and McLaws from Hooker's front, sure that the Union commander would remain passive. His forces were still heavily outnumbered, yet he felt secure enough to divide them to strike at Sedgwick's slowing approaching force.

Sedgwick found himself assailed by Anderson and McLaws on his front, as Early overran Marye's Heights in his rear and cut him off from his line of retreat over the pontoon bridge at Fredericksburg. Although he gave a good account of himself in the subsequent action, any thought of fighting his way to Hooker's relief quickly evaporated as his main concern became to save his command. What is striking is that Hooker—who apparently was informed of what was happening to Sedgwick and of the departure of two of Lee's five divisions on his front—did not seize the opportunity to now attack the few remaining Confederate divisions facing him and march to Sedgwick's relief. Late afternoon of the day before, the signal station on the north side of the Rappahannock had reported the beginning of Lee's move, noting a large force with seven regimental battle flags marching east. Butterfield, in his transmission of the report to Hooker, pointedly asks if this force is meant to attack Sedgwick, already alerting the army commander that forces were leaving his front.[77]

On the 5th there is a cryptic reference in a wire from Babcock to Sharpe that suggests he was aware of the forces closing in on Sedgwick when he mentioned only the divisions of Early, Anderson, and McLaws and stated he would send the "regiments by Manning." The message was probably in response to Sharpe's request for information. The fact that Babcock was sending them by hand was another indication of the failing field telegraph system.[78]

May 4 would not have been complete without the continuing merry-go-round of telegrams between Butterfield and Peck over the location of Longstreet. Butterfield cited the cavalry report that 20,000 of Longstreet's men had arrived at Gordonville. Peck responded by stating that he had the hard intelligence from captured documents and intercepted telegrams of May 2 that D. H. Hill and his division were in the process of joining Longstreet in the siege of Suffolk. One wonders how long Butterfield was going to keep on refusing to take no for an answer.[79] The next day Babcock was communicating with Sharpe on the same subject once again:

> Am daily making examinations regarding re-enforcements from Richmond. None have arrived, to my belief, in our front. We have prisoners from about Fredericksburg at all hours of the day, and many taken late last evening. None from Hood's, Pickett's, or Ransom's divisions have yet been found. If they are up, they have gone over in your direction toward Culpeper.[80]

The non-arrival of Longstreet's three divisions on the field at Chancellorsville was surely the most famous dog that didn't bark in the Civil War.

The same message revealed that Stoneman's cavalry had done enough temporary damage to the railroads to make the near-term arrival of 20,000 men by rail an impossibility. Whatever damage had been done, however, was repaired within two days, not enough time to deplete what supplies Lee had on hand. Nor did it disturb Lee's equilibrium. Whatever he learned about damage to the railroad was not serious enough to distract his focus on going for Hooker's jugular. Babcock had sent out the scout, William Chase, who had secreted himself in a good observation post near Guiney Station, 12 miles south of Fredericksburg on the RF&P. He reported to Sharpe that there was no traffic on the line except for two small engines that only made short trips, indicating the line to the south had been cut. Babcock took this opportunity to state that among the numerous prisoners he had been examining, none were from Longstreet's three divisions.[81]

By this time these issues had become moot. The game was up. Pressed against the Rappahannock, Sedgwick saved his command by crossing the river at U.S. Ford on the 5th. Informed of this, Hooker threw in the towel. Despite a council of war's recommendation to stay and fight it out, he ordered his forces back across the river. He was so eager to escape that he abandoned the severely wounded to the clemency of the enemy. The army crossed on the night of the 5th–6th.

Lee had been planning a killing blow for the 6th. He was much put out when he discovered that Hooker had flown.

Sorting Out the Pieces

Back across the river, almost the first thing Hooker did was to send a message to Lee requesting permission to send physicians and medical supplies to care for the wounded left behind. He offered to replace any medical supplies the Confederates had used to treat his wounded. Lee graciously agreed to assist, but the rain-swollen Rappahannock could not be crossed by ambulances to carry off any of the stricken men.[82]

The stunned Army of the Potomac settled into back-biting recriminations over a battle that should not have been lost. Desperately trying to put a good face on the disaster, Hooker issued General Order No. 49: "We have taken from the enemy 5,000 prisoners; captured and brought off seven pieces of artillery, fifteen colors; placed hors de combat 18,000 of his chosen troops; destroyed his depots filled with vast amounts of stores; deranged his communications; captured prisoners within the fortifications of his capital, and filled his country with fear and consternation."

Two days later Patrick met with Hooker, who told him that Dix had captured a dispatch of Lee's that admitted he had suffered 18,000 casualties, the origin of his claim. Patrick wrote, "I don't believe it at all."[83]

Behind the scenes, Sharpe and Babcock were working on calculating Lee's actual losses. Less than a week after the battle, they obtained a copy of the *Richmond Whig*, in which a surgeon claimed a loss of 900 killed, 7,000 wounded, and 1,200 missing, for a total of 9,100 casualties.[84] That was the first piece of information they had, but it was probably believed to be too low. It took the rest of the month collecting more information, weighing and comparing it all, before Babcock was satisfied. His letter of May 30 estimated that Lee had suffered 14,348 casualties. Lee had in fact reported only 13,460, a difference of only 7 percent.[85] By then the armies were in motion to a place called Gettysburg.

Renewing the work they had done to prepare for the Chancellorsville Campaign, Sharpe had also put McEntee to work to draw up another analysis of the fords over the Rappahannock Rapidan which was finished on May 13, in a report in the captain's hand but signed by Sharpe.[86] Sharpe did find time to arrange a meeting, either in camp or in Washington, with his old friend and former Congressman John Steele.[87]

Although the armies were recuperating from their bloodbath, Sharpe's staff continued to work, interrogating the occasional deserter. To prove that serendipity is also a factor in intelligence, Brigadier General Patrick was surprised to find in the correspondence he received from the other side "under flag of truce" a letter from Jefferson Davis to a Mississippi colonel.[88]

Patrick had a problem closer to home. His paymaster, Capt. George D. W. Clinton, had just been arrested in Washington by Lafayette Baker, head of the War Department's Secret Service, for selling commissary stores. Knowing how powerful Baker was, Patrick noted, "I shall not interfere, in any way, in these operations of Bakers." Eventually, Clinton would be cleared. As Provost Marshal Department paymaster, he was responsible for paying the BMI. Apparently, for reasons unknown, he would come to harbor some grudge against Sharpe.[89]

The great intelligence gap of the battle was still unanswered. Had Longstreet joined Lee yet? Longstreet had indeed personally reported to Lee at noon on May 9; his divisions were in Richmond.[90] On the 10th Sharpe forwarded a report of the interrogation of a deserter, James McMillem from 2nd South Carolina, Kershaw's Brigade, McLaws's Division. He stated that no reinforcements had come up during the battle and that Hood and Pickett were still south of Richmond. The scouts were kept busy on their own to discover if and when Longstreet arrived. On the same day that McMillem was interrogated, Sharpe dispatched scout Ernest Yager. "You had better go to Culpeper before coming here. Learn whether Lee's Army has been reinforced or not—and if so, by whom and which way they have come. Learn also position & strength of Cavalry. Then come to us." Yager would not be heard from for four days.[91]

Apparently, Sharpe was receiving information that Longstreet's three divisions had left Suffolk, sufficiently credible for Hooker to wire Lincoln as part of a lengthy message on the 13th: "I am informed that the bulk of Longstreet's force is in Richmond. With the facilities at hand, he can readily transfer it to Lee's army…"[92] Late on that same day Sharpe reported the seemingly credible interrogation results of a deserter. Hooker immediately wired President Lincoln at 10:30 p.m.: "A deserter from the Third Alabama reports Pickett and Hood arrived. The provost-marshal's department [read BMI] seem to place confidence in his statement. I have not seen him." The late hour of the telegram meant the information had not gone through Sharpe, who was detached on a special mission.[93]

Yager returned on the 14th with definite news. "Longstreet's forces are guarding the Rapidan. The bridge will be done by to-morrow. They expect Longstreet's division [Corps] at Culpeper soon." This report would have been forwarded either by McEntee or Babcock to Butterfield since Sharpe was still absent.[94] Yager's observations were only a little premature. Longstreet's two divisions had left Richmond. Hood was approaching Gordonsville with Pickett a day's march behind. The identification of Culpeper as Longstreet's destination revealed that his corps would not return to its old positions around Fredericksburg but would be deployed further north along the Rapidan. It was the first inkling of Lee's plans to invade Pennsylvania through the Valley.[95]

Even though no longer in day-to-day command of his regiment, Sharpe remained ever solicitous of the welfare of its men. The day before he had written to his uncle to discuss his transfer of his regiment's payroll to the Kingston bank from which their families would be paid:

> I now write & enclose a check for ten thousand one hundred & thirty nine Dollars ($10,139) being a part of the pay of my regiment. The whole amount sent home this time is about $18000—the balance being forwarded by other officers—principally by the Major. The regiment was very badly paid—the payment having commenced after the beginning of the march on the late move. Four companies were paid before going into battle—and this money I managed to send back from the field to Wash.
>
> I hope you will charge for collection only the actual cost, and let me be informed what it is; when I can be repaid out of the regimental fund.

Like most every other married man in both armies, he missed his wife. In the same letter, on a more personal note, he wrote that he looked forward to seeing his wife again shortly. She had stayed in Washington and would leave soon, as the weather warmed oppressively. "I am expecting to go to see Carrie now every day—and after that I suppose she will make her way home—as the weather has already become very warm here. I hear from her nearly every day."[96]

Isaac Silver had less to look forward to. On May 1 he found his home was in the middle of the fighting for that day as "Confederate troops swept across his fields and camped on his property that night." They stripped his farm of posts, rails, and stored planks for their campfires. Had they known he was a Union agent far worse would have happened. Instead, he boldly put in a claim to the army for damages. A board of officers visited his farm to investigate the claim, ruled that Silver should be paid for his fencing, and ordered the quartermaster to pay him $923. Silver claimed he could not identify the units that had damaged his farm because he "was taken by the Yankees." A pass dated May 8, for him and fellow Unionist Jackson Hardinge, written by Sharpe and signed by Patrick indicates that he had been at army headquarters during the battle.[97]

Saving the Wounded

A week after the Army of the Potomac had trudged back over its pontoon bridges over the Rappahannock, Hooker turned to Sharpe for what was probably the last act in the Chancellorsville Campaign—retrieving the large numbers of severely wounded Union soldiers abandoned to the Confederates. He had been advised by Dr. Letterman that the army "should lay a bridge at the United States Ford for the passage of our ambulances after our wounded in the vicinity of Chancellorsville." A Union officer sent to make arrangements to retrieve the wounded was told that the flag of truce for such matters had expired.

Hooker, on May 13, then appealed to Sharpe to try. "I would like to have you go, but I cannot ask you to," Hooker told him, an admission from the army commander that the mission was so hazardous that it called for a volunteer. Sharpe saw his expected leave with his wife evaporate and accepted on the spot.[98] His orders were hurriedly drafted and read:

> I am directed by the commanding general to say that he learned, through Drs. Letterman and Taylor this afternoon, for the first time, that we should be allowed to lay a bridge at the United States Ford for the passage of our ambulances after our wounded in the vicinity of Chancellorsville. Instructions have been given to throw a bridge across the river early to-morrow morning at the United States Ford, and the commanding general wishes you to make whatever arrangements may be necessary with the officer commanding the Confederate forces at the ford with regard to laying the bridge, and to have it taken up when no longer required for the purpose indicated.[99]

Sharpe was obviously becoming the man for those special missions that come up at headquarters that no line officer seemed suited for. There was no doubt that Sharpe was the officer in charge of this operation vested with the full authority of the army commander.

The next morning Sharpe and his orderly found a rowboat and were crossing the river, thinking that Hooker had arranged with Lee for an extension of the truce, when a bullet whizzed overhead. When they landed, they were taken prisoner. A Confederate colonel informed him that the truce no longer protected him and that they were bound for the infamous Libby Prison in Richmond.

Sharpe now had only his wits between himself and spending the rest of the war in that infamous hellhole. His knowledge of the grim state of Confederate rations now served him well. He said, "Well if we must go to Richmond, let us have one good square meal first and perhaps you will be willing to enjoy it with us. I have on the other bank some extra fine porterhouse steaks and a basket of champagne. If you will allow my orderly to row back and bring them over, together we will have a good supper." The Confederate readily agreed, and as they ate steak and drank champagne Sharpe discoursed on the humanity of treating the wounded of war properly. His captor resisted Sharpe's suggestions through the first bottle, worrying about his authority and the prospect of court-martial, but the second bottle had a wonderful effect upon his fears. He finally exclaimed, "Damn the authority, whether I have it or not, those wounded and dying men shall be cared for. You may use the pontoon, but at five o'clock in the morning they must be taken up."

That night, by lamplight, Sharpe scribbled a note to Hooker. Such was the seat of the pants nature of this operation that Sharpe could only find small scraps of paper on which to write to the army commander:

> I have been over the river. The Confed officers do not object to our using the ford but the ford is now impracticable. A horse would now have to swim, ambulances would be swept away. The river is falling now, but 2 hours of rain would raise the ford again. We may possibly be able to use it in the morning, but it is doubtful. The work here is very slow. Almost 250 came over today. The Confed officers say there are 1000 of our men there yet—our surgeons say there are 800 or more. The two pontoons at Banks ford were sent for this A. M. but have not yet arrived. I shall send to see what is the matter & in the morning will try the ford again.
>
> We might have a bridge or in default of it, 6 more pontoons, so as to make 3 more rafts. There is only one raft here now. I beg you will send a fresh orderly back to me saying what will be done.
>
> I shall be during the night with the ambulances of the 3rd Corps, after daybreak at the river.[100]

The next morning he sent another scribbled note on a small piece of paper:

> Shall be beyond the cliffs in this side of the river. I tried the ford this a.m. The water was high—I got over one ambulance as an experiment safely, but they were picked horses & behaved well. Otherwise it would not have succeeded & the jolting in the water would have been most painful for the wounded. I managed to have the ford well reconnoitered when the shower visibly raised the water this p.m., it would have been impracticable. The bridge will save many a life. I will try to send word to our nearest force of about the time when the bridge will be "beyond the cliffs." We might finish today, but they object to our working after sundown.[101]

By 3:30 p.m. he was writing from U.S. Ford that the situation was under control and proceeding smoothly:

> The pontoon bridge was completed at 2 ½ p.m. The delay was due to the [word indistinct] state of the road in the woods between the Warrenton and the high ground here, & I think was unavailable. Things are going grandly now, but we can hardly expect to get all over tonight. I hope we shall have the pontoons up and started down by noon tomorrow. We have a written memorandum of the truce under which the bridge is laid, in duplicate. I have no paper to send you a copy, but the stipulation on my part is that the bridge shall be inviolate and the truce shall not cease until the bridge, ambulances, attendants etc. [last part missing.][102]

Sharpe coordinated the movement with army headquarters which ordered the Cavalry Corps commander to "direct your forces in that vicinity to cover the river, and prevent any passage, except under proper authority, after Colonel Sharpe, now in charge there, has ordered their withdrawal."[103] In the end, 1,200–1,500 severely wounded men were brought back. Sharpe's performance of duty was such that today he would have been awarded the Distinguished Service Medal, the highest non-combat-related military award. Hooker was to say, "Sharpe you are the best man I know that could successfully accomplish that business. I am sure that you would get into a scrape, but I was just as sure that you would wriggle out of it." Speaking in later years, Sharpe would say often that the act in which he took the greatest satisfaction was the rescue of all those wounded men.[104]

CHAPTER FIVE

The Gettysburg Campaign: Movement to Contact

Opening Moves

After Chancellorsville, Lee did not rest on his laurels. He sought to follow on the heels of his victory with an invasion of the North that could settle the war by defeating the Army of the Potomac on its own ground, seize Baltimore or Washington, and at worst strip the rich fields and barns of Pennsylvania in order to spare a ruined Northern Virginia another levy to support his army in the coming year. With Jefferson Davis's permission, he reinforced the Army of Northern Virginia by 50 percent to 75,000 men, with brigades and divisions that had been in garrison of the ports and forts along the eastern seaboard of the South. On May 30, he increased the number of his corps from two to three, by creating III Corps and assigning Maj. Gen. A. P. Hill to its command. In Jackson's old II Corps, he appointed Richard Ewell, who had been out of action for more than a year after losing a leg in battle.

Lee's invasion plan was strategically elegant but simple. He would march his infantry corps up the Shenandoah Valley, cross the Potomac, and march through western Maryland and into the heart of Pennsylvania. His march would be shielded by the Blue Ridge Mountains in Virginia and its continuance in Maryland and Pennsylvania called South Mountain. His cavalry would ride east of the mountains to block the passes to shield that movement. Once in central Pennsylvania, he could threaten the state capital, Harrisburg, as well as Philadelphia, Baltimore, and even Washington. With any luck, he would steal such a march on the still-stunned Hooker and be in Pennsylvania before the Army of the Potomac stirred from its camps just south of the Potomac between Alexandria and Leesburg.

He would be doing that, however, with a reorganized and expanded army that had not had time to shake down into a cohesive force. Two of his three corps commanders and half his division and brigade commanders would be new in command of their formations. He had not made the mental adjustment in his command style that such a cast of new leaders required. He continued to rely on the very personal and intuitive relationship he had had with Stonewall Jackson and Longstreet, whose well-judged initiative could be consistently relied on. He would find that Lt. Gens. Ambrose Powell Hill and Richard S. Ewell did not measure up to that standard.

Hooker still smarted from his drubbing at Chancellorsville. That drubbing had made him shy of another go at Lee in the immediate future. Bad timing, then, is probably a good reason why Hooker turned down his young aide-de-camp's idea of a raid on Richmond. Captain Dahlgren submitted the outlines of such a plan to Hooker on May 23 at Falmouth. He wanted to wait until the Confederate cavalry was otherwise engaged and take the 6th U.S. Cavalry, cross the Rappahannock and Rapidan, dash south to Richmond, burn the arsenal at Bellona, and ride through Richmond, then south to Petersburg and to the safety of Union forces around Suffolk. The plan did not seem to have any great objective other than counting coup on the Confederacy itself by riding hell bent for leather through its capital. Interestingly, he added, "I know several men in the provost marshal's service who feel confident of guiding such an expedition, and have offered to do so." Dahlgren's association with the BMI was obviously more than just the casual acquaintance of men on the same staff if he was discussing such an operation with them. It has the ring of just the sort of derring-do that men like Cline and Carney would relish. It is doubtful that Dahlgren would have introduced the willingness of BMI men to participate in the adventure without the at least tacit approval of its director. A lack of boldness was not one of Sharpe's failings.[1]

As this episode indicated, the command's reluctance to contemplate aggressive action did not extend to Sharpe. He continued to actively scout the enemy and to run his agent line behind enemy lines in Virginia. On the same day Dahlgren submitted his plan to Hooker, Patrick, turned over some $3,300 in Confederate currency captured by Pleasonton to Sharpe, "to use on the other side." He would need the cash to keep the "other side" productive. Something was up.[2]

Sharpe was on to the reinforcement of Lee's army between mid-May and mid-June. Sharpe's first definite information came from a deserter who alerted him that the enemy had received orders for a long march. Surprisingly, the deserter was a fellow New Yorker, a recent immigrant to the South, and from Sharpe's hometown as well. Sharpe's suspicions had been aroused because Lee had been sending bogus deserters with false information in the form of men born and raised in New York in the hope that Butterfield and Patrick would find fellow Empire State men more believable. Information from other sources, such as Southern newspapers and reports from signalmen, balloonists, and agents, flowed in to form a corroborating picture. On May 27 Sharpe presented Hooker with a comprehensive and accurate assessment of Confederate troop movements, but the most important information was his assessment of the enemy's intent. It was an impressive all-source effort. (See Appendix J for the full report.)

> The Confed. Army is under marching orders and an order from General Lee was very lately read to the troops announcing a campaign of long marches & hard fighting in a part of the country where they would have no railroad transportation.

All deserters say that the idea is very prevalent in the ranks that they are about to move forward upon or above our right flank.[3]

What Sharpe was not able to do at this time was produce an accurate update of the order-of-battle and strength of the Army of Northern Virginia. The scale and speed of its reorganization, reinforcement, and movements created a situation that was too fluid to fix. At the same time, his right-on assessment of the enemy's intent failed to have any timely impact on the authorities in Washington because there was an inexplicable delay of almost two weeks from its dispatch to its arrival in the capital. Lee, at least, was in a worse situation. He wrote to President Davis of the near total failure of his intelligence operation. But his security effort was working well. His picket system around his main infantry corps was so thickened that Sharpe's scouts could not penetrate it.

That itself was an indicator, as Babcock would have noticed, since the same ploy had presaged a successful attempt in 1862 to steal a march on the Federals. Although Sharpe's scouts could not penetrate Lee's picket barrier, his other all-source elements filled the gap. Balloonists, Signal Corps observers, and Union pickets began noting extensive movement of Rebel forces. On June 5 a contraband claiming to be the body servant of Major General A. P. Hill, commander of the newly formed III Corps, was captured and interrogated between Hagerstown and Frederick, Maryland. He revealed that he had overheard Hill tell his officers of the planned invasion of Pennsylvania by a route west of the Blue Ridge Mountains. Sharpe was skeptical at first but became more convinced when the contraband's story proved unshakeable. With no other information to corroborate the story, he tucked it away as a puzzle piece that might find its place a little later.[4]

Years later another scout, William J. Lee, would recall that "In order for Lee to get his army across the river it was necessary for him to take his pontoons from Richmond to Staunton, and from there on to the old ferry site…" He had learned that "Every engine, freight car, and coach in Northern Virginia was pressed into service to move the army and the supplies." Lee made three trips between Richmond and Mineral City, now called Tollersville, gathering information that he thought would be useful. He would meet scout Edward McGee in Staunton, and from there McGee would take the information to the Potomac and pass it to a waiting steamer, which took it to Washington. On the way, McGee would pass his Unionist father's farm and get a fresh horse. Whether or in what form this information reached Sharpe and Hooker is unknown, but it would have clearly contributed to the general picture that Sharpe had presented.[5]

Sharpe's life was not entirely consumed by the observation of Lee. With his family in Washington, he found opportunity to visit them. He was also able to bring his wife, Caroline, to camp for visits on occasion, much to the distress of Patrick who noted how his deputy flaunted the regulations on bringing wives to camp. They

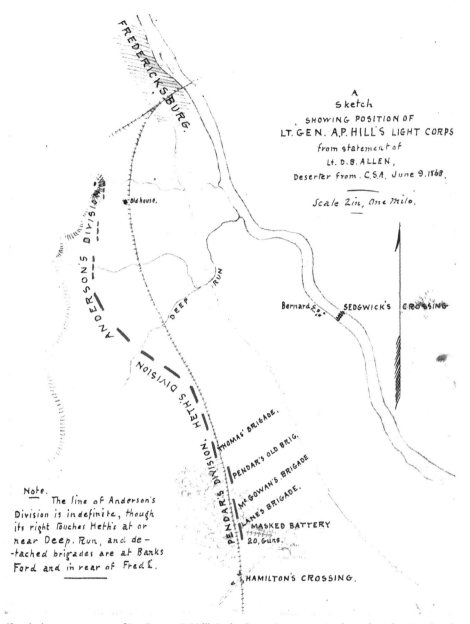

Sketch showing position of Lt. Gen. A. P. Hill's Light Corps, June 9, 1863, drawn by John C. Babcock, BMI. Courtesy Huntington Library.

made the rounds of friends, and in the manners of the time, both left their calling cards, as Colonel Gates noted when they dropped by his headquarters in his absence.[6]

Spoiling Attacks, Contrabands, and Cavalry

Ominously, reports of a heavy concentration of Stuart's Cavalry Division at Culpeper were piling up as well. The build-up had all the signs of presaging one of Stuart's great cavalry raids that has so often humiliated the Union army. On June 6 McEntee had reported that Stuart had held a grand review of his cavalry at Brandy Station. On June 7 Sharpe reported to Hooker, "I respectfully suggest that a force of the enemy's cavalry, not less than 12,000 and possibly 15000 men strong are on the eve of making the most important expedition ever attempted in this country." Interestingly, a correspondent for The *New York Times* wrote a letter dated, "Headquarters Army of the Potomac June 8," that repeated much of the details of Sharpe's report and speculated that Stuart's intention was to "make a grand raid into the North ... Of the direction of Stuart's march my information is not definite," but then goes on to say whatever it is will take him "into Maryland and Pennsylvania." It appears that Sharpe or someone else at headquarters had taken this correspondent into his confidence enough to brief him and show him the report with the intention that it be published.[7]

Hooker resolved to launch a spoiling attack on Stuart, and his timing was unintentionally perfect. The Cavalry Corps, under its new commander, Major General Alfred Pleasonton, attacked Stuart in his camps at Brandy Station on the morning of the 9th, the very day Stuart had planned to cross the Rappahannock at Beverley Ford. Noteworthy, in this, the greatest cavalry battle ever to be fought in North America, was the conduct of one of Sharpe's fellow staff officers, the 20-year-old Ulric Dahlgren. He received the honor of being "praised in dispatches." Pleasonton's after-action report was effusive in its description of his conduct:

> Captains Dahlgren and Cadwalader, aides-de-camp of Major-General Hooker, were frequently under the hottest fire, and were untiring in their generous assistance in conveying my orders.
> Captain Dahlgren was among the first to cross the river and charged with the first troops; he afterward charged with the Sixth Pennsylvania Cavalry when that regiment won the admiration of the entire command, and his horse was shot four times. His dashing bravery and cool intelligence are only equaled by his varied accomplishments.[8]

Dahlgren wrote his father of the charge:

> We charged General F. H. Lee's brigade up to General Stuart's headquarters, and within one hundred yards of their artillery ... This brigade was drawn up in mass in a beautiful field one-third of a mile across—wood on each hand. On their side was a ridge, upon which was posted the artillery, and near a house in which Stuart had his headquarters. We charged in column of companies. When we came out of our woods they rained shell into us, and, as we approached nearer, driving them like sheep before us, they threw two rounds of grape and canister, killing

as many of their men as ours; upon which they stopped firing and advanced their carabineers. All this time we were dashing through them, killing and being killed; some were *trampled* to death in trying to jump the ditches which intervened, and, falling in, were crushed by others who did not get over.

Dahlgren and the regimental commander were jumping a ditch when both their horses were cut out from under them by canister. Stunned for a moment, Dahlgren gathered his wits quickly enough to see the regiment turning about as the Confederates converged to surround it. He gave his horse a "tremendous kick," which brought the animal to its feet as he spurred it out of the trap barely in time to avoid capture. More would be heard of this *beau sabre* in the coming campaign.[9]

Stuart's planned departure on the eve of Pleasonton's attack, however, was not the precursor to a great raid but to shield the movement of Lee's infantry into the Shenandoah. The Union cavalry completely surprised Stuart, who was lucky to pull off a draw. But Hooker's spoiling attack had succeeded in two ways. First, it delayed Stuart's departure by a week. Second, it had brought down such criticism on Stuart for his handling of the affair that he was determined to redeem himself in the subsequent drive north, a motivation that would trump his good judgment. Sharpe was about to add injury to insult by personally going to Alexandria, Virginia, to interrogate and parole prisoners captured by Pleasonton at Brandy Station.[10]

On June 11 McEntee reported on a contraband captured and brought through the lines by one of his scouts. "A captured contraband, who was at Culpeper Court-House last Monday [June 8], states that Hood's division was there, and that infantry was arriving in great force. The enemy have infantry picket all along the river to-day."[11] The next day he discovered another contraband that had come over from Culpeper. To his amazement, the young man, named Charlie Wright, had a surprisingly good knowledge of a dozen enemy regiments which McEntee cross-checked and confirmed. Wright reported the concentration of Lee's infantry corps around Culpeper. This was corroborated by another contraband that had been brought through the lines by one of Sharpe's scouts. On the 12th he reported: "A contraband captured last Tuesday [June 9] states he had been living at Culpeper CH [Court House] for some time past. Saw Ewell's Second Corps passing through that place destined for the Valley and Maryland. That Ewell's Corps had passed the previous day to the fight [Brandy Station] & that Longstreet was then coming up."[12]

A second, then third, message from McEntee, each with more impressive detail of Wright's knowledge of the troops passing through Culpeper, finally convinced Hooker that the army must be put in motion to the east of the Blue Ridge, thus paralleling Lee's movement on the other side of the mountains. The result was that on June 13 the Army of the Potomac began to respond to Lee with a general movement north, even before two of three of Lee's corps (Hill's and Longstreet's) were yet to pass through Culpeper on their way to Pennsylvania.[13]

Now, with Sharpe desperate to make sense of the enemy's movements, Hooker's failure to convince all his major commanders that they were part of the same intelligence system was again about to harm the army's ability to respond to the enemy. McEntee found that his scouts were being arrested by the cavalry when they tried to return through Union lines even with the proper passes and that his access to prisoners and captured documents was restricted. The priceless Charlie Wright was lost to further possible use as an agent when he disappeared into the cavalry's POW system. McEntee was beside himself as he watched cavalry officers reading captured mail for laughs before discarding often valuable documents such as company rosters. He also found his scouts commandeered by the corps commander to act as guides and couriers.

An Expanding Theater and Patriotic Initiative

Sharpe's task had become immensely more difficult now that the theater of operations had been vastly expanded. The limits of the BMI's ability to function had been exceeded simply by the geographic scale of operations. A corresponding intelligence organization at the national level in Washington was needed to coordinate intelligence across the entire Middle Atlantic states region. Its absence would be sorely felt. Secretary Stanton and Chief of Staff Halleck, and even Lincoln, at times, became personally involved in attempting to coordinate intelligence to support the army, but the absence of a trained staff at the national level was painfully obvious. Stanton wired Hooker, "You shall be kept posted upon all information received here as to the enemy's movements but must exercise your own judgment as to its credibility." Lincoln himself followed this up with a wire that said the superintendent of the telegraph office was sending everything he received to Hooker.[14] In other words, without a trained intelligence staff to conduct proper analysis, Washington would be dumping a huge amount of raw information on Hooker and Sharpe. At this time, for want of a Washington-level patron, the Balloon Corps was disbanded. Its absence at Gettysburg would narrow victory's margin. Nevertheless, even in its absence it proved an advantage, for the Confederates went to extraordinary measures to conceal their artillery and infantry march routes because of the fear of observation they had acquired from the Balloon Corps' efforts.[15]

At this juncture the personal initiative of those outside Hooker's direct command came to the rescue. Brigadier General Daniel Tyler, commanding the garrison at Harper's Ferry on the Potomac in Maryland, with great initiative and zeal was employing every collection means at hand to gather and forward much useful information to Hooker's headquarters.[16] Major General Darius Couch, who had been Hooker's second-in-command at Chancellorsville, and now commanded at Harrisburg, also was determined to reinforce the intelligence effort. Among the numerous groups of scouts he organized in Pennsylvania was one under the leadership of a local notable,

David McConaughy, the founder of the cemetery around which the coming battle would be fought. By June 16 McConaughy had found and reported Lee's cavalry advance at Greencastle in Pennsylvania, barely 25 miles from Gettysburg. Scouts sent out from the military commander in Baltimore also found Lee's cavalry the next day. Uncoordinated as their efforts were, the aggregate of patriotic and intelligent initiative started to pay off.[17] Other citizens were showing their patriotism in acts of defiance, which, though they did not add to the intelligence picture, at least reminded the Confederates they were in hostile territory. One woman had pinned an American flag across her bosom and flaunted it to the passing Rebel ranks. As the Texas Brigade marched by, one man cautioned her, "Take care, Madam. For Hood's boys are great at storming the breastworks when the Yankee colors are on them."[18]

Sharpe also determined to break through Lee's security. He sent off Sergeant Cline and a party of scouts to pass through the Union cavalry and find their way into Warrenton to locate Longstreet. So far Stuart's men were doing a better job. On June 17 they had captured Meade's acting signal officer, Captain B. F. Fisher, out on a reconnaissance near Aldie right under Pleasonton's nose.[19] The opportunity to turn the table on Stuart arose with the arrival of Hooker's orders to Pleasonton also on the 17th which directed that "you leave nothing undone to give [to Sharpe's men] the fullest cooperation." His orders also repeated the verbal message he had already dispatched through his aide, Captain Ulric Dahlgren. It directed, surely at Sharpe's urging, the cavalry to break through the enemy's pickets regardless of loss "to give him information of where the enemy is, his force, and his movements." Cline and his party arrived at the same time and were quickly integrated into the attack plan. The cavalry promptly attacked the Confederates at the pass through the Bull Run Mountains at Aldie, Virginia. In the fighting they assisted Cline and his scouts surely in Confederate uniform to join the rear of a retreating Confederate cavalry brigade. Sharpe had achieved the penetration of Stuart's cavalry that Lee's tight security had so long prevented.[20]

Sharpe employed another artful expedient this time. In a lecture after the war, Brigadier General Kilpatrick recalled the tension in the army as events were unfolding and Sharpe's anxiety to pin down Lee's intentions. Sharpe personally crossed the Rappahannock below Fredericksburg to make contact with a "colored washerwoman, whose cabin was in sight of our most powerful field glasses." The woman's husband sold food in the Confederate camps of Hill's III Corps.

> [T]he instant he saw any signs of the enemy breaking camp he was to hurry home and tell his wife to put up red cloth for artillery, a blue one for infantry, and a white towel for cavalry, his wife to place them on the north end of the clothesline if they started north, in the middle if they went west, and at the southern end if going south. Taking a favorable outlook, Gen. [then colonel] Sharpe waited with the breathless anxiety the result of his daring scheme, and just at daybreak saw a red cloth on the north end, then another, then a blue one, and then a towel, until the whole north end was full, when he hastened to headquarters with the news that the whole rebel army was marching north. This timely information was afterwards confirmed by scouts…[21]

The movement of Hill's Corps was especially important because its camps south of Fredericksburg were the furthest south of Lee's army. Once they moved, he knew that the entire army was in movement.

Hooker Shows the Strain

In the midst of this fluid and highly charged situation, Sharpe found he had to deal with an increasingly difficult commander who disregarded his analysis and began to treat him in a contemptuous manner. Hooker, whose confidence had never recovered from the beating Lee had given him in May, was showing the strain and becoming more and more erratic as he lashed out at the very man who then had put victory in his grasp. Brigadier General Patrick noted that Hooker could not make up his mind what to do to counter Lee's movements. An order had gone out on the morning of the 17th to put the army in motion but was then countermanded. He wrote in his diary on the same day:

> [Hooker] acts like a man without a plan and is entirely at a loss what to do, or to match the enemy, or counteract his movements. Whatever he does is the result of impulse, now, after having failed, so signally, at Chancellorsville … He has treated our 'Secret Service Department' which has furnished him with the most astonishingly correct information, with indifference at first, & now with insult.[22]

This was not staff backbiting but the observation of a man who was in daily contact with both Hooker and Sharpe. In fact, all three shared the same sleeping tent. Sharpe, who was in daily close communication with Patrick, must have unburdened himself to his nominal boss.

By June 20 the picture of Lee's deployment was becoming clearer. A mass of confusing information was yielding to painstaking all-source cross-checking and corroboration. Important pieces of information came from Sharpe's scout, Mordecai P. Hunnicutt, who had slipped into Richmond. Hunnicutt was a perfect example of the type of man Sharpe picked for his scouts. He spent his early years in the area south of Richmond and joined a volunteer regiment to fight in the Mexican War. Ten years later he joined William Walker's failed filibustering expedition to Central America and instead ended up as a pastry chef for the president of Costa Rica. Back in the United States, he took part in the fighting in Bloody Kansas before the Civil War and later enlisted in an Ohio infantry regiment in 1862.

Finding regular soldiering not to be of his taste, he positively leapt at the chance to volunteer for Sharpe's scouts. And Sharpe had the good sense to snap him up. Sharpe had sent him earlier on a mission to penetrate Richmond and learn what he could. Posing as a Union deserter, he enlisted in a Tennessee regiment in Virginia which got him to Richmond. He left on June 9, and in order to skirt the moving mass of Lee's army, moved by way of western and southwestern Virginia to Charleston in West Virginia, where he reported in to the local Union commander. That officer was so suspicious of him that he wired Sharpe for confirmation of his identity before forwarding Hunnicutt's report. Sharpe was able to filter out the errors in reporting Pickett's order-of-battle, but found several pieces of extremely useful information. The defenses of Richmond had been stripped to the bare minimum to defend the city from any attack by Maj. Gen. John Dix at Fort Monroe. Lee's strength had been increased to 85,000, which was about 10,000 too high. The third item was of a higher order than the order-of-battle numbers he had discovered. It addressed Lee's intent. He overheard from a corps staff officer that "The present move is to divide our forces and dash into Washington." This last would have to be weighed as more became known of the enemy's movements.[23]

Sharpe wrote his uncle that "I need scarcely add that the two armies are maneuvering for the best position, and that Lee was "trying to get upon the old field of Manassas. He must whip us before he goes in force to Md. or Penna. If he don't, we propose to let him go, and when we get behind him we would like to know how many men he will take back."[24] But the one element of the picture that remained opaque was the location of Longstreet's Corps, which was the key to discerning Lee's objective. This only added to Hooker's stress, for Longstreet's Corps was the mightiest offensive force in American history. Hooker's mental state continued to distort his judgment. Patrick's diary entry for the 19th became even more scathing:

> We get accurate information but Hooker will not use it and insults all who differ from him in opinion. He had declared that the enemy are over 100,000 strong. It is his only salvation to make it appear that the enemy's forces are stronger than his own, which is false & he knows it. He knows that Lee is his master & is afraid to meet him again in fair battle.[25]

By now Sharpe apparently had lost all confidence in Hooker. He had already sent his family home to Kingston from Washington. Some clash with Hooker may have been reflected in Patrick's diary entry. Now Sharpe asked to be returned to the command of his 120th New York. He may well have felt that his contribution at army headquarters was so circumscribed by Hooker's state of mind that his usefulness was over He wrote his uncle that he had not replied to his recent letters, "but I have not the heart for it. I am too 'near the throne' to say much and yet I cannot help feeling what transpires so closely to me and all of which I know so well." Sharpe was clearly trying to write between the lines because his natural sense of prudence and loyalty prevented him from going into detail about what was going terribly wrong at headquarters. Hooker may have had a keen appreciation for intelligence, but in his state of mind he forgot that in Sharpe he had an intelligence chief with many talents, and one of them that especially worked in Hooker's favor at this time was that he could keep his mouth shut. Unlike so many officers in the Union army who thought the service was fair ground for cutthroat politics, Sharpe, who had sound political instincts himself, was also profoundly loyal. He concluded that, if Hooker would not let him do his job, then at least he could find useful duty in command of his Ulster and Greene

Counties men. Twice he requested to be returned to his regiment. Each request was denied, and Sharpe found himself shackled to a commander fast losing his nerve.[26]

Hooker's state of mind may be partially explained by the flood of mostly inaccurate information he was getting from the cavalry who continued to operate in competition with the BMI. However, a major cavalry attack on Stuart on June 21 allowed Sergeant Cline and party to slip back into Union lines. He was able to identify Longstreet's concentration near Berryville, 20 miles south of Harper's Ferry.

The day before, Butterfield had taken a vital step in creating a near real time communications and intelligence system.

> On 20 June, by direction of the chief of staff, two signal officers were assigned to each army corps. Communication was opened by flag signals between the First Corps headquarters, at Guilford Station, the Eleventh Corps at Trappe Rock, and the Twelfth Corps at Leesburg. The officers at the last-named point worked successfully also with the signal station at Poolesville, Md., and through it with those at Sugar Loaf Mountain, Point of Rocks, and Maryland Heights direct to the commanding general at Fairfax Court-House, giving to him at the same time a rapid means of communication with all the corps named above. A reconnaissance was made for General H. W. Slocum by the signal officers attached to his command.[27]

Lee had nothing like this system.

Stuart and Pleasonton Spar at the Gaps

Sharpe was finding out that the trouble with Pleasonton was that sometimes his reports were accurate. In the mass of confused reporting there were the occasional flawless gems. He reported to Hooker on June 20, "I have been attacking Stuart to make him keep his people together, so they cannot scout and find out anything about our forces." He reported that cavalry east of the Blue Ridge was a covering force. "Longstreet has the covering of the gaps, and is moving up his force as the rebel army advances toward the Potomac.... Lee is playing his old game of covering the gaps and moving his forces up the Shenandoah Valley." Pleasonton was full of confidence in his men's performance and requested on June 20 the permission "to take my whole corps to-morrow morning, and throw it at once upon Stuart's whole force, and cripple it up."[28]

Hooker approved and ordered Maj. Gen. George G. Meade, commanding V Corps, to provide infantry support. Pleasonton pitched into Stuart the next morning and "steadily drove him all day, inflicting heavy loss at every step. I drove him through Upperville into Ashby's Gap and assured myself that the enemy had not infantry in the Loudon Valley... I never saw the troops behave better or under more difficult circumstances. Very many charges were made, and the saber was used freely, but always with great advantage to us." Pleasonton had just hammered Stuart back into the gap he was supposed to block in any case, but Stuart had resisted the temptation to replay Brandy Station and instead had stuck successfully to his blocking mission.

He reported to Lee that since the day was the Sabbath, "I recognized my obligation to do no duty other than what was absolutely necessary," and to rest his men. He had a more practical reason as well, noting that had he attacked, he would have met not just the Union cavalry but a strong force of infantry and artillery as well, "and the result would have been disastrous, no doubt." Pleasonton admitted that Stuart still held the gap, noting, "Stuart has the Gap covered with heavy Blakelys and 10.-pounder parrots."[29]

In the same message announcing his success, he stated that "Ewell's Corps went toward Winchester last Wednesday." Every newspaper in the country had already reported that Ewell had overrun the Union garrison in Winchester in a stinging defeat on June 15, something Pleasonton was obviously unaware of. Hooker's penchant for holding information close to the vest was keeping his corps commander seriously uninformed, which was especially dangerous for the Cavalry Corps screening the army and attempting to penetrate the enemy's own screen.[30]

Pleasonton's haphazard intelligence collection was now to drop some appalling analysis on Hooker and Sharpe. On June 22 he reported, based only on the statements of two deserters, that "Lee is at Winchester and that Longstreet's troops were on their way to that place; that A. P. Hill's corps was on the road up from Culpeper, on the other side of the mountains…" Lee was actually at Berryville, southeast of Winchester. Longstreet was still some distance from Winchester, having just withdrawn from the Blue Ridge, where he had come to support Stuart's defense against Pleasonton's attack. Hill's lead division had already arrived in Berryville to fall in behind Ewell on the march north. Pleasonton had already placed Ewell near Winchester, when Ewell had Rodes's Division already across the Potomac between Hagerstown and Sharpsburg. That same day Lee gave Ewell orders to cross the rest of his corps over the Potomac and head for the Susquehanna River in northern Pennsylvania. He himself with Hill's Corps would depart Berryville the same day.[31]

Babcock and a Narrow Escape

While McEntee was finding Charlie Wright, Babcock had arrived in Frederick, Maryland, on June 19 with a detachment of scouts on a special mission. He had assumed the cover of a reporter for the *New York Herald*. It was a good cover, for the *Herald* was an intensely antiwar and anti-Lincoln newspaper and one that Sharpe thought maintained a "usual character for lying." Sharpe had determined on the 17th that he needed a trusted agent and executive on the spot to report on the crossing of Lee's army into Maryland. Officially, Hooker exercised no command north of the Potomac, but Sharpe was taking the initiative to put his people in place. Frederick was a regional communications center, and the nearby South Mountain range gave vital observation for the area. On June 20, Hooker sent him detailed instructions which he had already put into effect. He was anxious that Babcock "employ only such persons as can look upon a body of armed men without being frightened out of their senses" and "Send me no information but that which you know to be authentic." He need not have worried; Babcock knew his business and wired Hooker back that he had already anticipated those instructions.[32]

That afternoon, at 3:30 p.m., Babcock again wired Hooker, this time that Rodes's Division of Ewell's Corps and Jenkin's Cavalry Brigade were all the forces that had crossed the Potomac at Williamsport, with most of the infantry at Charlestown. Ewell had left Williamsport for Harper's Ferry. The rest of Lee's army was not within supporting distance. Two hours later he sent a hurried wire that "Signal corps just driven in; and are flying through the town. Report that the enemy are 3 miles out. Everything in an uproar, and everybody leaving. I suppose I must go too." He added that he would go to Monococy Junction and return when he could. Even in a crisis he smelled advantage. "It is only a raid, and may prove beneficial to me, as I can learn much on returning after they have left."[33]

But things were about to get worse. He found himself trapped in Frederick. With the telegraph too dangerous to use, he sent off a letter to Sharpe:

> [T] wenty-five of the 1st Maryland Cavalry made a dash into the city. I tried to get out but found all the approaches picketed and gave it up as dangerous. I have been dogged about all day as a suspicious character by several notorious rebels... I had sundry papers about me stating in very strong terms my business here. Being at the time the rebel cavalry entered, in front of the Central House, a notorious rebel hole, I could not hide my papers and had to carefully destroy them by piece-meal and throw them away. A large crowed having collected I made my escape from the parties on my track and put up in a private house in a remote part of town.

The danger did not dampen his sense of humor, as he penned, "I am not over-anxious to be _____," putting in place of the blank a sketch of a man on the gallows. Nevertheless, the danger was real. The Confederates that had ridden into town were Maj. Harry Gilmore's 1st Maryland Battalion, attached to Fitzhugh Lee's Brigade. Gilmore's men shifted back and forth between partisan and regular warfare and were particularly hard on anyone they discovered as a spy. Babcock was certainly not going to put them to the test. The next morning he slipped through the pickets on a railroad handcar in the direction of Baltimore, hired two men to take him further until he could find a telegraph office to communicate with Sharpe through the War Department in Washington.[34]

His efforts had not been entirely in vain. He had performed the vital service of locating Ewell's movement across the Potomac into Maryland. Pleasonton had located Longstreet's brigades supporting Stuart's attempt to shut off the gaps to prying Union eyes. The greatest coup was carried off by Sergeant Cline and his scouts. After having slipped into the enemy rear in civilian clothing, they had moved freely among the Southern troops masqueraded as Confederate partisans, and four days later slipped out again with a wealth of information and were in Sharpe's tent in Fairfax late at night on June 22. Sharpe reported the next day that Cline had found "Divisions of Pickett and Hood lying in rear of Snicker's Gap, in position to defend it. Three companies of infantry at Millwood, opposite Ashby Gap, and the rest of Longstreet's corps between Front Royal and Winchester." To top it off, "they heard that Ewell was establishing a line, so as to draw stores from Maryland and Pennsylvania. Learned from a Confederate soldier, disabled in a house, that A. P. Hill was also in the Valley." All three Confederate corps were now located and the direction of the movement clarified. His scouts also reported that Ewell's Corps had concentrated and camped in Boonesboro Valley, in the area of the Antietam battlefield.[35]

On June 22 Lee ordered Ewell with the rest of his corps, with Hill following directly behind, to cross into Pennsylvania. By the 24th, Sharpe was able to trace a 40-mile column of the Army of Northern Virginia, though the location of particular units remained unclear. A major contributor to this all-source intelligence was the signal system set up only four days before which reported, "Large trains are crossing at Sharpsburg. Artillery and general trains are passing near Charlestown toward Shepardstown."[36] The anxiety level would have risen in the Union army headquarters had they been able to actually witness the enthusiasm with which Lee's regiments crossed the Potomac, ringing out "Dixie" and "Nellie Gray" as they approached. As the regiments tramped across, their bands burst out with "Dixie." Major General John Bell Hood would note, "Never before, nor since, have I witnessed such intense enthusiasm as that which prevailed throughout the entire Confederate Army." Undoubtedly it was helped along by the whiskey ration he issued on the occasion.[37]

Unfortunately, for Hooker and Sharpe, the level of uncertainty was already high; heavy reporting from other commands dumped a good deal of erroneous information on Hooker, information that was not subject to Sharpe's all-source processing. A telling part of that information was based on a Confederate deception that had Hill's men in Maryland pretend to be Longstreet's men. Hooker thus believed that Lee's entire army was across the Potomac on the road to Pennsylvania when, in fact, Longstreet's Corps was still in Virginia. Based on this unverified information, Hooker put his entire army in motion once again. By June 27, the blue columns had completely cleared the Potomac even ahead of the Army of Northern Virginia and began the northward movement to parallel Lee on the other side of the Blue Ridge and South Mountains across the Potomac. Hooker now had stolen a march and got the inside track that would allow the Army of the Potomac to intercept its opponent. It would be a tremendous advantage in the coming crisis; ironically, it was based on bad intelligence, which in turn was based on a Confederate deception that worked far too well. All in all, it was a telling example of the law of unintended consequences in high gear.

Beauregard and Stuart—On and Off the Stage

Lee was not finished with disinformation. In a series of letters to Jefferson Davis dated June 23 and 25, he elaborated on a plan he had obviously been thinking about for over a month. He urged Davis to assemble a small army under General Beauregard at Culpeper Courthouse to threaten Washington from the south while he threatened it from the north. Shortly after Chancellorsville, Lee had suggested bringing Beauregard to command a new force because "the little Cajun's" reputation was strong in the North. As early as May 14, one of Sharpe's agents traveling through Lee's forces around Culpeper had picked up the rumor which Lee had probably planted. By early June Lee was discussing the plan with Longstreet. That plan called for scouring the Confederate Atlantic coast and Richmond garrisons of their brigades. At that time in the Department of North Carolina, there were six brigades and another body of troops at Cape Fear as well as three cavalry regiments. With these forces and what could be scrapped up in South Carolina, he thought a credible IV Corps could be created that could move on Washington. At the same time, though, he wanted Corse's Brigade of Pickett's Division—which had been left in Richmond as part of the garrison—to join him as well as one of the North Carolina brigades (Micah Jenkins's). He was hopeful that such a force would pull at least one corps if not more from the Army of the Potomac to defend the national capital.[38]

As the armies crossed into Union territory, Sharpe began to receive a flood of information from his scouts. The length of Lee's column loosened his hitherto tight security. At this time, Stuart was given an independent mission to cross the Potomac east of the Blue Ridge and keep in contact with Ewell's right flank. His first problem was that in attempting to cross the Potomac River he had to move further and further east to avoid collision with the mass of Hooker's army on its movement north. Hooker's interposing army effectively put him out of range of supporting Ewell. At the same time, Stuart began to turn a flank security mission into another great raid that would reestablish his Brandy Station-tarnished reputation. Stuart had done Sharpe a great service in removing his cavalry from Lee's flank. Up to this point, Stuart had done a splendid job keeping Union eyes off Lee's unfolding operation. Stuart was not entirely to blame, as Lee left two of Stuart's brigades guarding gaps in the Blue Ridge long after his army had passed north.[39]

Stuart was responsible for selecting Brig. Gen. Beverley Robertson (commanding his own brigade) as the overall commander of both brigades. Longstreet for one had had no confidence in him and wished Brig. Gen. John Imboden assigned this mission. Robertson's instructions from Stuart, dated June 24, were clear:

> Your object will be to watch the enemy; deceive him as to our designs, and harass his rear if you find he is retiring. Be always on the alert; let nothing escape your observation, and miss no opportunity which offers to damage the enemy.
>
> After the enemy has moved beyond your reach, leave sufficient pickets in the mountains, withdraw to the west side of the Shenandoah, place a strong and reliable picket to watch the enemy at Harper's Ferry, cross the Potomac, and follow the army, keeping on its right and rear.[40]

These instructions were so clear that, had Robertson executed them with alacrity, Stuart's subsequent absence at a critical time of the campaign would not have deprived Lee of his eyes and ears. The cavalry he left with Robertson would more have compensated for his absence. In fact, the junior of the two brigade commanders, Brig. Gen. "Grumble" Jones, was considered the finest outpost officer in the Army of Northern Virginia. Instead, Robertson lingered over a week in the quiet mountain passes after both armies had moved on, far too long for the cavalry to play any significant role after they were finally recalled to join Lee.

Lee had a few other intelligence assets with him. In June he had appointed Major John H. Richardson, commander of the 39th Battalion, Virginia Cavalry, of 200 officers and men, to his staff. The battalion's duties included scouting enemy positions and finding efficient routes in the army's line of march. At least one company accompanied Lee's headquarters, with the other companies assigned to each of the three corps headquarters.

The 1st Battalion, Virginia Infantry, of 250 men, was assigned as the army provost guard and marched behind the army, rounding up stragglers and deserters. Lee assigned its commander, Capt. David B. Bridgford, as his acting provost marshal. In addition to its military police duties, the battalion was charged with collection and interrogation of prisoners of war. The battalion was to collect order-of-battle information by collating from prisoners and deserters the "names, regiments, brigades, and corps." When Lee reached Winchester on June 24, he could not ascertain the whereabouts of the 1st Maryland Battalion with which he had intended to garrison the town. Instead, he left the 1st Virginia Battalion as its garrison. This effectively took his provost guard out of the operation. Thomas J. Ryan comments, "In the absence of his headquarters provost guards, Lee would have to rely on those units at brigade, division, and corps level to interrogate prisoners and acquire order of battle and other intelligence. He thus lacked direct control over the process that would be needed to derive timely intelligence in a combat situation."[41]

Lee's ad hoc provisions for his provost marshal operation are in stark contrast with those of the Army of the Potomac. Lee's provost marshal was a captain commanding a battalion of 250 men. His Union counterpart, Patrick, was a brigadier general with the equivalent of an infantry brigade—1,787 officers and men—in his provost guard.[42]

Enter Meade

As Lee was blinded by Stuart's ride around the Army of the Potomac, Sharpe began receiving more and more accurate information. The wires were pouring in reports from 13 separate army and government sources. Even more important was the information from refugees and patriotic citizens, such as those in Chambersburg, Pennsylvania, who set out to gather information even while under occupation. Amazingly, about 75 percent of it proved accurate, which Sharpe's all-source methodology was able to substantiate. One citizen provided a highly accurate count of Lee's artillery and an overall strength figure that was also very close to actual strength as of June 27. Other reports located Lee and his subordinate commanders at Chambersburg and marked their departure on the road to Gettysburg. On that same day, Hooker, who had demanded control of the Harper's Ferry garrison on threat of resignation, got his subliminal wish. Lincoln relieved him.

His replacement was the V Corps commander, Maj. Gen. George Gordon Meade. Lincoln passed over his first choice, Maj. Gen. John Reynolds, because the general had stipulated that he wanted a completely independent command, but he had recommended Meade. When the assistant adjutant general of the army woke him in his tent well before dawn on June 28, Meade thought it was to arrest him, his mind racing over what he had possibly done to merit this. At first he protested that the command should go to Reynolds, his respected senior. But the bearer of his promotion insisted that the president wanted him, and Meade dutifully accepted. It would be a sound choice. This Pennsylvanian was a consummate and reliable professional who had the confidence of the army. He was also a friend to the intelligence effort and a man McClellan rated as "an excellent officer; cool, brave, and intelligent."[43]

Unfortunately, Hooker's habit of keeping his senior commanders in the dark not only on operational matters but also on the coordination of intelligence required Meade to spend a day being intensively briefed by Sharpe. The experience established a mutual self-confidence and certainly removed the load of anxiety Sharpe had been bearing. After the increasingly erratic Hooker, the cool-headed Meade was an enormous relief. Meade immediately put Sharpe's analysis to good use by fanning the army corps out over a 60-degree angle between Emmitsburg and Westminster in Maryland, with the aim of intercepting at least part of Lee's army. Information from the Gettysburg group of citizen scouts had identified the march of Early's Division of Ewell's Corps through their town and northward. Meade aimed to cut right through it. At this time Babcock and his scouts returned from the Frederick area; Butterfield personally introduced him to Meade and fairly sang his praises and received the compliments of the new commander for the value of his service. Meade, at this time, was welding a team and certainly won Babcock over.[44]

As Stuart rode east of the Army of the Potomac on June 29, he severed all the telegraph communications with Washington. However, scouts had already reported on that day that the Confederates had marched out of Hagerstown and marched toward Chambersburg, Pennsylvania.[45] Loss of the telegraph cut off Sharpe from sources of information in-theater. He was now thrown on his own resources, but Meade was working closely with him and ordered all of the BMI's scouts out to gather more information. Butterfield's order to Sharpe read: "The major-general commanding desires that you send to Gettysburg, Hanover, Greencastle, Chambersburg, and Jefferson to-night and get as much information as you can of the numbers, position, and force of the enemy, with their movements." Unbeknownst to Meade, that had already been done by Sharpe's intrepid scouts. Sergeant Cline again had slipped in among the Confederates in Hagerstown and was forwarding valuable information. Another of his scouts, Ed Hopkins, had ridden ahead with the cavalry and entered Gettysburg, where he sought out McConaughy's group and established liaison with Sharpe. It was a decisive action. Hopkins's report, which he delivered to Reynolds at Emmitsburg, was amazingly accurate:

> … a scout of Sharpe's, has just returned from Gettysburg, with a statement of affairs in that quarter yesterday. Early's division passed there in the direction of York, and the other division (Gordon's, I think), with the trains, was in the Valley, and moved along a road nearer the mountains. Another division (Rodes') of Ewell's was up by Carlisle, and Hill (A. P.) was said to be moving up through Greencastle, in the direction of Chambersburg. The cavalry with Early was sent off to Hanover Junction, and up the railroad to York.[46]

McConaughy's efforts and those of other citizen groups in Chambersburg were telling Meade the location of Hill's and Ewell's Corps. Sharpe had already appreciated the great value of McConaughy's earlier information as had Meade, who would write in a circular on the first that "All true Union people should be advised to harass and annoy the enemy in every way, to send information, and [be] taught how to do it; giving regiments by number of colors, number of guns, generals names, &c."[47] Sharpe now pressed the Gettysburg agent for more in a letter on the 29th:

> The General directs me to thank you for yours of today. You have grasped the information so well in its directness & minuteness, that it is very valuable. I hope our friends understand that in the great game that is now being played, everything in the way of advantage depends upon which side gets the best information. The rebels are shortly in advance of us—but if thro' the districts they threaten our friends will organize & send us information with the precision you have done, they may rest secure in the result—and we hope a near one. The names of the Generals, the number of the forces, if possible, are very important to us, as they enable us to gauge the reports with exactness.
>
> The General begs, if in your power, that you make such arrangement with intelligent friends in the country beyond you to this effect, and that you continue your attention to us as much as your convenience will permit.
>
> Hoping at some future day to have the pleasure of meeting you, I am, dear sir, yours very truly,
>
> Geo. B. Sharpe
> Col. and of Gen's Staff, Army of the Potomac.[48]

McConaughy's reports more than any other source drew Brigadier General John Buford and his cavalry division toward Gettysburg on June 30. Buford was an experienced and aggressive commander with a keen appreciation of the intelligence role of the cavalry. He also firmly believed in the timeliness of information, as his rapid stream of dispatches to higher headquarters showed. His division was guarding the army's left flank as it moved north. These were the three corps (I, III, XI) under the operational control of the I Corps commander, Maj. Gen. John Reynolds. Reports on the enemy—which was closer to Reynolds and Buford than army headquarters itself—were arriving from Sharpe because they had come directly from McConaughy.

Lee at Chambersburg was oblivious to the flurry of intelligence that was concentrating the Army of the Potomac against him. He fully shared the invincible enthusiasm of his men. He had heard of Meade's appointment at least by this time and commented to Major General Hood, "Ah! General, the enemy is a long time finding us; if he does not succeed soon, we must go in search of him."[49]

It was a reflection of hubris that was about to be quickly answered. By June 29 Buford had reached the village of Fairfield about 5 miles south of Gettysburg where he received an order from Pleasonton, based on Sharpe's intelligence, directing him to move to Gettysburg by the following night. That very night, while still in Fairfield, his scouts captured a Confederate courier near Oxford with a dispatch from Confederate Major General Early that showed his location and the rest of Ewell's Corps north of Gettysburg. Buford was especially exercised that he had missed the opportunity to bag two Mississippi regiments camped nearby because of the complete lack of cooperation from the townspeople:

> The inhabitants knew of my arrival and the position of the enemy's camp, yet not one of them gave me a particle of information, nor even mentioned the fact of the enemy's presence. The whole community seemed stampeded, and afraid to speak, often offering as excuses for not showing some little enterprise, "The rebels will destroy our houses if we tell anything." Had any one given me timely information, and acted as guide that night, I could have surprised and captured or destroyed this force…[50]

Happily, the citizens of other towns, such as Chambersburg and Gettysburg, were made of more patriotic stuff.

The last day before the collision of the armies at Gettysburg was June 30, a day when all-source intelligence had already fused a coherent picture of the enemy. Scouts, civilian informants, and the cavalry were all contributing to Meade's intelligence summary of that day, which he sent to all his corps commanders. "[F]rom present information, Longstreet and Hill are at Chambersburg, partly toward Gettysburg; Ewell at Carlisle and York. Movements indicated a disposition to advance from Chambersburg to Gettysburg." With this order, he put his corps in motion, directing I and XI Corps to Gettysburg and the others to within supporting distance.[51] Meade was also being served by the synergistic effect of the determined initiative and efficiency of his sources, of which, at this point, John Buford would outshine all others.

Buford rode into Gettysburg, arriving at 11 a.m., well ahead of schedule. He was preceded by a detachment of scouts of the 3rd Indiana Cavalry, Hooker's old Horse Marines, as well as men of the 8th Illinois Cavalry, led by Sgt. Harry B. Sparks of Company C. They charged "into the streets in a full, pounding gallop, surprising and capturing several Confederate stragglers from their earlier expedition into the town four days prior." Buford arrived to find the town in a state of hysteria generated by the imminent arrival of a Confederate force. It was barely a half-mile away. Buford wrote that the local civilian description of the enemy force "was terribly exaggerated by reasonable and truthful but inexperienced men." He had no trouble driving the Confederates back toward Cashtown when apparently he made contact with McConaughy. "On pushing him back toward Cashtown, I learned from reliable men that one of Hill's divisions was marching in this direction heading for York to the east of Gettysburg." He immediately sent out patrols, one of which found a pass signed by Lee that day putting him at Chambersburg.[52]

That night, at 10:30 and 10:40, he wrote two highly accurate reports that he sent to Reynolds and Pleasonton who were with Meade at Taneytown. He identified Hill's Corps at just west of Cashtown with his pickets only 4 miles from Gettysburg. "Longstreet, from all I can learn, is still behind Hill." Finally, he fixed Ewell's movements, "Near Heidlersberg today, one of my parties captured a courier of Lee's. Nothing was found on him. He says Ewell's corps is crossing the mountains from Carlisle, Rodes's division being at Petersburg in advance."[53] In effect, he had identified all three of Lee's corps and their evident movement in the direction of Gettysburg.

That same evening in Emmitsburg, the commanders of I and XI Corps met to discuss the intelligence they had received throughout the day. Major General Howard recalled that the reports "were abundant and conflicting. They came from Headquarters at Taneytown, from Buford at Gettysburg, from scouts, from alarmed citizens, from all directions. They, however, forced the conclusion upon us that Lee's infantry and artillery in great force were in our neighborhood."[54] Intelligence clearly was pulling the Army of the Potomac to Gettysburg like a magnet. Reynolds would have had a better grasp of the situation because John Babcock and Captain McEntee and a number of his scouts were traveling with the headquarters to provide collection and analysis support.[55] That night, Meade ordered the two corps to the little crossroads town in Pennsylvania.

CHAPTER SIX

Gettysburg and Sharpe's Three Golden Gifts To Meade

July 1

Lieutenant Jerome in the Cupola

The next morning, at 7:00, the young signal officer recently attached to Buford was gazing intently from the cupola of the Lutheran Theological Seminary. Lieutenant Aaron B. Jerome had ridden in with the cavalry the previous day, having supported them on the ride with intelligence from observation and flag signals. Now through the lifting haze he could see the enemy pickets of Maj. Gen. Henry Heth's Division of Hill's Corps advancing from Cashtown. Jerome quickly sent a courier to Buford, who joined him in the cupola. It was a force considerably stronger than his, but he would have to hold them. He rushed down the stairs to organize his two brigades to meet the attack and sent a message to Reynolds to come up fast.[1]

Buford rejoined Jerome in the cupola to control the battle from the best observation point. Jerome identified a large Union infantry column approaching from the south as Reynolds's I Corps came just in time. It was about 10:00 a.m. On his approach Reynolds had been kept informed of the situation at Gettysburg by his signal station on the flank of the mountain behind Emmitsburg. Now on the field Reynolds immediately threw in a bruising punch with his 1st Division that threw Heth's men back, only to fall from a sniper's bullet as he was waving the Iron Brigade into the attack. This elite unit inflicted heavy casualties on Heth's men and took hundreds of prisoners, many from the regiments trapped in the railroad cut as they tried to use that sunken way to slip through Union lines. Those hundreds were quickly shunted into the hands of Babcock and McEntee, who had arrived on the field with Reynolds's staff.

This engagement quickly took on a life of its own as it drew more and more forces from both sides into it. About 11:30 a.m. Jerome spotted Howard and his XI Corps command staff arriving on Cemetery Hill to the rear of the fighting. He immediately signaled him, "Over a division of the rebels is making a Bank movement on our right; the line extends over a mile, and is advancing, skirmishing… There is nothing but cavalry to oppose them."[2]

Howard assumed overall command and deployed his corps to the right of I Corps just in time to stop another attack, this time by Ewell, with Robert E. Rodes's Division attempting to lap around I Corps' flank. At least twice that morning Jerome had supplied Union commanders with real-time intelligence that allowed them to counter Confederate attacks. But Confederate numbers were to eventually overcome the intelligence advantage, as Early's Division of Ewell's Corps arrived on the field from the north with the power of an avalanche to turn the XI Corps' right flank, triggering a general collapse. Jerome moved his observation station to the steeple of the Gettysburg Courthouse as Union troops attempted to get away through the streets of the town. From his vantage, Jerome could see the XI Corps signal station set up on East Cemetery Hill. That signal station moved to West Cemetery Hill and became the main signal station through the rest of the day.[3]

Meade's Reservations

Although Meade had identified Gettysburg as the enemy's point of advance, he had great reservations about fighting there. He had already ordered his engineers to build field fortifications at Pipe Creek just over the Maryland line. It was there he preferred to fight. Sharpe, who was constantly at his side at the time, noted years later, "Nor had Meade designed or desired to fight at Gettysburg. The line of Pipe Creek between Middleburg and Manchester was better adapted to cover Baltimore and Washington, and his depot, Westminster, would be in the direct rear of this centre."[4]

A half-hour after Howard's Corps joined the battle, Meade, unaware that his two corps had become decisively engaged, issued a circular which ordered Reynolds to withdraw from Gettysburg and, along with the other corps, to pull back across Pipe Creek. He intended for Reynolds to conduct only a holding operation.

> If the enemy assume the offensive, and attack, it is his [Meade's] intention, after holding them in check sufficiently long, to withdraw the trains and other *impedimenta*; to withdraw the army from its present position, and form line of battle with the left resting in the neighborhood of Middleburg, and the right at Manchester, the general direction being that of Pipe Creek… The time for falling back can only be developed by circumstances.

He had concluded "from information received" that his maneuvering had caused Lee to abandon his further invasion of the north and that Lee would follow him to ground of Meade's choosing. He also ordered his acting signal officer, Captain L. B. Norton, to extend field telegraph lines to points in northern Maryland along a general line of withdrawal. Norton promptly complied, which resulted in the field telegraph being unable to operate on the Gettysburg battlefield itself.[5]

When Buford's news of Reynold's death arrived, Meade sent his most reliable and able general officer, Maj. Gen. Winfield Scott Hancock, commanding II Corps, to take overall command on the field and to ascertain whether to continue fighting at

Gettysburg. Hancock arrived about 5 p.m. His powerful and charismatic personality quickly beat new life into the dispirited survivors of the fighting as he organized them for the defense of Cemetery Hill and Culp's Hill. One of his first actions was to send his own signal officer out on two reconnaissance missions. Hancock's report of the scale and importance of the fighting there and the critical nature of the ground now drew Meade as an unwilling participant from the ground he had chosen to offer battle. For that reason, he would leave most of his trains at Westminster, the nearest railroad terminus to Gettysburg, except for ambulances and ammunition. The army would fight hungry at Gettysburg for that.[6] Had he pulled out as he originally intended, the one-day battle of Gettysburg would have gone down in history as another brilliant victory for Robert E. Lee.

When Hancock's courier rode into army headquarters, Sharpe remembered:

> I was laying on the ground in a corner of General Meade's tent at Taneytown, when Hancock's reply came, partially approving this line. The advantages of Pipe Creek were thought to be counter-balanced by the moral effect of joining our brave comrades who had fought here, instead of withdrawing them, and giving the impression of a retreat.
>
> Meade boldly decided to advance his converging corps, and as soon as the orders could be written and forwarded, he mounted and with his staff rode rapidly to the front. It was a moonlight night. We started before midnight and covered the distance of fourteen miles by one o'clock in the morning. And I recall with distintness [sic] the solemnity of our reflections and discussions.[7]

Meade found the survivors of I and XI Corps had been hammered back into a defensive position on the high ground of Cemetery Hill. Hancock already had ordered the garrisoning of neighboring Culp's Hill just in time to throw back a Confederate assault. As reinforcements arrived, the Union line started to extend down Cemetery Ridge. Following Sharpe was the rest of the BMI to join Babcock and McEntee, who had been at work with prisoner interrogations from the moment they arrived with Reynolds that morning. Prisoners were then passed to Provost Marshal General Patrick at Taneytown, who had spent the morning "overhauling trains [traffic control] & examining prisoners etc. sent down from Reynolds & Cavalry." He would join Meade later that early evening after setting up a depot for prisoners. The fighting that day, especially the attacks of I Corps early in the day, netted 600 prisoners, and Babcock and McEntee had made good use of the time to begin filling out the enemy's order-of-battle.[8]

Stuart Missed

Meade may not have realized it, but the value of the BMI would be multiplied because the comparable Confederate effort was dysfunctional. For Lee, Stuart embodied the intelligence function of the Army of Northern Virginia. Stuart's famous absence until the late afternoon of July 2 effectively blinded Lee, who, because of his personal reliance on Stuart, made little reconnaissance use of the 800 cavalry that remained with him. Lee realized that he was in the midst of a hostile population, unlike

Virginia, where the geography and people were on his side. In his eyes a darkness had fallen around his army that he felt he could not penetrate without Stuart, which explains his refusal to let Longstreet boldly maneuver around Meade's flanks on the second day of the battle. When Stuart's cavalry finally stumbled, exhausted, into Gettysburg from their ride around the Army of the Potomac, they were unfit for vigorous reconnaissance the next day. Lee had thus fixed himself to a battle of position. Lee was also suffering from a self-inflicted wound, the absence of his provost guard. There are few indications that any interrogations of Union prisoners were taking place at Lee's headquarters that night nor any attempt to prepare a comprehensive order-of-battle other than the brief summary in Lee's official report of the campaign:

> It was ascertained from the prisoners that we had been engaged with two corps [I and XI Corps] of the army formerly commanded by General Hooker, and that the remainder of that army, under General Meade, was approaching Gettysburg. Without information as to its proximity, the strong position which the enemy had assumed could not be attacked without danger of exposing the four divisions present, already weakened and exhausted by a long and bloody struggle, to overwhelming numbers of fresh troops. General Ewell was therefore, instructed to carry the hill occupied by the enemy, if he found it practicable, but to avoid a general engagement until the arrival of the other divisions of the army, which were ordered to hasten forward.[9]

What information Lee was getting must have been that obtained by his subordinate corps and divisions and fed to his overworked staff. His intelligence picture was only barely further illuminated by the capture of a courier whose dispatch revealed the presence of another corps and the arrival of another Union corps early the next morning.[10] The official reports of Lee's three corps commanders revealed scarcely more order-of-battle information than Lee's report, indicating that his headquarters had derived its information from these sources. Ewell reported that he had broken Barlow's Division (XI Corps) on the first day and that the captured dispatch, mentioned by Lee, was from Major General Sykes, commanding V Corps, to Major General Slocum, commanding XII Corps. Hill's report only stated that the first day's fighting resulted in the total destruction of the Union I Corps, an exaggeration. Longstreet's report contains no order-of-battle information at all. Thus the official reports of the commander and his corps commanders contained only information about four of the seven Union corps (I, V, XI, XII) and no information about the enemy's Cavalry Corps.[11] There are no indications that interrogations to build an order-of-battle took place on the next two days of fighting. While some efforts must have been taken on July 2 that surely revealed the presence of Hancock's II and Sickles's III Corps, Lee failed to mention any further discoveries of the Union order-of-battle in his official report. Sharpe could not have asked for more.

Meade could not have asked for more as well. From his statement above, Lee as much as admitted that he was fighting blind. He had gathered from prisoners that the rest of the Army of the Potomac was on its way to the battle, but the timing of the arrival of its corps was so complete a mystery as to induce a case of severe caution in one of the boldest risk-taking generals in American history. Only four of his nine infantry divisions were on the field, and he feared to continue the fighting to storm the heights behind Gettysburg held by the already-beaten survivors of I and XI Corps, because a much larger Union force might arrive to surprise and overwhelm his exhausted divisions. That fear had settled upon him because Stuart's superb reconnaissance capabilities were entirely absent. Had Stuart been with Lee on July 1, his cavalry would have been actively probing the approaches to Gettysburg, drawing for Lee a clear picture of the arrival of the rest of the Army of the Potomac. With that in hand, he surely would have been bolder in driving the Union from Cemetery Hill that night.

July 2

"Not Mere Bookkeeping Problems"

As the Army of the Potomac concentrated at Gettysburg early on July 2, the Cavalry Corps' mission became to guard the army's flanks. The next two days would see Meade's intelligence assets shrink largely to the efforts of the BMI and the Signal Corps because the cavalry was devoted to flank security rather than reconnaissance. All day Meade would employ Sharpe as a primary staff officer to help him fight the battle. Such a senior staff officer is charged with carrying the commander's instructions to the corps commanders and giving orders in the commanding general's name, just such a role Sharpe himself describes below and which was mentioned in a eulogy after his death: "At Gettysburg he was Meade's mouthpiece, his representative..." The BMI staff was on its own, but the team Sharpe had created was fully capable of operating without a chief in a crisis.[12]

As Edwin Fishel described the situation early on the second day of battle, the men of the BMI were diligently at work:

> Sharpe, Babcock, and McEntee began their battlefield labors expecting that the face-to-face proximity of the enemy would enable them to fill in most or all of the gaps in their organizational records. Some of the recently added regiments were still unidentified; the brigades to which many regiments belonged were still unknown; and this dearth of information may have extended to the division assignments of a few brigades. These were not mere bookkeeping problems ... the presence of a mere regiment would indicate the presence of an entire corps, provided its subordination to the larger units—brigade, division, corps—had been determined.[13]

As the fighting men surged across the field and men fell by their thousands, a stream of Confederate prisoners was flowing to the rear that at the end of the day would add another 660 to the bag of prisoners, a further rich opportunity for Babcock to flesh out his order-of-battle. As their signal counterparts struggled amid shot and shell to keep communications open to transmit operational information and intelligence, the BMI men worked patiently and deftly, taking one man at a time from the long lines of Confederate prisoners into the seclusion of an interrogation tent. In addition to the interrogations conducted on the field by Sharpe's staff, interrogations were also being conducted by BMI staff and provost guards at the prisoner collection point, established by Patrick at the army's base at Taneytown the day before.[14]

The weight of intelligence collection and analysis fell on Sharpe's staff because the head of the BMI was being used by Meade as senior staff officer to help him fight the battle. Messages delivered by such senior staff officers carried more authority than notes carried by couriers or aides-de-camp. Equally important were the practiced observations they made, as well as the decisions they could make in the commander's name. That left the order-of-battle analysis to Babcock, McEntee, and Manning. It was in good hands.

That morning Meade was looking to attack Ewell's II Corps on his right, facing the army's positions on Culp's Hill. He wanted to employ his XII, and V Corps and VI Corps as it came up from Manchester. But his information that Ewell was attacking was dead on and was confirmed by a Signal Corps observation report at 9:30 a.m. "The enemy are moving a brigade of five regiments from in front of our center to our right, accompanied by one four-gun battery and two squadrons of cavalry, at a point east-southeast of Second Division, Twelfth Corps, and in easy range. A heavy line of enemy's infantry on our right. Very small force of infantry … visible in front of our center." Major General Slocum, commanding XII, also conducted a reconnaissance of the proposed ground of attack and recommended against it. In the decision and planning to conduct this attack, both corps and army commanders were fully supported by an all-source system that included order-of-battle and signals intelligence as well as reconnaissance. This support prevented Meade from making an attack over unfavorable ground against a strong enemy.[15]

If any word other than professionalism described the efforts of both groups, it was initiative. That characteristic would be found throughout the Army of the Potomac during the battle and would be one of the chief causes of its victory.

The Signal Corps Goes into Action

The night before, Butterfield had directed the signal officer to report to headquarters at Gettysburg with the signal officer reserve. He would report:

> On July 2, I reported at an early hour at the point selected for headquarters of the army for that day, but found the signal officers who had been previously assigned to the different army corps, already on the field, and that through their exertions the general commanding had been placed in communications with nearly all the corps commanders.
>
> Before 11 a.m. every desirable point of observation was occupied by a signal officer, and communications opened from General Meade's headquarters to those of every corps commander.[16]

These desirable points of observation included the Culp's Hill spur now known as Steven's Knoll, Power Hill (where Slocum had his wing headquarters), Cemetery Hill, Little Round Top, and the Widow Leister's house (behind Cemetery Ridge), which Meade was using for his headquarters. Because these signal stations could reach his headquarters so easily, Meade was to become attached to it as a hub of information and the point from which he could best stay informed. In addition to the active signal party at Leister House, a constant stream of couriers was arriving and departing. The efficiency of the signal stations made an effective substitute for the missing field telegraph.

This day would see some of the most desperate fighting of the war, in which the army fended off one Confederate hammer blow after another. Meade acquitted himself with great distinction as he fulfilled the primary role of the commander in battle—the allocation of the reserves that time and time again blunted an enemy advance on the point of a breakthrough. A vital part of his ability to do so was due to the timely reports of enemy movements rapidly sent to him by signal corps officers. Probably the greatest warning he received was from the station on Little Round Top.

Lieutenant Jerome was there with his signal team. By 11:45 a.m. he was reporting to Butterfield, "Enemy skirmishers are advancing from the west, one mile from here." Ten minutes later he reported that the Confederates were driving Union skirmishers back and that 1 mile from his station the woods were full of the enemy. These were men from Anderson's Division of Hill's III Corps. Unfortunately, he departed soon thereafter as Buford's Division, to which he was attached, was departing the battlefield.

It was not long before Captain Norton arrived on his tour of the battlefield signal stations accompanied by Captain P. A. Taylor, the junior XI Corps signal officer. They found the site unoccupied and quickly began to search the field for the enemy. They signaled information on the enemy, also from Anderson's Division, to the senior corps signal officer, Capt. James Hall, stating it was "a good point for observation." Hall then joined them on Little Round Top. Norton now departed, and Hall assumed command of the signal station as the senior officer present.

"Order, Counter-Order, Disorder"

Hall and his flagman, Sgt. John Chemberlin, were watching the field to their front just as two divisions of Longstreet's I Corps were making their approach march to strike the Union left-center. Longstreet was not happy about this assignment, fearing a direct assault on Union high ground. He had taken thoroughly to heart the lessons of slaughter in marching troops across wide open ground against strong defensive positions manned by determined defenders armed with rifled weapons. Malvern Hill and Fredericksburg, the first a Confederate bloodbath and the second a Union one, had made indelible impressions. He had preferred to maneuver completely around the Union flank, but Lee had pointedly refused and directed him to attack in the direction of Cemetery Ridge. Lee had made this decision upon a poor reconnaissance conducted by a member of his staff, Capt. Samuel R. Johnston, which produced, in Stephen Sears's words, "utterly false intelligence on the Union position." Johnston "left an indelible impression that the Yankees' left flank was exposed, in the air, without an anchor, susceptible to being rolled up. This immediately roused memories of Chancellorsville and another unsuspecting Yankee flank in the air. No sooner than Johnston confirmed the target's vulnerability than Lee turned to Longstreet and said, 'I think you had better move on.'"

Lee then asked Maj. Gen. Lafayette McLaws, commanding a division in Longstreet's Corps, "I wish you to get there if possible without being seen by the enemy. Can you do it?" McLaws said it was possible, but he wanted to conduct his own reconnaissance with Captain Johnston, but was forbidden by an increasingly disgruntled Longstreet who insisted that McLaws stay with his division. Longstreet then directed McLaws to place his division in a specific location along the Emmitsburg Pike. Lee intervened to give him his own orders to position it perpendicular to the Pike. McLaws once again asked to be allowed to conduct a personal reconnaissance, but "General Longstreet again forbade it." Lee did not contradict him. As they left, McLaws noted that "General Longstreet appeared as if he was irritated and annoyed." Longstreet was going to launch the major Confederate attack of the day, but that plan was based on false intelligence accepted by Lee. Longstreet had also brushed aside an opportunity to correct that mistake with another reconnaissance by McLaws out of a sense of pique at Lee's disregard of his advice.[17]

For some reason, Lee did not employ his initial reconnaissance elements of Jenkins's Cavalry Brigade, which had accompanied Ewell on the march into Pennsylvania to screen his movements and gather information. That brigade remained guarding Ewell's flank. That morning, Imboden's Brigade of cavalry, which had been guarding the army's western flank, was ordered to relieve Major General Pickett's Division of Longstreet's Corps in garrisoning Chambersburg. Robertson's and Jones's brigades had been ordered to rejoin the army as soon as it was learned that the Union army had passed into Maryland. They arrived on the field on July 3, in time only to guard the rear from a cavalry raid but too late to add weight to Stuart's attack on the Union rear that same day. One of the great mysteries of the campaign was Lee's reluctance to use the considerable cavalry assets he still had under his control to enhance his intelligence picture.[18]

Another mystery is why signal parties were not used in the reconnaissance of Longstreet's route. Their employment would have certainly shortened the time taken in reconnaissance and improved its quality. Throughout the battle the preferred method of communication for the Confederate commanders was by courier, transmitting either a written or verbal message. For an army that was occupying exterior lines, it meant that the distance covered was twice that faced by their counterparts in the Army of the Potomac. Only three signal messages survive from the Confederate side as opposed to hundreds from the Union side. Of course, "the absence of evidence is not the evidence of absence," but a message from Ewell indicates there was, indeed, an absence of flag signal communications between corps.

> Before the beginning of my advance, I had sent a staff officer to the division of the Third Corps, on my right, which proved to be General Pender's, to find out what they were to do … I then wrote to him (it being too late to communicate with the corps commander) that I was attacking with my corps, and requested that he would co-operate. To this I received no answer, nor do I believe that any advance was made. The want of co-operation on the right made it more difficult for Rodes' division to attack, though, had it been otherwise, I have every reason to believe, from the eminent success attending the assault … that enemy's lines would have been carried.[19]

Meade had his own difficult subordinate in Daniel Sickles. The III Corps commander was unhappy at the position Meade had assigned his corps along Cemetery Ridge tying into Little Round Top. From his vantage point, the position appeared to be lower ground than that to his front and presaged a replay of Chancellorsville, where Hooker had pulled his corps off dominant terrain. The enemy had quickly occupied that high ground and savaged his corps with massed artillery. He was not about to allow that to happen again and violated Meade's specific orders by advancing his corps into a salient that reached three-quarters of a mile to the Emmitsburg Pike. His corps now had a frontage that was double what it should have been defending. Unfortunately, Sickles's observation had been deceiving; his new position was not on dominant terrain but was exceptionally vulnerable. Longstreet's approach march was taking his two divisions directly against the flank of Sickles's salient.

McLaws was still wary of the route that had been designated for his approach march. Lee had sent the feckless Captain Johnston with him as a guide. As soon as the head of his column approached Herr Ridge, he rode to the top and ordered his column to stop. He had seen the Union signal station on Little Round Top and Sergeant Chemberlin waving his large white signal flag. Unable to find another nearby route, he found Longstreet and said, "Ride with me, and I will show you that we can't go on this route, according to instructions, without being seen by the enemy." If there was any man in the Confederate army other than E. Porter Alexander who was as aware of the danger posed by the signal station, it was Lafayette McLaws. Before the war he had commanded the unit that had conducted the western field trials of Major Myers's new flag signal system. Longstreet agreed with McLaws that a countermarch was the only solution. Longstreet would write in his after-action report, "Engineers, sent out by the commanding general and myself, guided us by a road which would have completely disclosed the move. Some delay ensued in seeking a more concealed route." "Some delay" was an understatement. The fear instilled by the single signal station on Little Round Top would now add another two hours to the march and allow Sickles's III Corps to establish its salient. Initially, Longstreet had simply wanted to reverse the order of march and have Major General John Bell Hood's Division, which was following McLaws's Division take the lead. By simply having his two-division column do an about face, much of that ensuing delay would have been cancelled. McLaws objected so strongly that Longstreet let the order of march stand, which added a great deal of time to the countermarch.[20]

For just such a situation of self-induced friction, the great German field marshal, Helmuth von Moltke, had coined a famous aphorism—"Order, counter-order, disorder."[21]

Longstreet's precaution to travel by a concealed route was in vain. Captain Hall observed the countermarch and sent off to Butterfield a message that said, "A Heavy column of enemy's infantry, about 10,000 strong, is moving from opposite our extreme left toward our right." Forty minutes later, he sent another message updating Butterfield on Longstreet's movements. "Those troops were passing on a by road from Dr. Hall's house to Herr's Tavern, on the Chambersburg Pike. A train of ambulances is following them."[22] What Hall had described in both messages was Hood's Division in its countermarch. From Hall's vantage, it looked as if it was marching from the Union left to the right. What the signal officer did not see was its turnabout that took it back toward the Union left.

Unwittingly, the signal station was sowing confusion in both armies in what must be a classic case of friction in war. The station's very presence had already thrown off Longstreet's plans and caused him to countermarch. That countermarch had been observed by the signal station but only that part that gave the misleading impression that the large column was heading to the Union right. By the time the column had turned to the Union left, it was marching by a concealed route. It is no wonder that Butterfield did not take the message too seriously. Nor did Meade, who would later state that he had no advance notice of an imminent threat to that flank.[23]

Meade's signal officer, Captain Norton, would later report a third message: "… at 3:30 p.m., the signal officer discovered the enemy massing upon General Sickles' left, and reported the fact to General Sickles and to the general commanding." By then, Longstreet was only minutes from launching his attack on the Union left from the point of Sickles's salient at the Peach Orchard to Little Round Top.[24]

Meade's chief engineer, Brig. Gen. Gouverner Warren, was worried about Little Round Top. From an engineer's point of view, it was evidently dominant terrain, and it was unguarded. He may also have been aware of the messages from the signal station there. He requested Meade's permission to investigate as Meade's command group was riding to Sickles's salient. Meade replied, "Warren, I hear a little peppering going on in the direction of that little hill off yonder. I wish that you would ride over and if anything serious is going on, attend to it."[25]

Riding up the hill, Warren found only Hall's signal party and was briefed on what had been observed. Warren concluded that Little Round Top was the key to the entire Union position and that Sickles's men positioned below in the salient would be taken unawares by an enemy approaching through the woods. He ordered a gun fired into the woods, which caused the enemy's line of battle to be revealed. Another account has Captain Hall arguing with him, unable to convince him that the enemy lay to the front of the Round Top. A shell burst near the party, wounding Gouveneur Warren, whereupon Hall said, "Now do you see them?"[26]

In any case, Warren sent a captain for immediate help to Sickles, who should have been holding Little Round Top as Meade had ordered. Sickles refused, and the captain rode back to find the V Corps commander, Major General Sykes, who was conducting his own reconnaissance in order to place his units in support of Sickles. Sykes promptly wrote out an order to Brig. Gen. James Barnes, commanding the corps' 1st Division, to send a brigade. The captain dashed off with it. The division commander, as usual, was nowhere to be seen on the field that day, but luckily the 26-year-old Col. Strong Vincent, commanding the lead brigade of Barnes's Division, saw the excited exchange with Sykes and the messenger and rode out to intercept the captain. It would be one of the most dramatic exchanges of war.

"Captain, what are your orders?"

The captain replied, "Where is General Barnes?"

Vincent said, "What are your orders? Give me your orders."

"General Sykes told me to direct General Barnes to send one of his brigades to occupy that hill yonder," shouted the captain.

Vincent said, "I will take the responsibility of taking my brigade there."[27]

Vincent rode ahead to reconnoiter the hill while his brigade followed quickly. They were just in time to stop Hood's Division from overrunning Little Round Top.

Had the Confederates been only minutes earlier, the entire Union position at Gettysburg would have become unhinged and the army's line of retreat threatened. The army's signal intelligence capability had delayed the attack by its very presence, forcing Longstreet into a time-consuming countermarch. But pure chance caused the observation of the countermarch to be misinterpreted, thus allowing Longstreet's attack to be delivered with little warning. Ultimately, III Corps collapsed under Longstreet's bludgeoning blows, and its survivors fled over Cemetery Ridge. By that time the mighty Confederate I Corps had exhausted itself and was unable to break over the ridge in the face of Union reinforcements.

On balance, the countermarch delay for Longstreet was the more serious of the consequences emanating from the signal station on Little Round Top. The lost two hours were irreplaceable. Had a competent reconnaissance been conducted that provided a covered route of approach, he would have struck Sickles half deployed and rolled right over his corps and then crested over Cemetery Ridge into the Union rear. Meade's and Butterfield's confusion as to the meaning of the signal station messages prevented a timely intervention by the army commander to repair that flank's building vulnerability. But Meade's tardy presence was enough to ensure that strong reserves would be fed into the battle to make it one of attrition. Patrick played an important role by throwing his provost guards across the rear of the fighting front to "[K]eep the Troops from breaking.—It was hot work & I had several lines formed, so that very few succeeded in getting entirely through." It was not until early evening that he could set up a local POW holding area. By early evening when Sickles's III Corps finally broke, Longstreet's own corps had shot its bolt and could do no more.[28]

The rapid acquisition and transmission of intelligence on the Union side was in bright contrast to the poor use of intelligence made by the Southern leaders. Lee based his major blow on this day on amateurish reconnaissance. Stuart's absence was telling. On no other field with Stuart present would Lee have resorted to such a careless reconnaissance. Inexplicably, Lee also failed to use the cavalry brigade guarding Ewell's flank, which would have provided a much faster and practiced reconnaissance. Compounding this, both he and Longstreet refused to allow McLaws to conduct his own, despite his request. Hood would indeed make his own reconnaissance that showed Little Round Top empty and the enemy trains vulnerable right behind the hill. In the face of this priceless information, Longstreet refused to use his initiative to alter Lee's orders, and the opportunity vanished.

Longstreet's frustration at having come within an ace of smashing through the Union left would have been intense. Yet he probably would have been amused to learn that the Confederate prisoners were telling their interrogators that he had been killed, with his body in Union hands. It was convincing enough to be passed up to Meade, who had it included in a dispatch he sent off at 11:00 that night. Longstreet would have been less pleased at the accurate admission of his captured men that his corps and A. P. Hill's "were both much injured … and that many general officers were killed. Gen. Barksdale, of Mississippi, is dead. His body is within our lines."[29]

The story of Longstreet's death spread quickly. The next day Brig. Gen. Herman Haupt, chief of U.S. Military Railways, reported at Westminster, Maryland, the terminus of the railroad supporting the army, that information had arrived that Longstreet had been killed. The press picked this up in a flurry of articles. On the 4th Meade sent a dispatch in which rebel prisoners claimed that Lt. Gen. A. P. Hill had been killed in the fighting of the 3rd. As of the 5th, the press was saying that "reports concerning the death and capture Generals Longstreet and A. P. Hill are still conflicting. By the 6th the BMI had been able to ascertain that both generals were still alive. The *National Republican*'s retraction on the 6th noted with some chagrin that the reports of Longstreet's death "were apparently well authenticated, and fully believed." This chain of events is a good example of how initial reporting, even though seemingly authenticated, can be wrong.[30]

Dahlgren and the Band of Angels

While the BMI labored through its interrogations, another intelligence operation was playing itself out with a bang that would be heard in Washington. On the 30th Captain Dahlgren, as he recorded in a small notebook, approached Meade with a proposal, "to take some men and operate on the rebel rear. He, then anxious about the movements of the army, did not give the matter much attention. Then applied to General P[leasanton] who ordered a sergeant and fifteen men to report…"[31]

It was apparent that Sharpe and Dahlgren, being in close proximity on the staff, had come to know each other well. Dahlgren was the son of Rear Admiral John

Dahlgren, already known as the father of naval ordnance. He was a good friend and advisor to Lincoln and on good terms with Stanton, who the year before had given the 19-year-old Ulric a captain's commission based on his leadership and initiative in the Philadelphia Home Guard and in conveying naval ordnance to reinforce the garrison at Harper's Ferry.

Dahlgren was more than worthy of the rank. He was an impressive young man, a *beau sabre* with dash, brains, and an instinct for the main chance. Tall, lithe, with fine features and blond hair and bright blue eyes, he was a magnificent horseman and the epitome of vigorous young manhood. He was assigned to Major General Sigel's Corps as an aide but so quickly proved his knowledge of artillery that Sigel requested his appointment as chief of corps artillery with a promotion to major, but as so often happens, it was lost in the limbo of army administrative routine.

Dahlgren had a nose for a fight and repeatedly volunteered to accompany the cavalry into action or on outpost duty. In early November 1862, Burnside ordered Sigel to conduct a reconnaissance to ascertain Confederate strength in Fredericksburg; Dahlgren led 160 cavalrymen in stealthy approach, forded the Rappahannock unseen, and rode into town with such audacity as to scatter much larger Confederate forces and take 35 prisoners from the 9th and 15th Virginia Cavalry Regiments.[32] At Brandy Station, he had rallied the 6th Pennsylvania Cavalry to cut its way through the surrounding Confederates. He was also what would be called today a perfect "special operator". On such a small headquarters staff, Sharpe naturally would have been well aware of Dahlgren's unique talents. Just as naturally, Dahlgren would find in Sharpe's activities the opportunity for action. That opportunity arrived in the guise of Sergeant Cline, "who had by some stratagem ridden out of Salem with Stuart's raiders on 25 June." He slipped away and rode hard to report to the army at Frederick with exciting news.[33]

Cline related to Sharpe that important dispatches from Richmond for Lee would be carried by a courier across the Potomac at a specified hour on July 2. The courier and escort would then ride north up the Confederate main supply route through Greencastle. The timing could not have been more perfect for Sharpe. The day before he had been ordered by Meade, "to send to Gettysburg, Hanover, Greencastle, Chambersburg, and Jefferson to-night and get as much information as you can of the numbers, position, and force of the enemy, with their movements." It was important enough for Sharpe to keep as a personal souvenir.[34] That Sharpe approved the attempt to intercept the courier is evidenced by the next line in Dahlgren's diary, "with these [the 10 cavalrymen] and four scouts under Sergeant Cline, we started out."[35] Sharpe was not about to part with five of his best scouts at this critical moment, especially Cline, if he had not been a party to the plan. He especially would not have parted with them had he not had great confidence in Dahlgren.

The 10 cavalrymen given to Dahlgren were from the 1st, 2nd, 5th, and 6th US Cavalry Regiments, the best men on the best horses. Early on the 1st, Dahlgren

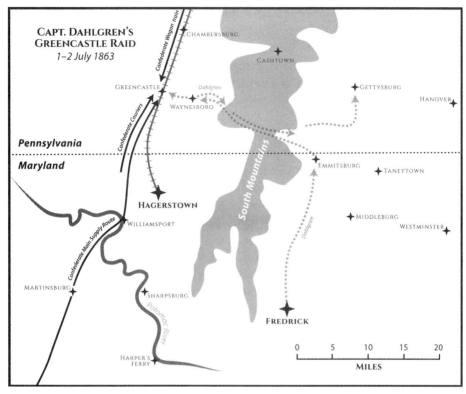

CAPT. DAHLGREN'S
GREENCASTLE RAID
1–2 July 1863

Captain Dahlgren's Greencastle Raid July 1–2, 1863. (After Jespersen)

and his group departed from army headquarters in Frederick at daybreak disguised in civilian clothing.[36]

Carefully wending their way through Confederate patrols through Monterey Pass to Waynesboro, Pennsylvania, Dahlgren was able to learn of the fighting of July 1 and the death of Reynolds. That same day they picked up a local guide, a recently discharged Union soldier and a native of Greencastle, who agreed to guide Dahlgren there. The next morning, now back in uniform, the group entered the town. Seeing blue uniforms for the first time in two weeks, the population poured into the streets in celebration. "If a band of angels had come down into town, they could not have been more unexpected or welcome," one resident wrote. Another would note that, "though a mere youth, he [Dahlgren] had the entire confidence of his men, and seemed to handle them with perfect ease and skill."[37]

Dahlgren cut short the adulation and ordered the people back into their homes and positioned his men around the Dutch Reformed Church in the town center. He climbed to the belfry to discover he was just in time. To the south he saw a cavalry company riding toward town—the couriers and escorts. He rushed down to join his men when, to his surprise, a Confederate wagon train, escorted by several infantry companies and loaded with the loot of Pennsylvania, entered the town from the north at the same time as the cavalry. Dahlgren realized that with the train guards and the cavalry he was outnumbered many times over. He told his men that there was something important in the approaching Confederate party, and then asked, "Boys, how shall we take them? Will we take them with the saber or shall we depend upon our pistols and carbines?" Every man drew his saber and shouted, "We will take them with this!"[38]

When the two columns met in front of the church Dahlgren attacked. The quiet scene was suddenly rent with shouting horsemen hacking with their sabers. Dahlgren led the charge in among the wagons as Cline rode into the cavalry pistol in hand and captured the couriers. The panicked Confederates fled without a fight, leaving 17 prisoners to the 16 Federals.[39]

Dahlgren's exultation quickly gave way to disappointment as he emptied mailbags of nothing but soldiers' mail. Then he noticed one of the couriers nervously looking at his saddle. Dahlgren found the official dispatch case hidden under the saddle. He opened it immediately and found two letters for Lee, one from President Davis himself and the other from the adjutant general of the Confederate army, General Samuel Cooper. He broke the seals and read them on the spot. In this he was doing exactly what any good intelligence officer should do, for the knowledge of their import is necessary to guide the next step. So stunning was the information in the letters that he said, "Boys, here is an important dispatch from Jeff Davis to Gen. Lee. I must leave you and endeavor to place it in Gen. Meade's hands as quickly as possible. Serg't Cline, take charge of these men; make your way to Emmitsburg and deliver all the prisoners to the nearest Union force. If any of these fellow attempt to escape, shoot them."[40]

He alone would ride the 30 miles around the Confederates to bring the prize to Meade. He rode relentlessly through the afternoon and evening and into the night, asking civilians along the way where the army headquarters had moved to until he arrived at Gettysburg about midnight and turned the dispatches over to Butterfield.

The *New York Times* correspondent attached to the army reported the incident differently, giving the entire credit to Cline. "A party of Col. Sharpe's gallant scouts, only nine in number, headed by Sergt. M. W. Kline [sic], dashed into Hagerstown this morning, in the very rear of the enemy, and captured ten prisoners and large rebel mail, which was on its way from the South to Lee's army." If Cline was the source of the story, he was careful not to mention the capture of the dispatches to Lee among the mail.[41]

Meade and the Council of War

While Dahlgren was still in the saddle several hours from headquarters, another meeting was taking place. It was in the lull after the day's horrific fighting, when the body's adrenalin is drained. Meade was in his headquarters, a single farmhouse room in Leister House, as his exhausted staff arrived one by one. Sharpe left a vivid account:

> I think the hardest day I ever experienced during my entire service in the civil war was the second day at Gettysburg. We were kept from daylight until darkness, and were all over the extensive battlefield, taking General Meade's directions to the various army corps. But of the stirring and awful sights that I beheld that day none comes to me more vividly than an unchronicled little scene that occurred when the fighting was over for the day.
>
> In the evening, just after dark, we of the staff came straggling in one after another to General Meade's headquarters, a plain little farmhouse. When I entered the room the general was seated at a table, with his chin resting in his hand, and evidently deep in thought. He returned my salute, but said nothing.
>
> In a few minutes another of the staff came in, then another and so on until we were all present. We were all covered with dust, and my face felt as though it had a thick incrustation of mud on it.
>
> Presently the servant came in and spread upon the table a few crackers or hardtack, some pieces of bacon, and if I recollect, a little fruit—perhaps they were cherries, although where he could have got them I do not know.
>
> General Meade looked smilingly although it was rather a dry smile, at our humble repast. Then, doubtless realizing how worn out we all were, he said: "This is one of the occasions when I think a man is justified in taking a drink of whiskey."
>
> General Meade was himself a very abstemious man, rarely drinking any spirituous liquor, and the same was true of every member of the staff.
>
> "I will see if there is any whisky here," he added. Again he spoke to the servant, who, a moment or two later, brought in a bottle of whiskey and set it upon the table.
>
> General Meade glanced casually at the bottle.
>
> "General [sic—Colonel at the time] Sharpe," he said, won't you take a glass of whisky? I think it will do you good."
>
> I took up the bottle and a tumbler, although I never knew how that tumbler got upon the table at that time. Without pouring out any whisky, I said to General Meade, "General, I think you ought to take a drink. You need it more than any of us."
>
> General Meade, without taking the bottle, looked at it, and, in the dim light of the two candles that were on the table, was able to see exactly how much whisky it contained. There was not enough for one moderate drink.
>
> The general again glanced casually at the bottle. "NO," he said, "I don't think I care for any whisky. I would like a cup of coffee."
>
> Then he urged one of the staff to take a drink, but he, also having discovered by this time that there was only one drink in the bottle, shook his head and passed the bottle along. In similar fashion the whiskey was refused by each member of the staff, and in the middle of this table the bottle stood, with its scanty contents, untouched while we ate our hardtack and bacon.
>
> To me that bottle has always told a perfect story of the devotion and unselfishness of the commanding officer and the members of his staff. I don't remember any incident of the war that more impressed me with the real unselfishness which desperate experiences develop in a true military man than this renunciation of the drink by General Meade and his staff under conditions that would have warranted a teetotaler in foregoing his pledge.[42]

Eventually most of the staff except Sharpe left the commander alone. On the table the plate of hardtack for Meade and the whiskey remained, all still untouched. The hardtack was Meade's dinner, his punishment of sorts for leaving his supply trains at Winchester.[43] Major Generals Hancock and Slocum came in and found a seat on a cot. Slocum promptly fell sound asleep. Meade had called for a meeting of all his corps commanders at nine that evening, and these two were the first to arrive. Before the meeting, though, he wanted to talk to Sharpe again. The ability of his army to continue fighting after the terrible ordeal it had gone through that day was uppermost in his mind. Tugging at this mind was the option of pulling out to the prepared positions at Pipe Creek. He had arrived on the field deeply unhappy with this battlefield. He had even had Butterfield prepare a contingency plan for withdrawal. Major General Doubleday, who met him when he arrived on the field at one in the morning of this very day would write later that "It was an open secret that Meade at that time disapproved of the battle-ground Hancock had selected." Meade's circular of the day before had made that clear.[44]

Nevertheless, by the time the fighting had ended on July 2, Meade felt himself committed to fighting at Gettysburg. Too much was at stake, but his confidence in the outcome was anything but sure. He wired Halleck at eight in the evening, "I shall remain in my present position to-morrow, but am not prepared to say, until better advised of the condition of the army, whether my operations will be of an offensive or defensive nature."[45]

The condition of the army hinged on that of the enemy. He turned to Sharpe and said, "I must have more detailed information of the strength of the enemy. Can you get reliable information of the number of troops that were engaged today and whether he has any fresh troops in reserve? Can you also get information of one of our own corps which is expected?" Sharpe excused himself to confer with Babcock, telling Meade he would have the information within an hour or two.[46]

Two hours later Sharpe was back and produced a report prepared by Babcock on the enemy's order-of-battle that he had signed for Sharpe. It was astounding, the results of interrogations of hundreds of prisoners by Sharpe's staff. Seldom in all of military history has a commander received such a golden report. It read:

> Prisoners have been taken today, and last evening, from every brigade in Lee's Army excepting the four brigades of Pickett's Division. Every division has been represented except Picketts [sic] from which we have not had a prisoner. They are from nearly one hundred different regiments.[47]

Babcock had signed for Sharpe.[48] Sharpe summarized it by saying, "All of the Confederate troops have been in action except Pickett's division and a small body of cavalry. Pickett's division has arrived." Sharpe explained the painstaking efforts Babcock had made to compare the information taken from prisoners against his order-of-battle charts. He also added, "Our own corps has come up and is now in bivouac and will be ready to go into action fresh tomorrow morning."[49]

With that, Hancock rose from the cot and announced forcefully, "General, we have got them nicked!" He was loud enough to rouse Slocum from his sleep.[50]

Hancock had seized the essence of the situation. Sharpe had answered that question that hovers over the mind of every senior commander in battle—what does the enemy have left to throw onto the scales of battle? Such a question unanswered breeds doubt, and with doubt comes lack of resolve. A commander who is ever looking over his shoulder for a way out is half-defeated.

Sharpe had answered that question with a precision and surety that was hard to match. So impressed was Meade that he exclaimed, "By God, I'll stay here." Babcock proudly recorded these words in a summary of his military service. It had been a virtuoso performance under conditions of the highest stress for Babcock, who was known to have been wounded in the battle but on which day was not certain. As a civilian no records were kept of his injury.[51]

Meade realized that his own reserves, in the shape of the uncommitted VI Corps and other elements, far exceeded the strength of Pickett's Division, which was the weakest in Lee's army. It was actually weaker than Babcock realized. The latest update of his order-of-battle on June 22 showed Pickett's Division with four brigades. It had actually had five brigades, but two had been transferred to Lieutenant General D. H. Hill's command in North Carolina before the Gettysburg Campaign began. But without prisoners or deserters from this division, Babcock would not have known that Pickett had only three brigades of fewer than 5,000 men on the field. In contrast, VI Corps, which Meade had in reserve, numbered almost 16,000 men present for duty in the returns of June 30. One V Corps Division and two brigades of XII Corps had not been heavily engaged as well. Meade could look forward to the next day's fighting with at least four times as many fresh men in reserve as Lee.[52]

A great weight was lifted from Meade. He could fight tomorrow's battle with confidence, even though there was only one day's worth of supplies, and some corps had none at all. Meade used the conference with his corps commanders that followed to test the fighting spirit of his senior officers. That fighting spirit, already strong from the conduct of their men that day could only have hardened as Meade shared Sharpe's information. Slocum typified the response of these men when he said, "Stay and fight it out."[53] The army would indeed fight it out to victory the next day. Six of the officers present at the meeting would later state that "Meade never uttered any word about wanting to retreat or even gave the appearance of being unsure of what to do."[54]

But the night was not finished. About midnight Dahlgren rode his exhausted horse into the headquarters and delivered his captured dispatches to Butterfield. Upon examination, Meade's new confidence in the outcome of the next day's struggle became adamantine. Where Sharpe's intelligence had filled in the tactical situation, these dispatches supplied the operational and strategic-level intelligence that presented an unprecedented look at the enemy's capabilities and vulnerabilities.

The letter from General Cooper, dated June 29, gave Meade a priceless look at the operational level of the campaign. Cooper denied Lee's request for reinforcement with the stray brigades left in Virginia because of an imminent threat to Richmond by Maj. Gen. Benjamin Butler's army on the Peninsula. "Every effort is being made here to be prepared for the enemy at all points, but we must look chiefly to the protection of the capital." He continued, "I would suggest for your consideration whether, in this state of things, you might not be able to spare a portion of your force to protect your line of communication against attempted raids by the enemy." It was a cogent and most unintentionally ironic comment in light of the loss of the dispatches to lack of security on Lee's main supply route. With this information, Meade now knew that Lee would be receiving no reinforcements. There was nothing in the pipeline. Lee would have to fight with just what Sharpe had told him was on the field.[55]

The letter from Davis, dated June 28, filled in the strategic picture. Davis reviewed the situation with the armies in the west, the threat to Richmond, and the evident need to keep all the remaining brigades in the region.

> Do not understand me as balancing accounts in the matter of brigades; I only repeat that I have not many to send you, and enough to form an army to threaten, if not capture, Washington as soon as it is uncovered by Hooker's army. My purpose was to show you that the force here and in North Carolina is very small, and I may add that the brigades are claimed as property of their command. Our information as to the enemy may be more full and reliable hereafter. It is now materially greater than when you were here.[56]

Meade's eyes must have become saucers as he read further as Davis listed all of the remaining brigades in the eastern theater and their missions, to justify their retention. After reading these letters, Meade turned to Dahlgren and asked what he could do for him in the way of reward. The captain asked to be given a hundred men and be sent out again to raise hell among the rebels.[57]

The Three Golden Gifts

Arrayed alongside Babcock's order-of-battle report, these two dispatches gave Meade an unprecedented look at his enemy at the tactical, operational, and strategic levels. Meade now knew that Lee not only had a small, uncommitted reserve but also that there were no theater reserves coming to him. This would allow him to fight the next day with complete confidence and without reservation in his ability to meet any challenge. It also gave him the confidence to think that he could even ruin Lee the next day should the opportunity arise. Meade had achieved the priceless moral ascendancy in his contest with Lee. He had come a long way from distrusting the battlefield and preparing contingency plans for withdrawal. It would be a crucial addition to his moral armor—the ability to commit himself and his army wholeheartedly. The evidence suggests strongly that he would have stayed and fought it out in any case, but then it would have been a decision based on the shifting ground of desperation.

The dispatch from Davis gave him another sort of peace of mind. Few things can undermine the confidence of a commander in the field than an anxious and interfering political authority. Lee's invasion of the North and the rumors of Beauregard's army threatening Washington from Culpeper had succeeded in driving Meade's political superiors to a state of near hysteria. On July 3 the *New York Herald* reported that a member of Longstreet's staff had been captured on his way to Culpeper, "to ascertain what had become of Beauregard's army."[58]

The last thing Meade needed to worry about was fighting both front *and* rear. Davis's dispatch was telegraphed to Halleck probably from Winchester. Their effect can be judged by Stanton's awestruck comments as he retransmitted Cooper's and Davis's letters to all senior Union commanders in the eastern theater: "We have sure information … Davis' dispatch is the best view we have ever had of the rebels condition, and it is desperate. They feel the pressure at all points, and have nothing to spare in any quarter, so that Lee must fight his way through alone, if he can." One of the first to see the telegrams was Maj. Gen. Samuel P. Heintzelman, who commanded the forces in the defenses of Washington. He noted in his diary the very next day, July 4, "The news from General Meade is good … We captured very important dispatches from Jefferson Davis to Lee and from General Cooper. The letters go into minute details of the situation. With the knowledge we have of our situation and this information of theirs, our prospects are decidedly flattering."[59]

A Burden of Grief

A burden of grief had fallen on Sharpe that day. His beloved 120th New York had been in the forefront of the fighting in Sickles's III Corps and had paid the price of its courage in holding off attack after attack. Of the 383 men that had deployed with the corps that afternoon, 203 had been killed, wounded, or taken prisoner—a loss rate of 53 percent. At the crisis of the fighting, as the rest of III Corps gave way, the acting corps commander, Brig. Gen. Andrew A. Humphreys, stayed with his men:

> [He] placed himself in the rear of our ranks, standing alone on a line which had been stripped for the salvation of others, he proclaimed in the most affirmative manner that this was then the vital point; and while he was powerless to afford relief except by his presence and example; while death stared him in the face, and it did not seem possible to those who watched him slowly riding in the rear of our formation, that he should escape, he chose to take his part with "the men that held the line."

Lieutenant Colonel Westbrook had fallen with two severe wounds, and would carry the bullet from the second for more than 10 years. At the Peach Orchard, Major Tappen was in command. He fought the regiment back to Cemetery Ridge in a stubborn and skillful fighting retreat as the corps rearguard, to the cheers of the "scattered remains of other regiments."[60]

The regiment had been Sharpe's child, and even though detailed to the army staff, he had stayed in close touch with the men, helping them with their problems, advancing money in need, and making sure families were supported.

Twenty-six years later, Sharpe would describe that sacrifice in more graphic terms. "The eye could not be turned in any direction along our line without seeing men fall at every moment. All the details to those colors … were successively shot down, yet none shrank from the honor of carrying them." But that would be long in the future. This evening he focused on the duty before him—the report he must deliver to Meade.[61]

July 3

While Lincoln and Stanton rejoiced in this coup, Meade was planning to take full advantage of it the next day. As the council had broken up about midnight, he took Brig. Gen. John Gibbon, commanding a II Corps division on Cemetery Ridge, by the arm and said, "If Lee attacks to-morrow, it will be upon your front." Taken aback, Gibbon asked why. "Because he has made attacks on both our flanks and failed, and if he concludes to try it again it will be on our center."[62] But Meade's thoughts were already moving on to the counterblow. The next day, before Lee attacked, he spoke with Hancock of "the probability of an attack by the enemy on the center of the Union line, and decided, in the event of such an attack being made and repulsed, to advance the V and VI Corps against the enemy's flank."[63]

The man who had not wanted to fight at Gettysburg had been so bolstered by his precise knowledge of his opponent's capabilities that he was now planning on taking the offensive. As the Confederates retreated on the 4th he attempted to put the army in readiness to counterattack but found his corps and divisions so mixed up due to exigencies of the battle that he concluded the moment had passed before he could properly organize such a major effort.[64] History can only speculate what a powerful Union attack into Lee's disorganized, depleted, and demoralized center would have achieved.[65]

Early on the morning of the 3rd, Butterfield sent Babcock a hurried note: "Are you satisfied that there are only two Divisions of Ewell in front of Slocum and how strong do you think they are—If the General was pretty sure of this he would make an attack there. Write me soon." Babcock and Sharpe replied in a report written on the back of Butterfield's note at 8:00 a.m. Babcock listed the number of prisoners taken from all of Ewell's three divisions. As good as Babcock's information was, it did contain one error and that was based on sheer chance. According to Edwin Fishel:

> Babcock's reply named twelve brigades in Ewell's Corps, four to a division. But Rodes's Division, like only one other in Lee's army, had five brigades; the fifth was missing from the bureau's records. This was Junius Daniel's North Carolina brigade, 2,200 strong, one of the three brigades Lee had added shortly before marching north. That Babcock had received no deserters from Daniel's ranks in those weeks of tightened picketing is not surprising, but the brigade also suffered no losses from captures in the two days' fighting; none of its members turned up on the lists of prisoners the provost marshal officers were turning over to Babcock.[66]

Babcock also listed the estimated strength of each of Ewell's three divisions computed from prisoner accounts of the strengths of their own regiments and brigades:

However, Babcock and Sharpe thought these figures were far too high based upon their understanding of the enemy's order-of-battle balanced against the estimated number of casualties. In other words, they employed analysis to reach a much more accurate conclusion. They appended a note to the report "expressing the opinion that the figures they had been given were exaggerated. Those figures probably represented pre-battle strengths. Overall, those figures were within fewer than 100 men of Ewell's overall corps strength on July 1, an order-of-battle bullseye.[67] A look at the actual numbers at the beginning of the battle showed their skepticism as to the current strength of Ewell's Corps to be justified.

Table 6.1. BMI Estimates of Ewell's Corps Based on Prisoner Estimates

Division	Strength
Early	7,000
Johnson	7,000
Rodes	7,200
Total:	21,200

Table 6.2. Pre-Battle Strength and Casualties of Ewell's Corps Based on Confederate Returns[68]

Division	Strength	Casualties
Early	5,458	1,188
Johnson	6,308	1,873
Rodes	7,499	2,853
Artillery Res	644	22
HQ Escort	125	0
Total:	20,034	5,936

Sharpe added an appraisal to the report on the damage done to the other two Confederate Corps on July 2: "A further examination shows that Ewell's whole corps was on our right yesterday—is now attacking. All prisoners now agree that their whole army is here, that A. P. Hill & Longstreet's forces were badly hurt yesterday, & that several general officers are injured."[69]

That morning, Capt. E. C. Pierce and Lieut. George J. Clarke, signal officers attached to VI Corps, had taken over the signal station in the rocks of Little Round Top occupied by Captain Hall the day before. The Confederate sharpshooters in Devil's Den made the normal use of the station lethal. Seven men near the station would be killed or wounded that day. They were joined by Lieutenants J. C. Wiggins and N. H. Camp from I Corps, and together the four officers used their couriers to relay the information gathered from the station. About two in the afternoon, just as the great Confederate artillery bombardment of Cemetery Ridge was concluding, Warren returned to the hill and ordered the signal officers to closely observe their front and report directly to Meade. Shortly thereafter, they observed Longstreet's regiments appear in preparation for the charge that would bear Pickett's name. Their couriers sped away to Meade.

At the same time, the commanding general had reluctantly abandoned his headquarters at Leister House. The Confederate artillery, which was largely passing over the II Corps defenders of Cemetery Ridge, was falling over the ridge to land among the reserve artillery and trains, and directly around Leister House. At his staff's urging, Meade very reluctantly transferred his headquarters to Slocum's XII headquarters at Power Hill which had a signal station.

However, the friction of war intervened again. At Power Hill Meade immediately sought out the signal officer to get back in contact with his Leister House headquarters signal officer, Capt. David Castle. The XII Corps signal officer reported he could not communicate with Leister House. Meade assumed Castle had abandoned his position and immediately returned there. There he found Castle, who was still at his post; unfortunately, Castle's staff with their signal equipment had ridden off with Meade's entourage. The signal officer attempted to use a makeshift bed sheet as a substitute. Meade returned despite the danger because he realized that with modern signal intelligence and communications, he could effectively control the battle from that spot. As soon as the Confederate artillery ceased fire in preparation for the advance of the infantry attack, the Leister House signal station was back in operation.[70]

Although Meade did not realize it amid the shot and shell falling around Leister House, he was the first commander in history to tie himself to a modern signal intelligence and communication system in order to more closely control a battle, a system that did not rely on the speed of a man on foot or horseback to relay information and one that, in fact, provided near real-time information.

At the crisis of the battle Meade rode forward to Cemetery Ridge. As he came up the reverse slope, he was stunned to see a column of Confederates double-timing toward him. His first thought was to order up reserves until he noticed they were unarmed and guarded by men in blue. He arrived at the top to see the II Corps men waving their fists at the retreating survivors of the attack as they yelled, "Fredericksburg, Fredericksburg!"—the field where they had been slaughtered in as hopeless a charge. Meade took in the entire scene. At this moment, victory offered even greater laurels. Sharpe had told him the night before of how slim were Lee's reserves. Now he saw its ruin. He had 20,000 fresh men. The unblooded, tough VI Corps waited. Twenty-five years in the future, at the reunion of the blue and gray on that same field, Longstreet would gaze upon it and remark:

> That was a fatal error. After the failure of Pickett's charge—and there were some of us who expected it to fail—there were men who stood on Seminary Ridge who expected to see a general advance by Union forces. We were for a time in great trepidation. Our lines were very thin; they were in no condition to withstand an attack if it were made with any vigor. I am convinced that had we been then vigorously attacked there would have been an end to the war.[71]

How generals command is one thing. How the men in the ranks fight is another. Sharpe's old friends in the men of the 20th New York State Militia were in the direct path of Pickett's Division as it made its immortal charge across the mile of open ground in front of Cemetery Ridge. The New Yorkers flung them back from their toehold on the fence line, cheering as they advanced, and fired. It had been three hard days for the Ulster Guard. Of the 287 men Colonel Gates had taken into battle on July 1 he would lose 35 killed, 111 wounded, and 24 prisoners for a total of 170 or 59 percent. Added to those of the 120th New York, Sharpe would mourn many friends.[72]

Four days after the battle Sharpe penned a painful letter attaching to a report for the local newspaper of the losses of the two Kingston regiments.

> MY DEAR ROMEYN—I send you the enclosed memoranda by our surgeon of the losses in the 120th, in the late battles. It is not complete, except as to officers, but is correct as far as it goes. I shall try and send you more full accounts by tomorrow.
>
> I send you by same mail a letter from Col. Gates, with the losses of the 20th.
>
> Our Regiments have fought together upon a field of great glory, but the counties of Ulster and Greene have sadly contributed to its accomplishment.
>
> When you look over the list you will see that my heart is too full to write more.[73]

Last Act

After the collapse of Pickett's Charge on the 3rd, Meade moved quickly to occupy Gettysburg as the Confederates withdrew. Sharpe had unleashed his scouts, who reported that night that the enemy was already retreating by the Greencastle road toward Hagerstown.[74]

The Army of the Potomac greeted Independence Day while trying to shelter from a great downpour that descended upon the battlefield and the entire region. Through the rain they could see Lee's wounded army withdrawing back the way it came. Meade, already forewarned of the withdrawal, had prepared for the pursuit. This was the cavalry's moment, and Meade sent them in pursuit at first light. With them went Dahlgren, leading the hundred men Meade had given him. He was to play a daring role in the pursuit of Lee's army through the mountains over the next few days where he suffered the wound that resulted in the loss of his leg. "Among the first to sit by his bedside, with kindly words of heart-felt sympathy is Mr. Lincoln." As a reward for his intrepidity, he was jumped three grades to full colonel. Stanton personally came to present him with his promotion. When he found him so ill that he could not understand, Stanton closed off the street to wheeled traffic so as not to disturb his recovery and posted a military guard to turn away all visitors except medical personnel.[75]

And with the cavalry went Sharpe's scouts to follow Lee's every move. Their reports flowed back in almost real time, and Sharpe was at Meade's elbow with them, figuratively waving opportunity under his nose. But Meade was spent.

Since assuming command on June 28, Meade had slept hardly at all and then gone through the enormous stress of the battle. He was in desperate need of rest and recovery. His pursuit was not conducted with all the vigor of a fresh man. In justice, his victory had been at such a cost as to lay a heavier burden on him. His best and most aggressive corps commanders were dead or wounded—Reynolds, Sickles, Hancock. His best corps were broken or badly cut up—I, II, III. And XI Corps had been broken beyond redemption. Reinforcement units and commanders were not up to the standards of the men they replaced. He would be justified in feeling that it was a blunt sword now in his hands. And if the sword was blunt, the swordsman himself was tired and slow, and that meant caution loomed more and more important in his mind.

Nature had conspired at this time to present this tired, cautious man with a priceless opportunity. The deluge of July 4–5 had swelled the Potomac River to make it impassable at just the time Lee needed to get his army across it at Williamsport. The rearguard of his army had closed on Hagerstown on the morning of July 7, and he immediately began to inspect with an engineer's careful eye the approaches to the river on the Williamsport-Hagerstown Pike for the defenses he knew he would need with a swollen river at his back.[76]

By the next morning, Sharpe had received information from his scouts on the enemy's preparations for crossing. Scout Greenwood reported that at Williamsport the river had risen 9 feet, and the current was running rapidly. The enemy was reduced to crossing with only two boats. At Shepardstown the enemy was trying to man a ferry and had set up a new rope the night before. Sharpe noted, "Our scouts will cut it at all hazards to night unless a force is sent to destroy it."[77]

The next day he presented two more reports that detailed the enemy's dire problem at Williamsport. The Confederates were desperately trying to cross their wounded on two flat-bottomed boats—"and making poor progress. Mules and horses saddled are occasionally coming down the river drowned." "The current has increased so since yesterday that crossings are made with difficulty, & the flat boat is unable to make the opposite point so as to connect with the road on the other side & the boat had to be towed up stream after crossing on both sides." The scouts accurately identified the main body of the enemy between Boonesboro and Hagerstown. Sharpe also threw in that the scouts, for want of the requested force, cut the new ferry rope at Sherpardstown.[78]

On the 10th Sharpe reported that the river's level had fallen a foot but "must fall three feet more until it is fordable." He also noted that no pontoons had arrived at the crossing. The enemy was still passing its wounded to Virginia over the slow flatboats, and tellingly, bringing ammunition over on the return trips. It was a hint that Lee might need to fight things out on the Maryland shore. The clock was ticking for Meade, who was more worried by any surprise Lee might have for him than on the opportunities Sharpe was reporting.[79]

It was only the next day, the 11th, that Lee's engineers began marking out the defenses extending from Downsville to 1 ½ miles south of Hagerstown around the bridgehead at Williamsport. The Confederates threw themselves at the task with great energy. Edward Coddington noted tartly, "By the morning of 12 July the Confederates had almost finished preparing their fortifications, and at this exact time Meade finally brought up his forces to confront them." Within the next two days Lee had brought all of his army within the fortifications, as Meade hesitated.[80]

The night of the 12th, Meade held another council of war at which the loss of his fighting corps commanders was felt. The majority of corps commanders were adamantly against assaulting such strong positions. Meade went with the majority, an act from which his reputation never recovered and which threw Lincoln into despair. Lee's opinion the next morning when he saw that the Union troops were digging entrenchments was brutal. "That is too long for me; I can not wait for that." Then, he added, "They have but little courage." Within hours Lee's engineers, in a superb achievement, had repaired the pontoon bridge, and the river had fallen to a fordable level. Lee ordered an immediate retreat. By the next morning almost everyone but the rear guard was over the river. The cavalry fell on this force as it was waiting to cross the river and took about 500 prisoners. How Sharpe felt at this meager trophy, when his intelligence reporting had presented Meade with the entire Army of Northern Virginia, he kept to himself.[81]

Rewards and the Satisfaction of Duty Done

Sergeant Cline was rewarded for his role in seizing the dispatches with the honor of conveying them to Washington, where he was "showered with praise (and gold) by Secretary of War Stanton."[82] The men of the BMI could not refrain from recognizing their contribution:

> All their lives Sharpe and Babcock believed it was their reports that brought the decision to remain at Gettysburg. Former intelligence officers would not have been as much given to telling "war stories" as other veterans, and neither man is known to have told relatives and friends a great deal about his intelligence service ... but neither man held back this one story. They both seem to have regarded the night of July 2, 1863, as the high point of the secret war they fought.[83]

Reflections

It would be hard to disagree. In the fewer than 120 days of its existence the BMI had become, from a standing start, a fully functioning all-source intelligence operation, a professional and personal triumph for all involved. Unfortunately, it would be an accomplishment that would not be replicated again by the U.S. Army at field army level until 1918 in World War I.[84] Sharpe and his staff played a decisive role in two major campaigns by providing the commanders of the Army of the Potomac with consistently accurate all-source intelligence on the strength, movements, intentions, and vulnerabilities of the enemy. That Sharpe was able to find so many talented people, coordinate their efforts so efficiently and harmoniously, and create a fully functioning all-source intelligence operation in so short a time where nothing comparable had existed anywhere before, in the United States or worldwide, makes him a major, albeit unsung, hero of the art of intelligence, even had he resigned after the battle.

To Hooker goes the credit for having a keen nose for intelligence and the sense to recognize the powerful synergy of a gathering together of all sources of information to create all-source intelligence. To Hooker also goes the credit for the creativity to formalize that function as a primary staff function. It is important to realize how truly innovative this step was, because heretofore generals had been their own intelligence officers. George Washington was the last commanding general in U.S. history to be able personally to fulfill such a task well.

Hooker's great achievement was to realize the army's intelligence function would have to be raised to a state of professionalism comparable to the improvements in logistics, ordnance, and communication—all hallmarks of the industrialization of war. In doing so, Hooker was responsible for an American innovation unequalled elsewhere in the world of intelligence gathering. He was truly a transformational figure. Such individuals are extremely rare who are able to step boldly from an exhausted paradigm into another, racing along the crest of change. History is littered with the ruins left by those who could not.

Hooker could not have stressed the importance of the BMI more than when he ordered that Sharpe report directly to him. He established the principle that the commander is an active participant in the intelligence effort. That Hooker failed to fully exploit the advantages given him by the BMI at Chancellorsville did not invalidate his creation. And it reflected nothing on the achievement of Sharpe and his men. Hooker's nerve failed him at the crisis of his life, and no amount of intelligence could steady a man already beaten in his own mind. Nevertheless, in the balance of Hooker's service to the Republic, a reasonable observer would conclude that the creation of the BMI would more than balance the loss at Chancellorsville.[85]

Meade, however, was made of plainer but sterner stuff than Hooker. He assumed command on June 28 of an army that had been repeatedly beaten by a veritable Mars—Lee—whose reputation alone had undone his predecessor. He took that army into the greatest battle of the Civil War three days later, fought that terrible three-day battle, and broke the heretofore irresistible tide of Southern valor. In all this time he hardly slept and ate little. It would have been natural for his confidence to have shown the strain. And it is true he did not want to fight at Gettysburg and would have preferred to fall back to Pipe Creek even as the battle of Gettysburg bled into its second day.

But here Meade surpassed Hooker. In one day Meade had to bring himself up to date on the situation, learn the capabilities of the BMI, and then determine to trust it. To Meade's credit he immediately grasped the value of his intelligence staff and assumed that direct hand in its mission guidance that marks a successful commander. On the terrible field of Gettysburg Meade would prove himself a great commander. He was the first commander in history consciously to tie himself to modern signals and all-source intelligence in order to control and fight the battle. Of equal importance, he steeled his nerve because Sharpe and his staff came through for him—they cast a bright and revealing light across the battlefield, and on that would hang the fate of the Republic.

CHAPTER SEVEN

"The Period of Inaction"

July–December 1863

Meade smarted from his failure to crush Lee when the Virginian was trapped at Williamsport with his back to the rain-swollen Potomac. Now he pushed his own army across the receding river quickly toward the gaps in the Blue Ridge, but his army was worn out. Sharpe observed to his Uncle Jansen in a letter of July 18, "We must stop soon, as horses & mules are dropping dead every day—& the men are nearly exhausted."[1]

Sharpe had made the same observation Homer did 2,600 years before—"Past his strength no man can go." Courage in battle is a factor of energy, and energy is an accumulated resource. The exertions of the forced march to Gettysburg, the exertions and trauma of battle, and the pursuit had seriously drained the army of that moral and bodily energy upon which success in battle is based. If the men in the ranks were exhausted, so too were their officers, line and staff. Meade himself had almost no sleep in the three days after he assumed command and little more in the three days of dreadful battle. That applied to most staff officers and Sharpe himself. Field Marshal Bernard Montgomery may have said as a subaltern in 1915, "If bread is the staff of life, what is the life of the staff? One big loaf." On the contrary, the staff on active campaign works early and late into the night after the soldier, his duties at bay, slumbers. Sharpe had had the advantage of being an energetic and active man, but even that by this point had its limits after a month of continuous effort.[2]

Taking Care of Friends

That limit had just been reached by an intimate friend of Sharpe's. Just before the headquarters crossed the Potomac, Sharpe and Patrick were presented with a family problem of sorts. Colonel Gates of the 20th NYSM passed his resignation to Patrick on July 17 as he boarded a train with 727 Confederate prisoners destined for Washington and with most of the survivors of his regiment as guard. Apparently, his regiment's heavy losses had been too much for him. On his return to the army four days later, he found that his resignation had been refused. That night he had dinner with both Patrick and Sharpe. He pressed his "personal application" for his resignation. As friends, Patrick and Sharpe must have struggled with a decision. It is significant that Sharpe played such a role in this matter when it was Patrick's decision. Gates evidently relied on Sharpe as a friend and fellow veteran of the old 20th NYSM for advice. Sharpe recommended a rest to clear his mind of too many ghosts. A week later Sharpe wrote Gates a letter, which Gates described in his diary as stating that "he [Sharpe] & Gen. Patrick had concluded that my resignation had better not be pressed at present but that I had better go home on the conscript detail." Patrick arranged for this detail and that of two officers and six enlisted men to train conscripts on Riker's Island in New York Harbor.[3]

It would be light duty for Gates, who took frequent leave to visit his family in Kingston. He was ordered back to his regiment and arrived on December 18 to "cheers and pleased faces." The next day he called on Patrick and Sharpe, who must have been pleased to see that he was his old self again. On Christmas Day Sharpe and the other officers of the 120th New York arrived at Gate's tent with the regimental band to serenade an old friend. They stayed to party until one in the morning and "had quite a jolly time."[4]

This story reveals Sharpe as a concerned brother officer and friend. He realized how much the trauma of Gettysburg had affected Gates. He also realized that allowing Gates's resignation to be approved would both lose a good officer and forever destroy the man's self-esteem. By his action he saved Gates, and on Christmas Day welcomed him back in a handsome style that told Gates all was well; he was back among friends.[5]

No sooner had the broken Gates been sent home to recover than another personal tragedy hit the provost marshal's official family. Fred Manning's father had recently visited his son at the army's camp at Germantown and then had gone on to visit another son, who had lost a leg at Chancellorsville, at the Mount Pleasant Hospital in Washington. Upon leaving, the elder Manning died suddenly of a stroke. Lieutenant Manning asked for 15 days' leave. Sharpe approved it immediately and authorized Manning's use of the army telegram service to expedite his leave. Patrick was equally supportive, noting that Manning's father had lived near Patrick's own family in New York.[6]

This is another example of the band of brothers attitude that Sharpe consistently demonstrated toward subordinates, whether in the 120th New York or the BMI. Those that worked for him knew he would be sensitive to their concerns, loyal to them as comrades, and would do his utmost to be fair. It would be reciprocated with devotion and an intelligent and aggressive initiative to excel that broke down the many barriers that crop up in armies at war. The reciprocal bonds of affection that Sharpe induced in his subordinates produced a determination never to let "the old man" down.

Mum on the Draft

The opposition to the draft that summer, particularly the riots that engulfed New York City, July 11–16, had stirred up strong feelings in the army. Sharpe's Uncle Jansen apparently had written him that his name had been associated with a strong opinion on the draft and that he would be bringing his regiment home to enforce the draft. Aghast, Sharpe had replied on July 28 that he had not written a word to anyone on the subject of the draft or his regiment's use to enforce it. He commented that reticence was due to larger considerations. "I have uniformly tried to be very prudent in what I said in my letters—I know of no one more so—& I have to be—for my position is a very confidential one—& I am informed of all the movements of both armies." Sharpe was a natural-born politician, but he also possessed a good lawyer's ability to keep his client's affairs entirely opaque.

Trying to unravel the story, he said that a local Kingston dignitary, Dr. Dawes, had suggested to him that if he brought his regiment home to recruit, it "could be filled up by volunteers." Dawes had stated that "he and other gentlemen of standing were authorized to guarantee it." Sharpe had given the matter much thought and concluded that "it could be done—because the friends of each Company—raised as my Companies were, in distinct localities, would have done it… I should like to see the draft averted from our County." Volunteers would fill the counties' draft quota.

He then formally requested of Meade that his regiment be sent home for recruitment. Meade replied that "not a man could be spared from this Army." Sharpe was disappointed because he believed that an important opportunity had been lost. The best he could do now was to repair his reputation on the matter and perhaps effect an end run around Meade. "I shall write to [Congressman] Steele immediately on the subject of your letter—to get him to set me straight in certain quarters. Perhaps a strong paper from leading citizens of our district—backed by Steele might get our 2 regts sent home to recruit & save the dft in the district—It can only be done from Wash."[7]

But the pressure on Meade to fill up his depleted regiments was too great. The historian of the 120th wrote, "The ranks of the regiment had grown greatly depleted through losses of the Gettysburg campaign, and its one crying need now, was a fresh supply of men. This need, indeed, it shared with nearly all the army." Companies that a year before had numbered 100 men now could only muster 20; at one brigade parade the regiment could only put out 83 men. "Accordingly, efforts were at once put forth to supply this demand. A detail of officers and men was sent North to obtain what was so urgently required. The several rendezvous of drafted men were resorted to, to secure the necessary supply, it being found that voluntary enlistments were insufficient…"[8]

"The Regiment is under the command of Capt. Abram Lockwood. Major Tappen has gone to New York, with a detail of men from the Regiment to aid in enforcing the draft, and to bring on the conscripts—three hundred and fifty-five of whom will be placed in the 120th."[9]

What Sharpe had feared had come to pass. The draft had fallen on Ulster County. Sending details from the regiment to bring back drafted men seemed the worst solution. Had Sharpe been able to bring the entire regiment home to actively recruit among communities, his enthusiasm, his reputation, and his ability as a public speaker probably would have filled up the ranks without resort to the draft.

The draft issue would continue to bother Sharpe but from a different angle. Enforcement of the draft was in the hands of the provost marshal general of the U.S. Army, Col. John B. Fry. Unfortunately, civilians in Sharpe's county associated him with the effort because he was the deputy provost marshal general of the Army of the Potomac. As he was at pains to explain on occasion, "I do not wonder that there is some misunderstanding regarding the particular work assigned to Provost Marshals of whom so many have been created since the war. Our pro Mar Genl Department is a purely military organization forming part of the army in the field—and having nothing to do with Drafted men…" Nevertheless, he would always do what he could for someone with an appeal, either by directing them to Fry's office or researching the matter as far as he could.[10]

Meade Steps Backwards

Irony of ironies but Meade, the very man whose reputation rested on his timely receipt and use of intelligence, now ordered Sharpe to deal only with the sources under his own direction—espionage, scouting, document exploitation, and interrogation. Meade was enough of a traditionalist and a scholar to think he could coordinate the remaining sources himself. At a stroke, he undid the all-source miracle. Sharpe ceased to use any name for his organization, now using only "Office of the Provost Marshal General." The coordination that Sharpe had conducted directly with the signals and cavalry now had to go "through channels." The chief signal officer of the army, Capt. Benjamin F. Fisher, went so far as to suggest that his reports be shared with the "secret service."

His new chief of staff was the recently promoted Maj. Gen. Andrew Humphreys, who had stood behind Sharpe's old regiment on the second day at Gettysburg when only it held the line against the Confederate tide. He was also the same topographical engineer whose maps had been so outclassed by Babcock's efforts in the Peninsular Campaign. Sharpe had to make Babcock scarce for quite a while and even have subordinates prepare the order-of-battle reports that had normally been in Babcock's hand. Nor was it possible for Babcock to sign Sharpe's name. It was Humphreys who would now collect all the information from all the non-BMI collection sources, Sharpe's former task.[11]

Meade was far more directly involved in the analysis of information than he should have been, even of those areas of responsibility retained by Sharpe. Captured newspapers were brought to him first before Sharpe and his staff could analyze them. Sharpe had to beg for them back. "The papers brought by our men—Richmond dates of the day previous—are included—We would like to examine them carefully, when the General himself have done with them." Again in December Manning, signing for Sharpe, had to plead to Meade in a way that indicated this was a constant problem, "Much information can be gleaned from them for our records should you see fit to return them."[12]

It also appears that Meade was taking a lot of the reports from deserters and prisoners far too literally, without Sharpe's analytical filter. He was also known to personally interrogate them. This would have consequences later on.[13]

At the same time, Meade's constant ill-temper was alienating everyone around him. Grant's characterization was again on the mark when he wrote that Meade "was unfortunately of a temper that would get beyond his control, at times, and make him speak to officers of high rank in the most offensive manner... This made it unpleasant at times, even in battle, for those around him to approach him even with information." Meade's tongue was just as sharp with his own general and personal staff.[14] We shall see later that Sharpe on at least one occasion became the quiet spokesman to Patrick of the army staff's unhappiness.

Meade's scholarship did make a significant contribution to the art of intelligence by resurrecting the meaning of the word "intelligence" to mean processed information about the enemy, in which sense it had been used by George Washington. Meade deserves the credit for returning its meaning to Washington's original sense of the word.[15]

After Meade clipped Sharpe's wings, he reserved the right unto himself to answer the ultimate question of military intelligence, "What does all this mean?" He had gone from being not only the primary consumer of intelligence but the ultimate military intelligence analyst. As Sharpe was confined to rely on only the four lanes that were left to him (and we have seen with the latter it was only contingent, and at times Meade conducted his own interrogations), he could not incorporate the equally valuable information received from the Signal Corps and the cavalry. Whatever intelligence Sharpe was providing was no longer fully all-source.

Despite Meade's disruption of the all-source effort, Sharpe made the most of the assets that remained to him, and his continuing control of interrogations allowed him to state in late 1863, "We are entirely familiar with the organization of the rebel forces in Virginia and North Carolina." The BMI had become familiar "with each regiment, brigade, and division, with the changes therein, and [with] their officers and locations." With the coming of the new year, he could state confidently, "the state of our information has been such as to form a standard of credibility by which these men were gauged, while each was adding to the general sum." Babcock would also note that after Gettysburg, "Much was done in perfecting Lee's organization, selecting guides for country to be operated in, location of enemy on map. Etc."[16]

Despite his problems with Meade, Sharpe was having some success in creating the concept among the various staffs and commands within the army that everyone had a part to play in the development of intelligence. The two other traditional collection arms were the Signal Corps and the cavalry. It is evident that Sharpe and the signal officer had a close working relationship. Doubtless the signal officer was providing his reports under the table to Sharpe. It was a natural relationship.

It was the cavalry that had to break old habits and ideas that it was the primary collection means of the army. Sharpe in the last two campaigns had shown he was the new game in town, and the cavalry resented his treading on their traditional mission. An example of the attempt to play it alone was Brig. Gen. George A. Custer, commanding a brigade in Kilpatrick's 3rd Cavalry Division. He bypassed Kilpatrick and sent a letter dated August 13 directly to the corps commander, Pleasonton, in which he at some length went over his collection and analysis efforts. He referred to a Richmond newspaper which he enclosed and to the contents of an Army of Northern Virginia mailbag he had captured. He did not forward the letters, and it appears that army headquarters learned nothing of them.[17]

On the morning of the 17th it appears that Kilpatrick's command captured another mailbag but forwarded only two letters and a newspaper to Pleasonton who, in turn, sent them on to Meade's headquarters the next day. It took another 10 days for the matter of the various mailbags to come to Meade's attention, an indication of the confusion attendant in the headquarters, with Meade and Humphreys trying to substitute themselves, already burdened with heavy workloads, for the single-mission dedicated BMI. In his response, it is not clear whether Meade was referring to the mailbag captured on the 13th, if he ever learned of that one, or to the one captured on the 17th. He sent a preemptory order that "hereafter ... anything of that kind that is captured be forwarded at once."[18]

The BMI was no threat to the cavalry; rather, it complemented it, although there was some natural overlap in the use of scouts. Cavalry patrols and scouts largely functioned at the tactical level to warn of enemy movements and threats against the army, and to answer the questions of what and when. Although cavalry and BMI scouts went out in small numbers or singly, Sharpe's men were frequently in civilian clothes or Confederate uniforms that allowed them to pass unobtrusively among the enemy, and here is an important difference—to interact with Confederate soldiers and civilians. For example, in the episode described above, scout Skinker posing as a Confederate civilian was able to elicit important information from an influential man who assumed he was also a rebel. They also worked with a network of Union agents in the enemy countryside and regularly brought back written reports. Isaac Silver was only the most important of Sharpe's agents. The most telling limitation of the cavalry is its inability to answer "why." That was Sharpe's forte even with the limitations forced on him by Meade.

In Meade's defense, there is no evidence that he discouraged the collection of information from any source. If anything, he gave collection his complete support. That meant not only the cavalry but the major corps commands as well. The corps now knew that it was just not enough to forward prisoners and deserters to the provost marshal general but to conduct initial interrogations to be able to alert the BMI to promising sources. Deserters, in particular, usually had something to offer and were up front about it. Sharpe would have been the one to coordinate with corps staffs and commanders. He was very much a hands-on staff officer who would brief pickets on what information to worm out of their counterparts. He would have worked closely at lower levels essentially to train the staff and line, and to gain the goodwill of the corps commanders to smooth the way for his message. Since he was regularly providing the corps commanders with Lee's order-of-battle down to regiment, he ensured himself a positive reception. Slowly but surely the army was learning that everyone had a role in the creation of intelligence.

Filling in for Patrick

On August 11 Patrick suddenly took leave for 15 days; he had angered some powerful authorities in the War Department and saw his removal as imminent. The only thing that seemed to be staying their hand was finding a qualified successor. In the meantime, both Meade and Patrick thought it advisable for him to take leave as things sorted themselves out. Sharpe had already had his own leave approved for what he had called "this period of inaction," and wrote his uncle that Patrick suddenly had to take leave because of a severe illness in his family. The illness was either an amazingly timely coincidence or a public face on why Patrick had to leave, one that Sharpe does not appear to have known.[19]

Shortly after Patrick took leave, the threat of his relief seems to have blown over. Reports in the press indicated that rumors of his replacement were unfounded, and "although should the exigencies of the service require him to take command of a division, the ability and experience of Col. Sharpe would point to him as the next Provost Marshal General." The correspondent was evidently picking up the high regard in which Sharpe was held at headquarters.[20]

Patrick's sudden departure on leave meant that Sharpe had to immediately step into the provost marshal general's demanding job while continuing to do his own, even as it began to pick up again. One of the first issues he had to deal with was the policy on allowing sutlers to bring liquors into the army, a matter of no little concern given the hard-drinking attitudes of the period and the effects on good order and discipline of uncontrolled access to such. He instructed Captain Beckwith on the provost marshal general's staff to produce a summary of the current policy, and based upon that, he recommended, "It is quite important that the system of bringing goods to the Army should be fixed, and that it should harmonize not only with rules established here, but also with such as Major General Martindale [military governor of Washington] feels called upon to make…" In other words, he had arrived at a common sense solution that would prevent the ongoing friction between the army and its rear.[21]

A good part of his time was taken up in dealing with the Virginia civilians in the army's area of operations. There were constant appeals for redress of grievance over animals seized by the army. Each case was the subject of inquiry and adjudication. Another critical issue was the overall treatment of civilians. Sharpe wrote out a memorandum stating that citizens who refused to take the oath of loyalty had only to expect the protection of their lives and property and not expect to be given passes into Washington or Alexandria, travel on the roads, come within the army's lines, or be allowed any favors or indulgences. Sharpe concluded, "Each case should rest upon its individual merits but the Oath of Allegiance should always be a prerequisite."[22]

A normal responsibility of the provost operation was dealing with criminal matters within the army, which entailed numerous investigations, even down to claims of stolen horses. Of far more importance was the problem of desertion, which plagued both Union and Confederate armies, particularly among drafted men. In one case Sharpe requested lists of names and descriptions of deserters from the 15th Massachusetts Volunteers to aid in their apprehension. Sharpe lamented, "Conscript deserters are being brought in every day and are using every device possible to escape identification." Eventually, Patrick and Sharpe would hit upon a foolproof method of forcing a confession from such deserters.[23]

There was also a lot of humdrum and detail in the provost duties Sharpe had to deal with. One of them was in confiscating the significant amount of pornographic material being sent to the army through the mail. A serious sex scandal in the army may have provided some dramatic if not comic relief. A teenage prostitute, Anne (Annie) E. Jones, had joined the army as "a daughter of the regiment," a term for a female mascot, and gone on to ensnare a number of general officers, including cavalry Brig. Gen. Judson Kilpatrick, who put her up in his tent and flaunted her about his command. Jealous that she boasted also of bedding Brig. Gen. George A. Custer, of the flowing blonde locks, he accused her of being a spy.[24] She brazenly applied to remain with the army. Sharpe was the one who, in accordance with Meade's orders, denied her application, ordered her to headquarters to expel her from the army, and sent her to Washington. She would eventually spend three months in prison as a suspected spy, but would be pardoned and released.[25]

Patrick returned on August 26 and immediately approved Sharpe's leave. Upon Sharpe's return, Patrick surprised him with some news:

Genl Patrick asked me on my return what I would like best in case of his soon leaving. I replied that I would rather do something for my regiment than myself & he said he could apply for it to be ordered on duty with me at H. Q. immediately—he has since told me that Meade has consented—but the order is not out as yet. I hope it may come.

At last, it seemed that Sharpe would succeed in having the 120th transferred to the provost guard—or so it seemed. Nothing came of it in the end.

At least the middle of August found the 120th with comparatively easy duty. One of the soldiers wrote home, "At present our Regiment is doing picket duty along the Rappahannock, between Beverly and Freeman's Ford.—I assure you we enjoy ourselves along this beautiful stream, and in the cool shade. It is just the placs [sic] for our wearied soldiers, after long marches over dusty roads, and through the hot sun." He also took the opportunity to vent: "Great indignation is felt by the members of the Brigade at the dastardly conduct of the Copperheads in our native State. We have some respect for the rebel soldiers who will stand up, face the bullets and fight like men; but words cannot express the contempt with which we regard those home traitors, who seek to stab in the dark and fire in the rear." It was a sentiment actively held by Sharpe and one he would not fail to express after the war.[26]

Babcock's Journal

A detailed insight into the workings of the BMI at this time is found in what can only be described as John Babcock's daily journal of intelligence operations. It covers the period from August 24 to December 6, 1863 and is a day-by-day account of interrogations and scouting activities. That it was meant to be a journal of only those issues on which Babcock concentrated is evidenced by the absence of Sharpe's dealings with spies and counterintelligence and interaction with other agencies such as McPhail's provost marshal general's office in Baltimore.

The journal reflects the rhythm of the BMI's order-of-battle and scouting operations for that period. Throughout the interrogation reports are brigade-level orders-of-battle, and here and there are elegant hand-drawn maps in color. Given the precision and order of this journal, which clearly reflected Babcock's approach to his duties, it is a reasonable assumption that this is the only surviving volume of a series that covered the entire history of the BMI. The disappearance of the other volumes remains a great loss to the study of military intelligence in the Civil War.

In the 75 days covered by the journal, Babcock shows that he interrogated 80 POWs/deserters, 20 civilian refugees, and 20 contraband slaves. These were among the subjects that Babcock thought worth interrogating. Given that the army headquarters moved 13 times in this period during which interrogations were not conducted, Babcock was conducting about two interrogations a day. Separating this wheat from the chaff required a careful sorting process that included almost all POWs and deserters. Because of his selectivity in choosing his subjects, reports generated by them were often lengthy. Great care was especially given to determining how genuine were the motives of deserters in seeking to be sent North.

Babcock also reports that there were 19 scouting expeditions composed of at least two and often more scouts which often lasted three or more days. That amounted to a constant scouting effort against the enemy. Babcock mentions the names of the most stalwart of the scouts: Cline, Brown, Anson B. Carney, Hogan, McGee, Plew, McCord, Dodd, and Hunnicutt.[27]

Pasted at the end of the journal are a number of newspaper clippings from Northern and Southern newspapers, the latter showing how much important order-of-battle information was available "open source," as the term is used today. For example, there was Lee's official report of the Gettysburg Campaign as published in the Richmond papers; a *Richmond Enquirer* account of Pickett's Charge and its losses; a list of Confederate general officers who had been killed, wounded, or resigned; and a list of senior officers confirmed by the Confederate senate. All of these, processed and analyzed, ended up in the growing files of the BMI. Of the Northern papers, the *New York Herald* printed in early September a complete order-of-battle of the Army of Northern Virginia down to regiment that it claimed originated from the office of the Confederate adjutant general. It was hugely inaccurate and bears little resemblance to the actual return of the Army of Northern Virginia for the end of August, except such publicly known information as the corps and divisions and their commanders. For example, the article shows a strength of 112,000, whereas Lee's returns for that time show only 61,202 officers and men present for duty. It has all the earmarks of a deception operation—just enough accuracy to be believable, and the inaccuracies cleverly woven to seriously mislead and alarm the enemy. That it appeared in the *Herald*, a newspaper despised by Sharpe for its antiwar positions, indicates that the newspaper may have been carefully chosen as a platform for the deception. It must have caused Babcock to shake his head at what nonsense got into the Northern press. It would not be the last time the BMI and the Provost Marshal Department would protest such consistent cupidity and error.[28]

Confederate Disarray

The Army of the Potomac and the Army of Northern Virginia would fight no more major battles until the spring of 1864. Essentially the armies left each other alone for August and September in order to recover from the bloodletting at Gettysburg. The relatively calm situation was ideal for scouts, and Sharpe had his "constantly on the move. One group ranged as far eastward as the Potomac, its members posing alternately as Confederate soldiers and as local civilians, and repeatedly encountering enemy picket lines." Communications were reestablished with Isaac Silver, who had been waiting to hear from Sharpe's men. He had a report ready on Lee's right wing.

On August 4 Sharpe reported on "a most important expedition, conducted by Cline, attended by the highest results. Cline in another bravura performance had slipped into Spotsylvania County and through his own observations and information from agents such as Silver had reported on the severe problems affecting Lee's army. The country he traveled through was swarming with cavalry patrols searching for deserters. Desertion had become so rampant in the Army of Northern Virginia as to cause a crisis in morale. Lee reported to Davis that "Great dissatisfaction is reported among the good men in the Army at the apparent impunity of the deserters." He issued general orders to implement Davis's August 1 proclamation of amnesty to any deserter who would return to the ranks within 20 days. It backfired, and as Lee explained, "many presumed on it and absented themselves from their commands choosing to place on it a wrong interpretation." Lee was forced to institute a system of furloughs. Cline's report was dead on, an amazing insight into the crucial morale of the enemy.[29]

Cline also reported on the attempted resignation of Robert E. Lee in response to the barrage of criticism over the failure of the Gettysburg Campaign. Sharpe wrote:

> An extraordinary state of excitement is pervading all classes of Southern society in regard to the late retreat of General Lee. A disagreement has sprung up between himself and the Confederate cabinet, and General Lee has tendered his resignation. He desires to retire to the line of the James River, and Mr. Davis urgently insists upon his defending the line of the Rappahannock. Much recrimination exists in regard to the immense loss occasioned by the advance into and retirement from Pennsylvania. All agree that the line of the Rapidan will only be defended for the purpose of retarding our movements.[30]

In fact, Cline's information had anticipated Lee's resignation, which was not made until August 8. But the crisis in the Southern command was as genuine as Lee's heartfelt attempt to resign.

> The general remedy for the want of success in a military commander is his removal... I therefore, in all sincerity, request Your Excellency to take measures to supply my place. I do this with the more earnestness because no one is more aware than myself of my inability for the duties of my position. I cannot even accomplish what I myself desire. How can I fulfill the expectations of others? In addition, I sensibly feel the growing failure of my bodily strength. I have not yet recovered from the attack I experienced last spring. I am becoming more and more incapable of exertion, and am thus prevented from making the personal supervision of the operations in the field which I feel to be necessary. I am so dull that in making use of the eyes of others I am frequently misled.[31]

Sharpe apparently had already personally briefed Meade on these issue, but added in his official report that this information had been "obtained from such sources as to make it entirely reliable—the details hereof being personally communicated to the Commanding General." Sharpe had delivered a remarkably accurate report of the political-military state of the enemy at this time, a state of shock and demoralization after the ruinous failure of the Gettysburg Campaign. It was strategic political-military assessment that today might be the subject of a National Intelligence Estimate (NIE).[32]

In addition to reporting accurately on the enemy's morale and command crises, Sharpe had another morsel of operational importance. However garbled the reason, he had identified the importance of the Rapidan to Lee. When Meade finally took up a position on the Rappahannock, Lee settled down along the Rapidan. And settle down he could, recovering his health, and resting his army and restoring its morale for the rest of August and September, largely undisturbed by his opponents. Meade was doing essentially the same thing. There was an alarm, however, on August 15 that most of Lee's army was on the march from Culpeper Court House along the Fredericksburg road with the intent to cross the Rappahannock at U.S. Ford. The press attributed the alarm to the story of Curtis Merritt, a black drummer boy who had deserted and come into Union lines that day. Humphreys informed the I Corps commander of the movement, citing the evidence of "scouts and other sources." There are no BMI supporting documents of this event to include an interrogation of the drummer boy, but the files are incomplete. Nevertheless, the story has the ring of authenticity. Charlie Wright before Gettysburg is the most noteworthy example, but there were many more, a rich and often reliable source of excellent information. Humphreys was clearly alluding to Sharpe's reporting. It is hard to explain, then, Meade's comment in a letter to his wife of August 19 that "it is very difficult to obtain any minute or reliable intelligence of his [Lee's] movements." Sharpe had done just that with the reports of his scouts and possibly the interrogation of the drummer boy. In the end, Lee's movement was seen to be a demonstration to warn Meade off any offensive action by threatening his left flank.[33]

If ever there was a time to strike when the iron was hot, this was it. However, neither Meade nor Army Chief of Staff Maj. Gen. Henry Halleck saw that the combination of rampant desertion, drop in morale, and crisis in confidence in the highest levels of command was a reason for offensive operations. They were to be similarly unresponsive to an even greater opportunity. One wonders what Lincoln, who haunted the War Department's telegraph office reading everything that came through, would have thought of this had Meade forwarded it to Halleck. Surely the content would have resonated politically in showing an especially vulnerable enemy and prompted a prodding inquiry to Meade. Unfortunately, there is no evidence that he saw or responded to Sharpe's report in either the Lincoln Papers at the Library of Congress or the Official Records.

Sharpe was looking deep into the battlefield beyond his own immediate responsibilities. He understood that the ability of Lee's army to sustain itself was as vital as its order-of-battle; he had passed the threshold out of parochial concerns—the old saw about tactics are for amateurs, logistics for professionals. Grist for his mill came also from McPhail on August 17, whose man in Richmond provided insight into Lee's very ability to sustain his army with this report on the Tredegar Works in Richmond, the largest single source of ordnance for the Confederate armies:

I have been able to obtain in relation to the Tredegar works Situated between the canal & River on the west side of Richmond. They are now in full operation, employing about 600. men, making all kinds of shot & shell and cannon from six to fifteen inches, and are making arrangements for Rifling larger sizes, the workmen form a battalion of five hundred as infantry and artillery having two batteries. The works turn out from nine to ten field pieces and from three to four large guns per week, a number of shops attached to the works, making smaller work. Lester's factory for making small arms employ at least 200—hands. Iron and coal are scarce. Thousands of pounds of shot, shell & old scrap iron are at the works which cannot be used for want of proper fuel… The convicts in the penitentiary are making gun carriages, and nearly all the shops in the city are on Govt work. Three ironclads are nearly finished have a larger ordnance than the Merrimack had, three guns on the side, if one bow & one stern.[34]

The report also described how the employees of the works had been formed into reserve militia formations to supplement the defenses of Richmond.

Richmond included not only the Tredegar Works but enough other war industries to make the city along with Atlanta the largest sources of war materials for the Confederacy. Sharpe eagerly collected on Richmond's war industries to supplement what he obtained from McPhail. On August 23 he reported the information provided by James Edgeworth, a conscript deserter, formerly an employee of the Tredegar Works. Edgeworth stated that the works were frequently disrupted and shut down while the employees were called up to man the defenses of Richmond. He also related how munitions works had been transferred from the works to Manchester and Belle Island to accommodate the female employees. Both Union and Confederate munitions makers found it more efficient to employ women and children, whose smaller hands and finer motor control were an advantage with sensitive explosives.[35]

Another feature of Sharpe's reporting, supporting Cline's report of the 4th, was on the increasing numbers of deserters who wished to take the oath of allegiance and be transported north. Twenty-five men from Benning's Brigade deserted in one night. Most spoke of "hard treatment" and constant deprivation of food and clothing. Sharpe was "quite certain that almost all the men who originally enlisted from Western Va are secretly going to their homes within our lines." There were almost no replacements, and the only men arriving were convalescents. Sharpe was identifying the phenomenon of men deserting once their homes fell beyond Union lines. Deserters were frequently being found in their own homes, now under Union control, such as the four men from the 49th Virginia taken at their homes in Rappahannock County and who had deserted the previous December.[36]

Perhaps most revealing was the statement of an officer deserter, Lieutenant Clair Mayfair, whom Sharpe judged intelligent and truthful:

The feeling among the troops differs a good deal. The men are very anxious for the war to close. Many of our men are sorry they did not desert in Maryland. The Tennessean and N. Carolinians desert in droves. Most of them go home but would come here if they knew how they would be received and treated.

I think that an order from General Meade similar to that issued by General Rosencrans [sic] would do Lee's Army more damage than any battle that could be fought. This I know to be so. For I have talked with many of the men, who would desert if they had not heard that they would be badly treated here.[37]

Certainly this supported Sharpe's advocacy of the psychological warfare effort to encourage desertions, an advocacy that would be transformed later into a very effective policy.

Mayfair also pointed out another problem that Lee was facing that was not reflected in the deserters that the BMI interrogated. Large numbers of Confederate soldiers were deserting in the opposite direction—homewards within the Confederacy, just the painful point President Davis was making in his amnesty proclamation of the month before.

"Quo Vadis, Longstreet?"—Again!

Sharpe's greatest achievement in these fallow months was to learn that Longstreet had departed to reinforce Lt. Gen. Braxton Bragg's Army of Tennessee, which was being outmaneuvered by the Union's Army of the Cumberland under Maj. Gen. William S. Rosecrans. Lee was spending an extended period in Richmond and had left Longstreet in command in his absence with the instructions to take offensive action if the opportunity arose. Longstreet replied that the offensive action would only have utility if it could be made north of the Potomac, but that the army did not have the strength to ensure a decisive outcome. Instead he added:

> I know little of the condition of our affairs in the West, but am inclined to the opinion that our best opportunity for great results is in Tennessee. A few could hold the defensive here with two corps and send the other to operate in Tennessee with that army, I think that we could accomplish more than by an advance from here.

Longstreet had not crassly recommended his own corps, but the suggestion clearly hung in the air. Davis approved the plan on September 9.[38]

The plan was already being talked about openly because two deserters from Hood's Division had come into the Union lines on the 8th and reported the rumors of a move to Tennessee. Babcock had noted in his journal for the 9th, "Can't locate Pickett's or McLaws's Divisions," and that "Hood's Divn is reported to be moving south!"[39] In the same entry he underlined this information as important in his interrogation report of two Georgian deserters that went to Meade the same day Davis approved Longstreet's plan.

> It was the opinion of many, that a corps of Lee's army would go west as soon as the Yankee army advanced in Tennessee. Hood's Division had marching orders to leave yesterday at 3 a.m.
> This was before informants left but they say they heard drums beating about that time. Think they are going to Richmond. Do not know however. Orders to cook three days rations.[40]

Two days later, on the 11th, Babcock noted in his journal that scouts Carny and Hogan had reported that farmers and slaves were all stating that there were large troop movements heading south.[41]

On September 14, Babcock reported that prisoners had revealed, "That Longstreet's Corps had gone to Tennessee, and left the position in and about Fredericksburg in the following order: McLaws' Division first, Hood's next and Pickett last. They have all passed through Richmond and are taking the Richmond and Knoxville R. R." That same day two more sources reported. An Italian refugee and resident of Richmond came into the lines on the 14th and reported the next day that he had witnessed Longstreet's entire corps passing by rail through Richmond. Scouts McGee and Plew, who had been operating near Chancellorsville, came in the same day as the refugee and reported the departure from their own observations and from news from "reliable sources," probably meaning Silver and the other Unionist agents in the area. Their only mistake was to report that all three of Longstreet's divisions had departed for Tennessee. All three had gone to Richmond, the departure point for the long roundabout train journey to Tennessee, but Pickett's Division had been retained there, not having recovered from its bloodletting at Gettysburg. Deserters from Virginia regiments suggested another reason. Pickett's Division was entirely composed of Virginia regiments; they had simply refused to leave their home state. "The Virginians say if General Lee evacuates Virginia, they will not go with him. The Virginians in Longstreet's Corps were on the point of refusing to go to the west. Think many of them will desert." McGee and Plew's report was the final confirmation of Lee's strategic reinforcement of Bragg.[42]

Meade properly forwarded the intelligence to Halleck at 10:30 that morning and followed it up with a 10:30 p.m. letter reinforcing his opinion. "My judgment, formed on the variety of meager and conflicting testimony, is, that Lee's army has been reduced by Longstreet's corps." Meade's sour phrase, "meager and conflicting testimony" was unwarranted. Sharpe had provided his analysis based on multiple scout reports, the interrogation of a refugee, and the information gathered by Silver.[43]

For his part, Halleck immediately forwarded Meade's warning to Rosecrans, where it arrived on the 16th. His chief of staff, Brig. James Garfield, reported, "A dispatch from General Halleck this morning confirms our reports that Longstreet has joined Bragg, or is on the way to do so, with three divisions." Although it was only two divisions. Longstreet's divisions had to travel by rail through North Carolina and Atlanta before moving north to join Bragg, arriving in increments over three days, 17–19 September. On the 18th Sharpe was almost boastful as he related to his Uncle Jansen, "General Lee has tried to cheat us as to his movements—but failed. He has sent off one corps, Longstreet's, south and west." Sharpe would not have felt so smug had he known that the mighty I Corps under its great commander was at that moment coiling to strike Rosecrans's flank.[44] However, Sharpe, by alerting Rosecrans four days before the battle, had done as much for him as military intelligence could do.

Knowing Longstreet would most likely be in the enemy's array in the next battle in itself was not decisive. What Rosecrans did with that information was. It allowed him to fight a better battle. He fought Bragg to a standstill on the 19th and was doing well even when Longstreet's forces entered the battle the next day. In the end, it was just plain bad luck. Longstreet found an unexpected hole in Rosecrans's left flank and charged through it, to put half of the Army of the Cumberland to flight.

With his army beaten, Rosecrans fled back to Chattanooga. Bragg followed slowly and put Chattanooga under siege. Halleck was now roused to send the XI and XII Corps from Meade's army to help break Rosecrans out of his trap. Joe Hooker was given command of the relief force and brought Butterfield with him as chief of staff. Butterfield requested that Meade's aide, Captain Oliver, who had recovered from wounds at Gettysburg, accompany him. They sang such praises of George Sharpe to the desperate Rosecrans that he requested from Meade any intelligence that might apply to his theater, writing on October 18, "Please ask Colonel Sharpe to advise me of rebel movements affecting us here." Edwin Fishel observed, "In a Hooker regime, Sharpe himself would have sent it himself or written it into a telegram for Butterfield's signature, but he may not even have been informed of Rosecrans' request."[45]

Now it's A. P. Hill's Turn

The continuous refinement of the enemy's order-of-battle and deployments by the BMI allowed Sharpe to present to Meade on October 1 with as good an estimate of the enemy situation as possible. He stated, "That two corps, Ewell's and A. P. Hill's comprise all the force now in our front…" and then laid out the deployment of each of the subordinate divisions and identified the whereabouts of the detached elements of the army. "That no reinforcements have been received, or any of Longstreet's Corps returned since they went away. That Pickett's is at Shaffer's Bluff just below Richmond on the James River and two divisions at Chattanooga. No information as to what force is at Gordonsville but think there are none there."

He ended the report with the general comment on the enemy's intent: "Informants all agree that Lee's present position is one of great strength, and has been fortified with a great deal of consideration. Also that they are anxious for us to make an attack, and exhibit much impatience at our inactivity. They state that deserters have put our army at 78,000 strong (infantry)."

Lee had indeed heavily fortified his positions and would have liked nothing more than for Meade to impale himself on them. That Confederate deserters had attributed a strength of 78,000 infantry to the Army of the Potomac may reflect indirectly the reason why Lee had entrenched so heavily. He had perhaps learned a painful lesson at Gettysburg on the power of the defensive. The enemy might have felt more confident had they known that Meade's present for duty infantry strength was about 55,000.[46]

In early October another controversy arose over the question of whether A. P. Hill's Corps and Ewell's Corps had also been sent to Tennessee. It was an issue that would provoke Lincoln himself to weigh in with his own opinion. On October 4, a summary report written by Babcock and signed by Sharpe related the assertion of a deserter that Anderson's Division of Hill's Corps had been transferred to Tennessee and been replaced by Pickett's Division from near Richmond. The report stated that this was "very probable."[47] The same day McPhail forwarded information obtained by an agent in Richmond to Sharpe that "Lee advancing with fifty-five thousands (55,000) men. Hill and Longstreet cannot return."[48]

The story began to gather its own momentum when Meade wired Halleck on the 7th that two deserters repeated the camp rumor that a division of Hill's Corps had been sent to Tennessee and that he had sent out scouts to confirm this. Two hours later Halleck wired back an inquiry from Secretary of War Stanton, "if a part of A. P. Hill's Corps has gone west, a portion of your army cannot be spared..." One can see an edifice being built on camp rumors. The next day Sharpe, as part of ongoing analysis, expressed doubt on the issue and informed Meade of another camp rumor from three deserters that Mississippi brigade was breaking camp for transfer to Tennessee, but Sharpe comments that they were recent conscripts who knew little of their army's organization. That same day he sent over a summary of the results of interrogations of a large number of deserters from both Ewell's and Hill's Corps who uniformly said that there had been no transfers of parts of Hill's Corps from the Army of Northern Virginia.[49]

On the 10th Sharpe presented another report to Meade based on the observations of his scouts and in coordination with an agent who had freely traveled to Richmond. He stated categorically, "There is not the slightest evidence that any reinforcements whatever have been received by General Lee nor that any troops have left his army since Longstreet's movement but all the evidence is to the contrary." And that the "main body of the enemy was lying between Orange Court House and Rapidan Station," in an inactive state. Later that day, Meade wires Halleck, "From a deserter and prisoners I learn that A. P. Hill's whole corps and part of Ewell's are turning my right flank, moving from Madison Court-House to Sperryville."[50] Enough prisoners and deserters acquired during the Bristoe Campaign (October 13–19) confirmed beyond doubt that A. P. Hill's Corps was present with Lee's army. Seemingly the issue of transfers to Tennessee had been laid to rest. However, now rumor mills would be fed by the story that it was Ewell's Corps that was being sent west.

At this same time, Sharpe received a stream of telegrams from Michael Graham, formerly a spy for Maj. Gen. Robert Milroy. He was a Virginian and former railroad builder based in Martinsburg, West Virginia. Apparently he had been retained in some official capacity in both collecting information and conducting counterintelligence. The fact that Graham ran his own scouts and acted in the provost marshal capacity indicates he may have been leading a subordinate activity created by Sharpe for the Shenandoah Valley. Sharpe quite clearly had no problems giving him orders in both his capacity as chief of intelligence and as deputy provost marshal. Martin again and again warned of a new invasion of the North by Lee in dramatic terms.

All my scouts who came in and reported to me say that General Lee has a large army, and if he cannot capture Washington, Baltimore, and redeem Maryland, that he will fortify South Mountain, and will winter in Washington County, Md., and draw his supplies from the richest parts of Maryland and Pennsylvania. I am satisfied that they are coming. They have had the Union force weighed and counted, and found them wanting. Prepare for the storm.[51]

There is no evidence that Sharpe ever took these claims seriously. Graham's estimates of Lee's strength were too far out of line with what his own order-of-battle analysis told him. Graham's order-of-battle estimates were so wide off the mark that Sharpe had to admonish him, "What regiments & brigades are the prisoners from who tell you the stories of last night? If you see the prisoners at all, you can ask them from what regiments & brigades they are; and I don't want what they say, without knowing who they are—answer immediately."[52] Sharpe was instructing Graham on an essential element of collection—ascertaining the knowledgeability of the source.

Graham also kept Sharpe up to date on the activities of Imboden's Cavalry Brigade of Lee's army operating independently in the Valley. Martin appears to have at some point around the 20th stated that Imboden was in retreat down the Valley to Harrisonburg. Though this particular message cannot be identified, it will be referenced by Lincoln.

McEntee reported on October 21 that two refugees arrested near Warrenton had reported seeing 2 miles from Culpeper Court House long columns of troops heading south and were told they were Ewell's Corps going to Tennessee. Two days later Meade immediately forwarded to Halleck Sharpe's report based on what his scouts had brought to him.

Our men returned this morning. The old man [Isaac Silver] says that Ewell's corps went to Tennessee last Monday. He did not have time to go to the army himself, but yesterday he saw a man from Fredericksburg who had gone up to Culpeper on Monday as claimant to get certificates for damages done to his property and that of citizens around Fredericksburg. These certificates were to come from officers in Ewell's corps. The claimant returned to Fredericksburg on Tuesday, and said that he was unable to complete his business, because Ewell's corps had left for Tennessee on Monday. This is the authority, and the old man thinks it straight.

This was the first time Silver had based his report on secondhand information. The scouts on their return had come across an Irish refugee from Richmond who asserted that Ewell's Corps had not passed through the city and that the governor had appealed to the citizens of the capital to volunteer to defend the salt works. Notably Sharpe did not confirm Silver's assessment from other sources. In fact he included the contradictory statement of the Irish refugee. This was the type of single-source report that an intelligence analyst will let sit for a while until it gets company that confirms or disproves it, or offers a third explanation. But in this case, there had not been time because Meade wanted it sent immediately, even though he said in his endorsement that he had ordered confirmation. It was amateurish to alarm Washington with such unfinished intelligence. Given his established methodology, Sharpe undoubtedly would have waited to let the issue ripen as more information came in, But Meade was acting as his own chief intelligence officer and made the judgment that it was accurate. It was he who decided to forward Sharpe's unconfirmed report to Washington.[53]

Lincoln, who often haunted the War Department telegraph office next to the White House, had been following the issue and focused on this last report which had been sent at 6:30 p.m. The next day he shot back his own analysis of the enemy situation to Halleck who must have forwarded it to Meade by 11:00 a.m.

EXECUTIVE MANSION,   Washington, October 24, 1863.

Major-General HALLECK:

Taking all our information together, I think it probable that Ewell's corps has started for East Tennessee by way of Abingdon, marching last Monday, say, from Meade's front directly to the railroad at Charlottesville.

First, the object of Lee's recent movement against Meade; his destruction of the Orange and Alexandria Railroad, and subsequent withdrawal, without more motive, not otherwise apparent, would be explained by this hypothesis.

Secondly, the direct statement of Sharpe's man that Ewell has gone to Tennessee.

Thirdly, the Irishman's statement that he has not gone through Richmond, and his further statement of an appeal made to the people at Richmond to go and protect their salt, which could only refer to the works near Abingdon.

Fourthly, Graham's statement from Martinsburg that Imboden is in retreat for Harrisonburg. This last matches with the idea that Lee has retained his cavalry, sending Imboden and perhaps other scraps to join Ewell. Upon this probability what is to be done?

If you have a plan matured, I have nothing to say. If you have not, then I suggest that with all possible expedition, the Army of the Potomac get ready to attack Lee, and that in the meantime a raid shall, at hazards, break the railroad at or near Lynchburg.

Yours, truly,
A. LINCOLN.[54]

Upon receipt of this telegram, Meade must have burst into one of his fits of profanity and lashed out at Sharpe as was his well-established habit. No general in the field likes the commander-in-chief monitoring his operations so closely. There surely was an intensive relook at the issue in order to prepare a reply. (It is amazing how contemporary this sequence reads.) McEntee had already submitted a report that morning in which a deserter identified at least two of Ewell's divisions nearby at Rappahannock Station. Meade then promptly replied at 2:00 p.m. and blamed Sharpe. "The information given in Colonel Sharpe's dispatch is disproved by two deserters just in, who report Ewell's corps in my immediate front on the Rappahannock, with one division (Anderson's) on this side at the railroad crossing." He discounted the interpretation of Imboden's movements, attributing them to simple defensive repositioning.

Sharpe had been thrown to the wolves by the one report of Isaac Silver that he had not based on the "old man's" own personal observations. Nor had time allowed him to check that information against other sources. Meade, as his own ultimate military intelligence analyst, had made the decision to send the telegram to Halleck, which meant it would also be seen by Secretary of War Stanton.

The incident is revealing of the perils inherent in basing a conclusion on one source. Ironically, it was Silver's high reputation for accuracy that made it easy to do so in this case. This lesson applies to the longer controversy on whether Lee had detached another corps to Tennessee. Individual reports can be and often are misleading or just plain wrong, but a constant checking of information from other sources eventually teases out the right answer. It was also proof against Lee's efforts at disinformation in the form of carefully primed deserters. So it did, by putting to rest all the initial reports of A. P. Hill's Corps being dispatched to the west. Nothing could be less likely. Lee lamented to Longstreet that it was his absence that prevented the Bristoe Campaign from being more decisive. "But I missed you dreadfully and your brave corps. Your cheerful face and strong arms would have been invaluable."[55]

The wolves in this case did not devour Sharpe. He was one of the only staff officers whose reports were regularly sent to Halleck and Stanton by name. Lincoln read them and was familiar with Sharpe as the phrasing in his telegram above indicates—not an unwelcome situation for a man who realized that if he did not blow his own horn, someone would use it as a funnel, a method of self-promotion he would use successfully the rest of his life.[56]

No Rest for the Scouts

Sharpe worked his scouts hard all through the end of the year. In late November, the odds finally came close to catching up with Sergeant Cline.

> Cline is just in. He went first to Chancellorsville, where he found a detachment of the enemy's cavalry observing the roads leading to Fredericksburg. They belonged to Rosser's brigade. Being pursued, Cline retired, and at the forks of the plank road another party of the enemy's cavalry pursued them. They (Cline's party) then came to Parker's Store and there tried to get through the Wilderness by some of the wood roads but found them all full of the enemy's cavalry, apparently observing every approach to Fredericksburg and the Catharpin road. Cline tried to reach the Catharpin road but was unable to do so.

Along the Plank Road, Cline came across a woman who told him that the pickets were all over the roads between Spotsylvania and Chancellorsville. Cline and party slipped out through the Wilderness and snatched five prisoners on the way out, whose interrogation revealed that Heth's Division held the right of the Confederate line at New Verdierville.[57]

Although Sharpe and Patrick had worked out a professional relationship that allowed them both to work well together, Sharpe's style continued to rankle Patrick, who wrote in his diary on October 5 that "Col. Sharpe is not a man to place much reliance on, so far as business in a *business* way is concerned—He is quite too fond of a nice time, loves fun and is very irregular in all his ways…" All in all, it was a poor recommendation for a run of the mill staff officer, much less military policeman, but it was a great recommendation for a master of intelligence. The sort of personality that Patrick preferred as businesslike would not have had the imagination, flexibility, or intuitive feel for intelligence that Sharpe possessed.[58]

Sharpe continued to press the collection of intelligence at all times, especially during the lulls in active campaigning when the best work was done in refining Lee's order-of-battle. He was not above roaming the picket lines to encourage the men to elicit from their counterparts in gray the names of their units. On one occasion near Culpeper he encouraged a little Rhode Island soldier to get all the information he could from the Rebels while on picket duty.

> The young fellow, quite elated with the importance of his mission proceeded to his post and, hailing the picket of the opposing force, only a few hundred yards away, the following dialogue ensued:
>
> "Hello, Johnnie, what regiment to you belong to?"
>
> The ready answer was: "I belong to the Twenty-Fourth South Carolina," and in a moment, came the natural inquiry: "Well, yank, what regiment do you belong to?"
>
> Said the Rhode Island boy smartly. "I belong to the One Hundred and Thirty-seventh Rhode Island."
>
> Quick came the repartee: You are a _____ liar. There are not 137 men in that state.[59]

Sharpe, however, was loathe to let the Confederates know what a fruitful source the picket banter was. The day after Patrick returned, the Army of the Potomac issued a press release, printed in the Lincoln friendly *National Republican*, in which the hand of Sharpe is evident. It stated that the Union and Confederate pickets along the Rappahannock "hold daily friendly interviews, but no intelligence of importance is obtained through that channel." Sharpe knew that Lee read the Northern papers and wanted to cast a cloak of disinformation over this very useful source of information.[60]

A Bad Day for the 120th NY Volunteers

On October 10 a catastrophe fell upon the object of his constant paternal solicitude. The 210 men of the 120th New York under Captain Lockwood as acting commander had been sent forward as infantry support for the cavalry on October 8. The next day Lee put his army in motion, hoping to catch Meade at a disadvantage and deliver a surprise blow. Meade considered this only a feint.

Lockwood found the situation to be the reverse of what had been intended. Instead of being in support of a large body of cavalry, he found his regiment to be isolated from any sort of serious body of Union cavalry or infantry by at least 5 miles. He found himself supported by barely three companies of cavalry. Hampton's Cavalry Division hit them near James City on October 10. Lockwood recounted the skirmish:

The cavalry pickets were soon driven in, the enemy advanced upon me in heavy force, attacking on both flanks and in my front. No support coming to my assistance, I was forced to order my regiment to fall back, skirmishing, as the only means of preventing our being captured in a body. We fell back, keeping up a skirmish fire until we emerged from the woods in sight of James City, where I got a position behind a fence, and checked the advance of the enemy.[61]

Lockwood failed to say that the 120th was on the point of being overwhelmed when the belated order to fall back was given, as Private Wilbur Hale recalled:

in the disorder consequent upon it, the rebel cavalry rode through our numbers in all directions, with the cries of "surrender." Instances of personal bravery and persistent refusal to surrender were very common and marked, but we were overwhelmed by numbers, and under the persuasive argument of from two to half a dozen loaded carbines, most of us thought discretion the better part of valor, and one after another threw down his arms and gave up the fight.[62]

Despite severe combat at Chancellorsville and Gettysburg and numerous smaller engagements, the regiment had never lost a prisoner until this day. Almost the entire regiment was captured, and all would have marched into captivity had not a spirited counterattack by the 5th New York and the 5th Michigan Cavalry been able to free many of the prisoners. As it was, the regiment had been cut in two, with one man killed, nine wounded, and 104 taken prisoner, for a loss of 114 men or 54 percent. Barely 97 men staggered out of the fight. Lockwood carefully noted that his losses were two assistant surgeons, one hospital steward, and 10 sergeants missing; two sergeants wounded, 11 corporals missing, two corporals wounded, one private killed, five privates wounded, and 80 privates missing.[63]

Sharpe was stunned at the news and demanded and obtained a formal investigation from the chief of staff. He wrote to his uncle, "This investigation, I shall certainly have—it is promised me by Genl Humphreys … and there is a general feeling of indignation about the matter on the part of all officers at head quarters." If there was a silver lining, he was at pains to explain that, of the number lost, "Very few of these men are killed or wounded, and they will be returned to us, soon I hope, by exchange. This should be known for the benefit of the soldiers families, & I would be glad if you would let your courier make the above statement of the facts."[64]

Sharpe put far too much faith in the cartel for the exchange of prisoners. The two assistant surgeons were exchanged in December. It would not be until December 1864 that only 25 men were exchanged, 32 having died in captivity.[65]

For Sharpe the entire episode left a bitter taste. He contemplated trying to get the regiment transferred to Sickles's command if, as seemed likely, in mid-October, his old division commander would be given command of the forces defending Washington. "I think," he wrote Uncle Jansen, "they & I have done such a share of campaigning as to be entitled to some of the immunity which all get that can." Between the lines it is easy to read Sharpe's exasperation with Meade, who had promised, through Patrick, to have his regiment transferred to the provost guard a month ago. Had Meade followed through with his promise, the 120th would not have suffered its catastrophe. It would not be the end of rancor.[66]

"We have lost so many men trying to take"

Sharpe had opened an office of sorts in Washington where his scouts and others could meet, exchange information, and coordinate activities. That location offered easy access to sources that seemed to converge on the capital, much as others did under McPhail's watchful eye in Baltimore. From there Major General Martindale, one of the BMI's original members, sent Sharpe a startling message on November 1. He stated that he was "reliably informed ... that there is no one now defending the [Marye's] heights beyond Fredericksburg, that we have lost so many men in trying to take. I am well satisfied that a second demonstration of one or two thousand might succeed without much loss."[67]

Sharpe rushed it to Meade, satisfied with who Humphrey's reliable sources were. Meade jumped at the opportunities inherent in the report. By the next day he had worked out a plan of campaign that would allow him to steal a march on Lee. He wired Halleck a well-reasoned plan:

> From the best judgment I can form, his army is massed between the Rappahannock and Culpeper, prepared to contest the crossing of the river ... I have determined to attempt the movement by his right, throwing the whole army rapidly and secretly across the Rappahannock at Bank's Ford and Fredericksburg, and taking a position on the heights above the town.
>
> The success of this movement will depend on its celerity, and its being kept from the enemy. From my latest information, he had no force below the junction of the two rivers. My present position, and repairing the railroad, has doubtless induced him to believe I shall adhere to this line, and if my movement can be started before he is apprised of it, I have every reason to believe it will be successful, so far as effecting a lodgment on the heights in advance of him; and if he follows and gives me battle, my object will be accomplished.[68]

It was a sound plan that would have forced Lee to attack him by threatening his flank and communications, especially the Richmond, Potomac, & Fredericksburg Railroad—putting him at great disadvantage. It was a plan suggested by fruits of the BMI's relentless efforts to gather information.

Unfortunately, the plan was dashed by Halleck the next day in what Meade thought were insulting terms. His response was measured and simply stated that Halleck's disapproval "caused an immediate abandonment of the plan." He added that he was "anxiously endeavoring to see my way clear to make some movement, which, by tactical maneuver on the enemy's flank, would bring my army in contact with his, without giving him all the advantage of defense and position." Unspoken here was the reproof that the plan Halleck had dismissed was the very one that would put him on Lee's flank without giving them the "advantage of defense and position."[69]

On the 10th Sharpe reported an unusual capture. B. Hammond, one of Lee's special scouts, had been captured near Buckland Mills. "When questioned as to his orders he states that they were to proceed in the rear of our army and when any movements worthy of note took place to report them immediately at the headquarters of General Lee." He had had a pass signed by Lee himself but had eaten it "that it might not fall into our hands and be used to the detriment of the rebel service." Sharpe recorded Hammond's account of how he penetrated Union lines.

> That he left Orange Court House about the time our army was advancing across the Rapidan with orders to go around by Fredericksburg in our rear and find out what he could relative to the movements of our army. At Fredericksburg he understood from the cavalry there that our infantry was crossing at Germanna Ford. Being provided with a pass from General Lee outside the lines he crossed the river at Fredericksburg and came around by Brentsville crossing the Orange and Alexandria R. R. between Collette and Bristow Station. After leaving Fredericksburg he was accompanied by a scout of General Stuart's whose name he refused to give. He also refused to give the names of those he had been stopping with since he has been within our lines… He stated that at the time he crossed the railroad it was guarded by infantry pickets which he eluded by running his horse.

It was a story that any of Sharpe's scouts could have verified since they were doing exactly the same in the other direction. Nevertheless, since he had been captured in civilian clothes, Sharpe recommended he be tried as a spy. The next day Cline and his men captured another member of Lee's scouting establishment, a soldier of "Randolph's Company (the black-horse) of the 4th Va. Cavalry taken by the scouts seven miles beyond Culpeper C. H. [northwest] toward Sperryville." He was as uncommunicative of his contacts as Hammond. To Cline it was clear he was scouting in that direction. Cline and his party had found no Confederate forces either.[70]

Hammond was part of an extensive scouting mission that Lee had set in motion. He reported to President Davis on the 12th his conclusions that Meade was concentrating for offensive action and that it would be logistically impossible to follow him.

> The country through which he will have to pass is barren. We have no forage on hand and very little prospect of getting any from Richmond. I fear our horses will die in great numbers, and, in fact, I do not know how they will survive two or three days' march without food. I hope every effort will be made to send some up, and I think it would be well to stop the transportation of everything on the railroad excepting army supplies.[71]

The same day he wrote to Secretary of War James A. Seddon on the perilous stated of his railroad lifeline:

> The condition of the Virginia Central Railroad, on which we depend almost entirely for our supplies, seems to become worse every day. Colonel Corley reports the frequent accidents of cars running off the tracks, and that the track, in many places, is very bad. I beg you to consult with the president and superintendent of the road as to what measures can be taken for its repair before the winter fairly sets in. To make details from this army for the purpose, in the present reduced condition of our regiments, is next to impossible. I hope, however, something may be done to put it in good repair, so that it may be relied on for the regular transportation of our supplies. If this cannot be done, the only alternative will be to fall back nearer to Richmond.

> This would leave not only the railroad, but the richest portion of the State of Virginia at the mercy of the enemy… It is of great importance that the work should be done while the good weather lasts.[72]

The general also wrote in what appears to have been even stronger terms of the want of proper clothing for his ragged men. Lee's stress may have found an echo in the story that a Mr. Smith told the commander of the Cavalry Corps, Maj. Gen. Alfred Pleasonton, on November 15, that "it is reported and freely talked about in Richmond of abandoning Virginia, and they are now moving things quietly from the different parts of the State."[73]

Two days after Lee's messages to Davis and Seddon, on November 14, three contrabands who had left Orange County the day before reported that Lee's army was on the move south to Louisa Court House, some 30 miles away, and probably as far as Richmond. They were repeating what their master said as well as his observations of empty camps and troops marching south in the direction of Orange Court House with Rodes's Division the last to go. "They overheard an officer say to their master that if he wanted to keep his negroes, he had better carry them off at once, as the army was falling back." They seemed credible to Sharpe. They also had the testimony of a deserter who claimed Lee was retreating to establish a new line "from Hanover Junction to the James River." He had been dismissed initially as a half-wit.[74]

Events moved rapidly. Humphreys late that night telegraphed Meade who was in Washington that there was overwhelming evidence now that Lee was on the move. Meade received the wire at 1:15 on the morning of the 15th:

> A deserter from the 15th North Carolina, Rodes' division, was brought to headquarters this evening. He states that he deserted early last night. His regiment was on picket at Raccoon Ford yesterday, and at night moved off without being relieved. That the orderly that brought the order to move said that cavalry pickets would take their place. That the brigade had already marched, and that the whole division was in motion. He says they moved toward some court-house, but does not know whether it was Spotsylvania Court-House or Orange Court-House. Believes the whole army has fallen back. This deserter came into Kilpatrick's pickets. General Davies' report, just received, corroborates these statements. He states the enemy's pickets are not so numerous as they were yesterday, and their infantry posts have been relieved by cavalry, and he believes that their main force has been withdrawn from the river.
>
> There was a good deal of noise about midnight on the other side of the river and at Morton's Ford; reveille was at 3 o'clock this morning, and the noise of wheels and the shouting of men was heard. The cavalry on our front is ordered to push reconnaissances close in on the enemy not later than daylight to-morrow morning.

There had been no reporting from scouts, and the day had been so hazy the signal stations could see nothing. Yet, the evidence was so overwhelming just from Sharpe's interrogations, now suddenly confirmed by the noise of an enemy in movement. Humphreys put the army's corps in readiness to move. Then he noted, "If the enemy is falling back, it is not from any military necessity, but in consequence of a policy adopted at Richmond." It was an idea that Sharpe would have brought to the table.[75]

On the 16th the scouts that had been sent out to gain further information returned. As soon as they contacted Silver, he made a special effort to answer their questions. Security was so tight around the Confederate center at Orange Court House that he had to go around it and approach it from the rear. He affirmed that Lee had received no reinforcements and that his two corps were roughly deployed from Orange Court House to Rapidan Station and along the Rapidan River to Fredericksburg. They were strongly entrenching at the station. Another agent at Fredericksburg told them that the enemy cavalry was "greatly reduced in condition they have little or no forage and now that the grass is gone are seeking it wherever it may be found," confirming Lee's own assessment of the 12th. A third informant, a Mr. Clay Rowe, of Fredericksburg, strongly vouched for by Scout Skinker, said that all the talk of Richmond was that "General Lee would be compelled to retire" and that he was investing all his Confederate money in tobacco to be sold to the North. Apparently unknown to Skinker and Sharpe, Rowe, who had been a strong Unionist just before Virginia seceded, had done a complete about-face to champion secession. In 1862 he had spent several months in Washington's Old Capitol Prison as a hostage for comparable Union men held by the Confederates. He did not change his politics upon release. Skinker as a resident of the area surely knew this. The most plausible explanation is that Skinker obtained the information from Rowe surreptitiously, posing as a loyal Confederate.[76]

The conflicting accounts of Silver and Rowe could only be resolved by further inquiry, although the benefit of the doubt must have been with Silver given his reputation for reliability. Sharpe sent Cline out again to get Silver to find an explanation. Cline returned with it on the 19th. He reported that the Old Man "says that he learned from the major commanding Staunton brigade, that a week ago yesterday orders were issued to General Lee's army to fall back, but were afterwards countermanded." This episode is a good example of the careful checking and examination of inconsistencies that goes into intelligence analysis.[77]

The explanation partially may be in the bomb that Lee had dropped in Seddon's lap in the form of a forceful letter about his want of supplies. Seddon had shaken up the Quartermaster Department and given priority of supply to the Army of Northern Virginia. The quartermaster general, A. R. Lawton, responded immediately to Lee, informing him that between rounding up all available stocks and the large foreign shipments just received, he would be able to immediately dispatch to Lee's army over 20,000 pairs of shoes, 15,000 overcoats, about 8,000 blankets, much clothing and leather accoutrements.[78]

The Mine Run Campaign

Stung by repeated urging from Washington for offensive action, Meade saw an opportunity to strike a blow at Lee before the weather closed campaigning for the winter in late November. It does not seem that he had appreciated the warning in Sharpe's recent reports. Sharpe reported on the 19th that his scouts had returned with information from Silver:

> Agents of the rebel government have been lately gathering up in the counties before named [Louisa, Orange & Spotsylvania], as well as in Fauquier, and Prince William, all axes, picks, and shovels. The old man saw five teams pass up plank road to the rear, loaded with these articles at one time. Even a load of horse shoes left by us in old camps was gathered and sent to the rear. The country about Fredericksburg is being stripped of every material of war...

All cattle were also being either slaughtered or sent to the rear of Lee's army. Silver quoted a Confederate major visiting a home nearby. "Damn the Yankees—they can't get much now even if they do come at us, our trains have all been sent to the rear between Orange Court House and Gordonsville." Three days later, a deserter would report having seen a cattle park in Gordonsville. Other reports confirmed the large wagon park.[79] Lee was clearly gathering his resources with some urgency from as close at hand as possible; he could not rely on Richmond for much material support. The authorities in the capital were so desperate, reported one refugee, that "an order was issued by the authorities, prohibiting the use of any meat whatever by the citizens, that it must be reserved exclusively for the army." Most importantly, Lee was concentrating both his subsistence and his transportation in his rear, a clear statement that no offensive operations were near at hand.[80] This must have jumped out of the reporting and encouraged Meade to think that Lee would be vulnerable.

Sharpe was also reporting an increase in conscript deserters—men who had recently been conscripted and bolted for Union lines shortly after joining their units. There were also conscripts who had only recently been held in the Castle Thunder prison as Union men, an indication of how desperate were the Confederates for men. There were no reinforcements coming to Lee other than this trickle of less than enthusiastic conscripts. One conscript deserter, John Wieman, whom Sharpe deemed intelligent and reliable, was from Mitchell County, North Carolina. He stated that he came with 16 other conscripts from his county, and "there was very few left to be got." He also revealed that rations "were a quarter of a pound of bacon or a pound of beef and two pints of flour daily. They once had sweet potatoes..."[81]

Meade led the army south across the Rapidan on November 26, hoping to turn Lee's right flank. He hoped to conduct a campaign of maneuver to pry Lee out of his strong positions and force him back to Richmond. Surprise was lost by the lack of celerity displayed by the III Corps commander. Meade was fuming that this had given Lee 48 hours' warning. The weather had turned on the night of the 26th, adding to the army's misery. On the 28th it began to rain as the army edged up to Lee's strongly fortified positions along Mine Run. The cold and wind dried out the mud enough to drag up siege guns, but the cold had become more of an obstacle to operations than the rebel fortifications. "Winter had set in," wrote Patrick who reported that some of the wounded of III Corps had died of the cold, and that supplies were so short that the horses were becoming debilitated from being on half-rations. Everything seemed to be going wrong. And Lee had clearly stopped Meade's offensive in its tracks with formidable field fortifications, with a hearty assist from General Winter. It was now clear what use all those confiscated tools had been put to.

Meade probed for a weak spot to begin his assault. On the 30th Major General Warren, commanding V Corps, called off the attack on his own initiative given the strength of the enemy defenses. Meade flew into a rage and there was a terrible encounter with Warren who gave as good as he got in the exchange. But the troops had learned that their generals had opposed the attack.

Patrick observed the collapse in morale as the army shivered in front of those formidable Confederate field fortifications. "A general feeling of disappointment & despondency had, on Monday night, taken possession of the whole Army—I have never seen the Troops in as good spirits as they had been up to about Sunday..." Early the next morning Sharpe approached him. "There seemed to be so strong a feeling of the hopelessness of an Attack, that Colonel Sharpe, on behalf of the others, came to me to ask that I would go & talk with Meade, to dissuade him from further attempts to attack." Sharpe had become the spokesman for the army staff. He stated frankly that Meade had become so exasperated with his corps commanders that he was "like a Bear with a sore head & no one was willing to approach him—that I was one of his [West Point] Class Mates, and one to whom he had never spoken unkindly I ought to use my influence to carry this point." Convinced of the united opposition of the staff which had surely been in touch with the corps staffs and commanders, Patrick determined to see what was going on. He found that a council of war had just broken up in which Meade had agreed to abandon the campaign.[82]

Winter Politics & Psychological Operations

The army settled back into its camp near Brandy Station. Sharpe's political connections now became a source of information not of the enemy but of machinations in Washington. On December 12 he informed Patrick that Sickles was expanding his confrontation with Meade over events at Gettysburg, that he had shifted his target from Meade to Halleck, demanding an inquiry, and that it was expected that he would replace Halleck as chief of staff. "He is all powerful at the White House & is the Gallant of Mrs. Lincoln, going there at all times. Although the President is Sick—too ill to see persons on business, he is said to call on him at any time." In this reporting, Sharpe showed less of a fine touch than he did with analysis of rebel goings-on. Lincoln was not sufficiently charmed and bluntly told Sickles that no inquiry was necessary. Whatever hopes Sickles had to resume an active command deflated with that, an immense relief to Meade, whom he had made a mortal enemy.[83]

At this time Sharpe took an initiative in formulating and proposing a policy for what would be today called psychological operations. On December 12, while in Washington on the Sickles matter, he recommended in a penetrating memorandum to the military governor of Washington, Brig. Gen. J. H. Martindale, that the Federal Government "adopt a policy of preferential treatment of Confederate deserters or prisoners who wished to stay in the Union" to encourage desertion. The document is so extraordinary and ahead of its time as a subtle and effective example of psychological operations that it is included in its entirely in Appendix K.

Sharpe had put his finger on a bleeding wound of the Army of Northern Virginia—the flood of deserters and the information they were providing the enemy. On April 7, 1864, Lee directed that the men were to be instructed that they were "to preserve entire silence with regard to everything connected with the army, the positions, movements, organizations, or probable strength of any portion of it." Perhaps aware of the enemy's order-of-battle operation, he also ordered that the men be instructed, "not to disclose the brigade, division, or corps to which they belong."[84]

> Sharpe first established his credentials by stating that since January all prisoners, deserters, refugees, and prisoners of state had been the subjects of examinations more or less extended… These examinations have on manifold occasions, and sometimes by request been extended into long and repeated interviews in which the mind and heart of the plain people of the South had been revealed.

He explained that military necessity had caused him in order to obtain valuable information to "hold out to numbers of these prisoners a hope of their speedy liberations, upon their making full discovery of their knowledge of the enemy." He told them that the "Government only desired the insurgents to lay down their arms, and return to their allegiance… Large numbers have gladly embraced these assurances… I am led to express the opinion, carefully formed, that more than a majority of the prisoners of war now held would gladly accept such conditions for their release."

He explained that a significant number of prisoners had been Northern men resident in the South and forced into uniform, as well as Union men from North Carolina and Tennessee. It would be most unwise to return these men to the Confederate ranks through the cartel for the exchange of prisoners. He had also received many letters from prisoners applying for release whose credibility had been established.

A stumbling block that prevented even more men from deserting was the stories told by their officers that they would be immediately pressed in Union uniforms and sent to fight their own people. He recommended that a clear distinction be made between those prisoners who had come over voluntarily or wished to remain with the Union and those who insisted on being exchanged and that such a policy would have the following positive benefits:

That it would create a disorganizing influence within the rebel army, particularly at this juncture, when their conscription is about to be made extreme – that it would create a healthy Union sentiment among the families of those who are set at liberty and permitted to go to work in the North that it would prepare those men to be better citizens when they return south with some of the rewards of labor in their hands and that it would in a considerable measure replenish the field of labor in the North.

Sharpe noted that the "air of confidence and defiance" that had met them last winter at Falmouth was gone and even officers were deserting to them now. Then, as the clever politician, he added, "the President's proclamation would seem to be the fitting opportunity for the action proposed." Lincoln had declared the Proclamation of Amnesty and Reconstruction on December 8, which issued a full pardon and restoration of property to individuals who had taken part in "the existing rebellion," except the highest officers.

Sharpe cautioned that a considerable effort had to be made "in determining the good faith of the men who shall decide not to return to the ranks of the rebel army." There were a significant number of Union army deserters passing themselves off as Confederates in order to escape military service. Many had come by way of the Valley. He then volunteered the BMI as uniquely able to separate the wheat from the chaff.

You will permit me to remark General, not I hope with too much confidence, but what is thoroughly understood by General Patrick and such distinguished officers as have noted our work within the past year, that we are able to give considerable means to assist in determining the good faith of the men who shall decide not to return to the ranks of the rebel army.

We are entirely familiar with the organization of the rebel forces in Virginia and North Carolina, with each regiment, brigade, and division, with the changes therein, and in their officers and locations. These and many other data which have been carefully collected will throw light upon the credit to be given to professions [of loyalty]…

The very day of Sharpe's recommendations Martindale wired Meade requesting the extension of Sharpe's leave in Washington. Lincoln was intensely interested in the success of his proclamation and was frustrated that the Confederate authorities had done so much to ensure no word of it was published. A major reason he would approve Kilpatrick's raid on Richmond next March was the general's promise that the proclamation would be scattered liberally along the way. It is conceivable that his memorandum was brought to the president's attention, though there is no evidence to support it other than circumstantial. Perhaps not so coincidentally, Sharpe's recommendations were embodied in General Order No. 64 issued on February 18, 1864 and would prove to be highly successful.[85]

Both armies had now settled down for the winter, a time of inactivity for everyone but the BMI. Although Sharpe and McEntee would be able to take considerable leave, Babcock and Manning remained to diligently interrogate deserters that the cold and poor rations of the enemy were driving through the Union picket lines. By December 9 they had confirmed when and where the elements of the Army of

Northern Virginia went into winter quarters. The frequency of North Carolinian deserters in particular was an indication of the bottoming enthusiasm for the war in that state which had only reluctantly seceded. Two deserters "reported a strong feeling against the Confederacy by all the N. Carolinians—and a general despondency throughout the South." Sharpe noted, "a disposition to desert is prevalent in many of the N. C. regiment, and only fear of detection and the dishonor attending it, prevents nine tenths of the N. Carolinians coming to the north."[86]

Deserters repeated a consistent story of poor rations—a daily ration of 1 pound of beef and flour each, frequently only half of which was issued. Despite the best efforts of the Confederate quartermaster general, there was a general want of clothing and especially overcoats and blankets. Being cold and hungry with no sign of improvement were compelling inducements to desert, even more so to men whose homes were behind Union lines.

On December 12, Babcock interrogated Chris Latham, a member of the Black Horse captured near his home in Jefferson (today West Falls Church, a Washington suburb). He freely admitted "That the Black Horse company had him scout up in this vicinity, and the members allowed to go to their homes and collect information concerning the movement of General Meade's army." The company had been recruited in Fauquier County, now inside Union lines. Latham most emphatically was not interested in taking the loyalty oath and wanted to be exchanged. That fit in with the knowledge that the entire 4th Virginia—known to be largely from Madison County just to the west of Culpeper—had been disbanded temporarily and the men allowed to go to their homes to "recruit their horses and refit," probably due to the scarcity of fodder for their horses. It was a double-edged problem for Sharpe; it took most of the 4th Virginia out of the game for the winter but left its most effective company within Union lines with the mission to gather intelligence. Not all of the 4th Virginia was as ardent as Latham. David Mulligan of Company B gave himself up after his company was detached for service in the Valley, but he was a rare exception to the 4th Virginia's reputation for loyalty.[87]

Ironically, some of the BMI's most cunning and dangerous opponents also found their homes behind Union lines—Company H, 4th Virginia Cavalry, the famous Black Horse—and they had no intention of deserting. The 4th Virginia fulfilled for Lee the scouting and reconnaissance missions that the BMI shared with its own cavalry. Within that regiment, the Black Horse was an elite, with 80 to 100 men on active service at any one time. The scouts of the BMI had had plenty of encounters with Black Horse patrols in the no-man's land between the armies. Scout Anson Carney had repeated encounters, such as this one, at the end of May along the Rappahannock:

> Carney shot a bushwacker dead and brought his sword and pistol with him but the horse and horse equipments were nor worth bringing along. They sent this man alone and [Carney] tried to capture him alive, but he attempted to get away and he [Carney] shot him through the back. He lived long enough to tell him that he belonged to the 4th Va. Cavalry.[88]

The tables were turned on him in late September in a report written out by Lieutenant Manning:

> When about six miles the other side of Kelly Ford at a place called Crittendon's Mills, about 2 o'clock yesterday after noon Kearney [sic Carney] was surprised by five of the Black Horse Cavalry who had concealed themselves by the roadside. They compelled him to surrender and took away his horse and arms—They also robbed him of his goods, his pocketbook containing $100 in greenbacks & $15 in Confederate money, together with every article of value about him. They then carried him to Elk Run where they halted at a house—Three of them went inside leaving him under charged of the other two—Kearney [sic Carney] was allowed to [walk] to the well under pretence [sic] of getting a drink, when he ran for the woods about 40 yards distant. The guard fired upon him wounding him slightly in the arm but he succeeded in making his escape—He crossed the river near Kelly Ford and came into our lines this morning.

Cline also brought back information on an operational security breach. Humphreys reported the following:

> A scout who was captured by a guerrilla party on the road to Hartwood Church from Warrenton, and has just escaped reports that there is a Lieutenant Embrey [CSA], whose mother lives near Morrisville, whose house is frequented by the officers of our army; that their conversations he overhears, and that he gets newspapers there that are left with his mother by our officers, and that a colonel, particularly leaves newspapers there daily.[89]

The band that had waylaid Cline was part of a group of at least 50 men that was hanging about the lines of Meade's army. Brigadier General Judson Kilpatrick, commanding the 3rd Cavalry Division, reported that they also "have furnished accurate information of our movements to the enemy." The Black Horse and the guerrillas, sometimes indistinguishable, were like a cloud of bold stinging flies, hanging about the Army of the Potomac, raiding, killing pickets, ambushing patrols and were bold enough to pose a threat to the army's main supply route, the Alexandria & Orange Railroad. The correspondence of the army is filled with references to the toll taken by the enemy. It is through this cloud that Cline and the other scouts of the BMI had to carefully make their way. Information on the Black Horse was at a premium. For that reason Sharpe personally interrogated a 10-year-old escaped slave boy who had fled from his master, an officer in the Black Horse. He eagerly offered to show where his hideout was.[90]

Cline and his men were out in all weathers relentlessly gathering information, often using the homes of agents such as Silver as bases. As skilled as he was as a scout, Cline did not seem to run a taut ship. He was letting his men get away with a lot. Patrick, ever a stickler for regular army order and discipline, came down hard on him in a special order on December 23.

> It is ordered that hereafter Milton W. Cline, Chief of Scouts, will be held responsible for the presence of the scouts and guides employed in this Department. All applications for leave to be absent from quarters for any length of time whatever, must be made through him.
>
> The scouts and guides will be held to a more rigid responsibility in care of their horse and equipment in future, and the unserviceable condition of their animals will not be received as an excuse for their being unprepared for duty, unless the same has been properly reported.

> In the absence of the Chief of Scouts, Sergts. Plew and Cole will assume command in the order named, and will perform the duties accordingly.
>
> The Chief of scouts will report any failure or neglect of the men to comply with orders that they may be discharged or ordered back to their commands.[91]

That the order completely bypassed Sharpe could only be seen as a rebuke. But then Patrick had already noted how lax Sharpe was in running his operation in what he considered a businesslike manner.

The only active operation that the BMI could follow in the latter half of December was the recent detachment of Maj. Gen. Jubal Early and several brigades from the Army of Northern Virginia to the Valley. Brigadier General William Averell's Cavalry Division was sweeping through on a destructive raid. Brigadier General Imboden, commanding the only Confederate brigade in the Valley, asked Lee for help. He in turn chose two infantry brigades from Hill's Corps and Fitz Lee's Cavalry Brigade to send and designated Early to command all the forces in the Valley to run Averell down and capture his force.

On the 21st Meade was able to report the BMI's findings so far to Halleck. The scouts had returned with the information obtained by Silver at Orange Court House that Averell had wrecked the depot at Staunton and damaged the railroad. In response, Lee had sent Fitz Lee's and Wickham's cavalry brigades to the Valley. The report was only partially correct on the last item—only Fitz Lee's Brigade had been sent. There was no information on the two infantry brigades or Early yet.[92]

Comings and Goings

One of the major pressures on citizen soldiers such as Sharpe and McEntee is that they left behind business and legal affairs for which they remained responsible, a dilemma that is all too apparent to today's citizen soldiers as they spend extended periods on active duty in the Global War on Terrorism.

On October 17, McEntee had requested 20 days' leave to visit friends in New York, stating that he had been 28 months in service without leave. That was approved, even though the two armies were skirmishing heavily across Bull Run. Sharpe may well have thought he could get along without a subordinate who desperately needed leave. With the end of the campaigning season—after the Mine Run Campaign petered out in late November—active campaigning effectively ceased until the spring. The army encouraged leaves to boost morale and get men out of the winter camps where disease was always a great risk. On December 28 McEntee asked for 15 days to settle his affairs with a business partner. Not even 15 days later he was requesting another 20 days, "for the purpose of being married," a natural response for a soldier who had had so little leave. That too was approved.[93]

The last day of the year ended with an embarrassment for Sharpe and McPhail in the person of George Smith, one of the handful of legacy agents Sharpe had inherited from the army's previous intelligence activities. He was a Northern-born resident of Culpeper County and had originally been working with a topographical unit under Major General Pope. One of his colleagues would say later that George was a "damned rascal; when you are done getting information out of him, turn him over to the Provost Marshal." Sharpe had had reservations about him and designed his missions so that he would "not compromise" the BMI. McEntee became especially suspicious, and Sharpe said to him, "It is well to watch Smith and give him no information, but use him." McEntee later concluded that Smith, as a gentleman, was offended to have to live and comport with scouts, "men with whom he would not have let his negroes associate." A few weeks before Gettysburg, as every hand was needed, he left the BMI claiming he could be of no further use.[94]

He returned later to Sharpe's employ, placed with McPhail in Baltimore to facilitate communications between the two despite some reservations on Sharpe's part. There Smith expressed the hope that his services would be "beneficial and appreciated." The Baltimore Provost Marshal now ruefully admitted, "I have found out what you have expressed, that Smith is very indefinite, and visionary, and I would add very extravagant…" Smith's mission appears to have been to expose espionage in New York City that had tendrils in Baltimore. He kept expressing his great desire to accomplish this mission, yet found ways to postpone it. To McPhail's mortification, "I had all things arranged, and on the evening he was to leave, I found he had run to Washington to consult the highest authority in the Government. President Lincoln plainly told him he had done wrong for he did not want to know anything about such business as he had intrusted it to proper and competent hands, and depended upon them for the results, &c." That was enough for McPhail to state, "I do not consider his services necessary to the interchange of communications which may be needed between us."

This had not been the sort of presidential exposure army officers seek. Fortunately there were no repercussions coming down the chain of command. The next day McPhail sent another message that Smith, who had acquired a War Department job, was on his way to Sharpe to render his resignation. At this point Sharpe could only have been relieved.[95]

Sharpe dealt with civilians on a more frequent basis where his intelligence and provost marshal duties overlapped. A security threat in Virginia was the doubtful loyalty of many civilians living near the army and the possible assistance they could provide the enemy. As a result, Sharpe frequently interrogated arrested civilians and consistently demonstrated a humane and fair approach. All too often, though, he had to admonish arresting officers for careless or unfounded arrests often with no supporting evidence. On December 18, he reported:

> I don't see what Henry Bryant citizen—taken, where he lives, near Union Mills, and where he has lived forever, is arrested and sent here for, without charges of any kind. I have carefully examined him. He seems to be a very inoffensive man, professes to be earnestly attached to

the Union, has been often in the employ of our folks and I believe is honest, when he says he don't know what he is arrested for. He is a simple minded body, has a large family of little ones waiting for him...

He was clearly annoyed at the arresting officer for the harm he had caused an innocent man. Apparently it was an all too often occurrence that needed to be turned around. "I think the officer making the arrest should be called on to toe the mark with a report & that report ought to be followed up, no matter what it is. I believe there to be a good case for a test one."[96]

It would be a slow process. The next month he was reporting that a Mr. Weaver be returned to his home because the arresting officer had provided no reasons for his detention or supporting reasons. He had been arrested despite having on his possession his signed loyalty oath, much to Sharpe's exasperation.[97]

Enter Van Lew

Although December found the armies snug and inactive in their winter quarters, espionage continued its active campaign. On December 8, at the encouragement of sympathetic Unionist visitors, two Union prisoners, Captain Harry S. Howard and John R. McCullough, assistant surgeon of the 1st Wisconsin, escaped from the Libby Prison hospital. They found refuge with Unionists and met one of the most remarkable women of the Civil War. Elizabeth Van Lew was a small, pretty, blonde of iron will and enough guile to rival Ulysses. She and her mother were part of Richmond's wealthy society, but her sympathies and loyalty were with the Union. She was also an ardent abolitionist who had freed the slaves whom she inherited from her father and kept them on as paid employees at her home and farm. Her strength of character had kept the persecuted Unionist minority together in Richmond. Later she and Sharpe would create a partnership that did much to secure victory for the Union. There is no better description of her efforts in the period to date than the testimony Sharpe wrote on her behalf in 1867.

> From the beginning, the family, with all its influences, took a strong position against the rebel movement, and never ceased fighting it until our armies entered Richmond. Their position, character and charities gave them a commanding influence over many families of plain people, who were decided and encouraged by them to remain true to the flag and were subsequently able during the war to receive our agents—assist our prisoners—to conceal those who escaped and to convey information to our armies.
>
> By her talents and enthusiasm Miss Elizabeth L. Van Lew became the leader of the little union party in Richmond, and indeed in Virginia. By her attractive manners and free use of money she soon gained control of the rebel prisons, and our officers and men felt the effects of her care. Regular reports were taken to her of the conditions of our prisoners, and for all and each according to his necessities, she obtained indulgences; for one additional food, for others raiment and bedding, for some a few hours a week more in the fresh air, and for others escape and protection to our lines.

She influenced rebel surgeons to send our men to the hospitals, and when she got them in the hospitals, she alone went from cot to cot where lay a sufferer in blue, while all the other women of Richmond attended the men in gray. In these visits she was attended by her colored servants having beautifully laden baskets, whose contents have been the means of returning many a man to his northern home.

For a long, long time, she represented all that was left of the power of the U.S. Government in the city of Richmond. John Minor Botts wrote from prison for her advice and protection and Franklin Sterns took her orders.

Not only clothing and bedding but even furniture was sent in to prisoners, and I was informed in Richmond by the plain union people that the Van Lews marketed as regularly for Libby Prison, as they did for their own house. They put their hands on whatever of their patrimony they could realize and expended it in what was substantially the service of the U.S. Government.[98]

Her loyalty to the Union demanded action. By the summer of 1862 she was assisting Union prisoners to escape and to make their way to Union lines. On August 14 the *New York Herald* published the account of four Union men, soldiers and civilians, who had escaped. They related how after their escape they "visited a house occupied by a lady of the most thorough going Union sentiments, who furnished us with food and clothing. We also met other Union friends here who did everything in their power to aid our escape." Three days later *The New York Times* wrote that the same men recounted that "Through means of numerous Union sympathizers, our officers in Richmond are kept thoroughly versed in all facts known to the public there."[99]

Harris and McCullough similarly escaped Richmond on December 17 through the help of the underground Unionists who made clothing for them from gray Confederate blankets. By the 19th a letter from Van Lew was in the hands of Maj. Gen. Benjamin Butler, commanding the Army of the James with his headquarters at Fort Monroe. Surgeon McCullough was the likely courier. Captain Harris—who was actually Harry Catlin, one of Butler's scouts—surely guided McCullough to Butler. Both would have briefed Butler on the extent of the Richmond underground. Butler was more than impressed; he was excited at the prospect of acquiring an agent in the heart of the Confederacy from someone he described as "a true union woman as true as steel."[100]

CHAPTER EIGHT

Enter Grant

January–May 1864

Winter Quiet and Regimental Business

The new year found both armies locked into their camps in the deep cold. Things were quiet enough so that Sharpe felt he could also take leave while McEntee was away and leave Babcock in charge. This time Sharpe mixed family and business, the latter being the need to settle an estate in Delaware County for which he was the executor. He obtained an extension of that leave for 30 days from January 19, during which time both Colonel Gates of the 20th NYSM, also on leave, and he spoke at a dinner held at the Second Reformed Dutch Church in Kingston. While in Kingston, he still attended to the needs of his regiment. He was wired from the army to substantiate the claim of Sgt. Silas Deyo for compassionate leave on the death of his father, which he promptly did.[1]

Six weeks after he returned to the army, his mother, Helen Hasbrouck Sharpe, was making herself famous for her services on behalf of the war effort. The Metropolitan Fair was held in New York from late March through April to collect funds for the Sanitary Commission, which did so much to support the troops with medical care and other necessities. Helen Sharpe ran the Knickerbocker Kitchen and gained a "national reputation" for her efforts in support of the troops.[2] The kitchen sold a large number of antiques donated by the people of Kingston, including a portrait of Mrs. Sharpe at age 12. What drew the large crowds were the rooms showing life in earlier, less luxurious times —"the simple articles of household use" that were an intriguing window into the past. "Mrs. A. Bruyn Hasbrouck plied the needle to the old-style calico be[e] quilt, while Mrs. H. Sharpe did the honors at the small spinning wheel." In addition, the kitchen sold meals as they were known in earlier times which were enormously popular. Under Mrs. Sharpe's direction, the kitchen brought in a major part of the funds collected at the fair.[3]

Concern for the 120th was never far from Sharpe's mind, and he continued to involve himself closely with the well-being of his regiment. He was therefore surprised when returning from his leave that Lieutenant Colonel Westbrook had sought and received a medical discharge on February 20, without notifying him. Westbrook had not recovered from his wounds and remained in Kingston, his medical leave being repeatedly extended. On March 15 John Tappen was promoted to lieutenant colonel to take his "place which he has long desired." Captain Lockwood succeeded to his majority. Sharpe confided to his uncle on March 16 that with Tappen in acting command of the 120th, "I shall feel less hesitation about resigning at the end of another campaign—and indeed hope that such successes will be vouchsafed to us as will not make it improper to do so." The sentiment reflected the optimism that attended Grant's arrival. The long, bloody months ahead would put thoughts of resignation aside. Come what may, he concluded, "I shall go straight on and do my duty."[4]

Sharpe was not the only one going on furlough. Both armies used the period of weather-enforced inactivity to furlough a large number of men. It was a vital morale measure and got men out of the cold and poor sanitation of the camps where disease was more likely to fell a man than at home. The Confederates had a more pressing reason the Union armies did not have: the more men on furlough relieved the army of the need to feed them. Lieutenant Manning signed this report for Sharpe on New Year's Day of information brought in from Isaac Silver by the scouts. "Large numbers of furloughs are being granted in General Lee's army and the country on the enemy's right was full of men going and returning. The old man is quite certain that the whole of General Lee's army is on half rations. No movements are talked about or expected."[5] Things were so quiet that Patrick sent Cline and two of his men to Washington to obtain new horses for his scouts on requisition from the quartermaster general.[6]

As the new year began, the only active operation collection priority since mid-December remained refining the strength of enemy forces in the Shenandoah Valley under Maj. Gen. Jubal Early. Initial reporting that month missed most of those forces. By January 5, though, more accurate information had come in from Silver who identified the two infantry brigades. This was supplemented by information provided by deserters and contrabands who continued to brave the brutal weather to come into the Union lines for food and to take advantage of Lincoln's amnesty proclamation. Sharpe was then able to confidently tell Meade, "we know that Walker's [Stonewall] Brigade [Johnson's Div] and Thomas' [George] Brigade]Wilcox's Division] are with Early." He was less accurate on the cavalry, still overestimating the units that had been sent to the Valley including Rosser's, Wickham's, and Jenkins's brigades.[7]

Sharpe's relationship with McPhail not only served his intelligence collection needs but his counterintelligence ones as well. From his perch in Baltimore's nest of intrigue, McPhail often came across information vital to the security of the Army of the Potomac. The army in its winter encampments was in constant need of extra comforts that only sutlers could provide. These small-scale merchants were frequently attached to specific units with whom they had long-term relationships. Their constant presence in the camp and familiar relations with many soldiers made them the ideal cover for both criminal behavior and espionage. On a number of occasions, McPhail was able to warn Sharpe of suspect sutlers who were known to be "sesech" who had no respect for their oath.

McPhail was also able to follow up on a previous warning with more definite information about a Confederate signal station operating across the Potomac that dealt with both messages and merchandise. He provided the details of the operation and its location as well as the houses where the crews were living. The records are silent, as they so often are, of what action was taken, but presumably the sutlers were either arrested or denied the camp and the signal station and its crews seized. Sharpe's own assets were also actively collecting on subversive activities in the army's rear. McEntee reported to Patrick on February 2 of citizens supplying Confederate forces with supplies between Brentsville, Dumfries, and Occoquon, in Prince William Country only 15 miles south of Alexandria, as well as the name of the detective in Alexandria who had vouched for the loyalty of all of them.[8]

Warnings worked both ways. Sharpe was to inform McPhail of Confederate agent William Croft in Baltimore. McPhail responded that the information came just in time. He took two deputies to the hotel Sharpe had identified and arrested Croft and his men 10 minutes after receiving Sharpe's letter.

> I found on his person a certificate for ten shares stock in the Virginia Volunteer Navy Co. of $300 each, a memorandum or cipher, a copy of each of which I enclose. He also had about $900 rebel money and a deed of property in Hanover County, Va., made in Richmond … 1863. He claims to be a British subject, and states that he has been three times since last spring taken then by the conscripting officers and released on his British protection. I have confined him in jail and await the order of the war Department, how to dispose of him.[9]

McPhail and Sharpe did not confine themselves to counterintelligence in this period. McPhail was still running his agent Maddox in Richmond and came up with an ingenious collection operation. McPhail approached Sharpe in a letter of February 14 on a tempting opportunity presented by his agent in Richmond. He said that he could create a level of credibility from senior officials by providing them with a large shipment of uniforms and stationery by running a ship through the blockade for which he could obtain the Navy's cooperation. McPhail needed Sharpe to push the plan through Meade and the War Department. He concluded, "You know my views as we have often talked the subject over. In a word what would it matter to this government if we uniformed a [Confederate] brigade so we gain a point that might cost us hundreds of lives." In middle March he was apparently still pursuing the same proposal, postponed by his go-between with Maddox in Richmond who had been ill. He wrote:

> General Grant would appreciate it, and give such authority as will be necessary to send him in safety. I will arrange with navy Dept. It could be well in case you can get the required paper from General Grant, to send me as you have done before memorandum of the information desired by you for the army, I will make all efforts to obtain it.[10]

The cold, want of clothing, and starvation rations continued to drive Confederate deserters into the Union picket lines. These miseries made taking advantage of the president's amnesty all the more compelling. A deserter from the 14th Alabama related in a report of January 10 that "five men of his company came out on picket barefooted on the snowy ground. Rations of late have been one pint of flour, 1/4 pound of pickled beef, daily, and sometimes bacon." Sharpe's interrogations were reflecting a growing breakdown in the Confederate Government's ability to sustain its armies. Lee wrote to Davis on January 11, describing his army's "crying necessity for food, and the evil may extend further than has been brought to my knowledge, and may exist on distant lines of communication." Quartermaster invoices on rail showed a loss of 5,000 pounds of bacon (20,000 rations) on route just between Richmond and Orange Court House. His investigation showed no real security on the trains, which evidently were being plundered along the way. He feared that if the loss was so great on such a short run, how much greater must it be on lines further south leading into Richmond.[11]

On March 1 Sharpe produced an analysis of the 402 interrogations from 222 deserters and 180 prisoners of war that had come into the army's hands December through February. They were broken down by command and by arm of service. A. P. Hill's Corps accounted for 72 losses and Ewell's 112 (here Babcock makes an error in addition, totaling only 177 when the correct figure is 184) and Stuart's Cavalry Corps only 19. By arm he showed:

Infantry	177 (should be 184)
Cavalry	19
Artillery	8
1st Virginia Bn	12
Scouting Commands	6

The last two figures were of special counterintelligence value. The 1st Virginia Battalion, also known as the Irish Battalion, was Lee's provost marshal unit assigned to his headquarters, which dealt with prisoners of war and other security matters. The scouts would also have been sources of the enemy's collection priorities and agents within Union lines. If they were from Lee's own select group of scouts, such as the man Hammond described in the previous chapter, they may have been of great value. Unfortunately, it is not known how many from this last group were genuine deserters and how many prisoners of war, most likely unforthcoming like Hammond. The men from the 1st Virginia were surely deserters.[12]

Beginning in January, the abstracts from the field return of the Army of Northern Virginia included strength figures for its headquarters provost guard as well as an entry for "battalion scouts, guides, and couriers." These were organizations analogous to Patrick's provost marshal brigade and the scouting and guide elements of the BMI. Whereas Patrick's brigade numbered about 2,000, the 1st Virginia Battalion rarely exceeded 300. Stonewall Jackson had designated the battalion as his corps provost guard in October 1862, and it was transferred after Chancellorsville to Lee's headquarters to fulfill the same function. It was notorious for desertion and poor discipline. The number of scouts, guides, and couriers goes from about 100 in January to 230 in late April.[13]

In comparison, Sharpe never had more than 60–70 men in the BMI at any one time, of whom 40–50 were scouts and guides. Meade had refused Sharpe's attempts to increase the size of the BMI, citing reasons of economy. He did make an exception when his chief of orderlies, Sergeant Patrick McEneany, requested to join the scouts. Both Generals Meade and Humphreys recommended him to Sharpe. McEneany was to prove this worth in the succeeding campaigns to the end of the war.[14]

A unique group of four deserters from the 17th Battalion Provost Guard at Orange Court House came in late February. Their duty was to control the new conscripts to the Army of Northern Virginia who would come by train every day from Richmond. They would all be immediately put in the general confinement facility of the basement of the court house along with men awaiting court-martial sentence and men apprehended absent without leave. The next day they would be sent to their regiments on their own, all except the men from North Carolina who had to be sent under guard. After close questioning, they estimated that Lee had received 5,000 conscripts since the fall, at a rate of 30–40 a day.[15]

Also in late February, Capt. Jacob Rotte, Company E, 48th Mississippi, Posey's Brigade, who was officer of the pickets for his regiment, deserted with his first lieutenant and most of his own company. He was able to give a precise strength of the brigade (1,180) by regiment. The 48th Mississippi, which had been reduced to 128 men, had not received any conscript replacements since the fall until 22 had recently arrived, four of them cripples. Rations had improved and "now are 1 ¼ lb corn meal & 1 ¼ lb pork—which they say is enough. Occasionally a little coffee, sugar & rice are issued—but this is very rare." The reports of Confederate rations never mention fruit or vegetables. The winter season would have been especially barren, contributing to the breakdown of health caused by vitamin deficiency. Rotte stated it was the opinion of the army's officers that Longstreet's Corps would never return to the Army of Northern Virginia.[16]

Maintaining and refining order-of-battle estimates was a continuous process. Sharpe would later attest, "Throughout the last years of the war, a roster of the strength of the rebel Army of Northern Virginia was kept at the Union head-quarters, and there was not a regiment, Brigade, or division of the Confederate forces whose position and numbers were not known to us through the various sources of information…"

Unfortunately, there are no extant tables from the BMI with the details of those in April and May 1863, but there are references to such estimates being regularly provided to the corps commanders. McPhail through his agents in Baltimore contributed to those estimates, and in one case precisely enough to conclude that his information was obtained from official Confederate sources. In a letter in cipher to Sharpe dated February 14, he provided strength figures for a number of Confederate commands. For January he gave a strength of 46,000 to the Army of Northern Virginia. The returns for that army of January 10 showed 46,313 men present for duty. Currently, because of 6,000 furloughs, detachments, and disbandment of cavalry units due to lack of forage, Lee's strength had fallen to 35,000. His army's returns for January 31 showed a strength of 38,604 men present for duty. It does not get much better than that. An additional interesting piece of information had 19,000 Confederate troops concentrating around the Union enclave in New Berne less to threaten that place than to "overawe Union sentiment" in North Carolina.[17]

Beginning this year the BMI maintained a file on all Southern newspapers that came into its hands. These files—along with the other various documents such as captured letters and journals, as well as order-of-battle files—required a significant increase in the number of wagons and teamsters allotted to the BMI.[18]

Unknown to Sharpe at this time, Butler was about to find the permanent source of information in Richmond that had eluded both Sharpe and McPhail. After securing Van Lew's bona fides, he sent his scout Harry Catlin into Richmond in January to ask for her help in securing information. She accepted eagerly, and Catlin provided her a cipher and taught her how to use "a peculiar kind of ink and writing materials." Butler now had a regular source of largely accurate information in the heart of the Confederacy as Van Lew organized the Unionists in Richmond for the task.[19]

Van Lew responded quickly in a ciphered letter dated January 30, which Butler received on February 4 and passed on to Stanton the next day. Butler closely questioned the messenger, probably the son William S. Rowley, Van Lew's closest associate. Most of the information was from two sources, a man who insisted on being called Quaker and Charles Palmer, who advocated a rapid descent on Richmond. Palmer was one of the wealthiest men in the Unionist underground and a slaveholder.

Van Lew opened the letter, however, with the notice that the Confederate authorities would shortly transfer the Union prisoners in the city to Georgia. The message would lead to two major actions by Union forces.

DEAR SIR

It is intended to remove to Georgia very soon all the Federal prisoners; butchers and bakers to go at once. They are already notified and selected Quaker knows this to be true. Are building batteries on the Danville road.

This from Quaker: Beware of new and rash council. Beware! This I send you by direction of all your friends. No attempt should be made with less than 30,000 cavalry, from 10,000 to 14,000 infantry to support them, amounting in all to 40,000 or 45,000 troops. Do not underrate their strength and desperation. Forces could probably be called into action from five to ten days 25,000, mostly artillery. Hoke's and Kemper's brigades gone to North Carolina; Pickett's in or about Petersburg. Three regiments of cavalry disbanded by General Lee for want of horses. Morgan is applying for a 1,000 choice men for a raid.[20]

Butler seized upon the vulnerability of Richmond and wrote to Stanton, "Now or never, is the time to strike." The additional objective of freeing Union prisoners was also cited, and that was something that would interest Lincoln.

Butler had appealed to Maj. Gen. John Sedgwick, acting commander of the Army of the Potomac during Meade's illness, in a cipher message to threaten Richmond at the same time. It is clear from Sedgwick's reply on February 4 that Butler's message had included the strength figures supplied by Van Lew. There is no evidence that he also communicated information on the source, although it is likely if Halleck simply forwarded the messages Butler had sent Stanton. The message was shown to Sharpe for comment. His report was incorporated into Sedgwick's reply:

> The only troops sent from Lee's army on the Rapidan to North Carolina are two brigades of infantry and one or two regiments of cavalry, numbering in all between 3,000 and 4,000 men. No portion of Lee's army is in Richmond, unless some of the troops mentioned above have been stopped there… Two brigades from Pickett's division have been sent recently from James River or the vicinity of Richmond to North Carolina.

Sedgwick underlined the accuracy of Sharpe's figures, "The information upon this head is exact and positive." Meade's aide, Lt. Col. Theodore Lyman, described the interchange in a letter and commented that Butler had claimed that "large reinforcement had been sent from the Rapid Ann to North Carolina…" Van Lew did not state that large reinforcements had been sent, only two brigades. Butler may have been embellishing Van Lew's information, and Sharpe's citation of the low strength of those two brigades was meant to correct Butler's assertion.[21]

Interestingly, Sharpe confirmed some of the essentials in Van Lew's letter. They agreed that two brigades had been sent by Lee to North Carolina, and Sharpe was able to add the detail of their strength; that the Pickett's division was in the vicinity of Richmond/Petersburg, although Sharpe had the important detail that two of his brigades had been sent to North Carolina. Sharpe added that no part of Lee's army was in Richmond, probably a reference to Van Lew's assertion that the garrison could probably be increased to 25,000.

Sedgwick closed by stating that Lee was so firmly entrenched so close to his army that a demonstration would have no effect. Butler then appealed to Halleck, who ordered Sedgwick the next day to assist Butler anyway. As Sedgwick predicted, his demonstration failed to have any effect on Lee.[22]

Butler's plan, however, was revealed by a deserter from his army, and the Confederates were able to frustrate the Union attempt on the city on February 7. The second Union action triggered by Van Lew's notice about the transfer of prisoners would not take place until the end of the month. This effort would require the full cooperation and participation of the BMI.[23]

If Sharpe did in fact see Van Lew's figures, he probably was impressed. He had received valuable information from McPhail's agents in Richmond, but they were not permanent sources, and probably not connected to the Unionist underground. The prospects inherent in an organized underground in Richmond could only have excited Sharpe's interest. However, Van Lew was Butler's asset, for now.

The Scouts Who Came in From the Cold

A hard winter blew in with the new year, dropping temperatures below zero. As the armies on both sides huddled and suffered in their winter quarters, Sharpe kept the BMI, and especially its scouts, busy. It took a steely resolve to send men out into that cold again and again, especially when he knew that they would be crossing the Rappahannock repeatedly and lying out in the weather at all hours. Some would suffer permanent impairment to their health as subsequent appeals for pensions would attest. The effects were immediate as well in some cases. In May Sharpe would send a scout to Major General Hancock with a request that the man had "to ride in an ambulance having lost part of one of his feet while lying within the enemy's lines during the late snow-storm." To make the crossing less brutal and more efficient, he acquired a special inflatable rubber boat for them. Sharpe never forgot the quiet sacrifice and did everything in his power to secure pensions for these men after the war, particularly the civilian scouts for whom special acts of Congress were required to add them to the pension rolls. Among these would be Judson Knight and William Lee.[24]

The scouts had set up a hide-out or depot, as they called it, across the Rappahannock near Isaac Silver's home. On one occasion at this time, they were surprised to find three men using their tent when they arrived. Two of them claimed to be Butler's scouts, who had been unable to leave Richmond by way of the Peninsula but had been directed by Unionists to Silver who could help them back to Union lines through the Army of the Potomac. The third was a young Confederate deserter they had picked up on the way. The small shelter was overcrowded, and the newcomers refused to cooperate and share information and in general made themselves obnoxious. In order to get them across the river, two of Sharpe's scouts stayed behind. Butler's men, refusing to follow instructions, swamped the old boat in crossing the river and drowned the young deserter. On arriving at Sharpe's office, they apparently made themselves equally obnoxious to him and refused to answer any of his questions. Undoubtedly to the glee of his own scouts, who had had enough of these two, he promptly threw them into the Bull Pen, the nickname for the prisoner-of-war cage, until communication with Butler verified their identities.

Sharpe had a more immediate problem—half of his scouts were stranded on the enemy side of the river with no boat to fetch them. He immediately ordered the carpenters of one of the provost marshal regiments, probably his old 20th NYSM, to build a new boat to get the two scouts out that very night. The boat was speedily finished and carried in the dark through the picket lines to avoid civilian eyes.

Nevertheless, they came across one man and passed the boat off as a coffin. They slipped the boat into the icy river and saw it disappear with its rescue crew into the dark for the other side. The other scouts waited with their own picket reserve through the next day and at night returned to the shore. Their worry increased as no boat appeared. As light began to break, they again moved back through the picket line, but their fears were dispelled when a cavalryman shouted, "Your boys are in!" They had arrived earlier than expected.[25]

During this fallow period of late winter and early spring, Sharpe's scouts had been continuously working back and forth across the Rappahannock, picking up information from Isaac Silver. Judson Knight described the concealed point of entry through the enemy pickets that nature had provided across the river:

> Coming down to the edge of the river from the south was a ravine, which commenced about half a mile from the river, and gradually grew steeper and narrower as it approached the river, until at the river's edge the sides of the ravine were very precipitous and at least 100 feet high. At some time in the past, and not many years previous to the war, a wind-storm had thrown nearly all the trees down, and they now lay across the ravine, some broken in two, so that one had to crawl under them; in a few places you could stand upright. The place was considered utterly impassable, and no attempt was made to have any pickets in the ravine, they always being stationed on the top on each side. The boys went through and came out a half mile inside enemy lines.[26]

The Dahlgren Affair

In late February the path of the *beau sabre*, Colonel Dahlgren, crossed Sharpe's again. He recovered from the loss of his leg with none of his aggressiveness dimmed. Visiting his father commanding the Southern Blockading Squadron at Charleston that fall, he volunteered to lead a raid on the Confederate coast. Admiral Dahlgren pointed out that being an army officer and on crutches with a cork leg disqualified him for command of the naval landing force. But he did let him go along as a volunteer, with four boatloads of Marines that cut out an enemy schooner and left her in flames on New Year's Day, 1864.[27]

While Dahlgren was visiting his father, a document came into Sharpe's possession. It occurs alone in the BMI files with no note of explanation of its origin or its date, but it is mixed with the correspondence from James McPhail, provost marshal in Baltimore, and was most likely one of his agent reports that he regularly sent to the BMI. Sharpe thought it important enough to copy part of it out in his own hand, label it "extract," and cover its origin with four x's centered on top and bottom. From its viewpoint and the events discussed it appears to have originated from a Union sympathizer in Richmond and may have been written in late November or early December, 1863. It boldly advocated a coup de main to "capture Richmond," and "burn the government buildings, release the federal prisoners, and carry off Jeff Davis." It provided details on the small guard forces in Richmond and routes to be used as well as a knowledge of the economic and transportation dynamics of

Richmond and surrounding regions vital to the Southern war effort. Speculation on its originator centers on Samuel Ruth, the superintendent of the Fredericksburg Railroad and a strong Unionist. Ruth had been born and raised in Pennsylvania and had moved to Richmond at the age of 21 and was highly regarded in Richmond both for his loyalty to the South and his efficiency in directing railroad operations despite complaints from J. E. B. Stuart on the mysterious slowness of his trains in the transportation of troops at critical times.[28]

Ruth was to become one of Sharpe's most valuable informants, but that would not be for almost a year, when the armies had settled into the siege of Petersburg. Ruth had, however, made contact with Brig. Gen. Judson Kilpatrick, now commanding the 3rd Cavalry Division, "on May 4, 1863 at Ayletts King William County and stayed with him two days." The two appeared to be on friendly terms. It is not unreasonable to assume that the two discussed the possibilities of such a raid.[29]

The issue of the fate of Union prisoners in Richmond had become urgent with the arrival Van Lew's letter announcing the imminent transfer of Union prisoners from Richmond to Georgia. Georgia was the hot button, for it signified transfer to the already infamous death camp at Andersonville. But she counseled against rash action and that any attempt to rescue the prisoners be conducted by an extremely strong force because the Confederates would be able to concentrate 25,000 men around the capital in five to ten days. "Do not underrate their strength and desperation," she advised. Butler's cover letter to Secretary of War Stanton on February 4 endorsed Van Lew's suggestion of rescue but without any of Van Lew's cautionary statements. Butler's failed attempt to take Richmond on the 2nd was partially due to the neglect of this warning.[30]

The issue of the mistreatment of Union prisoners in Richmond had become notorious in the North, and Lincoln was under great pressure to take some action. Butler was considering such an attempt and requested Meade's assistance to launch a diversionary attack. It was probably from this request that Kilpatrick's ambition was ignited over the fame that such an enterprise would bring him if he led it instead of Butler. It is at this point that Sharpe may have become involved. Kilpatrick and he apparently were on friendly terms that lasted long after the war; Sharpe would invite Kilpatrick to be the guest of honor at the 1879 reunion of his regiment in Kingston. Both Kilpatrick and he had a taste for special operations of this sort. It was Sharpe's support of the raid made by Dahlgren and Cline that snatched the dispatches from Cooper and Davis meant for Lee on July 2 that had contributed to the victory at Gettysburg. That could not have been far from his mind. He may well have encouraged Kilpatrick that such a raid was feasible. Knowing that going through the chain of command with his plan would see it killed, Kilpatrick went directly to political friends with Lincoln's ear, chiefly Senator Jacob B. Howard. Before his machinations could bear fruit, Butler made the attempt on February 6 with a force under the command of Maj. Gen. Isaac Wistar from the Peninsula, but the plan was betrayed by a deserter and failed.

The pressure to do something about the prisoners increased for Lincoln with this failure and with the news on February 11 that a large number of Union officer prisoners had broken out of Libby Prison in a daring escape (aided by Van Lew). Now, on the evening of the 11th, Lincoln recalled Senator Howard's recommendation of Kilpatrick's plan. He telegraphed Kilpatrick to report to him in Washington immediately. The next day he presented his plan to Lincoln who approved of its general objectives. Kilpatrick was surprised to find that Lincoln had a competing motive. He had been disappointed that his amnesty proclamation of December had not brought more Confederate defectors and thought that it was due simply to the failure of the news to reach the Southern population. Kilpatrick quickly seized on the opening to include in his plan the distribution of leaflets on the way to Richmond. Lincoln was pleased and approved the outline of the plan and sent him to Secretary of War Stanton for more precise instructions.[31]

Meade must have gone into one of his tantrums when he received the order to support Kilpatrick's scheme. Nevertheless, though he and Pleasonton looked askance at the plan and distanced themselves from it immediately, they provided as ordered all the resources required. Those resources included not only the 4,000 cavalry Kilpatrick wanted but the active participation of the BMI. Sharpe concentrated the efforts of the BMI on this mission. At this point Dahlgren joins the expedition. He had just returned from his stay with his father's squadron. He called on Lincoln, who was delighted to see the engaging young man and learned from the president of the raid. It was just the sort of glorious adventure he was seeking. He traveled to army headquarters at Brandy Station to meet with Kilpatrick on February 24 to offer his services. Kilpatrick was pleased to obtain the services of the famous young colonel, especially one who was in such favor with the president and secretary of war.[32]

Ominously, Babcock shared Meade's clear dislike of the plan and referred to it negatively as a "scheme" rather than a plan. Strangely, for a man normally so concerned with counterintelligence, Sharpe confided in a letter to his wife about the raid, which she freely related to Patrick when he encountered her at Willard's Hotel in Washington on the night of February 27.

Babcock identified Confederate defenses and the forces of the Richmond garrison, and McEntee would personally accompany Kilpatrick's larger part of the expedition. Just before the expedition departed, a man delivered this message to Dahlgren from Babcock: "At the last moment I have found the man you want; well acquainted with the James River from Richmond up... Question him for five minutes, and you will find him the very man you want." This was the freedman Tom Heath, a bricklayer from Goochland County.[33]

On the 28th Sharpe sent Dahlgren a note in which he stated that he had delivered Confederate uniforms to two men the young colonel had sent. In addition to

McEntee, Sharpe sent some of his best scouts on the expedition of which he also informed Dahlgren.[34] Sergeant Cline, his chief of scouts, accompanied McEntee and Kilpatrick with several other scouts. Of those that accompanied Dahlgren were Sergeant Anson B. "Gus" Carney, his cousin Phil Carney, Jake Swisher, a man named Dykes, and Martin Hogan, a 19-year-old Irish immigrant who had been in the country only three years. Dykes is a shadowy figure whom Dahlgren for some unknown reason distrusted. Sharpe in his note states, "We have no reason to doubt Dykes. You can inquire fully about him from Cline and others of our men, who consider him above suspicion."[35]

They proved their worth almost immediately on February 28, in the words of the BMI's future chief scout, Sgt. Judson Knight:

> [Hogan, with] a few of the Headquarters scouts … with some volunteers from the cavalry comprising the raiding party of Kilpatrick and Dahlgren, volunteered to wade the river at Ely's Ford, carrying their arms over their heads to keep them dry. Hogan was in the advance, and he crept up to the first rebel picket, surprised, disarmed, and made him show the way to the next post telling him to answer properly when challenged, or he was a dead man; and from him to the third and last post, whom he also captured without a shot; after which exploit the house where the reserve picket was quartered was surrounded, and Hogan told the boys when they heard a shot inside the house to smash the windows and cover the party inside with their carbines. Then boldly marching to the door he threw it wide open and sprang inside, shouting, "SURRENDER, YOU REBEL SONS OF A GUNS!" firing his pistol into the floor as he said it. Instantly several carbines were thrust through the glass and over 20 men, including a Captain and Lieutenant of a South Carolina cavalry regiment surrendered. Taking his prisoners to the river Hogan told them that as he and his men had waded the river to pay their respects to them, they might wade it back, while he and his men would ride their horses across which they did, and the Confederate captain complained bitterly to Gen. Kilpatrick of the indignity of his treatment.[36]

Cline sent back a report that Dahlgren was at Spotsylvania as of 2:00 a.m. on February 29, when Kilpatrick's column was 2 miles beyond Chancellorsville and that no alarm had been given by the enemy. Meade ordered Sharpe to pass the information to the Cavalry Corps commander to keep him informed. Hampton's Cavalry Division was below Richmond in anticipation of an attack from Butler's Army of the James. Sharpe thought that the plan was off to a good start. He could not have been more wrong. Two Confederate scouts had joined the end of the column and rode with it until they could break off and give the alarm.[37]

Sharpe found himself carrying the entire load of the BMI as this operation unfolded, with McEntee riding off with Kilpatrick and Babcock sent on another mission. He would write, "I was worked night and day during our late operations." He tried to follow the course of the raid as best he could, but the technologies of the time did not allow for the rapid transmission of information in the midst of active operations. He would not have been gratified had he been able to track the operation. As it was, his scouts were picking up surprisingly accurate echoes of the chaos behind Confederate lines. His scouts just back in reported that Silver had got into Orange Court House on March 1 and discovered that two cavalry brigades had been sent in pursuit and that the telegraph wires had been cut and the Virginia Central disrupted, and that Lee's army was ordered to prepare three days of cooked rations. Fifteen hundred Union troops were supposed to be at Madison Court House. He tried to return that night but was turned away by tightened security. Other rumors spoke of 6,000 Yankees rampaging through Walker's Tavern [Walkerton Tavern) in Henrico County right outside Richmond.[38]

Because of Kilpatrick's poor planning and bad luck, the raid collapsed into disaster. Dahlgren's luck finally ran out, and on March 2 he was killed attempting to exfiltrate his command from enclosing Confederate forces. Of the five BMI scouts with Dahlgren, four (Phil Carney, Swisher, Dykes, and Hogan) were captured, along with freedman Heath, another freedman from Goochland County who had joined the expedition. Only Gus Carney escaped, though badly wounded; the ball that went through his right hip nicked his spine. He was immediately evacuated from White House to a hospital near Washington. McEntee would blame Cline's unexplained disobedience of orders for the capture of these scouts. After their capture, Martin Hogan was so distressed at the condition of Dahlgren's body that he begged for a coffin but was ignored by the Confederate soldiers. A friendly schoolteacher helped him find a coffin, and Martin carved a headboard with the fallen colonel's name.[39]

On Dahlgren's body were found orders that would ignite a firestorm of Southern outrage. The orders were an exhortation to his men to burn Richmond and kill Jefferson Davis and the Confederate cabinet. The orders were a clear violation of the rules of war at the time. Kilpatrick authenticated the main body of the orders but denied having seen or approved of the lines exhorting arson and murder. Meade responded to Lee's direct enquiry denying any official approval of such actions, but he had deep suspicions of Kilpatrick's honesty. Captain McEntee, who accompanied Kilpatrick on the raid, had doubts about him and openly called him a liar to Provost Marshal Patrick, who recorded in his diary, "He has the same opinion of Kilpatrick that I have and says he managed just as all cowards do. He further says, that he thinks the papers are correct that were found upon Dahlgren, as they correspond with what D. told him." Babcock was equally clear in comments which were probably based on his own conversations with McEntee. "Letters found on Dahlgren's body published in the Richmond papers—authentic report of contents."[40] Given McEntee's reputation for probity, the indictment of Kilpatrick is damning.

Another scandal also surfaced but quickly fell out of sight. According to a cavalryman writing 30 years later, when Dahlgren ordered the destruction of a store of whiskey they had come across, the men, including the guide Martin, helped themselves, and Martin helped himself so much that thereafter "he lost his head, and the right road." Dahlgren, who was not aware of Martin's condition, repeatedly asked him when they would arrive at the crossing, and Martin answered that they would come to it soon—a big swinging gate leading to the ferry. Instead he led them up to a Confederate fort. Other, more contemporaneous, accounts state that when they arrived at the James River ford, the water level had risen so much a crossing was impossible. In a rage, thinking he had been deceived, as he saw it, Dahlgren turned to Carney and ordered, "Carney, have that nigger hung alongside of the road within 15 minutes." Carney had the man swinging in less than 10. Carney related this event 30 years later in a story in *The National Tribune*. Shortly after the raid, the *Richmond Examiner* made much of the hanging in its headline, "Murder of Their Negro Guide by the Raiders," referring to it as a "barbarous atrocity" discovered a few hours later by Dahlgren's Confederate pursuers. This reporting was supported by Kilpatrick's chief of scouts, John W. Landegon, who questioned the Dahlgren survivors and was convinced that "the hanging of that poor black man was a cruel and cowardly murder," and wrote, "My experience with Southern blacks during the war proved to me that they were truly loyal to us, and were ever ready and willing to peril their lives to aid a Union soldier."[41]

Nevertheless, Dahlgren had legal justification for his actions. General Orders No. 100, dated April 24, 1863, stated, "Guides, when it is clearly proved that they have misled intentionally, may be put to death." How well that justification could have held up under scrutiny is another question. Clearly, Dahlgren was under great stress. He saw his chance to fulfill his mission in ruins at that point, and in his mind the man's guilt was "clearly proved" by the unfordable river. Whatever his reasons, his order to hang Robinson left a blot on an otherwise sterling reputation.[42]

Meade suspected the worst but did his best to distance himself from the fiasco. In this he was able to truthfully assert that the plan to release the prisoners had originated with Kilpatrick. Using a friendly senator as a go-between, the cavalry general had been invited to brief Lincoln, who approved of the raid solely to liberate the prisoners and sever Confederate communications. Lincoln then directed him to Secretary of War Stanton. There is no record of their conversation, but Stanton was clearly a far more ruthless and brutal man than the president. On occasion, in referring to Davis he had quoted Henry II's wish about Thomas Becket, "Will no one rid me of this man?" Kilpatrick was just as eager to curry favor and just as unscrupulous as Henry's barons 600 years before. Conceivably, Stanton could have given Kilpatrick secret instructions which he then passed on to Dahlgren. The young colonel may well have had serious reservations about them because the only man he shared them with was McEntee, someone whose confidence he valued. This would have been right before the departure of the expedition because McEntee rode with Kilpatrick's column.[43] No other member of his command, including his second-in-command, knew of the orders for arson and murder. In fact, the second-in-command, Captain Mitchell, affirmed exactly the opposite, "I know that it was not Colonel Dahlgren's intention to kill Jeff. Davis, in case he should be captured."[44] Further critical testimony was given by Lieutenant Bartley, a signal officer and Dahlgren's only staff officer:

I knew all his plans, what he intended to do and how he intended doing it, and I know that I never received any such instructions as those papers are said to contain. I also heard all the orders and instructions given to the balance of the officers of the command. Men cannot carry out orders they know nothing of. The colonel's instructions were, that if we were successful in entering the city, to take no life except in combat; to keep all prisoners safely guarded, but to treat them with respect; liberate all the Union prisoners, and destroy the public buildings and government stores, and leave the city by way of the Peninsula.[45]

Given Dahlgren's upstanding and chivalrous reputation, and Bartley's account mirrors it faithfully, it is difficult to reconcile the orders with his character and the fact that officers and men of his command had already been given exactly the opposite instructions. The most likely explanation is that the orders contained instructions given by Kilpatrick, which originated or were approved by Stanton without Lincoln's knowledge. Dahlgren had dutifully recorded them, but his reservations were such that he had decided not to execute them. He may well have kept them as evidence of the calumny of his superior officers. History will never know, for his intentions died with him. Significantly, after the war Stanton ordered all documents concerning the raid found in Confederate hands—to include the original orders and Dahlgren's notebook—to be brought to him. They have never been seen again. Yet, doubt remains and may never be resolved, for the mask of chivalry fell from this hero and let loose the worst angel of his nature when he hanged Martin.[46]

Even in death Dahlgren and the BMI retained a connection. Reports that his body had been mutilated prompted Sharpe's future chief spy in Richmond, the redoubtable Miss Van Lew, to organize a team of agents to recover and hide it until after the war when it was recovered and returned to his father.[47]

Meade had wisely kept his distance from this ill-starred adventure. He had no love for Kilpatrick, and in a letter to his wife, summed up the outcome. "You have doubtless seen that Kilpatrick's raid was an utter failure. I did not expect much from it. Poor Dahlgren I am sorry for."[48]

Meade had his own reputation to worry about. He wrote to his wife on April 18 as the pot continued to boil over what was to be called the Dahlgren Affair. Lee had sent him photographic copies of the documents found on Dahlgren's body, and asked pointed questions:

... whether these papers were authorized, sanctioned or approved by the Government of the United States, or Col. Dahlgren's superior officers. This is a pretty ugly business; for in denying having authorized or approved "the burning of Richmond, or killing Mr. Davis and Cabinet," I necessarily threw odium on Dahlgren. I, however, enclosed a letter from Kilpatrick, in which the authenticity of the papers was impugned; but I regret to say Kilpatrick's reputation, and collateral evidence in my possession, rather go against this theory. However, I was determined my skirts should be clear, so I promptly disavowed having ever authorized, sanctioned or approved of any act, not required by military necessity, and in accordance with the usages of war.[49]

Meade was anxious to get his surviving scouts back, though, a mark of their value to him. On March 11 Sharpe wired McEntee at Fortress Monroe, "The general commanding desires you to return to headquarters with such of our men as are unhurt." They were to travel through Washington and leave Kilpatrick to come as he may.[50]

The four captured scouts were thrown into the Confederate prisons in Richmond, destined for Andersonville. Tom Heath, however, was due a special fate. P. H. Aylett, the Confederate District Attorney of Richmond, wrote to Major General Winder, in charge of the POW prisons in the city, "He has clearly been guilty of the crime of communicating intelligence to the enemy, giving him aid and comfort and holding intercourse with the enemy without necessity and without the permission of the Confederate States, he may therefore be imprisoned and denied all recourse to the writ of habeas corpus." He would recommend hard labor in addition to the summary imprisonment, because, "The crime with which he is charged is one of such frequent occurrence that an example should be made of Heath. It is a matter of notoriety in the sections of the Confederacy where raids are frequent that the guides of the enemy are nearly always free negroes and slaves."[51] Ironically, no better witness to the truth of that last sentence would have been Sharpe himself.

Enter Grant

The fiasco was happily put aside upon the arrival of Ulysses S. Grant to his headquarters at Brandy Station on an official visit on March 10. Grant had just been made general-in-chief of the armies and promoted to lieutenant general on March 1. The promotion required the momentous revival of the rank held only once before in American history—by George Washington himself. Grant had intended to replace Meade, but their meeting was so cordial and Meade so willing to put the good of the country over his own ambition that Grant decided there and then to retain him in command. At that time Grant informed Meade that he would accompany the Army of the Potomac in the upcoming campaign of 1864. Grant was determined not to sit behind a desk despite the fact that he knew that his presence with the Army of the Potomac would on occasion infringe on Meade's authority. His primary concern was to ensure the destruction of Lee's army, and that required his presence.[52]

He would quickly become acquainted with the work of the BMI and developed a healthy interest in it. Sharpe began visiting his headquarters frequently.[53] In the process he naturally came in contact with Grant's staff, all of whom had come with him from the west. They were not part of the Army of the Potomac fraternity. Sharpe could see that they were protective of Grant, and he must have realized it was up to him to get along with them so that they would facilitate and not hinder his budding relationship with Grant. When it came time to join that staff in July, he apparently found no enemies there. The Sharpe charm had worked.

On April 8, 1864, Grant announced his staff:

Brig. Gen. John A. Rawlins, chief of staff
Lt. Col. T. S. Bowers, assistant adjutant-general
Lt. Col. C. B. Comstock, senior aide-de-camp
Lt. Col. O. E. Babcock, aide-de-camp
Lt. Col. F. T. Dent, aide-de-camp
Lt. Col. Horace Porter, aide-de-camp
Lt. Col. W. L. Duff, assistant inspector-general
Lt. Col. W. R. Rowley, secretary
Lt. Col. Adam Badeu, secretary
Capt. E. S. Parker, assistant adjutant-general
Capt. George K. Leek, assistant adjutant-general, in charge of office in Washington
Capt. P. T. Hudson, aide-de-camp
Capt. H. W. James, assistant quartermaster-general on special duty at headquarters
1st Lieut. W. M. Dunn, Jr., 83rd IN Vols., acting aide-de-camp[54]

The most important staff officer was Brevet Maj. Gen. John A. Rawlins, Grant's chief of staff and his closest and most influential friend and confidant. Shortly after taking command of the 45th Illinois Volunteer Infantry in 1861 Grant had asked him to give up his law practice and become his aide-de-camp. They had been through everything together. Rawlins was a natural chief of staff with great attention to detail. There was no man that Grant trusted more. When his appointment as chief of staff of the Armies of the United States was before the Senate, Grant wrote an influential senator that Rawlins "comes the nearest to being indispensable to me of any officer in the service."[55]

Cyrus B. Comstock had so impressed Grant at Vicksburg when he stood in for the ill chief engineer that he made him his senior aide-de-camp, and by the time Grant arrived in Washington, he was after Rawlins, the most influential member of the staff. Orville E. Babcock was an 1861 graduate of West Point whose excellent engineering at Vicksburg and Knoxville earned him a position as aide-de-camp when Grant assumed command of the Armies of the United States. Horace Porter, West Point Class of 1860, was an ordnance officer who distinguished himself at Fort Pulaski and Chickamauga. William R. Rowley had been a friend of Grant's in Galena; he made him a first lieutenant in his 45th Illinois Volunteer Infantry and promoted him to his staff when appointed major general. Adam Badeau, a newspaper editor and writer before the war, had served with Sherman and been wounded at Port Hudson, returning to New York to be nursed back to health by his friends, the famed tragedian Edwin Booth and his obscure younger brother, John Wilkes. He recovered in time to receive an appointment on Grant's staff with the vague intention to write a military history of the coming campaign.[56]

Lieutenant Colonel Ely S. Parker was a highly educated, full-blooded Seneca Iroquois. Grant had met Parker before the war in his hometown of Galena, Illinois, where the latter had been working as an engineer. Besides engineering they shared a common interest, as Bruce Catton put it, "in horses and silence." Refused a commission by the Secretary of the Army, he heard Grant needed engineers and applied to him and was accepted. After excellent work at Vicksburg, Grant appointed him to his staff. During the coming campaigns he would become Grant's military secretary.[57]

Theodore S. Bowers and Capt. George K. Leet were assistant adjutant generals. Bowers had enlisted as a private in 1861 and was detailed as a clerk in Grant's headquarters in January 1862. He performed so well he was speedily commissioned. He showed great presence of mind and intrepidity during a raid on district headquarters in Grant's absence. Like Bowers, Leet had joined the army as a private and fought with Sherman at Vicksburg. He was then detailed to work at Grant's headquarters and promptly promoted to captain on Grant's recommendation. Leet was the cousin of Grant's wife, Julia.[58]

Grant had come east to take command of all the Union armies trailing a string of victories in the west. Meade observed to his wife that "Grant is emphatically an executive man, whose only place is in the field." He also observed, "[A] s I understand he is indoctrinated with the notion of the superiority of the Western armies, and that the failure of the Army of the Potomac to accomplish anything is due to their commanders." The men who came with him boasted that they had only seen the backs of the Rebels, to which the weary men of the Army of the Potomac responded, "Well. Grant has not met Bobby Lee yet."[59]

Grant would find this observation a painful one. His style of command heretofore had relied on his intuitive sense of the enemy's intentions as well as his own aggressive seizure of the initiative. Coupled with his innate combativeness and cool determination, it had stood him in good stead against lesser commanders than Lee. In fact, bold exercise of the initiative can at times be a substitute for intelligence of the enemy. But as Grant was to discover, against Lee it was not as successful as against the Confederate generals he had faced in the west. Lee was also a firm believer in seizing the initiative and striking first. Five months later, Meade would put his finger on Grant's problem in a remarkable character sketch:

> Grant is not a mighty genius, but he is a good soldier, of great force of character, honest and upright, of pure purposes, I think, without political aspirations, certainly not influenced by them. His prominent quality is unflinching tenacity of purpose, which blinds him to opposition and obstacles—certainly a great quality in a commander, when controlled by judgment, but a dangerous one otherwise. Grant is not without his faults and weaknesses. Among these is a want of sensibility, an almost too confident and sanguine disposition…

It was a shrewd and balanced appraisal that led him, despite Grant's refusal to see obstacles, to conclude: "Take him all in all, he is, in my judgment, the best man the war has yet produced."[60]

For his part, Sharpe had been impressed with Grant's unpretentious manner from the first time he saw him on his visit to army headquarters. Meade would have introduced him to Sharpe along with the rest of his staff.

Grant has been down here—came in a very unostentatious way—declining a special train—said he didn't want a review—looked and talked like a very plain man—was very decided however and evidently means "to run the machine"—kicked over everybody's preparations to fête him and left unexpectedly the next morning—what is best of all, *he has sent three horses* down to this Army, which is taken as a pretty sure indication that he means to move with us. He said he would move with the army which was first ready—& we suppose that after his return the fur will fly in these diggings.[61]

Four months later, in the midst of some of the worst bloodletting in the history of American arms, Sharpe's opinion would not be shaken.

Grant made a good impression on the men as well. The comment heard from the 20th NYSM was "Boys, the next campaign means business; Uncle U. S. is going to travel with the Army of the Potomac." Headquarters had been refurbished for Grant in Washington, but he had no intention of using them. Instead, he left Captain Leet there to have charge of them. Leet was to later play an important part in Sharpe's operation based in those headquarters. By March 23 he had set up his headquarters at Culpeper Court House, only a few tactful miles south of Meade's headquarters. Sharpe would become very familiar with those few miles.[62]

Between Grant's visit on the 10th and running up his flag on the 23rd, Sharpe had become even busier than usual, and he had Grant to thank for it. The new lieutenant general must have been impressed with him. Sharpe did not mention in his letter to his uncle that he had met Grant on his visit, but the evidence exists in a subsequent letter Patrick wrote to Grant through the War Department's assistant adjutant general, Brig. Gen. Edward Canby, on March 16. In that letter, Patrick refers to "your suggestion to Colonel Sharpe, with reference to auxiliary bureaus of information." Undoubtedly Sharpe informed Grant of his theater intelligence problems, particularly the nonexistence of an intelligence operation in Sigel's Army of the Shenandoah. And like a good staff officer, Sharpe would not have raised a problem without a recommended solution. Canby's earlier letter embodied Grant's approval of that solution. Patrick's letter detailed that solution, and he recommends the assignments of Captain McEntee to the Valley District and First Lieutenant Manning to the Peninsular District, with the Army of the James, to set up subordinate bureaus. He ended by writing that the memorandum had been made brief because it was hoped that "success and a hearty cooperation will be best obtained by a fuller exposition, which it is intended Col Sharpe shall make."[63]

The decision to create BMIs in Sigel's and Butler's armies was rapidly executed. Secret War Department orders sent McEntee to report to Sigel at Harper's Ferry on April 13, with instructions to go anywhere necessary in the Valley to "give the greatest facilities for the employment of scouts, and for the prompt examination of persons coming within my lines."[64]

That same day that Patrick wrote Grant, Sharpe was already planning the theater-level expansion of his intelligence operation. He mentioned in his letter to his uncle that "I am arranging branches of my establishment in the valley, at Fortress Monroe & Washington—and shall be backwards & forwards a good deal." It seems that the possibility of posting Sharpe with Grant's headquarters in the field, along with Patrick's Provost Marshal Department, was given serious thought. There were great possibilities to establish the national-level intelligence office able to coordinate and direct the intelligence operations of all the Union armies—a capability that the Union had so sorely missed. Brigadier General Patrick supported the idea, but Sharpe wrote home, "Whether it will result in my being personally in Washington I can scarcely yet judge. General Patrick wants me there—& think Meade is afraid that I will get away from him entirely. I shall go straight on and do my duty." In the end the idea would come to nothing at this time. Had Grant then had the appreciation for Sharpe's abilities that he would gain in the months to come, it may well have been done.[65]

At this time, Sharpe decided that there was no need to additionally antagonize Meade by pressing this issue. He had come back from his extended leave in February to find himself in a potentially difficult situation with Meade. Sickles had applied to the War Department to have Sharpe detailed for duty with him on his political-military tour of the Mississippi, Gulf coast, and eastern seaboard. Lincoln had found a good use for this troublesome general whose feud with Meade over Gettysburg had stirred up too much bitterness. "I was passive about the matter," he wrote. To have shown any enthusiasm for it would have aligned himself with Sickles, a man Meade despised for his vicious attacks on his conduct of the battle of Gettysburg. Sharpe let nature take its course. If Sickles wanted Sharpe, Meade would do everything he could to keep Sharpe, and that is the way it worked out. "Meade fought it—said I couldn't be spared from here—& here I am." With McEntee and Manning detailed from the BMI, the reassignment of Sharpe would have left only Babcock, and a civilian would not have been allowed to take over. In the end, in addition to Meade's possessiveness, there were just not enough experienced and talented officers to go around. Unfortunately, Meade, so possessive of Sharpe, would make poor use of his talents in the coming campaign.

At the end of his letter home Sharpe hinted at some ambivalence in continuing to run the BMI, despite his successes and no doubt fueled by the difficulty of working with Meade: "... now that Tappen is Lt. Col of my regt I shall feel less hesitation about resigning at the end of another campaign—and indeed hope that such successes will be vouchsafed us as will not make it improper to do so."[66]

CHAPTER NINE

The Overland Campaign

April–June 1864

Blue & Gray Intelligence Preparation of the Battlefield

After planting his flag with the Army of the Potomac in March, Grant concluded that he had two critical intelligence problems. The first was the disposition of Longstreet's I Corps, which had been dispatched the previous year to Tennessee where "Old Pete" had been the chief cause of the Confederate victory at Chickamauga in September. The presence or absence of Lee's most powerful offensive arm in the upcoming campaign against Lee was central to his planning. For that reason, keeping track of Longstreet and especially learning of his return to Virginia became a collection priority for Sharpe.

Grant's second problem depended largely on the answer to the first—how would he approach Lee's army to come to grips with it? The Army of Northern Virginia lay south of the Rapidan River, a southwestern tributary of the Rappahannock River. Grant had to decide whether to turn to its right or left as he penetrated south. Beyond that, he would trust to combat to achieve a decision, for his intention was to bring Lee to battle and destroy his army. He had rightly concluded that the Confederacy would collapse when its main military strength was shattered. What he had underestimated was how adamantine that strength was.

As soon as Grant set up his headquarters, barely a mile away from Meade's, in the last week of March, Sharpe became a frequent visitor to the general-in-chief's tent. Sharpe's first summary that Grant saw was dated March 31. Sharpe stated that there was no movement detected in the Army of Northern Virginia and no word in the immediate future of any, according to agents; that Early had returned from the Valley with his forces; and that the forces remaining in the Valley numbered only 3,350 by Babcock's analysis, almost all cavalry and partisan rangers. With Early's return and the order-of-battle of forces in the Valley fixed, Grant and Meade could be sure that there were no reinforcements available from that area. It also told Grant that the Valley would be especially vulnerable and likely to draw resources from Lee.

By April 2 Sharpe was able to present Grant with a remarkably accurate estimate of Lee's present-for-duty strength. He had just interrogated two deserters from the Stonewall Brigade, and one of them was "intelligent, and well informed of the strength and organization of their own division" (Johnson's Division, Ewell's Corps). With the reliability of the source verified, Sharpe added another piece of information that now had credibility: "That no considerable number of conscripts have been forwarded to Lee yet, and it is generally understood by officers and men that his army does not number 50,000 men of all arms." Lee's own field return for March 20 was 47,045 present for duty. Lee's strength was so low because Longstreet's Corps had not rejoined the Army of Northern Virginia.[1]

On April 5 Lee informed Davis that the Union's main effort would be made in Virginia, but "Nothing as yet has been discovered to develop their plan ... but all the information that reaches me goes to strengthen the belief that General Grant is preparing to move against Richmond." In this he was only indirectly correct. Grant's objective was Lee's army and as that army would always try to protect Richmond, the capital became a byproduct target.

Lee did not need any subtle intelligence to conclude that a mighty offensive was in the making. A blind man would not have missed the massive reinforcement of the Army of the Potomac as well as Grant's personal presence in the east, not to mention the constant buzz to that effect in the Northern press. Lee was just as intent on discovering Meade's strength, and surprisingly his old-fashioned intelligence operation was able to keep its fingers constantly on the pulse of the Army of the Potomac. In a letter of the 13th to Braxton Bragg (kicked upstairs after his failure at Chattanooga, to the figurehead position of commanding the armies of Confederate States), Lee stated that his scouts had learned that the three reorganized corps of the Army of the Potomac (II, V, VI) numbered "75,000 men, and that he [Meade] will move with 100,000 men." His scouts and agents were accurately reporting the continuous reinforcement of the Army of the Potomac. The army's returns for January showed 64,010 for duty, organized in its original five corps. The army's returns for March already showed a strength of 93,158 for duty. The return for April 30 showed 74, 356 in the three Union corps and a total of 102,329 for duty four days before Grant initiated the Overland Campaign. In an intelligence summary of April 22, Sharpe reported, "The rebels boast that they get news from Culpeper court-House every other day, and sometimes every day." He was all too correct. Lee was very much in the intelligence game and still a formidable opponent for Sharpe.[2]

What Lee did not gather was that the 19,250 men of the reorganized IX Corps under Burnside assembling in Annapolis would be fighting alongside the Army of the Potomac. They were not included in the army's order-of-battle because Burnside technically ranked Meade, and to avoid complications so common in a rank-conscious army, Grant had decided that Burnside would report directly to him. Grant had also thrown Lee off track by allowing both Burnside and the War Department to think until the last moment that IX Corps was to land on the Virginia coast south of Norfolk to operate against Richmond. It was a clever bit of disinformation that caused the Confederates to plan for a stronger defense of Richmond than would be necessary and to underestimate the strength of the force crossing the Rapidan by a full 20 percent.[3]

Where Sharpe had an advantage was in the much greater flow of deserters willing to share what they knew about the Army of Northern Virginia. They painted a detailed and harrowing picture of the level of privation throughout the army. The men were reduced to a pint and quarter of corn meal and a quarter pound of bacon a day and complained about the rations that "they get not better very fast." Sharpe would have been even more encouraged had he been able to read Lee's desperate letter to Davis of April 12 on the matter of provisions. It was apparent that the trickle of supplies had not allowed him to accumulate an operational reserve, and he had to depend on almost on a day-to-day delivery. "Any derangement in their arrival or disaster to the railroad would render it impossible for me to keep the army together, and might force a retreat into North Carolina. There is nothing to be had in this section for man or animals."[4]

More importantly, Sharpe was learning of Lee's anxiety over what he knew to be a hemorrhage of information from deserters and prisoners. A number of deserters told of Lee's general orders being read on dress parade, admonishing the men that if they fell into the hands of the enemy to reveal only the letter of their company and number of their regiment and not to give any information on their brigade, division, or corps. The steady stream of deserters made it clear that the resolve of the South was beginning to fray seriously. Deserters included a large number of recent conscripts who had barely arrived in their regiments before they slipped over the Rapidan into the waiting arms of Union pickets. Sharpe was also interrogating a surprising number of veterans who had had enough.[5]

In the surviving records Sharpe and Babcock interrogated at least 60 deserters and prisoners of war from the following units. There are references to many others but not by regiment.

Late in April Sharpe dispatched Sergeants Cline and Knight and another scout named Forrester to activate contacts with the BMI's civilian agents across the Rappahannock. They had not used the covered crossing through the ravine since January, but the agents were alert and visited them in their hiding place the night after they arrived. Silver had just arrived from a visit to Orange Court House, where Lee kept his headquarters. He had obtained Lee's ration strength. The scouts agreed that the information had to be taken back to Sharpe immediately. They agreed that Knight would take it while the other two continued to work with the local agents.

> When about half way through the ravine, in a place where one could stand upright, I suddenly ran against a man who was coming up from the river. It was very dark, and I had not been taking any heed or keeping still, and I judged the one I met was in the same fix as myself—neither of us knew that anyone was near until we came breast to breast. To say I was not frightened would

be untrue. I actually felt my hair rise, and thought of the "quills upon the fretful porcupine." I have always thought he recovered from the shock sooner than I did, for I heard him almost instantly trying to scramble up the side of the ravine. As soon as I heard that I thought to myself, "You are as much frightened as I am; let me alone and I will you," and immediately went on my way. Neither of us spoke. When I had gotten on the north side of the river and told the boys of my adventure they said they had heard from a citizen that day that a mail was going to cross the river that night for Richmond.

It was the Confederate courier of that mail that Knight had collided with in the dark. The experience was a healthy reminder that the enemy was also an active participant in intelligence collection. It is unlikely that Sharpe did not use this information to set a snare for later Confederate couriers.[6]

Table 9.1. April 1864 Interrogations by the BMI

Date	No.	Regt.	Brigade	Division	Corps
April 2	2	4th Va.	Walker	Johnson	Ewell
April 3	2	9th Al.	Perrin	Anderson	Hill
April 13	2	1La.	Stafford	Johnson	Ewell
April 17	2	White's Bn	Rosser	Stuart	
April 18	1	16th Ga.	Gordon	Early	Ewell
April 19	7	10th Al.	Perrin	Anderson	Hill
April 19	2	12th Ga.			
April 20	6	48th Ms.			
April 20	2	28th NC	Scale	Wilcox	
April 21	1	10th Va. Cav	Rosser	Stuart	
April 21	1	Mosby's Cmd			
April 21	1	9th La.			
April 21	1	45th NC.	Daniel	Rodes	
April 21	5	48th Va.			
April 21	1	12th Va. Cav.	Rosser	Stuart	
April 21	1	37th NC.	Lane		
April 22	1	6th Va.	Jenkins	Stuart	
April 23	1	21st Va.	Jones	Anderson	Hill
April 24	2	9th Va. Cav.	Fitzhugh Lee	Stuart	
April 24	2	12th Va. Cav.	Fitzhugh Lee	Stuart	
April 24	1	13th Va. Cav	Fitzhugh Lee	Stuart	
April 24	1	49th Va.			
April 24	3	42nd Va.			
April 24	12	50th Va.			

Even before Grant raised his flag at Culpeper, the War Department had issued a confidential order on the establishment of equivalent BMIs in the forces in the Valley and the Army of the James at Fortress Monroe. Manning, now promoted captain, departed for assignment with the Army of the James in April. On April 7, McEntee received orders to set up a BMI "for the purpose of acting in that district in accordance with Confidential Order, War Department, Washington City, March 21, 1864." He was authorized to take two men and his servant. A week later his orders were clarified by the War Department to read that he was "authorized to proceed to such other points in the Shenandoah Valley, as will best serve the purposes of the orders, and give the greatest facilities for the employment of scouts, and for the prompt examination of persons coming within our lines." It was a tall order with only two assistants. That would be the least of his problems.[7]

Sharpe's analytical resources had now shrunk to Babcock and himself. He had received a number of applications to join his scout force which needed an increase for the coming campaign. He was very selective and turned down most. However, there is no indication in the surviving records of replacement officers assigned to the BMI. An unidentified individual is now writing out the interrogation reports that Manning used to prepare. Whether this is a clerk or an officer is unknown; the historical record is silent, and that silence is a strong indication, given Meade's penny-wise, pound-foolish penury, that there were no officer replacements. It was now all up to Sharpe and Babcock, only a little less than a month before Grant would launch the most relentless and bloody offensive of the entire war. A list of the 49 officers on the staff of the Army of the Potomac as of May 2 shows no other officers working for Sharpe. Meade had not seen fit to replace the two detailed officers.[8]

Where is Longstreet—again?

In the middle of March Sharpe's scouts brought in Herman Lohman, an employee of the RF&P run by Samuel Ruth; he was a German immigrant and secret Unionist. Sharpe was to find that German and British immigrants were common in the underground. Lohman had been sent by Unionists in Richmond to make contact with Meade's army to provide information. He had gone to Isaac Silver's home, where he made contact with the scouts. This would be Sharpe's first direct contact with the Unionist community of Richmond that would ultimately be of the greatest value. Sharpe hurriedly wrote up the results of his interrogation on March 15 and briefed it to Meade, who in turn telegraphed it next day to Halleck and the day after to Grant. That same day Lohman was sent to Washington for further interrogation.

Lohman had presented a wealth of information. The most important item was that Longstreet was expected back in Richmond and was to be given command of an attack on Norfolk. Heavy drafts of men from Pickett's Division were working night and day on three gunboats at Richmond. A feint was being prepared against Williamsburg. The eminent early 20th-century biographer Douglas Southall Freeman thoroughly reviewed the discussions of Longstreet's options prior to his return to Lee. None of them had anything to do with an attack on Norfolk.[9] Meade alerted the Cavalry Corps to prepare to meet the raid, but on March 21 Brigadier General Kilpatrick reported that there was some cavalry at Fredericksburg, but Stuart was simply collecting his people from furlough; ordered to return on the 15th of this month.[10]

It is clear that however enthusiastic were the Richmond Unionists to help the army, their collection methods left much to be desired. That problem, however, was correctable with proper guidance. Sharpe saw that the real importance lay in the fact they represented an established network that could be exploited. That it represented direct access to the operation of the railroad that was Lee's main supply route was of enormous importance.

Lohman also told Sharpe that he "came by direction of Union citizens in Richmond—Mr. Charles Palmer, Mr. John H. Van Liew [sic], Franklin Stearns, Mr. [Frederick William Ernest, Herman's brother] Lohman—Mr. Graham." Presumably, Lohman explained who these people were. Van Lew would have figured in prominently. This is the first time that Van Lew's name appears in a document of Sharpe's. If Butler had shared Van Lew's name with Meade, this would have been an "Aha!" moment for Sharpe. It would have told him that the Union underground was broad and overlapping and that Van Lew was its unofficial leader.

Useful as the scout's information on Lee's ration strength was, it was the patient work of Babcock's interrogations that gave Grant the answer to his first great question—where is Longstreet? This was the dominant question in almost every interrogation report of deserters, prisoners, and contrabands, and it yielded a steady stream of surprisingly accurate camp rumor. At first it was downright inaccurate, perhaps reflecting Lee's increasingly strong demands to Davis for the return of his most able corps commander. It also reflected the concern among all ranks of the Army of Northern Virginia for the absence of the mighty I Corps. It would be difficult to contemplate the major campaign they knew was coming without Lee's Old Warhorse in the fray. Ironically, Grant had set Sharpe to finding Longstreet when Lee was not even sure where he was. On the 5th Lee wrote Davis that he had to infer Longstreet's location in the absence of accurate information. In the strongest terms he asked for Longstreet's return to his command. Early in the first week of April contrabands and deserters reported I Corps was entrained and halfway from Tennessee to Virginia with advance elements in Lynchburg, when Longstreet would not even receive his orders to move until April 7, orders triggered no doubt by Lee's remonstrations of two days before.[11]

But from then on the information kept getting more and more accurate until it built a coherent, reliable picture. Longstreet was concentrating slowly at Charlottesville because of the limited capacity of the railroads and informed Lee on the 16th that not all of his men would reach that point until the 21st. On the 17th Sharpe reported the camp rumor that elements of I Corps had arrived in

Charlottesville the previous week. On April 22 Lee ordered the corps moved to Gordonsville because of a lack of good camping sites in the Charlottesville area, a transfer that the BMI quickly picked up on the same day from deserters. Nevertheless, it is clear from the tone and wording of Sharpe's reports that he was not satisfied with the camp rumors being reported by deserters. Like a good intelligence officer, he kept hunting for more concrete evidence, but his nervousness was palpable as his evidence remained only wispy camp rumors.[12]

At the same time, Babcock's interrogations were also picking up another constant camp rumor entwined with the others reported from the BMI's civilian agents. Lee intended to maneuver Longstreet through the Valley to attack the Union right at Culpeper while he attacked across the Rapidan. The origin of this rumor was probably the letter Lee wrote to Davis on March 30, in which he recommended, "Longstreet should be held in readiness to be thrown rapidly in the Valley if necessary to counteract any movement in that quarter, in accomplishing which I could unite with him, or he with me, should circumstances require it on the Rapidan." Even the very reliable agent Silver, the "Old Man," was reporting the intertwined rumor—one true and the other not—that Longstreet's "corps was at Charlottesville. And it is supposed that Longstreet will join Early at the head of the valley, and when General Stuart and Fitzhue [sic] Lee starts from Fredericksburg, Longstreet will start down the valley, to commit depredations on the west side of the Union army." The reporting was as persistent as it was consistent and had therefore to be taken seriously. It is one of the vagaries of the art of intelligence that intelligence of the discussion of a plan will trigger counter-planning by the collecting side. The latter will take on a life of its own, as it did in this case, even when the original threat never, in the end, materialized. When the truth and an untruth come wrapped around each other, it is nearly impossible to untangle them, as Sharpe was not able to do in this instance. The importance of Longstreet's arrival outweighed the misinformation of his movement to the Valley.[13] It was better that both be believed than both disbelieved.

The misinformation would have important consequences. What was clear at the time to Grant was that Lee was attempting to forestall him. He had accurately read Lee's intent of the proposed Valley maneuver, and fearful of losing the initiative, he set the date for the Union advance for May 4.

The location of Longstreet remained a collection priority. Braxton Bragg on the 16th had ordered Longstreet to move his corps at Charlottesville, but then, since the area had no good camping grounds, he was to bivouac in the vicinity of Gordonsville where Lee's headquarters was located. Lee had informed Davis on April 23 that he was retaining Longstreet at Cobham 6 miles southwest of Gordonsville until the remainder of his troops arrived. That would be slow because the trains could only deliver 1,500 men a day. Sharpe was closely following the move of I Corps. On April 25 the weight of testimony from deserters and agents was such that Sharpe was able to confidently state that "the arrival of Longstreet's advance at Charlottesville is fully corroborated." That was only 12 miles southwest of Cobham. Two days later Sharpe identified Longstreet at Wolftown, 21 miles from Cobham to the north in Madison County. That same day Meade ordered cavalry reconnaissance in brigade strength to confirm that report. The brigade found none of Longstreet's infantry there. McEntee, who was in the Valley with Sigel's command, was still reporting on April 28 Longstreet in the valley, but the next day corrected that assessment and reported Longstreet in Gordonsville, definitely outside the Valley, with the vital observation, "in easy supporting distance of Lee." Longstreet himself in his memoirs cites a location just south of Gordonsville. Notwithstanding the erroneous identification of Wolftown as occupied by some of Longstreet's Corps, the BMI had accurately located Longstreet in the vicinity of Gordonsville.[14]

At this point it was clear that Longstreet was not moving to the Valley; Lee had concentrated his II and III Corps along the Rapidan, with Longstreet's Corps the furthest west of the three corps but within easy supporting distance of the others. Lee had placed Longstreet in a position that would shield Richmond while at the same time giving him a mobile reserve while he awaited Grant's first move.

Grant had more than one army to employ in the coming campaign in eastern Virginia. Major General Benjamin Butler's Army of the James was ideally poised for a rapid descent on Richmond, while Lee would be focused on Meade's army. While planning was underway for the coming campaign, Butler had come across a pearl of great price, the news of which reached Sharpe. A Richmond lady named Elizabeth Van Lew had made contact with him, volunteered to provide valuable military information, and had done just that. In his planning for the Army of the James's share of the general offensive of all the Union armies, he had identified Fort Darling protecting Richmond on the James River as a key obstacle to be overcome. He passed a request through the lines for information on the fort. Van Lew responded with a complete set of drawings from Union sympathizers most likely in the Confederate war department.[15]

For Sharpe, Van Lew's potential as an agent would have been immense. He must then have been horrified to read that the *National Republican* on April 12 published an article that did all but identify Van Lew by name. The nightmare of any intelligence officer is that the feckless press will compromise agents. It was an especially dangerous revelation because the Confederates had a rapid conduit for information from Washington to reach Richmond. Fortunately, the Confederate authorities did not connect the article to Van Lew.[16]

It was not long before Sharpe sent a request for information that was passed through Butler to Van Lew. There were three issues:

1. Is there any powder under the Capitol at Richmond?
2. Money sent by Hughes for Hancock's benefit (Hancock was a prisoner at Libby. Hughes was a scout)

3. Send immediately correspondence between Early and Barksdale after the battle of Chancellorsville.

The use of the Capitol as a possible headquarters after the fall of Richmond prompted the first item and was probably prompted by a rumor that must have caused some senior officer—Meade, Humphreys, or Grant—to request confirmation. Van Lew's reply assured Grant's headquarters that there was no powder under the Capitol. The third item was expected to have topographical and other information useful to the planning for the coming Overland Campaign. How Sharpe knew there was such correspondence is unknown but intriguing. That correspondence had already been published and was also included in her reply. Barksdale's Brigade of Early's Division occupied the area of Fredericksburg after the battle of Chancellorsville. Barksdale was the officer charged with cleaning up that part of the battlefield and in sending Union wounded back across the Potomac. The Early-Barksdale correspondence would have discussed the Fredericksburg area, the terminus of Lee's main supply route. What specifically Sharpe was looking for is unknown, but intelligence casts a wide net in support of operational planning. However, there is nothing in official records to substantiate this story.[17]

Van Lew also provided Sharpe with a startling report obtained from one of her agents at the War Department—that Davis and his cabinet considered the Confederacy "to be in a state of collapse." In April Sharpe received a report from McPhail's well-placed and reliable agent Maddox that supported that report.

> An order has just been issued ordering the quartermasters throughout the land to seize all provisions in the possession of the people except ¼ pound per day for every grown person. Lee's army has not meat twice a week. They are subsisting entirely on cornbread and molasses. The cold spring has thrown back the corn crops in the South and the whole country is apprehensive of an early famine. Lee cooped up in Richmond could not subsist an army 30 days. The Petersburg Railroad could not supply him.

Perhaps this explains Grant's optimism in the coming campaign that if he kept hitting Lee hard and often enough, the Army of Northern Virginia would simply collapse.[18]

The Other Side of the Hill

Lee's intelligence collection efforts and his own analysis were also serving him well, as Douglas Southall Freeman pointed out:

> Lee studied with utmost care the reports that came from his spies [scouts] during this period of waiting, and on April 16, he was satisfied that three attacks were in the making—a main assault across the Rapidan, a diversion in the Valley of Virginia, and an attack on the flank or rear of the Army of Northern Virginia, probably directed against Drewry's Bluff on the James River, so as to expose the ware-line to Richmond.

Lee's reports of the activities of his scouts is worth recounting at length to show how his scouts were operating and how effective they were. Sharpe's BMI was not the only game in town. As early as April 7, Lee was able to inform Braxton Bragg, now figurehead commander of all the Confederate armies, that "I think it apparent that the enemy is making large preparations for the approaching campaign in Virginia." You can almost see him rolling his eyes as he recounts how a source named "Potomac," as of the 1st, had reported, "60,000 troops marching from Washington to Point Lookout I suppose intended for wit." Point Lookout was the large Union POW camp located on the tip of the long stretch of ground separated by the Potomac River and Chesapeake Bay. Lee thought it a poor unintended joke that a Union army would be marching to a cul de sac and POW camp.

He discounted rumors of Union reinforcements coming from the west, "but none of my scouts have seen them. I therefore think it is doubtful." He had two scouts observing the Orange and Alexandria Railroad, on either side of the tracks, with no communication between them. They were providing him the same information that the railroad was extremely active and that troops were constantly arriving from Alexandria. "They think they are recruits and furloughed men. Their clothes are too new and overcoats of too deep a blue for old troops. They estimate that from 20,000 to 30,000 men have been transported by the railroad in the last ten days." Lee than insisted on the return of his two detached brigades and the forwarding to him of every available recruit.[19]

On the 18th he wrote to President Davis:

> I received yesterday reports from two of our most reliable scouts, upon whom I have depended for information. One was dated the 4th and the other the 6th. The writer of the former had been near Alexandria, had communication with persons inside the town every day, and had watched the Alexandria and Orange Railroad four or five days. He states that a large number of recruits are being sent to the Army of the Potomac, and expressed surprise at the number of troops conveyed on the road, but that no additional corps had yet passed up. The general impression was that the great battle would take place on the Rapidan and that the Federal army would advance as soon as the weather is settled. All the white troops had been taken from the intrenchments around Alexandria and ordered to General Meade, and their places supplied by negroes. It was reported that the troops from Charleston were to be brought to Fort Monroe. The writer of the latter was in Culpeper in communication with the C. H. watching the enemy's movements. Among the reports in circulation was that the Eleventh and Twelfth Corps were expected. That may be, however, to encourage their men, who were deserting in expectation of a fight.[20]

Lee wrote again the very next day to Davis. His scouts had identified the concentration of IX Corps at Annapolis, and the *Washington Chronicle* had identified its strength at 30,000, but he correctly noted that it was an exaggeration—Burnside had about 20,000 men in reality. The Washington newspapers had rumored that this force was to be used in some special operation on the coast, the deception planted by Grant.

Scout Thomas N. Conrad was sent on a special mission to pin down Burnside's mission. His War Department contacts did not know. So far Grant's security was working. He was keeping Burnside's mission to himself. Then Conrad traveled up to Annapolis and walked around the city dressed in his preacher's suit, chatting up a number of people, and discovered that no one expected any coastal adventure. The only logical alternative mission was to reinforce Grant in the coming campaign. He wrote out a dispatch to Lee: "Burnside will reinforce Grant, and that at an early day." The next day he sent it out through the "doctor's" line to the Potomac where it was taken across to camp on the Virginia shore called the "Eagle's Nest" and from there to the Fredericksburg telegraph which sent it directly to Richmond. To ensure that Lee got the information, Conrad crossed back into Virginia and rode breakneck to Lee's headquarters, where he discovered that his first message had been forwarded to Lee the day before. Lee was now sure that Burnside's IX Corps would array itself against his Army of Northern Virginia in the spring.[21]

His scout at Culpeper also continued to report the arrival of large numbers of troops, not in organized units but in squad size that reported to different commands, presumably replacements and or convalescents. He, however, erroneously reported that the XI and XII Corps were expected, and rumor had them arriving in Alexandria. Lee then noted that the *Washington Chronicle* had also written on the 4th, "that General W. F. Smith has been ordered to the command of the troops around Fortress Monroe … if true, would indicate that operations are contemplated from that quarter, which they did not wish to trust to General Butler." He was correct in this. Grant had put Smith in command of XVIII Corps in Butler's Army of the James precisely because he did not trust the latter's ability but was forced to keep him for political reasons.[22]

Three days later he wrote Davis another summary. Mosby reported that no reinforcements had been sent to the Army of the Potomac despite the deception measure of the enemy to assert that it had to dismay the local population. Lee did not believe this, concluding that this information came from citizens and because his scouts from personal observation have reported otherwise. He does accurately report that troops from the defenses of Washington were being replaced with the Invalid Corps. An especially trusted scout, Lt. Channing Smith reported security measures and indications of preparations for movement. "[T]he sutlers, traders, and all persons not connected to the Army of the Potomac are ordered to leave. All extra baggage, &c., has been ordered to Washington." Smith then adds that XI and XII Corps had been ordered to join Meade. The *Washington Chronicle* continued to be a good source of information; Lee noted that it reported that the two corps had been consolidated under the command of Major General Hooker and that Maj. Gen. P. H. Sheridan has been assigned to the command of the cavalry of the Army of the Potomac.

Scouts on the Potomac on the 9th observed 10 steamers carrying an estimated two brigades of infantry. In a shrewd appraisal, Lee drew the appropriate conclusions:

> They may be merely sick, &c. If they are preparing armed transports and launches for disem-
> barking troops I think they can only be intended for the James River. I see no other place where
> they would be required. We should be prepared in that quarter. A landing may be intended at

City Point to capture Drewry's Bluff. I think it probable that at the appointed time operations at Charleston will be suspended and certain troops and iron-clads be transferred to James River, as I see it stated in the Northern papers that General Gillmore has been assigned a part in the proposed campaign in Virginia.[23]

It was another shrewd appraisal. Gilmore and a large number of his troops were indeed being transferred to the James from the siege of Charleston.

In his April 18 letter to Davis, Lee persisted in the error that XI and XII Corps had returned to join Meade. His sources were also unsure of the numbers of the corps, an indication that his order-of-battle analysis was not nearly as detailed as Sharpe's. His most important conclusion was to divine Grant's intentions in the Valley.

A scout just from the valley reports that Averell left Martinsburg last Tuesday, and moved up the Baltimore and Ohio Railroad, taking with him all the cavalry that could be spared from that region, leaving only a garrison at Martinsburg… I think it probable that Averell will move upon the Virginia and Tennessee Railroad, or Staunton or some point west, at the time of the general movement upon Richmond, from some point beyond the North Mountain. I think, too, General Grant will rely upon his flank movement upon Richmond to draw this army back.

One day later he was alerting Maj. Gen. John C. Breckinridge, commanding in the Valley, to Averell's cavalry threat, though he incorrectly discounted it as a deception of a major advance up the Valley. He added that "General Meade's army is reported ready to advance. His sick, invalids, sutlers, &c., have been sent back to Washington, his troops rationed, and only waiting for the roads to become passable." On the 29th Lee cited another trusted scout, Frank Stringfellow, as reporting the movement of Burnside's Corps through Washington and Alexandria and concluded it was destined to be employed on the Rappahannock front. He received a report dated April 27, probably from his clandestine agent, Walter Bowie, which gave an "extremely accurate account … of the forces and strategy General Grant expected to employ" in the coming campaign.[24]

Finally, on the 30th Lee wrote to Davis again to tell him essentially that the Union forces were uncoiling from their camps and moving across the Rappahannock. He quoted a *Philadelphia Inquirer* of the 26th that said that "all their available forces are being advanced to the front. They are also apparently drawing troops from Florida and the Southern coast." On the 28th Mosby was at Centerville, between Alexandria and Manassas, and watched Burnside's IX Corps training south. Prisoners told him there were only convalescents left in the camps in Annapolis. That same day "loyal citizens" reported Burnside had arrived at Rappahannock Station. *The Washington Chronicle* of the 27th stated that XI and XII Corps would not return from Tennessee to reinforce the Army of the Potomac. His scouts reported that V Corps, which had been guarding the Orange and Alexandria Railroad had been relieved by negro troops. They also reported that Meade's engineer troops, pontoon trains, and all his cavalry had crossed the Rappahannock. "Everything indicates a concentrated attack on this front…" He also identified that Union forces would "demonstrate" north or south of the James River and that Sigel and Averell would strike the Virginia and Tennessee Railroad to Stanton.[25] How quickly he acquired enemy newspapers is a testament to his intelligence collection network in the Union rear.

Lee's scouts were an operational security challenge for the Union forces. They had the uncanny ability to infiltrate camps and even headquarters and gain the most valuable information simply from listening to conversations. Lieutenant Colonel Theodore Lyman, Meade's aide, observed, "A secret expedition with us is got up like a picnic, with everybody blabbing and yelping. One is driven to think that not even the prospect of immediate execution will stop Americans from streaming on in their loose, talking, devil-may-care ways."[26]

Lee had security problems of his own which he expressed in a letter to Secretary of War Seddon on the 30th. He objected to the publication of official military reports of operations:

> It is no little advantage to our opponents to know how we are affected, or what action is induced by movements of theirs, or by any other state of circumstances. Particularly is this the case at the present time. The operations of his campaign are likely to cover many localities that have been the scene of some of the events narrated in my reports, and it is by no means impossible that we may have to deal with combinations of circumstances in all respects analogous to some that have already been encountered, and I feel that I should be embarrassed if the enemy knew the line of conduct pursued by me on former occasions and the reasons that governed me.
>
> I am afraid that much injury has already been done by these publications. I should be well pleased to have as accurate information as to the strength, means, and difficulties of the enemy...[27]

It would have been bitter vindication had Lee known that Sharpe had acquired a train of about 20 wagons for this campaign—dedicated to carrying his growing valuable files of newspapers and other captured documents. It represented a unique database in the history of war.

Taken all in all, Lee had orchestrated an effective intelligence collection effort; his scouts appear to have been able to penetrate just about anywhere in the Union rear. He made full use of their information, shrewdly analyzing the results, despite the errors in reference to XI and XII Corps and a major move down the Valley. Confident that he had fully grasped Grant's strategy, he concluded in his last letter to Davis, "If that movement can be successfully met and resisted, I have no uneasiness as to the result of the campaign in Virginia."[28]

The Wilderness

With this information, Grant could decide which enemy flank to turn, and that decision turned largely on logistics and the need to get between Lee and Richmond. Attacking Lee's left or western flank would severely overextend the supply lines of the Army of the Potomac and offer an easy target to Lee. An attack from that direction would also engage Longstreet directly and would break communications with Butler's Army of the James near Richmond. It would also violate another working principle of Grant's—try to get between Lee and Richmond. Grant decided to maneuver around Lee's right or eastern flank, and at this juncture, Sharpe's scouts found that the necessary fords over the Rappahannock were unguarded. Meade's chief of staff, Major General A. A. Humphreys, was given the task of planning the movement, and he relied on Lee's reaction to Meade's similar maneuver the previous fall in the Mine Run Campaign as a guide. Then Lee had taken over 30 hours to develop the situation against Meade and had retreated behind his fortifications along Mine Run to the south of the Rapidan. The unguarded fords, however, were not an unalloyed gift. On the other side lay the Wilderness, the same tangle of jungle-like thickets and woods that had enmeshed Hooker at Chancellorsville the previous May. The problem would be to rapidly push through the Wilderness and debouch into the open territory to its south in order to maneuver against Lee. This done, he would let opportunity guide his actions. As he wired to Halleck, "My own notions about our line of march are entirely made up," because "circumstances beyond my controll [sic] may change them."[29]

Grant was not too concerned with the enemy's probable course of action as long as it allowed him to engage Lee in the open while guarding his logistics. For him, the essential point was to know that the enemy was in the area of operations and to bring him to battle through the use of bold initiative. Unfortunately, precise intelligence on enemy dispositions and movements and especially on the terrain to be traversed was exactly what was needed to facilitate Grant's grand movement to contact. None of these were to be forthcoming.

Maps of the terrain of the Wilderness area prepared by the army's topographical engineers were so devoid of detail as to be essentially useless. Both Meade and Grant bungled the use of cavalry for reconnaissance over this difficult ground. It would be Meade's infantry and not his cavalry that would warn him of the approach of Ewell's men in the battle on May 5. Apparently the cavalry was not used to gather intelligence on the most useful routes through the Wilderness before the army was set in motion. During the movement to contact, two-thirds of the Cavalry Corps were employed guarding the trains, and the other third performed poorly in reconnaissance.

Aside from his excellent order-of-battle reporting, Sharpe's scouts and agents mainly reported on "fortifications protecting certain fords, the strength of the Mine Run defense, and Longstreet's latest whereabouts." The latter was critical because it indicated to Grant where Lee's reserve was located as well as its movement in the direction of Orange, which was bringing it closer to Grant's intended battlefield.[30] Sharpe did, however, attempt to do what the cavalry did not and that was provide local guides through the Wilderness, but his resources were limited. On May 2 Sharpe wrote to Hancock, commanding II Corps, promising to send "two good men as guides. One of them may have to ride in an ambulance having lost part of one of his feet while lying within the enemy's lines during the late snow-storm."[31]

Lee's scouts and signal corps would serve him much better, though there would be a barb in that service. On the very morning that the blue columns were in motion over the Rappahannock fords, the Union signal station on Stony Mountain, north of the Rapidan, intercepted and deciphered a signal report of 9:30 a.m. to Ewell. "From present indications everything seems to be moving to the right, on Germanna and Ely's Ford roads, leaving cavalry in our front." At 11:00 another intercepted message read, "We are moving." Grant was delighted. "That gives me just the information I wanted. It shows that Lee is drawing out from his position, and is pushing across to meet us." That was confirmed again by a further signal station observation at 3:00 p.m.: "Enemy moving infantry and trains toward Verdierville. Two brigades gone from this front. Camps on Clark's Mountain breaking up." The giant meeting engagement he had wanted was about to come to pass.[32]

As the blue masses snaked toward the Rappahannock that morning of the 4th, many of them set fire to their winter quarters, a clear statement that they did not intend to return. The army's headquarters was at one end of a small valley, and the provost marshal and BMI headquarters at the lower end. In the distance the huge plumes of smoke from the burning camps of the Cavalry Corps filled the sky. The scout Daniel Plew set his own hut on fire just as Brigadier General Patrick rode into the camp. He flew into a rage at Plew, striking him repeatedly with his riding crop and shouting, "Do you want to let the enemy know we are coming?" He promptly arrested Plew and kept him in confinement for three more days. It was not difficult to see why the scouts thoroughly detested Patrick. By inference it seems Sharpe was not present but probably with the army command group at the upper end of the Valley. Given his paternal care for his men, he doubtless would have intervened.[33]

Patrick could have spared Plew the abuse had he known that Fitzhugh Lee's cavalry scouts had infiltrated the Union camps and galloped back to inform their commander of the enemy's movement. Fitzhugh Lee informed Robert E. Lee immediately. The latter divined Grant's intentions from these and the signal reports and put his army in motion to meet him.[34]

Sharpe had his scouts out, crossing the Rapidan at Germania Ford and fanning out along the roads. They found the dense scrub hard going and eventually most of them were held near the army headquarters to be available for any special missions. The next morning, at 7:30 a.m., Meade notified Grant that the enemy had appeared on his front still within the Wilderness. Grant ordered him to pitch in, and the terrible battle of the Wilderness had begun. In the first day's fighting on May 5, Sharpe discovered from an intercepted message and prisoner interrogation that the Confederates were aware of Grant's build-up on their right and that Longstreet would be arriving to stop him the next day. Scouts Knight and McEneany also discovered that "the bulk of the rebels, in our belief, had moved to the left, and the results showed that we were right," and reported this finding immediately to Sharpe at headquarters.

The role of the BMI becomes more difficult to follow, because for the battle of the Wilderness there is only one report by Sharpe for May 5 and another by Meade to Grant on the same day in which he cites what Sharpe told him. "It appears to be the general opinion among prisoners that Longstreet was not in the action to-day, though expected, and that his position was to be on their right or our left. His force supposed to be about 12,000. He probably will attack Hancock to-morrow."[35]

Grant's build-up on his left was meant to cover his communications, and Longstreet or no Longstreet, he would be committed to that attack regardless of the fact that it meant a brutal fight in the jungle-like growth of the Wilderness where his advantage in numbers would be cancelled. The next day his attack, led by Hancock's II Corps, just ground away at the Confederates opposing his attack until their front began to unravel. The crisis was such that Lee himself rode to the front to lead a last desperate defense. It was then that Longstreet's I Corps double-timed onto the field, shouting, "General Lee to the rear!" as Lee tried to join them in their charge and threw the victorious Union advance back. The battle ended on that flank as a stalemate while hundreds of the wounded burned to death in the fires set among the thick brush.[36]

The battle had one last act. The Confederate II Corps overlapped the Union VI Corps flank on the right. Lee authorized an attack late in the day by Early's Division. Sharpe was a direct observer of Grant's *sang froid* as the Confederate attack struck.

> Well, one of the very critical periods of that battle—I might say its crisis—occurred on the second day, May 6, 1864, when General Early was hurled in a vigorous attack against the Union right wing, then in command of General Sedgwick, who met his death three days later while planting some guns in an advanced position at Spottsylvania [sic]. At the height of this attack I know that General Mead was greatly disturbed that Lee should turn our right flank. That done, in all probability we should have been driven back over the Rapidan, and the country would have said it was a case of Bull Run, Chancellorsville and Fredericksburg over again.
>
> We were standing in a little group around Meade, observing his anxiety, when, casually turning my eyes toward the place where I had seen General Grant standing some time before, I failed to locate him. However, I did see a soldier sitting under a tree and whittling a stick. I thought that was a curious attitude for a soldier to take, and I looked again. Then, for the first time I saw that the man in question was General Grant. You know, at that time, our eastern officers were not as familiar with his peculiarities as we became later. This was the first battle we had been in with him.
>
> There sat the great general, actually whittling on a piece of pine, and apparently perfectly unconcerned as to the outcome of the attack on Sedgwick or the fortunes of the battle anywhere else along our front. I think Meade also must have observed Grant's apparent indifference, for at last he approached him, and the rest of us went with Meade. As we neared the tree, I noticed that Grant wore no uniform with which would distinguish his rank. He had on a private's blouse and thick boots and, so far as I could see, no stars.
>
> He looked up at as Meade came within speaking distance and waited patiently for the latter to speak. I did not catch exactly what Meade said, but I know its purport, Meade intimating to Grant that he was very apprehensive that Lee was turning our right and it seemed to him that reinforcements should be sent to Sedgwick.
>
> Grant stopped whittling, with the knife blade buried half way down the wood. "I don't believe it," he said. Slowly, quietly and very decisively. Then he began whittling again.

General Meade and the rest of us drew off a few paces, but after a minute or two Meade repeated his anxiety to Grant, who once more stopped shaving down the piece of pine just long enough to repeat in the same quiet, determined way: "I don't believe it."

But despite the assurance from our commander we stood around apprehensively, and Grant, finally noticing our doubt, apparently added a few words to his stock sentence as he whittled away. "Don't worry about our right," he said. "Sedgwick is there. No one will be able to turn him; nobody can get by him. Besides, Lee can't afford to send reinforcements from other parts of his army to his left. Don't worry, gentlemen."

I could see that General Meade was not at all convinced that he was, in fact, beginning to lose his temper—you know, he was a quick-tempered man. But just then occurred an extraordinary incident. An officer rode up, saluted General Grant, and the next moment was declaring that he had the honor of reporting for Sedgwick that the right was holding its own and was in no danger.

"I thought so," said Grant quietly, more to himself than to us, as he resumed whittling.

I think from that moment we never lost our confidence in the accuracy of Grant's judgment.[37]

Confidence in Grant had also permeated down through the ranks. On June 19 Grant, Meade, and Butler were riding along the lines of the VI when Grant stopped before Drummer Bill and asked, "Drummer, where do you belong?"

Seeing all the stars on the group, Bill snapped to attention and saluted, "To the Sixth Corps."

Grant then asked, "Well, Drummer, where is the Sixth Corps going?"Bill shot back, "Deed I don't know, sir. Gen. Grant ought to know!"[38]

Sharpe's information about Longstreet had been spot on. Unfortunately, there were no other BMI reports to illustrate the role of intelligence, other than those two, for the rest of the battle. Meade's report to Grant of the 5th shows that there was more BMI reporting. If those reports survive, they have not yet come to life; a diligent search of the National Archives has proved fruitless. The next extant report from Sharpe would not be until May 9, after the army had already reached Spotsylvania. Most of Sharpe's reports during a battle would have been delivered in briefings; there was no time to write out official reports. What reports that have survived in the Official Records are in the form of prisoner interrogations by the capturing corps which contained an important piece of information. The word had spread like wildfire through the Confederate ranks when Longstreet had been badly wounded, and, through prisoners, quickly came to the ears of Meade and Grant. Lee appointed one of his division commanders, Maj. Gen. Richard A. Anderson, to replace him. Sharpe picked this up from a Richmond newspaper and briefed it to Meade and Grant because the latter cites Longstreet's wounding in a message to Halleck on the 7th as did Rawlins in a letter of the same day. About the same time Butler found Lee's official report of Longstreet's wounding.[39]

As the fighting was raging, Sharpe had sent his scouts out to find the enemy's rear. Scouts Knight and McEneany found their way blocked and reported back to Sharpe. They also reported the ludicrous flight of the new 22nd New York Cavalry, in which half the men had fallen off their horses so green were they after only two months' service. Sharpe immediately took him to Grant and Meade to repeat the story. Grant replied, "Take their horses away and give them to better men, if they don't behave better." Luckily for the 22nd NY, the order was never carried, and with experience they became a good regiment.[40]

In one of the bitter ironies of war, one of Sharpe's most valuable agents, Isaac Silver, whose farm was on the Plank Road, suffered the ruin of his farm at the hands of Sheridan's cavalry, which had "settled down on his place like a flight of Egyptian locusts." Sheridan had concentrated his cavalry divisions around Silver's home on the night of May 8 during the battle of Spotsylvania in preparation for his strike into the Confederate rear that would lead to the battle of Yellow Tavern and the death of Stuart. Silver served Sheridan as his guide.[41] He would find little gratitude from the cavalry.

Later, Sharpe had sent Knight and other scouts to rescue some Union wounded in the hands of the Confederate sheriff. Before their arrival the sheriff had sent the prisoners to Richmond and then fled. On their return to BMI headquarters they stopped at Silver's farm. Knight remembered that a few days before he had been there and had never "seen a nicer farm … growing crops, with young apple and peach orchards. Now it was the desert of the Sahara, orchards, fences, growing crops all had disappeared from the face of the earth." He asked why he did not explain that he was a Union agent. Silver replied, "I did, but no one would believe me, and it seemed to me that they have treated me worse on account of what I told them than they would have done had I said nothing." One can imagine Sharpe's wrath had he come across the scene. The perpetrators had already departed with Sheridan on his great ride through the Confederate rear.

> The only troops at the farm were from the Quartermaster Corps. Knight sought out the commander.
>
> I told him who Silver was, and what he had done for us, the condition he was now in, and what he would be in when our people left, and asked him to furnish rations enough to keep the family for some time. His answer was that he was sorry he could not do it, but there was no law or regulation by which he could. After thinking the situation over, I asked if he could issue rations to me, and he said he could; also, that he would be pleased to do so. I made a requisition for a great many more men than I had with me for 10 days, and turned the things over to Silver.
>
> The scouts visited the man over twenty years later and found he had forgotten the desolation of his farm as old age had fallen upon him. They were to note that "His wife, however, remembered."[42]

What was manifesting itself at Wilderness in the dearth of intelligence reports and subsequently was the consequence of Meade's inattention to the BMI. He had allowed the detail of McEntee and Manning to the Valley and Fortress Monroe and provided no replacements. The entire burden of BMI analysis fell upon Sharpe and Babcock alone. As the campaign continued he would find other duties to further divert Sharpe from his primary mission.

Spotsylvania

If Grant had been checked by Longstreet's timely arrival on the field on May 6, he had not been deterred. The indecision of the battle and its heavy losses, while disappointing, had not dulled his relentless objective to hang onto Lee until he had ground him to bits. His men were not so sure. That evening gloom enfolded the army that had gone into the battle with such high hopes. It was Chancellorsville all over again, almost literally—the same field and approximately the same number of casualties—15,000—and the same failure, for Bobby Lee had bloodied them badly. On the morning of the 8th, the army was on the road again with black failure hanging over it, bitterly expecting to march north to lick its wounds one more time. Grant and his staff rode past the troops of Hancock's II Corps, aides shouting, "Give way to the right!"

> And suddenly the soldiers realized that the generals were riding south. South: that meant no retreat, no defeat, maybe the battle had been a victory after all even though it had not exactly felt like one … and the men of the Second Corps sprang to their feet and began to cheer, and kept on cheering as long as they had breath for it. For the first time, Grant won a spontaneous applause of the Army of the Potomac.[43]

Grant kept moving southeast around Lee's flank, reaching for Spotsylvania Court House, but Lee, unbeknownst to him, was quicker off the mark. Even after Maj. Gen. Gouveneur Warren's V Corps had captured several of Longstreet's men in skirmishes on the roads leading to the Court House, as William Feis observes, "the army commander brushed off Warren's report, remarking, 'I hardly think Longstreet is yet at Spotsylvania.'" Even by the next morning the report had not filtered down to Hancock, who was at Todd's Tavern beyond the army's right flank.[44]

As it was, Grant's advance corps nearly got to the Court House first, but Lee's men beat them by a hair to the surprise and chagrin of everyone, not least of all Grant. It was also only dawning on him that V Corps, which should have seized the Court House, was commanded by a man who would prove time after time that he was habitually a day late and a dollar short—Warren. An initial attack to bounce the fresh Confederate positions failed. Grant planned a direct assault on the increasingly formidable Confederate defenses for the 10th as his army closed on Spotsylvania. His chief of staff and alter ego, Maj. Gen. John A. Rawlins, wrote on the 9th, "The feeling of our army is that of great confidence, and with the superiority of numbers on our side, I think we can beat them notwithstanding their advantage of position."[45]

Babcock and Sharpe, now reunited at a fixed headquarters, intensified their interrogations to provide critical information prior to the attack. They found themselves at this time deprived of the supplementary information that would have been provided by the Cavalry Corps had it been with the army. Unfortunately, it was absent, the result of a violent argument between Meade and Sheridan. Meade had wanted the corps to continue to guard the army's flanks and trains. Sheridan wanted to hunt down the Confederate cavalry and had got into a violent shouting match which Meade reported to Grant. The lieutenant general decided to let Sheridan have his chance, and Sheridan galloped off with almost the entire corps to raise hell deep in the Confederate rear. The raid's greatest achievement was the mortal wounding of Stuart at Yellow Tavern, but it deprived the army at Spotsylvania of an aggressive reconnaissance effort that would have added immeasurably to Sharpe's own efforts.[46]

Lee's army had the amazing ability to throw up deadly field fortifications in almost no time, and that is what faced Grant as his corps arrived on the field. The key to the works was a formation called the Mule Shoe or the Salient in front of the Union VI Corps. Grant decided to strike there. If it cracked, Lee's entire position would be untenable. The reinforced regiments of Col. Emory Upton's brigade of VI Corps were massed one behind the other on a narrow front to assault a position in the center of the Confederate line called the Salient or the Mule Shoe, while Hancock and Warren attacked the Confederate III Corps to the left of this position. The Salient formed the apex of a right angle with Ewell's Corps packed inside. The assault was scheduled for just after 6 p.m. The other two Union corps would attack two hours earlier to fix the enemy's reserves. Grant figured that the enemy could not be strong everywhere, and that his superior numbers would eventually crack the enemy line. Just before the assault Meade wrote to Grant that "a scout just in from the right says there is no infantry beyond Barlow's right but a cavalry force at Corbin's Bridge." He then dispatched one of Hancock's divisions to shore up the flank.[47]

At 3 p.m. Sharpe rushed an interrogation summary to headquarters that identified the enemy forces in the Salient as well as the nature of its defense, confirming and amplifying the visual reconnaissance conducted by Upton and his officers. The report stated Rodes's and Johnson's Divisions were defending the perimeter of the Salient and that hidden fortifications made the position extremely strong. The report was precisely accurate. The two divisions in fact defended a perimeter of about 1 mile with a third, that of Gordon, in reserve in the hidden fortifications that cut across the base of the Salient. The prisoners further said that divisions of Hill's Corps were in deeper reserve to the south, and in fact Hill's troops manned the right of the Confederate line that dog-legged south from the Salient putting them effectively in supporting distance.[48]

The VI Corps attack, as described by Major General Humphreys, went in at 6:10 p.m. from the shelter of a wood only 200 yards from the Salient. At command, from its concealed position, the brigade rushed forward with a hurrah under a terrible front and flank fire, gained the parapet, and had a hand-to-hand desperate struggle, which lasted but a few seconds. Then the column poured over the works, capturing a large number of prisoners. Pressing forward and extending right and left, the second line of entrenchments fell into Upton's hands.

At this moment the VI Corps division held in reserve to exploit just such an opening was stopped cold by heavy Confederate artillery fire as it moved forward. At the same time, Gordon's Division in Ewell's reserve line counterattacked. Upton's men held on but were finally evacuated after dark. He lost a thousand men, but had left the Salient filled with Confederate casualties and brought away 1,000 to 1,200 prisoners. Knight was there to see Upton's men return in a drizzling rain, especially Upton's old regiment, the 121st New York, in which he had many friends. "When they came out they could scarcely have been distinguished from negroes, their faces and hands had become so black by biting cartridges and getting the powder smeared on their wet hands and faces."[49]

Grant was implacable in his determination to keep striking until the Army of Northern Virginia finally collapsed. The near success of the 10th encouraged Grant to plan an even greater blow on the 12th. Hancock's II Corps crashed through the Mule Shoe. The fighting was in close quarters between two implacable masses of men that seethed and killed back and forth over the fortifications, leaving heaps of dead and wounded, probably the most intense combat of the war. In the end, Lee was able to throw in enough reserves to push the Union troops out. The men in blue had suffered 9,000 casualties and the Confederates 8,000. Among the 3,000 prisoners was almost the entire old Stonewall Brigade. Scout Anson Carney was there with Grant's and Meade's command groups:

> … the prisoners were marched into a large open field, being soon after sent to the rear under a strong guard. Half an hour or so later I was ordered to ride after them in haste and secure information if possible with regard to the correctness of a rumor that the enemy had destroyed or burned a large portion of our wagon train. I rode rapidly to the rear. The prisoners had been halted on a hill for a brief rest. I made known my orders to the proper officer in charge. I questioned several of the Johnnies and found there was no truth in the rumor, I returned and reported. But our officers were uneasy, and believed there was something in the rumor, and presently another member of the bureau was dispatched after the prisoners on the same errand. When he returned he corroborated my report.[50]

In this episode is an indication of the problem that plagued the BMI for the rest of the campaign. With only Sharpe and Babcock left as analytical staff, they now had to rely on talented and perceptive scouts such as Knight to conduct interrogations. The other members of the bureau who corroborated Knight's assessment could only have been Babcock since there was no one else available.

Right after the horrendous fighting at Spotsylvania, Sharpe found time to write to the *Kingston Journal* of the casualties suffered by the 120th NY as well as a breathless account of the fighting.

> A partial culmination was reached yesterday in the capture of over 3,000 prisoners and 19 guns; making the whole number of prisoners sent to the rear so far 7,800. Extravagant reports are in circulation, but the above figures will be more than borne out by the official returns. This morning General Lee was found to have retired from our front, only to occupy a very strong position a few miles father on. Large numbers of his wounded are now being brought in by our stretcher-bearers, while piles of his dead encumber our front.

He then addressed the unique nature of the continuous fighting since the battle of the Wilderness. No longer were there brief individual battles between long periods of inaction or maneuver. He was identifying the first occurrence of that hallmark of the modern wars of the Industrial Revolution—continuous operations without let up.

> I must leave you to form an idea from the army correspondents, loose and inaccurate as they are, of the series of operations which have attended us since crossing the Rapidan on the morning of the 4th instant. The situation, I believe, is unparalleled in history. Two large armies, substantially representing the fighting forces of immense populations, lying for nine consecutive days in each other's presence, and throughout that time continually fighting each other with a determination evinced only at rare intervals by great nations in the crisis of their fate. No result is yet reached, and as I write, cannon and musketry have again opened.

He appended a list of the all the regiment's dead (5), wounded (48), and missing (8). "We hope, but only that, that the heaviest is over. God grant that our own regiment, singularly brave among the foremost, may have offered its last tribute to the work!"[51]

As Grant prepared to attack the Mule Shoe, Sharpe dispatched his scouts to scour the area of operations. One group rode east from the army's left in the direction of Guiney's Station supported by a detachment of the 13th Pennsylvania Cavalry and came upon the plantation of a Dr. Boulware which was a collection point for Confederate taxes in kind. While enjoying a square meal, gladly prepared by the plantation's slaves, the scout leader noticed a nearby Confederate signal station in operation about a mile away on the other side of the Mattapomy River. He dispatched the news to Sharpe immediately and requested a signal officer to read the traffic. The signal officer came and harvested a wealth of information. The scouts thought they had found a comfortable billet for the time being and suggested the signal officer relay what an important vantage point it was. His glowing reports, animated by his own fine meal, to headquarters resulted in orders for them to stay where they were and await further orders.

In the meantime the scouts were using their initiative to the best advantage. Scouts Knight, Cole, and Plew spotted a train from Richmond on the way to Guiney's Station. The slaves pointed out it was the mail train. With the help of the 13th Pennsylvania, the scouts tried to capture the train, but it got away. They did capture the mail which had been dropped off. Among the personal letters was one from the "flying artillery" attached to Stuart's cavalry.

> If the writer had tried to give Gen. Grant the information of what Sheridan had done, and what success he had, it would have been impossible for him to have done any better. He told the young lady the day and date where they had met the Yankees, and how they had got whipped; how his battery was lost, all owing to the cowardice of their cavalry, and wound up by advising her never to marry a cavalryman.[52]

For Grant the knowledge of what Sheridan had been up to was his first information since the Cavalry Corps commander had disappeared behind Confederate lines on his deep raid. Knight's report of his raid alerted Sharpe to the fact that Guiney's Station was a supply depot as well as a telegraph station. It now had a guard force after Knight absconded with the mail. On the 18th, a larger raid by 300 cavalrymen led by the scouts drove off the guards, "captured telegraph operators and apparatus, rebel mail, etc. The station was destroyed, besides a large quantity of supplies." Secretary of War Stanton was impressed enough to give it out as a press release, attributing the raid to the scouts.[53]

Grant was plainly impressed when Sharpe presented this intelligence and asked him how many scouts there were that got this information. When Sharpe replied that this particular find was due to the initiative to only a few men, Grant remarked that "he never had any information while he was in the West that would compare with what he had" been receiving on this campaign from Sharpe's organization.[54]

The acquisition of papers through the picket lines also showed that Lee's orders forbidding the pickets to communicate with their Union opposites was simply not being obeyed. For that matter, similar orders of General Meade for the pickets to have no communications from the enemy was more honored in the breach. Meade knew the value of the newspapers Sharpe was bringing him and surely granted him exception for their collection as well as the information on order-of-battle gleaned from casual conversation with Confederate pickets.[55]

Knight was harvesting mail from the Confederate flanks and rear. He rode into one village directly to the post office.

"No one was in at the time. I made a clean sweep of all newspapers and letters but touched nothing else." Just as he was about to leave a woman walked in from the back room and said with genuine astonishment, "Mister, what are you doing?"

"Helping to sort your mail."

"You will assort yourself into jail if you are not careful."

"I reckon not. At all events, I'll risk it."

The scouts had to deal with frequent contact with the elite 9th Virginia Cavalry who were also roaming the flanks and skirmishing with any Union force they met. After capturing a large group of footsore infantry stragglers on the Union right flank at Spotsylvania, who thought the scouts were in larger number than they actually were, a man exclaimed, "'Well, if I have got to be a prisoner I know of no body of men on God's earth I would sooner be a prisoner of then you all.' He had recognized Cline, Plew, and Cole. He been captured by our party the year before in the Gettysburg Campaign."[56]

While his scouts were constantly probing the flanks and rear of the enemy, Sharpe and Babcock were not only keeping track of the enemy's order-of-battle, but providing actionable intelligence for combat operations.

Sharpe had seen the importance of the crossroads at Corbin's Bridge over the Po River behind the Confederate right flank and had sent Knight there repeatedly to observe the enemy during the Wilderness fighting. On the 7th his waiting paid off as he observed a Confederate cavalry regiment come up the bridge to act as a blocking force. At the same time, he witnessed the evacuation of Confederate field hospitals toward Spotsylvania Court House to the southeast followed by the cavalry. A friendly slave delivered to him a good map of the area dropped by a Union topographical engineer from which Knight was able to ascertain the direction of the Confederate movement. The slave told him also that the few men left on the other side of the river were cavalry and would pull out at night.

Knight had been a witness to Lee's reaction to Grant's decision to sidestep the Army of Northern Virginia and steal a march to Spotsylvania Court House which would put him behind Lee's right and between Lee and Richmond. Grant had dispatched his trains first earlier in the day, and it was this movement that the local inhabitants had reported to Lee. Lee, in turn, instantly saw what Grant intended and reacted quickly to steal that march from Grant. He set his army in motion to get the Court House first. It was this movement that Knight observed.

While Grant and Meade assumed the movement of the trains would be too obvious to go undetected by Lee, they were confident that they still had enough of a head start to reach the Court House first. Warren's and Sedgwick's Corps were in the lead, with Hancock left behind to hold the right flank. A few miles to the south across the Po River, the Army of Northern Virginia was streaming toward the Court House. Knight arrived at the BMI camp after dark and was immediately summoned to army headquarters. He stated, "Our reports were always made to Col. Geo. H. Sharpe in person, if he was present." Entering Sharpe's tent he found only Babcock, who asked him how things were going on the Confederate right. Knight replied that "there was nothing going on except that they were evacuating and moving off to our left." Babcock was stunned and immediately began to write out the scout's report—"Knight reports the enemy leaving their left." Then he turned to Knight and said, "This is one of the most important reports we have received in the campaign, and it is in direct conflict with reports received all day from officers along the lines. They report the enemy massing on our right, and the II Corps has been sent out there."

Knight replied, "Yes, I met them as I came in, and there is no use of their going, for I tell you the last one of them [the enemy] have left there before this." Babcock then closely debriefed him. "Then by a series of cross-questions as to what made me think as I did, he learned everything I had to tell. I showed him the map the contraband had given me—in fact left it with him, and fully committed myself to the report." It was a nervous Knight who wandered back to the scout camp.

> After leaving him I began wishing that I had not been quite as positive. I thought to myself, "Suppose these people fully realized what your presence there meant, and took that way of deceiving you. If they had troops where you could not see them, and should make an attack out there tonight, what will be thought of you." To make the thing short, I will state that no sleep visited my eyes that night.[57]

What Knight had reported seemed to confirm Sharpe's report of 8:00 a.m. that morning.

Twenty prisoners brought in this a. m. were taken partly on the enemy's skirmish line but mostly in its rear, asleep in houses. They only know that their line has fallen back; don't know where. Their rations were out last night and were to have been issued last evening; but neither to those who were on the skirmish line nor to those who were with or near the main body of the troops were any rations issued. The prisoners represent four divisions: Anderson's, Rhode's, Early's, and Wilcox's.[58]

These four divisions represented both Confederate corps on the field (Anderson and Wilcox's III Corps, and Rodes and Early's II Corps).

Within minutes of receiving this report, Meade sent it to Grant by the hand of his own son and aide, Capt. George Meade. Grant replied at 8:40 a.m. "I do not infer the enemy are making a stand, but simply covering a retreat, which must necessarily have been slow with such roads and so dark a night as they had last night. I think it advisable to push with at least three good divisions to see beyond doubt what they are doing."[59]

The results of Knight's reconnaissance were included in the following report submitted by Sharpe at 6 p.m. that night to General Meade:

GENERAL: Knight reports he left Tinder's Mill on Po River 1 ½ miles Corbin's Bridge at 3 p. m. Saw a small squad of rebel cavalry (15 men) on this side of the river at the mill. They recrossed on seeing our party. On other side of the Po, one-half mile below mill, on a large clearing, were 75 to 100 cavalry horses grazing. No indications of other force. Not as much rebel cavalry up that way to-day as yesterday. Our men went 2 miles beyond, some of our cavalry picketing in that direction, and saw nothing except as above.[60]

On the same day Cline reported on his reconnaissance of the army's left:

I have followed the line of troops at Anderson's plantation. Came on to rebel cavalry 2 ½ miles from Massaponax Creek. It consisted of two regiments. There is nothing at Hamilton's Crossing; the iron is all taken up from Fredericksburg to Hamilton's. The bed of the road is good except in places where it has been converted into rifle-pits. The bridge across the creek at this place is burned. I shall graze my horses and try what I can find to-night.

Anderson's plantation was 2 miles north of the Spotsylvania and directly behind Union lines. From there northeast to the Massaponax was another 3 ½ miles, and from the creek to Hamilton's crossing 4 ½ miles. The crossing itself was 4 miles south of Fredericksburg on the RF&P Railroad. The two cavalry regiments were what would be expected of Lee covering an open flank. That flank was wide open.[61]

That report also would have found a very receptive audience in Grant, who was intensely frustrated enough to telegraph Halleck that "The enemy are obstinate and seemed to have found the last ditch." That very night, the Army of the Potomac was sent in motion to the left as Grant wrote:

I was afraid that Lee might be moving out, and I did not want him to go without my knowing it. The indications were that he was moving, but it was found that he was only taking his new position back from the salient that had been captured…

The night of the 13th Warren and Wright were moved by the rear to the left of Burnside. The night was very dark and it rained heavily, the roads were so bad that the troops had to cut trees and corduroy the road a part of the way, to get through. It was midnight before they got to the point where they were to halt, and daylight before the troops could be organized to advance to their position in line. They gained their position in line, however without any fighting… This brought our line east of the Court House and running north and south facing west.[62]

As much as Knight believed his report had been the cause of Grant's deciding to move the army to the left, the special order putting the army into motion was dated at 5:45 p.m., but Sharpe's summary of his scouting report was dated at 6:00 p.m. If anything, it was Sharpe's report of that morning that may have made Grant apprehensive that Lee was beginning to move, as he indicated in his memoirs, as well as the cause of dispatching Knight for a special reconnaissance. Knight's report then would have both confirmed Sharpe's original observation and confirmed Grant that he had made the right decision. An alternative explanation based on Knight's description of Babcock's surprise was that his information was briefed orally by Babcock or Sharpe with the latter's written account completed later.

Grant as usual never made a direct reference to Sharpe, the BMI, and intelligence operations. His references were oblique as in this case when he said, "I was afraid

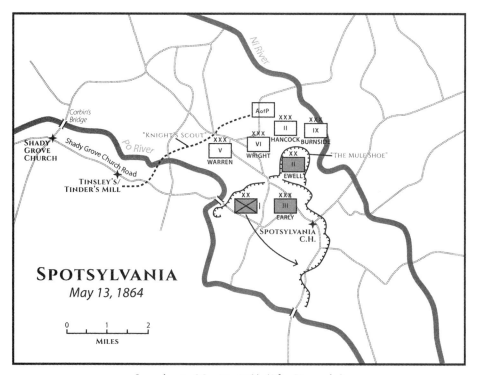

Spotsylvania, May 13, 1864. (After Karamales)

that the enemy was moving out." From Sharpe's report on Knight's observations made at 6 p.m. Grant and Meade would have known they were in a faster race than they realized with a general as swift as fleet-footed Achilles. It gives some credence to Knight's belief written some 30 years later that he had something to do with that.[63]

In any event, the attempt to outflank Lee failed again, and the armies settled down to glare and skirmish with each other for another week. Lee ordered every brigade to thoroughly scout its front. On the night of May 16 a scout of the 1st South Carolina, Sgt. Berry Benson, attempted to pass through the Union pickets by declaring himself a Union scout, relying on the dark to hide the gray of his uniform. It was a daring ruse, but the light of a candle made him a prisoner. He was taken first to an interrogation the next day at the headquarters of the provost marshal general on the very spot he had infiltrated only six days before. Patrick would have been mortified had he known. He was next taken to army headquarters where he was interrogated by a colonel that could only be Sharpe. Benson's postwar account is the only one known to describe one of Sharpe's interrogations from the prisoner's point of view, although some 20 or more years after the fact. Benson was no ordinary prisoner, but a man whose success was due to daring and wits. He would prove no easy subject for Sharpe's probing. Unfortunately, there is no surviving record of Benson's interrogation to balance his memory of it.

Sharpe had already read Benson's diary before he walked out of a tent and immediately accused Benson of being a spy. Benson asked him "what grounds he had for making such a charge, which I denied." Sharpe had to be aware by this point how easily Confederate scouts had penetrated army lines, which explains his further line of questioning.

Sharpe then produced Benson's diary and asked him if it was his and was this his writing. Benson confirmed both questions. Sharpe then asked, "Are you detached from your regular company?" Benson again said yes. "As what?" Sharpe asked.

"In a corps of Sharpshooters, sir."

"Are these Sharpshooters mounted?"

"Not as a general thing, sir. A few have horses that they use sometimes in scouting. I have one, now in charge of my quartermaster."

Sharpe then showed Benson a strip of paper and demanded to know what it meant. It was a receipt for a rebel prisoner dated the 10th. Benson explained that it was the receipt for him from the Union pickets. But, Sharpe, retorted, he was captured on the 16th. Clutching at straws, Benson said the 0 was actually a badly written 6, which Sharpe did not entirely accept.

Then Sharpe asked, "What were you doing when captured?"

"Scouting, sir."

"For what purpose?"

"I was ordered to learn whether you were moving, sir." This was a truthful answer which Benson felt could do no harm to the Confederacy.

"Then, upon being hailed, why did you claim to be a Union scout?"

"I hoped, sir, that they would not order me in, but would let me remain outside the picket lines." Here Benson was dissembling. He had fully intended to penetrate the camp and had already done so on the 11th.

"But upon being brought in you represented yourself to Colonel Switzer also as Union scout." It was Sweitzer's pickets who had picked him up, and their colonel, despite the darkness, had recognized him by his accent as a son of the Palmetto state where he had once worked. Sharpe had obviously already spoken to him about Benson.

"True, sir. But I had to be consistent. I hoped there was a chance *he* might let me go."

Sharpe thought for a moment and then said, "Inside a Federal camp, you misrepresented yourself as a Union scout. Is that not spying?" This was a gambit to frighten Benson.

Benson protested. "Colonel, I was taken *outside* your lines, armed with my regular arms, dressed in full grey uniform, as a Confederate. Was it wrong of me to make use of this accidental advantage? Wouldn't your scouts have done the same thing?" Sharpe may have had trouble keeping a straight face since his scouts did exactly the same thing—Cline, Knight, and Anson Carney among the most brazen and cool.

Benson recalled that he had never been more eloquent in his life and that his interrogator seemed to soften to him. Sharpe said that Benson would probably be tried by court-martial as a spy. He said he felt kindly to Benson, would do all he could for him, and hoped things would turn out well. The scout, now in a state of high anxiety, was placed with other prisoners, one of whom told him that in his interrogation he had been asked what motive Benson could have had for claiming to be a scout. The man claimed he was just a frightened greenhorn. He gathered from the conversation of his interrogators that Benson would be classified only as a prisoner of war.[64]

"Virginia and Lee's army is not Tennessee and Bragg's army"

All along the gory trail from the Rappahannock to the James, Grant had been expecting the imminent collapse of Lee's army. Smelling blood he had kept attacking, turning the Overland Campaign into the most costly period of the war, willing to lose two men for every one of Lee's. His expectations were fed by his experience against the Confederate armies in the west and by an uncritical assessment of information from prisoner interrogations that painted a picture of despair and breakdown. His picture at times verged on wishful thinking, as he continually confused Southern tenacity with the last surge of effort before the death rattle. He pointed out that Lee's refusal to meet him in the open field since the Wilderness and fight only from behind entrenchments showed a collapsing morale. He did not stop to consider that the defense was a common-sense tactic by Lee who was fighting outnumbered and out-resourced and that in the hands of a brilliant engineer like Lee, the defense evened the odds considerably. Grant confused this with how the Confederates in the west had behaved, and to him it bespoke a loss of fighting spirit, a recognition of looming defeat. Lee's men would be no different, he believed. Meade, with his long familiarity with Lee and his army, would write home in despair, "Virginia and Lee's army is not Tennessee and Bragg's army." He realized that for Grant, the wish had become father to the thought.[65]

It is difficult to imagine Sharpe and Babcock, with their seasoned interrogation skills, giving undue weight to the tales of woe from deserters and prisoners. That's what prisoners often do to curry favor with their captors. But even these reports were far thinner on the ground than would be imagined from Grant's enthusiasm. On May 17 Sharpe reported the results of an interrogation of one deserter.

> We have a deserter who came into our lines last night from Forty-fifth North Carolina, Daniel's brigade, Rodes' division, which he left lying on the enemy's left near where Hancock charged the corner. Thinks his whole division is there. Loss in his brigade very heavy. General Daniel killed. This man thinks that within a few days the spirit of the men has somewhat failed. Rations issued for two days Saturday night, which is the last he was in the way of knowing about. Knows nothing of re-enforcements or communications.[66]

Grant received these reports through channels from Meade and did not have the opportunity to be briefed personally by Sharpe or Babcock. He appears to have read what he wanted into them. On May 23 on the North Anna he would write Halleck, "Lee's army is really whipped. The prisoners we now take show it."[67]

Confusion and the North Anna

By the last week of May, Sharpe was able to inform Meade and Grant that Lee had been receiving important reinforcements. On May 24 his scouts had identified Kemper's Brigade of Pickett's Division as the force opposing Hancock the day before and reported that civilians had said that the rest of the division had arrived at the Chesterfield Station just north of Hanover Junction on the RF&P Railroad. That brigade earlier had been detached to serve under Maj. Gen. Robert F. Hoke in the capture of Plymouth, North Carolina, in April. Scouts now reported as well that 2,000 men passed through Milford, barely 10 miles south of Spotsylvania, on the 20th. He added:

> [W]e have a prisoner from Forty-third North Carolina, which has been with Hoke in North Carolina and is now back with three other regiments (Twenty-first North Carolina, Fifty-seventh North Carolina, and the Twenty-first Georgia), having left Richmond day before yesterday early, marched from Milford toward Lee's army and back again yesterday. This man says three trains left Richmond with the troops, and he heard Ransom's brigade was on the way…

Barton's Brigade of Pickett's Division had also marched through Milford about this time to Spotsylvania but, finding the army falling back, marched to Hanover Court House where the rest of the division assembled and was joined by Pickett himself on the 27th.

Sharpe was faced with one of the most difficult problems for an intelligence officer—to make sense of an enemy's order-of-battle that was in the immediate process of both heavy reinforcement and significant reorganization. The following explanation keyed to the previous report presents the scope of the problem.

Sharpe was correct that the 43rd North Carolina had been indeed with Hoke at Salem as one of the regiments in his original brigade. The 21st North Carolina and 21st Georgia were also part of Hoke's original brigade and fought at Drewry's Bluff in the defense of Richmond against Butler's army. Once transferred to the Army of Northern Virginia, they were assigned to three brigades of Early's II Corps: The 43rd North Carolina went to Grime's Brigade and the 21st Georgia went to Dole's Brigade, both in Rodes's Division; the 21st and 57th North Carolina went to Lewis's Brigade, Ramseur's Division. The 57th had originally belonged to Lewis's Brigade before being sent to North Carolina, and was the only one that would have fit into Sharpe's order-of-battle records.

In April Hoke had been promoted to major general after his victory at Plymouth in command of an ad hoc division. To complicate things for Sharpe that was not the division with which he joined Lee. It had been cobbled together from four brigades that had originally been stationed along the coast but recently transferred to Richmond. In early May Hoke now commanded a division in the defenses of Richmond. It helped repulse Butler on May 16 and was ordered to join Lee but dropped two of its brigades and picked up two new ones from two other divisions in Richmond. The division joined the Army of Northern Virginia on May 18, about the same time as Pickett's Division began arriving. Hoke's Division's returns for May 21 showed 7,125 men present for duty. The records do not indicate whether Sharpe knew the composition or the strength of the division. He would have seen Hancock's report of the 21st in which slaves reported that Hoke's Division with 10–13,000 men had arrived at Milford 2 miles south of Bowling Green to reinforce Lee. Given the source, Sharpe would have discounted the number but not necessarily the unit.

In the same report of the 22nd, Sharpe also cited the dispatches captured by Cline that gave information on Sheridan's Cavalry Corps raid and the enemy's movements directed at the Union army. They also brought in Richmond newspapers with more information on Sheridan's approach to the capital. That report had one more useful piece of information.

A prisoner from Longstreet's Corps described with a certain rough accuracy the shape of the positions occupied by Lee's army on the North Anna. It was in the shape of a V. Hill's Corps ran between the North and South Anna Rivers then curved up to run along the North Anna until it joined Longstreet's Corps, which ran diagonally southeast of the river where it joined Ewell's Corps. The genius of this position was that the rounded apex of the V shape rested upon the river. Reinforcements then could be easily shifted within this triangle and just as importantly it ensured that the enemy would have to divide his forces in order to attack both long sides of the V. Warren's Corps arrived on the 23rd and crossed the river, only to run into a strong attack from Hill. Hancock arrived later and took a bridgehead over the river as Anderson pulled his I Corps back. Sheridan returned with the Cavalry Corps on the 24th. While Grant was staring at the Confederate position across the river, Lee was prostrate with diarrhea, Hill was sick, and Ewell exhausted, none of which was known on the enemy side. Again as at the Wilderness, the absence of BMI reporting tells us nothing about the intelligence support of the Union operation.

On the 26th Sharpe's scouts also brought in the information that with the arrival of troops from the Valley and the opinion of civilians, no Confederate forces had been left in the Valley. This was undoubtedly Gen. John C. Breckinridge, former vice-president of the United States under John Buchanan (1857–61) and Lincoln's opponent for the presidency in 1860 and now fresh from his victory at New Market in the Valley on May 15. Sharpe believed he was there personally. The day before Grant wired Halleck based on Sharpe's reporting that "Breckinridge is unquestionably here. Sixty-six officers and men have been captured who were with Hoke in the capture of Plymouth."[68]

Sharpe confirmed that Breckinridge's Division had joined Lee's army. A deserter from the 23rd Virginia Battalion, Echols's Brigade, had left his camp at Hanover Court House right after they arrived on the 24th. He identified the division's two infantry brigades correctly but mistakenly included Imboden's Brigade of cavalry with it. In the same report he described prisoner testimony of trains leaving Richmond filled with furloughed men returning to their regiments in Lee's army. There were, however, no organized units, only individuals. Sharpe also reported the position of Lee's right flank held by Ewell's Corps.

Sharpe would have a lot to do to keep track of all the organizational and command changes in the Army of Northern Virginia caused by heavy casualties to include division and brigade commanders. Normally, this was the work of months to untangle all these changes in a stable base. The BMI had neither the time nor the base. The army had been on the march between the Wilderness and Spotsylvania for two days (May 7–8), between Spotsylvania and the North Anna for four days (May 20–23), and between the North Anna and Cold Harbor for five days (night of the 26th to the first of June)—a total of 11 of the 28 days since the campaign began on May 4 to the army's arrival at Cold Harbor, or almost 40 percent of the time. It is amazing that the BMI accomplished as much as it did. Brigadier General Patrick emphasized this same problem when he prepared a prisoner-of-war summary for Grant at the beginning of November after the armies had settled around Petersburg. "It is impossible to tell with any degree of definiteness, on what occasions the captures were made... In consequence of the manner in which we moved, no permanent record of the prisoners taken was kept, until after the 27th of July, when the office at this place [City Point] was established."[69]

Johnson's Division of II Corps had disappeared from the order-of-battle, its remnants consolidated into a single brigade after the carnage at the Salient. Two new divisions, those of Breckinridge and the other entirely new division under recently promoted Maj. Gen. Robert F. Hoke, were added to the army but not subordinated to any of the corps but under Lee's direct control. Pickett's Division, which had been detached since last September, rejoined I Corps as well. Sharpe would have a lot to do to keep track of all the organizational and command changes in the Army of Northern Virginia. Wilderness and Spotsylvania had reaped a heavy harvest of Lee's regimental, brigade, and division commanders.[70]

Not counting the individuals returning from furlough, Sharpe had informed his commanders that Lee had received in the space of less than a week reinforcement in three new divisions and a number of separate regiments, and that the defenses of Richmond and the Valley had been stripped to provide them. However, the flow of reinforcements did not even begin to make up for the losses of the Army of Northern Virginia. On May 31 Lee issued the following order:

> ... to get every available man in the ranks by to-morrow. Gather in all stragglers and men absent without proper authority. Send to the field hospitals and have every man capable of performing the duties of a soldier returned to his command. Send back your inspectors with instructions to see that the wishes of the general commanding are carried out. Let every man fit for duty be present.[71]

Running Dispatches

By the time the army was moving to Cold Harbor, Grant had cut loose from his overland communications. While the army was self-sufficient for the near term in everything it needed, it had become more than difficult to communicate with Washington in a timely manner, especially since the 9th Virginia Cavalry carefully patrolled the areas to the army's rear and snatched up any small parties they came upon. Sharpe's scouts were now entrusted with dispatches. Anson Carney and another scout tried to go by land through the Wilderness but had to turn back.

> Cline and Phelps made their way to the Potomac River, constructed a raft and got across to the Maryland side, where the river was several miles in width; got aboard a schooner where they had smallpox. They had to draw their pistols and threaten to use them before they could make the crew get underway.[72]

At the end of May after the army had crossed the Pamunkey River, Knight was told to report to the command group. Patrick told him that Assistant Secretary of the Army Charles Dana, who had accompanied Grant's headquarters since Wilderness, wanted to see him. When he reported to the command tent, Grant and Col. Rufus Ingalls, the quartermaster general of the army, were there too. Dana introduced himself and said, "You are a scout. We want to send dispatches to Yorktown. That is the nearest point we can reach a telegraph." Knight thought to himself that "Yorktown was about 70 miles away, and the country between in full possession of the enemy. I am free to confess that there was no craving on my part for the job." All he knew of the area to be crossed was what he remembered as an infantryman in the Peninsular Campaign.

> Two years had elapsed since. I thought over our guides, and the different scouts; not a man of them knew a thing of the country, and told Mr. Dana that were was not a horse in our party in fit condition to make such a trip, and said my own horse had a sore back—in fact, they all had. Gen. Grant, I could see, was listening to our conversation. When I mentioned the condition of the horses in our party, he said: "Ingalls, haven't you got fresh horses in the corral?" "Yes," said he. Then he said to me: "When you get through here, I will go with you to the corral, and show you what I have." That settled it, and I could see there was no way to get out of it, and might as well put on a cheerful air as any other. Mr. Dana then showed me a lot of dispatches, and marked them, saying, "This is to be telegraphed, and this is to be mailed," until he had all but three marked.

Now well-mounted and with trusted companion James Hatton he set out. They encountered Brig. Gen. George Custer, who remembered Knight from their service with Brigadier General Kearny two years before and inquired of their mission. When told, he replied, "I should not care to take such a trip." Custer was more than right. That very day a Pamunkey Indian warned them of heavy Confederate patrols. Before long they were seen and chased but escaped. Hiding out that night, they held their

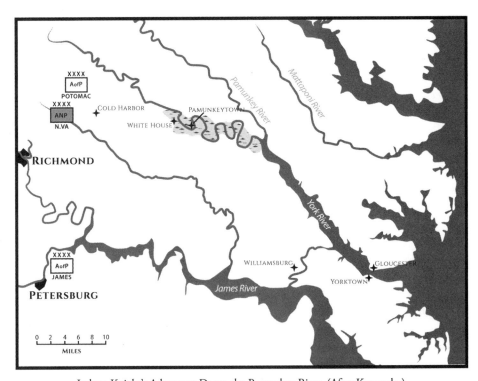

Judson Knight's Adventure Down the Pamunkey River. (After Karamales)

horses in silence in the woods as the patrol stopped within earshot to discuss their escape, sure they were couriers. That decided Knight that the job was only for one man on foot, and he sent Hatton back with the horses. The next day he was chased into a swamp by the enemy and hid all day.[73]

The following day he made his way to the Pamunkey River and encountered several slaves fishing. He tried to pass himself off as a Confederate soldier with the group that had just tried to catch him. A slave told him outright that he was a Yankee:

> "Oh, you don't talk like our folks does."
> Up to that time I had imagined I was playing the part of a Confederate rather successfully, and to be detected by this fellow so easily made me ashamed. I had played the part of a Confederate surgeon only the previous Winter, and knew that there was no suspicion on the part of several families of white people of my being anything than what I represented myself to be. It lowered me several pegs in my own estimation.

They asked him if was true that Yankees cut off the arms of black people as their masters had told him. He replied that it was nonsense, and they were immensely relieved, fed him, and sold him a boat.

He paddled down the river and eventually climbed a bluff to make his way inland to White House, when he was stopped by Union pickets who escorted him to Major General Smith, commanding XVIII Corps. The general put him on the first steamer and sent him to Yorktown where he delivered his dispatches to the telegraph and post offices. It had taken him two days. He treated himself to a good meal and new clothes and regaled the troops there with stories of the fighting. He made his way back to army headquarters on foot and horse, arriving on June 2, the day before grand assault at Cold Harbor.[74]

Cold Harbor

Even Grant considered Lee's position on the North Anna too dangerous to attack, and on the night of the 26th the army once more moved out to its left, crossing the Pamunkey River marching southeast to wrap around Lee's right flank. Meade sent Sheridan ahead with cavalry divisions to take the crossroads village of Cold Harbor. Lee quickly joined the race but found the cavalry there first on June 1. Anderson's Corps attacked with force but recoiled at the firepower of the repeater-armed Union cavalry. The Confederates drew back and immediately set about building their field fortifications. An attack late in the day by Union infantry nearly cracked the Confederate line; Grant planned for the killer stroke to be delivered two days later. There is an absence of BMI reporting from May 29 until right after the assault, so there is little to base what intelligence support Sharpe could have provided. Whatever the loss of documentation, it appears that the senior officers were pleased with what they were getting from the BMI.

On June 2 a Union signal station reported that the enemy's positions had remained unchanged, and Sheridan's cavalry was hovering on the Confederate flanks. There was little more that Sharpe could have added that would have prevented the horrendous loss of 7,000 men to Lee's 1,500. Grant ordered a second attack, but the army from private to general simply refused. Grant would later write that his decision to attack was what he regretted most in the war. In a speech Sharpe gave after the war in 1876, however, he stated, "The general commanding always maintained that we should have continued the contest even at a further loss of thousands, and if we had only known, as we know now, that their Army was practically destitute of ammunition when we withdrew, how much subsequent slaughter and expense would have been saved." Unfortunately, the exhaustion of Confederate ammunition was not something the BMI was able to uncover at the time.[75]

The evening after the attack, Sharpe made a report based on a pool of about 300 prisoners taken that day. "Their examination shows that to-day Ewell held their left, Longstreet next, Breckinridge next, with a new division of four brigades on their right, and that the greater part of A. P. Hill's corps was in reserve near the right." He was precisely correct in every detail except he had not yet learned that Ewell had been replaced by Early.[76]

The day after the last attack, Sharpe had a fruitful opportunity to glean information through the picket line. Lieutenant Colonel Lyman was an observer as he came over to the Confederate side to seek a truce in order to pick up the wounded who lay thick on the line. "The pickets were determined to have also a truce, for when a Reb officer went down the line to give some order, he returned quite aghast, and said the two lines were together, amiably conversing. He ordered them to their posts, but I doubt if they staid." Lyman was back on the 7th, when Lee finally granted the truth after most of the wounded were dead. Both sides came out onto the field now as burial parties.

> Round one grave, where ten men were laid, there was a great crowd of both sides. The Rebels were anxious to know who would be next President. "Wall," said one of our men, "I am in favor of Old Abe." "He's a damned Abolitionist!" promptly exclaimed a grey-back. Upon which our man hit his adversary between the eyes, and a general fisticuff ensued, only stopped by the officers rushing in.[77]

In all of this carnage, Sharpe and Knight still found time to help out a forlorn soldier. Knight remembered:

> My old regiment (2nd NJ) went home from Cold Harbor, and a day or two afterward one of the guards at the "bull-pen," a member of the 20th NY, came to me and said: "There is a man in the bull-pen who says he belongs to your old regiment, and wants to see you."
>
> I went back with him, when a young fellow who was on the inside of the line of guards pressed forward as far as the guard would let him, and said: "Don't you know me, Sergeant?"
>
> I took a good look at him, and answered: "No; I can't say that I do."
>
> He said: "Sergeant, I used to belong to your old regiment."
>
> "What company were you in?"
>
> "G, and yours was H."
>
> "Yes; that is right. So you were in Capt. Close's Company. How did you get in here? The regiment has gone home, and I can't see how you should be in the bull-pen."

He then told me that he was in one of the Wilderness fights, and was wounded; had been sent to Washington to a hospital, and as soon as he could leave it applied to be sent to his regiment; had come down the Potomac to Port Royal, and had helped to guard a wagon-train from there to Army Headquarters; when he got there his regiment was gone. His story had not been believed, and he had been brought up in the pen. After listening to his story he said: "You remember me now, don't you, Sergeant?"

I could not recollect him, and said so. Tears came into his eyes as I turned away and walked to Col. Sharpe's tent, who at that time was Deputy Provost-Marshal-General of the Army of the Potomac. I went in and told the story to Sharpe, and when I got through he said: "Do you remember him?"

"Hardly; but I know he tells the truth."

"Well, said he, "it is a shame, and we will have him out."

He then wrote out an order to turn the boy over to me, and told me to go and get him. When he came the Colonel questioned him for a few minutes, gave him an order for transportation and the paper he would need to keep him out of trouble with military authorities, and turned him loose. He was one of the most grateful boys I ever saw.[78]

Even after the disastrous assault, Grant's determination to fight it out with everything he had was clear to everyone. Writing his Uncle Jansen, Sharpe noted that Grant had ordered that no officer could go to Washington except the wounded. Sharpe was wistful since his wife was living in Washington solely because of its proximity to him, "and I must have her there as long as she desires it."

But his attention was only briefly distracted. The bloodbath at Cold Harbor had left Sharpe with a sobering idea of what lay ahead:

I can scarcely say whether we shall push on to Richmond direct from this point or not. The Chickahominy is deadly—but it would probably cost us from 20 to 30,000 men to fight our way thus to the James—& we should be that much weaker on getting there, without perhaps being able to inflict equal loss on the enemy, as we have thus far done.

He then weighed the options. It was all speculation but informed speculation since Grant was keeping his plans close to the vest. "We are now 12 miles from Richmond by the roads—& in swinging around to the James, every step would put us farther off. The country around the James is more healthy—we would have good communications & the gunboats."

While the next move hung in the balance, Sharpe's faith in Grant was only growing. "You see it is difficult to decide—but Grant has decided I have no doubt. His determination is immense—& I begin to think him a considerable of a man." Sharpe's confidence had survived the huge casualties of the campaign so far; he could see the long-term effects on the enemy. "We have certainly not been whipped—we have whaled Lee considerably twice, without routing him, to be sure—and we have sent many guns, colors, & 12,000 prisoners to the rear. The Va Central [railroad] is destroyed & we are in front of Richmond." Then in a bit of overconfidence he would have cause to rue, he wrote, "[I]f he [Lee] want now to go to Penn, I think Grant would hail the opportunity."[79]

As chief of the BMI and deputy provost marshal, Sharpe's writ ran to identifying and suppressing subversive activities and espionage among the local population in the army's area of operations. He was appalled when an overzealous commander sent him two local women accused of providing information to the enemy:

> They are ignorant and simple-minded people, and I have failed to discover the slightest evidence of any intent on their part. I think they had no idea that they were doing any harm, and that they would have given us information about the rebels with equal readiness had the occasion offered. Mrs. Bowles is very far gone with child, and General Patrick approves a respectful recommendation to the commanding general that they be returned home.[80]

That writ, however, ran rougher when the examination of seeming Confederate deserters indicated that they were after all originally Union deserters who were trying to escape service by claiming Lincoln's amnesty. Patrick wrote about the method used to winnow out these characters:

> The usual practice of this office in examining prisoners has been to let them tell their own stories until by their own falsehoods and impossible statements we know they are deserters when we tie them up to trees and keep them without food until they tell their regiments. Colonel Sharpe, Capt. Leslie and myself are the only persons who do this and among the vast numbers thus treated no mistake has ever been made.[81]

This and only one other piece of correspondence, to be shown later, so far discovered in the official records of the National Archives identifies what might be called in today's more sensitive if not overwrought times "enhanced interrogation methods." Surely, if such methods had been common, the Southern newspapers and literature, both during and after the war, would have been rife with graphic descriptions.

Although Meade forced Sharpe's reporting to go through channels, it was being read and acknowledged at the highest levels. On June 9 at Cold Harbor, Assistant Secretary of War Dana wrote to Stanton, forwarding "a communication just send [sic sent] from Colonel Sharpe, deputy provost-marshal-general, to chief of staff, Army of the Potomac," noting "Principle facts above are confirmed by various other evidence, and are most probably correct." The reference to the authority of all-source confirmation is telling.[82]

Sharpe's continuous acquisition of Richmond and other Southern newspapers allowed Grant to remain informed of the progress of other commands in a far more timely manner. By this point, he was largely cut off from overland communication with Union territory. Enough Southern forces filled in behind his armies made it dangerous, as Knight's adventures on the Pamunkey showed, to try to get information this way. Southern newspapers, on the other hand, had the advantage of interior lines connected by telegraph and, over short distances, couriers. Rawlins would be sure to mention these finds in his letters to his wife. On June 7 he wrote he was reading a *Richmond Inquirer* of the same day, a feat of timely intelligence on Sharpe's part. That issue related welcome news. Union Maj. Gen. David Hunter had defeated and killed General W. H. "Grumble" Jones at the battle of Piedmont 12 miles beyond Staunton. Rawlins described it as "a triumph which will inure greatly to our interest in this campaign." He continued, "Hunter is doing what we expected Sigel to do some time since. Hunter and a heavy force, under General Crook, will meet now without doubt at Staunton if they have not already done so. Their combined forces will be sufficiently strong to enable them to strike a staggering blow to the Confederacy."[83]

On June 10 Grant's chief of staff, Maj. Gen. John Rawlins, wrote a letter in which he stated that Richmond newspapers brought Grant his first news of General Hunter's continued progress and successes in the Valley, a full three days before Hunter's dispatch arrived with the news. Grant had every right to be pleased with Sharpe and his men. He was now clearly getting detailed information from Sharpe on the state of Confederate logistics at the strategic level. That had concentrated his attention on Lynchburg, the nexus of two vital railroads and the James Canal. His orders to Hunter embodied that appreciation. Hunter was to seize Lynchburg and Charlottesville to ensure that the railroads and canals "should be destroyed beyond possibility of repair for weeks."

Grant would write in his memoirs of the source of some of that information—the Richmond newspapers Sharpe's scouts were bringing through the lines or acquired by trade from the pickets.

> About this time word was received (through the Richmond papers of the 11th) that Crook and Averell had united and were moving east. This, with the news of Hunter's successful engagement near Staunton, was no doubt known to Lee before it was to me. Then Sheridan leaving with two divisions of cavalry, looked indeed threatening, both to Lee's communications and supplies. Much of his cavalry went after Sheridan, and Early with Ewell's entire Corps sent to the Valley. Supplies were growing scarce in Richmond, and the sources from which to draw them were in our hands. People from outside began to pour into Richmond to help eat up the little on hand. Consternation reigned there.

Again on the 15th Rawlins wrote that Richmond papers reported Hunter's capture of Lexington. On the 21st and 22nd he cited Richmond papers that announced the defeat of Hunter at Lynchburg on the 18th. This was the first news to reach Grant about an important Union setback in the effort to destroy a vital Confederate transportation hub. All of this information was courtesy of George Sharpe and his BMI.[84]

Toward the end of the Overland Campaign, Knight would encounter a refugee from Richmond whose information would lead to a great opportunity for the BMI in the months to come.

> At Cold Harbor I met a citizen who was sent to our quarters with orders for us to take care of him. He was with us, I should think, three days, then he came over from Gen. Grant's and Gen. Meade's headquarters and said to me:
> "Good-by; I am going to leave you."
> "Well, sir, good-by. Where are you going?"

"To Philadelphia."

He then told me that Grant and Meade had not made him take the oath of allegiance; and when I asked him the reason, he said it was not expected from him, so that the Confederates should have no excuse, if they heard of it, for confiscating his property. Before I got through talking with him, I learned he was from Richmond; that his name was John N. Van Lew; that his family were from Philadelphia, originally; that his father had been a successful hardware merchant in Richmond for many years previous to the war; also, that he was in the same business; that his mother and sister were both living on Church Hill; that the family were known as Union people; also, that the rebel Provost-Marshal-General Winder was boarding at their house, and that they gave him his board as an equivalent for the protection he afforded the family. As soon as he told me he was from Richmond I began importuning him to join our party, and he inquired what we were. As soon as I told him he declined, saying that the life would not suit him.[85]

When we parted, he said to me: "I will tell you something that may be of value to you. If you can ever get into communication with my mother or sister, they are in a position where they might furnish you with valuable information. Their names are both Elizabeth Van Lew." I walked with him several miles and urged him to stay with us, for patriotism if nothing else, but did not succeed.[86]

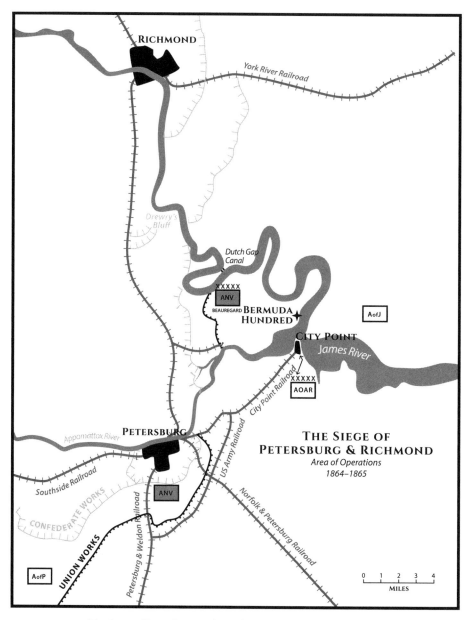

The Siege of Petersburg-Richmond Area of Operations 1864–65.

CHAPTER TEN

Petersburg and Intelligence Overhaul

June–August 1864

Stealing a March

Blocked again by Lee north of Richmond and with dangerously extended supply lines, Grant sought to steal another march on the night of June 12. This time the army would cross first the Chickahominy then the James River below Richmond to seize Petersburg and cut off the Confederate capital's communications and force Lee into decisive combat. His supply lines would then be reestablished by sea and the James River.

Sharpe had been reporting on the state of the garrison of Richmond and Petersburg. On June 10, the interrogation of North Carolinian deserters indicated that the "force for the protection of Richmond is altogether too small. It is not believed that their new troops and conscripts will make a good fight, and but few of the old troops are left." The next day Sharpe reported that one of his scouts who had infiltrated an enemy headquarters had overheard Confederate Brigadier General Scales speaking to a number of officers:

> ... a large number of [Union] scouts are employed to continually approach and reconnoiter our lines in front, as it is their momentary expectation to find our lines withdrawn for the purpose of being passed to the left to the James River. For this, it is claimed, full preparation has been made, and it is given out in the rebel army that a portion of General Beauregard's forces have occupied and intrenched [sic] Malvern Hill, and that their lines are sufficiently prolonged to connect with Malvern Hill from their present position in our front.[1]

This information could have had a chilling effect on the resolve of anyone but Grant. Instead it beckoned with opportunity. He had learned that sidestepping to his left to get around Lee's flank in order to bring him to decisive battle simply was not working. Lee was just too good a soldier and engineer to let that work.

Grant worried that trying to maintain a line of supply for operations northeast of Richmond "would give us a long vulnerable line of road to protect, exhausting much of our strength to guard it," while allowing the enemy to be supplied by the network of railroads south of the James. "I now find, after over thirty days of trial, the enemy deems it of the first importance to run no risks... They act purely on the defensive..." The enemy also had an enormous new advantage of position. "Lee's position was now so near Richmond, and the intervening swamps of the Chickahominy so great an obstacle to the movement of troops in the face of an enemy... Without a greater sacrifice of human life than I am willing to make," something else would have to be done to cut this Gordian knot. He concluded, "I determined to make my next left flank move carry the Army of the Potomac south of the James River."[2] His objective was Petersburg, just south of Richmond, where all the railroads that could supply Lee and sustain the Confederate capital converged.

Leaving Warren's V Corps to demonstrate in front of Lee, Grant put the army in motion on the night of the 20th, a full 8 miles north to the rear. Security was so good that Lee was not to discover that his opponent had slipped away until the next day. Even then, Lee did not comprehend the audacity of the move. He thought Grant would attempt another, shallow envelopment that would directly threaten Richmond from the north or east. This he planned to forestall as he had the other such moves. The operating element of the intelligence obtained by Sharpe was that Lee would only put his move into action when his scouts had revealed another attempt to outflank him. To meet that threat Lee threw cavalry out initially to cover the line from Malvern Hill to White Oak Swamp Creek, a southern tributary of the Chickahominy. With one flank resting on Malvern Hill which itself frowned over the James River and the other flank on White Oak Swamp, he felt assured that he had a powerful defensive line of little over 5 miles' length.

Sharpe's report did contain a positive error—Beauregard had not garrisoned Malvern Hill with infantry. That hill had been held by McClellan's men in the 1862 Peninsular Campaign against repeated bloody charges by Lee. It could serve such a purpose for the Confederates this time. Grant encouraged him to think defensively by aggressively screening this line with V Corps before Warren slipped off to join the rest of the army assembling on the north bank of the James. Brigadier General James H. Wilson's Cavalry Division continued the screen on the 13th after Warren withdrew, which prevented Lee from discovering the massive movement of the Army of the Potomac about 8 miles to Wilson's rear.

Lee was further inhibited from offensive action by his dispatch of II Corps, to save threatened Lynchburg in the Shenandoah, on the same day that Grant slipped away from him. He had a further mission to threaten Washington to force Grant to thin his forces to defend the capital. Lee's security emphasis was on his own left to make sure that Grant did not learn he was sending Early off. It worked perfectly; no word leaked out. Grant and Lee had successfully deceived each other on the same day in what both thought would be a decisive strategic move. It was one of those very rare examples in military history in which both sides attempt the same maneuver simultaneously and in opposite directions. Both sides were so intent on their stratagems that they did not detect each other's departure.

Grant cut loose his overland communications and ordered the army to be supplied up the James River with his base at City Point. In three days 115,000 troops in five corps and one cavalry division passed over a pontoon bridge thrown across the James River. At over 2,100 feet it was the largest ever built, and it was built in less than a day. The 49 batteries of artillery of almost 330 guns were accompanied by their 1,200 caissons and ammunition wagons and followed by an enormous supply wagon train that together stretched 35 miles long, and was trailed by 3,500 beef cattle. The transfer of the army had been a triumph of staff work and a superb performance by the quartermasters and engineers.[3] "Grant had done the near-impossible and had completely out-witted Lee. The Federal movement had been complicated and dangerous, and had been handled with rare skill."[4]

For Grant this maneuver was meant to be the killing stroke. He was showing the strain of this great movement so fraught with perils. He lit his cigars over and over, again and again, letting them go out. He was short with his staff officers, and his aide, Col. Horace Porter, wrote that he was "wrought up to an intensity of thought and action which he seldom displayed." By seizing Petersburg, he would cut the three southern railroads that tied Richmond to the rest of the Confederacy. It would force Lee to abandon his endless entrenching to come to the rescue of the capital and logistics. It meant Lee would have to fight in the open where Grant's numbers would be decisive. It should have been done. It could have been done. The Confederates had erected for the defense of Petersburg the strongest fortifications seen by the Union army in the war, yet there were barely 2,200 men to guard them.[5]

The Army of the Potomac had massed on the northern bank of the James behind the Wyanoke Peninsula by the 14th. Lee by now had sensed that Grant was somewhere on the James. Yankee stragglers stated Grant was heading for Harrison's Landing where McClellan had had his base camp in the Peninsula Campaign of two years ago. McClellan's fortifications were still intact, and Lee did not think it wise to attack Grant there. At the same time, Sharpe's scouts were actively looking at Harrison's Landing and reported back that it was guarded by a picket line with mounted infantry behind.[6]

The Army of the Potomac started to cross the next day. At the same time, Grant had ordered Butler to send Smith's XVIII Corps with Maj. Gen. August V. Kautz's cavalry in the lead. His cavalry overran the outer line of works in a great rush, but the infantry would be needed to take the more imposing lines behind. Smith and his corps reached it first on June 16—and stopped. The sheer might of the fortifications and the dread of the slaughter at Cold Harbor gave him pause that he must mount a deliberate attack as did the rumor that Lee's troops were arriving on his front. Beauregard, in command of the defenses of Richmond and Petersburg, had stripped the latter of defenders to send reinforcements to Lee and recently to counter an attack by the Army of the James at Bermuda Hundred on the 10th, the very diversion that Grant had counted on when he ordered the attack. But Beauregard had just thrown the bumbling Benjamin Butler back into his works at Bermuda Hundred, something Grant had not planned on. Now Beauregard began shifting his meager forces south to Petersburg while begging Lee for help. While Smith contemplated his next move, Hancock's II Corps, which was supposed to support the attack, was uselessly countermarching because of erroneous orders. Grant had not taken Meade into his confidence that Hancock was supposed to throw his weight into Smith's attack, and this mission was not included in Meade's ordering. Wright's fresh VI Corps, which could have made the forced march to Petersburg in good time, displayed no sense of urgency in its approach.

Grant could share the blame with Smith for his failure to closely control this vital operation. Beauregard showed no such lack of celerity that day. He had played his bad hand with skill. It would be one of the great lost opportunities of the war. Sharpe's senior scouts, Cline and Knight, had ridden ahead, and Knight would later record the surreal moment when the fate of Petersburg, Richmond, and the war itself hung in the balance:

> About 4 p.m. we came out on the high ground to the east and in full view of Petersburg. No Confederate troops were to be seen, and the outer line of works captured by Gen. Kautz a day or two before were standing there unmanned. The troops in the advance were halted and bivouacked for the night. It could not have been over two and half miles from the heart of the city. A little before dark, Cline and I rode down the Prince George Courthouse road, through the works captured by Kautz very nearly to the top of the hill. Some gasworks were just to the right of us. A few shots, not over a dozen altogether, were fired on us. Cline said to me if we had a hundred men we could go in and do what we pleased. My belief was that we could, but next morning it was too late.[7]

The recriminations over the failure to seize Petersburg had begun. On the surface, the blame could be described as an intelligence failure. Had Smith known that so few men held the lines at Petersburg, he most likely would have swept over them. He was not a timid man, but the lessons of Missionary Ridge and Cold Harbor tugged at his sleeve. The fact was that Sharpe's operation had begun to break down. Sharpe was now facing a series of major intelligence failures largely outside his control. A good part of the Petersburg fiasco could be laid at the feet of Butler; Petersburg was in the area of operations of his Army of the James, and he had not had a clue as to the depletion of its defenses to pass onto Grant through Sharpe.

A host of circumstances had whittled away Sharpe's ability keep his hand on the enemy's pulse. The continuous movement of the army since early May had deprived the BMI of the stable base it needed. Meade was doing nothing to facilitate Sharpe's work either. On June 8 Sharpe had requested the detail of a Pvt John Smith from the 22nd New Hampshire Cavalry to his scouts. He had heard good things of the man's abilities and wanted to test them. The next day, the adjutant general responded tartly that "the Commanding General considers that the interests of the service will not admit of an increase at the present time of the force which has been placed at the disposal of the Bureau of information." Adding insult to injury, Meade had also directed that Patrick report the number of men Sharpe had working for him. In terms of military politics it was a crude demonstration of an utter lack of regard for his services. It was also the type of offhand small-minded insult Meade was wont to throw at his subordinates. Sharpe was not a man to look for an insult, but he knew one when he saw it. In that he was much like the rest of Meade's increasingly unhappy staff.[8]

That was also demonstrated as Sharpe himself found his time being consumed by provost marshal duties assigned by Meade. For example, Sharpe had been assigned by a court martial on June 8 to defend, "a negro for Rape on a White Girl…" Apparently Sharpe's considerable legal talents were insufficient or the evidence overwhelming for the man was convicted and hanged on June 20. Tempers were also fraying. A confusion about the disposition of prisoners threw Meade into "a great stew," and like the proverbial substance that rolls downhill in a military environment, Patrick blamed Sharpe but later found it was another of Burnside's bungles.[9]

McEntee had been sent off to the Shenandoah Valley in a fruitless attempt to stand up an intelligence operation there. Banks simply would not cooperate. That left Babcock alone to control the entire operation which was beyond any single man. In addition, the flat topography had made the heretofore valuable signal intercept system of observation towers useless, and the cavalry was also not being efficiently used to gather information, both sources already out of Sharpe's responsibility. In addition, Meade had not been too eager to share intelligence with his superior, insisting that reports all go through time-consuming channels from his headquarters to Grant's. On Grant's part, his gullibility in reading the raw intelligence derived from prisoners declaring the enemy to be on their last legs had colored his judgment. The absence of an intelligence chief at Grant's elbow was telling.

Over the next few days the overriding collection requirement for Sharpe was to determine when Lee's men would enter the fight. The constant movement of the army meant that Sharpe was not able to prepare any reports on the crucial 15th and 16th of June. Only very late on the night of the 17th with the establishment of a base does he resume his reporting. His summary of that day's interrogations revealed that only Beauregard's troops appeared to be in the defense. Though there were rumors of reinforcements about to arrive, especially of Hill's Corps, there was no proof of it; on the contrary, that fact that Beauregard's forces remained in the front lines without relief was proof that no reinforcements had arrived.[10]

The next day unleashed a flood of BMI reporting in at least six summaries based on the examination of 863 prisoners and deserters. About a third of these were taken by Butler's Army of the James, which under Lt. John L. Davenport direction was also extracting information. Now with a secure base, Sharpe's system could begin to function efficiently, as large numbers of the captured enemy could be processed through the BMI and its Army of the James daughter BMI's interrogation mills.

The picture began to show that none of Lee's corps had arrived yet. II and V Corps had taken prisoners only from units under the command of "Beauregard and part of which were sent from General Lee's army (as Hoke's division), and represent nearly the whole of Beauregard's force, at least nine brigades in all. None of them have seen any of the forces properly belonging to any one of the three corps of General Lee's army." In a postscript to one of the summaries, he wrote, "I keep steadily inquiring for any of Lee's army proper, and have so [far] failed to find indications of it." In the next report, he states, "There is no evidence whatever of General Lee's having sent any of his own forces to our present front, but all the indications are to the contrary." He also observed that Beauregard's brigades were much stronger than any of Lee's battle-worn ones, averaging 3,000 to 3,500 men. Most of the prisoners taken by Hancock been found asleep while away from their regiments, possibly indicating those units had been dropping exhausted men as they moved.[11]

At 4:00 a.m. on the 18th Grant struck the eastern defenses of Petersburg with four corps. The attack faltered and then halted, confused by Beauregard's sudden withdrawal to a second line. When the army did eventually attack, Beauregard stopped it with heavy loss for small gains. Late the previous night Lee was brought word that Grant was definitely on the south side of the James. He immediately ordered Hill and two of Anderson's divisions to force march to Petersburg. In the late afternoon, the two I Corps divisions filled in on Beauregard's open right flank just as Warren's V Corps attacked. Confederate fire swept the field and broke the attack. Grant's window had finally closed. Lee had arrived. Lee had moved so fast that his coming outran the intelligence that Sharpe had been analyzing. His last report at 9:00 p.m., which reported no proof of the arrival of Lee's troops, was proven wrong four or five hours before, but Warren's men had not taken any prisoners to show otherwise.[12]

About this time Scout Anson Carney returned from a mission but was immediately given new orders by Sharpe:

> "General Butler has captured some prisoners near Petersburg. Now, Carney, get on your horse and gallop all the way there and all the way back, even if you kill your horse and see that you don't get gobbled up, for I want you to get back and let me know what troops have been fighting General Butler to-day; also, whether General Lee's army has arrived there."

Carney described his new mission:

> I rode rapidly away, some shells passing high over my head enroute. I found the prisoners in a sheep pen guarded by colored troops. Explaining my orders to the proper officer, I jumped over the fence and commenced talking to the rebs something after this fashion: "Well, Johnny, you had quite a skirmish to-day?"
>
> "Yes, we did; and when Uncle Bob [General Robert E. Lee] gets here he will pay you back for it."
>
> "Hasn't he got to Petersburg yet?"

"No, but he is coming."

"What regiment do you belong to?" The regiment was named and then I passed on to another prisoner. In this way I ascertained that only rebel General Kershaw's brigade had been fighting Butler's troops, but that this brigade would soon be re-inforced from Lee's army. I returned to headquarters with the information. It was thought by many officers at headquarters at the time, that if the information had been obtained a little earlier, Petersburg might have been captured that day.[13]

Sending a scout to interrogate prisoners was another example of how short-handed Sharpe still was at this point.

The next day, on the 19th, Sharpe sent out his scouts to find the enemy's flank. They followed the Jerusalem Plank Road south to an intersection with a western-running road (probably the Weldon Road) where they were engaged in a fire fight with Confederate pickets. They observed the enemy busily building "a considerable earth-work or fort … about a mile and half south of Petersburg." At 9:00 that night he was able to report that his scouts had successfully found the enemy's flank. The next day, based on the scouting report, Meade wrote to Grant to tell him that he was going to move two corps to the left and endeavor to stretch to the Appomattox. He also passed on from Sharpe that he had questioned a deserter from the 3rd Georgia Sharpshooters Battalion, Wofford's Brigade of McLaws's Division, I Corps, who admitted that they had come into the line late on the 18th. He rated the man's credibility highly. It appears that the forced march to reach Petersburg had utterly worn out the troops. Surgeons were forbidden to excuse a man from duty save for wounds. In another report of the same day, the BMI had also ascertained that A. P. Hill's III Corps had arrived on the evening of the 18th. Within a day and a half of their arrival the BMI was able to discover that I and III Corps were now manning the Confederate flank. Sharpe was also actively gathering information, through his scouts and interrogations of local civilians, on the location of important facilities such as water works and reservoirs supplying Petersburg, information which was quickly passed down to the corps commanders.[14]

The army was now about to profit from the initiative of Sharpe's resourceful scout Knight, as he would recount:

After we had been in front of Petersburg for a week or two, although we had been busy and done some hard work, it seemed to me that it was time something tangible should result from our service. Both armies were extending their lines to the left. There was no reason that all of us should stay in camp every night, and I concluded to make a night-trip and see if I could learn anything of importance.

He left headquarters on the night of June 21 without permission or a pass and slipped out the same way a rebel scout within their lines would take to return to his own lines. In crossing the Jerusalem Plank Road not far south of Fort Hell, he observed B Battery, 2nd New Jersey (II Corps), whose commander he knew. II and VI Corps were preparing to move forward the next day to tear up the Weldon and

Petersburg Railroad. Halfway to the railroad, he turned north and approached the Confederate lines and bedded down in a place that would give him good observation. The next morning he watched in amazement as Hill's III Corps assembled. It was obvious that they were planning an attack. Knight realized he could never get back to headquarters in time to deliver a warning. He realized he had no credentials and that he was unlikely to be recognized by any of the senior officers in II Corps. He did know Capt. Judson Clark commanding the guns of the 2nd New Jersey. The ground was so open he had to snake or low crawl a considerable distance before he could rise to his feet and rush to find Clark.

Clark believed him, but an infantry colonel commanding a regiment who was present dismissed him out of hand. Only Clark put his command in readiness to meet an attack. The Confederates fell upon the unsuspecting II Corps like a hammer, driving it back and taking several thousand prisoners. Only the steady and courageous action of Clark's battery prevented a greater debacle. It was a perfect example of the fact that a necessary predicate for surprise to be sprung is that the victim refuses to believe evidence of its approach. After returning to camp, Knight heard the noise of what would be called the battle of Jerusalem Plank Road erupt from the direction of II Corps. He decided to keep the entire episode to himself. Nevertheless, it was an example of the consistent resourcefulness that marked him to Sharpe as a man worthy of greater things.[15]

Now that the armies had settled down around Petersburg and Richmond and Lee's I and III Corps had been identified in the lines, a BMI collection priority became to answer the question of where was II Corps. Sharpe did not yet know that Early had replaced Ewell. Sharpe's intelligence summary of June 17 to Meade was the first he had been able to prepare in over a week, but it did not warn of II Corps' absence. There had been such tightened security and such thick lines of pickets to mask the departure of II Corps the previous week that deserters found it impossible to slip away.

Sharpe would not obtain the first evidence that the corps were missing from the front until June 20. That same deserter from the Georgia Sharpshooters also gave a clear and accurate account of just what had happened. "He says that Ewell's corps [apparently the prisoner did not know Ewell had been replaced either] left General Lee at Cold harbor; that it was understood to be going toward the Valley or Lynchburg; at all events, he has not seen any part of it since, and is quite certain that no part of General Ewell's corps is in our front." By the time Sharpe learned this, Early had already defeated Hunter at the battle of Lynchburg and begun to drive him out of the Valley, fulfilling the first part of Lee's orders. On the 21st there was more confirmation from prisoners of the presence of I and III Corps with information on the location of their divisions, and more evidence that II Corps was absent. "They agree that Ewell's corps is nowhere near them, but say that it left them at Cold Harbor, and they have not seen it since. They think from all they have heard it has gone to Western Virginia." There was also the news that "Anderson has been made a lieutenant-general, and now commands Longstreet's corps." The next day the interrogation of more prisoners showed that "They know nothing of Ewell" but could identify most of the divisions of the other two corps.

Sharpe felt worried enough to send off his chief of scouts to find II Corps in the lines around Petersburg. Cline had just come in from a reconnaissance on the 23rd, when Sharpe sent him back to obtain evidence and not to confine himself to the environs of Petersburg and Richmond. He had every confidence that Cline could handle a long-range mission. In his summary of that day, he stated emphatically, "I can hear nothing of Ewell's corps." On the 24th Sharpe summarized another prisoner interrogation. "I am satisfied from examination of this man, who is a great talker and blow-hard, that no part of Ewell's corps has returned or is in this vicinity. He says he heard, a day or two ago, that Ewell's corps had captured Hunter, but he does not seem to believe the report."[16]

It was only on the 28th that news of the Confederate victory in the Valley trickled in from McEntee. His report was the first accurate information on the size and whereabouts of Early's Corps. Trying to put a good face on it, he added, "By hard marches, closely pursued by the enemy, we got off without disaster. We have marched farther into the Confederacy, and injured the enemy more, than any column that has ever marched in West Virginia." Unfortunately, McEntee opined that Early was already returning to Lee's army at Petersburg, and Grant agreed, as William Feis argues:

> Grant agreed with the assessment, perhaps based upon the conviction that Lee needed every man to defend Richmond and Early had departed before the danger posed by the movement across the James had become clear. Given the circumstances, Lee would have little choice but to recall the detachment, making McEntee's conclusion provable. And before long, more intelligence emerged to support the captain's assessment.

That was in the form of a report from Hancock of the statement of three deserters who reported that "Ewell's [Early's] corps arrived yesterday [June 30th] and that part of it was marching to [the Confederate right]. He was so satisfied in mind that this was so that he brushed off Halleck's telegram of the same day that the enemy was now positioned to raid Maryland or Pennsylvania. Grant replied that "Ewell's [Early's] corps had returned here."[17]

On July 1 as well, McEntee wrote Sharpe a long, revealing letter from Charleston, West Virginia. It is not known when or if Sharpe received it:

> I telegraphed you on the 28th giving you the results of our Lynchburg fight and the forces we engaged there. The only prisoners taken by us were from the 54th N. C. Infantry. They all stated that the whole of Ewell's Corps was there. We had other information that they were there, but at the same time I seemed to be much doubted by the general and his chief of staff, and for that reason I stated that a part of that corps was at Lynchburg... I am at present A. D. C. in General

Hunter's staff, but as I have drifted entirely out of my [?] as the means of communicating with you have been so imperfect I have asked to be relieved here and ordered to the Army of the Potomac.

It appears that McEntee's assessment of June 28 had been heavily influenced by Hunter and his staff and that although he had arrived at the correct enemy order-of-battle it had been disregarded. Other communications he subsequently sent which might have clarified his comment that Early was returning to Richmond had not been received by Sharpe. The intended positive relationship between the commander in the Valley and his new BMI had failed to materialize to the point where McEntee was desperate to return to the Army of the Potomac. He provided another piece of information that would be of use later. He had encountered many Union deserters who were using the Valley to attempt to get back north.[18]

By the first few days of July, alarmed reports from Union commanders in the northern Valley of Early's continued advance had reached Washington. Lincoln, Stanton, and Halleck consulted Grant, who insisted Early was still in front of him at Richmond. He again asked Meade if he could confirm Early's presence. Clearly briefed by Sharpe, Meade replied cautiously. "The only information I have as to Ewell's corps was derived from deserters, who said it had returned from Lynchburg. No prisoners have been taken from any of the divisions of that corps or any other information obtained than above. It was never reported as in our front, but only that it had returned from Lynchburg."[19]

In the midst of this unfolding intelligence crisis, Patrick, in response to direction from Meade, sent Sharpe and Colonel Gates of the provost guard's 20th NYSM on July 3 to investigate the report of the rape of two "young ladies" by some of Sheridan's cavalry at Douthat's Landing across the James from City Point. Sharpe left immediately for City Point, and the next morning Gates and he took a tug across the James. After questioning the locals, they found the report was unfounded. Sharpe did add, "There were excesses with the negro women there, but they rested upon evidence which I considered secondary and conflicting and that I was not authorized to investigate." This assignment was indicative of the lack of priority given to Sharpe's intelligence mission, especially since he was gone for two days as the crisis over the whereabouts of Early's Corps was reaching the boiling point.[20]

Back at work on July 4, Sharpe learned from a deserter whom he judged reliable that rumors in the Confederate camp placed Early on Arlington Heights overlooking Washington and ready to pounce on the capital. Grant chose to discount Sharpe's judgment and wired Halleck the same day in words of studied denial:

A deserter who came in this morning reports that Ewell's corps has not returned here, but is off in the Valley with the intention of going into Maryland and Washington City. They now have the report that he already has Arlington Heights and expects to take the city soon. Of course the soldiers know nothing about this force further than it is away from here and north somewhere. Under the circumstances I think it advisable to hold all of the forces you can about Washington, Baltimore, Cumberland, and Harper's Ferry, ready to concentrate against any advance of the enemy. Except from the dispatches forwarded from Washington in the last two days I have learned nothing which indicated an intention on the part of the rebels to attempt any northern movement. If General Hunter is in striking distance there ought to be veteran forces enough to meet anything the enemy have, and if once put to flight he ought to be followed as long as possible. This report of Ewell's corps being north is only the report of a deserter, and we have similar authority for it being here and on the right of Lee's army. We know, however, that it does not occupy this position.[21]

In a letter of the same day, Grant's alter ego, his chief of staff, Maj. Gen. John Rawlins, wrote that General Hunter should be able to concentrate enough forces at Harper's Ferry to forestall Ewell's (Early's) descent upon Washington. He did unintentionally compliment Sharpe by citing the strength of Ewell's (Early's) army at not much than 15,000, a most accurate BMI calculation.[22]

The next day Grant's complacency begins to change. He must have reconsidered his hasty conclusion and wired Halleck at 12:30 p.m. "If the enemy cross into Maryland or Pennsylvania I can send an army corps from here to meet them or cut off their return south. If required, direct the quartermaster to send transportation." The situation in Washington had changed overnight. Halleck wired him at 1:00 p.m. of chaos along the upper Potomac from Harper's Ferry to Monacacy. The enemy had cut the wires and destroyed the bridges. What few Union forces there were in the area were falling back.

> We have nothing reliable in regard to the enemy's force. Some accounts, probably very exaggerated, state it to be between 20,000 and 30,000. If one-half that number we cannot meet it in the field till Hunter's troops arrive. As you are aware, we have almost nothing in Baltimore or Washington, except militia, and considerable alarm has been created by sending troops from these places to re-enforce Harper's Ferry.

He then begged Grant to send him all his dismounted cavalry.[23]

By 10:30 that night Halleck now felt the situation was easing. Thirteen hundred troops from Hunter were expected in time to deal with any problem. His earlier apprehension seemed to fade behind the conclusion that only an enemy raid had occurred.

> As Hunter's force is now coming within reach, I think your operations should not be interfered with by sending troops here. If Washington and Baltimore should be so seriously threatened as to require your aid, I will inform you in time. Although most of our forces are not of a character suitable for the field (invalids and militia), yet I have no apprehensions at present about the safety of Washington, Baltimore, Harper's Ferry, or Cumberland.

Like a good planner, however, he recommended Grant subordinate all the water transportation assets at Fort Monroe and the James River be placed under Meade's quartermaster, Ingalls.[24]

Sharpe added more grist for Grant's mill on this subject during the flurry of telegrams between Washington and City Point where Grant had set up his headquarters. Sharpe's summary from the interrogation of two deserters from the

20th Georgia Battalion Cavalry stated, "it was currently reported within their lines, both at Richmond and in Petersburg, that General Early was making an invasion of Maryland, with the intention of capturing Washington, having under his command two divisions of Ewell's [Early's] Corps…" At 1:00 p.m. Meade sent Grant what appears to be a summary of this report, with a few more details: that the force consisted of two divisions of Ewell's Corps, with Breckinridge's command and other forces, to capture Washington, "supposed to be defenseless. It was understood Early would reach Winchester by the 3rd instant."[25]

At 11:50 p.m. Grant wired Halleck in response to his telegram of 1:00 p.m., stating he had ordered the dismounted cavalry and an infantry division to be followed by the rest of VI Corps, "if necessary. We want to crush out and destroy any force the enemy have sent north. Force enough can be spared from here to do it." Then for the first time he admitted that it could be Ewell, probably based on Sharpe's last report, by ending his message with "I think now there is no doubt but Ewell's corps is away from here."[26]

On the 6th Sharpe prepared another summary about information obtained from a deserter from the 2nd North Carolina Cavalry, with the type of information that just leaps out at an experienced interrogator and analyst.

> Very little is known in their army of the whereabouts of Ewell's corps. It was reported to be operating in the Valley. Informant thinks it is certain that it is not here, for convalescents and furloughed men belonging to Ewell's corps are under charge of the provost-marshal at Petersburg awaiting its return.

Early's convalescents and furloughed men would have been returned promptly to the corps if it had been in the lines at Petersburg. The fact that they were collected all in one place by the provost marshal was a statement that the corps was far too distant to have sent them. Another less credible deserter who admitted knowing nothing about II Corps thought Ewell was with his command down the railroad. He had probably heard about Ewell being in the area as he was on other duties.[27]

Sharpe also reported that another deserter brought a Richmond newspaper of the 6th, which reported the capture of Harper's Ferry by Early. That caused some confusion since Grant had been in communication with Harper's Ferry that very day, and it was in no danger. In fact, Early bypassed the town, and the newspaper report was just inaccurate reporting. This did not stop Grant from ensuring that the promised forces were dispatched that very day to Baltimore—2,500 dismounted cavalry and 5,000 men of Rickett's Division of VI Corps. His staff had been working through the night, and orders were issued before daylight. At 3:30 p.m. Grant wired Halleck, "I think there is no doubt but Early's corps is near the Baltimore and Ohio road, and if it can be caught and broken up it will be highly desirable to do so." This is the first indication that he had fully accepted Early's presence on the Potomac.[28]

Halleck next wired Grant that the situation had worsened. Sigel had no scouts and could only guess that the enemy numbered 7,000 to over 30,000. He had other estimates that placed them at 20,000 to 30,000. "I think there is no further doubt about Ewell's corps. Probably, also, Breckinridge's, Imboden's, Jackson's, and Mosby's commands. If so, the invasion is of a pretty formidable character." He had lost contact with Hunter, and the railroad that would have brought his troops had been wrecked. He then asked Grant to send him a good major general to command the troops to command in the field. Unfortunately, this message was not received until the next day.[29]

The reinforcements arrived by the 8th. Halleck sent Ricketts on to join Maj. Gen. Lew Wallace's green troops at Monacacy to stop Early if they could. He complained that of the 3,000 dismounted infantry that had arrived, 2,496 were sick. When Meade had passed on Grant's orders to send dismounted cavalrymen to Washington, he apparently did not explain the reason. Sheridan had that many sick who were by definition dismounted and rid himself of them. Though he informed Meade through Humphrey, no one seemed to notice.[30]

Captain McEntee had arrived in Baltimore on the 7th, where he wired Sharpe for instructions. The wire eventually got through but took so long that Sharpe's reply—which told him to report to Wallace if he felt he could be of use and was addressed to his Baltimore hotel —never got to him; he was long gone. The next day McEntee had not heard from Sharpe and became alarmed at the reports of Early's force being in much greater strength than Hunter had opined. Then, on his own initiative, he took the last train into Harper's Ferry to be able to monitor events, presumably with his two scouts. He could not communicate with Sharpe again until the 12th because, as he wrote, "I am surrounded by rebels and torn-up railroads." Despite that he was able to construct an accurate order-of-battle of Early's command. He identified the three II Corps divisions commanded by Rodes, Ramseur, and Gordon, and the one composite one. As well, he identified how Early had split his force into two small corps by uniting Gordon's Division with the composite one and giving its command to Breckinridge. Early made these changes on June 24, changes that McEntee picked up within two weeks. McEntee was less accurate when he put Early's strength at 20,000—25,000 men. He thought Early's Corps was 12,000 strong and that the other elements of his overall command added another 10,000. Early, however, had only 8,000 men in his II Corps when he departed for Lynchburg. Altogether the Army of the Valley amounted to only 14,000 men. Since McEntee did not have access to Babcock's painstakingly kept order-of-battle records, it was an excusable error.

McEntee had put the order-of-battle together by interrogating prisoners and through information from a useful agent, but there were limits to what he could do.

> I would have gone out today but General Howe objects as he wishes me to remain with him until General Hunter arrives thinking I can do him more good than I can you. I can neither get a horse here for love nor money or would have followed the enemy up. Probably you know more of their whereabouts than I can tell you as I only give you the most reliable rumors.

I have seen many of the prisoners and have their organization. The local commander refused to let me go scout personally.[31]

In all this confusion over Early's location, the same question was now asked of Anderson's I Corps. Sharpe provided the answer. Two contrabands, servants at Anderson's headquarters, had been captured when they tried to graze their horses between the lines. They identified the location of Anderson's headquarters and affirmed that the entire I Corps was indeed in the lines at Petersburg and then proceeded to identify the location of each division. They identified Beauregard's Corps on the left and Hill's on the right of their own corps. They also stated that probably Heth's Division had moved out onto the extreme right near the railroad. This is some of the most accurate reporting Sharpe had seen. The Confederates paid no mind to their servants as security risks, thinking of them as merely furniture. Yet time and time again observant slaves had noted in detail what was going on around them. Charlie Wright in the Gettysburg Campaign was one such piece of furniture whose retentive memory set the Army of Potomac in motion. Meade immediately forwarded Sharpe's report to Grant and followed it up by writing, "I have no doubt Longstreet's corps is here."[32]

Sharpe's multiple collection sources now provided incontrovertible proof of what the interrogation reports had been saying. On July 9 Sergeant Cline, whom Sharpe had sent out from Petersburg to find II Corps wherever it may be, reported Early's exact location. He had conducted another of his scouting miracles by riding through Early's camps located on South Mountain between Hagerstown and Frederick, Maryland. That same day Early defeated Lew Wallace's scratch force at the battle of the Monocacy near Frederick. At that time Grant had no idea how much he owed to Wallace's desperate delaying action. Cline's report and a wire from Halleck who reported on Wallace's defeat at Monocacy and his estimate that he faced one-third of Lee's army drove Grant to decisive action. He immediately sent Maj. Gen. Horatio Wright and the rest of his VI Corps to Washington and directed that XIX Corps, which had earlier been ordered up from Louisiana to reinforce his Armies Operating Against Richmond, also be sent.[33]

The pot had come to a boil outside Washington on July 11 as Early completed his reconnaissance and ordered an assault which broke down under a combination of exhaustion of the troops and the discovery of whisky barrels in the looted mansion of Preston Blair. VI Corps troops arrived the same day to stiffen the defenses. The next day growing Union strength decided Early against an attack. He withdrew that afternoon and was south of the Potomac the next day. On the 11th Grant dispatched Sharpe to Washington and Baltimore to supervise the intelligence operation from closer to the crisis. His presence brought some calm to the civilian leadership of the government. He joked to his Uncle Jansen that his "coming was well timed to allay" his wife's "fears about the invasion!" He knew the size and nature of the threat precisely. "The two infantry divisions under Early, & one under Breckenridge [sic] with the scattering of odds & ends left in W. V. numbered from 23,000 to 25,000 men. I knew every regt and had an estimate of them by regimental strength." That calm assurance steadied the nerves among the civilians in the War Department which "was not stampeded." He had great faith in the competence of Maj. Gen. Christopher Columbus Auger, the commander of the District of Washington, as did Grant, but realized that he had few competent subordinates. Grant had combed the district thoroughly of able men to replace his losses. "But," explained Sharpe, "in the desire to provide for incapables & politicians there was not a live man near Washington to handle the troops."[34]

Sharpe closed his letter by venting a soldier's common complaint of the cost of political favors and deal-making. "When we shall relentlessly cut off the head of every failure, without regard to tickling Republicans or propitiating Democrats, then will the enormous preponderating resources of the north close up this thing & not before. And while we are waiting, we must pay."[35]

Sharpe had the last laugh, though, and possibly a windfall from the matter. Lieutenant Colonel Theodore Lyman of Meade's staff wrote in his diary on Sharpe's return, "Col. Sharpe has been to Washington where they all were sweating with fear! He told them Early had not over 25,000 men; they swore he had 92,000 including all A. P. Hill. He offered a heavy bet they would all fall back the moment the VI Corps reappeared in front of Washington; and it came to pass!"[36]

Lincoln was not so assured. Perhaps it was nearly getting shot at Fort Stevens which Early's men had taken under fire on the 12th that caused him to wire Grant that same day. "Vague rumors have been reaching us for two or three days that Longstreet's corps is also on its way to this vicinity. Look out for its absence from your front." Halleck wired also that, though the capital was now "pretty safe" for the present, prisoners and civilians were claiming both Longstreet and Hill were expected. Sharpe's reporting had clearly shown that both corps were in the defenses of Petersburg. The same day, Meade was fuming about the problem of keeping track of the divisions of those corps.[37] Lee kept them busy, regularly relieving divisions in the forward lines with divisions in reserve and in shifting them to extend his flank. Meade vented to Grant, "I send you the latest information received. It shows how conflicting is the information we receive, and how accurately the enemy is posted in our affairs. Mahone's division, of Hill's Corps, has now been positively placed in our front, on our left and rear, and on its way to Pennsylvania." If Meade had not insisted on being his own senior intelligence officer, his staff might have given him a better answer.[38]

Nevertheless, nailing down that Longstreet had not left Lee's army became a collection priority for the next three days. Then as now, presidential inquiries were taken with great gravity. On July 12 Babcock provided the definitive proof. The next day Rawlins was writing, "It is positively asserted [in Washington] that Longstreet's corps is on the way there, but we have the best of evidence that it remains here, and it is here I have no doubt. We have deserters from it daily and also make captures of prisoners from it. This latter evidence has never failed us." Based on a report from Babcock, Meade informed Grant on July 15, "There is no evidence in the provost-marshal's department of any part of Longstreet Corps having left Lee's army." But it is clear from Rawlins's letter that Sharpe had already shown Grant and Rawlins the results of Babcock's analysis.[39]

On the day after Monacacy Lee wrote to Jefferson Davis, sending him a copy of the July 8 issue of the *New York Herald*, with the note:

> You will see that the people in the U.S. are mystified about our forces [Early's expedition] on the Potomac. The expedition will have the effect I think at least to teaching them they must keep some of their troops at home & that they cannot denude their frontier with impunity. It seems also to have put them in bad temper as well as bad humor.[40]

It did indeed put Grant in a bad humor. He had learned a lesson. His inattention to intelligence had nearly allowed Early to seize the Federal Capital. It was the sort of near-death experience that provokes a fundamental reassessment of what went wrong.

Wright's timely arrival to forestall Early was not the end of alarm in Grant's command over the threat to Washington. There was plenty of "bad temper as well as bad humor" within the Union high command at City Point. The same day that Wright reached Washington, Babcock, in a report of that morning, informed Meade that a just- interrogated deserter, from the 8th Alabama of Mahone's Division of Hill's Corps, revealed that his division had left its position while he was in Richmond on pass. He stated that Hill's entire corps had left the lines at Petersburg at 5:00 p.m. the day before (the 10th) and moved toward the Weldon Railroad. Civilians in Petersburg told him they were headed to Pennsylvania. Meade immediately forwarded Babcock's report to Grant at noon with the following postscript: "There is no doubt that Hill's corps or portion of it moved last evening, but there is nothing to indicate the direction taken. It may prove a movement on our left flank due to the withdrawal of the VI Corps. I have directed the cavalry on our left to push scouts out in all directions."[41]

At 1:30 p.m. he reported anxiously to Grant that he had personally interrogated the deserter. "He says Heth's division left about the same time, and that he heard in Petersburg a report that Hill's Corps was going to Pennsylvania." He was careful to note that his signal officer reported, *per contra*, that two trains filled with troops and artillery had actually come *into* Petersburg that same day. Nevertheless, he concluded, "I think there is no doubt Hill has moved, but in what direction is as yet uncertain. It may be on our left flank or it may be to join Early." The story had all the earmarks of one of Lee's disinformation operations, in which he sent deserters into the Union lines with carefully constructed stories meant to mislead and confuse. This would have been the perfect time to capitalize on the now extreme Union sensitivity to Washington's security as he had pointed out to Davis in his letter of the 10th.[42]

If it was a trap, Meade fell right into it. If not, he simply fashioned a rod for his own back by accepting without corroboration the deserter's story. In either case, Lee would have been pleased because the story that Hill had departed to join Early in another invasion of Pennsylvania took on a life of its own. Grant smelled an opportunity here and replied almost immediately. "If Hill's Corps has gone we must find out where it has gone and take advantage of its absence." He discussed a major turning movement of the enemy's right at Petersburg combined with a heavy assault on their lines to fix them in place. Meade responded the same day that though there was "no further information … of the enemy's movements … I conclude they have been sent to re-enforce Early." He continued, "Intelligence of Early's success, combined with knowledge of the departure of the Sixth Corps, together with a confidence in the strength of his lines and his capability to hold them with a diminished force, has doubtless induced Lee to send Hill in hopes of thus transferring the seat of operations to Maryland and Pennsylvania, by drawing the greater portion of your army there to defend Washington and Baltimore."[43]

Meanwhile, Sharpe was trying to throw a net over this growing general officer speculation. He interrogated another deserter, from the 48th Mississippi, on the same day as the wires were humming between Meade and Grant. This man stated that as of the previous night, both Mahone's and Heth's Divisions of Hill's Corps were still in place in the defenses of Petersburg. He stated that Heth's Division was under marching orders, but his own, Mahone's, was not. Sharpe then confronted the deserter, who had told Meade of the departure of Hill's entire corps for Pennsylvania, "why their statements were so opposite." Sharpe then speculated that they were both right and that the latter, whom he thought a man of "considerable intelligence," may have well thought that to reveal Hill's departure would have been dishonorable. This was a mistake. Sharpe was giving in to the old trap of "making the wish the father to the thought." Nevertheless, he was still in the process of cross-checking this information and later in the day sent his scouts to Petersburg to see what they could learn. Meade was anxious for any new information, and on the 11th asked, at 10:15 p.m., if Sharpe had heard from them. Sharpe replied that they should be back in the morning.

That morning another deserter who had come into Union lines the night before stated that a friend had told him all of Heth's Division and Wright's Brigade of Mahone's were on the move to counter a Union move to cut the Weldon Railroad. Scout Carney also reported in that morning. He had contacted a Union agent at Ennis's farm the day before who was cradling oats all day in sight of the railroad. In the afternoon he saw troops, about division size, passing south on the Halifax Road, passing Ream's Station and then onto the Jerusalem Plank Road. The agent had been watching the train for the last several days and stated clearly that no troops had passed on it. Babcock commented that the scout had tasked the agent to find out what he could about the troop movement and where the division had gone.[44]

On the morning of the 13th, Babcock reported that deserters from Mahone's Division said that Wright's Brigade and Heth's Division had arrived back in their original positions at daylight the day before. Babcock provided a drawing of the positions of all of Mahone's brigades, including Wright's in reserve. New deserters corroborated this story. Shortly after receiving this, Meade wired Grant to put the entire matter of Hill's disappearance to rest.

> The above dispatch forwarded for your information. It proves Hill's two divisions are still in our front. It confirms the movement of Heth previously reported, and is in conformity with Gregg's report [from the cavalry] that he could find no infantry at Reams'. I now think the enemy having heard of Wright's movement sent Heth to Reams' to meet an attack on the road, which not being made, he was brought back...

It had certainly been an exciting two days but unnecessarily exciting. Meade had rushed to conclusions based on a single report—which had one statement picked up by a soldier from civilians in Petersburg that Hill was on his way to Pennsylvania—without waiting for his analysts to cross-check and confirm its accuracy. In other words, he immediately lent great credence to a major threat to the North based on civilian rumors, or, as it is facetiously called today in the Intelligence Community—RUMINT (Rumor Intelligence). After summoning this monster from the Aladdin's lamp of rumor, he had to turn to Sharpe's analysts to confirm or deny it.

New Missions

The near loss of the capital had a sobering effect on Grant. Whatever his wishful thinking had contributed to the intelligence failure, he could see that things needed to change. Clearly, he needed better intelligence support, and he saw Sharpe and the BMI as the solution. He was faced with Meade's touchy truculence in guarding his prerogatives as commander of the Army of the Potomac. Grant resolved Sharpe's awkward command relationship in a typical general officer fashion. Even before Early's raid on Washington had turned back, on July 4 he redesignated the provost marshal of the Army of the Potomac as the provost marshal of the Armies Operating Against Richmond, making it directly subordinate to himself. He was killing two birds with one stone. He did need a single staff to control provost marshal functions among the several armies he commanded. Undoubtedly, it also hid his other priority—to wrest Sharpe and company from Meade.[45]

By this time, Grant had not only become a believer in the value that Sharpe offered but had become personally fond of him. Sharpe was an attractive and engaging personality and a great storyteller. It was a talent that enlivened the moments between battles and one that no doubt relieved the burdens of command for Grant. It was also a talent that Sharpe consciously used to establish his relationship with the general-in-chief.[46]

The change quickly became common knowledge as Gates noted that Patrick traveled to City Point on the 5th to make arrangements, "to establish his Hd Qtrs here as Pro. Mar. Gen. of the Armies operating against Richmond and the lines of communication."[47] On his arrival he had an interview with Grant, who was trying to have it both ways. Patrick wrote of his interview, "The Object is, to have a Central power to regulate Butler & others, but, as Grant expressly says, not to take me from the Army of the Potomac." Patrick returned that night to see Meade, who was in a fury, not with his provost or with Grant but with "every body & thing. He had learned that his Staff would, all, gladly leave him, on account of his temper, and he had become desperately cross." He told Patrick he would find a replacement for him and "that he would not have any partnership with Grant, etc. etc."

Contributing to Meade's foul temper was his constant crucifixion in the press, stemming from an incident at Cold Harbor in early June. Meade had claimed that a reporter from the *Philadelphia Inquirer*, Edward Crapsey, had libeled him. He ordered the man, in Patrick's words, "placed on a horse, with breast & back boards Marked 'Libeller of the Press'—& marched in rear of my flag, thro' the Army, after which he was sent to White House & hence North—He was completely cut down—It will be a warning to his Tribe." It was the sort of warning that backfired. The reporters with the army agreed to never mention Meade's name again in the press in a positive light and ascribed advance to Grant or the Army of the Potomac.

Meade's anger had already been stoked over the BMI. A few days before the blow-up on the 5th, there had been another knock-down, drag-out argument between Meade and Patrick, and this was over the BMI. Meade had said that "the whole Bureau of Information was good for nothing—that it furnished no information not already received thro' the Cavalry—that it ought to be broken up & that Genl. Grant thought so, too." Patrick leapt to the defense of the BMI. "I disagreed with him entirely and told him that he had refused to let us do what was desired & which we knew to be for the best interests of the Service—I therefore told him, that I proposed to transfer that Bureau to Genl. Grant's Head Quarters & there give it a trial, when, if it still proved worthless, it should be disbanded."

That just fanned the flames of Meade's anger. He said that "he would not permit the transfer, but that he *would* allow it to be broken up." Patrick vehemently took issue with Meade's treatment of his staff as if they were personal servants.[48]

On the 6th Patrick rode back to City Point and had an interview with Brigadier General Rawlins, Grant's chief of staff. He agreed to relocate his operation to Grant's headquarters at City Point. It was agreed that "The Scouts, Guides, etc. with [Col.] Sharpe & [Capt. John C.] Babcock, remain here, until the questions now at issue between Meade & Grant are settled."[49]

Patrick next day then sought advice from Burnside, whose opinion, as a former commander of the army, he valued. Burnside strongly insisted that on no account should Patrick resign as provost marshal general of the Army of the Potomac, unless Grant proposed it. He also advised with a great deal of shrewdness, "to run the machine for the A. of P. to the best of my ability, taking such members of my Staff & of my Organization, as were necessary to carry out the orders of Genl. Grant, & let Meade do what he thinks his dignity demands." It was common sense advice that Patrick adopted. He simply decided to carry on his duties without reference to anyone's jurisdiction. On the 7th, Patrick actually set up shop at City Point. Sharpe joined him that evening. The old provost marshal was playing it by ear, and Sharpe was shrewd enough to take his cue from him. And that ear told Patrick to return to Meade's headquarters when Meade sent him a cutting telegram on July 9, stating his departure for Grant's headquarters at City Point was unauthorized. He returned and had dinner with Sharpe. Meade would not see him. The dispute had already become public; Gates recorded the Meade summons in his diary, and predicted, rightly, another row.[50]

Grant went to great lengths to placate Meade. He was well aware of how touchy Meade was and did not seek an open confrontation which would likely have led to the latter's resignation. He did not actually publish the order appointing Sharpe as assistant provost marshal of the Armies Operating against Richmond until December 2. In the meantime, most of the BMI operation remained with Meade's headquarters, in a classical compromise of military turf, described by Edwin Fishel: "Sharpe had desks both there and at AOAR headquarters at City Point ... in addition to meeting with Grant almost daily, he spent hours there working with Lieutenant Colonel Theodore Bowers, a member of Grant's staff, who by this association would become familiar with the details of the Sharpe-Babcock operation."[51]

Sharpe explained to his Uncle Jansen how he was dealing with the problem. "I am now by the way alternating in my duties at H. Q. Army of the Potomac & here at H. Q. Armies of the U.S. in the field, of which [the] latter Genl Patrick is the Pro Mar Genl. He comes down occasionally for a day or two, & then I return to represent him. My interviews with Genl Grant are frequent—generally every day." It was a situation in which familiarity did not breed contempt, rather just the opposite. "I have a strong liking for his entire simplicity & truthfulness of character united to a great firmness & decision." His budding case of hero worship went so far as to agree with the hated *New York Herald* that "Uncle Abe" should step aside for Grant in the 1864 election.[52]

The result of this keeping a foot in both headquarters to placate general officer egos, according to Fishel, was:

> Thus there were now two intelligence centers; deserters and other suppliers of information were received at both, reports issued from both, and Sharpe and Babcock spent as much time writing telegrams and notes to each other as they did in face-to-face discussion. At one point when McEntee was substituting for Sharpe at City Point, he and Babcock made estimates of Lee's strength, each unaware of the other's calculation; the two figures differed by only 600. The two totals, about 50,000, were 12 percent below the number of effectives shown on Lee's rolls.[53]

In practice, Babcock replaced Sharpe in Meade's eyes as his chief intelligence officer, and Babcock reported directly to him as the notes from the one to the other demonstrate. Babcock considered that he served under Grant through Meade. That meant he also worked for Sharpe. It was a deft juggling performance that he carried off with aplomb. This arrangement would have confounded the maker of an organization chart, but it worked.[54]

Meade continued to act out the charade of his control over Sharpe's bureau by sending Grant copies of its reports that the latter was already receiving from Sharpe. There was a distinct difference in how the two commanders treated the BMI. Meade for over a year had limited Sharpe to only the collection sources under his direct control. Grant expected Sharpe to use an all-source approach to prepare his intelligence reports and briefings. This situation continued to play out for the rest of the war. While it formed a sort of grudging truce between Grant and Meade, it certainly made the work of Sharpe and his staff much more difficult. While this is a common outcome when general officers lock horns and then back off, their subsequent jury-rigged compromise rarely makes the work of their subordinates easier. The fact that the provost marshal and BMI team were able to work with this situation and prosper, is a credit to both their talent and professionalism.

Although Sharpe reported to Grant for intelligence operations, he responded to any order Patrick might give him since he remained deputy provost marshal. He recognized that Patrick had repeatedly acted as his benefactor and repaid him with good will and friendship. He managed to take in his stride any additional duties required by Patrick. Gates recorded that on the 8th, Sharpe, another officer, and he had composed "a board to examine into the circumstances of the sinking of the Schooner *Ashland* by the Steamer *Tappahonnock*." They held their board on the steamer *Young America* in the James River; the proceedings took most of the day.[55]

Despite the general officer politics, Sharpe indisputably worked for Grant first and foremost from that time on. Almost immediately, he dispatched a senior scout, Judson Knight, with instructions to take 10–12 of the best scouts and commandeer quarters for the group at the City Point headquarters of the Armies Operating Against Richmond. He chose a small frame building that had been used as a marine hospital and within two days was ready for new missions. Sharpe's choice of Knight clearly showed his growing appreciation of the man's abilities. He may have been grooming him as a replacement for Cline when the man's enlistment would expire the next month. The change of headquarters breathed new life into Sharpe's staff, which started to use its own BMI letterhead stationery for the first time.[56]

As Sharpe was settling happily into his new role, he received startling news from a Kingston visitor that his name was being prominently discussed as a candidate for Congress. He claimed to Uncle Jansen, "This is the first time I have heard a thought of such a thing—& while I don't desire and would not manipulate for it, I would not kick away a thing that comes in a proper way, with good chances of success." Sharpe was an ambitious man and to say that he had never even thought of Congress, given his social and growing prewar political activities, might have been a case of "Methinks the lady doth protest too much." In any case, his candidacy would put him squarely in opposition to the sitting Congressman, his former law partner, friend, and benefactor, John Steele. That was something he would not do. Nevertheless, the idea was flattering, and despite his statement that he would speak to no politician about it, he asked Uncle Jansen to "tell me if you really think there is anything to it." The coming heavy combat would drive thoughts of running for office from Sharpe's mind, though the political bug would end up biting his friend, Colonel Gates of the 20th NYSM.[57]

New Missions

Grant now came to have an even keener appreciation for Sharpe's services, and soon the colonel was spending half his time at the general-in-chief's headquarters. Grant knew that doubt always remained even with the best intelligence, but his genius was that he was able not only to deal with ambiguity but to profit from it. He valued intelligence but would never be paralyzed by the lack of its perfection. Sharpe found Grant's command style more than congenial, epitomized in his most famous statement, "The art of war is simple enough. Find out where your enemy is. Get at him as soon as you can. Strike him as hard as you can and as often as you can, and keep moving on."[58] Grant quickly became aware of how vital Sharpe was for executing the first part of that definition—"Find out where your enemy is."

By this time, Sharpe was briefing Grant on almost a daily basis at his City Point headquarters and had drawn the all-source net back into his hands. When the armies had settled down to the grinding siege of Petersburg, beginning on July 9, Babcock was able to perfect his enemy order-of-battle by the careful coordination of excellent Signal Corps observation, the interrogation of deserters, and the breaking of the latest Confederate signal flag alphabet. Had anyone in the chain of command given thought to rebuilding the defunct Balloon Corps, it would have been a powerful addition to intelligence collection the flat terrain around Richmond and Petersburg.

Immediately on assuming duties at City Point, Sharpe focused on detecting transfers of forces between Lee's army at Petersburg and the Valley. His timing was right on. In late July Early made another raid north and burnt Chambersburg in Pennsylvania in retaliation for Union depredations in the South. The need to protect Washington and the opportunity to disrupt the interior lines that allowed Lee to shuffle his troops back and forth became obvious. Sharpe realized he needed more than his core BMI staff. He needed more scouts and spies. At the same time, Grant gave him two missions. The first was to coordinate intelligence operations between his headquarters and the Army of the James south of Richmond in order to keep track of Early. The second was to "get into Richmond." Patrick did his best to help Sharpe with these missions by seeing him off to City Point on July 21 to set up his new offices there and at Bermuda Hundred with Butler's headquarters, and about "sending off Scouts etc[.] in the direction of Orange Court House, to watch Early and get into Richmond."[59]

Expanding Control

Sharpe partially accomplished the first mission by sending Babcock to Washington to set up a system to keep track of the main railroads that Early would have to

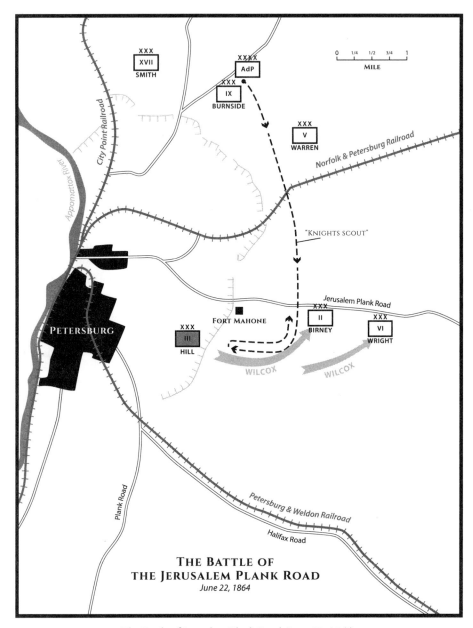

The Battle of Jerusalem Plank Road, June 22, 1864.

use to shuttle troops back and forth. Sharpe had proposed this idea to Meade who had rejected it earlier, but Grant was more appreciative of this sort of imaginative initiative. Sharpe was able almost immediately after relocating to City Point to begin organizing this collection system. Because Grant's forces around Richmond

The Senate House of Kingston, built in 1676, acquired its name when it housed the New York State Senate in 1777, in which year it adopted the state's first constitution. Young George Sharpe would attend a private school then located in the building. Today it is The Senate House Historic Site and serves as a museum of the history of Kingston. (Courtesy Walt Witkowski)

Castillo Morro in Havana, Cuba, showing its capture by the British in 1762. Here in 1850 on vacation after graduating from Rutgers, a far-too-curious Sharpe was arrested and questioned. His quick talking won his release. (Author's collection)

Above left: A prewar photo of George H. Sharpe when he had set up his shingle in Kingston as a new lawyer after his return from Europe. (Courtesy Walt Witkowksi)

Above right: Sharpe as captain in the 20th New York State Militia Regiment in 1861, wearing the double-breasted coat of a field grade officer that he perhaps bought in mistaken anticipation of being elected to the vacancy of major in the regiment. (Courtesy Seward Osborne)

Left: First Lieutenant Jacob Sharpe, George Sharpe's first cousin, as a captain in the 20th New York State Militia Regiment in 1861. He would rise to the rank of brigadier general. (Courtesy Seward Osborne)

Sharpe's first battle was at Fredericksburg in December 1862, where his regiment, although not heavily engaged, behaved credibly. Painting by Carl Röchling, (Author's collection)

Major General Joseph Hooker, commander of the Army of the Potomac (front row, seated second from right) founded the first professional military intelligence staff, the Bureau of Military Information, in February 1863 and put it in the hands of Col. George H. Sharpe. (Library of Congress, LC-DIG-ppmsca-34097)

Above left: Major General Daniel Butterfield, chief of staff, Army of the Potomac, under Hooker's command. (Author's collection)

Above right: Brigadier General Marsena R. Patrick was provost marshal general of the Army of the Potomac throughout its existence. The BMI was one of his subordinate activities. He was a strict disciplinarian much disliked by the army scouts who worked under him. Nevertheless, he supported Colonel Sharpe and the work of his bureau. (Author's collection)

Below: The temporary office of the provost marshal general, Army of the Potomac, at Acquia Creek, Virginia, February 1863, supporting the Army of the Potomac nearby at Falmouth. (Library of Congress LC-B8184-10418)

Above left: Colonel George H. Sharpe as chief of the Bureau of Military Information (BMI) for the Army of the Potomac. He certainly fulfilled the Prussian Field Marshal Helmuth von Moltke's admonition to staff officers to "Be more than you appear." He did not cut a dashing figure but was the creator of American all-source military intelligence and a brilliant staff officer. (Courtesy Seward Osborne)

Above right: Colonel George H. Sharpe wearing a double-breasted frock coat of a field grade officer and the heavy cavalry boots of the accomplished horseman that he was. (Courtesy Walt Witkowski)

Below: Sharpe's orderly, Private Philip Elmendorf, 120th NY Vol. Inf., holding the colonel's horses, Captain and Baby, at Falmouth, VA, April 1863. (Library of Congress LOT 4172-F, no. 9 [P&P])

The dapper John C. Babcock, the most famous scout in the Union during the Peninsular Campaign, and his equally famous horse, Gimlet. He was to become Sharpe's master civilian order-of-battle analyst and deputy. (Library of Congress LC-DIG-cwpb-00293)

Below left: John C. Babcock, standing with his hand on the tentpole, with John Pinkerton, seated on right, and staff. (Library of Congress LC-DIG-cwpb-01150)

Below right: Captain John McEntee of the 20th NYSM Regt. was transferred to the BMI at Sharpe's request to become one of his two deputies. (Courtesy Seward Osborne)

A detachment of the 3rd Indiana Cavalry, known as Hooker's Horse Marines, shown here at Petersburg in 1864, provided some of the best of the BMI's scouts, to include the first chief of scouts, Sergeant Milton Cline. (Library of Congress, LC-DIG-cwpb-03682)

Below left: Daniel Cole, 3rd Indiana Cavalry, one of the best scouts in the BMI. (Library of Congress Lc-B811-1211)

Below right: BMI Scout William Wilson. The scouts of the BMI numbered between 30 and 50 men at any one time. They were paid according to their proven experience and effectiveness. (Library of Congress, LC-USZ62-108336)

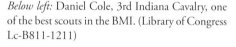

Michael Silver, Stafford, Va.

Above: The intrepid and ruthless Anson B. Carney was one of the boldest of the BMI scouts, whom Judson Knight considered the bravest man he ever knew. (Author's collection)

Below: The Richmond bread riots on April 2, 1863, by starving working-class women. This was the type of innovative political intelligence on the staying power of the Confederacy that Sharpe began reporting to his superiors. (Library of Congress LC-USZ62-42028)

Above: Isaac Silver, one of Sharpe's most effective agents in the collection of accurate information, owned a farm on the Orange Plank Road near Chancellorsville. This native of New Jersey had moved to Virginia in 1850 but remained a loyal Unionist. (Courtesy Michael Silver)

Below: The highly accurate order-of-battle of the Army of Northern Virginia prepared by John C. Babcock as the Chancellorsville campaign began. (Library of Congress, John C. Babcock Collection)

The right wing of Hooker's army crossing the Rappahannock at Kelly's Ford. Sharpe's intelligence preparation of the battlefield (IPB) for the Chancellorsville Campaign included a complete analysis of the fords over the Rappahannock and Rapidan rivers such as Kelly's. (Library of Congress LC-USZ62-10824)

The Germanna Ford on the Rapidan River. The photograph shows how the terrain at the time was denuded of trees unlike today. (Library of Congress, LC-B815-701)

Pontoon bridges over the Rappahannock, May 1863, over which Sharpe helped evacuate thousands of wounded left behind in Hooker's precipitous retreat from Chancellorsville. Sharpe would later say he was prouder of his effort here than anything else he did during the war. Alexander Gardner, (Library of Congress LC-B8184-10331A)

The Reliable Contraband by Edwin Forbes. Contrabands were an excellent source of intelligence for the BMI. The information provided by contraband Charlie Wright was instrumental in Sharpe's ability to identify the movement of Lee's army for the invasion of the North that ended at Gettysburg. (Library of Congress LC-USZ62-15833)

Above left: Major General George G. Meade, commander of the Army of the Potomac, was a competent professional, but his sharp tongue and determination to be his own chief intelligence officer put a strain on his relationship with George Sharpe and degraded the overall intelligence effort after the battle. (Library of Congress LC-B8184-B29)

Above right: Ulrich Dahlgren was jumped from captain to colonel personally by Lincoln for his brilliant and daring service at Gettysburg. He was bold and adventurous but was killed in the ill-starred raid on Richmond in March 1864, in which a number of the BMI scouts were killed, wounded, and captured. (Author's collection)

Below: Here Dahlgren leads the saber charge on July 2, 1863, at Greencastle, PA, that panicked the Confederate couriers who were carrying vital dispatches for General Lee. (Library of Congress)

Above: Longstreet's men captured at Gettysburg. The interrogation by the BMI's John C. Babcock and Capt. John McEntee of Confederate prisoners taken on the first two days of Gettysburg yielded priceless intelligence. (Library of Congress LC-USZ62-14654 300)

Below right: Major General George Meade and Colonel Sharpe at Gettysburg on the night of July 2, 1863. Sharpe had just presented him with one of the most priceless intelligence reports in American military history. (Author's collection)

Below left: Major General George Meade and his corps commanders at Gettysburg on the night of July 2, 1863 in the famous council of war in which they decided to fight it out, largely based on Sharpe's intelligence report. (Author's collection)

July. 2. 1863 - 4½ P.M.

Major General Butterfield
Chief of Staff.

Prisoners have been taken to-day, and last evening, from every brigade in Lee's Army excepting the four brigades of Pickett's Division — Every division and has been represented except Pickett's from which we have not had a prisoner. They are from nearly one hundred different regiments.

Respectfully,
G. H. Sharpe
Col &c

One of the most important intelligence reports in U.S. military history—Sharpe's report on Lee's strength at Gettysburg on the night of July 2, 1863. (Fishel Collection, Georgetown University Library)

Major General Andrew A. Humphreys. After Gettysburg, Meade replaced Butterfield with Humphreys as chief of staff, Army of the Potomac. (Author's collection)

Major George Meade and 34 members of his staff at Brandy Station, winter 1863–64. Colonel Sharpe is in the last row to the right of seated Meade, with a moustache and wearing a kepi. (Library of Congress, Matthew Brady Collection LC-DIG-ppmsca-34114)

The analytical heart of the BMI—seated left to right: its chief, Col. George H. Sharpe; its order-of-battle and interrogation expert, civilian John C. Babcock; Lieut. Alfred Tanner, a visitor from the 20th New York State Militia; and Capt. John McEntee, who supervised the scouts. (Library of Congress LC-DIG-cwpb-03707)

Select scouts of the BMI in winter quarters at Brandy Station, 1864. Standing left to right: James Doughty, James Cammack, unknown, Henry W. Dodd, unknown, unknown. Seated: John M. Irby, Milton Cline, Dan Cole. On ground: Dan Plew, Milton Cline's son, W. J. Lee, unknown, James R. Wood, Sanford McGee, John W. Landegon. (Photography by Alexander Gardner, (Library of Congress LC-DIG-cwpb-03959)

Thirty-five scouts, guides, and cooks of the BMI in winter quarters at Brandy Station, 1864. These may have been close to the entire complement of the BMI other than clerks and officers at this time. All of these men were paid from a special secret service fund. (Library of Congress, LC-DIG-cwpb-03707)

John C. Babcock and possibly Capt. John McEntee at Sharpe's BMI headquarters at Brandy Station, winter 1863–64. (Courtesy Walt Witkowski)

Headquarters of the BMI, Army of the Potomac, in winter quarters at Brandy Station, 1864. The bull pen is in the distance. (Library of Congress LC-DIG-cwpb-00721)

The Bull Pen was the name for the prisoner-of-war stockade at the headquarters, provost marshal general, Army of the Potomac. (Alfred R. Waud, Library of Congress LC-DIG-ppmsca-21194)

Pickets exchanging coffee for tobacco. Sharpe was aware of this fraternization and briefed the Union pickets to elicit useful information from their Confederate counterparts. (Library of Congress)

Lieutenant General Ulysses S. Grant, after he decided to accompany the Army of the Potomac in the Overland Campaign, quickly came to appreciate the combat multiplier represented by Sharpe's BMI and especially its scouts with whom he frequently dealt. (Library of Congress LC-USZ61-903)

Confederate prisoners from Johnson's Division taken at Spotsylvania on May 12, 1864. Army of the Potomac standard operating procedure called for prisoners to be quickly forwarded to the BMI for interrogation. (Library of Congress LC-DIG-ppmsca-33763)

Tinder's or Tinsely's Mill toward which Sharpe sent Knight to discover any movement on the Confederate left at the battle of Spotsylvania, as depicted by Edwin Forbes. (Library of Congress, LC-USZ62-79165)

Confederate prisoners taken at the cavalry fight at Aldie, Virginia, in June 1864, and destined for the Bull Pen and interrogation by the BMI. (Library of Congress LC-DIG-ppmsca-33762)

Fort Mahone, known as Fort Damnation, one of the major forts in the defenses of Petersburg, after its eventual capture. Knight found the defenses nearly empty when Grant stole a march on Lee to strike at the city, but the Union commanders hesitated while Confederate reinforcements rushed to man them. (Library of Congress, LC-B811-3211)

Right: Elizabeth Van Lew, the Union spy mistress of Richmond, upon whom Sharpe relied for priceless information on the Confederate defenses. (Author's collection)

Below: The Van Lew mansion in Richmond, the center of Union espionage, to which Judson Knight was a frequent visitor. (Library of Congress, LC-DIG-det-4a12640)

Ulysses S. Grant's headquarters at City Point during the Siege of Petersburg. John C. Babcock, Sharpe's deputy and master order-of-battle specialist, is seated second from right. (Library of Congress LC-USZ62-46635 300)

Headquarters of the BMI scouts at City Point established in July 1864. It was from here that Sharpe and Chief of Scouts Judson Knight planned the scouts' missions behind enemy lines during the siege of Petersburg and Richmond. (Library of Congress, LC-DIG-cwpb-02158)

Scouts and local black guides at the headquarters of the BMI at City Point during the siege of Petersburg. (Library of Congress LC-B811- 2676 [P&P])

Officers of the 20th New York State Militia Regt., Sharpe's old regiment and part of the provost guard, Culpeper Court House, October 1863. (Courtesy Seward Osborne)

Above: The explosion of a supply ship at City Point on August 9, 1864 was the work of Confederate saboteurs. Sharpe's counterintelligence operation was on their trail but not fast enough to prevent the explosion. (Library of Congress LC-DIG-ppmsca-21253)

Below: U.S. Navy gunboats such as this carried Judson Knight and his scouts up and down the James River to land them on the Confederate shore to slip in and out of Richmond with intelligence gathered by the Van Lew ring. (Library of Congress, LC-B811- 2547)

Chief of Scouts Judson Knight's depiction of a Confederate torpedo placed in the James River, which appeared in *Scientific American*, and Captain McEntee's sketch. Copies of the sketch were distributed to the fleet in the James, and one was dropped into the box of the Confederate Secretary of the Navy, causing work on the torpedo to stop. (Courtesy *Scientific American*)

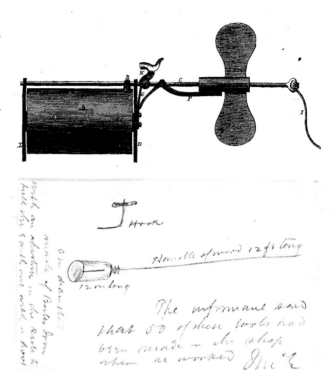

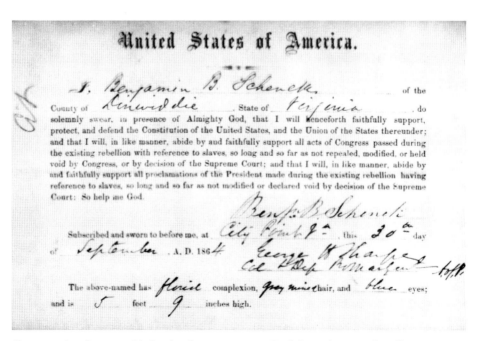

Sharpe was largely responsible for the plan to encourage Confederate desertions by offering generous treatment, a clever and effective psychological operation. Here is a loyalty oath signed by a Confederate deserter and countersigned by Sharpe. (Author's collection)

Above left: Major George K. Leet, Asst. Army Adjutant General at the War Department, conducted intelligence collection operations in Northern Virginia for the BMI after the Armies Operating Against Richmond settled into the siege of Petersburg. (NARA, 526681)

Above right: Captain and later Brig. Gen. Paul A. Oliver was an important addition to the BMI in the last months of the war. (Author's collection)

Left: Sharpe's portrait photo taken after his promotion to Brevet Brigadier General in February 1865. (Courtesy Walt Witkowski)

Lee's surrender at Appomattox. Sharpe was present as a member of Grant's staff and able to provide an accurate estimate of the number of rations Lee's army would need. He would also write an astute account of the proceedings. (Author's collection)

Sharpe's prize souvenirs from Appomattox—the two brass candlesticks he bought from the owner of the McLean House and the pass signed by Robert E. Lee to allow him access to his army, the last order he was ever to issue as commander of the Army of Northern Virginia. The pass appears to have been as faint when the photo was taken as it is now. (Courtesy Kingston Historical Society)

Clover Tavern at Appomattox where Sharpe conducted the paroling of the Army of Northern Virginia. (Library of Congress HABS VA, 6-APP0, 5-4)

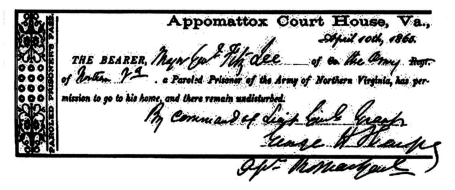

The parole of Henry Kyd Douglass issued by Sharpe at Appomattox. (Courtesy Antietam National Battlefield)

Sharpe's sword, which he wore as part of the general officer honor guard around Lincoln's body lying state in the East Room of the White House, still wrapped in its black crepe. (Courtesy New York Historical Society)

Sharpe was chosen to be one of the general officer honor guard around Lincoln's body lying in state in the East Room of the White House on April 18, 1865. There was one general for every state in the Union, including the former Confederate states. Sharpe represented Georgia. (Author's collection)

On May 23, 1865 a "grand review" of the Army of the Potomac was held in Washington. Sharpe proudly rode at the head of his beloved 120th New York Volunteers as their colonel. (Author's collection)

Above: Sharpe's mansion, The Orchard, with its fashionable second-empire mansard roof which he built after the Civil War. He would host President Grant here in 1873. (Courtesy Walt Witkowski)

Left: Charles Nast cartoon showing Boss Tweed as a ruined emperor in 1871. It was Sharpe's efforts as U.S. marshal to ensure that an honest election to the House of Representatives was conducted in New York City in 1870 that began Tweed's downfall. (Author's collection)

Below: Senator Roscoe Conkling's inability, as leader of the Grant Stalwarts, to be the kingmaker at the 1880 Republican National Convention allowed delegate Sharpe to maneuver his friend, Chester Arthur, into the nomination for vice-president. (Author's collection)

Above: George Sharpe (center) and veterans of his 120th New York at the 1888 Gettysburg reunion. (Courtesy Seward Osborne)

Below left: On October 17, 1896, Sharpe dedicated a statue to the "rank and file" of his beloved 120th New York Volunteer Infantry Regiment in his hometown of Kingston. Sharpe was the only commanding officer to erect a monument to his men rather than the other way around. (Courtesy Walt Witkowski)

Below right: Portrait of George H. Sharpe commissioned by his son, Severyn, after his father's death, hung over the mantel of his mansion, The Orchard. (Courtesy Kingston Historical Society)

Above: Gravestone of George H. and Caroline Sharpe in Wiltwyck Cemetery, Kingston. (Courtesy Seward Osborne)

Below left: The brass plate dedicated to George H. Sharpe by his regiment in the Old Dutch Church, Kingston, NY, 1926. (Courtesy Seward Osborne)

Below right: Reunion of the 120th New York Volunteers on the 50th anniversary in 1922 of the birth of the regiment, surrounding the statue Sharpe built to honor them. (Courtesy Seward Osborne)

did not have direct overland contact with this area of Virginia, this mission had to be controlled from the War Department in Washington. Babcock organized three of his spies living west of Fredericksburg, including old Isaac Silver, to travel to the railroad depots conveniently near their homes to monitor movement. Silver had moved from his ruined farm above Fredericksburg to a place below the town and near the railroad terminus. It is a tribute to Silver's patriotism that he continued to work as actively as an agent even after the devastation of his farm by Sheridan's cavalry.

Sharpe sent the scouts Dodd, McCord, Phil Carney, and S. McGee, among others. They were based in Fredericksburg and would meet the agents several times a week. Tugs were provided to shuttle them with their information to Washington from which Babcock would send their information to Grant and Sharpe. Once this new network was in place, Babcock returned to Petersburg, leaving the direction and coordination of the scouts in the hands of one of Grant's assistant adjutant generals in Washington, Lt. George K. Leet, who in effect became a member of Sharpe's team. He was responsible for intelligence operations between Washington and Richmond, in which Confederate authority had been reintroduced after the Army of the Potomac had passed and established its communications by the James River instead of overland. Leet had the authority to send the reports of these scouts to any command that required the information. By September, the hidden southern agents were supplying information "as often as five times in two weeks."[60]

Sharpe now essentially operated a branch BMI office, with Butler's Army of the James under the control of Lieutenant Manning. He was assisted by Lieutenant Davenport, Butler's military secretary, who would become an important element of the effort. Butler's enthusiastic support of this office would ease the coordination of intelligence considerably. McEntee would continue to operate out of Meade's headquarters south of Petersburg, and most of their reporting concentrated on the enemy opposing the Army of the Potomac. No matter where they worked, the members of the BMI were constantly exchanging information and coordinating their analysis through Sharpe by telegram over the efficient lines set up by the Signal Corps. Davenport, Babcock, and McEntee concentrated on the enemy's order-of-battle as Sharpe drew all the collection sources together.

"Get into Richmond"

To accomplish the second mission Sharpe had given Sergeant Knight instructions on "establishing daily communications between the Capital of the Confederacy and Gen. Grant's Headquarters at City Point." Two days after a scout group had set up at City Point, Knight was ready to try. Sharpe sent him his own orderly, a man named Powers, a native of Richmond and Unionist, thinking his knowledge of the Richmond area would be useful. Upon questioning him, Knight learned that Powers had fled Richmond to escape Confederate military service and had been secreted out of the city by another Unionist named Alexander Myers. The more Powers described Myers, the more Knight found him a potentially valuable contact. Myers was a New Jersey native who had spent time in jail in North Carolina for his Unionist sympathies but had moved to Richmond where he found a job with the Quartermaster Department. He had a roving commission to move anywhere about the state to confiscate any Union military property that had been left behind. Apparently, the Confederate Secret Service was behind on its background investigations.

Powers, it seemed, had also been a clerk for John Van Lew, which instantly reminded Knight of the conversation he'd had with him before the Overland Campaign, to the effect that his mother and sister would be able and willing provide a great deal of useful information if contacted. The Van Lew ladies were also known to Sharpe through Major General Butler, but Butler had apparently not been able to reestablish reliable contact with the women. The quality of information they had provided convinced him that they were the key to penetrating Richmond. He now gave Knight a letter for Elizabeth Van Lew. He was to give it to Myers, whom he hoped would deliver it. Powers, unfortunately, refused point blank to return to Confederate territory to guide the scouts to Myers. Knight would have to settle for closely questioning Powers about the terrain across the James from City Point. A steamer put Knight and scout Anson B. Carney ashore at night. Sharpe's bureau had an unquestioned priority for the use of any vessel they required. They crept inland, and slipped through enemy pickets, careful to leave no hint of their passage. Knight had been duly impressed by Sharpe's inflexible instructions to that effect that they "could neither kill nor take prisoners on night expeditions." There must be no trace of their comings and goings.

They came to a house. Knight knocked on the door and identified himself as Captain Phillips of the 5th North Carolina Cavalry but was told by a woman that she would not open it at night but to come to the back of the house where they could speak through a window. He explained that he was looking for Myers on official business; she knew Myers, who was scheduled to come by and drop off a barrel of flour. The woman was joined by another and both obviously had Southern sympathies. The second woman was suspicious why the authorities in Richmond would send out an officer who knew nothing of the area to look for Myers and who had passed through the pickets outside.

Knight went right into action, employing the cool effrontery that was the scout's best weapon:

> Putting on all the dignity I could muster, with as much hauteur as I could possibly assume, I sternly said: "Mrs. Slater, has not the war been going on nearly four years, and have you not learned by this time that a soldier, when he receives an order from his superior officer, has but one thing to do, obey it? Now, I can't say why Myers is wanted in Richmond, what he had done, or why he is wanted. I know nothing. I simply know that Gen. Winder, the Provost-Marshal of the Confederacy, ordered me about sundown to come down here and bring Myers to Richmond with me. Why I was sent on the errand I know not. Why he did not send some one who knew the country better than we do it is impossible for me to say. Your insinuations

as to how we passed the pickets lead me to suspect you don't believe what I have told you. I supposed we were talking to a woman with intelligence enough to know that an officer of Gen. Winder's rank and ability would not send a man off on an errand of that kind without papers that would pass him anywhere, and that is what I have got. Perhaps I had better show them to you, and possibly, after seeing them you will believe I have not been telling you a pack of lies. Sergeant, have you a match?

The woman's suspicions were quashed. Knight had the women raise their right hands to pledge that they would reveal nothing of this conversation to anyone, including Myers. Twenty minutes after Knight and Carney had left Myers arrived. The women rushed down the walkway to the gate to tell him to "Look out for Capt. Phillips of the 5th NC Cav." who was out to find him.[61]

Their steamer was waiting to take them back to City Point before dawn. That morning Knight briefed Sharpe who concluded that the proper guide for that area would be a local black man. He had found that they knew the areas they had lived in intimately. He issued orders allowing Knight to acquire the services of any black man native of Charles County and working for the Quartermaster at Bermuda Hundred. He found such a man in a free black named Lightfoot Charles. As with Powers, no inducement could get Charles to cross the river back into "Rebeldom." But with much cajoling and encouragement, he eventually and reluctantly agreed. Knight could have saved all the effort, for Charles turned out to be a very bad guide in the night, but in his defense, he had warned them that "it's rather a blind place to find, in fact."

During their next attempt, it was clear they were lost with Lightfoot as a guide, but what Sharpe called Knight's "topographical instinct" got them back to the wharf and waiting steamer. That instinct, Knight explained, was that he "was like a mule—could find my way to the place where I was last fed." Charles had at least provided one service by identifying the house of a Union sympathizer named Hill, an English immigrant.

Knight reported his failure to Sharpe just as a steamer brought over 10 Unionist refugees from Richmond. They had come through exactly the same area that Knight, Carney, and Charles had wandered around all night. He was thoroughly perplexed how they could have missed such a large party. Knight returned across the river, now without Charles, and questioned several slaves who also told him of Hill's sympathies. He then approached Hill. Evidently, the new Union uniform he was wearing this time took Hill much aback. He asked about the road to Richmond to test the man who encouraged him to return to the Union army immediately. Knight assured him he was not a deserter and that he had heard of his Union sympathies from local blacks. Hill admitted as much and agreed to go into Richmond. "I wanted him to find out from what States the different regiments he saw were, and their numbers. I also asked him to go to a market gardener, an Englishman like himself … and who I believed was a Union man." Having failed to find Myers, he would try to use Hill.

Returning to report to Sharpe, Knight was aggravated to find out that Myers had just sent another larger party across the river. Sharpe recognized that Myers was the key to Van Lew, whose reputation Major General Butler vouched for. He gave Knight orders to find Myers and tell him to stop sending people across the river because sooner or later the Confederate authorities would find out and "Myers' goose would be cooked." Knight returned to see Hill the next night to find that he had accomplished none of his tasks, but he had brought one of every Richmond newspaper, themselves of great value. At least they were some evidence of his otherwise fruitless attempts to penetrate Richmond.

Obviously, the problem in finding Myers was the absence of good directions to his house. Sharpe sent Knight off to see Major General Hancock, who was fighting north of the James, with a request to turn over a map found on the body of Confederate Brigadier General Chambliss. Hancock replied that he had sent off the map to be photographed. He suggested that the cavalry division on his right might have some prisoners who knew the area and sent him off to see Major General Gregg. Knight was again stumped when he found no useful prisoners until he asked Gregg if he had any cavalry near Malvern Hill. As it turned out, the 17th Pennsylvania Cavalry, which had accompanied Knight on several missions before Spotsylvania, was there. Its commander, Major McCabe, was a venturesome sort. He suggested that Knight request Gregg provide him the services of the 17th PA to break through the enemy's strong pickets to facilitate the insertion of the scouts into the enemy's rear. This effort too ultimately failed.[62]

Knight was now forced to go back to retrace his steps again with Lightfoot Charles and Carney. It was an embarrassing admission of failure and desperation. Again they found themselves going in circles with Charles in the lead. Coming across a crossing they had come through before, Knight noticed that Charles was about to go down the same path he had already taken once before. He put his foot down and said they would go the opposite way. Before long, they had come to the farm they had been seeking for the last week. They entered at gunpoint and found the elusive Myers sound asleep. Knight woke him and took him outside into the cornfield for a quiet conversation. He explained who he was to dispel Myers's fears and then passed on Sharpe's instructions to desist from sending any more refugees across the James because of the danger to him. Myers, now convinced of Knight's story, told him that the night he had made contact at the Slaters's, two Confederate scouts had been in the house, and out of fear of being revealed had begged the two women not to open the door but to only speak through the back window. Knight's bravado apparently convinced them as much as the Slater women that he had been a real Confederate officer.

At this point Knight gave Myers Sharpe's letter to Van Lew and made him promise to deliver it and "and meet me in the woods the next night if Miss Van Lew answered the letter." The next night Myers delivered Van Lew's reply, which contained information and a promise to send more whenever she could. Within days Sharpe's scouts were visiting Myers every night to receive information from Van Lew. At the same time, Knight was working on another contact given him by Hill—Charles Carter, who could do the work far better than Hill. Carter had been a recruiting officer in the "old army" in Richmond and was eager to meet Knight. Hill put them together, and Knight gave him a letter from Sharpe to Van Lew. Sharpe was now running two lines to Van Lew, each without the knowledge of the other. Knight would be the primary conduit for Van Lew's information. For Van Lew, who had become fearful of the poor security of Butler's contacts with her, her sudden access to Sharpe was a godsend. "As the war advanced and the army closed around Richmond, I was able to communicate with General Butler and General Grant, but not so well and persistently with General Butler, for there was too much danger in the system and persons. With General Grant, through his Chief of Secret Service, General George H. Sharpe, I was more fortunate." It was to be one of the great and most effective relationships in the history of espionage. One of the world's great spymasters had just stepped upon the stage of history and, figuratively, into the arms of George H. Sharpe.[63]

The day after setting up his own office at City Point on July 21, Sharpe was able to inform Patrick that he "has organized a system of information to Richmond."[64]

In addition to Van Lew, Sharpe had established contacts that allowed him to run two parallel sources of information from Richmond. One was run by the superintendent of the RF&P Railroad, Samuel Ruth, who since before the battle of Chancellorsville had been doing his best to sabotage the efficient logistics support of Lee's army. Scout William J. Lee brought Ruth's name to Sharpe's attention. Sharpe authorized him to be the single contact with Ruth. As Lee would later write to Grant after the war, "I was the 1st man and the only one to mention *Mr. Ruth's* name to *Genl Sharpe* & the only one that Mr. Ruth would have had anything to do with on the subject of information from the enimies [sp] lines." A third source was the abolitionist baker named Thomas McNiven with city-wide contacts.[65] Yet Van Lew remained the most important.

Elizabeth Van Lew was a wealthy member of Richmond society. The famed singer Jenny Lind, at the height of her career, sang in the great parlor; Edgar Allen Poe read aloud there "The Raven." She maintained an abiding loyalty to the Union and to the abolitionist cause. She was determined to provide information to Union forces and at the same time spent large sums of her own fortune to bring food and care to the thousands of Federal prisoners at Libby Prison as well as help many escape. One of those she aided was Colonel Revere of Boston, a descendent of Paul Revere of Concord and Lexington fame in the War for Independence. She used bold but effective methods to secure access to the military prisons—plying the warden of Libby Prison, Lieutenant Todd (brother of Mrs. Lincoln) with his favorite buttermilk and gingerbread, shamelessly flattering General Winder, who controlled the prison system, and by boarding at her home Libby's new warden and his family. She found that Union prisoners were an excellent source of military intelligence, which she was quick to exploit. The prisons were situated to give the inmates an excellent observation of the arrival and departure of Confederate units and supply trains. The prisoners also skillfully picked up information from their guards. All this they gladly shared with Van Lew.[66]

Her efforts to help the Union cause began soon after Virginia seceded, when she established contact with Federal officials in Washington in order to pass information, but it was only in the second half of 1863 that she established regular contact with the Union army in the person of the commander of the Army of the James, Benjamin Butler. The proximity to Richmond of the Army of the James made Butler a natural though dangerous contact.

Sharpe would say of this heroic woman and her family:

> Their position, character and charities gave them a commanding influence, and many families of plain people were decided and encouraged by them to remain true to the flag, and were subsequently able during the war to receive our agents... For a long, long time, she represented all that was left of the power of the United States government in the city of Richmond.

She was the *primus inter pares* among the three networks, coordinating their efforts. Her own sources were as varied as they were prolific, from clerks at the War and Navy Departments to a servant she was reputed to have placed in Jefferson Davis's employ at the Confederate White House. She held the Unionist community in Richmond together and actively employed its members in the full range of her activities—espionage, safe-houses, couriers, informants, and more. Her cover was as audacious as it was clever. She openly declared her Union and abolitionist views but then masked them by creating a persona of simple-minded eccentricity that earned her the disarming nickname of "Crazy Bett."[67]

Sharpe's Richmond espionage ring was quickly providing the most revealing information on the internal collapse of the Confederate economy and war production of which Grant and Lincoln were kept abreast. It consisted of a strong web of contact of five secret stations, meeting places for Richmond agents and Sharpe's scouts. Oral and written reports, many in BMI-provided ciphers, were given the scouts who in turn often forwarded requests for specific information from Sharpe and Grant. Often it was Knight and Lee who met directly with Van Lew and Ruth. As Feis points out, "Scouts met with agents two to three times a week using the 'upper' (along the James) or 'Lower' (along the Chickahominy) routes to reach the depots."[68]

There was no little risk attendant on these rendezvous. Both sides conducted operations such as cavalry raids through these areas. In November McEntee reported that the appearance of a Confederate cavalry force sent to counter Union cavalry raids made it impossible to use their depots on the Chickahominy route. The following January Sharpe made the following report:

Scouts having been interfered with, went yesterday afternoon under the cover of a scouting party, which was entirely successful. We believe that the enemy have a line of communication with the James River by substantially the same route as our own, of which we hope to give more complete information by the end of the week, in order that it may be broken up. Our scouts do not desire to interfere with it, as thereby their own business would be apparent.[69]

Presumably, Sharpe came down on the side of his scouts, valuing the preservation of contact with Richmond far more than a temporary interruption of enemy activity on one route.

The closer Grant's grip tightened on Richmond the more important became Miss Lew's organization, to the point where Sharpe was receiving same-day courier reports. Shape commented after the war that Grant asked repeatedly for "specific information" and she "steadily conveyed it to him." So efficient was her courier service that one source asserts "that flowers from the Van Lew gardens often arrived fresh and dewy on Grant's breakfast table!" More realistically, a second source says, "Flowers cut in her garden in the morning found their way to Grant's table at City Point." The important point is that couriers were able to pass in or out of the city to deliver their messages in one day. Two of the couriers were her servants, the brothers John and Peter Roane. Van Lew freed them and sent them to Grant's headquarters where they worked as tent-servants for Grant and Gen. Babcock of his staff. Sharpe did not stint his praise of her contribution to his espionage network. "[T]he greater portion in its collection and in a good measure in its transmission, we owed to the intelligence and devotion of Miss E. L. Van Lew." Grant himself would say, "You have sent me the most valuable information received from Richmond during the war."[70] Sharpe made sure to personally control this collection source.

Sharpe's intelligence collection efforts were not solely devoted to the Confederacy. He had a special talent for ferreting out information of the professional struggles within the leaders of the U.S. Army. Soon after moving to City Point in July, Sharpe was reporting to Patrick about the disfavor in which Butler was held by Grant and that the general-in-chief was worried that if he replaced him with Maj. Gen. Christopher C. Auger, currently commanding the garrison in Washington, Sickles would backfill his slot and thus be able to exert a baleful influence over the army. By August, the headquarters feared Butler's plotting against Grant. They worried particularly about the allegations that the general-in-chief had been drunk twice in the presence of the "Beast," as Butler was called North and South for his odious tactics as military governor of New Orleans. Butler had a record of noncompliance with orders from Grant's headquarters, including the transfer of prisoners, which fell in both Patrick's and Sharpe's areas of responsibility.[71]

It was not long before Grant began to rely on Sharpe for political intelligence of the ongoing struggles for power in Washington.

CHAPTER ELEVEN

The Siege of Petersburg

June–December 1864

Settling in for the Siege

Early's near capture of Washington had been deeply embarrassing to Grant, but it did not deflect him from his main purpose now that he had Lee's army pinned down in the siege of Petersburg. Neither did he let the criticism in the Northern press that labeled the 1864 Overland Campaign a failure bother him. His objective was the destruction of the Army of Northern Virginia. His immediate purpose was to keep Lee's troops pinned to the defense of Petersburg under increasing pressure that would prevent any more detachments such as to Early in the Valley or to Georgia to reinforce General Joe Johnston defending Atlanta against Sherman.

By forcing Lee to commit himself to the defense of the capital of Richmond and the railroad nexus at Petersburg, he had denied his Confederate nemesis his greatest advantage, the ability to maneuver with boldness. Instead he compelled Lee to fight a stationary battle of attrition in which all the odds were against the South. With three times the population of the South and a vastly superior industrial base, Grant rightly calculated that time was on his side. Keep the pressure up and Lee would inevitably crack. But Grant had already painfully learned that Lee would extract every advantage to be found even in this losing formula. He had discovered that he faced in Lee the greatest military engineer in the history of the United States. Lee threw the spade and shovel into the scales of battle and bought month after month of precious time. Lee was playing the bad cards well.

To break Lee in this war of attrition, Grant found the BMI's ability to build and update a precise enemy order-of-battle invaluable. The BMI's interrogation of prisoners and more importantly deserters was reinforced with information flowing in a steady stream from "our friends" in Richmond. "Systematic interrogations provided information on the whereabouts and movements of brigades and divisions, which were then plotted on 'information maps' distributed to field commanders.

Captives also told of brigade consolidations and changes in command and offered insights on morale within the ranks."[1]

The BMI's order-of-battle analysts did not just keep track of the organization and location of the enemy's units but of their strengths as well. For example, interrogations of an intelligent deserter from the 21st South Carolina revealed that when the regiment had been transferred from Charleston in May, its brigade numbered 3,700. In early September its commander was quoted by the source as stating, "Yes, if the sick and slightly wounded were with the brigade I suppose it would number 800 men." Another example was the comparisons in Confederate cavalry regiments of the number of mounted and dismounted men due to lack of horses. In Cobb's Legion there were 100 mounted men and 400 dismounted, while the 7th Georgia had 40 mounted and 350 dismounted. Information such as this was invaluable in discerning the weakening of the Confederate cavalry as the South exhausted its supply of horses.[2] In August the BMI made the interesting observation that fewer South Carolinians deserted than men from any other state.[3]

Assisting the BMI were the numerous signal station observation towers set up by the Signal Corps that gave them a bird's eye view within the Confederate lines during daylight as Lee constantly shifted regiments and brigades. Babcock matched these reports with information from interrogations to confirm his order-of-battle conclusions. The telescopes of the Signal Corps contributed more to the intelligence effort when they began to intercept Confederate signals from the Petersburg Custom House on June 21. The Signal Corps officer who was intercepting the messages quickly concluded that the Confederate code was similar to the one they had broken in 1863. By the 24th he could read the entire code and began to decipher messages that showed his Confederate counterparts could observe Union troop movements. The Signal Corps continued to read Rebel traffic throughout the rest of the siege.[4]

As the armies settled down to siege warfare in mid-June, Grant attempted to stretch Lee's forces by maneuvering repeatedly south of Petersburg against the railroads feeding Petersburg and Richmond and drawing Confederate forces away from the siege lines. At the same time, Sharpe's men were interrogating deserters who were coming over by the dozens every day, an indication of the creeping sense of despair in the Southern ranks. Three of Sharpe's intelligence summaries for June 18 are given at length below as models of careful assessment.

> Forty-two prisoners received so far this morning from Second Corps from none but the brigade properly of Beauregard. None of them know of re-enforcements from Lee. A part of Martin's brigade was brought down from six miles out toward Richmond yesterday a.m. and sent to the enemy's right. An apparently honest man among them says that in passing through Petersburg and out to the front no second line of works or of battle was passed, and the others, though less frank, confirm it. The prisoners do not seem willing to admit that their troops have left here. The greater part claim that they have fallen back only about one line to a position just this side of the town, but they are unable to describe any position of strength there, or any preparation to do so.[5]

We have received 4 officers and 36 men from the Second corps this morning, and 26 officers and 329 men from the Ninth Corps. These prisoners are all from the brigades which were under Beauregard and part of which were sent from General Lee's army (as Hoke's division), and represent nearly the whole of Beauregard's force, at least nine brigades in all. None of them have seen any of the forces properly belonging to any one of the three corps of General Lee's army. The men taken by the Ninth Corps on the enemy's extreme right this morning, at what they term a farm-house, were told by their officers, when asked to hold the ground, that re-enforcements were coming up and they must of good courage; others understood that Ewell was close at hand, but careful examination has failed to show us that any one we have taken has seen any of these men. Even the men who were unwilling to make statements as regards the force speak generally of the force as not being heavy. The nine brigades spoken of, however, are very much stronger, all of them, than the average of brigades in General Lee's army. We know some of them to be 3,000 to 3,500 strong. The prisoners state that in the attack last evening 500 prisoners were taken from us. (General Patrick has been informed that 275 men are reported to have been sent in to General Butler yesterday from the Eighteenth Corps.)[6]

In a further examination of the prisoners (42 in number, sent in by General Hancock this morning and heretofore reported) I find that a portion of Martin's brigade, two regiments of Gracie's (Alabama) brigade, and the whole of Evans' (South Carolina) brigade, were withdrawn early yesterday morning from a position about four to six miles from Petersburg toward Richmond, along a little creek which they are unable to name (perhaps Swift Creek), but where they understood they were placed to prevent the advance of General Butler. These men all seem to think, at least such of them as are willing to talk, that the whole infantry force in that direction was withdrawn yesterday, leaving nothing but cavalry there. When brought here they were put on the right of the enemy's line. The greater part of the prisoners taken this morning are such as having fallen asleep away from their commands, were picked up by our men this morning. They, consequently, cannot tell how far their forces have receded. Some of the most intelligent think that Martin's brigade is holding a position in the rear of what was the extreme right of the enemy's position yesterday, but that Martin's line is not prolonged on either side.[7]

A Little Scout Free-Lancing

As it became obvious that the golden chance was gone, Sharpe put his scouts in motion. Knight remembered:

We were now in a part of Virginia where none of us had ever been, and the first thing we set about was to learn all we could about the country. About the second day after our arrival several parties started out, some going east and south, while I started with a party toward the southwest… After we crossed the Norfolk & Petersburg Railroad we kept on until we came to the Jerusalem Plank road, which led directly south from Petersburg.[8]

Lee could read a map better than most. It told him that the roads and railroads leading south from Petersburg were seriously vulnerable. Three railroads ran through Petersburg to Richmond, keeping the capital and arsenal of the Confederacy alive. Military supplies run through the blockade to Wilmington were sent to Richmond and Lee's army by these routes. The three railroads were, from east to west, the Norfolk & Petersburg, the Weldon, both of which went due south, and the Southside, which paralleled the Appomattox River westward before turning south. The latter was the only one of the three that was not immediately threatened. The Norfolk & Petersburg was already overrun within a few days by Hancock's II Corps. Lee's eyes focused on the Weldon. He warned Secretary of War Seddon, "It will be almost impossible to preserve the connection between this place and Weldon."[9]

His apprehension was well founded. As Knight stated, Sharpe's scouts were already criss-crossing this vital line of communications preparing the way for Federal attacks. Already movement westward by Meade on the day Lee had made this statement had been rebuffed by a Confederate counterattack, but it would not be the last. Lee rode up that day to speak to Major General Mahone, who recalled that the commanding general, "expressed a desire that something should be done to arrest the progress of the Federal prolongation." Mahone was the right man for the job. As a Confederate officer commented, "Whenever Mahone moves out, somebody is apt to be hurt."[10]

At this point, part of the unsuspecting Army of the Potomac was about to benefit from the bold initiative of one of Sharpe's scouts. Judson Knight had worked hard since watching the great opportunity slip away from the army, but the nights brought no relief, and on June 20 he "concluded to make a night trip and see if I could learn anything of importance." Without permission or a pass that would get him through the lines he was off and crossed the Jerusalem Plank Road before dark. He thought to himself that he was acting in just the same way as a Confederate scout trying to get out through Union lines. Along the Plank Road, he came across Birney's Division, II Corps, and spotted the men and guns of Clark's B Battery, New Jersey Artillery, but gave them a wide berth. After traveling west beyond the army's left flank, he turned north toward Petersburg. Approaching the enemy's lines, he bedded down in a pine thicket for the night. In the morning he watched as a large number of men came out to work on the fortifications; he was amazed that the Confederates were using white men to do a job for which he had always seen blacks employed. He was even more amazed at how hard they worked. By 11:00 a.m. a large body of troops moved into the space in front of the working parties. Knight thought he would be treated to brigade and then division drill as the forces grew, but then the men sat down and waited.

It dawned on Knight that this was no drill but the assembly of an assault force. He knew that he would not be able to get back to headquarters in time for his report to do any good. Instead, he resolved to find the nearest unit and give the warning. Now he realized the consequences of leaving camp without permission or a pass that would authenticate his identity. He was most likely to be insulted or accused of being a Rebel spy as had often happened before, even with his identification. His penchant for making as few acquaintances as possible would mean he was unlikely to be recognized as a scout. He headed for B Battery, where he was luckily known, managed to avoid any other troops, and slipped unseen into the camp and went straight for Clark's tent. Luckily he was known there; Captain Clark's brother in the same battery had offered Knight a drink at one time which he had declined. The captain saw him as he entered his quarters and greeted him with the query, "What's the news?" As soon as Knight collected on the previous offer of a drink (surely he needed one by then), he warned Clark of the impending attack. An infantry colonel who was present sneered and said that Knight was more scared than hurt by his experience. Insulted, he walked out without a word, to be pursued by Clark's brother who said the captain wanted to know if he had been serious. "Certainly I meant it. You are sure to be attacked either this evening or early in the morning, and when it does come it will be from the west. You ought to have a strong breastwork thrown up facing that way instead of the one your guns are in now facing Petersburg."

Clark wasted no time in telling his own officers that the bearer of the news was a scout at army headquarters known to him and put the battery to work building new breastworks to the scorn of the infantry officers nearby. He would write 20 years later to Knight stating that his warning was what saved the battery from the storm of the Confederate attack that fell on II Corps soon thereafter on June 22. Hancock's command disintegrated from the blows of the divisions of Mahone and Wilcox and lost 650 killed or wounded and 1,742 prisoners. For a very short time Lee had saved the precious Weldon Railroad.[11]

If Sharpe had been caught blindside by the attack of June 22, it was because his scouts already had been given a priority mission for that same day—to support the great cavalry raid by Kautz's and Wilson's cavalry divisions to wreck the Southside and Richmond & Danville Railroads, the remaining routes that connected Lee's army and Richmond with the rest of the Confederacy. Just as the Confederate attack on II Corps was kicking off, Sharpe reported to Meade that his scouts had been out looking over the Weldon Railroad, several miles to the south of the impending attack, and had been overtaken by Wilson's cavalry and gone as far as Reams Station when they left to return to headquarters at 10:30 p.m., while the troopers stayed behind to wreck the station. One can only speculate what he would have given had he known of Knight's findings in time.[12]

That night Sharpe and his men interrogated prisoners from Wilcox's and Mahone's attack who admitted that they had been badly cut up in front of the Union positions, Clark's Battery B no doubt doing great slaughter behind its breastworks. They also admitted that their commands had pulled back after dark to their own lines. Early the next day Sharpe sent out as large a body of his scouts as he could, led by Cline, to confirm that the enemy had, indeed, withdrawn back. Three quarters of a mile west of the railroad all that Cline could find was a weak line of enemy pickets, and on the way back he came across men of the Union VI Corps, "engaged in destroying the railroad." Lee's problem was that the best he could do for a short while was to keep the enemy off only that part of the Weldon nearest his lines. The length of the railroad which ran along the Union flank made it vulnerable along a line the Confederates could never hope to defend. His attack had saved it for barely one day.[13]

The consequences were apparent within a week. On June 29 Sharpe reported that his scouts had found a party of four slaves on a plantation near the Weldon Railroad. They belonged to officers of the 17th North Carolina and had been given passes to take them home. "They stated that all the negroes who could possibly be spared were being sent from the army to their homes, and only such as were indispensably necessary were kept; that it was understood the want of provisions had led to the step." One of them said that he had heard General Martin and their colonel in conversation state that if the Yankees kept the roads cut for 10 days longer, "they (the enemy) would have to dig out." That same day Lee informed President Davis of his plans to bring in supplies:

> As before stated, my greatest present anxiety is to secure regular and constant supplies. At this time I am doing well, but I must look to the future. I have started today a train of wagons, via Dinwiddie Court House to Stony Creek Station, Petersburg and Weldon Railroad, for corn to be brought there from Weldon. This, with the standing crop of clover & oats, will subsist our horses for the present.

This was just the sort of information Grant wanted. He knew that while the order-of-battle was vital, it was equally vital to know if the soldiers in those figures were well fed or on starvation rations. It would make all the difference.[14]

Of more immediate concern for Meade and Grant was the fate of the cavalry expedition, consisting of the cavalry divisions of August Kautz and James H. Wilson, dispatched to cut the railroads between Petersburg and Lynchburg. They had disappeared behind Confederate lines, with only rumors of disaster filtering through. The broken fragments of Kautz's division had filtered in after a 335-mile eight-day ordeal. Despite the fact that their horses were in poor condition, the expedition had gone well until June 26, when Lee's cavalry arrived to harry the returning and exhausted blue cavalry. Wilson's and Kautz's commands began to disintegrate when they found the points at which they had intended to cross back into Union lines blocked. Sharpe was interrogating every prisoner that could shed light on the fate of Wilson's horsemen. One man from the 10th Virginia Heavy Artillery Battalion laid out the disaster in painfully accurate detail:

> He claims that the enemy have three divisions of cavalry concentrated against Wilson—Hampton's, Fitz. Lee's, and W. H. F. Lee's divisions. He says that part of them came from Richmond; that yesterday, the enemy having destroyed a bridge over Stony Creek, and Wilson being driven back upon it, when the bridge was found to be gone large numbers of our men surrendered themselves. He thinks they had taken, up to the time he was sent back with prisoners and horses, from 600 to 800 horses, a large number of prisoners—he does not know how many—all the artillery and ambulances of General Wilson, which, however he says were not many, and his baggage wagons. He says the woods were full of our men, who had abandoned their horses, and were scattering in every direction, and that the horses taken from us were found to be very badly knocked up.[15]

By the next day the survivors had crossed back into Union lines and the cost was calculated. Wilson had lost 33 killed, 108 wounded, and 674 captured or missing; Kautz had lost 48, 153, and 429 respectively, for a total loss of 1,435. On the other side of the ledger, Wilson would enter the claim that "Every depot, turn-table, water-tank, and trestle-work between the Sixteen Mile Turnout on the South Side Railroad to the Roanoke bridge on the Danville road was destroyed." The Confederate chief of railroads entered in his own debit column the fact that it took 63 days to repair over 60 miles of track Wilson and Kautz had destroyed. Lee's optimism on the state of his commissariat in the short run had been misplaced.[16]

Sharpe was having his own doubts about the near collapse of Lee's army as the month wore on.

> 50 odd days of fighting & marching have reduced the effective force of both armies to an incredible extent. But the enemy have their last man in the field.—It is literally true, as a Confed Col told me this week, that 100,000 men could now march anywhere on the continent, except within 10 miles of Richmond or Atlanta—I have a captured letter showing there were just 2 regiments within reach of Charleston last week. And every road leading to Richmond was cut last night. A French officer of artillery sent by Louis Napoleon told me last night he did not see how they could stand it long—I don't either—but they stand a good deal.[17]

An understatement, indeed. If anything, the last year of the war would show the Army of Northern Virginia's almost superhuman ability to "stand a good deal." And now that Lee's men were in the entrenchments of Petersburg, it seemed unlikely that any assault could storm through. "In front of Petersburg & fearfully hot! The enemy tried to attack our right yesterday—but altho' he showed three lines of battle, it was utterly impossible to induce his men to advance. I know this to be so—& should we attempt to assault him, I think we would be whipped beyond a peradventure [doubt]."[18]

Daring Escapes and an Interrogator with a Wooden Leg

The information brought by escaped Union prisoners was providing Sharpe a new source of information. On June 25 Sharpe got a welcome surprise. Phillip Carney, one of the four BMI scouts captured in the Dahlgren raid, had escaped in June as the siege closed in on Petersburg. He and another soldier were assigned to nurse the Union wounded in Richmond's Shockoe Hospital.[19] On the 19th the guards at the prison were called away to the defenses of Richmond, their places taken by militia boys so young they could barely carry a musket. With the audacity for which Sharpe's scouts were known, Carney and the other man put on "Confederate jackets, pretended to be clerks, took up the books as if they were such, and passed the guards." Carney gave a good report of the roads and bridges across their route of escape and noted that his fellow scouts, Dykes and Jake Swisher, had been sent to Georgia while Hogan was still in irons. He would join the other two scouts in Georgia but would also escape. Carney said that 1,000 Union prisoners had been sent to Georgia, and that there were 1,100 remaining in Richmond, of which 900 were sick and wounded. Significantly, he noted that he had found help from a Union man in Richmond during his escape who said that there were many of such sympathies there and that it would not be difficult to find them. It would not be long before Sharpe found out for himself when he activated the Van Lew ring in Richmond.[20]

The next month, McEntee, who had returned from his assignment in the Valley, reported the tale of four escaped Union prisoners who had made their way through Confederate lines. What was interesting was McEntee's reference that these four men, all from Hunter's command in the Valley, were "all personally known to me…" Although McEntee had served with Hunter, the odds that he would have known four random escaped prisoners from that command are very low. The likelihood that they were some of Hunter's scouts is much more possible, especially so as McEntee described one of the men as captured "while on his way to Georgia," an unlikely destination for an ordinary enlisted man at the time. The man had escaped and then been recaptured and placed with the other three in the Confederate POW camp in Lynchburg, Virginia. The observations of the four men after their escape also read like a running intelligence collection mission and is worth recounting to give an idea of the sort of report trained scouts would turn in. While being transported by rail on the Danville Road, they jumped from the cars and escaped.

> They saw two regiments of infantry and a battery of artillery at the High Bridge. They were at work throwing up strong fortifications on this end of the bridge and were building one large redoubt. The west end of the bridge is fortified with breast-works. The railroad has been repaired at the junction by laying down rails that had been burnt and afterward straightened. The road was in running order from Lynchburg to Petersburg. About ten miles of the Danville road south of Meherrin Station [where they left the road] has not yet been repaired… After leaving the Dansville road they came in nearly a direct course to Blacks and Whites Station, on the South Side road. The Second Virginia Cavalry was stationed at that point. There is there a very large shop for building and repairing Government wagons, also a corral of disabled horses. From that point they marched to Dinwiddie Court-House, hence toward Reams' Station on the road running from Dinwiddie Court-House to Reams' Station; where the road crosses Rowanty Creek they saw two camps. They were told by negroes that there were 5,000 men there—infantry, cavalry, and artillery. While lying in the woods there on the night of the 28th [June] they heard tattoo sounded by five different bugles [indicating five regiments]. These troops had been camped at that place since Wilson's raid. On the morning of the 29th they crossed the Weldon railroad three miles below Reams' Station. After crossing the railroad, they secreted themselves in the bushes near the railroad, where they remained all day of the 29th. They saw one train of about ten cars pass going toward Petersburg loaded with troops. There were troops in the cars and on the top of them. The cars run very slowly, and do not blow a whistle when they stop or start.

They finally made it into Union lines, guided by the sound of fighting. McEntee notes that they also had the foresight to bring lists of captured Union soldiers in Lynchburg.[21]

Trained scouts such as Phil Carney were not the only escaped prisoners who could provide valuable information. In early July a servant of a Union cavalry brigade commander was captured in a raid on the Confederate supply depot at Stony Point on the Weldon Railroad. He escaped to describe both the garrison, the defenses, the number of locomotives, and the amount and type of supplies in storage there. He also described being interrogated by a general officer. Babcock reported:

> He was asked a number of questions relative to the strength and movements of our army, particularly about the strength and organization of Wilson's Cavalry. He was told by the soldiers that it was General Ewell. He describes him as being a tall, spare-built man, with heavy mustache and no beard; thinks he had a false leg, as one foot appeared larger than another.

It was indeed none other than Lt. Gen. Richard Ewell himself, now commander of the District of Richmond, famous for his wooden leg which took a number of bullets at Gettysburg, to his amusement. The encounter showed how generals on both sides actively interrogated prisoners. Lee recounted how Hill had interrogated an intelligent prisoner, "A New Yorker, sharp & shrewd, from whom but little could be gained." But he had on his person his diary which revealed the presence of the Union IX Corps at Petersburg, filling one of his most pressing intelligence gaps. Meade, especially in this period, frequently interrogated prisoners himself, despite the presence of real experts in the BMI on his staff, a throwback to the days when commanding generals were their own intelligence officers.[22]

Confederate deserters were not only providing information on order-of-battle but were now an excellent source for operational information of the greatest tactical importance. July 17 was another hot, humid Virginia summer morning, and the men of the 44th Alabama and other units were sweating as they cleared the brush from a ravine. They were surprised to see their division commander, Maj. Gen. Charles Field, four brigadiers, and the colonel of the 44th Alabama pass up to the picket line. They had field glasses and were closely observing the Union lines. One of the Alabamians was close enough to overhear them speak. The colonel remarked that his regiment would be seen moving into the attack once they left the ravine in which they were to be sheltered. Field replied that there would be enough time for him to deliver his attack.

It did not take a genius to realize that the 44th was the point of a major attack by the entire I Corps of the Army of Northern Virginia. The eavesdropping soldier promptly deserted.

Having seen too much glory already to look forward to another attack, he was joined by a flood of other men from I Corps who began giving themselves up to Union pickets. Their stories under interrogation were consistent down to small details. At least a corps-level attack was planned by I Corps and possibly III Corps as well. A ravine had been cleared of brush to hide the assault parties; the attack would begin late at night or early in the morning before dawn. Five to seven days' rations had been issued. Babcock's summaries were confirmed by field interrogations of incoming deserters conducted by the various corps.[23]

Meade immediately began preparations to defeat the attack and then counter-punch. Burnside and Warren were ordered to prepare to receive and counterattack the enemy, and Hancock was to hold his corps in readiness to assist. Meade was almost looking forward to it as he reported to Grant, "I most earnestly hope they will try the experiment, for I think it will relieve us greatly."[24] Dawn came and then the morning wore on, and no attack materialized.

A deserter who came over about midnight revealed more of the extraordinary plans for the attack:

> He states that orders were issued to the pickets last evening to fire on any man seen going beyond the picket-line. These orders were peremptory and have never been given before; that his colonel said no attack would be made on our lines, as so many deserters came into our lines yesterday and told us all about it. They did not leave the trenches.

Reading the same report Grant commented, "so many deserters had come into our lines and exposed their plans." Another deserter provided an additional reason for the cancelled attack. "We learn from one of them that a deserter from our army went over yesterday afternoon and gave himself up to their regiment. We cannot learn what regiment he is from. One of the informants thinks he communicated something of importance concerning the attack and our preparations for it." Thus you see an operational merry-go-round driven by the intelligence provided by deserters from both sides.[25]

Fiasco at the Crater

By the next week Grant had formulated another plan to overstretch Lee. Sharpe's Richmond agent, Samuel Roth, had reported that the rail lines north of Richmond were critical to the feeding of the city population and part of the army. Grant proposed to send Sheridan's cavalry north of the James to destroy the railroads while sending Hancock's II Corps from Bermuda Hundred to cross the James at Deep Bottom ford to demonstrate against the eastern Richmond defenses. Although he did not intend Hancock to forcefully assault the city's fortifications, he wanted his commanders to be sure to take advantage to break into the defenses by coup de main if the opportunity presented itself. Grant hoped that Lee would take the bait and rush so many troops north to defend the capital that his lines could be broken at Petersburg. Grant had full confidence that the BMI would be able to tell him just when Lee snatched at the lure. He wrote to Halleck on July 26, "Deserters come in every day, enabling us to keep track of every change the enemy makes."[26] That day he dispatched Hancock.

While these plans were underway, Meade approached Grant with a daring plan from Burnside. Burnside recommended that a mine be driven from his IX Corps front under the opposing Confederate defenses and then detonated. The obliterated Confederate works would be a highway for the IX Corps to pour through and collapse Lee's entire position at Petersburg. Burnside's engineers were fearful that a second line of fortifications existed that would stop the penetrating force cold. Sharpe had been reporting since the army arrived in front of Petersburg that there was no second line of fortifications, but he put Babcock to work to conclusively determine whether this second line existed or not. He reported that "there is no second line of works to the rear ... between their present line and Petersburg. This is the repeated statement of all deserters." At the same time, according to Meade's chief of staff, "very careful examinations were made of this second line from a newly erected signal station, and it was found that the enemy had detached works, batteries probably, along the road in front of Burnside, but not a connected line."[27]

For a time the issue of the mine, as it was being dug, receded into the background as Grant pinned his hopes on Sheridan and Hancock. Presented with overwhelming evidence of Grant's major redeployment, Lee swallowed the bait hook, line, and sinker. He reinforced the Richmond defenses so strongly that neither Sheridan nor Hancock would be able to succeed. Babcock reported that Longstreet's and Hill's corps had left the trenches to reinforce Richmond, leaving only three divisions behind.

> A deserter from the Second Florida came in about 10 o'clock last night. He brings the following additional information: That Wright's brigade moved last evening to the right, and relieved Heth's division, which marched to the north side of the Appomattox. This was generally understood in informant's brigade. Does not know of any other movement. The following telegram has been received from Colonel Sharpe, at City Point:
>
> Received last night one captain and nine men from Second Corps. They were from Kershaw's and Bryan's brigades, McLaws' division. Marched from Petersburg over the James Monday evening. McGowan and Lane, of Wilcox's division, Hill's corps, were also there as well as the Tennessee brigade, of Beauregard's corps... [28]

By the time these reports came in on July 28, Sheridan and Hancock had already been thwarted outside of Richmond the day before by Lee's massive reinforcement. Meade was determined to help Lee maintain his error by further deceptions. He carefully informed his remaining corps commanders the next day to feign a withdrawal by all troops that could be spared from holding the siegeworks. The columns were to march into the woods in daylight and return at night.[29] Sheridan and Hancock had neither cut the railroads north of Richmond nor been able to break into the city by coup de main. Those had been secondary objectives all along. Their primary objective had been to draw Lee's forces away from Petersburg. In that they succeeded completely. Lee had only a third of his overall command left in the defenses. Grant was quick to shift his sights to the opportunity of the mine now that Babcock's report had assured him that only open country lay behind the Confederate works and that Lee had no reserves to throw into the breach. This was actionable intelligence of the first order.

Lee's intelligence was also working well, though not with the specificity of Sharpe's operation.

> From mysterious paragraphs in the Northern papers, and from reports of deserters, though those last were vague and contradictory, Lee and Beauregard suspected that the enemy was

mining in front of one of the three salients on Beauregard's front, and the latter officer had in consequence directed counter-mines to be sunk from all three, meanwhile constructing gorge-lines in the rear upon which the troops might retire in case of surprise or disaster... But the countermining on the part of the Confederates was after a time discontinued, owing to the lack of proper tools, the inexperience of the troops in such work, and the arduous nature of their service in the trenches.[30]

Burnside had been training his new all-black division for weeks as the first wave of the assault, but Meade and Grant both forbade it for race-sensitive political reasons. It was a new and untested division, and they had no idea what conditions it would have to face. The last thing they wanted was to be exposed to the vituperations from the radical abolitionists that they had carelessly sacrificed black lives. The white divisions would lead. That took the enthusiasm right out of Burnside, who sleepwalked through the rest of the operation. In picking the lead division he drew straws which awarded the honor of first through the breach to Brig. Gen. James Ledlie, who had no combat experience and had only risen recently to division command from that of a stationary artillery regiment. His division also had a poor reputation for aggressiveness. In doing so, Burnside overlooked the solid combat records of the other two division commanders. He overlooked far worse. Bruce Catton wrote, "Ledlie was a cipher. A brigadier who served under him said that Ledlie 'was a drunkard and an arrant coward... It was wicked to risk the lives of men in such a man's hands.'" Major General Humphreys stated later that Ledlie was "an officer whose total unfitness for such a duty ought to have been known to General Burnside... It was not known to General Meade."[31]

On July 28 the mine was finished. It ran 500 feet under the beaten zone between the siege works and then perpendicularly another 75 feet under a Confederate fort. It was packed with 320 kegs filled with 8,000 pounds of gunpowder. Two days later the order was given and the charge to set off the mine was lit. An enormous explosion obliterated the fort and a quarter-mile of Confederate fortifications. A nearby Confederate artilleryman would write:

> A slight tremor of the earth for a second, then the rocking as of an earthquake, and, with a tremendous blast which rent the sleeping hills beyond, a vast column of earth and smoke shoots upward to a great height, its dark sides flashing out sparks of fire, hangs poised for a moment in mid-air, and then hurtling downward with a roaring sound showers of stones, broken timbers and blackened human limbs, subsides—the gloomy pall of darkening smoke flushing to an angry crimson as it floats away to meet the morning sun.[32]

Immediately 160 Union guns opened fire to sweep any approach a Confederate counterattacking force would take. Meade's instructions to Burnside had been flawless in their design—attack through the gap in a column of divisions with the first peeling its brigades right and left to secure the edges of the penetration. In that first hour after the explosion, the Confederates were capable of little or no reaction. It was the moment the Army of the Potomac had waited years for—the killing stroke that would bring their mighty rival down into defeat. Then nothing happened.

If Meade's plans had been excellent, Burnside's execution was execrable. The troops had not been properly prepared to get through the shambles in front of them. Instead, they packed into the deep crater formed by the explosion in their thousands and milled there. Ledlie stayed behind in a dugout royally drunk. Burnside did not closely supervise the man either. Not one of the four brigade commanders was up with their men at this critical time as they jammed tighter and tighter into the crater. Their inaction gave the Confederates just enough time to rush to the lip of the crater and begin a slaughter of the trapped men in blue. Four thousand men were lost before Grant stopped the attack. Meade wrote bitterly to his wife:

> Our attack yesterday, although made under the most advantageous circumstances was a failure. By a movement to the north bank of the James, Lee was completely deceived, and thinking it was a movement of the whole army against Richmond, he rushed over there with the greater portion of his army, leaving his works in our front held by only three out of the eight divisions of his army.

Although Meade kept a discreet silence on intelligence matters in all his private correspondence, he does reveal here that the BMI had given him not only Lee's order-of-battle but his maneuvers on the battlefield with those forces as well.[33]

Grant wrote to Halleck that the attack "was the saddest affair I have witnessed in this war... Such an opportunity for carrying fortifications I have never seen and do not expect again to have." He understood that he had been handed a victory on a silver platter by the BMI. He shouldered the blame later when testifying before the Committee on the Conduct of the War: "I blame his [the lead division commander] seniors also for not seeing that he did his duty, all the way up to myself."[34]

He could well say it. For the second time in its history, the BMI had provided the clearly actionable intelligence that would have been of decisive importance to the success of operations had they been properly executed. The first failure was Hooker's at Chancellorsville; the second was Grant's at the Crater. In Grant's defense, it could be said that had a corps in the armies he commanded in the west been given this assignment, the outcome would most likely have been a success. Grant had winnowed the chaff from those superbly confident fighting formations. When he came east, he had to deal with the strange lack of alacrity and the pockets of incompetence that persisted in the Union armies in the east. Lieutenant Colonel T. S. "Joe" Bowers had come east with Grant and was to be blunt about the difference, when he commented that the troops "may yet accidentally blunder into Richmond." His friend, Capt. George Leet, another officer brought from the western theater, echoed the theme: "If we only had some of our old Western troops, with their own generals to command them, down here just now, we could smash Lee most effectively. Joe has not much confidence in the Army of the Potomac, either soldiers or officers. He says there appears to be no vim or snap."[35]

In all fairness, had the armies of the west gone through the bloodletting of the Overland Campaign, they may not have retained much vim or snap either.

Breaking Lee—Carefully

Grant was not only having to deal with a different army but an army that had turned over its personnel through combat wastage several times for which he bore no little responsibility. Rear areas had been combed and combed again for garrisons, too-long used to comfort to have had any fighting spirit or skills. From these backwaters came the incompetent officers like Ledlie, whose failings had not been exposed by action. Into the army also came the sweepings of the draft, often the men bought as substitutes. Mingling with them were the large numbers of foreigners, German and Irish mostly, recruited right off the docks after landing as immigrants. Ten percent of this growing wave of male immigrants changed into Union blue in their first days ashore. Colonel Theodore Lyman, one of Meade's staff officers, expressed the sentiment of the army's old hands at this flood of low-quality replacements:

> By the Lord! I wish these gentlemen who would overwhelm us with Germans, negroes, and the offscourings of great cities, could only see—only *see*—a Rebel regiment, in all their rags and squalor. If they had eyes they would know that these men are like wolf-hounds, and not to be beaten with turnspits. Look at our "Dutch" heavy artillery: we no more think of trusting them than so many babies. Send bog-trotters, if you please, for Paddy will fight—no one is braver.[36]

A certain amount of war-weariness had also settled in among the long-term veterans. So if Lee's army was wasting away from irreplaceable losses, Grant's was losing its tone and spirit.[37]

This meant that the troops had to be used more carefully, and this in turn meant that their objectives had to key on verifiable enemy weaknesses to ensure greater chance of success. Good intelligence was the key to maximizing the effectiveness of operations; the better the intelligence, the less requirement there would be for unnecessary sacrifice.

Through the summer and fall, Grant gave up the idea of grand assaults and concentrated on stretching Lee to the breaking point by working against his flanks, particularly to the south, which covered the Weldon Railroad that connected Lee's army and Richmond with the port of Wilmington, North Carolina, the primary entry for blockade runners bringing irreplaceable mostly British weapons, munitions, and other supplies. Sharpe's intelligence web grew denser and denser in support of these operations. At the center of the web were Sharpe, Babcock, and a much-needed McEntee, who finally returned from his bootless efforts in the Valley. They drew in an endless stream of information from interrogations, couriers from the Richmond espionage rings, and BMI subsidiary offices with the Army of the James and Sheridan's Army of the Shenandoah. All this was reinforced with an equally dense web of signal station reports, including one that was 125 feet high.

Finished intelligence was shared freely throughout the Armies Operating Against Richmond, an example modern intelligence agencies still have a problem with. A level of trust had been built such that Babcock no longer had to sign Sharpe's name but freely communicated his reports under his own name, as did McEntee with Humphreys and even Meade. Of particular interest, besides the circulars that Sharpe sent around, were Southern newspapers supplied by the espionage rings in Richmond. The army learned of Union victories at Atlanta, Savannah, Fort Fisher, and Mobile Bay faster by Southern newspapers supplied by Sharpe than they did through their own channels.[38]

Sharpe did not confine himself solely to all-source intelligence. He assumed the counterintelligence role as well. On August 9 at City Point, according to Grant's aide, Col. Horace Porter, he briefed the general-in-chief, who was sitting in front of his tent, that he was convinced that Rebel spies were in the camp and that he had devised a means of capturing them. No sooner had he finished and turned away when "A terrific explosion shook the earth, accompanied by a sound which vividly recalled the Petersburg mine, still fresh in the memory of every one present." Porter continued his account:

> Then there rained down upon the party a terrific shower of shells, bullets, boards, and fragments of timber. The general was surrounded by splinters and various kinds of ammunition, but fortunately was not touched by any of the missiles. Babcock of the staff [O. E. Babcock, not John Babcock of the BMI] was slightly wounded in the right hand by a bullet, one mounted orderly and several horses were instantly killed, and three orderlies were wounded.

In the ensuing confusion, everyone on the staff ran over to the bluff overlooking the James River. Below was a vivid scene of destruction. An ammunition barge had blown up, killing 43 and wounding 126. Among the casualties in the provost guard were five dead and 17 wounded of Sharpe's old 20th New York State Militia. Six hundred feet of warehouses and 180 linear feet of wharf were knocked down. Body parts were found a half-mile away. Grant appointed Porter to chair a commission of investigation. Blame was laid on the careless handling of ammunition, but Porter thought that Sharpe's suspicions of enemy agents was a more likely explanation. Van Lew subsequently confirmed that the explosion had been caused by a Confederate agent. After the war, Halleck reported that the explosion had been caused "by a horological torpedo [time bomb] placed on the barge by John Maxwell and R. K. Dullard" of the Confederate Secret Service's torpedo bureau, "under the direction of Brigadier General G. J. Rains and Captain Z. McDaniel." During Grant's presidency, Porter met the same John Maxwell who explained how he had infiltrated the camp to plant the time bomb that led to the explosion. He had simply handed the disguised bomb to one of the black stevedores with instructions to place it in the hold. Sharpe's suspicions were entirely correct, but as the story shows, he was unable to capture the Confederate saboteurs.[39]

Grant was the only one to remain in his chair during and after the explosion, completely calm and safe amid the shower of debris and munitions. Major General Rufus Ingalls, his chief quartermaster, noted that "The lieutenant general himself seems proof against the accidents of flood and field."[40]

A Deception Gone Awry: Second Deep Bottom, Weldon Railroad, Reams Station

Minor events, like exploding ammunition barges, would not deflect Grant from his relentless purpose of stretching Lee until his entire position broke down. But the lesson of Washington's near capture had been well learned also by Grant. He would not hesitate to subordinate operations around Richmond to prevent Lee from sending reinforcements to Early, still prowling in the Valley.

For Lee, the Valley also was a priority, but of a different sort. Sheridan's appointment to command the Army of the Shenandoah had caught his attention. Sheridan was a known favorite of Grant's, and an indication of the Union general-in-chief's sensitivity to that theater. He was also worried by the dispatch of two more Union cavalry brigades to Sheridan. Writing to President Davis on August 4, he said that he could only send two divisions to the Valley, which would leave him no reserves outside the trenches. "If it is their intention to endeavor to overwhelm Early I think it better to detach these troops than to hazard his destruction and that of our railroads, &c., north of Richmond." On August 7 he ordered the acting I Corps commander, Lt. Gen. Richard H. Anderson, to march to Culpeper with Kershaw's Division, with instructions to be prepared to move into the Valley. Lee instructed Anderson, "Any enterprise that can be undertaken to injure the enemy, distract or separate his forces, embarrass his communications on the Potomac or on land is desirable." Four days later Lee told Wade Hampton, commanding his cavalry, to take a cavalry division (Fitzhugh Lee's) to join Anderson in Culpeper, explaining, "It is desirable that the presence of the troops in that region be felt."[41]

Grant was not the only one who could bait the hook of war; Lee carefully released the disinformation that the rest of I Corps was to follow Fitzhugh Lee's cavalry. Fitzhugh Lee himself was under the impression that Anderson specifically "was selected to produce the impression, the remaining divisions of his corps were to follow, in order to induce Grant to send troops to Sheridan equivalent to the whole I Corps. In that case Lee would again re-enforce Early and transfer the principal scene of hostilities to the Potomac, just as he had drawn McClellan from the James and Hooker from the Rappahannock at Fredericksburg by similar movements."[42]

On August 7 Babcock prepared for Grant a remarkably complete report of the deployment of every one of Lee's divisions.

> The following is the latest information relative to the position of the different divisions of Lee's and Beauregard's commands: Longstreet-Pickett's division, in front of Major-General Butler; Kershaw's division, in rear of Pickett's in reserve; Field's division, at New market, near Deep Bottom. A. P. Hill-Mahone's division, right of (enemy's) line, south of the Appomattox River; Heth's division, joining the left of Mahone's; Wilcox's division, at Chaffin's farm. Beauregard-Hoke's division, on left of Heth's; B. Johnson's, on left of Hoke's, and extending to the Appomattox, in front of the Eighteenth Corps. It is not thought that any force by division has been sent away from Lee's or Beauregard's commands, though accoutering brigades may have left, escaping our notice. The above information is corroborated from all quarters.

The only mistake was to identify Kershaw's Division in reserve. It was an understandable error due simply to time-lag, given that Kershaw had only departed the day before.[43]

Lee's deception had not had time to catch up, but catch up it did. The next morning at 3:00 a.m. a Confederate lieutenant and private crossed into the Union lines and revealed that the "Corps of Longstreet, or two divisions, Field's and Kershaw's, have not returned to our front, and it was understood that all or the greater part of them had been sent to reinforce Early or Hood." As a postscript he added, "Information from a reliable source shows that a considerable force of infantry has been sent to Early and passed through Staunton, Va. (Friday, July 29), via Lynchburg; also that no trains are running on the Virginia Central Railroad from Richmond beyond Beaver Dam Station."[44]

Sharpe learned on August 9 from a refugee escaping Richmond that on August 6 a considerable infantry force had boarded Virginia Central trains and departed for the Shenandoah. He judged the source to be highly reliable because he was a friend of a "Richmond man in our employ." Grant's headquarters sent the information to Washington with instructions that Sharpe's detachment there should direct its attention to the Virginia Central. The next day Shape's BMI detachment at Butler's headquarters learned that at least a cavalry brigade had been sent to Early. On August 11 Babcock reported that Kershaw's Division had been seen passing through Orange Court House, destined for the Valley by another deserter. The same day, Sharpe's old agent around Culpeper, Isaac Silver, reported astounding news—that the entire I Corps had passed through on the way to the Valley.

The BMI was now scrambling to find out exactly what forces Lee had sent to the Valley. At 2:30 p.m. on the 11th, Babcock reported that deserters were saying that Kershaw's Division had passed through Orange Court House on the way to the Valley; that camp rumor had said one of I Corps' divisions had gone to Hood and another to the Valley. Trying to sort out the status of I Corps, Babcock then reviewed the last time each of its divisions had been confirmed in the defenses of Richmond: Field—August 8, Kershaw—August 7, and Pickett—August 7. He also noted that the location of Wilcox's Division of Hill's Corps was uncertain, though Butler reported it between City Point and Richmond. He noted that this needed to be confirmed.

The preponderance of information showed clearly that Kershaw's Division had been sent toward the Valley. It had been repeatedly identified. No other piece of information identified any other particular division being dispatched with Kershaw. That fine distinction did not trouble Grant. Five hours after Babcock wrote his last summary, he informed Meade, "There is strong evidence, aside from that brought in by deserters, that the enemy are sending troops north. I think one division each from Hill's and Longstreet's corps have gone. Is our line now in a position to be held by two corps?"[45]

Since Grant had no direct communication with Sheridan, he passed the warning through Halleck in Washington. Sheridan responded that his own sources, probably the BMI detachment with his army, had also heard of the enemy's approaching reinforcement. He suspended his own attack on Early on August 15 and withdrew back down the Valley.

In the meantime, Grant had decided to give Lee a painful reminder of the consequences of sending forces off to the Valley. Early on August 14 he transported Hancock's II Corps by steamer up the James to land at Deep Bottom and attack the weakened Confederate defenses there. At the same time, Maj. Gen. David B. Birney's X Corps would march north from Bermuda Hundred and cross the James on pontoon, to join the attack. Lee was aware of Union movement but confused as to its purpose. He was distracted by Butler's pet project to cut off 4 ¾ miles of navigation in the James River by cutting a canal across a loop called Dutch Gap just to the north of the Union lines at Bermuda Hundred. Work had begun on August 10, and Lee seemed to take it as a special act of effrontery aimed at turning Pickett's flank. One of his division commanders noted, "The general did not seem in remarkably good humor … with … this impudence of the Yankees in crawling up behind us." Butler's effort had nothing to do with Grant's plans, but it drew Lee's attention to just the area that Hancock was to attack. A deserter stated that both Butler and Grant had been seen at Dutch Gap on August 11, seeming to confirm the importance of the concentration of forces to the Union general-in-chief. It would not be the first time that Butler's reach had exceeded his grasp and got Grant in trouble. Lee wrote his wife the same day that Hancock's corps was steaming up the James:

> I have been kept from church to-day by the enemy's crossing to the north of the James River and the necessity of moving troops to meet him. I do not know what his intentions are. He is said to be cutting a canal across the Dutch Gap, a point in the river—but I cannot, as yet, discover it. I was up there yesterday and saw nothing to indicate it. We shall ascertain it in a day or two.[46]

Grant was personally on the scene as the fighting progressed that morning. He noted at 10:00 a.m. that prisoners showed that Field's Division had not gone to the Valley. When added to the known location of other divisions, he concluded, probably with some relief, "This leaves but one division of infantry to have gone to the Valley. I am now satisfied that no more have gone."[47]

That would be the sum of his satisfaction in the operation itself which bogged down after some initial success. The attack, though lacking drive, had worried Lee. He recalled Fitzhugh Lee's Cavalry Division on its way to join Kershaw's Division still waiting at Culpeper when a Union cavalry division began to cross the pontoons over the James on the 14th. Grant would have been happier had he known that his attack had done more than just confirm that only Kershaw had been dispatched to the Valley; it had actually pulled back part of the force Lee had concentrated at Culpeper. But it was Kershaw's Division that continued to fix his interest.[48]

Grant had effectively fixed Lee's attention in the fighting north of Petersburg. Lee had gone to Chaffin's Bluff on August 15 to direct the operations himself. That same morning the two brigades and a cobbled-together brigade he had ordered up from the lines at Petersburg, as well as W. H. F. Lee's Cavalry Division, also arrived to reinforce Fields.[49] The BMI outdid itself that day in providing actionable intelligence to the Union commanders. That evening, based on the BMI reports, Grant warned Hancock that a division-sized reinforcement had joined Fields. But Sharpe's efforts now concentrated on supporting Warren's V Corps operation against Petersburg with an intensive collection and interrogation effort culminating on August 16, two days before the attack began. The location and number of Confederate units on their right was checked and checked again.

> Sharpe to Babcock: Our cavalry took prisoners this a.m. from Fitz Lee's division; Chambliss killed; his body in our hands; fight on Charles City road two miles from White's Tavern. Prisoners taken this a.m. by Tenth Corps report Wright's brigade, of Mahone's division, and Lane's brigade, of Wilcox's division, on General Birney's front; supposed they came over last night.[50]
>
> Babcock to Sharpe: We believe the two brigades, Wright's and Perrin's of Mahone's division, to have moved from the enemy's extreme right before yesterday at 2 pm., that Heth's division and the two divisions of Beauregard remain here as usual.[51]
>
> Sharpe to Babcock: I refer to W. H. F. Lee's [cavalry] division as having crossed to the north side of the James—the one in which Chambliss, who was killed this morning, and Barringer, were brigade commanders.[52]
>
> Babcock to Sharpe: Deserters from three different brigades of Mahone's division received this a.m. report that Wright's and Perrin's brigades moved to Drewry's Bluff day before yesterday at 2 p.m. As far they know Heth's division remained unchanged, though we only hear from Davis' brigade, which is on the right of the division.[53]

All three divisions of Hill's III Corps had been identified, but by the next day two of them, most of Mahone's and all of Wilcox's, were shown to be north of the James. Of Heth's brigades, only the one on the extreme right, Davis's Brigade, could be clearly identified. Clearly Babcock had keyed on the weakness of Heth's Division holding the end of the Confederate right which covered the Weldon Road, and that is just the direction Warren's attack would take. Captain Fisher, the chief signal officer, confirmed their findings on the same day from direct observation, reporting that there was a "decrease in the enemy's camps all along the woods west of the city," and that, "my lookouts convey the impression that the enemy has to a very great extent weakened their lines in our immediate front within the past three or four days."[54]

Grant was even more pleased with the intelligence picture when Sharpe confirmed that Lee's reinforcement of his forces fighting north of the James left only three divisions defending Petersburg—Heth's, Hoke's, and Johnson's. Intelligence reports from the BMI and the signal observation stations now presented Grant with a new option. The BMI had been tracking the movement of forces from the lines at Petersburg to the fighting to the north. With Hancock and Birney diverting Lee north of the James, Grant sought to put more pressure on Lee south of Petersburg to pull Kershaw back from the Valley.

Grant reached an immediate decision. On August 17, the same day that the intelligence picture had clarified, he ordered Warren and his V Corps, "to destroy as much of the Weldon Railroad as practicable." Grant stated, "I want, if possible, to make such demonstrations as will force Lee to withdraw a portion of his troops from the Valley, so that Sheridan can strike a blow against the balance."[55] The Weldon Railroad was the main logistics artery for Richmond and Petersburg. It fed massive amounts of foreign, particularly British, munitions and supplies from Wilmington, the last major Confederate port open to blockade runners. After the fall of Fort Fisher the next year, Grant would send Secretary of State Seward a present of British manufactures that had come through Wilmington.

> With this I have the honor of forwarding to you specimens of fuses captured at Fort Fisher, N. C., together with the certificate of Lieutenant Colonel O. E. Babcock, aide-de-camp [no relation to John Babcock of the BMI] on my staff, that they were so captured, and the statement of Colonel Tal. P. Shaffner that the same were manufactured at the Woolwich Arsenal, England, an arsenal owned and run by the British Government.[56]

Grant sent a stream of messages to Meade, noting the enemy divisions and brigades now north of the James. He commented to Meade, "This leaves the force at Petersburg reduced to what it was when the mine was sprung." What he had considered to be merely a glorified raid to cut the railroad suddenly had wider possibilities, as he wrote to Meade, "Warren may find an opportunity to do more than I had expected." Meade, in turn, expanded Warren's orders "to strike the railroad close to the enemy's works, to extend and reconnoiter to the left, and, if he finds a weak spot, to attack."[57]

Warren was now armed with an accurate picture of the enemy he would be opposing as well as the opportunities for vigorous action. He brushed aside a cavalry brigade to cut the railroad on August 18 in an attack that took the Confederates by surprise. Warren's attack on this vital artery alarmed Beauregard, though he was not sure of the size of the attacking forces. He ordered Heth to retake the road with two brigades. He actually employed three. Beauregard was so concerned about how the Petersburg defenses had been so thinned out that he ordered Heth to return to his defensive works after the attack. Heth's attack drove Warren back but did not retake the railroad. The Confederates were not about to let the matter rest with the Union advantage. Colonel Lyman observed, "It is touching a tiger's cubs to get on that road!"[58]

The next day, the 19th, Lee lashed back with five brigades of Mahone's and Wilcox's Divisions brought back from north of the James, as well as W. H. F. Lee's Cavalry Division. Determined to regain the railroad, Lee attacked again on August 21 with eight brigades. But ultimately the railroad stayed in Union hands when the fighting ended that same day. The impact was not lost on Lee, who informed Jefferson Davis the same day, "Our supply of corn is exhausted today." He said he would do everything in his power to accumulate supplies at the Stony Point depot below the cut made by the enemy and wagon the supplies to the army. He had already sent one train out. He appealed to Davis to energize the Quartermaster Department, notorious for its lethargy.[59]

Grant was also unhappy, but with Warren's performance. "It seems to me that when the enemy comes out of his works and attacks and is repulsed he ought to be followed vigorously to the last minute with every man. Holding a line is of no importance whilst troops are operating in front of it." Much more could have been done, especially since McEntee had kept the command closely informed of the transfer of enemy brigades from north of the James. On the 21st, he listed the Confederates by unit from the enemy's right to left. Warren had chosen to remain on the defensive after repulsing attacks when the enemy was weakest. Thereafter the enemy in his front only grew stronger. Grant thought that, in such circumstances, a corps commander should have shown a more instinctive aggressiveness and attacked. Warren had thrown away the priceless advantage of knowing exactly what forces the enemy had available.[60]

On August 25 Sharpe presented very welcome news:

> One of our agents left Richmond about noon of day before yesterday, having arrived there on Monday afternoon about 4 o'clock. By direction he inquired from many different sources, and seemed to be entirely satisfied that no troops had been sent either to the Valley or to Atlanta, but understood, on the contrary, that it was considered necessary, and that the order had already gone forth, that one of the cavalry divisions sent to Early should return.

Sharpe also reported on Union prisoners taken in the fight and Confederate reactions supplied by couriers from his espionage rings in Richmond:

> Twenty-seven hundred prisoners are claimed to have been taken in the fight on the Weldon railroad, who are now on Belle Isle, but are to be shortly sent to Georgia. It is claimed that the Weldon railroad is to be retaken at whatever cost. A very large number of wounded men were brought into Richmond from the direction of Petersburg after the railroad fight, and the agent thinks that the trains running on Monday from Petersburg to Richmond and returning were loaded with the wounded going up, and going down were conveying the troops which had been operating on the north side of the river. He could not learn of any new movements of troops, except of the return of those which had been on the north side of the James.[61]

A report the same day from McEntee detailed the confusion among the Confederates opposing Warren along the Weldon Railroad and even noted that Lee and Beauregard had been riding down the line with great urgency. The day was filled with flurries of intelligence reports by McEntee and Sharpe, detailing organization, movement, and intentions of the enemy to concentrate so strongly to regain the road that they had left the Petersburg trenches manned only one man deep. One deserter accurately revealed that a three-division attack was planned with the destination of Stony Creek, below Warren's present position astride the railroad. Signal reports were confirming the movement of large numbers of troops as well. Hancock, now back south of Petersburg, and Warren were warned to expect heavy attacks, and Meade reinforced Hancock with another division. The attack came late in the afternoon of August 25 in a violent assault by eight brigades mostly of Hill's III Corps and two of Wade Hampton's cavalry divisions against Hancock's II Corps. Hit front and rear, II Corps was beaten and partially driven from its entrenchments in the battle of Reams Station. Despite this, Hill's victory had not been sufficient to recover the railroad. Hill's men returned elated to their trenches after the attack, carrying nine of Hancock's cannon, 12 stands of colors, and 3,100 small arms. They had inflicted 2,600 casualties and claimed to have lost only 720.[62]

Hancock complained bitterly about the conduct of his corps, saying that had his men behaved as they had in the past, he would have defeated the enemy. He attributed their performance to fatigue after a long campaign, the loss of many fine officers, and to the large number of recruits and substitutes. In one regiment some of the officers could not even speak English. Had not the confirming intelligence from the BMI and the Signal Corps resulted in the alert and reinforcement of II Corps, Hill's attack might well have resulted in a complete rout and the recovery of the railroad by Lee.[63]

In the end, the army's tactically inconclusive attacks throughout August had resulted in a strategic victory for Grant. As a member of Meade's staff remarked, "The Rebels licked us, but a dozen more such lickings and there will be nothing left of the Rebel army!"[64] He was more accurate than he knew. Sharpe's informants in Richmond were reporting that the "carnage is understood to have been severe. They say that the Union men in Richmond consider it he severest repulse the Rebels have had during the year, and that it was remarked that the 'Yankees had finally got the knack for firing low enough,' as almost all of the wounded were struck in the legs and lower part of the body."[65]

Lee had been too clever by half. He thought to stir things up by placing Kershaw at Culpeper where he could easily intervene in the Valley and thus draw Union forces away from Richmond-Petersburg. Grant had not obliged. By attacking Lee instead, he put the Virginian on the horns of a dilemma. The longer Grant attacked, the more Lee hesitated to send Kershaw to the Valley. At the same time, the prospect of reinforcing Early still seemed profitable and so he kept the division in Culpeper just in case. In the end, he did neither, and Kershaw was effectively out of the fight for a critical five weeks. The BMI played a central role in confounding Lee. Despite Lee's deception, the BMI had been able to sort out the Confederate dispositions and provide Grant with the intelligence he required to make the decisions that kept Lee on the horns of his dilemma. For Lee his dwindling strength closed off too many options and denied him too many opportunities. He realized that Grant had outmaneuvered him. He wrote to Davis: "This was fully illustrated in the late demonstration north of the James River, which called troops from our lines here, who if present might have prevented the occupation of the Weldon Railroad. These rapid and distant movements also fatigue and exhaust our men, greatly impairing their efficiency in battle."[66]

The end of August saw the departure of the legendary Sergeant Cline as the chief of scouts when his regiment, the 3rd Indiana Cavalry, was mustered out of service. Sharpe replaced him with Judson Knight, whom he had clearly been grooming for the job. Knight was to remain a primary intermediary between Sharpe and Van Lew's spy ring in Richmond. Knight also remained in touch with his initial contact, Alexander Myers, through whom he was introduced to Henry Roach, who coincidentally was the cousin of one of Knight's scouts, John Roach. Henry Roach was a goldmine of information about the torpedoes (mines) being manufactured in Richmond. Knight got Myers to actually bring out through the lines one of the men engaged in manufacturing the torpedoes along with an exact description. Knight had a precise drawing made and along with a description submitted it to *Scientific American* on September 21. It was published on October 8.[67]

Knight ensured that numerous copies were supplied to the fleet in the James River, and then decided to have a bit of fun with the Confederate authorities. Through Van Lew, and surely with Sharpe's permission, he had a copy dropped into the box of Confederate Secretary of War Seddon. The work on the torpedoes came to a complete stop, and after Richmond fell, Knight was able to find many of the devices in various stages of completion where they had been left.[68]

Roach had also worked as an engineer and pile driver for two years and was the source of a lengthy and detailed analysis of the Confederate obstacles in the James River prepared by Sharpe. It was a priceless piece of intelligence for the 5th Division of the North Atlantic Blockading Squadron supporting Grant in the James River.[69]

September would be mostly a quiet month, as both sides avoided major offensive operations. The Confederates continued to transship supplies by wagon from the Weldon Railroad south of where the Union army had cut the lines. The BMI monitored this activity, noting on September 11 that all the forage for the enemy cavalry was coming by that route. Babcock also passed on an informant's opinion that "it would take only a small raiding party to capture these trains."[70]

Made aware by the BMI of the importance of the Weldon Railway as a logistical lifeline for Lee's army and Richmond, he looked beyond merely cutting as he already had. The Confederates, with some logistical effort, had largely negated his control of the railway below Petersburg. He concluded that it would be far better to cut off the source of the supplies by taking Wilmington. On September 12 Grant informed Rear Admiral David Dixon Porter of his intention of sending an expedition to seize the port. Grant had expected the expedition to get underway about October 5, but it took longer to organize the joint army-navy expedition than expected, and the start date kept moving forward.

September also saw Sharpe involved in the hunting down of a counterfeiter. Early that month the presence of counterfeited greenbacks passing through the armies around Richmond and Petersburg became apparent. Lafayette Baker was called in but failed to find the source of the bills. Sharpe relentlessly pursued the counterfeiter and his accomplices until they were rounded up. The ringleader was a Captain McDonald, 1st Pennsylvania Cavalry, an English immigrant who had enlisted a week after arriving in the United States. The *Daily National Republican* newspaper was quite clear about who was chiefly responsible for breaking up the ring when it wrote that "great credit is due to Gen. Patrick, Provost Marshal General, and to the indefatigable exertions of his assistant, Col. Sharp [sic]."[71]

Before the onset of winter weather, Grant tried once more to cut the Southern Railroad. Before the attack, Babcock was focused on refining the enemy's order-of-battle in the area of operations, confirming that it consisted of Mahon's and Heth's Divisions of Hill's III Corps, the locations of brigades, so far as noting that one brigade moved a mile and a half down the line, and the identification and location of cavalry.[72] On October 27 Grant threw 17,000 men of II and V Corps toward the Boydton Plank Road and Hatcher's Run. Hill's Corps again stopped the attack, helped by a lack of cooperation between Hancock and Warren.

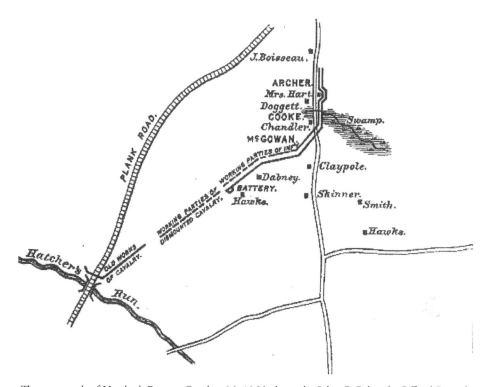

The area north of Hatcher's Run on October 24, 1864, drawn by John C. Babcock. Official Record.

A Sword, a Denunciation, and a Resignation

Sharpe's old associations with the 20th New York State Militia Regiment still remained strong and allowed him to do Patrick a good turn in September. Sharpe had written the old provost marshal a note on September 7 that the men of the regiment had, as Patrick recorded in his diary, "purchased, some time ago, a very handsome sword & 'fixings' to be presented to me, as they are about to leave for home." The 20th was about to be mustered out. The old puritan, in an act of self-effacement, had written back to Sharpe that he thought the presentation ought to be deferred until they all were out of service. Sharpe was disturbed because he knew how devoted the regiment was to Patrick, who considered them to be the only reliable regiment he had ever had in the provost guard and actually part of his military family. He also knew that Patrick, who was acting with the best intentions, could be a bit tone-deaf at times, and this was one of them. It was probably Sharpe who informed Grant who insisted to Patrick that he receive the heartfelt gift and that if he were "to decline it, the men would be chilled to death & would not re-enlist." Patrick put on a good face and received the soldierly tribute—and the 20th re-enlisted to serve out the war with him. He would bring them to Richmond when he reestablished the police function of the city after Lee's surrender.[73]

There was an unfortunate side to Sharpe's relationship with the 20th. Its commander, Col. Theodore B. Gates, apparently had developed a grudge against Sharpe, and one that he carefully hid. In a diary filled with references to his cordial relationship with Sharpe, he wrote on September 26 that he "had a long talk with Gen. Patrick about G. H. S." Patrick's recorded diary was more descriptive of Gates's well-chewed scrape of bile. "He [Gates] tells me that the Colonel [Sharpe] is known, at home, and by *his* Regt [,] as a man on whom little reliance can be placed—Tricky and full of all sorts of policy [politics] ..." Well, the "Tricky and full of all sorts of policy" are characteristics of a good intelligence officer. But the reference to lack of reliance runs against the devoted nature of the men of his own 120th New York, whose interest Sharpe had always furthered. He had gone so far, Patrick commented at this time, as to write to ask that his regiment be transferred to the provost guard. Patrick noted that "I have not, yet, asked for it." Nor would he. Sharpe had been equally solicitous of the men of the 20th NYSM; he had been the one, not Gates, to tell Patrick that his refusal to accept their presentation sword would be a mortal insult. Whether Gates's spite had influenced him, Patrick's diary withholds comment, but there is little else in his diary to show that he shared these sentiments except an irritated entry of September 20. Sharpe had applied for leave, which Patrick approved, then noted, "I hope he will now cease plotting—at least so far as I am concerned." If he had had sufficient cause, a man of Patrick's rectitude would have moved to replace Sharpe long before, yet there is nothing more in his diary to indicate that was ever contemplated. Reading between the lines, it seems that Sharpe was a serious player in headquarters politics, something his subsequent career would support but also something that Patrick and Gates would have found distasteful.[74]

Gates's secret denunciation of his friend reflected more on him than Sharpe. It is difficult to explain how Gates could have held such feelings for Sharpe then accept the hospitality of the man's home in Washington a few months later and in postwar years sit cordially with him on the dais at reunions of their regiments. Perhaps the best comment on his secret denunciation was that Patrick did not mention it again, nor did he take any action against Sharpe.[75]

Two months later, Patrick was interceding for Sharpe with Grant just before the general left for Washington. "I had a talk with Genl. Grant about Col. Sharpe, and have that matter all fixed right." There is no mention of what the matter was. Whatever it was, apparently it was enough to provoke Sharpe's resignation. Two days later, on November 18, Patrick sent up Sharpe's resignation to Meade. Three days after that Meade replied that he declined to act until he had a chance to discuss the matter with Grant on his return from Washington. Sharpe did not in the end resign. Grant had found him simply too valuable to lose.[76]

Sharpe again requested leave on October 12 for 12 days, again to attend to the settlement of a large estate of which he was the co-executor. Apparently a suit had been brought against the estate, and Sharpe's co-executor was not an "experienced business man. The time which an appeal can be taken in the suit ... had nearly expired, and a decision as to the course of action ... is deferred for my decision."[77]

Perhaps the best reason that Grant retained Sharpe was that he had been sufficiently impressed by him to include him in the small circle of staff officers that he had come to trust. Proof is found in Grant's use of Sharpe to help him monitor what Butler was up to. For Grant, Butler was an increasingly dangerous subordinate. He was a toxic mix of military incompetence and political ambition. Unfortunately, he was too powerful as a protégé of the Radical Republicans for Lincoln to dismiss with the election looming. He was also, in Patrick's words, "a very troublesome man to work with. I wish he was out of the way." He had had to intercede with Grant in late July because Butler refused to forward his prisoners to City Point. Already, Grant was trying to replace him, and Sharpe informed Patrick that "Butler's removal is hanging again by the ears in consequence of complications at Washington." Certainly Halleck hated Grant and relentlessly connived to remove him, something of which he was certainly not ignorant, courtesy in some degree to Sharpe. Yet, Butler's political allies were too powerful to offend by dismissing him.

In August Sharpe informed Patrick that "Butler has gone to New York ... to look out for the Convention." Grant was coming to see Butler as a postwar rival. This was heightened just after the election, when Butler accepted Rev. Henry War Beecher's acclamation as the next president without tactfully naming Grant as the rightful candidate. Also after the election, a possible shuffle in Lincoln's cabinet seemed imminent. Chief Justice Taney had died the month before, and Stanton wanted the appointment. Butler's name was seriously raised as his replacement. This so alarmed Grant that he turned to Sharpe. Patrick wrote on November 16 that Sharpe was "off to Washington .... with a view to head off Butler as Secretary of War." What influence he did have is unknown, but by the 28th Grant was able to tell Patrick that there was no chance that Butler would be made Secretary of War. This would not be the last time that Grant would use Sharpe in a sensitive political mission.[78]

CHAPTER TWELVE

Settling with Early in the Valley

September–November 1864

If events around Petersburg and Richmond remained largely quiet after the battles of late August, Grant had plenty to occupy his attention in supporting Sheridan with intelligence in support of his operations in the Valley. On September 6 he informed Sheridan, perhaps a little too eagerly, "From reports of deserters coming in at different times, and on different parts of our lines, we learn that Kershaw's division arrived in Petersburg last night. I think there is no doubt but some troops home arrived from the Valley." Sharpe was able to dismiss that conclusion the next day with information from a spy in Richmond. McEntee confirmed this by unraveling the source of the earlier error. From interrogations he learned that several deserters had seen I Corps brigades moving through Petersburg at the time which "gave rise to the rumor" of Kershaw's return from the Valley. Sheridan's capture of prisoners also confirmed this assessment, as he wrote on September 8, "I am to say positively that no troops have left."[1]

Early and the issue of his strength were clearly frustrating Sheridan's attempts to lay waste the Valley and deprive Lee of his main food supply, the mission given him by Grant. The Valley's farms and mills were the granary of the Army of Northern Virginia and Richmond. Early's presence in the Valley was to protect the granary. The Confederate general dodged Sheridan's attempts to bring him to battle in a series of maneuvers through the lower Valley. Yet Sheridan approached Early with caution; he had concluded erroneously that both sides were equivalent in strength at 40,000 men each, when Early had barely 14,000 men. Sheridan had another even more pressing concern. He would write later, "The Presidential campaign in the north was fairly opened ... under no circumstances, could we afford to risk defeat." He would wait until Early returned a sizeable part of his force to Lee. Early, looking at the same situation, arrived at a completely different conclusion—that Sheridan "possessed an excessive caution which amounted to timidity." At the same time, Early was aware of Lee's desperate need for more men. On September 15 he felt secure enough to put Kershaw on the road back to Lee. Three days later, Kershaw was in Culpeper. On the same day, Sharpe was reporting, "Nothing is known in Richmond outside of official circles of the position of Early." And Sheridan was anxiously asking Captain Leet, "Have you any information from your scouts from Culpeper or other points south? Please answer."[2]

Sheridan's own scouts now enter the picture. He had been impressed by the reputation of the "Jesse Scouts" serving with cavalry general Averell in West Virginia. The term "Jesse Scouts" had originated in the west in the command of John C. Fremont and were named in honor of his wife. Jesse Scouts not only gathered information in Confederate uniform but would gather in larger numbers to carry out raids. They were a forerunner of special operations. Over time they came to mean any Union scout operating in Confederate uniform. The effectiveness of the scouts in Sharpe's organization of the Army of the Potomac could not have been lost on him in his service with them in the Overland Campaign. When Sheridan took command in the Valley in early August, he concluded that "... I felt the need of an efficient body of scouts to collect information regarding the enemy, for the defective intelligence-establishment with which I started out from Harper's Ferry early in August had not proved satisfactory." This was evidence of Sigel's obstinate refusal to cooperate with McEntee to establish a BMI-type operation in his command. Sheridan now ordered Averell to send him his oldest scouts. These six men and one from the Army of the Potomac he put under the supervision of his provost marshal.[3]

Sheridan's new scouts quickly proved their worth. He had been frustrated by the conflicting information about Early's reinforcements. Two of his new scouts found Tom Laws, an elderly former slave and produce vendor, who had a pass that allowed him to enter Winchester three days a week. The scouts had sounded out this man, and, "finding him both loyal and shrewd, suggested he might be made useful to us within the enemy's lines." The next step was to find a reliable contact in Winchester; he called on General Crook, who responded that he had met such a person in a young lady he had met in the town—the 26-year-old Quaker school teacher and Unionist, Rebecca Wright. Sheridan then ordered Laws brought to his headquarters, where he interviewed the man himself. "I was soon convinced of the negro's fidelity." Sheridan discovered that not only did Laws know Wright but that he would gladly carry a message. Sheridan wrote the message himself:

> I learn from Major-General Crook that you are a loyal lady and still love the old flag. Can you inform me of the position of Early's forces, the number of divisions in his army, and the strength of any or all of them, and his probable or reported intentions? Have any more troops arrived from Richmond, or are any more coming, or reported to be coming?
>
> I am respectfully, your most obedient servant,
>
> P. H. Sheridan, Major-General Commanding. You can trust the bearer.[4]

On September 16 Laws drove his vegetable cart into Winchester with the message wrapped in tinfoil and hidden in his mouth. He delivered it to Wright, saying that he would wait for an answer. She nervously hesitated but steeled herself and replied that she had no communication with the Rebels but would tell what she knew. And here luck fell on the Union side. The night before she had been speaking with a convalescing Confederate officer who told her, "The division of General Kershaw, and Cutshaw's artillery, twelve guns and men, General Anderson commanding, have been sent away, and no more are expected, as they cannot be spared from Richmond." Laws put the reply in Sheridan's hand the same day. The general made immediate plans to move against Early.

Early on September 17 Sharpe reported in a summary to Meade that there was no sign of Kershaw's return: "Nothing is known in Richmond of the return of any part of Early's forces from the Valley." But earlier that same day, Babcock reported to Sharpe, "A large force of infantry, at least four or five brigades, from some point north of the Appomattox, passed through Petersburg on Wednesday eve and Thursday morning last." Sharpe's summary explained, "The infantry seen passing through Petersburg day before yesterday by deserters may have been Pickett's division, as it was stated it came from the north side of the Appomattox."[5] At 2:30 p.m. Meade, acting as his own chief intelligence officer, apparently drew his own differing conclusions and telegraphed them to Grant at Harper's Ferry on his way to confer with Sheridan:

> Yesterday I informed you signal officers north of the Appomattox reported the movement into Petersburg of troops on the Richmond road, and a deserter stated he had about the same time seen troops marching through Petersburg, said to be part of Early's forces, who, it was stated, had sent back 6,000 troops. There may be nothing in all this, but so many reports from different sources would lead to the conclusion that some movement is on foot—whether it be offensive, or whether it is, that seeing in our journals the reports of large accessions daily received by the army, Lee is merely preparing for an anticipated extension of our lines, I am unable to say; but the existence of those reports and the movements known to have combined to produce caution on my part during your absence.[6]

Combined with Sheridan's own reports, this message determined both Sheridan and Grant to go for the kill. However, the Union intelligence was only half right. Meade, taking counsel of his fears, had been wrong to suppose Kershaw was back in Richmond. Sharpe was right all along that there was no proof that Kershaw had returned, but he offered no evidence of where that division was. Meade's error, however, was benign. In a way, he was right for the wrong reason. What was important was that Kershaw was no longer with Early but had been withdrawn to an intermediate position at Orange Court House between Winchester and Richmond on September 14 as reported by Rebecca Wright. The critical information, though, was that his division no longer was available to Early. On September 17, the same day that Meade had told Grant that Kershaw was in Richmond, Lee wrote Early confirming that Kershaw was not in Richmond:

> I have been very anxious to recall General Anderson with Kershaw's Division to me. But a victory at this time over Sheridan would be greatly advantageous to us, and I feared that your

> corps would be insufficient for the purpose. General Anderson is more necessary here than in the Valley, and I have written to him to return with his staff if circumstances permit, and to direct General Kershaw with his division to report to you for the present.

Nevertheless, Lee throughout the message refers again and again to his desire to return Kershaw to Richmond so that he could take the offensive. He was clearly wanting it both ways—for Kershaw to be able to reinforce Early to beat Sheridan and for Kershaw to return to Richmond to take part in offensive action there.[7]

Sheridan was faster off the mark. Before Kershaw could rejoin the Army of the Valley as per Lee's letter, Sheridan attacked and defeated Early at Winchester on September 19, inflicting 3,921 casualties on Early's much smaller force for 4,018 of his own. Three days later Grant noted that Sharpe's friends in Richmond reported there was no news of Early's disaster at Winchester. That same day Sheridan beat Early again at Fisher's Hill. Sheridan wired Grant the next day, "Do not think that there ever was an army so badly routed. The Valley soldiers are hiding away and going to their homes." Grant responded enthusiastically, "I have just received the news of your second great victory and ordered 100 guns in honor of it. Keep on, and your work will cause the fall of Richmond." The whole lower Valley was now in Union hands as Sheridan proceeded to waste it, burning crops, barns, and mills. Not only was the Valley denied to Lee's quartermaster, but Grant could take immense relief that there would be no future threats from that quarter. He thought he had laid to rest the ghost of Early's near capture of Washington. The trigger of Sheridan's twin victories was the knowledge obtained by his scouts and Rebecca Wright that Kershaw was no longer with the Army of the Valley, reinforced by Meade's happy error confirming that that division was absent.[8]

Upon receipt of the news of Fisher's Hill on September 23, Lee telegraphed Anderson at Orange Court House. "Early has met with a reverse, falling back to New Market. Send Kershaw's Division with a battalion of artillery through Swift gap to report to him at once. You will report there in person with your staff…" Kershaw's trains were stopped near Gordonville and turned around. As he dictated the telegram, Lee may even have heard the ripple of Grant's hundred-gun salute. The irony was that had Lee committed Kershaw to Early in August, Winchester and Fisher's Hill could easily have swung against Sheridan. Joseph Kershaw was a formidable fighting man, and his presence on a battlefield was a combat multiplier. He would have the chance to prove his reputation.[9]

This time the BMI simply lost track of Kershaw's Division. The odds were going to look a lot better for Early. Lee could not have picked more favorable circumstances for his redeployment of Kershaw. Sharpe believed the division was on the way back to Richmond if it had not already arrived. None of his sources were able to pick up anything definite on its arrival or location. The same day Lee turned Kershaw's Division around at Gordonsville, Sharpe's friends in Richmond reported a rumor "that Early was eighteen miles this side of Gordonville." That was a garbled reflection of Kershaw's men on their way to Richmond. The only other news he received from his friends was that none of Early's wounded had arrived in Richmond. The next day, his friends reported that the news of Fisher's Hill was known in the city. On the 25th, Babcock concluded that they, "Are not aware of any re-enforcements arriving, or any troops sent away." That same day Sharpe reported that only the day before had the second of Early's defeats become known in Richmond. Two days later Grant wired Halleck that "No troops have passed through Richmond to re-enforce Early." The same day Babcock reported the Confederates, "have sent Early no re-enforcements," and that a camp rumor suggested one regiment from each brigade in Hill's Corps would be sent to Early. On the 28th a deserter stated that Field's and Hoke's Divisions had gone to Early. Another report suggested it would be Johnson's Division. Finally, he received an accurate piece of information that a Mississippi brigade went to Early five days before on the 23rd. Babcock concluded this was Humphreys's Brigade of Kershaw's Division, which had been left behind when the division had originally been sent west. That was a key to why they had seen no reinforcements going to Early. They had been looking at Richmond as the source for reinforcements. Kershaw's Division was not considered because it was on its way back to Richmond. There were scattered reports that it had actually returned. Being "in transit" put it out of mind. The only Richmond source for the information would have been Lee's telegram to Anderson and that simply did not leak.[10]

President Lincoln's instincts were better. With the election coming up, he was loath to risk a defeat and became worried that Sheridan's all-out pursuit of Early might lead to a reverse. As Grant would later summarize the situation, "The President was afraid that Sheridan was getting so far away [from communication with Washington [and Grant] that reinforcements would be sent out from Richmond to enable Early to beat him. I replied to the President that I had taken steps to prevent Lee from sending reinforcements to Early, by attacking the former [Lee] where he was."

Grant was working on the premise that with Early so badly beaten, he could withdraw Sheridan's VI Corps and return it to the Army of the Potomac. At this time Sheridan was wasting the Valley and trying to come to grips with Early's remnant. Grant and Sheridan both thought his remaining XIX Corps would be sufficient.[11]

The certain steps that Grant "had taken to prevent Lee from sending reinforcements to Early" would be a major two-pronged attack, "to retain Lee in his position." On the 27th Babcock produced a detailed sketch of the enemy forces from the Appomattox River on the east to the Weldon Railroad on the west. The sketch showed, in Babcock's fine architect's hand, the location of every division and brigade, to include those in the entrenchments and those in reserve. The latter were Hoke's and Field's Divisions and two of Heth's brigades. A 21st-century order-of-battle map would find it hard to improve upon it. In addition to the detailed tactical array, Babcock's sketch showed that six of the Confederate divisions were defending Petersburg—Heth, Mahone, Wilcox (all III Corps), Field (I Corps), Johnson, and Hoke (Beauregard's command).

That only left Pickett's Division (I Corps), a few stray brigades, and Hampton's cavalry north of the James defending Richmond. Grant did not have to be Alexander the Great to figure out that by striking here he would draw Lee's reserves like a magnet.[12]

It was interesting that deserters at this time were identifying Field's and Hoke's Divisions in reserve as having been sent to reinforce Early. Babcock began to have doubts about the two reserve divisions he had shown on his sketch map. He reported to Humphreys based on the information from one deserter, "From the fact that Hoke's division was to have relieved Johnson's yesterday at 5 o'clock and did not, it seems probable it may have gone to Early. Field's division has been lying in reserve on the right—enemy's right." He then notified Sharpe that a deserter from another regiment had stated Field's and Hoke's Divisions had gone to Early. "We have indications going to substantiate that." Sharpe, in turn, ordered Davenport to check on Babcock's report with his operation." By the morning of September 30, it had all been sorted out and Babcock reported these reserve divisions operating with Lee north of the James. On October 1, Sharpe was closing the loop with Davenport. "We think that Hoke and Field have gone up in front of you; that Bushrod Johnson and Mahone hold the line from the Appomattox to the lead-works, and that Heth and Wilcox are on the enemy's right. Can you give us anything to prove or disprove, or can you locate any part of the enemy's force?"[13]

The importance of this contretemps was not to show that Babcock could make mistakes. Even the finest intelligence analysts make mistakes. It offered an insight into the professional workings of the BMI as it collected, sifted, analyzed, checked, and confirmed information. It also showed Sharpe's central role in

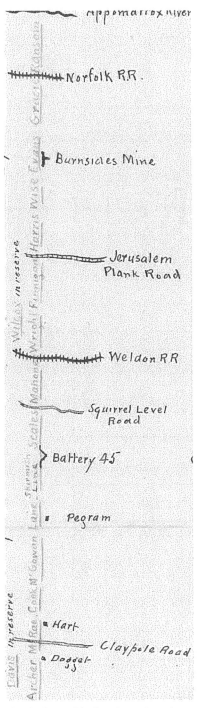

Sketch of part of the front line at Petersburg, November 6, 1864, drawn by John C. Babcock. Courtesy Huntington Library. p. 5

coordinating and cross-checking the reports of his subordinates. Most importantly, it showed the self-correcting process vital to any first-class intelligence analysis operation.

On September 29 Grant suddenly attacked Lee north of the James. Union troops of Major General E. O. C. Ord's XVIII Corps of the Army of the James stormed Fort Harrison, an important point in Richmond's defenses. The contest at Fort Harrison was considered so vital that both Lee and Grant were there personally directing operations. Lee recalled Hoke's and Field's reserve divisions for an attempt to recover the fort, and the next day threw them into an attack that failed with great loss.

The defenses of Petersburg were now largely denuded of reserves except for Heth's two brigades on the western end of the line. Lee had even ordered Wilcox's three brigades in the lines at Petersburg to be, "packed up and rationed, and under march orders," so desperate was the fighting around Fort Harrison. As Lee's attacks on the 30th crested in bloody waves on the fort, Meade lunged westward with 16,000 men of the V and IX Corps to cut the Southern Railroad running along the Appomattox River, one of the last major lines leading out of the city. The march orders to Wilcox's brigades were countermanded. Hill counterattacked with his two reserve brigades of Heth's Division and Wilcox's brigades in the battle of Pebbles Farm and saved the Southern Railroad, though he had to withdraw back into his entrenchments as the fighting ended on October 2. But Meade had inched his left wing closer to the artery and extended his lines 3 miles, forcing the Confederates to do the same. With shrinking manpower, every foot of new entrenchments the Confederates had to man was increasing the strain on the Army of Northern Virginia. Once again, Sharpe's intelligence preparation of the battlefield (IPB), to use a modern term, had prepared the way for Grant's one-two punch.[14]

In addition to order-of-battle analysis, the BMI was also keeping up with its biographical intelligence. As the second day of the fighting began, Babcock reported that Beauregard had been reassigned to Georgia. Beauregard's sense of grievance had been growing ever since Lee had given command of the Valley to Early and not him. Serving under the shadow of the great Lee had not been good for his ego or his reputation. Aware of his dissatisfaction, Davis arranged a transfer. Douglas Southall Freeman put his finger on the problem when he wrote, "Every soldier is on the wane from the moment he begins to think more of reputation than of opportunity." Now Grant would have to face Lee, in undisputed command of the entire Confederate force, as Beauregard's two divisions were incorporated into a new IV Corps for the Army of Northern Virginia.[15]

The intelligence log jam about Early's reinforcements started to break up on September 30, the day after Grant's offensive had begun. That day Babcock learned that Rosser's Cavalry Brigade had been sent to Early a few days before. Then, Maj. Gen. Benjamin Butler reported, undoubtedly on Lieutenant Davenport's findings, that a Confederate officer who had taken the loyalty oath to the Union identified the location of every one of Lee's divisions, placing Kershaw with Early.[16]

Early the next month Sharpe's scouts, working out of Northern Virginia, reported that Longstreet had joined Early with 5,000 men, besides Pickett's Division and Rosser's Cavalry Brigade. The figure of 5,000 was an exaggeration; Early would later state that Kershaw's Division arrived with only 2,700 effectives. The only other error was the identification of Pickett's Division. Halleck immediately notified Grant, who replied with a highly accurate review of enemy forces. Sharpe's BMI had made a good start in sorting out the muddle. Grant summarized the intelligence situation in an October 5 message to Halleck:

> Longstreet has been reported as having gone to the Valley, but took no troops. Kershaw's Division of his corps started back to Richmond before Sheridan's first fight, but was turned back from about Gordonsville. Rosser's brigade of cavalry has gone, but no other troops of any kind. We have had prisoners and deserters, I believe, from every brigade of Lee's army within the last few days, and know the location of every division at this time.[17]

With the exception of Longstreet's presence, which apparently was a deception, every other piece of information was accurate. In fact, Rosser's Brigade joined Early the day Grant sent the message. The Longstreet deception was to take on a new life. Lee had sent Early a strong encouragement to go on the offensive. "I have weakened myself very much to strengthen you. It was done with the expectation of enabling you to gain such success that you could return the troops if not rejoin me yourself."[18] Three days later, knowing that the enemy could read Confederate signals, Early borrowed Longstreet's reputation to intimidate Sheridan with the following deception.

> Lieutenant-General EARLY:
> Be ready to move as soon as my forces join you and we will crush Sheridan.
> LONGSTREET,
> Lieutenant-General.[19]

Sheridan left his army at Cedar Creek for Washington on October 15 for a meeting with Grant. He left Major General H. G. Wright, commanding VI Corps, in command. The next morning a courier sent by Wright rode up to where he had spent the night to give him the message about the signal intercept. He was skeptical and rightly considered the message to be a "ruse," but to be on the safe side he ordered the cavalry division he had detached for a raid to return to the army. He opined that if the presence of Longstreet was true, Old Pete would be working on the premise that Sheridan's cavalry was still detached.

> [S]o I abandoned the cavalry raid toward Charlottesville, in order to give General Wright the entire strength of the army, for it did not seem wise to reduce this number while reinforcement for the enemy might be near, and especially when such pregnant messages were reaching Early from one of the ablest Confederate generals.

In response to Sheridan's transmission of the "Longstreet" message to Washington, Halleck responded by relaying Grant's summary but added somewhat snidely, "I have very little confidence in the information collected at his headquarters." Nevertheless,

Sheridan left with a great sense of uneasiness but concluded that Longstreet would not be able to join Early before he returned to the army.[20]

On his return, Sheridan stopped at Winchester for the night of October 18–19. The next morning he could hear cannon fire coming from the direction of his army at Cedar Creek. The sound quickly reached the thundering rumble of a battle, and Sheridan was off to rejoin his army in a famous ride on his horse Rienzi. As he approached, "there burst upon our view the appalling spectacle of a panic-stricken army—hundreds of slightly wounded men, throngs of other unhurt but utterly demoralized, and baggage-wagons by the score, all pressing to the rear in hopeless confusion, telling only too plainly that a disaster had occurred at the front." Early had attacked his unsuspecting army that morning in its camp just as the men had started to wake. Homer's "panic, brother to blood-stained rout," unraveled the army and set it streaming to the rear. Early's men had overrun Sheridan's own headquarters with the purpose of capturing Sheridan himself.[21]

Sheridan galloped forward. His presence alone turned men in their tracks to march back toward the battle and rejoin their units. Sheridan found that substantial portions of both corps were still in good order and turned them around to face the enemy. The line held and beat off attacks growing stronger as men thronged back to their units. Sheridan needed this time to ascertain whether the formidable Longstreet was actually on the field. Lee's Old Warhorse had been responsible for too many Union routs from Second Bull Run to Chickamauga for him not to be concerned that he faced a far more able opponent than Early. So far, Longstreet's reputation was still serving Early well.

Table 12.1. Military Use Infrastructure and Supplies Captured or Destroyed by The Army of the Shenandoah, August 10–November 16, 1864

Infrastructure		Supplies	
Flour mills	71	Wheat	435,802 bushels
Woolen mills	1	Oats	20,000 bushels
Saw-mills	8	Corn	77,000 bushels
Powder mill	1	Flour	874 barrels
Saltpeter works	3	Hay	20,397 tons
Barns	1,200	Fodder	500 tons
Furnaces	3	Straw	450 tons
Tanneries	4	Beef-cattle	10,918
Railroad depot	1	Sheep	12,000
Locomotive	1	Swine	15,000
Box-cars	3	Calves	250
Rails	947 miles	Bacon & hams	12,000 pounds
		Tobacco	10,000 pounds
		Potatoes	2,500 bushels
		Cotton yarn	1,665 pounds

Sheridan was only waiting until his ranks swelled enough to call Early's bluff. He ordered his cavalry to attack an exposed enemy artillery battery expressly to take prisoners. This was speedily done, and the prisoner interrogations revealed that only Kershaw of Longstreet's Corps was on the field and not the great man himself. With that, he attacked. Early's line fell apart. Now it was the Confederate turn to experience rout, as Sheridan's exultant force pursued them into the night.[22]

With Early's army crippled, demoralized, and deserting away, it became a military cipher. Sheridan could now resume unimpeded the wasting the Valley with a thoroughness that would echo down the years and be known to the inhabitants as "the burning." The cost to Lee was enormous, as shown by Sheridan's report of the damage done to the resources of the Valley. Between August 10 and November 16, Sheridan's army destroyed or captured the following economic resources that Lee's hungry men would never see:[23]

The loss of military equipment and supplies also left a deep wound in the Army of Northern Virginia.

Cedar Creek had had another consequence. Sheridan's scouts had been critical to his victory at Winchester, but he felt they had not properly warned him of the impending attack at Cedar Creek the following month. He felt he needed a larger and more tightly organized unit. Sheridan decided to raise a special battalion which he announced would number 500 men, a form of psychological operations designed to magnify the Confederates' already healthy respect for the so-called "Jesse Scouts" and to throw off the Confederate spies Sheridan believed had penetrated his camp. He chose Maj. Henry Harrison Young of the 2nd Rhode Island Infantry to command and gave him the cover title of "Asst. Aide-de-Camp." Young's battalion never grew to more than 60 men, but he mixed scouting with a liberal amount of special operations. On their first mission, they joined a Confederate cavalry column, and when the unit had settled into a dozing ride, Young and his men galloped up the length of the column, firing into it with pistols and shotguns. Young also relentlessly hunted down enemy partisan leaders on Sheridan's orders. So effective was their scouting that Sheridan would comment that there was little he did not know about the enemy within a 50-mile radius of his base.

Table 12.2. Military Equipment and Supplies Captured or Destroyed by The Army of the Shenandoah, August 10–November 16, 1864

Pieces of artillery	94	Medical wagons	7
Caissons	89	Harness	1,134 sets
Limbers	8	Horse equipment	1,040 sets
Forges	6	Battle flags	40
Battery wagon	1	Small arms	19,230
Artillery ammunition	23,000 rounds	Small arms ammunition	1,061,000 rounds
Army wagons	131	Horses	3,772
Ambulances	137	Mules	545

CHAPTER THIRTEEN

Winter Hiatus

November 1864–March 1865

The action at Hatcher's Run in late October effectively ended major operations around Petersburg and Richmond until February of the next year as the troops settled into winter quarters, building fortifications, sniping here and there, doing picket duty, and patrolling. It was not a period of rest and inaction for the BMI but one of continued opportunity that required relentless effort, no matter the weather.

Deserters in Blue

The BMI's efficient interrogation process had some unique ways to cross-check the information gained and elicit information withheld. One of them was to plant BMI scouts in the guise of captured Rebels in the POW holding facility known as the Bull Pen or the Bull Ring. Babcock recounted to Meade how the scout Skinker had circulated among the prisoners to ascertain that they had lied when they had said there was a large Rebel force near where they had been captured. They also revealed that "prisoners think we could have easily taken the South Side Railroad to-day, there being nothing to prevent…"[1]

The BMI's emphasis on deserters gained a new twist in November. On the 11th one of Sharpe's scouts, I. M. Hatch, returned to report on his two-month special mission. He had been sent into Confederate lines on September 18 in the guise of a deserter to ascertain how the enemy was treating such persons. His was a most revealing tale, one of the strangest in the war. Upon surrendering he was taken through Petersburg to Richmond where he was put into the Castle Thunder POW camp. His interrogation was perfunctory, merely asking what unit he belonged to and some general questions on troop disposition. He was kept there for three weeks until enough prisoners had been collected to send "homeward by the usual route," as reported in the *Richmond Dispatch*, in a single party.[2]

While he waited, he learned that the "500 deserters had run through the blockade and shipped to some foreign port, nearly all them being foreigners by birth." He also observed that the black Union prisoners were forced to do the most menial work in the streets of Richmond and in the construction of fortifications.

After three weeks (October 10), when 137 deserters had been collected, they were sent to Abington in southwestern Virginia and from there were marched under guard to Pound Gap in the Cumberland Mountains on the Kentucky border, where they were joined by 20 more deserters from Sherman's army. At this point 30 of them joined a Confederate partisan command of Lieutenant Colonel Prentice operating in that region. "The principle incentive these men seemed to have in joining Colonel Prentice's command was for the purpose of getting mounted, stealing their horses, and deserting again from him." From Pound Gap, the rest of Hatch's party marched without guard to Louisa on the Big Sandy River, where they crossed through the Union picket line.

About 20 of them attempted unsuccessfully to pass themselves as Rebel deserters to get free transportation north. The rest of the party were transported down the Ohio River to Cincinnati and then to Lexington, where Hatch identified himself to the commanding officer who returned him to City Point. Hatch observed that the majority of his party simply deserted again.[3]

The problem with Union deserters was becoming serious. McEntee reported to Meade on December 11 that one of the BMI's agents on the north side of the James River had said that "a great number of our men are deserting and seem to have a regular run through Charles City County." Fifteen men had crossed the long bridge over the Chickahominy River two nights before. About 50 men a week were passing through, guided by a man named Bob Mattox. There was also a mail run following the same path. McEntee stated that "most of those connected with it are known to this department, and measures will be taken to arrest the parties."[4]

Grant took a personal interest in just how the Confederates managed getting Union deserters back home. He summoned scout Anson Carney and offered him a $300 bonus if he would desert and go through the system. He agreed and made his way to the Confederate pickets to give himself up. He was gone for seven weeks. After questioning he was sent to Libby Prison, until about two score deserters were collected and then marched west to the mountains and let go to find their way north. Carney found out that other deserters were shipped out through the blockade on British ships. In the mountains Carney was robbed of his clothes three times by "rebels, Union deserters, and bushwhackers, who had formed a sort of robber's gang in the mountains. The first time I was robbed I was told I wore too good clothes and must exchange. After the third robbery my clothes became too poor to excite the envy of any one, and I was allowed to proceed in peace."

Carney eventually reached Cumberland Gap, where he gave himself up to the Union pickets who thought he was a genuine deserter until he was taken to headquarters where he revealed his mission. He was sent on through Cincinnati and Washington and eventually found his way by steamer back to City Point, there to satisfy Grant's curiosity.[5]

Comings and Goings

Since his victory at Cedar Creek in October, Sheridan had continued to rely on Sharpe's agent and scout network in Northern Virginia working under the supervision of Captain Leet in Washington. Sheridan wired Leet on November 17, "Keep your scouts on the alert at Gordonville, or on the railroad in that vicinity. It is very necessary for the next ten days." Leet responded the next day to inform him that the scouts had been immediately sent out and would be kept active.[6]

The men of Kershaw's Division would be arriving in Richmond on November 18–19, as Lee had begun the process of writing off the Valley and withdrawing his forces. Their presence in the city was reported by one of Van Lew's agents whose market stall was robbed by several of Kershaw's men on the 19th. The next day McEntee reported that a deserter stated that Kershaw's Division would soon join Longstreet. Other deserters reported that two brigades were already "encamped at Chaffin's farm and the rest at Chesterfield," across from the Army of the James. Rumors also were rife in Richmond that the rest of Early's force would be arriving because the Virginia Central Railroad had been reserved for only military traffic and that Sheridan had arrived with his army to reinforce Grant. On the 22nd, Sheridan, still in the Valley, knew that Kershaw had returned to Richmond but asked Leet to keep his scouts at Gordonville for the next 10 days to watch the railroads. Early theoretically still had a powerful force, and Sheridan wanted to know its every move. Grant, for his part, was keeping the pressure on Lee to keep him from reinforcing Early again. Patrick wrote in his diary on December 3, "Nothing is going on here, *now*, excepting a heavy cannonading, much of the time, intended to keep Lee in the belief that we were ready to attack in case he should send off any more men.[7]

Lee was also keeping track of Sheridan in the Valley as a source of reinforcement for Grant. So it was with apprehension that he informed Davis on December 6 of the departure of the U.S. VI Corps from Sheridan's command. His own intelligence collection was working well. His agent, Lieutenant Cawood, had provided him with a stage by stage movement of VI Corps and an estimate of its strength at 10,000 men as it steamed by his station at 5:00 p.m. on December 3 in 21 transports. He did not know only two of its three divisions were on the move at this time. Lee had concluded accurately that they were destined to join Grant. He had already ordered Early to release Gordon's Division, which was scheduled to arrive the next night, and to have Pegram's Division ready to follow. This was the beginning of the recall of the entire II Corps to Richmond. As an aside to Davis, Lee thought the estimate of VI Corps' strength too large. Lieutenant Cawood was closer to the mark in estimating the strength of the two divisions steaming past him; the Union return for November showed 16,441 men in VI Corps; the December return showed 19,268 men. Splitting the difference would have had about 12,000 men in the convoy.[8]

Grant was equally concerned with enemy forces in the Valley. He and Sheridan had hoped that withdrawing VI Corps after Sheridan's victories in the Valley would cause Lee to also pull forces back to Richmond. As late as the 8th Sheridan was expressing his chagrin to Grant that his transfer of VI Corps had not prompted a return of the enemy's II Corps to Richmond-Petersburg. "I sent to-morrow morning the remaining division of the Sixth Corps. No troops of the enemy have left the Valley, except Kershaw's division. I did expect that the movement of the two divisions of the Sixth Corps would cause a movement on the part of the enemy, but to the present time it has not."

Sheridan was worried because Leet had wired him that same day the BMI's agent at Orange Court House and Frederick Hall Station on the Virginia Central Railroad had earlier that week seen or heard of no move of troops from Early since Kershaw left. Sheridan had only to bide his patience one more day.[9]

Sharpe's organization was fine-tuned to catch any evidence of the return of any part of Early's command. Almost immediately, the Richmond spy ring chimed in. Babcock reported to Meade on December 9 that he had just received the following information from Sharpe's office at City Point: "Agents from Richmond report the following: Early's command arriving in Richmond. Troops were coming in and going to Petersburg all night and day before yesterday evening [the 7th]." Amazingly, the Richmond agents were acquiring this information only later in the same day that Lee had penned his message to Davis. Babcock also stated, "Our latest information of the strength of this corps is 12,000 muskets." He was not too far off. II Corps' strength as of the returns of November 30 was 10,188, not a bad estimate for a force operating that far away. It was especially good when compared with Lee's underestimation of VI Corps, an error of over 50 percent compared with Babcock's overestimation error of 8 percent.[10]

Babcock continued to search for confirmation of the information from the BMI's Richmond agents. He collated more information from this source with information from deserters from Gordon's Division, two recent conscripts who estimated "the force that left the Valley at 7,000; could see the entire column, trains and all, at points on the way from New Market to Waynesborough, where they took the cars." Another deserter, Corporal Toohey, from the 6th Louisiana, "is a very intelligent Irishman and is well-posted on the strength of Gordon's and Pegram's divisions. He states that Gordon's division is only 3,000." The corporal was close; its strength on November 30 was 3,454. He also estimated Pegram's strength at 4,000, having been strengthened with conscripts and convalescents. That corresponded with Babcock's estimate. That would have added another thousand men to the November 30 abstract, making Babcock's 8 percent error about 5 percent instead. It was clear by the 11th that the divisions of both Gordan and Pegram had arrived and been sent directly into the defenses of Petersburg. The BMI's scouts were able to add a third point of confirmation. All-source intelligence does not get any better. Babcock was also able to accurately discover that both divisions were under Major General Gordon's command as the probable new II Corps commander.[11]

Babcock was aware that there was a third shoe that waited to drop—the location of Rhode's Division of II Corps. Would it stay in the Valley or join Gordon at Petersburg? Lee ordered it back to Richmond on December 13. In a letter to Davis the next day he explained that cold weather had closed operations in the Valley for the winter and that he had information that Sheridan's VIII and XIX Corps were moving out of the Valley, probably to reinforce Grant. Under the circumstances, he could not leave even one division of II Corps inactive in the Valley. He hoped that if the "Quartermaster's Department is active" (always a big "if"), Rodes's Division would arrive by Friday of that week. He further speculated that "General Grant may now be preparing to break through our center, as the canal at Dutch Gap is reported nearly completed." He explained to Davis that even with Rodes's Division, he would still only oppose one Union corps with one Confederate division.[12]

Lee had dropped the third shoe. How long would it take the BMI to find it? Babcock informed Meade on December 19 that BMI scouts from Richmond had learned that on the preceding Friday and Saturday (for once the Quartermaster's Department was on the ball) Rodes's Division passed through the city in the direction of Petersburg. The report had gone directly to Sharpe at City Point and been retransmitted to Babcock. For another three days, there was no further hard information on Rodes's Division, until December 22, when McEntee, who was working at City Point, informed Babcock that the division's presence had been confirmed. He also added, "They may have gone south, if they are not in your front." They were likely going to join the rest of Gordon's II Corps at Petersburg.[13]

Lee had little time to appreciate the addition to his strength with the return of his II Corps. Almost immediately he had to send off a force equivalent to more than half that reinforcement. Grant's plan to take Wilmington in October had foundered over poor planning, lack of army-navy cooperation, and, above all, Butler's insistence as privilege of rank on commanding the two divisions that would be the assault force to take Fort Fisher, the bastion that protected the great Cape Fear River port. The plan had had plenty of time to be compromised if it had not already leaked like a sieve. Wilmington was never far from Lee's thoughts; it was the last major port of entry for the blockade runners that brought vital war supplies to the dying Confederacy; it also brought in a great deal of Midwestern bacon purchased in New York by British agents, shipped to Bermuda, and then to Wilmington.

On the 13th Lee's commissary was informed by Richmond that there was no salt meat left at all. Lee wrote to Davis the next day, "Neither meat nor corn are now coming over the southern roads, and I have heard there is meat in Wilmington." Four days later he received a plea from Beauregard for reinforcements in the face of

Sherman's relentless march through the southern heartland. He begged for Hoke's and Johnson's divisions to defend South Carolina and Georgia. Savannah was on the point of surrender; Charleston was threatened. Yet, Wilmington and its precious stream of war supplies and bacon loomed far more important to Lee and Davis. Lee sent Maj. Gen. Robert Hoke and two brigades of his large division of 6,500 men to reinforce the defenders of Fort Fisher. Hoke's brigades were pulled out of the line to be replaced by Kershaw's men and then marched to the Danville station in Richmond to embark on December 21 and 22. One brigade would arrive in Wilmington just in time to frustrate the assault against Fort Fisher.[14]

On the 22nd McEntee reported, "Information from Richmond this a.m. to the effect that Hoke's division is now moving by the Danville Railroad. The last of it will be off to-morrow, and it is supposed that it is bound for Wilmington." Adding to the suspense, Richmond newspapers brought through the lines stated that "Butler and Porter's expedition against Wilmington has done nothing as yet...," according to a diary entry left by Major General John Rawlins, Grant's chief of staff. Yet again Van Lew's spy ring had hit a bullseye with an accurate near real-time report. The same day a deserter confirmed Hoke's departure, saying they went through Richmond, avoiding the more visible pontoon bridge. Sharpe's all-source system had confounded Lee's attempts at security. By attempting to avoid visual observation from Union Signal Corps stations, they had marched through the seeming cover of the Richmond urban area only to fall under the direct eyes of Van Lew's efficient band of Unionist agents. North of the James, the Confederates were trying to conceal the fact that Hoke's Division was gone by restricting the location of a flag of truce meeting with the Union XXIV Corps. It's commander, reflecting the rapid spread of Sharpe's intelligence circulars, commented to one of his officers, "I would suggest that if an officer goes out from the last-named place that he should tell them that they need not be so damned particular, for we know that Hoke is gone."[15]

When Sherman had left Atlanta to burn a swath across Georgia, Grant had accepted that he would be out of communication with his favorite general. Sharpe provided him with an alternate way to keep track of Sherman's march. The Richmond papers regularly reported his progress, and Van Lew was promptly sending them to Sharpe. Grant must have been amused to read in early December that the Confederates were "puzzled to know whether Sherman meant to strike Charleston, Savannah or Beaufort, or join General Grant in front of Richmond." On December 16 Sharpe was able to tell Grant that Sherman had reached Savannah and invested the city. By the 18th there was a palpable sense of expectation waiting on news of Sherman. To this was added the departure of the fleet for the attack on Wilmington.[16]

On the 23rd a telegraph operator from Richmond came through the lines and, as noted by Rawlins, stated that Beauregard telegraphed on the night of the 20th to Davis that Savannah had surrendered to Sherman unconditionally on that same morning. Also, papers of the 20th reported that Hardee had evacuated Savannah and Sherman had taken possession.[17]

Almost daily Babcock was reporting there was no official news until Christmas Day, when he wrote a number of reports on interrogations, all of which said that it was understood in the Confederate army that Savannah had fallen. On the same day Sharpe wrote to him that the Richmond papers said communications with Savannah had been broken. Then Babcock replied that it was now reported in the enemy army that Savannah had fallen, that Sherman was marching on Charleston, and had broken the Charleston-Savannah railroad in four places. Still, the next day Babcock can only tell Meade that there is nothing definite on Savannah. By the 27th the *Richmond Dispatch* announced the evacuation of Savannah. That same day Sharpe was reporting from his agents, "On learning the news of the fall of Savannah gold went up in Richmond from 36 & 40 to 50 Dollars for one—and greenbacks advanced from 10 & 12 to 20 for one."[18]

Unfortunately, there is often a downside to even the best all-source intelligence work. No apparent use of the intelligence was made by Grant. Neither were operations launched to take advantage of the absence of Hoke's brigades nor was Butler notified of the reinforcements sent to Wilmington. In defense of Grant, he may have concluded that the absence of 3,000 or so men from the defenses of Richmond was not sufficient grounds for offensive action since Gordon had just reinforced the garrison with almost 12,000 men. Also there simply may not have been time between the confirmation of the departure of Hoke's brigades on December 22–23 and the failure of the attempt on Fort Fisher on the 25th to notify Butler and Rear Admiral Porter who commanded the naval element of the attack.

Thus the year 1864 ended on a note of failure, appropriate for a year in which opportunity after opportunity was lost to end the war with one mortal blow. Instead, the armies had left a giant blood-trail from the Wilderness to Petersburg. However, if decisive victory was always out of reach, a more gradual one was at work in the form of attrition. While Lee's army lived hand-to-mouth on an increasingly starvation diet, Grant's army was getting hot bread every day. On October 25 Patrick was taken on tour of "the Bake Houses just completed—It will turn out 100,000 rations in 24 hours—Every thing is on a grand scale and of the most convenient & economical character—They make the most excellent bread." Enormous cakes were also baked by someone called "the Ice Cream Man." On the day before Thanksgiving (November 26), he would record that the first installment of Thanksgiving turkeys had arrived. The scale of support to the American soldier would set the standard for the next century and a half. Where Lee's horses were dying for lack of fodder as the South was also running out of horseflesh, each day almost 600 tons of grain and hay moved through City Point to supply Grant's vast herd of animals. As the Southern railroad infrastructure was creaking to a breakdown through a worn-out plant and Union destruction, Grant was reaping the fruits of industrial warfare. He had transformed City Point into one of the busiest ports in the world, the funnel for the industrial outpouring of the North. Trains were regularly shipped into City Point; one fleet of 90 steamers, tugs, and barges brought two dozen locomotives and 275 boxcars. This web of railroad support to the besieging armies was supported by a railroad construction brigade of 2,000 men.[19]

At the end of November an unusual prisoner fell into Sharpe's hands. Private Roger A. Pryor was one of Stuart's scouts. He had more than a private's past. He was a vociferous secessionist member of Virginia's Congressional delegation before the Civil War and had entered the Confederate army as the colonel of the 3rd Virginia Infantry, rising to command the Florida Brigade in Richard Anderson's Division in Longstreet's Corps. At Antietam he had replaced the wounded Anderson, but was so inept that Jefferson Davis denied him further promotion. In a pique he resigned in 1863. The next year he enlisted as a private and scout in August in Fitzhugh Lee's command, who worked out of General Lee's headquarters. He was captured by Union pickets while trying to exchange newspapers against Lee's orders forbidding any intercourse with the enemy. Sharpe suspected he was a spy, and he was confined to Fort Lafayette in New York. After the war he settled in New York City, established a law firm, and became a power in state Democratic politics and was known as a Confederate Carpetbagger. Remarkably he was appointed as a justice to the New York Supreme Court in 1890. He had intersected with Sharpe the year before when his son published a paper refuting a recent allegation that his father had actually deserted rather than been captured. Sharpe fully supported the story of his capture.[20]

The war had its own calendar which had nothing to do with the end of man's year.

Grant "has confidence in the Judgment of Colonel Sharpe"

Enigmatically, Patrick refers in his diary to tension with Sharpe at Grant's headquarters in the middle of November. On November 16, he wrote in his diary, "I had a talk with Genl. Grant about Col. Sharpe, and have that matter all fixed right." Apparently not. On November 18 he wrote that he'd sent Sharpe's resignation forward. The next day he wrote in his diary that Meade declined to accept the resignation until Grant had returned and he could confer with him. There the matter lay for the next 10 days. On November 29, Patrick wrote to Brigadier General Williams, stating that he wanted to send Sharpe to Washington on business, but that the letter of resignation was still pending and that he understood it was to have been acted upon in a few days. There is no copy of Sharpe's letter of resignation in his Military Service Record at the National Archives where such documents would have been kept along with their approval or disapproval. But such matters were considered sensitive, and after the matter had been settled and the letter of resignation withdrawn, it would probably have been disposed of. The army then, and now, does not always put everything in the public record. Most likely the matter that had sparked the resignation was the increasingly intolerable difficulty of working for both Grant and Meade at the same time. However, the record is opaque as to the circumstances. Whatever the issue was, the final decision was Grant's. The fact that Sharpe continued to work for Grant was an indication of his value to the general-in-chief. Grant put great store in the trustworthiness of his subordinates, and had this been the problem, Sharpe would have been gone.[21]

The visit of two British officers on November 12 would be the cause of an incident that Sharpe would relate 30 years later that would offer "some insight of the true Meade that lay underneath the coat of irritation that he so often wore." As a member of Meade's staff, Sharpe relayed the incident:

> I came to know full well that at times—in fact, a great deal of the time—he displayed a most peppery disposition to all with whom he came in contact, so that many of the generals of the Army of the Potomac did not personally like their superior…
>
> After the Army of the Potomac had taken up winter quarters … in the latter part of 1864, there appeared at headquarters [of the Armies Operating Against Richmond] one day two Englishmen who were recognized authorities in the British Army. They carried a letter from Lord Lyons, then British minister at Washington. In it the minister explained that its bearers were friends of his, they had come to this country for the special purpose of studying the movements of the Army of the Potomac, and he—Lord Lyons—would take it as a high personal favor if such assistance as was reasonable and proper should be given to them in their study.
>
> General Grant received the two strangers very courteously, told them that he would be glad to do all he could to help them, and then, after pondering a moment or two, turned to me.
>
> "General Sharpe," he asked, quietly, "Is there any general close at hand who is on good terms with Gen. Meade?"
>
> I replied that no one could be on better terms with him than myself. At that Grant's face showed the inward relief he undoubtedly felt. "Then," he said, "I wish you would escort these gentlemen to Gen. Meade's headquarters, and request him for me to give them such assistance as lies within his power."
>
> Arrived at Gen. Meade's headquarters, I requested the Englishmen to remain outside for a few moments, so that I might prepare Gen. Meade for their reception. Then I entered his tent and found him, as I was half afraid I might, in a very irritable mood. Something—possibility something most trivial—had gone wrong, and when I told him what my errand was, he let loose and swore like a trooper. But at least, he said: "Gen. Sharpe, bring your friends to me in about 15 minutes, I will receive them."
>
> Promptly at the specified time I entered Gen. Meade's tent with the two visitors, and what do you suppose I saw? Gen. Meade garbed in full dress uniform, ever handsome in appearance, and the acme of dignified and impressive presence. And when I introduced the Englishmen he received them with the utmost graciousness and put them at their ease at once. And this was the same man who had been swayed by passion a short quarter of an hour before.
>
> Well, for nearly an hour, Gen. Meade held those Englishmen in thrall while he discoursed on the strategy of the campaign. His courtesy, his thoughtfulness, his simplicity, his modesty, his patience at questions, completely captivated them, and when finally the interview was over and I rode away with them they could not sound his praises loud enough. You see, he gave those two men a glimpse of the Gen. George C. [G.] Meade that not many men of the Army of the Potomac got.

The intervening 30 years perhaps softened his memories, especially the row over Sharpe's transfer to Grant's staff, when he ended by saying, "But we of our staff knew right along that he had a tender heart, and our only regret was that, against his own good, he so often hid it behind those outbursts of irritability for which he has become famous in the personal history of our Civil War."[22]

Sharpe's perception was reflected more sourly in the contemporary diary of one of Meade's staff officers, Lt. Col. Cyrus B. Comstock. He was blunt at describing Meade's temper. "Some talk about Meade's quarreling with all his subordinates. Rawlins talks wildly. The truth is that Meade is a bear to his subordinates. I have heard him abuse Burnside, Hancock & Warren to their faces. Ingalls is glad to get away from him & under Grant & the Patrick wishes the same & talks about Meade." What tempered this for Comstock was not Meade's concealed affection for his subordinates but a grudging high respect for his abilities as a soldier. "Have talked with very different people—all snubbed by Meade. & think that while they all have private grievances, he would be first choice for Cmdg. Genl. Both among his staff officers & the Maj. Gen's."[23]

Grant was determined to keep his intelligence chief, and nothing more was said of the resignation, whatever its cause. The general-in-chief finally resolved the ambiguity over Sharpe's status in orders published on December 2: "Colonel George H. Sharpe, One hundred and twentieth Regiment New York Volunteers, is announced as assistant provost-marshal-general, Armies operating against Richmond, and will report to Brigadier General M. R. Patrick, provost-marshal-general, for duty."[24]

That same day, another set of orders was published by the Office of the Provost Marshal General specifically stating that Sharpe was "assigned to the special charge of the 'Bureau of Information' and will, with the least practicable delay, make such arrangements as will insure the utmost efficiency in that branch of the service." Of course, Sharpe was already doing this, but the order was a way to formally detach Sharpe from Meade and express Grant's confidence in him.[25]

An incident shortly before this was revealing for an expression of confidence Grant had in his chief intelligence officer. Sharpe had found that an inventor, Oliver Cox, had approached Grant months before to offer a new cipher system and signaling system. Grant had done nothing, but Sharpe had learned of the offer and asked for an interview. Sharpe endorsed the cipher system by stating that he had successfully employed it. Cox asked Grant for an acknowledgment of his cipher system, but Grant responded through his staff that he had not the time to personally review the system, "but has confidence in the judgment of Col. Sharpe."[26]

It was a simple statement but one that was high praise for the laconic Grant. It was indicative of the close professional relationship of the two men that was slowly evolving into a friendship that Grant would make good use of after the war in his presidency. Adam Badeau, one of Grant's staff that he had brought with him from the west, put his finger on the relationship when he wrote, "To some he gave a character of confidence not necessary to be given to others and not withheld from distrust, but because it had no relation to official duties and might not be interesting otherwise."

Grant just found Sharpe interesting. That he was a storyteller of Lincoln-esque talent also appealed to Grant the man.[27]

Colonel Theodore Lyman, one of Meade's aides, recorded a postscript to the visit of the two British officers. Left unsaid by Meade was the common knowledge that it had been the output of British factories and mills that had supplied the weapons, munitions, and supplies, without which the Confederacy would have collapsed in the first year of the war if left to its own resources. Meade's aide, Colonel Rosenkrantz—a Swedish immigrant—was the escort for these officers and less reticent. When asked by them what was the opinion among the Americans of the British, he said, "Vell, I can tell you that, so far as I have observed, some Americans do just care nothing about you, and many others do say, that, when this war is over, they will immediately very soon kick you out of Canada." The incredulous British asked why. "Rosie" replied, "Be-cause they say you have made for the Rebs very many bullets." More to the point, in March of the next year Grant forwarded to Stanton a captured ammunition box stamped, "Royal Arsenal Woolwich." Whether Sharpe had anything to do with this is unknown.[28]

Supporting the Navy—The Battle of Trent's Reach

The quiet of a winter siege was broken from an unsuspected quarter—the Confederate navy. The James River Squadron of rams and gunships lurked in the river to prevent a naval attack on Richmond. The low level of the river had prevented the ships from issuing out to attack the U.S. Navy protecting the vast logistics base at City Point. Heavy rain offered them a chance as the river rose. On January 21 Sharpe reported simultaneously to Grant and Meade:

> Our friends in Richmond send us word that the late freshet in the James River had so weakened and partially removed the obstructions placed therein that it was considered possible for the rebel gun-boats to pass them. An order was issued on Tuesday last that their fleet should go down the river, either pass or attack our iron-clads, and attempt the destruction of City Point. It was known in Richmond that we had two monitors up the river, but it was supposed that their vessels be numerous or strong enough for the attempt, it being claimed that now, in the absence of the larger part of our iron fleet, was the opportunity for their own; that upon the return of our iron-clads theirs would be permanently shut up in the upper James, and that even if the movement resulted in the loss of their vessels it could be no worse than what would eventually be the case, and might inflict incalculable damage upon us.[29]

This was actionable intelligence of the first order. The same day his report to Grant's headquarters transmitted the facts to Willian A. Parker, commander of the 5th Division, North Atlantic Blockading Squadron, defending City Point; he received it on the 22nd. "We have information from Richmond that on Tuesday last an order was issued that the rebel fleet should come down the river, either pass or attack our ironclads, and attempt the destruction of City Point." The letter recommended, "It would be well that you exercise more than the usual vigilance to defeat any plan the rebels may have in contemplation in the river." Unfortunately, the navy failed to make the most of it.[30]

Grant was not going to rely solely on the navy. He ordered Major General Gibbon to offer whatever assistance he could. In response to Gibbon's query on the 23rd Parker replied that the state of river obstructions was bad and that he did not consider his naval forces sufficient to prevent the descent of the enemy. He recommended that Gibbon strengthen the batteries at Trent's Reach, commanding the route the enemy must take with more heavy guns, to sink more vessels as obstructions, and plant more torpedoes (mines). At the same time he pulled most of his own vessels except for the *Onondaga* down river below City Point.[31]

On the night of the 23rd–24th the Confederate squadron slipped out, and almost immediately two of its ships went aground. One ship was sunk and the rest severely damaged by the army batteries and the heavy guns of the *Onondaga* in what was called the battle of Trent's Reach. The Confederate ships withdrew, and Parker withdrew *Onondaga* as well, even though another attack was expected. Grant was incensed at Parker's timidity and requested and received permission to give direct orders to the navy in the James. He tartly informed Parker, "The delay of the last few days in preparing for a visit from the enemy … was providentially prevented from proving fatal to us." He had every right to be incensed. His man Sharpe had given ample warning of the breakout of the James River Squadron. Parker's failure to respond energetically could have resulted in a catastrophe had those ships closed on the vast assembly of ships and stores at City Point. But by the time he wrote this, the crisis had passed. The heavily damaged James River Squadron had withdrawn back up river and would never emerge again.[32]

Departures and Promotions

Whatever problems Sharpe may have been having in November, it was a good month for John McEntee. Colonel Gates of the 20th NYSM had resigned effective the 22nd to run for Congress, which resulted in the elevation to command of the regiment's lieutenant colonel, Jacob H. Hardenburgh. That left the position of the regiment's lieutenant colonel open. On the evening of the 25th the officers of the 20th met to elect replacements for vacancies. While the rest of the volunteer regiments had long since dropped the election of officers, it seems the 20th had retained this old policy dating to its militia days. Captain John R. Leslie had been in line for the position, but the officers evidently preferred McEntee who, despite his detached service since April 1863, was the more popular and respected. McEntee had not allowed absence to let ties with his regiment fray, especially since they were in close proximity as the provost guard. Patrick noted in his diary of the next day that the officers referred the decision to him, but he told them to "make their own selection." They elected McEntee, and on December 19 both Hardenburgh and he received their respective

promotions to lieutenant colonel and colonel of the 20th NYSM. McEntee, of
course, stayed on detached service with Sharpe's Bureau. Sharpe's obvious trust in
McEntee may well have weighed in as a factor in the election. He probably was not
above some electioneering on behalf of his deputy.[33]

About the same time, Captain Manning was also promoted to lieutenant colonel.[34]
That would be followed by his transfer to the Army of the James as provost marshal
general on February 1, where he would continue to serve as an unofficial member
of the BMI, reporting on intelligence matters to Sharpe. That transfer, however, left
Sharpe's original BMI short and he sought and received a replacement in Capt. Paul
A. Oliver, who was serving on the V Corps staff. Oliver had been wounded twice in
the Seven Days battles in 1862, serving with the 12th New York, and later served as
aide-de-camp to Hooker and Meade. He had then followed Hooker when he was
transferred to the West. At the battle of Resaca in Georgia he had won the Medal
of Honor. He requested transfer back to the Army of the Potomac, and Meade
thought so well of him that he requested the governor of New York to promote
him to captain. Following him was an extraordinary letter of recommendation from
Major General Hooker dated February 7 of that same year, with whom he had served
in both the Army of the Potomac and the Army of the Cumberland. Hooker is at
pains to state that he had the opportunity to closely observe Oliver during both
periods, adding force to the following:

> Captain Oliver is an officer of uncommon merit. His services have been great and often
> brilliant. He is faithful and fearless in execution, sound in judgment, and quick in forming
> it. He rendered me invaluable service at Fredericksburg, at Chancellorsville, at Wauhatchie,
> and Lookout Mountain, and repeatedly on the Atlanta campaign. Without doing injustice to
> any I can say that I know of no officer of his rank who can point to a prouder record. He is
> qualified to exercise the rank of Brigadier General, and were I in the field I know of no officer
> that I would be more rejoiced to have at the head of a brigade.[35]

The letter had its intended effect. It was probably a subject of Hooker's cordial visit
to Meade on February 27. Oliver was promoted from captain to brevet brigadier
general on March 8, an extraordinary leap across the ranks even during the Civil
War. That promotion would prove to be entirely justified. The modern U.S. Army
would do well to accelerate the rise of talent rather than forcing everyone, from
genius to mediocrity, through the same promotion sequence.[36]

McEntee and Manning were not the only ones to celebrate a promotion that
winter. On February 7 Sharpe was promoted to brevet brigadier general. The brevet
was, in effect, an honorary promotion and not one reflected in permanent rank or
pay. It did entitle the bearer to all the dignities, privileges, and authority of that
rank. Socially, the brevet rank was that which a man would carry for the rest of his
life as a mark of honor. It was also a mark of Grant's favor.

Sharpe explained to his Uncle Jansen that his promotion was not for any specific
deed—"I did in fact nothing." It was a case of timing and the marshaling of influence.

Just after he had been officially transferred to Grant's staff, Meade had submitted a number of his staff for brevet promotions. The fact that he just missed the wave of promotions awarded to the men he had worked with for almost two years "irritated me a little, & I took steps to have it brought to the notice of Mr. Stanton, who very naturally recollected that I was one of the very few staff officers he knew, & with whose services he was personally acquainted—So the thing was set right in short order." Sharpe's numerous visits to Washington on official business over the last two years and especially his calming presence during the height of the Early invasion of the previous year certainly made a positive impression on Stanton. And Sharpe never failed to impress. He worked on the principle that if you don't blow your own horn, someone will use it as a funnel.

Before that contact bore fruit, he approached the prominent senior officers with whom he had served and received, "handsome testimonials" from Hooker, Humphreys, & Butterfield. "Hooker generously forgetting his defeat and recommending that I should be promoted for gallantry under fire at Chancellorsville." Meade heard about the promotion and wrote Sharpe a "capital letter" full of praises, a gracious concession. All in all, it was a display of military politicking of a high order and one to which today's "Perfumed Princes of the Pentagon," sophisticates in bureaucratic advancement, would tip the hat. He concluded that it had been worth it, for he was "much better off than if included with the others." His brevet would be backdated to December 20,, 1864.[37]

The Confederates had been clearly keeping track of Sharpe. On January 24, the *Richmond Dispatch* reproduced a telegram from "Grant's army" that can only have been a BMI product, describing news brought by Confederate deserters on the Danville Railroad. It appears to be a BMI product; however, although there is no copy of it in the BMI files at NARA or in the Official Records, the information in it appears to be correct. It should be noted that not all of the BMI reports made it into the National Archives. It was no accident that the article closed by printing, "Colonel Sharpe so long connected with the army in the capacity of deputy provost-marshal, and lately acting as deputy provost-marshal-general of the armies operating against Richmond, has been promoted to brigadier-general." The Confederates were thumbing their nose at Sharpe, in effect showing they had intercepted an intelligence report and then congratulating him on his promotion. That the enemy knew of his promotion two weeks before it became public should have given him pause. If he had a network inside Richmond, the Confederates had one in City Point.[38]

Even during the dreary months of the winter, when serious operations awaited the spring, there was much to do for an active staff officer. Sharpe explained to his Uncle Jansen on February 24 that "I am one of the hardest working men in the army, when we are lying still." Just keeping track of the enemy's frequent moves within the defenses of Richmond and Petersburg as well as elsewhere throughout the theater required constant attention. "My only relief is when we begin marching or fighting." Grant could see that Sharpe was working hard, but commanders expect staff officers to work hard. Douglas MacArthur summed up a commander's attitude in reply to a visitor to his headquarters in the Southwest Pacific who said he was working his staff to death. "Well, can they die a nobler death?" For all of that, Grant was impressed by Sharpe's hard work, his clever and perceptive intelligence, his positive personality, not to mention his ability to tell a good story to liven up the after-duty conversations. Gradually, he began to include him in his military family, the close staff officers he had brought with him from the west. Eventually, he would become one of Grant's family of generals in whom he placed his complete trust.[39]

Despite his heavy workload, Sharpe always seem to find time to show concern for those in distress, as he had during the Overland Campaign, when he retrieved a soldier from the bullpen who had been accidently arrested and provided for his discharge and transportation home. In late November he approached Meade in the case of Charles McCandlish, a Scottish immigrant and Unionist who had come through the lines in August desiring to take the oath of allegiance. He was such a skilled mechanic that he immediately found employment at the blacksmithing repair shop at City Point. He requested permission to slip back through the picket lines to retrieve his family, who had moved to a house nearby. Sharpe fully supported the request to Meade who approved it promptly the next day.[40]

The news of the fall of Wilmington had heartened the army as had the news of Sherman's continuing successes. Yet, Sharpe was not optimistic about a sudden end to the war; he had been impressed too many times with the resilience of the Army of Northern Virginia under the command of "Lee the Incomparable." He offered this assessment:

> If we begin fighting, I shall not leave as I have never suggested such a thing at any such time. "The end draweth nigh"—but I am not one of those who believe that the catastrophe is to be immediate. Lee's ability will not be denied now that he has been "tackled" by Grant & he has considerable resources yet at his command. When he takes a brigade of infantry and leads it in a desperate charge into the thickest of the volley firing—then, he will have given up and not before—and he will die on the field, with the reputation of being one of the ablest soldier the world has ever seen.[41]

Pay Problems and Bonuses

On a more prosaic level, funding for the BMI was experiencing problems. Babcock continued to be responsible for control of the BMI's funds. On November 19 he reported to Sharpe that the provost marshal general's paymaster, Captain Clinton, had not been able to issue pay for September and October, forcing Babcock to divert notes accumulated for four of the scouts captured during the Dahlgren raid to pay Anson Carney and the wife of another scout. Of his remaining funds ($400 or $500) he recommended to Sharpe that they be returned to Clinton, who was begging for help after improperly advancing his commissary funds, which "[he] had no business to do." He urged Knight to bring this situation to the attention of Brigadier General Patrick in the strongest terms.[42]

The next day Captain Leet was reporting to Grant that the scouts based in Washington and operating south of Fredericksburg had not been paid for some time. "I would respectfully recommend that positive orders be given to the proper officer to forward at once … funds for the payment of the men, who are sadly in need of money." He also requested more Confederate currency of the latest issue for the use of his scouts behind the line.[43]

Regular funding would remain a problem and not just for pay but was interfering with the conduct of operations. On December 15 Sharpe reported to Patrick, "General Ingalls' requisitions on the Treasury Department were honored yesterday. I respectfully ask that a messenger may be sent to me immediately with a portion of the money Captain Clinton may get as I am forced to admit that some our failures here have been owing to want of funds." The failures he refers to were no doubt associated with collection efforts in Richmond.[44]

In contrast to interruptions of BMI funding were the special awards for Judson Knight directed by Grant himself. So important had Knight become in the coordination of intelligence collection in Richmond, despite any interruption in operational funding, that Grant was rewarding him with handsome bonuses beginning in December. One cannot help but see Sharpe's recommendations in this unprecedented liberality.[45]

Despite the funding problems, Babcock had not neglected his own accommodations. They were enviously described by one of Meade's staff officers, Lt. Col. Theodore Lyman, who noted that "Babcock and the Captain [presumably Capt. John McEntee] have artistic cottages nicely papered within."[46]

The Siege Takes its Toll

The amount and quality of information coming out of Van Lew's network in Richmond kept getting better and better as the new year began. In a series of reports in the first two weeks of January, Sharpe painted a picture of the wasting effects of the siege both upon the Confederate war effort and the population of Richmond and Petersburg.

On January 9 he wrote, "We have information this morning from three of our agents in Richmond, coming by different sources," effective as of the previous morning. He repeated that the information "was derived from different and independent sources" which cross-checked each other. The picture painted was one of war industry grinding to a halt as vital machinery was being moved south and as the remaining shops and factories simply ran out of raw materials. One source reported that "At the Tredegar works there has not been a large gun cast for a month or more." The Tredegar works were the South's largest—and by this time last—major foundry.

"The people are in a deplorable situation," he went on. "There is neither food nor clothing to be had; the rations for the soldiers in hospital have even been reduced." The recent Union capture of the salt works had driven the price up by 150 percent. Flour had shot up to $600 to $700 (Confederate) a barrel, buckwheat $60 a bushel, and gold had risen to 50 to one.[47] This, of course, was all good grist for Grant's mill. In his mind, he was able to calculate over time the cumulative effect of economic disintegration on the ability of Lee to fight. Every such report burned another hole in Lee's coat as far as he was concerned. Time was working for him, but it could work against him, for he was in a race, too. If the South's war-making ability was falling apart, the North's patience and will were also perishable things. It would be a race to see which would give out first.

On the 13th Sharpe reported his agent had had a very difficult time getting out of Richmond. "It would seem that these extraordinary regulations were made for the purpose of preventing information going out of the real condition of the city, which is daily becoming worse. Gold has risen to seventy for one. Flour, according to the grade, is sold at from $600 to $800 a barrel; beef, salt, and all other articles steadily advancing [in price]." Sharpe could have been reading Lee's mail, which was reporting the same thing. Two days earlier he had written the Secretary of War, "There is nothing within reach of the army to be impressed. The country has been swept clear. Our only reliance is upon the railroads. We have but two day's supplies."[48]

While Lee was placing such reliance on the railroads, Sharpe was emphasizing collection on them. His January 13 report bore the result. His agent on the Danville Railroad, an engineer, reported that transportation over the last two weeks was provided for 16,000 of Lee's men and that it was intended to convey Hoke's and Kershaw's Divisions and Early's brigades to Wilmington. Sharpe was careful to state the man based his calculations on the number of men that could be loaded in a car and the number of cars. He had not actually seen the troop movement. The man also reported that one-third of the Danville line's 45 locomotives were out of use and had to be replaced by engines from other lines. Whatever the Danville was transporting, it was not any significant number of troops. The engineer was more accurate when he reported that heavy rains had seriously damaged the Piedmont Railroad between Danville and Greensborough, and it would take 15 days to repair. Two days before, Confederate Secretary of War Seddon had written Lee to tell him that the line had been washed out and was unusable for 20 miles and could not be used for several days to a week.

More consistently reliable information was coming in from Samuel Ruth, the superintendent of the RF&P. Sharpe took care to refer to him as one "whose name and position are known to the commanding general," to emphasize the reliability of the reporting as well as supporting his cover. Ruth estimated also that it would take as much as 10–15 days to repair the Piedmont Railroad, supporting the Danville

Railroad's engineer. Ruth was also privy to an extremely revealing episode at a board of directors meeting of his railroad. The president of the line was the father of General Breckinridge's assistant adjutant general. He met his son at the meeting, and his first question to him was, "What is the news?" The son replied, "Damned bad. If Sherman cannot be stopped, there is an end to this business." It was just the sort of anecdotal intelligence that gives a sudden clarity to a situation, and would have delighted Grant as he contemplated the sense of desperation the story imparted. Sharpe ended his report by saying, "Our friends quite naturally send us word that the Union sentiment is largely on the gain."[49]

Sharpe's network in Richmond was supplying more than strictly military information. It was reporting Confederate economic ties with northern business interests. On the 13th Sharpe reported for the second time, and this time from a second source, that the Confederate railroad companies had "contracted for block tin, zinc, and other necessaries of like nature to be sent to them in some way through Norfolk; it is understood that the supplies are to come from a firm or firms in Philadelphia; that the negotiation is to be perfected by the exchange of cotton, which is to go down the Blackwater in small boats."

On the 18th, Sharpe also reported, "Our friends tell us that they know well that the principal men in the Government and at Richmond are employing agents to go North, via the Northern Neck, for the purpose of changing everything they have into gold."[50]

Confederate Counterintelligence Gets Lucky

Sharpe did not confine his duties to City Point. When necessary he was in the field with his scouts. On several occasions he met with his Richmond agents at their meeting places with his scouts in order to directly discuss their operations. On at least one other occasion, on January 18, he personally accompanied the scouts because they had been interfered with by Union troops in passing through the lines. His presence set that problem right. He personally resolved this issue because of the sensitive nature of the expedition. He wrote Meade:

> We believe that the enemy have a line of communication with the James River by substantially the same route as our own, of which we hope to give more complete information by the end of the week, in order that it may be broken up. Our scouts do not desire to interfere with it, as thereby their own business would be apparent.[51]

Sharpe was sensitive to the survival of his agents within Richmond and did everything he could to protect their covers. He noted on January 21 that one of his agents had been arrested on suspicion for using Union greenbacks. Sharpe noted that the agent had been released and would be back at work for him, but the arrest had shown once again the danger of supplying Union currency to support operations in Richmond. He requested Confederate bills.[52]

Sharpe went to Grant for help, who, in turn, wrote to the Secretary of War:

> Two or three times a week scouts are sent from here into Richmond. The only funds the provost-marshal has for defraying their expenses is U.S. currency. These funds naturally would attract suspicion, and have therefore to be converted for their use. If, therefore, you have any rebel currency, I would respectfully request that from $20,000 to $50,000 be sent to Col. George H. Sharpe, assistant provost-marshal-general, at City Point.[53]

On February 8 Grant directed that $10,000 in Confederate money be turned over to Sharpe. The currency issue, as sensitive as it was, was only part of Sharpe's concern for his network at that time. The day before he reported the currency problem, the Confederates had dealt the Van Lew and Ruth rings in Richmond and Leet's agents in Northern Virginia a hard blow. On a tip, they had intercepted a group of refugees fleeing the Richmond area. Under interrogation, the refugees revealed the names of those who had helped them. It was a considerable counterintelligence coup and netted Ruth, F. W. E. Lohmann, John Hancock, and James Duke and his three sons in Richmond, and John H. Timberlake and old Isaac Silver in Spotsylvania County. Ruth stood his ground, proclaiming his innocence, and employed every ounce of his social prestige to have the charges dropped. Timberlake was acquitted, but the rest languished in Confederate jails until Richmond finally fell. Tellingly, none of them betrayed Van Lew.[54]

Unsafe and Unfit—Double Agent Benjamin C. Pole

On the heels of this blow to his agent rings in Richmond, Sharpe would inadvertently help inflict another. Picking agents has always been a tricky business, and on this occasion Sharpe erred badly. There was a long trail of events that led to this. The Confederates had penetrated the U.S. Government and were able to receive a steady stream of sensitive information within 48 hours. That conduit alerted Davis and his cabinet that was a constant source of intelligence in Richmond for Grant's armies. Efforts to ferret out the source were unavailing.

The frustration was the subject of diplomatic communications with James W. Mason, the Confederate representative in Great Britain. Mason had been pestered by a 19-year-old British mechanic and inventor named Benjamin C. Pole (misspelled as Pool or Poole subsequently) to obtain a contract for the manufacture of torpedoes. Pole may have been young, but he was "unusually bright and plausible," was a good-looking blue-eyed blonde, and appeared to be trustworthy. The most important thing he was to sell was himself and his promises.

According to a later statement, Pole said he had worked for John Laird & Sons shipbuilders in Liverpool. They had built in 1862 the famous Confederate commerce raider, the *Alabama*, and had nearly completed two armored, turreted rams before Lincoln threatened war, forcing the British government as a matter of state to seize them in September 1863. An engineer who worked at Laird Brothers was then a prize to be turned by U.S. agents. Pole later claimed he had been solicited by American consular official Moore to turn over documents "of value to the Confederacy" that he apparently had in his possession. Instead, he gave them to a Confederate who destroyed them.[55]

It occurred to Mason that such a man of Confederate sympathies could be employed as a double agent to penetrate the Union spy ring. He offered to send Pole through the blockade, but in the end he simply sailed for New York to make his way south. Much of what happened subsequently is based on Pole's statements, which are not entirely reliable. Upon his arrival in New York, he wrote a long letter dated July 29 to Secretary of State Seward, giving an extensive review of "rebel privateers in European waters" from the perspective of an engineer who had worked for the Confederates. Pole gave the letter to the U.S. Marshal, who promptly sent it to Seward. Given that the Union merchant marine was being crippled by these commerce raiders, such a letter was bound to arouse Seward's interest.[56]

On August 6, the assistant secretary of state wrote to the U.S. vice-counsel in Liverpool, enclosing Pole's letter and asking to be acquainted with him. Thomas Dudley, the U.S. consul, responded on September 22 and bluntly stated, "Mr. Pole is quite unfit and unsafe to be trusted with any important business." He further wrote that Pole had worked for them to gather information but had caused more harm than good. He talked a good game about providing information on the building commerce raider *Pompero*, but when pressed could provide nothing. As to the content of Pole's letter, "the information it contains was known to Mr. Moore and myself before Pole left, and was probably obtained from us."[57]

One would think that would be the end of any interest Seward had in Pole. The young engineer, however, would write a letter to Seward almost two years later, in which he refers to meeting the Secretary at the Astor House in New York, where he "presented to you certain plans and which you approved of." At the same time he wrote a series of demands in which he again referred to the meeting with Seward and intimated that the Secretary had been paying him at the rate of an engineer. He would also later intimate that Seward had recommended him to Assistant Secretary of War Dana.[58]

A month later Pole made his way to Washington where he would claim he met Dana. The first step was to join a regiment that was at Petersburg. He enlisted with the 11th U.S. Infantry at its recruiting station across the Potomac in Alexandria. He claimed to be broke, having spent the last three weeks vainly trying to get a government clerkship.[59]

Now in Union blue, Pole appears next in the historical record in his regiment, part of V Corps, at Petersburg. On the last day of January, he sent Sharpe a remarkable letter. Claiming to have been the principle in the seizure of privateers being built in Liverpool and Glasgow, he stated, "I shall have certain plans equally useful and more reliable. That I should go through to the Rebels for the purpose of gaining information all respects…" Then he laid out his bona fides.

> These Plans are known to the Hon. Secretary of State W. H. Seward and he is willing for them to be carried into effect and recommends me to the Hon. Secretary of War. However the mode of action I only communicated to the Assistant Secretary of War Dana…
>
> I have testimonials as to being an Englishman and an engineer. And for the truth of the rest I would refer to the Hon. Assistant Secretary of War. However delay is always bad in such undertakings and I am ready to proceed at one and would first like to make you acquainted with the secret correspondence.[60]

One can only imagine Sharpe's reaction to Pole's letter. It certainly must have triggered an interview with Pole and a review of the "secret correspondence." Sharpe was a very good judge of character and a skilled interrogator. It is hardly likely that he would have taken Pole seriously had he not had proofs of support from the highest levels of the government. Yet none of these proofs have survived in the official records of the government. Nevertheless, Pole was able to convince Sharpe of his good faith. Sharpe decided to employ him in the scheme to gather information about the Confederate rams in the James River Flotilla. Special orders were cut, detailing him for "special service in the Department of the Provost Marshal General."[61]

In February, Judson Knight visited Van Lew to tell her, "I am directed to tell you that that there will be an Englishman sent through the lines, whose duty it will be to oblige and bring you information to send through." He would be picked up, to be brought into Richmond by one of Van Lew's Union loyalists, Lemuel Babcock, to be later assisted by another Unionist, William White, who also was an English immigrant. Van Lew was instantly suspicious. "My heart sank for here was another avenue of danger," she wrote and rightly so. She had been careful to ensure that he not be brought to meet her at her home. She never had meetings at her home. Instead she used the shop of an English immigrant and Unionist named Clark for such meetings.[62]

The night of the 23nd Pole was given a message in cipher for a lady to whom he would be guided. He was taken to a point where he could easily reach Lemuel Babcock's farm. He presented Babcock a letter that confirmed his having been sent by Sharpe. That night Babcock took Pole into Richmond where they checked into a hotel and spent the night.

The next morning Babcock left Pole in their hotel to hastily arrange a meeting with Van Lew at Clark's shop, where he left the enciphered message. While he was gone, Pole rushed to the Confederate provost marshal and betrayed both Babcock and White. They were promptly arrested. A Confederate detective demanded of White, "tell all you know or I'll blow your brains out." This Englishman was made of cooler stuff than Pole and replied, "Blow away." Babcock was equally defiant. Both White and he were thrown into Castle Thunder prison where they were found after the fall of Richmond only a few days before their scheduled execution.[63]

Pole was questioned by the brutal Deputy Provost Marshal T. W. Doswell and immediately told everything, including the fact that Sharpe had provided Pole with $1000 in new issue Confederate bills to give to Babcock. Doswell confronted Babcock with that information, forcing him to admit that he had given that sum to another man, who, when questioned, turned the money over. Babcock and White were brought before a Confederate commission. Pole turned state's witness and testified against them. As White would later relate, Pole testified that it was Colonel Sharpe who had identified White to him and told him he would transmit information through White. "That he was employed as a spy for the U.S. by Col. Sharp [sic] who told him if could find Mr. White, that he—White—could communicate with Col. Sharp [sic] in twenty four hours."

Babcock also related more of Pole's testimony:

> That he came from England to N. Y. from there to Washington DC. Desired to go south, where his sympathies were. That he conceived the plan of joining the U.S. army for the purpose of deserting to the rebel lines, and joined the 11th U.S. Infantry. That he was selected by Col. Sharp [sic] to perform some confidential service and a plan was arranged that he should desert to the rebel lines, and return with what information he could gather.
>
> That he was sent by Col. Sharpe [sic] to Mr. Babcock's house, near the rebel picket line, with whom a plan had been arranged to take him into Richmond, and deliver him up as a deserter to the rebels.[64]

Pole also added that while at Sharpe's headquarters he had seen "several large boxes filled with Confederate (new issue) money, which was being freely distributed for similar objects which he had in view."[65]

His perfidy did Pole little good. According to Van Lew, "He offered to act in any way the Rebel Govt. had use, he had plans for torpedoes and gun boats, the highest commendation of self—but alas! For him, the days for Torpedoes and gun boats had well nigh passed the winter of 1865… His advent was late in the day for his own glory. His coming upon our sinking ship was suspicious…"

Unlike Sharpe, the Confederates did not trust him. They actually believed his story up to the point of his sympathies and charged him with "attempting to palm himself off as a Yankee deserter, in order to obtain his parole, give information of our situation, and communicate the same to the enemy." He was immediately consigned to Castle Thunder, though not in the solitary confinement of the men he had betrayed.[66]

Van Lew first heard of the arrests and of Pole's betrayal in the *Richmond Dispatch* of February 27. She would have ensured that Sharpe had a copy by the next day. She wrote in her diary that when Babcock had left the hotel on the morning of the 24th, Pole was afraid he had gone to betray him. In a panic, he had betrayed Babcock and White. She wrote in her diary:

> His regrets now were deep and vain that he had not apparently entered into the service of the U.S. Govt., and then betrayed the prisoners he was sent to. "There are eight or ten of them,"

he would say, "Oh, I could so easily have given them all up. What a fool I was." A paper Pole has written addressed to the Confederate Govt., on its way, was shown to me. I commenced in this manner: "When a man gives up principal, family, friends, country, everything for a cause you may know this, he is in earnest this one."[67]

Clearly, Benjamin Pole was no James Bond. Consul Dudley's appraisal of Pole had been spot on if not downright prophetic. He had indeed been "quite unfit and unsafe to be trusted with any important business" and had indeed done more harm than good. Eccentric and flighty, Pole was entirely out of his depth. He consistently made promises he could not fulfill. If Van Lew was correct in stating that he had betrayed Babcock before Babcock could betray him, it shows massive poor judgment coupled with an impulse to panic. He acted before he had had his meeting with Van Lew, who would have been the prize of prizes. Once caught, he was filled with remorse that he had not honestly worked for the U.S. Government in the first place. It was a remorse based on getting caught, not on his failure of judgment. This would not be the end, however, in Sharpe's dealing with Pole.

Despite this setback, Sharpe's network in Richmond was resilient enough to recover and continue to provide vital information. Key to this success was the critical role of Judson Knight, not only in establishing the connection with Van Lew but in maintaining and improving it. On a number of occasions Knight met with Van Lew to coordinate operations.

> Knight's successes were well thought of enough to award him for special services with cash grants of $300 in December 1864, $520 in January 1965, and $393.58 in February, a total of $1,213 or a little less than the yearly pay of a first lieutenant ($1,386). His monthly pay was already equivalent to a first lieutenant ($1,480). This would all be small change. The April 1865 payroll shows him receiving an astounding $6,000! That was more than the pay of a major general ($5,489). Only Grant as the Army's only lieutenant general, made more ($9,776). In June he authorized another payment of $2,500 for Knight. The BMI payrolls identify only two other men to receive cash grants. They were Ebenezer Halleck and Alexander Myers (one of Van Lew's Richmond couriers), both of whom were awarded $500.[68]

Nothing spoke louder of Grant's appreciation for the value of the intelligence derived from the Van Lew ring and others than cold, hard cash.

Patrick to the Rescue Again

Despite his fulsome letter of congratulations to Sharpe on his promotion, Meade may still have harbored resentment over the re-subordination of the provost marshal to include Sharpe to Grant's headquarters. On February 12 Babcock went on 20 days' leave which Sharpe had, out of courtesy, consulted Meade about. Oliver had been working with Babcock and would be able to fill in for him. The next day, according to Patrick, Meade sent Sharpe "an insolent letter" over the leave, which, according to Patrick, "comes like a thunderbolt." Patrick added, "He [Sharpe] will pay him off." Meade's irascibility continued to make him enemies. Patrick remained the only one who could coax a degree of rational dialogue from Meade. On March 6 he was able to get Meade to agree to the appointment of Brig. Gen. George N. Macy as provost marshal general of the Army of the Potomac. It had only taken from July 4, 1864 to March 6, 1865 for Meade to accept Grant's rearrangement of provost and intelligence functions. Grant was happy that the issue had finally been resolved without his having to confront Meade when he needed to maintain a close working relationship with his primary army commander.[69]

Although Patrick would consistently defend Sharpe, he felt no hesitation in putting his free-wheeling subordinate in his place, even when the chain of command between the two had become tenuous. On the night of March 15, he wrote, "I have had to talk to … Sharpe very unpleasantly, for meddling in matters that do not belong at all to him." Just what those matters were, Patrick did not say.[70] Given that Sharpe was functioning as the equivalent of the modern DIA as well as executing many of the functions of the CIA and FBI, in addition to being a political agent for Grant, it is not surprising that he would upset Patrick's strict sense of order.

Southern Hemorrhage

In February and March the rate of desertion had opened even wider another wound that the Army of Northern Virginia could not afford to suffer. Lieutenant Colonel Lyman was impressed enough to write home that in February—what can only be Sharpe's figures—almost 900 men had deserted to the Army of the Potomac and a proportional number from the Army of the James. On one day alone 134 came over with four commissioned officers, their NCOs, and arms. The startling fact is that they were Lee's formidable veterans.

> The remarkable point, also, is that these are *old* men—nearly all of them—and not the raw conscripts… Of course many more desert to the rear than to the enemy; so that I doubt not that Lee's losses from this cause during February were something between a large brigade and a small division. General Meade, after reviewing Lee's position and prospects, said: "I do not see what he is to do!"[71]

The rate of desertion among North Carolina troops, whose homes were just south of Richmond across the state line, was so acute that Lee cancelled all furloughs and leaves for North Carolina troops on February 18. The proximity to home, the strong Union sentiments in the western part of the state, and the fact that North Carolina had seceded with little enthusiasm all came together. On the 28th he reported to the Secretary of War that 1,094 men had deserted between the 15th and 25th of the month, with almost half coming mostly from the North Carolina brigades of Early's Division in Gordon's II Corps and Heth's and Wilcox's divisions of Hill's III Corps. That was a hemorrhage of almost 110 men a day. Lee was especially alarmed that the North Carolinians were veterans "who have fought as gallantly as any soldiers in the army." The receiving officer for this stream of deserters who chose to give themselves up, of course, was Provost Marshal General Patrick, who noted on February 24 that "The Rebs. Are getting very much depressed and the last 24 hours, 192 have come into my hands as deserters—Good men too." Wilmington had just fallen, and the Union troops had enthusiastically received the report, which they undoubtedly shared across the picket lines. Their exultation was salt in the wounds to the enemy, who had already received the news and may have done much to spur desertions. On March 8 Lee submitted another report for the 10-day period ending on that day that reported 779 desertions, again mostly from the divisions with North Carolina brigades.

Lee supposed that most of the men had gone to their homes, but an alarming number had gone over to the enemy. Many had left in bands with their weapons and ammunition. Adding to this loss, he had been forced to send a large detachment from Heth's Corps to North Carolina to apprehend them and a brigade to guard the ferries of the Roanoke River with little result.[72] That so many left with their arms and ammunition was an indication that the Union program that paid deserters for their weapons was having an effect.

Lee was forced to remind the army that the ultimate sanction "for advising or persuading a soldier to desert is death," and that even those engaging in such advice in jest would find it difficult to prove at court martial. He ordered that this order and "the 23rd Article of War will be forthwith read to every company in the army once a day for three days, and to every regiment at dress parade once a week for a month; and at such other times … as commanding officers may deem proper."[73]

Indicative of the withering away of morale was an incredible story Babcock reported after the penultimate military operation of the siege, initiated by Grant's attempt to extend the front to the Boydton Plank Road and Hatcher's Run with his II and V Corps on February 5. Lee struck back that afternoon with Heth's Division of III Corps. The battle whipped back and forth for two days as part of Gordon's II Corps joined he fight. It ended with the Union giving up attempts to cut the Boydton Plank Road but now firmly entrenched on Hatcher's Run. On the 9th Babcock interrogated "two very intelligent" deserters:

> [They were] from the 42nd and 26th Mississippi, Davis' Brigade, Heth's Division. One of them left camp, the other the picket line… On Sunday last General Lee addressed the three divisions of Gordon, Mahone, and Heth, which were drawn up in their lines of battle in front of the Second Army Corps. Informants state that the orders to charge were repeatedly refused, and that "General Lee wept like a child." Heth's Division afterwards made the charges, with two lines of two brigades each.[74]

The only division of the corps to attack that day was Heth's, just as the deserter described. A newspaper report, clearly based in part on this intelligence reporting, which can only have been provided by the BMI, stated that Lee, "notwithstanding his personal efforts to urge the men, they could not be induced to fight with anything like the spirit they formerly did. This fact was noticed by many of our own officers, who saw the rebel officers endeavor in vain to urge the men forward at different points." Whether the story of Lee's despair is true or not, one can only wonder whether, as Grant read it, did he think back on Cold Harbor when his own troops refused the order to attack.[75]

The South was not only hemorrhaging information from deserters such as this but from the newspapers Sharpe was collecting from his agents and from the picket line exchanges, which were brought to headquarters "as regularly as if they had been subscribed to," according to Grant's aide, Adam Badeau. Even more damaging was the increasing effectiveness of Sharpe's scouts, a field of contest in which the Confederates were worthy opponents.[76]

Confederate Lt. Gen. John B. Gordon in early February sent out his own "superb scout, young George of Virginia," on a mission to get as close as he could to Grant's headquarters and waylay someone carrying dispatches. Although wearing a Union pale blue overcoat, he always wore his gray uniform underneath to avoid the death penalty for impersonating the enemy if captured. He crept close to the headquarters when he saw two men in Confederate uniform passing by. He immediately made himself known, only to be surprised when they drew their pistols on him. He realized instantly they were Sheridan's "Jesse Scouts," so notorious had his scouts become in the Confederacy. He may have been mistaken since Sheridan did not join Grant until the middle of the next month, and Sharpe's scouts never hesitated to wear Confederate uniforms. The two marched him to the headquarters, where he was questioned by Grant himself. His gray uniform saved his life as he coolly maintained his cover story.

> His opportunity for escape came late one night, when he found a new recruit on guard at his prison door. This newly enlisted soldier was a foreigner, and had very little knowledge of the English language; but he knew what a twenty-dollar gold piece was. The Confederacy did not have much gold, but our scouts were kept supplied with it. George pulled out of his lining of his jacket the gold piece, placed it in the foreigner's hand, turned the fellow's back to the door, and walked quickly out of the guard house. George would not have dared to attempt such a programme with an American on guard.[77]

Apparently "George of Virginia" was not the only prisoner scout to escape. Patrick had already investigated the escape of two Rebel scouts who had cut through the floor of the Guard House in middle December. Even in captivity, scouts, both Union and Confederate, showed the most ingenuity and determination to escape which should not be surprising given the self-reliant and bold nature of the men who volunteered for such duty.[78]

The favorable treatment given to Southern deserters was actually prompting an increase in Union desertions. Grant had issued Special Orders No. 82 in August of the preceding year, which effectively updated the policy on deserters Sharpe had pioneered the year before, no doubt urged by Sharpe. It offered Southern deserters, in exchange for an oath of loyalty to the Union, subsistence and transportation back to their homes if now under Northern control. If their homes were still in the areas controlled by the Confederacy, they would be offered free transportation anywhere in the North. The order had been widely circulated across the picket lines to the enemy and was obviously helping to gnaw away at Southern resolve. Many Northern soldiers also found it of interest, and to Grant's alarm, an alarming number were masquerading as Rebel deserters, claiming their homes were in Confederate-occupied territory in order to win free transportation home. In response, Patrick dispatched McEntee to Norfolk, the collecting point for Southern deserters. His knowledge of the Army of Northern Virginia would allow him to ferret out the fake Rebels.

> You will examine all deserters from the enemy, and all refugees, and telegraph a summary of as much of their information as may seem to be immediately important, transmitting the other by correspondence. In so doing, you will be careful to see that no deserters from the United States forces pass through your hands purporting to be deserters from the enemy. Whenever you are convinced that such a case is brought before you, you will make a detailed report of the statement of the person thus falsely representing himself, and you will, in every case, proceed with the investigation as far as you possibly can in order to determine the status and regiment of the deserter. Every such person, with statement, will be forwarded to this headquarters.[79]

As Sherman burned his way through the interior of South Carolina with avenging zeal, he was out of communications with Grant, who worried that his brilliant subordinate might bite off more than he could chew. Sharpe, therefore, also gave McEntee the mission of tracking the progress of Sherman up through the Carolinas, for which Norfolk was "a proper base from which to send scouts southward," better suited than City Point. Southern newspapers, although a steady source of information on Sherman's scorching progress, were not enough to calm Grant's apprehensions, and Sharpe directed McEntee to select and direct a band of scouts to penetrate into the Carolinas to find more reliable information.[80]

Besides McEntee at Norfolk, three more officers were detailed to work for Sharpe as "examining officers" (interrogators) at subsidiary locations, although their duties were listed as provost marshal. Captain Alexander J. Dallas (12th U.S. Inf.) was sent to Washington to support Leet's intelligence operations. Captains J. S. Conrad (2nd U.S. Inf.) and Edson M. Misner (80th NY Vol. Inf.) were sent to Fortress Monroe. These are the only other officers known to work for Sharpe.[81]

Black Confederates

Any accretion of strength to Lee was a priority concern for Sharpe, and in the winter he was becoming particularly concerned about a most unusual and potentially serious reinforcement of Confederate manpower. He was reflecting Grant's own considerable apprehensions. As a great commander, Grant understood that wars not only have a rhythm to them but a culminating point, in which the point of greatest return is reached, beyond which everything is waste leading to exhaustion. He would later write, "Anything that could have prolonged the war beyond the time that it did finally close, would have probably exhausted the North to such an extent that they might have abandoned the contest and agreed to a separation."[82] That "anything" could have been the appearance of tens of thousands of freed slaves in Confederate uniform, a specter that haunted Sharpe through March.

Early in 1863 Confederate agents in Europe were discussing countering Lincoln's Emancipation Proclamation by taking blacks into the Confederate forces and granting them freedom. A rumor at the time to the effect that the South would free 500,000 slaves to serve in the army swept through London. Although the idea was circulating in influential Southern circles, no hint became public at home. In January 1864, the South's Stonewall of the West, Maj. Gen. Patrick Cleburne, was the first prominent Southern figure to openly call for the incorporation of black men into the Confederate armed forces, with the explicit granting of freedom as a prerequisite. As an Irish immigrant, he saw this country with different eyes and was open to possibilities that escaped those who had grown up in the system of slavery. He had presented this to the other senior officers in his corps in the Army of Tennessee in January 1864. Most had supported it; he read his manifesto to the assembled general officers of the army where it met with some approval as well. One hostile officer sent a copy to Jefferson Davis, who ordered the manifesto suppressed and forbade all further discussion.[83]

By November, the manpower crisis had become so severe that Davis himself put Cleburne's idea forward to the Confederate Congress. Sharpe, who perused every newspaper page printed in Richmond, would have been aware of Davis's move from the moment he proposed legislation. Luckily for the Union, the matter moved slowly through the legislative branch, but that did not lessen Sharpe's concern. He reported every mention of the subject obtained from his agents. "Our agent says he was present at the great meeting on the evening of the 6th instant [February 6th], and that in his speech, Jeff. Davis made use of an expression that every negro would be armed, which has been suppressed in the published accounts." Grant forwarded the message immediately to Washington.[84] Three days later there was another enthusiastic public meeting, this time at Richmond's First African Baptist Church of all places, in which whites crowded in to hear speakers on both sides of the issue. Secretary of State Judah Benjamin told the crowd that there were 680,000 black men capable of bearing arms. "Let us say to every negro who wants to go into the ranks, go and fight, and you are free… Fight for your masters and you shall have your freedom." He was met with cheers and cries of support. He boasted that the Army of Northern Virginia could be reinforced with enough black recruits to resume the offensive in twenty days. The opinion of the slaves does not appear to have been sought.[85]

Both Grant and Lee would have been annoyed at a civilian's blithe prediction of how long it would take to transform recruits into reliable soldiers, but both took the issue with great seriousness. Lee fully supported the idea of black soldiers but chafed that each day's delay put off the desperately needed reinforcement of his wasting army. Grant looked at it from the opposite perspective. He saw that if Lee could hold on for a few months longer, then black reinforcement would begin to bring his enemy back to life. He wired Major General E. R. S. Canby in the Western theater on February 23 a warning: "It is also important to get all the negro men we can before the enemy put them in their ranks."[86]

The issue was so uppermost in Sharpe's mind that the next day he commented on it in a letter to his Uncle Jansen.

> Now take the map and look at Gordonville, Richmond, Danville & Lynchburgh [sic] & see what a stretch of country they cover. Negro troops in intrenchments [sic] around each of these places, with a few white troops to hold them up to their work, will give Lee really the whole of his white forces for movable column—& all that is very formidable.[87]

As anxious as Lee for the arrival of black troops were the rank and file of Lee's army. Major General Gordon reported to Lee the reaction of his own II Corps troops to the measure deadlocked in Congress:

> I have the honor to report that the officers and men of this corps are decidedly in favor of the voluntary enlistment of the negroes as soldiers. But few have been found to oppose it. The aversion to the measure has in no instance been found strong. The opposition to it is now confined to a very few, and I am satisfied will soon cease to exist in any regiment of the corps. I respectfully suggest that these reports be immediately forwarded to the authorities at Richmond.[88]

On the 26th he was writing to a friend, sensing that the South had passed the point of no return.

> We have many desertions—caused I think by the despondency in our ranks. It is a terrible blow— the defeat of the negro bill in congress—troops all in favor of it—would have greatly encouraged the army—they are much disappointed in its defeat. What mean the national legislators? We shall be compelled to have them or be defeated—with them as volunteers & fighting for their freedom we shall be successful—But I presume we can hope for any assistance now from this class of our population—If authority were granted to raise 200,000 of them it would greatly encourage the men & do so much stop desertions. I can find excellent officers to take command.[89]

On March 13 the Confederate Congress finally passed a watered-down measure that would lead to the incorporation of up to 300,000 black troops into the Southern armies. Three days later Sharpe presented Grant with a remarkable analysis of the potential of black troops to not only extend the war but to put offensive power back into the Army of Northern Virginia. He stated that the South could eventually put 200,000 black men into the field and that, if 50,000 of them were to reinforce Lee at Richmond-Petersburg, they could assume the defensive role while Lee's white troops could be reserved for offensive action as a mobile striking force. Sharpe saw it as imperative to take measures now that would forestall and cripple the Confederate effort to bring blacks into Confederate ranks "before, by habit, discipline and experience with arms, they shall have grown to that aptitude of a soldier which will bring them to obey orders under any circumstances." He recommended a covert effort to sow discord and encourage desertion by sending into Richmond black Union soldiers in disguise. He thought this a workable plan unlikely to be betrayed, because "Negroes are an eminently secret people; they have a system of understanding amounting almost to a free masonry among them; they will trust each other when they will not trust white men."[90] (See Appendix L—Sharpe's Report on the Raising of Negro Troops for the Confederacy.)

The matter continued to loom large in the minds of Grant and Sharpe as would anything that would promise to prolong the war past the endurance of Northern public support. They could not know that the Confederacy had less than a month to live after the measure passed the Confederate Congress. Sharpe continued to give priority to reporting on this subject. Deserters on March 15 insisted that there were five regiments of black troops in training near Petersburg and that black troops had been put into the line that week. Sharpe reported on March 22 that "our friends" informed him that three companies of black troops were drilling in Richmond and were certain that no more were in training. The imminent collapse of the Confederacy was to hide the actual extent of such preparations in the ensuing chaos.[91]

Inaugural Interlude

With the weather still keeping active operations in abeyance, Sharpe found the opportunity to attend the inauguration of President Lincoln and Vice-President Andrew Johnson in Washington on March 4. It was a plum opportunity for Sharpe, who relished being in the center of great events.

His recent promotion gave him a pass for the swearing in of Johnson in the Senate chambers. It was not an edifying experience. Johnson was seriously drunk. He had come to Washington the evening before with typhoid fever and had drunk heavily that night at a party. The morning of the inauguration, he drank three straight shots of whiskey before proceeding to the chamber. Sharpe observed:

> After [outgoing Vice-President] Hamlin delivered a brief and stately valedictory, Johnson rose unsteadily to harangue the distinguished crowd about his humble origins and his triumph over the rebel aristocracy. In the shocked and silent audience, President Abraham Lincoln showed an expression of "unutterable sorrow," while Senator Charles Sumner covered his face with his hands. Former Vice President Hamlin tugged vainly at Johnson's coattails, trying to cut short his remarks. After Johnson finally quieted, took the oath of office, and kissed the Bible, he tried to swear in the new senators, but became so confused that he had to turn the job over to a Senate clerk.[92]

Sharpe's comment was biting. "I have witnessed many public ceremonies here & abroad—but have never been present at such an official disgrace before." Sharpe undoubtedly shared the feelings of Michigan Republican Senator Zachariah Chandler, who wrote home to his wife, "I was never so mortified in my life, had I been able to find a hole I would have dropped through it out of sight." The appalling situation even allowed Sharpe a backhanded compliment for his most hated newspaper when he wrote, "The Herald account was under drawn."

Stepping outside the Capitol to see Lincoln sworn in was a refreshing relief. "The presidential inauguration outside was a contrast—and in the simple dignity and earnestness of Mr. Lincoln went far to relieve the previous vice-presidential fiasco."[93]

CHAPTER FOURTEEN

The End

March–June 1865

Fort Stedman: The Last Offensive

In the first week of March the situation had become so dire that Lee held a conference of his corps commanders on the 4th. The full extent of the army's miseries and debilitation was grimly apparent. But Lee injected a note of humor at the end when he said, "By the way, I received a verbal message from General Grant to-day," as Lt. Gen. John B. Gordon remembered:

> He explained that General Grant had sent, under flag of truce, a request to cease firing long enough for him to bury his dead between the picket-lines. The officer who bore the flag of truce asked to be conducted to army headquarters, as he had a message to deliver to General Lee in person. Arriving at headquarters, he received General Lee's courteous salutations, and, having explained the nature of his mission, said: "General, as I left General Grant's tent this morning he gave me these instructions: 'Give General Lee my personal compliments, and say to him that I keep in such close touch with him that I know what he eats for breakfast every morning.'" … "I told the officer to tell General Grant that I thought there must be some mistake about the latter part of his message; for unless he [General Grant] had fallen from grace since I saw him last, he would not permit me to eat such a breakfast as mine without dividing his with me … I also requested the officer to present my compliments to General Grant, and say to him that I knew perhaps as much about his dinners as he knew about my breakfasts."

Gordon went on to explain by this anecdote that "This, of course, meant that each of the commanders, through scouts and spies, and through such statements as they could extract from prisoners or deserters, kept fairly well posted as to what was transpiring in the opponent's camp." The record is clear that however much Lee knew about Grant, Grant knew far more about Lee due to Sharpe's highly efficient operation. That was shown by the constant initiative Grant was able to employ against Lee in the pendulum battles from August to October of the previous year.[1]

Sharpe's efforts had struck Lee's sharpest sword from his hand—the ability to surprise. No great captain had employed that element of the art of war more successfully than Lee. Grant had reason to appreciate that quality as Lee had slipped away from him repeatedly in the Overland Campaign. But now Lee was fixed, and Grant could write confidently to Halleck, "The great number of deserters and refugees coming in daily enables us to learn if any considerable force starts off almost … as soon as it starts." There would be no repeats of Early's sudden appearance in the Valley or at the gates of Washington because Lee "could not send off any large body without my knowing it."

Yet, however much Grant knew, Sharpe would not be able to detect even the vaguest hint of the offensive operation that was the fruit of Lee's conference with his commanders. At that council, General Gordon had succinctly laid out the options remaining to the Confederates: (1) make the best terms possible; (2) abandon Richmond and unite with Gen. Joseph Johnston's army in North Carolina; and (3) "Lastly, we must fight, and without delay."

Lee fully agreed with Gordon but had been loath to exceed the traditionally accepted limits of his authority to recommend such courses of action embodied in the first two suggestions. But the state of extremity of the army finally pushed him to go to Richmond and lay these options before Davis and the Confederate Congress. He found that Davis and the Congress were living in a fantasy world that would not countenance such drastic measures and still held out hope for what could only be a miracle. Only the third of Gordon's recommendations remained. Lee instructed Gordon to prepare a plan for an assault that would shatter the Union front south of the Appomattox.

Lee knew time was running out. He was receiving reports at this time of Sheridan's approach from Winchester. That news quickly leaked to Sharpe's network. Manning reported to Sharpe on March 15 that the Union officer in charge of newspaper exchanges had been told "confidentially" by his Confederate counterpart that Sheridan had crossed the James on pontoons at Elk Island on the 12th or 13th. Deserters were telling similar stories.[2]

For next 18 days, Gordon put his plan together and evidently kept his own counsel. On the 22nd he briefed Lee who brought the entire body of his judgment and experience to bear as he examined the plan in a series of probing and often sharp questions. The next night he approved the plan. Gordon would have barely 30 hours to organize one-third of the Army of Northern Virginia for its do or die attack on its old enemy, the Army of the Potomac, in the lines of Petersburg. In that time, not a word leaked out for Sharpe's agents and scouts to pick up. The extremely short time between the approval of the plan and the beginning of the attack in the predawn hours of the 25th was the best operational security measure the Army of Northern Virginia could summon at this late date.

As speedy as Sharpe's intelligence cycle had become, Gordon had got inside it. Sharpe's report of March 24 stated that the most important news from Richmond was that of the construction by the Confederates of a tunnel under Fort Harrison opposite the Army of the James. There was also a report that the Confederates planned to evacuate in 10 days but nothing overt to indicate an attack. An attack could have been inferred as a necessary first move to facilitate an evacuation, but reports of the imminent evacuation of Richmond had been coming in since the middle of 1864 and were discounted. No hint of an attack came from deserters either. There simply had not been time for them to slip through the lines, be forwarded to Babcock, and interrogated, the last being a lengthy process in itself. Most of Gordon's Corps had been pulled from the trenches at the last minute to mass for the attack. The thinly held trenches did not leak any deserters in time to be of any warning.[3]

In February there had been reports from Sharpe's ring in Richmond that a major attack such as Gordon was now planning was in the offing, but nothing had happened. Samuel Ruth would claim after the war in seeking compensation for his services that he warned of the attack but could not tell when it would take place, "but understood that it would be as soon as the ground was dry enough to move artillery." Given the 30-hour window between approval of the plan and its execution, it is certain that Ruth was mistaken if his timeline was long enough to wait for the dryer conditions. He probably was referring to the February rumors of an attack.[4]

The day of the attack on Fort Stedman, Babcock submitted a report to Meade stating that Gordon's entire corps was south of the Appomattox. He identified 60 regiments in the corps with an average strength of 200 men, totaling 12,000. The Army of Northern Virginia returns for February 28, the nearest in time, showed Gordon with 64 regiments; Babcock had been off by only 7 percent.[5]

Before dawn on the 25th Gordon attacked. His men overran a number of batteries and Fort Stedman, but a determined counterattack drove them back with great loss. The pursuing Union forces seized the entrenched Confederate picket line. It was the last offensive action of the Army of Northern Virginia. President Lincoln had been visiting Grant at the time and did not even notice the attack, probably because he was still asleep before it ended. Later Grant and he rode past the thousand Confederate prisoners, one of whom recalled them riding by, "seemingly not the least concerned and as if nothing had happened." He and his fellow prisoners took note of this self-confidence and "with one accord agreed that our cause was lost."[6]

Lee drew the obvious conclusions. The BMI would now be picking up evidence of the actions he would be taking to prepare to save his army. The next day, March 27, Sharpe reported, "Our men, in making their way to the Chickahominy last night ran into a party of the enemy's scouts, with whom they had a little fight, one of our people was shot which caused the return of the men, who went out again at daybreak this morning. They have just returned, having met an agent who left Richmond yesterday."

The agent laid out the information collected from Sharpe's network that painted a picture of imminent evacuation.

> Our friends there send us word that large quantities of machinery are being sent from Richmond nearly every day, that some days as many as twenty car-loads of it go out, and there have been days when more than this quantity has been taken, & that it all goes to Danville and Salisbury.

> Numbers of men are being employed to work on pontoon boats; and these are finished with dispatch, and then sent away by the Danville road. Our friends are informed that the enemy is busily engaged in fortifying at Staunton, Danville, and on the Roanoke River—at what point is not stated.
>
> The information is repeated that all the sick in hospitals whom the surgeons report as not likely to be convalescent in fifteen days are ordered to Danville and Farmville. The information this time comes from a source different from that from which it was heretofore obtained.

Sharpe also reported that wealthy men were buying up slaves and selling them to Confederate enrolling officers.[7]

The end was coming in Richmond as desperation seized the Confederate Government. Every horse in the city was confiscated to shore up Lee's wasting army, but even here Van Lew did her best to thwart it. Warned by a War Department clerk that her last remaining horse was to be seized, she hid it in the smoke house. Warned again that this ruse had been discovered, she led the horse upstairs to her library where its hooves were muffled by the straw strewn across the floor. Van Lew wrote that he was "a good, loyal horse," which "accepted his position and behaved as though he thoroughly understood matters, never stamping loud enough to be heard nor neighing." The end was not far off.[8]

On the 28th Babcock's interrogations of deserters revealed that Lee was concentrating south of the Appomattox, leaving "only Kershaw's and Mahone's divisions [Longstreet's Corps] north of the James between the two rivers." The next day, on the 29th, Oliver reported that BMI's Richmond agents said that "Jefferson Davis has his things all packed up and was ready to leave yesterday at 9 o'clock." On the 31st the agent reported, "On Tuesday, General Lee and President Davis were together, the latter accompanying General Lee to the cars when he left." A hundred pontoons had been laid over the Appomattox River at Appomattox Station and the Tredegar Works had been completely shut down, with some of the remaining workers sent to Texas. The real gem and the one that explained all the information on evacuation, though, was the statement, "Our friends say that it is understood in official circles, that the forces of Lee and Johnston are to be joined."[9]

It was clear to Grant that Lee had shot his bolt at Fort Stedman. Lee had no other option but to escape Grant's grip at Petersburg and unite with Johnston, who had just evacuated Raleigh, North Carolina. Grant called his senior commanders including Sherman to plan the coup de grâce against Lee. When Sherman departed on March 28, Sharpe accompanied him by ship as far as Fort Monroe to brief him on the intelligence situation.[10]

Sheridan began the ball by crushing the Confederate cavalry at Five Forks on April 1. When Grant received the news, he scribbled out an order at 9:00 p.m. and then commented matter of factly, "I have ordered a general assault along the lines," by II, IX, VI, and XXIV Corps to commence in the early hours of the next day.

Earlier on the 1st, Oliver informed Sharpe that Knight had not yet returned from his latest foray into Richmond to work with Van Lew. An intriguing article would appear in the *Kansas City Daily Gazette* 24 years later. It was a brief story about Knight, who was then a watchman in the Post Office Department in Washington. "He was in Richmond as s spy one week before the Confederate capital fell; and upon information obtained by him, the movements of the army in these last successful days of fire were largely directed by the commanding general."[11] There is no indication in the article of what "the information obtained by him" was. The story apparently originated with him; his veracity was apparent in the numerous articles he wrote (1890–94) for the *National Tribune*. Fact-checking discovered very few errors in what he had to say. On a number of occasions, he described incidents with Grant that were substantiated by other sources. What, then, could have been this information? Whatever it was, it must have been of enormous value to Grant—how else to explain the princely $6,000 bonus paid to Sharpe by Grant shortly after the surrender?

In the confusion of the fighting on the 2nd, Lieutenant General A. P. Hill was killed trying to join his men. The relentless Union assaults were cracking the defense in place after place. By early morning Lee realized that any further attempt to defend Petersburg was hopeless. He notified the War Department that he was evacuating his army the next morning. A copy of the telegram was delivered to Davis in church. He left immediately, met with his cabinet one last time, and departed by train for Danville in the middle of the afternoon.

Here possibly is the circumstance that earned Knight his enormous bonus. Van Lew's sources in the War Department could have notified her of Lee's telegram. If she passed that to Knight and he left immediately he could have been back to City Point by that evening. Grant would have then been informed of Lee's decision to evacuate the next morning. This is all speculation, but it does explain Grant's open-handed reward to Sharpe.

When the word spread of the army's evacuation, the Confederate capital descended into chaos as the government fled. The burning of government property to keep it from falling into enemy hands spread fires to destroy the business district.

Elizabeth Van Lew saw the collapse of the Confederate Government as fire and chaos swept through Richmond after Lee abandoned its defenses. She had had a large American flag, 18 feet by 9, smuggled into the city, and now she and her servants climbed to the roof to lay it flat on the roof. It was the first Stars and Stripes to be raised in Richmond in four years, but the flag enraged her desperate neighbors.

> Richmonders glared, and a howling mob gathered. God damn the old devil; burn her place down! Men shoved toward her house, trampled the garden, and Crazy Bet stepped forth to confront them. "I know you, and you…" Her thin face contorted, she screamed their names and pointed them out. "General Grant will be in town in an hour. You do one thing to my home, and all of yours will be burned down before noon!"[12]

The mob cowered and broke up, and as she predicted Grant's troops began flooding into the city with the Stars and Stripes in plain view from the Van Lew mansion on

Church Hill, across from the church in which Patrick Henry had proclaimed, "Give me liberty or give me death!" Grant had sent a special detachment under Colonel Parker, his military secretary, straight to her house to ensure her protection but did not find her at home. They found her in the Confederate Capitol's archives, hoping to find useful documents in the debris and ashes left behind when the government fled. Grant called on her personally after the surrender to offer his thanks, an event she would always consider the highpoint of her life. While Van Lew was searching the debris in the Capitol, the news of the fall of Richmond reached the Confederate deserters confined in the Bull Pen, and they gave a great cheer. Seven hundred of the deserters volunteered to give the oath of loyalty.[13]

At this time Lincoln visited Grant with his young son, Tad. He watched the army in motion as it began its pursuit of Lee. When the troops recognized him, they cheered wildly. Lincoln finally reached Grant at the Wallace House. Grant extended his hand as the President said, "Do you know, general, I had a sort of sneaking idea that you intended to do something like this all along." While they talked on the porch, Tad was fidgeting. He had been so indulged that he had little self-discipline. Sharpe brought up a pouch and brought out some sandwiches and said, "You must be hungry." To the amusement of the watching officers, Tad replied, "Yes, I am, that's what's the matter with me."[14]

That same day Grant wrote to Sheridan to ask, "Do you hear of any movement on the part of Johnston? I have heard from a variety of sources that he had been ordered up to unite with Lee." Enough reports from Richmond in the last two weeks indicated that the union of Lee's and Johnston's armies was uppermost in Grant's mind. It was clearly a collection priority.[15]

With the armies now in motion, official BMI reporting disappears as it had so often during the Overland Campaign. The only surviving report of the BMI is a hurriedly scribbled note by Sharpe of the 6th, in which he reports the accounts of refugees coming into their lines from Danville. The most important news was that Jefferson Davis and his cabinet had stopped there and that Sherman was running Johnston to ground. This would be Sharpe's last known report of the war.[16]

As the Confederates were evacuating Richmond, Castle Thunder's commandant, Captain Callahan, put his prisoners, including Lemuel Babcock and probably the man who betrayed him, Benjamin Pole, on the road, presumably to follow the army and with the order to his men to shoot anyone who fell out. Nevertheless, Babcock escaped. Pole was captured 2 miles outside the city and apprehended on April 3. Perhaps Babcock pointed him out as a spy to Union troops.[17]

If the order-of-battle efforts were interrupted, the scouts were even more active. The chaos of the retreat was their element. In his message to Sheridan, Grant stated, "If you can get scouts through to Burkeville to ascertain what is there I wish you would do it."[18] On April 6 Gordon's scout, "George of Virginia," brought the general two prisoners he had taken that night counting the files of the Confederate troops in retreat. He insisted they were Yankee spies. Gordon questioned them closely but could find no fault with their story. They claimed to be from Fitz Lee's command and had a comprehensive knowledge of its organization and officers, but ordered them brought under guard. As soon as the light of a log fire along the road fell upon their faces, George exclaimed that they were the two men who had captured him outside Grant's headquarters. They scoffed at him and produced furloughs signed by Lee himself. Gordon said the signatures were authentic, but George insisted they were spies and asked permission to search them. Gordon assented and watched as George went through every article of clothing and equipment they wore. Finally, his search was rewarded when he found under the sole of the man wearing the lieutenant's uniform, an order from Grant to Maj. Gen. Edward Ord, commanding the Army of the James, directing his movement to cut off Lee at Appomattox.[19]

With that the man admitted the truth. Gordon told him to expect the fate of spies. Tomorrow he would have them shot. Yet he was impressed with their lack of nervousness. The one was barely 19 or 20 and the other a "beardless youth." The older said to him, "General, we understand it all. We knew when we entered this kind of service, and put on these uniforms, that we were taking our lives in our hands, and that we should be executed if we were captured. You have the right to have us shot; but the war can't last much longer, and it would do you no good to have us killed."

Of course, Gordon had no such intention but did not tell them. Instead, he sent the captured order to Lee who responded quickly to order him to march to Appomattox Station as fast as the physical strength of his men would allow. He also approved Gordon's suggestion to spare the "Jesse Scouts." Gordon had the pleasure of turning them over to Sheridan two days later.[20]

Sheridan's remaining Jesse Scouts were going to ensure that the armies converged on Appomattox Station. They had reported to him that railcars full of supplies for Lee were concentrated there. Sheridan reported to Grant late on the night of the 8th that he was headed straight there. He ended his message with, "I do not think Lee means to surrender until compelled to do so." Sheridan threw his cavalry in Lee's path to provide the necessary compulsion.[21]

The Surrender

On the 7th he still thought he had a chance to escape and declined Grant's offers to surrender. But on the 8th the crucial supplies he had relied on were captured at Appomattox Station. With Sheridan barring the way and the Armies of the Potomac and the James converging on the rear and flanks, Lee recognized the inevitable. Probably half of the men he had commanded just before the evacuation were now prisoners or had deserted to their homes on the march thereafter. Much of his trains and artillery had been captured or abandoned. When Grant again appealed to him on the 9th, Lee accepted.

Sharpe was riding with Grant and the rest of the staff when they stopped at the McLean House in Appomattox, where Lee waited to discuss the terms of surrender. Grant came in with Col. Orville Babcock and met Lee. They talked of having met in the Mexican War and wandered in their conversation. Babcock went to the door and called to the rest of the staff, including Sharpe, "The general says come in." Colonel Horace Porter would write, "We walked in softly and ranged ourselves quietly about the sides of the room, very much as people enter a sick chamber when they expect to find the patient dangerously ill." Sharpe noted that "gathered around the room were several officers, of whom I was one."[22] Other accounts do not mention him, but it was his nature as an intelligence officer to be unobtrusive. The artist Alfred Waud, who was accompanying the army, drew a sketch of where each man had stood in that room. Sharpe is clearly shown.[23] (See Appendix M—Sharpe's account of the surrender.)

The two generals were in great contrast. Lee had donned his finest uniform, a spotless gray with the bright gold stars of his rank, a beautiful formal sword at his side. Grant in great contrast habitually wore the blouse of a private adorned only with the shoulder straps of his rank. He had not changed his mud-stained and dirty garment, so anxious was he to meet Lee and settle the issue. He made a point of making sure Lee knew he had meant no insult. He was even more haphazard than he thought. Sharpe noted that "one button of his coat—that is, the buttonhole was not where it should have been—it had clearly gone astray."[24]

After the two generals had finished agreeing to Grant's chivalrous terms, Grant introduced his officers to Lee, who was unbendingly formal but without giving any offense. Sharpe noted that Seth Williams, "trying to relieve the awkwardness of the occasion, inquired: 'General Lee, what became of that white horses you rode in Mexico?' General Lee bowed coldly, and replied: 'I left him at the White House on Pamunky river, and have not seen him since.'" After these attempts at small talked died, Lee and Grant spoke privately. According to Sharpe, "There was one moment when there was a whispered conversation between Grant and Lee which nobody in the room heard."[25]

It only became apparent when Grant interrupted Sheridan, who had been chatting with Col. Charles Marshall, Lee's aide. "General Lee has about a thousand or fifteen-hundred of our people prisoners and they are faring the same as his men, but he tells me his haven't anything. Can you send them some rations?" Sheridan said he could.

Then Grant asked Lee "How many men have you, General Lee?"[26]

Lee replied that his army was so broken up that many companies were now commanded by non-commissioned officers and that he had not seen any returns for days. Porter writes:

> Grant had taken great pains to have a daily estimate made of the enemy's forces from all the data that could be obtained, and judging it to be about 25,000 at this time, he said: "Suppose I send you over 25,000 rations, do you think that will be a sufficient supply?" "I think it will

be ample," remarked Lee, and added with considerable earnestness of manner, "and it will be a great relief, I assure you."[27]

The "great pains" taken by Grant had actually been the work of Sharpe and his team. The figure of 25,000 men was an undercount of barely 4 percent. It was an amazing achievement to have conducted the analysis of an enemy army in the chaos of retreat and rout over a seven-day period. That undercounted 4 percent did not go without. Lee's own supply trains captured by Sheridan at Lynchburg shortly before the surrender were turned over to Lee's quartermasters. Grant also ordered that every Union soldier with three days' rations was to turn over two to the former enemies, now countrymen again. Haversacks were emptied of what now seemed like unbelievable luxuries for the Confederates. The scent of fresh-roasted coffee, the American soldier's joy, wafted among the hunger-pinched Johnnies for the first time in what seemed like an eternity.

Sharpe would have his memento of the occasion. Grant's staff bought just about everything in the parlor of the McLean House. Sharpe bought the brass candlesticks that had stood on the table at which Lee sat for $10 from the reluctant owner of the house. They are now in the Senate House State Historical Site in Kingston.[28]

Catching a moment in the proceedings that has escaped historians, Sharpe related that Lee "betrayed his agitation only when the roar of four hundred guns proclaimed the victory for the Union. Then General Lee glanced reproachfully at Grant, as though to say, 'You might have spared me this.'" Grant, of course, had no such intentions and speedily sent orders for all celebratory gunfire to cease.[29]

Paroling General Lee

But Grant had more in mind for Sharpe than merely being an observer of the historic moment. He placed him on orders to "receive and take charge of the rolls called for by the … stipulations" of surrender. He was to organize and administer the parole of all the remaining 28,231 men of the Army of Northern Virginia. Sharpe set up his headquarters in the Clover Hill Tavern, the oldest structure in the village of Appomattox Court House and immediately began work, which began early each day and finished late each night until completed on April 15. He was ably assisted by Brigadier General Oliver. A reporter observed, "There is an air of business about the place, and with the sauntering crowds in the streets gives the surroundings more the look of a town meeting or general election than one of the events of the war." Confederate officers were selling their horses to their Union counterparts and bargaining sharply for their fine animals. The reporter came away with the distinct impression that the Confederates rated the Maltese Cross men of V Corps as their most formidable opponents. Sharpe told the reporter that so far he had not had a single complaint from Rebel officer or soldier about the terms of the parole.[30] (See Appendix N—Sharpe's report on the parole.)

Lee issued probably what was his last order to allow Sharpe to do his work:

Headquarters, Army of N. Va.   11 April 1865

Pickets and guards;
    Permit Bvt. Brig. Gen. George H. Sharpe, Asst. Provost Marshall General to pass unmo-
lested from Appomattox Courthouse over to the federal lines with such officers, orderlies and
transportation as he may have with him.

R E Lee
Genl[31]

That order would be Sharpe's most treasured souvenir of the war. It would eventually be donated to the Senate House State Historical Site.

Shape complained of the difficulty of paroling an army due to its "very considerable disorganization," which made the work "difficult and laborious, and infinite pains were taken to reduce the same to some system…" He found that the increasing losses, transfers, and amalgamations of units of the Army of Northern Virginia in its last month had resulted in a situation in which "many of the rebel officers did not clearly understand their own organization." Sharpe "undoubtedly relished informing stunned Confederate officers" which brigade and division they belonged to.

Sharpe was more disturbed by the lack of concern of a number of Southern officers for their men. The terms of the parole stated that officers would sign their own paroles and then sign for their men if they were company or regimental commanders. Many of these officers simply departed after signing their own paroles. Sharpe found that other officers and the enlisted men "were found most willing to obey directions for the faithful carrying out of the terms of surrender, under the expectation that the same would result in personal benefit to them, and many of them while expressing thankfulness to our officers animadverted strongly upon their abandonment by their own officers." Sharpe had organized the parole by brigade, but apparently a number of senior officers in Gordon's Corps had departed early, requiring the issuance of parole by regiments. Sharpe also remarked that he had to apply to Fitzhugh Lee to appoint an officer to assist him in the paroling of his men, presumably since so many of their officers had already departed. Sharpe did state that Longstreet's Corps was paroled with accuracy and William H. F. Lee's cavalry command was paroled under the personal supervision of its commanders.[32]

Visiting the Confederate camp, Union Major General Crawford had an interview with Lee. Crawford told him that such was the respect with which he was held that should he visit the North, "he would view the President's treatment and consideration, and would find that [he] had hosts of warm friends there." Lee was clearly moved. As tears filled his eyes, he replied, "I supposed all the people of the North looked upon me as a rebel leader."[33]

At first Sharpe did not issue a parole to Lee, fearing that it would be presumptuous and disrespectful, but Lee's aide reminded him that his general was also a member of the paroled army. Lee was undoubtedly thinking of the political forces that would be baying for his prosecution for treason now that the war was over. After conferring with Grant, Sharpe issued paroles for Lee and his staff. Being an astute lawyer, he added a special annotation: "The within officers will not be disturbed by the United States authorities as long as they observe their parole and the laws in force where they reside." That parole and Grant's backing would save Lee from seemingly inevitable postwar persecution by the hard war Republicans who dominated Congress. On the advice of the Union commissioners of the surrender, Sharpe himself, as assistant provost marshal, signed the parole for Lee and his staff.[34]

With that task completed, the wartime mission of the BMI ended. All that was left was the victory parade in Washington and home. Sharpe had another cause for satisfaction before he departed. The suspected double-agent Pole was delivered to him. Sharpe then put him into the custody of the provost marshal of XXIV Corps, with instructions to return him to the new U.S. authorities in Richmond.[35]

As Sharpe was getting ready to ride north, he encountered a Rebel officer:

> a Confederate colonel stepped up to him and asked him whether he might ride with him. General Sharpe accepted his company with pleasure. They rode all day and as evening was falling arrived upon a lofty bank of the James River. In the valley ahead of them General Grant's army was encamped. Over its thousands of tents there was floating in the evening breeze "Old Glory" the flag of the United States. Standing silently and viewing this impressive scene the Confederate colonel turned to General Sharpe and with tears in his eyes said, "After all, General Sharpe, there is only one flag."[36]

With Sharpe's departure from the Army of the Potomac, the Bureau of Military Intelligence went out of existence, its members going in different directions. But Sharpe's military duties were not yet at an end. The day before he wound up the last details of paroling the Army of Northern Virginia, Lincoln was shot. The President died the next day. Sharpe left for Washington that same day to deliver the army's copy of the Confederate parole rolls to the assistant adjutant general, while Oliver went to Richmond to deliver a copy of the rolls to Lee's adjutant general, Col. Charles Taylor. Sharpe reported to Bvt. Col. T. S. Bowers in Washington on April 19 with the rolls. Sharpe was in time to attend the funeral the same day, and was delegated to represent, in the general officer guard of honor around Lincoln's coffin, the State of Georgia, now effectively back in the Union. He draped his sword in black crepe, which was never removed and still swathes the sword today in the Senate House State Historical Site in Kingston.[37]

Court Marshaling a Congressman

Twelve days later, while still in Washington, he was ordered to sit as a member of the military court-martial of Benjamin G. Harris, member of the House of Representatives from Maryland, elected as a Democrat to the 38th Congress (March

4, 1863). Harris was an antiwar, pro-Southern Marylander, not at all happy with the government's prevention of Maryland secession. He was also vocal and intemperate in his opinions and was censured by the House of Representatives on April 9, 1864, for treasonable utterances. Speaking in opposition to a resolution for the expulsion of Alexander Long, of the Second District of Ohio, who had expressed himself in favor of recognizing the independence of the Southern Confederacy, Harris said:

> The South ask you to leave them in peace, but now you say you will bring them into subjection. This is not done yet, and God Almighty grant it never may be. I hope that you will never subjugate the South. If she is to be ever again in the Union, I hope it will be with her own consent; and I hope that that consent will be obtained by some other mode than by the sword. "If this be Treason, make the most of it!"

Harris did more than just speak his mind. Toward the end of the war he was charged for harboring two paroled Confederate soldiers and in violation of the 56th Article of War, "advising and inciting them to continue in said army [Confederate army] and to make war against the United States, and emphatically declaring his sympathy with the enemy, and his opposition to the government of the United States in its efforts to suppress the rebellion."

Secretary of War Stanton ordered an immediate trial on May 1; that same day the members of the court were appointed. In addition to Sharpe, the president of the board was Major General J. G. Foster. Another member was Lieutenant Colonel O. E. Babcock, one of Grant's aides-de-camp, someone with whom Sharpe had worked. Harris was tried in Washington D.C. The defense, in a surprise move to discredit the claim of the two soldiers that they had been paroled, called upon Sharpe to testify. He was asked to present the parole rolls of the Army of Northern Virginia and prove that, as the prosecution claimed, the men were paroled soldiers.

> Q. "Do you find the names of Sergt. RICHARD CHAPMAN and Private READ as members of Company K on that roll?"
>
> A. "The names of CHAMPMAN and READ do not appear on the roll"; he had seen evidence which led him to think that one of the men had been paroled; on the roll of Company K there were the names of one corporal and two privates; many of Lee's men were absent, having run away at the time of the surrender. After they heard of the surrender, they returned for the purpose of being paroled. Just before the surrender, an attempt had been made to reorganize Lee's army, which created much confusion and many of the men did not know what they were with, the men of one command having been merged into another. Many of the men who had left Lee's army before the surrender, and who came back after the surrender, for the purpose of being paroled, found that the command to which they belonged had been paroled and gone home. Many of the general officers of the rebel army had left their commands before the surrender. Any commanding officer was allowed to take up the men who returned and have them paroled. The names of many of the men who were paroled might not be found in the company, regiment or brigade to which they belonged, but somewhere else among the different rolls, because of being paroled some time after the surrender. The fact that the names of CHAPMAN and READ did not appear in the rolls of Company K, 32nd Virginia regiment, was no evidence that they had not been paroled, as they might have come in afterwards and been paroled.

The judge advocate ruled that "it had been showed by the witness that the men might have been paroled, though their names did not appear on the rolls of the Thirty-second Virginia regiment. He thought that it should not be taken as evidence." The court was then cleared for deliberation, and after reopening, the judge advocate declared that the rolls would be accepted. Despite this, Sharpe's testimony, on which he was the recognized expert, had thrown a cloud over the defense's contention that there was no proof in the rolls that the two men had actually been paroled. Harris was convicted on the 12th and sentenced to three years' imprisonment and permanent disqualification from holding any office under the United States Government. President Andrew Johnson approved the findings on May 31 but then remitted the sentence.[38]

At the end of Congressman Harris's court-martial, Sharpe's official duties were essentially over. With the imminent disbandment of the armies, there was little need for his formal services. In fact, except for this note and the general order returning him to his regiment in June, he disappears from the *Official Records of the Rebellion* after paroling Lee and his army. Most of the BMI staff had already gone their separate ways; McEntee and Babcock were in Richmond working for the provost marshal of the city. Several of his scouts, including Judson Knight, were also in the city working for the provost marshal or other federal agencies. Sharpe had every reason to stay in Washington and await the arrival of his regiment and the victory parade. Instead, Sharpe suddenly traveled to Richmond. The reasons are opaque, but two issues awaited him there.

On May 9 the provost marshal of XXIV Corps turned Pole over to the officer in charge of Libby Prison, now under Union management. Oliver—still, though temporarily, working for Patrick, who had been redesignated as provost marshal general of the Department of Virginia—wrote, "the case of the man Poole [sic] is a special and peculiar one, which will come up for investigation as soon as General Sharpe arrives. He is suspected of having worked for the Confederate gov't under the plea of working for us, and is also supposed to have been the cause of the arrest and imprisonment of our friends in the city." The resulting investigation led to the leveling of charges of espionage against Poole in August.[39]

While in Richmond Sharpe wrote this note to Grant:

> Will Mosby be admitted to parole with the other officer of Rosser's command, to which he belongs? The question is asked to determine the action of Mosby and some others who would probably follow him out of the country if he goes. Shall a definite answer be given, or shall it be said that he and others will learn the action of the United States Government after they acknowledge its authority?

The wording of the note is curious—"the question is asked to determine the action of Mosby..." and "shall a definite answer be given." It is as if Sharpe were in communication with Mosby, who was wanting reassurance of his treatment should he offer himself up for parole. For someone with the precise legal mind and prose of

Sharpe, this sentence was carefully crafted and certainly no accident. The presence of key members of the BMI staff in Richmond also may have been the means by which communications were established, as their agent networks were still functioning. If Grant wanted a trusted agent to make this problem go away, who better than his chief of intelligence, a man of subtlety and discretion, who had already paroled almost 30,000 men in gray?[40]

In the end, The Gray Fox's innate caution caused him to take his good time and many assurances before he agreed to sign his parole. Mosby had been at the center of a controversy for over a month now. He had declined to surrender until he had ascertained to his own satisfaction that the Southern cause was hopeless, although he had allowed his men to offer their paroles. Secretary of War Stanton wanted Mosby excluded from the terms of parole offered to the Army of Northern Virginia. On June 13, "understanding that he would be paroled" if he surrendered himself, he tried to apply for a parole in Lynchburg but was refused. Later in the month, he tried again, and his parole was accepted. Grant was decisive in obtaining the parole over Stanton's objections about which Mosby was emphatic in his appreciation. "If he had not thrown his shield over me, I should have been outlawed and driven into exile." By then Sharpe had already gone back to civilian life.[41]

Victory Parade, Home, and One Last Battle

With that task completed, Sharpe rode directly back to Washington to join the delighted 120th, which gave him a royal welcome. He was in time to be with them at the great victory parade or "grand review" in Washington on May 23, as the Army of the Potomac marched in review past the new president to the "applauding shouts of the uncounted multitudes which had gathered to gaze upon them." He rode Babe at the head of his beloved regiment, sharing the honor with Lieutenant Colonel Lockwood, as the band played "Battle Hymn of the Republic," and the men marched in a perfect step that West Point could not better. As the regiment awaited transportation home, Sharpe received his final official orders—Paragraph 6, Special Orders 276, Headquarters of the Army, Adjutant General's Office, Washington, June 3, 1865, which tersely, as such orders do, marked the end of a remarkable accomplishment in the history of the U.S. Army as well as the art of intelligence: "Bvt. Brigadier General George H. Sharpe, colonel One hundred and twentieth New York Volunteers, is hereby relieved at his own request from duty at the headquarters Armies of the United States, as assistant provost-marshal-general, and will report for duty with his regiment."[42] A final gift from Grant was his promotion to brevet major general of volunteers to date from March 13, 1865. It would be confirmed by the Senate the following July.[43]

Moving the vast numbers of soldiers concentrated in Washington for the parades to their homes was a remarkable logistics feat, but it required the regiment to wait until June 4 for its turn. Sharpe was with them as they retraced their steps that had brought them to war in August 1862. "Packed like cattle in box cars the regiment rolled away from Washington," but they would not have minded the inconvenience, for every mile brought them closer to home. The first stop was Philadelphia where they were greeted with the same handsome hospitality of almost three years before, and "its progress from city to city was a continued ovation." In New York City, they marched down Broadway, the regiment marching splendidly on a company front, and the famous street, "quieted its bustle for a moment to look and applaud as we passed along." From there they sailed up the Hudson, "delightfully entertained on board," until they arrived at Rondout 2 miles from Kingston on June 9 for a glorious welcome.

> The town was out to greet the returning heroes. We were crowned with flowers; every soldier had a bouquet in the muzzle of his gun, and the officers were loaded down. The fire companies paraded, every bell in town was run, cannon were fired, and every possible demonstration of joy was indulged in. There was one grand triumphal arch with inscriptions of praise and welcome, over which a live eagle flapped his wings…The hotels, stores and private houses vied with each other in the profusion of their patriotic adornments. At the Academy green a banquet was provided, songs of welcome were sung, an oration of welcome pronounced and a fitting response made by General Sharpe.

Sharpe then presented, on behalf of the regiment, an elegant sword to Colonel Lockwood, who had commanded the regiment since Petersburg.[44]

The next day Sharpe was fighting for his regiment's interests one last time. The chief mustering officer in New York, one Lieutenant Colonel Dodge, assigned by the War Department to see to the mustering out of the 120th, refused them their final pay, even though a paymaster had accompanied them to Kingston for the express purpose of making their final payment. Dodge claimed that the regiment had failed to turn in its arms at Hart's Island, New York, on their passage through the city. By refusing to muster them out, the 120th remained on active duty and in limbo. On June 10, Sharpe wrote to Major General Dix, commanding the Department of the East in New York City, a telegram advising him of the treatment of his regiment and threatening to press charges against Dodge. He was seething at the treatment of his regiment. "The regiment after three years service and having received a magnificent ovation from the people of Ulster and Greene is lying at the mercy of Lieut. Col. Dodge unpaid and without rations." He assured Dix that the weapons were being turned in to an ordnance officer in Kingston at that moment. He asked that orders be issued by the War Department immediately to pay the men and to have them issued three days' rations. Sharpe threw in some political muscle by having the telegram endorsed at the bottom by Congressman John B. Steele, representing the local 13th Congressional District of New York.[45]

Dix forwarded a copy to Dodge, suggesting that the problem was being taken care of and said a "mustering officer should be sent to complete the mustering out of this regiment without further delay." Incredibly, Dodge replied the next day to Dix in a tone of snotty officiousness. He complained that the commanding officer of the 120th had violated explicit instructions to turn in the regiment's arms at Hart's Island, New York. "I cannot recognize or have anything to do with this regt (except by order of the War Dept) unless it is returned to my jurisdiction & control at Hart's Island without expense to the U.S." He ended his note with a reference to his taking the matter up the chain of command. "A full report of these facts had been made to the adj. Gen. office, Wash., DC." Little good it did him. George Sharpe was far more adept at bringing influence to bear and certainly was not about to march the 120th back to New York at the command of a puffed up bureaucrat in uniform. The matter ended quietly as the regiment was paid and mustered out.[46]

The Support Cast Departs

Maj. Gen. Joseph Hooker

Hooker recovered from his fall at Chancellorsville. Three months after Gettysburg, he was given the command of two army corps and sent to relieve the Army of the Cumberland besieged at Chattanooga, Tennessee, after the disastrous battle of Chickamauga. He served under the command of Ulysses S. Grant, who was also appointed overall commander. Hooker kept the supply lines open to the besieged army and performed brilliantly at the battle of Lookout Mountain that November, though Grant assigned much of the credit to Sherman.

Hooker performed with equal skill in the following Atlanta Campaign of 1864. His superior, the commander of the Army of Tennessee, was killed, and the command was given to Major General Howard, his junior in rank, who had commanded the ill-fated XI Corps at Chancellorsville and Gettysburg. Hooker saw it as a professional affront and asked to be relieved. Although acknowledging Hooker's superb performance, Grant stated bluntly, "I nevertheless regarded him as a dangerous man. He was not subordinate to his superiors. He was ambitious to the extent of caring nothing for the rights of others. His disposition was, when engaged in battle, to get detached from the main body of the army and exercise a separate command, gathering to his standard all he could of his juniors."[47] Hooker finished out the war as commander of a backwater military district. He suffered from poor health, was partially paralyzed by a stroke in 1866, and died in 1879.

Brig. Gen. Marsena Patrick

Patrick became provost marshal of the Department of Virginia, headquartered in Richmond after Lee's surrender, but in that position the old Democrat did not seem reliable to Grant and the administration. Unfounded rumors of pro-Democratic, pro-Southern sympathies had resurfaced in the wake of the hardening of attitudes after Lincoln's assassination. Grant wired Halleck on June 1, "Do you not think it advisable to relieve General Patrick? The machinery kept up in his duties is represented as heavy, and his kindness of heart may interfere with the proper government of the city." His relief followed on July 7.[48]

There may have been more to it than his kindness of heart. A Colonel J. W. Shaffer, formerly of the Army of the James, made serious accusations about Patrick based upon a visit to Richmond in late May. He stated that he had known Patrick during the war and had only the kindest feelings toward him. What he had seen in Richmond of Patrick's actions had outraged him. By early June upon his return to Washington he related them directly to Secretary of War Stanton. He alleged that among the Union officers in Richmond there was open disgust at Patrick's coddling of Confederate officers, many of whom promenaded defiantly in their uniforms. He stated that he had known these Union officers well during the war and vouched for their integrity. One of these officers was Col. Fred Manning, provost marshal of Richmond. He also stated that he met Sharpe in Richmond, who was there upon official business and saw him again on his arrival in Washington. At that he states that Sharpe confirmed these accusations as being entirely true.

What raised his anger to white hot was the story concerning the Van Lew ladies. A party of Northern ladies were visiting and wanted to call upon them to express their thanks for all they had done in the service of their country. Patrick is alleged to have discouraged them by saying, "Ladies, I would advise you not to call on the Misses Van Lews, as they are so notoriously radical in their sentiments, and, of course, very unpopular, and you will only irritate the Richmond ladies. Our policy is to conciliate, not irritate."[49]

Making matters worse for Patrick were the complaints of a Richmond freedmen's delegation to President Johnson complaining of harsh treatment by the provost guard. Their complaints to Patrick were dismissed when he told them that "he was acting under orders and did not wish to be told his business."[50]

In judging these allegations, it is interesting to note that Sharpe and Patrick went their separate ways after the war. They had worked closely together, mostly harmoniously, for over three years. Sharpe was a natural networker and maintained contact with just about everyone he met during the war. He would be corresponding secretary for the Society of the Army of the Potomac for over 20 years. He retained cordial relationships with officers who were Democrats such as Sickles. Yet there is not a single reference to contact with Patrick. If Schaffer's allegations of Sharpe's confirmation of his accusations are true, then that may explain the complete break between the two men. Sharpe was open to generous reconciliation but only on two conditions: (1) that former Confederates acknowledged the decision of the sword and the victory of the government; and (2) that there was to be no oppression of the freedmen. Again, if Schaffer's allegations had any merit, then Patrick, in Sharpe's eyes, had broken faith with both non-negotiable conditions.

After his relief, Patrick resigned from the army and ran unsuccessfully for New York treasurer on the Democratic ticket. He then resumed his career in scientific farming in upstate New York. In 1880 he was appointed governor of the Soldiers' Home in Dayton, Ohio, based on his reputation as a strict disciplinarian and as a man of integrity. He testified before a committee of Congress investigating soldiers' homes in 1884, "I am a man of strong convictions. I fear God and Him only. I shall not depart while the little life that is left to me shall remain, from the principles I have laid down through my life for my guidance." It was his own epitaph. He died of epilepsy while governor in 1888. The home, which subsequently was incorporated into the Veterans Administration as the Dayton VA Medical Center, is reputed to be haunted with the ghosts of Civil War veterans, including Patrick himself.[51]

Ulric Dahlgren

Ulric Dahlgren's body was returned to his father after the war. Miss Van Lew's agents had spirited it away to a secret resting place that was revealed after the fall of Richmond. A memorial service was held in Washington on September 1, 1865. In attendance were President Johnson, most of the cabinet, and a host of dignitaries. Two generals and six colonels carried the casket into the church, where the renowned abolitionist preacher, Henry Ward Beecher, gave the eulogy. From Washington, the casket was sent to Philadelphia the next day where it received the unique honor of lying in state in Independence Hall; he had been preceded there only by Lincoln himself. At the gravesite in Laurel Hill Cemetery, Major General Meade, his chief of staff, and a vast throng gathered. "The profound silence is broken only by the quick, clear click of muskets, and then comes the loud volley from a thousand muskets, repeated again and again."[52]

Elizabeth Van Lew

Grant had not forgotten Miss Van Lew. In the years after the war, she lived amidst the open hatred of her fellow Richmonders and in straightened circumstances. She was completely shunned. Within 15 days of his inauguration in March 1869, Grant rewarded her with the office of postmistress of Richmond for eight years during which time she initiated letter carrier service for the first time. To those who complained about women being given such a position, one newspaper commented, "A woman who was able to render 'important' services to her country during a time of war, is doubtless able to manage a post-office." She became known "as the former postmistress, who every year protests against taxation without the right to vote. As certain as her taxes were paid, the 'annual protest' was filed along with them. She was a strong believer in women's rights." President Rutherford B. Hayes declined to reappoint her due to pressure from Richmond's "reconciled" Confederate elites whom he wanted to accommodate, despite Grant's request as a personal favor to do so, because "she gave him valuable information about Lee's movements." Upon her departure, she "clenched her little hand and vowed that the proudest jewel in her crown would be that she had received the hatred of the Richmond people."[53]

She fell into destitution, having spent her considerable fortune in support of the war and much of her salary as postmistress on charities for black Americans. After two years she was given the position of clerk in the Post Office and transferred to Washington, where her independent character did not sit well within the bureaucracy and led to further demotions. She finally resigned and returned to Richmond to poverty and persecution. She wrote, "I tell you truly and solemnly that I have suffered for necessary food. I have not one cent in the world... I have stood the brunt alone of a persecution that I believe no other person in the country has endured who has not been Ku-Kluxed. I honestly think that the government should see me sustained."[54]

In 1869 Sharpe had written a strong letter asking the government to compensate her with $15,000 for the expenditure of her fortune in the cause of the Union, but Stanton hardened his heart, giving as an excuse that when Grant immediately after the surrender had awarded her $5,000, it had covered all claims due to her. Others had not forgotten. The men and families of those she had helped while prisoners of war came forward, especially the Revere family, to provide her a comfortable annuity in her last years. She died in September 1900. Her funeral was attended only by her servants, so hated did she still remain in Richmond. Her granite and bronze tombstone donated by the Reveres read:

> Elizabeth Van Lew
> 1818–1900
>
> She risked everything that is dear to man—friends, fortune, comfort, health, life itself, all for the one absorbing desire of heart—that slavery might be abolished and the Union preserved.
>
> ———
>
> This Boulder
> From the Capitol Hill in Boston is a tribute from her Massachusetts friends[55]

The tombstone was almost immediately vandalized. Later, the men she had rescued from Libby Prison paid off all the debts left by her estate. Among her papers was a note scribbled on a scrap of paper that was a more moving epitaph than the granite and marble of her tombstone.

> If I am entitled to the name of "Spy" because I was in the Secret Service, I accept it willingly; but it will hereafter have to my mind a high and honorable signification. For my loyalty to my country I have two beautiful names—here I am called "Traitor," farther North a "Spy"—instead of the honored name of the Faithful.[56]

Scouts and Agents

Milton Cline

The intrepid Milton Cline was discharged on September 7, 1864 in Indianapolis with the rest of the 3rd Indiana Cavalry. He moved to Illinois after his discharge and from there to Colorado in 1871 with his family, finally settling in what was to become Cimarron. He started the Cline Ranch on 480 acres and raised beef and wheat.[57]

He developed a closer friendship with the Ute chief Ouray, which proved critical to the rescue of the Meeker women and children held captive by the Utes after they attacked the nearby agency in 1879. It would be known as the last major Indian uprising. At this time Cline was still referred to by the rank of captain, and he went with the party to negotiate the release of the captives. He was chosen because of "his skill as a frontiersman and thorough knowledge of Indian character. No doubt his experience as a scout proved useful. The Utes tried to mislead the party on its departure, but "Here again Captain Cline was equal to the emergency." His knowledge of the trail led them to safety. It was a performance equal to those of his days scouting for Sharpe.[58]

Cline applied for a pension in 1904, which was approved for $12 a month and increased to $20 in 1907. He died on October 7, 1911 at the age of 84. His death certificate stated that the cause of death was due to service in the army. His government-issue white marble tombstone still proclaims him a member of the 3rd Indiana Cavalry as it tilts amid the sagebrush in the Cimarron Cemetery.[59]

Judson Knight

Judson Knight found life so attractive in postwar Virginia that he never wrote home much less went home. In early 1867, his worried brother wrote Meade asking about his whereabouts. Meade forwarded the request through channels to Sharpe who had kept track of many of the men in the BMI. He was able to state that Knight was paid off in the spring of 1865 at the end of the war and that he had "received some appointment under a treasury agency in Virginia. I heard of him somewhere in Southwestern Va during the last year, and I think he is there yet, tho' I am unable to recall the name of the place." He then suggested a number of prominent men in Richmond that would have knowledge of him. Sharpe may have been toning down Knight's activities for public consumption. Knight later admitted that he continued to work for the Secret Service hunting the "Ku Klux in Georgia."[60]

Knight finally settled in Washington, DC, and in 1992–93 wrote a series of articles on his derring-do scouting adventures for *The National Tribune*, the prominent Civil War oriented Union veterans' weekly. Ironically, these articles of his personal experiences as a scout in the BMI are the only extensive account by any surviving member of that organization. They are well worth the read for the glimpses into the risky world of the scout and for his occasional illuminating references to Sharpe, Babcock, Patrick, and Grant. They have been published by this author as *Scouting for Grant and Meade: The Reminiscences of Judson Knight, Chief of Scouts, Army of the Potomac* (Skyhorse Publications, 2014).

Within 20 years of the end of the war, Knight's health began to fail due to injuries sustained as a scout. Since he had served as a civilian, he was not legally eligible for pension. Only a special act of Congress could make an exception. His appeals for help led to the support of a number of senior general officers, with whom he had served in the war. Besides Sharpe, who appears to have had a leading role in the effort, their number included Major Generals Daniel Butterfield, Winfield Scott Hancock, and William S. Rosecrans.

Sharpe's hearty testimonial added the weight that pushed the bill through and was printed by both pension committees reporting the bill.

> During a considerable part of the time that I served on the general staff of the Army of the Potomac, and afterwards on the general staff of the armies operating against Richmond, in Virginia, Judson Knight was employed at these headquarters as a scout. He enjoyed an enviable reputation as a man to whom a bold enterprise could be intrusted without endangering the confidence of his superior officers. At times he rendered services that received signal praise of the major-general commanding [Meade] the Army of the Potomac and the lieutenant-general commanding the armies operating against Richmond [Grant].[61]
>
> When he came to the headquarters he brought high testimonials of his service with the late General Phil. Kearny. He was immediately engaged by me to serve with us. In 1864 he was made chief of scouts of the Army of the Potomac, and in that capacity, and until the close of the war, rendered the most efficient service. Throughout his service his reports were always relied on, and I take pleasure in saying he is a man who deserves well of his country. He is now crippled from the effects of these services, and it affords me pleasure to make this testimonial in behalf of one who was always faithful and gallant in the performance of his duty.

Sharpe then keyed on Knight's vital role in making and maintaining contact with Elizabeth Van Lew and her spy ring. "At a later date, and in preparing for the last campaign, he gave substantial aid in establishing lines of communication between Richmond and our headquarters."[62]

Major Generals Rosecrans and Winfield Scott Hancock added their endorsements. The latter wrote, "My remembrance of you is that you were a meritorious person and performed good service."[63] The bill was so heavily endorsed that it sailed right through the Senate on March 31 and the House on April 3, 1888, with the committee reports stating, "The pension laws do not cover this case, but it is evident that he had earned a pension and needs it." The bill was passed on July 9 and read:

> Be it enacted by the Senate and House of Representatives of the United States in Congress assembled, That the Secretary of the Interior be, and he is hereby authorized and directed to place on the pension-roll the name of Judson Knight, late chief of scouts at headquarters of the armies operating against Richmond, subject to the provisions and limitations of the pension laws, as though he had been regularly mustered into the United States Army, with the rank of captain of volunteers.[64]

Knight's health continued to worsen, and in 1899 he petitioned for an increase in his pension, only to be overwhelmed by the bureaucracy in a story that many of the wounded from the Iraq and Afghan wars today can appreciate. His attorney wrote in an appeal in 1902:

It should not be lost sight of that the reports of the several boards of examining surgeons are in as much uncertainty and confusion, and even the same report contains contradictions of what is stated before; surely there is as wide a difference as in the medical certificates of the physicians who have testified in the claimants behalf. When the doctors disagree who then is to say? This poor claimant has been examined until the doctors are all at sea, and we are no nearer the right of the matter. There must be a way out.[65]

For Knight there was no way out. He died at the age of 73 in 1902. The Bureau of Pensions had simply waited him out. His last appeal was overcome by events in the year of his death and simply stamped "dead."[66]

William J. Lee

Like Knight, William J. Lee had served as a civilian in the BMI. And like Knight, he had suffered the effects of repeated exposure after the war. He applied for a pension in 1879 to compensate him for the rheumatism he suffered in the war. As a civilian scout, he was not eligible for a military pension. To obtain a pension, a special act of Congress was necessary. He appealed for help to his old comrades to support his claim.[67]

Scout John Landegon stated that Lee's rheumatism was due to "crossing and recrossing the Rappahannock and Rapidan Rivers" in March 1864 and "that the duties we were obliged to performed incurred very great exposure, and in all kinds of weather." Sharpe wrote an affidavit on December 18, 1879 attesting to his service and stating that "Lee was constantly exposed while on said duty as a scout in crossing and recrossing the Rappahannock and Rapidan Rivers in Va: That his duties were hazardous; that he was frequently compelled to wade and swim the rivers referred to at all states of the winter in order to ascertain the movements of the enemy." Sharpe wrote another affidavit in 1881 in which he said, "His service was meritorious and attended with danger, and he was reckoned among the most effective and faithful men serving under my command in that capacity." Ulysses S. Grant also provided a letter supporting his claim. Lee finally was granted a pension by a special act of Congress on July 5, 1884, backdating his discharge to December 18, 1865.

Lee worked for the U.S. Army Chief of Engineers in Washington after the war until at least until 1913. He appeared to be a central government contact for the old scout network and the other BMI veterans. A newspaper article on him noted that "Rain or sun, there floats over it the Stars and Stripes, from the identical staff that bore the colors over Gen. U.S. Grant's headquarters when that commander had office where the depot quartermaster now holds forth at Seventeenth and F. Streets northwest." He passed away at the age of 79 on November 21, 1917 and was interned at Arlington National Military Cemetery.[68]

Anson B. Carney

Anson B. "Gus" Carney wrote an article about Dahlgren's raid for *The National Tribune*. His callous comment about hanging the slave guide provoked a contemptuous rebuttal from another scout, J. W. Landegon. Carney's response was "As to hanging the negro, any good soldier knows that the orders of a superior officer must always be obeyed," an argument only fully invalidated 51 years later at Nuremburg.

Carney, like so many other veterans, went west for many years. He returned to Kingston in 1915 for the reunion of the 20th NYSM and was happily recognized by many of the survivors of the regiment. He spoke of his pride in all the letters of recommendation he had received from senior officers in the war. Of them all, he was proudest of the letter Sharpe had written for him. He also in his reminiscences recounted the four bullet wounds he had suffered.[69] As with Knight, Carney's war wounds dogged him throughout the rest of his long life, contributing to eventual near total disability. In 1887 he appealed for a pension and was supported by a deposition from John McEntee. In 1912, again like Knight, he had appealed for a higher rate of pension. He was able to muster enough support for Congress to enact private legislation which ordered that he be paid a pension which was set by Congress at $40 a month. Carney lived to be 91, dying in 1932 in Canton, Pennsylvania, probably the last of the men that worked for Sharpe in the BMI.[70]

Isaac Silver

When the war ended, Isaac Silver went home to his farm after being released from the Confederate prison camp in Salisbury, NC. With his wife, Catherine, and their six children, he moved to Stafford County across the Rappahannock, perhaps because his neighbors did not approve too highly of his service to the Union. He died on Christmas Eve 1901 at the age of 91. The Fredericksburg paper wrote an obituary that would have pleased him, describing Silver as "a prosperous farmer and during the war of 1861 and '65 was conspicuous for his fidelity to the cause of the Union."

Benjamin C. Pole

Pole was arguably one of the most bizarre and sad characters thrown up by the Civil War. He penned a short biography of himself from his cell in Libby Prison that admitted he had intended to "come south" where his sympathies lay. This was seized upon by John C. Babcock, who wrote a detailed account of the witness statements of the men he had betrayed, William White and Lemuel E. Babcock, He also stated that Sharpe had told him that Pole had assured Sharpe before he was infiltrated into Richmond that he was acting in good faith.[71]

Charges were prepared for desertion, communicating with the enemy, and perjury. Then things became interesting. The witness list read like a who's who of the Richmond underground, with the notable exception of Van Lew, who had presciently avoided meeting Pole. The list included William White, Lemuel E. Babcock, Frederick W. E. Lohman, and John Hancock from the underground; and, from the BMI, Sharpe and McEntee. It also included the two Confederate commissioners that heard the case against White and Babcock.

The judge advocate general for the Department of Virginia wrote to the Secretary of State on December 11 about certain allegations made by Pole. Seward replied eight days later, "You also inform me that Pole alleges he committed these acts under instructions from myself," and that "this matter will engage my early and serious attention." He then asked for a "specification of his claim to have received from me authority to proceed in the measures related." If ever there was a hedged, lawyerly reply, this was one. One would think that if he had not had the meeting alleged by Pole, he would know it. A simple denial would have been dispatched. Had he had the meeting he would also have known it. If that were the case, he would be loath to admit that he had been so badly taken in.[72]

On Christmas Day Seward wrote another letter:

> Referring to your letter of the 11th … inquiring concerning the truth of the allegation of B. C. Pole that he was instructed by me to commit certain improper acts with which he is charged. I have now, in reply, to lay before you such information as I have been able to obtain upon the subject from the files of the Department from these papers it will be seen that the opinion entertained of Mr. Poles [sic] services was such as to prohibit me from giving him employment of any kind.[73]

Undoubtedly he was referring to the letter Dudley had sent him. Again he gave no outright denial. Instead, his argument was a model of artful and disingenuous indirection. Essentially he said there was no proof that he did what Pole alleged. That skirted his having to give a false statement.

There matters lay as Pole languished in jail into the next summer. He was himself delaying proceedings by claiming material witnesses on his behalf were not available. Finally, in early July he unleashed a torrent of complaints, turning the government charges on their heads. He claimed compensation for the time the Confederates had held him at Castle Thunder. In the first few days of July 1866, Pole was released from prison and sent back to his regiment at Camp Grant in Richmond to await trial. He then, on July 10, wrote letters to Seward, in which he wrote, "I will call you to remember that when you were at the Astor House [New York City] I presented you certain plans and which you approved of. I have carried those plans and have been arrested charged with 'Spy.' Shall upon trial require the circumstances to be substantiated by witnesses and shall call upon you to come forward…"[74]

One can only imagine Seward's reaction to being called as a witness, especially since he thought he had gaffed off the issue with his Christmas Day letter. Not surprisingly the government gave up the case against Pole shortly after this. He served out his enlistment with the 11th Infantry Regiment at Camp Grant in Richmond, being discharged on October 29, 1867. He stayed in the United States and became a citizen and patent attorney. His fascination with torpedoes had not waned. In 1871 he submitted plans for a "self-steering, time-firing, and plunging torpedo" to the British admiralty, and in 1887 submitted new plans to the U.S. Navy. In the 1890s he formed a company to market his invention of a perpetual motion machine. He married and had two children, and at some point claimed and received a military pension. He died in 1916, and irony of ironies, he was buried at the U.S. Military Cemetery at Arlington.[75]

The BMI Staff

Bvt. Col. John W. McEntee

John McEntee assumed command of the 20th NYSM after Appomattox until June, when he was ordered to Richmond as part of the Provost Marshal operation under Patrick that had to replace the collapsed civil authority. McEntee was appointed as the city's provost judge to hear "cases normally heard in a major police court." He was specifically retained in service in January 1866 by the order of the Secretary of War, ostensibly for duty with the Freedman's Bureau, until April when he was mustered out.

Upon his return from the war he was appointed to a lucrative position in the Custom House of New York. He later went into business in Boston but returned home to Kingston where he founded the company McEntee and Dillon, a foundry and machine shop for the repair and manufacture of boilers and engines that enjoyed a high reputation for quality.[76]

He was promoted to brevet colonel in the Volunteer Force, Army of the United States, on June 22, 1867, "for faithful and meritorious service during the war."

He took an active part in the civic life of his community, and served the City of Kingston "as an Alderman from the fourth ward, member of the Board of Water Commissioners and Trustee of the Kingston city library. He was also the local agent for the Society for the Prevention of Cruelty to Animals and a member of the State Charities Commission."[77] His wife and he had no children, but neighbors' children would recount in their own old age what a kindly man he was to them. The remaining productive years of his life were good to him, but, as with so many other veterans, old age brought infirmity which fell hard on him in July 1900 with a disease of the lungs. In May 1903 he applied for a pension, but his condition deteriorated and on December 19, 1903 he passed away from a pulmonary hemorrhage, a distinguished and much-respected citizen of Kingston.[78]

After his death, an article in the *Kingston Journal* said of him:

> Colonel McEntee was man of quiet nature, courteous manners, and a keen sense of honor. Whatever he did, in war or peace, and in public or private life, was well done. His was a useful and notable career, and the recollection of it, and of his agreeable personality, that of a gentleman of the old school, will long survive him.[79]

John C. Babcock

Babcock went on to become chief of police of Richmond and was joined by his wife, Mary, daughter of English and Irish immigrants. He retained the services of guide

Richard Johnson as his coachman and that of his wife, Sarah, as cook. Things in Richmond were unsettled enough for the chief of police and his coachman to have their carriage horses stolen, apparently at gunpoint. In early May Patrick sent him on a secret mission with a cavalry escort with carte blanche to seize the records of the Orange and Alexandria Railroad Company and the trunk of George N. Saunders. Saunders was the notorious Confederate agent in Canada who had duped Horace Greeley into pressuring Lincoln into peace negotiations in hopes of harming his chances for reelection. He had also been implicated in the Lincoln assassination. With the records and trunk secure, Babcock was then ordered to personally turn them over to Assistant Secretary War Dana. Secretary of War Stanton himself signed for them. Their contents have never been found.[80]

One of the first missions given Babcock as chief of police was to arrest Confederate Capt. Dick Turner, commander of the infamous Libby Prison, denounced for his cruelty to Union prisoners. "By some pretty sharp detective work," Babcock traced him to his home in a Richmond suburb. Surrounding the house, Babcock inquired of Turner's wife, but she denied knowledge of him. She freely agreed he could search the entire house but begged him as a gentleman not to disturb an ill lady in one bedroom. After searching the house, he forced the door on the forbidden room and found Turner in bed reaching for a brace of Derringer pistols. Babcock quickly subdued him and kept the pistols as souvenirs.[81]

Ironically he was thrown into Libby Prison, the same facility he had so cruelly run during the war. He shared close confinement with the Englishman Pole.[82]

Babcock left the service on September 1, 1865 and eventually moved to New York and resumed his career as an architect.[83] He founded the New York Athletic Club and became a noted yachtsman and racing judge and the inventor of the sliding seat used in shells. Over the years his wartime military title migrated from honorary captain to colonel. Within army circles he remained known for his work; in 1876, Meade's senior aide and author of an important memoir of the Army of the Potomac wrote to him asking, "if you still have … your notes … Estimate of Lee's army from your secret service…" "Our object," he wrote "is to get at the truth, as near as we can and to record the valuable testimony of men who knew these details and who are yet living." Babcock still retained an order-of-battle of the Army of Northern Virginia in the form of an index in a small leather notebook and a summary chart on a single sheet of ruled paper. They are available at the Library of Congress and are a wonder of his very small and precise by-hand printing, without errors, in ink, the work of a highly skilled draughtsman.[84]

About 25 years after the war, the reporter John A. Cockerill interviewed Babcock, who showed him an array of documents from 1861 to 1865 and told him of his plans to write a memoir. Unfortunately, this potentially invaluable work was never completed. His papers at the Library of Congress, while extensive, do not support the writing such a work.[85]

Mary and John would have one daughter, Jesse, in May 1867. She would be living at home with them in 1900. The 1880 census also showed that he had become the support of his widowed mother who also lived with them.

Through the network of old BMI veterans, he was approached by a law firm in late 1902 to help support the claims of the ailing Sarah, the widow of Richard Johnson, in her efforts to secure compensation for her husband's wartime service as a guide for the BMI. Patrick and Sharpe had already done what they could by referring the firm to the appropriate payroll records. Babcock gladly did what he could.

Babcock's help came at a cost of great effort. In December 1901 he had suffered a severe stroke that left him with intermittent paralysis on his right side. In January 1905 he applied for and received a pension and two years later applied for an increase after another severe stroke.[86]

The twilight years provoked a desire to tie up loose ends. In 1903 he contacted his old friend from the Peninsular Campaign, William Pinkerton, to help him run down his discharge from the Sturgis Rifles, which he had never received since he had not been with them when they were formally mustered out. That same year, now interested in writing a history of the BMI, he was inquiring fruitlessly for information from Ulric Dahlgren's relatives. He contacted Sharpe's son, Henry G., the next year, who wrote him back, "My father was very warmly attached to you, and always spoke of you with the greatest affection" and lamented that his father had never undertaken that task. He very much wanted Babcock to try, writing "I was anxious that an account of the operations of the "Bureau of Information" during the Civil War should be prepared and published & wish to counsel you on that subject. My father had a number of documents, and I intended writing to Miss Elizabeth Van Lew's representatives to ascertain if there was anything among her papers."[87]

Nothing came of it, and in 1905 the younger Sharpe expressed his own interest in writing an article on the BMI:

> I should have availed myself of the opportunity of running up and seeing you, and talking with you about matters connected with the Bureau of Information, hoping that I could get some assistance in preparing an account of operations of that Bureau during the Civil War, for an article which I think should be written. I understand that Captain Oliver is dead, and by the death of Colonel McEntee, I think you are the only surviving member of the Bureau. From your familiarity with all its operations, I am sure that you could give the information I am seeking.[88]

Babcock maintained that relationship with Sharpe's son and appealed to him, as an army general, to help him obtain a government clerkship. The years had taken the steadiness of his hands and thus the means to continue as an architect. Sharpe did his best, but government jobs had been completely locked up within the Civil Service that such appointments were impossible. The government could not be interested in hiring Babcock to write a history of the BMI either. The heyday of contracting was not yet on even the distant horizon. Sharpe suggested he work through the New York Commandery of Military Order of the Loyal Legion of the United States

(MOLLUS) to write a confidential report for the War Department or approach a prominent publisher of Civil War histories such as Charles Scribner's Sons with the project, but nothing came of these suggestions. The idea of writing receded in the face of his wife's death and his own bouts with illness.[89]

In 1908 he wrote a poignant letter to William Pinkerton:

> I am going to call on you again, for the sake of old times … for you and I are the only ones left of that famous party that left Washington in the spring of 1862 for the peninsular. Not a commanding general or a chief of staff is living of the five commands that started out for the front, and I find it difficult to think that we had any war, or that I had any part in it.

John C. Babcock died of pneumonia later that year at the age of 72 and with him the last central eyewitness of the story of the Bureau of Military Information.[90]

Bvt. Col. Frederick L. Manning

The War Department's records show record keeping in the 1860s was no less prone to error than today. Fred Manning was promoted twice to the rank of brevet colonel "for gallant conduct in the field," on August 22, 1865 and June 22, 1867. Both, however, dated his brevet to April 9, 1865, the day Lee surrendered at Appomattox. He stayed on active duty to serve as provost marshal of Richmond.

Like most of the other former BMI members, Manning returned to an active civilian life. An appreciative President Grant remembered his services in the Army of the James and appointed him to be the collector of internal revenue for the 24th District of New York on March 22, 1871. He lived most of his life in Waterloo, New York, where he practiced law and served as a public prosecutor. He was active in his community and served as the president of the Waterloo Board of Education. As the century came to a close, a local newspaper recorded his hearty welcome at the reunion of the old 148th New York on September 8, 1899. As with so many soldiers, these gatherings were poignant reminders that there was a time, as Oliver Wendell Holmes remarked, "Our hearts were touched with fire." Frederick L. Manning passed away in 1908 and the age of 77.[91]

Bvt. Brig. Gen. Paul Oliver

Oliver's last official duty was to hand over duplicate rolls of the paroled members of the Army of Northern Virginia to Lee's adjutant general, Colonel Taylor, in Richmond. Thereafter he submitted his resignation and was discharged on May 5, 1865.[92]

After the war Paul Oliver worked for a short time in the coal business with his brother-in-law. In 1869 he established a small powder mill in Wilkes-Barre, which caught fire, killing a number of his workers and badly burning himself. He then organized the Luzerne Powder Company—his buildings burned down and rebuilt only to blow up shortly afterwards, killing two men. He then bought out an old company and established himself at Laurel Run in Luzerne County on 600 acres in 1872. His mills went into full production six years later, reaching 1,000 kegs a day using machinery of his own invention which, given the motivation of his own experience, reduced risk of explosion to a minimum. Unfortunately, 1892 saw another fire and another explosion. A major competitor was Dupont, also located in Luzerne County, which made use of his patents for improved powder and powder machinery.[93]

The powder mills made Oliver a wealthy man and gave him the ability to be a philanthropist, active in both the Humane Society and forestry conservation matters. His grandfather had rescued a sucker from the "Treaty Elm," under which William Penn had signed his famous treaty with the local Indians after a storm had blown down the tree. The sucker became an enormous tree, which Oliver had moved to his own estate. He in turn sent a sucker in 1895 from that tree to be planted on the site of the original Treaty Elm. He was also lifelong Republican.[94]

Like almost all other former senior Union officers, Oliver was a member of MOLLUS as well as the Society of the Army of the Potomac. In the 1893 reunion at Gettysburg, he led one of the four divisions of veterans in parade. He was a local leader in raising a fund for the widow of Maj. Gen. Winfield Scott Hancock in 1886. Oliver stayed in touch with the fraternity of soldiers with whom he had served, including colleagues from the BMI. Like Sharpe he remained devoted to Grant. Upon Grant's death, he closed his mills in mourning, raised a 90-foot flagpole, and held a memorial service in the chapel he had built on the grounds of his mills. In 1889 he wrote a letter to the Secretary of the Treasury on behalf of John Babcock for a position in that department. He died in 1912.[95]

CHAPTER FIFTEEN

A Full Life: Sharpe's Progress

Like the men of the 120th, Sharpe settled back into his prewar pursuits in the law career and local politics. He made sure that his warhorse, Babe, was tenderly cared for on the grounds of his large home, The Orchard, at 1 Albany Street, "in green pastures so that he could pass his old days in peace and plenty." When Babe died in 1882, Sharpe showed his enduring affection by setting up a stone over the animal's grave. Upon the stone was engraved:

Babe

A noble, intelligent and resolute Horse, who carried his Master through all the marches and conflicts of the Army of the Potomac, from Fredericksburg to Appomattox, and faced the last enemy in October, 1882, aged 28 years, full of the fire and courage, he had shown on the field of battle.

———

One of my best friends.[1]

Sharpe did not disappear into the quiet anonymity of Hudson Valley gentry but retained powerful connections in Washington. For example, on the evening of March 21, 1866 he received an urgent telegram from Secretary of War Stanton to come immediately to Washington. Sharpe replied that the message had come too late to take the last train but that he would catch the first one in the morning. Interestingly, this telegram is found in the papers of the Secretary of State, William H. Seward, though addressed to Stanton. It apparently had been forwarded from Stanton's office to Seward. The trail on this intriguing moment then disappears from the historical record.[2]

Almost the first thing we hear of him after the war is a reference to a meeting he had in Washington with Brig. Gen. Cyrus B. Comstock. "When I saw you last in Washington, we conferred upon a matter, theretofore spoken of, and for sundry reasons delayed, which it was understood between us was to be put on paper by myself, and would then be presented by you to the consideration of General Grant."

He was referring to the compensation for Elizabeth Van Lew's war services. He had traveled to Richmond in the middle of May in 1865 on the issue of Mosby but apparently at the time had not met the woman he would eulogize as the "Lady of College Hill." He had made a trip to Richmond in the summer of 1866, when he finally met the remarkable Miss Van Lew. After the surrender at Appomattox, he had ridden directly back to Washington and not gone to Richmond. He wrote, "I became possessed of the facts many of which I had some knowledge before which tend to show that they [Van Lew and her mother] have a very strong claim upon the assistance of the Government." He had learned of her financial plight at the time and on his own urged the War Department to compensate her for having expended her fortune and property in the service of the Union. The letter was detailed, generous, and heartfelt. He obviously held Van Lew in great respect and did his utmost to obtain $15,000 as the minimum owed to her. He ended his letter by stating that hers was "the most meritorious case I have known during the war." His letter would have convinced a stone, but the letter had another quality of a stone—it sank like one in the mean-spirited offices of Stanton's War Department.[3] (See Appendix O—Sharpe's letter of support of Van Lew's claims.)

Sharpe closed his letter by saying that "I do this now without waiting for future reference because I am just leaving home to be absent some little time…" That was because the government, which ignored his generosity to others, had not forgotten his ability as an intelligence officer. In the wake of Lincoln's assassination, John H. Surratt, the son of Mary Surratt, one of the conspirators to be convicted and executed, fled to Europe and later Egypt where the local authorities delivered him into American custody in February 1867. In January 1866, with Surratt still at large, Secretary of State Seward sent Sharpe on a special mission to Europe "to ascertain if possible whether any citizens of the United States … other than those who heretofore have been suspected and charged with the offense, were instigators of or concerned in the assassination of the late President Lincoln and the attempted assassination of the Secretary of State." Unspoken in his official instructions but certainly communicated to Sharpe was Seward's belief that the former Confederate vice president, Judah Benjamin, who had fled to London, was implicated in the assassination.[4]

Sharpe followed Surratt's trail first to Liverpool and then to London, where he sought the assistance of the embassy secretary, Benjamin Moran. The secretary, a self-important busybody, had been at the embassy since the early 1850s and left voluminous diaries. He left a record of Sharpe's efforts which revealed that there was a greater prize than Surratt, one of such delicate importance that it was not stated in his official instructions. It was none other than the former vice president of the Confederacy, Judah Benjamin, who had fled to England as the Confederacy collapsed.

Moran's diary entry on February 11 stated, "Mr. George H. Sharpe, the detective, has been sent here to hunt up evidence against the persons implicated in the assassination of President Lincoln. He is a bullet-headed person and is determined to catch Benjamin if possible."[5]

His next entry was a week later: "General George H. Sharpe also called. He thinks he will be able to prove that Judah Benjamin was implicated in the assassination of Mr. Lincoln. I hope so."[6] Sharpe spent the next month pursuing this lead. On March 14, Moran recorded, "General Sharpe came up. He is on the track of George McHenry and Benjamin and thinks he will be successful."[7] The net had widened to McHenry, who been an assistant in Paris to Edwin DeLeon, a Confederate propagandist.

Sharpe evidently saw the value of Moran's knowledge of London and engaged his active assistance in the chase. On March 16 the two went to a hotel "to ascertain if J. P. Benjamin and George McHenry saw John Surratt and supplied him with money after Mr. Lincoln's assassination in London."[8] Five days later he was working on his own for Sharpe. "In the afternoon, I went to Fenton's for General Sharpe about Benjamin and Surratt, but could get no reliable information."[9]

Sharpe then traveled to Rome where the fugitive had enlisted in the Papal Zouaves, and even to Egypt where Surratt had fled last, before concluding his investigations. His report showed in detail how he had pursued every lead, but each had petered out. The only item of interest in his report was that "Surratt's passport showed that it was obtained by some influence from the provincial government of Canada, and had received the visé of the United States consul-general." That in itself was highly suspicious since the conspirators had frequently traveled through Canada and been well supplied with gold, a rare priority for the specie-starved Confederacy. This line of investigation too led to nothing. In July Sharpe made his official report to Seward while Surratt's trial was underway:

> Conscious that earnestness was brought to the attempt at identifying the loathsome instigators of the great crime, and that every possible assistance was received, I have to report that, in my opinion, no such legal or reasonable proof exists in Europe of the participation of any persons there, formerly citizens of the United States, as to call for the action of the government.

Surratt was acquitted by a Democrat jury. Seward would wait until December to acknowledge Sharpe's report but would thank him for his zeal in the matter, stating that the Department of State had approved all his actions, and that his report had been "communicated to the House of Representatives," the day before.[10] (See Appendix P—Sharpe's report to Seward.)

Sharpe's observations of the political situation in Europe during his visit were prescient:

> I took every occasion of talking with Frenchmen on their all engrossing interest of Luxembourgh [sic], and was surprised to find the unanimity with which war was desired with Prussia. The French are eminently an ideal[istic] people—they will fight more for ideas than interests, and they had all conceived the opinion that France had been grossly insulted, and by the people ... whose legions at Waterloo had turned the scale [Prussia].

He observed that the lull was entirely due to the fact that the Prussian Army had been fully equipped with the needle gun, the first breech-loading rifle as general issue to an army, and to the fact that if Louis Napoleon went back on his promises to the other great powers to submit to arbitration, the French people would not be able to pay the necessary war loans. Nevertheless, he concluded, "[T]hat Louis Napoleon will not try to reestablish his success by letting them fight the people they hate, is to believe him to be willing to let the empire take slow poison."

Sharpe thought that France would have been better off to have gone to war with Prussia earlier when Austria and Russia could have been paid off to support France. A French ambassador told him in Rome that "The only question now is one of alliances," surely an example of barring the barn door after the horse has escaped. When France did blunder into war with Prussia in 1870, it was because the Prussian foreign minister, Otto von Bismarck, was able to play upon the French eagerness for war. Sharpe did see a silver lining for the United States. He accurately predicted that U.S. securities would rise in value in Europe.[11]

He recounted how well he had been treated in Britain in the way of "receptions and compliments, one that a much more prominent officer could scarcely have hoped for." At one large dinner party, he met a former Confederate officer, Maj. Osman Latrobe, of Longstreet's staff, whom he had paroled at Appomattox. He had quite forgotten the officer, but Latrobe had not forgotten him. He announced to the room that the officer that had paroled him was also a guest, and, tongue in cheek, "that he must therefore conduct himself carefully." Sharpe was surprised at the great interest of the other guests to hear of incidents of the war that had "not struck me as being of particular interest."

> Then too these people did not believe that we could conquer the rebellion and having done it, we have risen immeasurably at one monstrous stride in their estimation. They are greatly struck with the bloodlessness of the end—that there is nothing like heads on Temple-bar—that there has been little or no confiscation—that that there is but one man [Jefferson Davis] in the United States restrained of his liberty, on account of the rebellion.

Sharpe then noted that he had just heard that Davis had been released and was on his way to New York. He could not resist writing, "I hope he will not find it necessary to visit Kingston." Returning to the seriousness of upper class sentiment in Britain, he noted, "But there are thousands of people here, who hate us because we have succeeded, and the ... support of the reform bill is ascribed to the pernicious influence of America, which in her success they look upon as a protest against the Aristocratic institutions of England."[12]

The most memorable event of his trip was his meeting with John Bright, the champion of the Union in Britain during the Civil War. Then he had been a member of Parliament and so determined in his support for the American cause that he was referred to by his fellow Parliamentarians as "the member from the United States." Sharpe was perhaps a bit star struck by the man beloved by the American public and whose portrait was the only such to hang in Lincoln's cabinet room (other than an old print of Andrew Jackson) as such a singular friend of the United States. He would fondly remember the moment in his speeches over the decades, and as in the following case to a meeting of veterans.

> I saw him once. It was after the war. I scanned his appearance very closely—as strangers will frequently do when they meet some famous man the first time—to see if he looked like what I had pictured to myself he was; if I could find in him what, it would seem, marks a very great man; and there, through an open door, I saw that splendid figure and that massive head; that head that seemed to resemble Webster's more than any other I have ever seen. Among others, I was introduced. "Now, Mr. Bright," said he who presented me, "I want to introduce to you an American officer who paroled Gen. Lee's army." John Bright replied, "I am glad to see you, and you treated them a great deal too well, too." That was the first thought that struck the mind of the man who would not have been a Minister of the Crown of England if these men here had failed.[13]

Upon his return to Kingston Sharpe settled down to a happy family and successful professional life. The 1870 census shows Sharpe claiming the value of his real estate at $15,000 and his personal estate at $4,000, a fall from the $30,000 he claimed in the 1860 census. Nevertheless, he was employing five servants at his home at the time, four women and a coachman, all apparently Irish. Two were born in Ireland, the rest native-born New Yorkers.[14]

Sharpe became an active member of the Society of the Sons of the Revolution and presented a number of erudite addresses on the history of his town and region in the American Revolution. He remained a devoted member of the Old Dutch Church in Kingston. He obtained and donated for the church two stones that were embedded on either side of the entrance. They originated in the "Old Middle Dutch Church on Nassau Street in New York City, erected in 1729 and given over to civic uses in 1844. With Biblical inscriptions in Dutch on the sandstone and in English on the granite, the tablets read, 'I have loved the habitation of thy house' and 'My house shall be called a house of prayer.'"[15]

Sharpe was a convivial man, at ease with others individually and in groups of even great size. He was also a man who could enjoy life in robust and enthusiastic style. Although he came from old Hudson Valley stock, he was at ease with everyone. He fit a definition of the gentleman as "Someone who shows respect for those who can do nothing for him." A quarter-century after his death, former Congressman Cornelius Van Buren would pen this remarkable character sketch of Sharpe:

> In one way or another I have been in touch with all the leading Ulster politicians of the time. If I were to name the best one of each of the great parties I would name General George H. Sharpe from the Republican… Sharpe was a college graduate, a scholar, widely read, a good talker, had travelled abroad, was in touch with all the prominent men of his day. Share could go to East Kingston when the brick yards were in full blast, enter the dance hall, grab the first pretty girl he saw, swing her in the waltz, take the whole crowd up to Garry's and buy the drinks, then call upon and smoke a cigar and drink a glass of wine with the priest, start for home and if it wasn't too late stop and express his absolute belief in the doctrines of election and predestination to the Dutch Domnie.[16]

This personal side of him may have been one reason he was to remain a popular figure so long in Kingston.

As might be expected, he was also a very public man and took an active part in the associations of his life. He was a "member of the Sons of the Revolution, The Loyal Legion [MOLLUS], St. Nicholas Society, Delta Phi Society, Union League Club, Metropolitan Club of Washington, Army and Navy Club, Society of the Army of the Potomac and that of the Third Army Corps." He was also a Mason. He remained attached to the educational institutions of his youth as well and served as a Rutgers College trustee from 1879 until his death in 1900. In 2006 he would be inducted into the roll of Rutgers distinguished alumni.[17]

Sharpe easily fit the ancient Athenian definition of a *politis* (citizen) by remaining deeply involved in the social and political life of Kingston. When any event required a gifted speaker, Sharpe was called upon. When civic leadership was needed, Sharpe was called upon. When positions of public trust were open, Sharpe was called upon. The following partial list of his efforts in public life in 1889 are illustrative of that involvement:

Jan. 8: Appointed President of the National Bank of Rondout.[18]

Feb. 20: Gave an oration at the dedication of the new lodge of the Knights of Pythias.[19]

Feb. 23: Appointed again as President of the 120th Regiment Union.[20]

Apr. 22: Served as Chairman of the design committee on a Soldiers' and Sailors' Monument.[21]

May 15: Called upon to deliver the oration at the dedication of the regiment at Gettysburg.[22]

May 17: Led the work of the Soldiers' and Sailors' Monument design committee.[23]

Jun. 7: Called upon by the mayor to lead the collection of funds for survivors of the Johnston Flood.[24]

Jun. 26: Led the veterans of the 120th Regt. to Gettysburg to dedicate their monument and delivered an oration.[25]

Jul. 20: Issued a report on the condition of the National Bank of Rondout.[26]

Sep. 15: Presented a eulogy at the Mason lodge for naval officer lost at sea.[27]

Sep. 19: Served as a pallbearer for funeral of Claude V. Quilliard.[28]

Dec. 23: Endorsed the election of Charles Preston as State Superintendent of Bank.[29]

His estate was known as "The Orchard" for its location in a vast grove. It had been in the family for over 200 years. There Carrie and he raised a happy, devoted family. Their two boys and a girl adored their father. His older boy, Severyn B., followed his father's example, graduated from Yale, and became a lawyer. He practiced law, served as an Ulster county judge, became active in New York Republican politics, and ran a successful law practice in New York City.[30]

The younger son, Henry, unexpectedly secured an appointment to West Point in the Class of 1880 through the good officers of President Grant. The appointment was never solicited and came as a complete surprise to father and son. "President Grant intended the selection as a compliment to the son and a delicate expression of regard for the father." Nevertheless, Henry had been inspired by his father's record in the Civil War and would find a fulfilling life in the army. He served for a few years with the 4th Infantry on the frontier, but in 1882 resigned his commission. Evidently he thought better of that and in the autumn of 1883 requested a return to active duty. President Arthur, no doubt to do a favor to his friend, recalled Henry with the rank of captain in the Commissary Corps. He married Kate Morgan on June 7, 1884 shortly after returning to active duty. For the next 15 years he provided subsistence support to a number of posts across the country. By diligence, hard work, and talent he established an impressive reputation. That apple did not fall far from the tree.[31]

Although the Sharpes were a close-knit and loving family, like so many fathers Sharpe doted on his only daughter, Katherine. When she married New York Congressman Ira Davenport on April 27, 1887, her father pulled out all the stops to give her, described as a "pretty and vivacious brunette," a storybook wedding. The church was engulfed in a sea of a thousand friends and admirers of Sharpe, a sign of not only his political but his personal popularity as well. Inside, the church was filled with flowers of every description and heady with their perfume. To the tune of Lohengrin's wedding march, he walked his daughter down the aisle as she leaned lovingly on his arm. He gave her away grudgingly, as all fathers do, to the groom who was flanked by her brothers as groomsmen.

A lavish reception followed at The Orchard which was also brightened with flowers everywhere. He feasted 250 guests to a wedding breakfast prepared by one of the great chefs of New York. At the end Katherine toasted her new husband in a massive, antique family silver loving cup. They departed on their honeymoon to Europe in the railroad president's own car. Sharpe saw his New York City guests off on a special train of the West Shore Railroad he had reserved for event.[32]

Severyn would wait until 1897 to marry. He and Frances Patynr were wed on February 17, 1897 at her parent's home in Kingston. General and Mrs. Sharpe gave the bride a family heirloom diamond necklace as a wedding present. Severyn and Frances would have one daughter, born in 1902, named Katharine after Severyn's little sister. She would be General Sharpe's only grandchild.[33] (See Appendix Q—Sharpe's Family.)

The Orchard was not only the site of a contented family life but was known for its hospitality as well, and Sharpe as a great host known for his splendid table and fine conversation. Sharpe knew the value of a rich, formal table as a setting for good manners and fine conversation. His family had a custom when they met for dinner. All would wait until Sharpe's wine glass had been filled. They then raised their own to him with the salute of "Hoste," to which he would reply, "Gramercy." The visitors to The Orchard included Presidents Grant and Arthur, Generals Sherman,

Thomas, Slocum, Hooker, Howard, Davies, Kilpatrick, Wilson (James H.), Sickles, McMahon, Varnum, Major Ulrich, and Judge Rawlins, Grant's former chief of staff. As the animosities of the Civil War faded, he would add a number of former Confederate generals to his wide circle of friends.[34]

Clearly a favorite of Grant's, the President appointed Sharpe to a number of critical positions, requiring a high degree of trust and ability, during his administration—to be addressed later. A highpoint in Sharpe's life was Grant's acceptance of his invitation to be his guest in Kingston in July 1873. His reputation as a host was already local common knowledge. *The Kingston Daily Freeman* wrote, "Whatever is needed or desired in the matter of entertainment may safely be trusted to the hospitable Gen. Sharpe." Indeed, Sharpe threw him a magnificent party at the Overlook Mountain House nearby. He did not neglect to include in the guest list his old deputy in the BMI, John McEntee. "As the guests went in to dinner a comely young lady hung on the arm of General Grant. To make conversation he said, 'Are you fond of Shakespeare?' She, never having read a line of that author, said, 'Why, General, I read his books as fast as they come out.'" There is no report of Grant's reaction to Sharpe's choice of his dinner companion.[35]

For Sharpe Grant's demonstration of his favor and friendship had been a personal and social triumph which burnished his reputation in Ulster County to a high sheen. He wrote Grant an effusive letter of thanks on July 1 that emphasized the effect of the visit on the people:

> It was an extreme kindness to our people, and so thoroughly appreciated by all classes of them that I find their gratitude extending somewhat to me—while to myself the mark of favor was so dear personally, and so brilliant from its conspicuousness, that I could not trust myself to thank you in words. How much good it is your power to do in this way! I know already that the tone of our people has been raised by your visit—they have more pride in themselves; and I am confident too that misconduct would be more difficult to me in the future than heretofore—I should have farther to fall.

As an aside, he reminded Grant that a large gift of wine he had presented the President was "safe, in a separate store-room of this building, ready to be forwarded anywhere as you may direct. And there is no reason why it should not remain here as long as you may direct."[36]

Grant's visit gave rise to speculation about Sharpe's future. He was thought to be Grant's choice to succeed Roscoe Conkling as senator and the power in New York if the latter were appointed to the Supreme Court. It would remain, however, only speculation, as Roscoe Conkling declined to his later regret, but its inspiration lay in Grant's high estimation of Sharpe based upon their wartime association and reinforced by Sharpe's dramatic triumph against the Tweed Ring, described in detail in the next chapter.[37]

At some point a deep friendship grew. It was understood that Grant was fond of Sharpe, enjoyed his company, and valued his advice. It is assumed that they did more than retell old war stories, although it appears that one of the things that had recommended Sharpe to Grant in the war was his marvelous ability as a storyteller. At one point he was a facilitator for Grant early in his presidency, a man who could be depended upon to take care of delicate political matters discreetly. On a visit to the White House in October 1870, he wrote to James McKean, whom Grant had just that year appointed Chief Justice of the Superior Court of the Utah Territory, that he had been asked by someone "in an important quarter" to persuade his brother not to run as a third candidate in a New York congressional district because it would endanger that district. Sharpe ended his letter with the pointed remark, "It is suggested that you must be deeply interested in the matter."[38]

Not only were Grant and Sharpe close but their wives and children were as well. Jessie Grant and Cary Sharpe had become good friends. In October 1874 Cary Sharpe was accompanying the Grants as their guest on a tour of Indian Territory.[39] Earlier that same year the Sharpes and their daughter were invited by the President to the wedding of his daughter Nellie in May to the English singer, Algernon Sartoris. Their gift was a ring set with a cameo surrounded by diamonds. Their daughter Kate and another little girl threw their slippers at the departing couple, a custom of good luck at the time.[40] In February 1875 the couple returned to the United States; when they returned to England it was with a new grandson of the President. When the couple returned to England from New York in September, Sharpe requested the honor of carrying their newborn son, Grant, on board their ship.[41] In June of the next year, it was the turn of the Grants to be guests of the Sharpes at the commencement exercise of Sharpe's daughter at the Notre Dame Academy in Baltimore.[42]

However much Sharpe was in New York City or Washington on business or politics, he remained a devoted son of Kingston, that pleasant town on the Hudson. His affection for his hometown found expression in a loving and fond address on the history of Kingston to the Kingston Young Men's Union on the evening of December 20, 1875. Reprinted in *The Journal* of Kingston and *The New York Times*, it stands as both a delightful and scholarly history of the town. His purpose, he said, in writing the history was to hand "down to those who are to come after to celebrate the second Centennial of the Republic, a distinct recollection of our forefathers." He paid homage to the original commander of the 20th NYSM, Col. George W. Pratt, who had begun the work but whose life had been cut short when he fell at the battle of Second Manassas in 1862. Sharpe said he was only picking up the fallen standard, a charge left behind by a gallant man. He closed by asking his audience to join him in the aspiration of that lovely version of the 23rd Psalm:

> Let goodness, and mercy, our bountiful God
> Still follow our steps, till we meet thee above;
> We seek, by the path which our forefathers trod,
> Through the land of their sojourn, they kingdom of love.[43]

CHAPTER SIXTEEN

A Public Life

Sharpe did more than settle into a comfortable life as the local squire. He jumped into politics and became one of the most influential and personally popular Republican Party figures in the Hudson Valley. With his hero Grant running for president, Sharpe rushed to his support and became a delegate to the 1868 convention. Grant's landslide victory would have a decisive effect on Sharpe's life.

By September 1869 Sharpe was appointed to the Central Committee of the Republican Party of New York at the state convention in Syracuse. In 1873 he was admitted to the party executive committee. Republicanism fit him like a glove. The head of the state party organization was the autocratic and imperious Senator Roscoe Conkling. Republican to the bone, Sharpe became an ally of Conkling and was joined by former state quartermaster general, Chester A. Arthur, and Alonzo B. Cornell. These four men were the Republican Party in New York.[1]

His quick mind, likeability, powerful personality, and distaste of politically driven animosities paved his way. He seems to have successfully followed the advice given by the Greek Polybius to Scipio Africanus: "Never leave the forum without making a new friend." He would have his inevitable enemies, but the circle of his friends constantly widened. Even his Democrat opponents would come to speak of his fairness, gentlemanly conduct, good nature, and probity. It was the vindictiveness of his own Republican opponents that would prove more dangerous.[2]

Despite that statewide prominence, he had to struggle to maintain his influence and power base in Ulster County for decades against the animosity of a rival, Thomas Cornell (no relation to Alonzo B. Cornell). That animosity was said to be born in the Sharpe family's prewar purchase of outstanding debts against Cornell when he was in straightened circumstances. While Sharpe was away in the war, Cornell stayed home, amassed a fortune, and "became a power" in Ulster County Republican politics. Sharpe's ambition to play a leading role in Ulster politics ran straight into both Cornell's grudge and his entrenched base. As the founder and owner of *The Kingston Daily Freeman*, Cornell would frequently use it to attack Sharpe.[3]

Another cause of enmity was their mutual involvement in the Rondout and Oswego Railroad, which was expanding through the Catskills. Cornell had been its first president but resigned in 1870 because of other interests competing for his time and an animosity to its president. He continued to attack the president in the pages of the *Freeman*. The next year Sharpe joined the board of directors. The president's mismanagement forced the board to lease the railroad to William B. Litchfield in February 1872. In April Sharpe was elected president of the company and promptly moved to reorganize the railroad and initiated a bill in the state legislature to authorize it as well as change its name to the New York, Kingston & Syracuse Railroad (NYK&S). He first fired the treasurer, Anthony Benson, a Cornell man. In July Sharpe and Litchfield sued Cornell for the "grossest malfeasance" as an officer of the railroad "such as misappropriation of bonds, theft of money from the treasury, etc." Cornell threatened a libel suit. Both sides then backed off. By the next year Sharpe and the board had become alarmed at the plundering of the railroad by Litchfield and put it into receivership to drive him out. An actual gun battle ensued in dispossessing Litchfield.[4]

Following on Litchfield's mismanagement, the depression of 1873 doomed the railroad and brought on a major lawsuit against Sharpe and the board the next year. In June 1875 at the request of the bondholders, the NYK&S Railroad was sold. Immediately thereafter Cornell assumed the presidency and the railroad was renamed the Ulster & Delaware Railroad. The stockholders, many of whom were ordinary working people, lost everything.[5]

Cornell's son-in-law, S. D. Coykendall, who had also been named in Sharpe's suit against Cornell, continued the feud that roiled Ulster Republican politics for decades. The *Times* reported:

> The two made it so lively for Gen. Sharpe that he has had hard work to convince politicians outside that he has much influence in the Republican Party in Ulster Country. The general, however, has not given up without a sturdy fight each year at the nominating convention. This has caused factional fights in the party, but few political plums have come from Ulster on account of the lack of harmony.
>
> On being asked the other day whey Coykendall and Sharpe did not pull together politically, an old Republican said: "They have been opposed to each other so long they would not feel natural if they did."[6]

Sharpe remained a strong admirer and supporter of Grant, and neither ever forgot the bond that had been formed as a member of that exclusive group, Grant's family of generals. He was an active proponent of the move to put Grant in the White House after the disastrous Johnson administration. As a member of the influential New York delegation to the 1868 Republican convention, he did much to insure Grant's nomination. As Grant's biographer, Jean Edward Smith, said of him, which could also be said of Sharpe, "loyalty to friends and benefactors was the pole around which his universe revolved..."[7]

Sharpe added his impressive oratorical skills to Grant's election. On September 17 the largest political demonstration in New York City's history was held on the anniversary of the battle of Antietam in support of the Grant ticket. Sharpe's rising political star put him on the podium as second speaker at this rally. He did not hesitate to wave the bloody shirt. To him, voting Republican and especially voting for Grant was a continuation of the struggle of the Civil War. Those who had either betrayed or failed the Union had reassembled under the candidacy of Horace Greeley, whose *New York Tribune* had been the country's most influential newspaper for 20 years. Greeley ran on the Liberal Republican ticket, splinter of the Republican Party, and was nominated by the Democrats as well.

Greeley came with enormous political baggage. He had attempted his own peace negotiations with the South in 1864, finding himself badly manipulated by the Confederate agents with whom he had been dealing. He had also refused to support Lincoln in that year's election. In 1866 he stood Jefferson Davis's bail and lost half his subscribers overnight. He was also a hopelessly inept campaigner. Much of his platform was seen as rewarding the South for secession. What particularly incensed Sharpe was Greeley's call for the end of Reconstruction, which he saw as a thinly disguised attempt to undo the decision of the sword. It would also be an assault on the 14th Amendment, which was vital to the protection of the liberties of all Americans, and throw the black population of the South to the tender mercies of their former masters, undisturbed by the interest or power of the Federal Government.

Sharpe's stay in London had helped crystalize his belief that the victory of the Union was a clear demonstration of American exceptionalism and the inherent strength of republican government. It was a belief that stayed with him for the rest of his life and was expressed in a speech he gave to the Grand Army of the Republic (GAR) 23 years later. The press reported that Sharpe said:

> Gladstone and Lord John Russell … were against the Union and they said that the end of the war would leave us with a military government, but they were wrong, as the farmer, the lawyer and the minister went back to their original occupations, thus showing that no government on the face of the earth was as strong as a republican form of government.[8]

In a speech to a veterans club on September 5, Sharpe also reminded his audience that a Greeley victory would result in the payment of Confederate debts and pensions to Confederate veterans by the Federal Government to be made on the backs of the loyal men of the North. Sharpe was fully in favor of reconciliation and honored the valor of the Confederate soldier, but he was damned if he was going to compensate them for the cost of the Rebellion.

> We intend to see to it that the men who were maimed at Spottsylvania Court-House and at Gettysburg shall not be pushed aside by the men who maimed them; and we don't intend to have a statue raised to Robert E. Lee in the capitol until the last of those hobbling me has joined the ranks of those who are gone before.[9]

His powers of oratory were impressive in an age when the standards were far higher than today. As would be said in another context, "by those unfamiliar with his stentorian voice, it might have been mistaken for the Angel Gabriel."[10] On September 17 he delivered another powerful speech. The crowds of veterans howled in approval at what was a brilliant political stem winder of a speech. He was throwing them the red meat that their memories of the war made so appealing. But he was also laying out what had become central to his political philosophy—the primacy of the victory of the Union in the life of the nation, the importance of the 14th Amendment to guarantee the result of that victory, and the necessity of protecting the rights of the black minority. The *New York Times* ended its report of his speech with the following words:

> Referring to the Democratic hatred of the poor, downtrodden African, he spoke of the assistance rendered by those humble patriots to our soldiers during the war, of the many marches and hardships in which they had borne our boys company; of the patriotic songs in which their voices had mingled with those of the "Boys in Blue," while on the march or in the tented field. He would never forget the inspiring song which he once heard those negroes singing on the march:
> "In the beauty of the lily Christ was borne across the sea.
> In the beauty of the lily he transfigured you and me.
> As he died to make us holy, let us die to make men free."

Applause thundered from the vast crowd as he ended.[11] It was the roll tide of victory. The Republicans crushed Greeley, who received only 40 percent of the vote.

Grant did not fail to remember Sharpe's political assistance or his abilities. He had something more arduous in mind than minister to Paris. In March 1870 Grant appointed Sharpe U.S. Marshal for the Southern District of New York as an important part of his plan to break the grip of the notoriously corrupt William Tweed and his ring of Tammany Hall politicians that were plundering the city of New York.[12] Tammany Hall had evolved from a fraternal organization to an arm of the Democratic Party and controlled the city through the patronage of the large immigrant population, especially the Irish. By easing their path to citizenship and providing food and jobs, Tammany had secured the loyalty of a large and decisive part of the electorate. William M. Tweed had risen to power as the Grand Sachem of the Tammany organization and gained control of the party apparatus from 1860 to 1870; he had great influence in the state legislature, and control of state judges, often by illegal means. Tweed had important allies in two financial buccaneers, Jay Gould and James Fisk, Jr., who had secured control of the Eire Railroad and plundered it into near ruin. Fisk had secured his position so well as to obtain the colonelcy of the 9th Regiment New York State National Guard. The state militia had been reorganized after the war into the new structure of the National Guard. Fisk and Gould's attempts at stock market speculation had led to the national financial panic of Black Friday in 1869.

In 1870 New York City had the most important governmental organization in the United States other than the Federal Government itself. The port of New York alone was the largest single source of revenue for the Treasury. For the city to remain in the hands of the Tweed Ring was a national scandal of the first order. It set the standard and precedence for other city machines and posed a direct threat to the concept and practice of representative government. The financial shock of Black Friday only served to emphasize the national threat the Tweed Ring posed. If Grant was to bring it down, he had to attack it at its foundation.

The Tweed Ring had stayed in office in good part by manipulating elections through a form of ballot box stuffing in which thousands of so-called "repeaters" voted again and again. Crowds of these ruffians would move arrogantly from one polling place to another, casting their ballots under different names. It was bad enough that city and state elections were corrupt. What roused Grant's ire was that Federal elections to the House of Representatives were also corrupted. This was a direct threat to the integrity of representative government.

Surprisingly, Sharpe received a handsome write up in the *New York Herald* which had so detested in the war. "General Sharpe ... is regarded by all who have had intercourse with him as a man of high attainments, unspotted personal integrity and the most genial address." The *Herald* was a Tammany Hall supporter and would have cause to regret its positive review.[13]

Sharpe quickly settled into the job and on the 15th appointed someone he had worked with in the war and trusted as his deputy marshal—General H. E. Tremain, former chief of staff of the Third Army Corps.[14] Sharpe's first task was to supervise the conduct of the 1870 census. He started by hiring 200 honest enumerators to spread out through the huge city to conduct the census. The actual enumeration was conducted "against violent opposition," some of it directed at Sharpe's own person. It was only Sharpe's unflinching use of U.S. marshals to protect the enumerators that the census was successfully completed. Its results clearly proved that the 1868 Democrat electoral victories had been based on brazen fraud. One electoral district counted 870 residents in the 1870 Census and 707 voters in the previous 1868 election.[15]

But the census was only the opening of the campaign against the Tweed Ring. The November 1870 elections for city, state, and Congressional offices was to be the showdown. Despite his federal office, Sharpe remained a Republican politician, and in that day and age, this was the norm. He saw no conflict between his advocacy of the Republican Party and his non-partisan role as a federal officer. A modern audience might be skeptical of the dichotomy, but Sharpe appears to have carried it off honestly.

An insight into his motivations appeared at the mass meeting of black voters at the Cooper Union Hall on October 12 at which Sharpe was a speaker. The black community had been consistently abused by the Democratic machine and was a natural Republican constituency. Sharpe was there as U.S. Marshal to defend their rights and as Republican politician to ensure that their votes reinforced the defense of those rights. He was preceded by the Rev. Butler who proceeded to tell his audience that any black man who was beguiled to vote the Democratic ticket was out of his mind and had forgotten it was that party that "had sustained slavery; which assisted in enforcing the Fugitive Slave Law; which had systematically opposed everything for the benefit of the black man, and hunted the colored people for three days in July [draft riots of 1863], burned their orphan asylum, and hung some of our fathers and brothers to lamp-posts." Sharpe spoke next as reported by *The New York Times*:

> He considered it a proud privilege to be present with them tonight, and welcome to the rights of citizenship the members of a race who have so long been deprived of their rights. As the representative of the executive authority of the United States he welcomed his audience on this auspicious occasion. After alluding to the heroism of the colored troops during the war, he referred to the duty of his hearers in this canvas and urged them for the sake of their brethren at the South and for themselves to vote rightly on this occasion, and adhere inflexibly to the principles of the Republican Party.[16]

Sharpe was being practical as well to seek allies to break the hold of corrupt machine politics on New York City. That had not been lost on the Democratic machine which rallied to oppose the next step in Grant's plan, now that a clean census had been taken—a strict registration of voters to be supervised by U.S. supervisors of elections under Judge Woodruff of the U.S. circuit court and protected by Sharpe's U.S. marshals. By September Sharpe was fending off clumsy and fraudulent complaints against the accuracy of the census by Tammany Hall cronies. On the 24th of the next month, Sharpe announced in a letter to *The New York Times* that all complaints against the census had been addressed and provided the census returns to the press which duly printed them. By making the returns public ahead of the elections, he challenged Tammany openly. Sharpe found time at least once in early October to confer with Grant in the White House on the developing situation.[17]

On October 18 the registration began. The *Times* observed that "It was generally characterized by quiet and orderly conduct unlike the acts of lawlessness perpetrated in former political campaigns." Sharpe's marshals were out in force which had a demoralizing effect on the Tammany toughs. The *Times* went on, "Very few of the gangs of repeaters who have been the chief features on election days during the last ten years, were observed in the streets; those who were seen did not conduct themselves in their usual arrogant manner, but were extremely cautious about the way in which they acted." Sharpe had made it more than clear that the U.S. marshals would extend the fullest protection of the law to the supervisors of elections. As the registration went on, the supervisors directed the arrest of a number of repeaters bold enough to try, including a member of the Tammany Hall General Committee, for having registered in three districts.[18]

The Tweed Ring was temporarily trumped but would come back with a snarl to defend its hold on the pocketbook of New York. As the registration continued over several weeks, their toughs grew bolder, attempting to intimidate federal officials.

Those officials did not back down, and arrests mounted. On occasion gangs of repeaters would rescue one of their number who had just been arrested. Sharpe's marshal's office was becoming more and more to resemble a command headquarters girding for battle. Tammany was prepared to attack from more than one direction and pressed suit in federal court, challenging the government's authority to supervise a local election. Judge Woodruff rebuffed that attempt by a ruling on November 2, stating that the House of Representatives' constitutional authority to judge the qualifications of its members included the authority to "crush any systematic effort to control those elections by fraud or violence."[19]

Not surprisingly, Sharpe's intelligence of Tammany's next step was crucial. The same day that Judge Woodruff ruled against Tammany, Sharpe's sources told him of the plan to call out the state National Guard to bully federal officials from properly supervising the election. It was a blatant threat of rebellion against the United States Government, something of which Sharpe had already had too much experience to tolerate in his own backyard. On November 2 he informed the Secretary of State, Hamilton Fish, who was in the city at the time, and named the three regiments to be called out—the 9th, 22nd, and 69th. NYSNG (New York State National Guard). Fish promptly telegraphed Grant. The 9th Regiment was commanded by Fisk, who had recruited Tammany Hall toughs to fill its ranks. On the 5th of the month Fisk issued a secret special order to his regiment to assemble at their armory on the morning of election day –November 8. It was an order which quickly found its way into Federal hands, probably through Sharpe's sources.[20]

In the meantime, Sharpe had been working the issue politically with both the Tammy-controlled governor and mayor. He appeared to have reached an agreement with the governor "looking to the non employment of any State Troops, & an agreement as to the mode of exercising their authority by the United States Marshals & Supervisors…" Sharpe was a man with a noted ability to negotiate in personal sessions. He was also a man who would not flinch at political hardball. Shortly thereafter, on November 7 Sharpe and U.S. Attorney Noah Davis, now armed with this agreement, had a hard-nosed meeting with the mayor A. Oakley Hall, and his superintendent of police in which the full force of the United States Government was thrown into the scales to, as it was diplomatically reported, "guard against any collision between the United States and City authorities to prevent fraudulent voting and false counting of votes…" Tammany flinched. A joint statement was issued in which both sides agreed to cooperate to ensure a fair election.[21]

Sharpe had driven Tammany into a corner, depriving it of its gangs of repeaters, corrupt officials, and friendly police. It had only one desperate ploy left, the very one that Sharpe had identified and warned against five days earlier—the use of the Tammany controlled National Guard. Despite his agreements with state and city officials, he was not convinced that he had fully forced Tammany's hand. Secretary Fish reported to Grant that "Genl Sharpe insists on having the U.S. troops in the

City, and distributed in small detachments," a measure with which he disagreed to the President. Sharpe's fears were well-founded. The same day Sharpe was meeting with the city's officials, the commander of the National Guard's First Division in the City, Maj. Gen. Alexander Shaler, issued a general order that stated that although city and federal officials had come to an agreement on the peaceful conduct of the election, "yet, as a measure of extreme precaution, it is ordered that should the services of this division be required to aid the civil authorities in the preservation of peace and order on election day," the Guardsmen would hold themselves in readiness to report to their armories in fatigue dress.[22]

Sharpe's intelligence sources picked this order up as soon as it was issued; he informed Grant immediately. The President, having crushed the rebellion of the valiant southern Confederacy, was not about to see the authority of the U.S. Government challenged by municipal thugs. He responded the same day with an order to Shaler:

> By virtue of the authority conferred upon the President of the United States to use the land, naval, and militia forces of the United States in maintaining the laws, you are hereby notified that the Division under your command is called into the service of the United States, and you are directed to hold it, or so much of it as you may deem necessary, in readiness to cooperate with the United States Marshal, and Brigadier General commanding the Military Department of the East, "to enforce the faithful execution of the laws of the United States," during the election to be held in the City of New York to-morrow the 8th instant.
>
> You will please acknowledge the receipt of this, and report your action.[23]

Grant wired the letter to Sharpe who passed it on to Shaler. Secretary of War Belknapp informed Brigadier General McDowell in New York City at the same time:

> An order from the President Calling out Genl. Shaler's Division or so much of as may be necessary goes to Marshal Sharpe for delivery to Genl. Shaler to-day by telegraph and Mail. Gen. Sharpe may consult with District Attorney as to the propriety of calling out Militia and if not recommended by them inform me by telegraph for further instructions. See Sharpe at once.

The last two sentences were in Grant's hand. Grant was making it clear to Federal authorities in New York, including the senior army officer, that Sharpe was his representative in the city in this crisis. His support was as full and confident as it had been for Sherman in his independent campaign that fought its way to the gates of Atlanta and then scorched its way to the sea. Tammany's last effort folded as Shaler, a political general, hurriedly withdrew his order, probably in sheer terror at the threat from the man who had broken Robert E. Lee.[24]

On election day, Sharpe in effect commanded a large Federal force of 5,000 deputy marshals and supervisors, all of them specially commissioned to make arrests for voting fraud. Sharpe had thoroughly organized this force. Each voting district had 10 men under the command of a sergeant, with a large number held in reserve at important points. The districts were subordinated to assembly districts under the control of a chief deputy marshal and chief supervisor, operating out of a central headquarters, who were prepared to give instructions on the disposition of prisoners. Sharpe chose for these offices "worthy ex-army officers, who have adopted excellent measures of discipline for the body men place at their disposal." Badges and batons were distributed the night before the election. Five thousand warrants were prepared for known repeaters, and long lines of carriages were parked outside polling places to be ready to transport them once arrested. It was a formidable organizational effort and a daunting show of force.[25]

Sharpe was determined to have a reliable military back stop to his marshals. *The New York Times* reported that General McDowell, commanding the Department of the East, had been ordered to place his troops under "Marshal Sharpe's directions," an order that could only have come from Grant himself. On election day, New Yorkers along Broadway were surprised to see five companies of the U.S. Army's First Artillery Regiment in campaign dress, normally stationed at Fort Trimble in New Haven, Connecticut, now marching through the streets to disappear into a building on Reade Street where they remained quietly all day. The press reported that they were under the overall command of Brig. Gen. Henry Hunt—the great artillerist of the Army of the Potomac whose guns had savaged the men in gray who charged with Pickett and others on the last day of Gettysburg. Three more companies from the First Artillery stayed quietly on the steamboat that brought them quickly down from Fort Adams at Newport, Rhode Island. Other bodies of troops also quietly entered the city. Sharpe had at his disposal about 3,000 regular army troops. "The frigate *Narraganset* was stationed in the East River near the foot of Wall-street, and it was understood that she would be used to sweep the street to protect the United States Treasury." The ironclad *Guerriere* was similarly placed in the North River. Marines from the frigate reinforced those normally stationed at the Navy Yard, and the other U.S. Army garrisons in the city held in readiness "for instant service." All Federal troops had strict orders to keep out of sight.[26]

The threat of the use of federal troops was already hanging in the air. The *Herald* was hyperventilating on October 26 when it wrote, "only the verbal request of Marshal Sharpe ... will be enough to precipitate upon the freemen of New York an army of paid mercenaries to occupy, sack, and slaughter in the holy name of the law."[27]

In the end, the repeaters stayed away and the troops out of sight, and the election went off quietly. Sharpe had accomplished the epitome of generalship according to the Chinese genius of the art of war—Sun Tzu. He had brought off a victory without fighting. His preparations covered every front—political, civic, organizational, military, and especially the psychological. At every step he outmaneuvered Tammany into impotence. Sharpe had fully justified Grant's faith in him for this delicate and vital mission. Great military partnerships are rarely able to reconvene in great crises after their time in history has passed. Not so with Grant and Sharpe. If anything, Sharpe exceeded in this crisis his performance during the war. In this case he had vastly more executive and command authority than he did as director of the BMI. In effect, he was his own commanding general, and he pulled off a flawless campaign. One can only speculate how he would have performed as a senior combat commander. Sharpe would be the first to give Grant the supreme credit for backing him up with judgment and resolve. It was proof that the greatest military collaborations are based not only on ability but on mutual trust and respect.

The election has a final irony—Tweed's Tammany ticket won after all. But it was a pyrrhic victory. Its margin had been much reduced as a result of a clean election. The Tweed Ring's grip on the electoral process had been broken. That was the beginning of the end for it as a threat to Federal authority in New York, although the Tammany machine would survive well into the 20th century when its patronage was dealt major blows by President Franklin Roosevelt.

Bill Tweed's control was about to run out much faster as reform candidates organized for the municipal elections of 1871. Sharpe actively campaigned for them. At a speech on October 26 at the Cooper Institute, he described in stark terms exactly what was at stake in the struggle against the Tweed Ring. After alluding to the threat to the cause of liberty posed by the Civil War, he spoke these challenging words:

> Is this not the same contest in a more insidious form? Is this not the same blow at the right of popular expression of the people's will? If this be so, then let me ask you to recollect how criminal you have been in time gone past in paying no attention to the first duty of citizens of a republican form of government.

He went on to call for Democrats and Republicans to unite in opposing corruption. His speech was enthusiastically received and described by the *Times* as a "brilliant address." The reform movement's moment had arrived. Sharpe's successful assault on Tweed's control of elections had given new strength to reformers. The *Harper's Weekly* cartoonist Thomas Nast was savaging Tweed with his cartoons that were especially effective among Tweed's immigrant base. Democrat reformer Samuel Tilden had been patiently gathering evidence against Tweed. Now events moved with a rush. That same October Tweed was arrested for corruption. Seventy reform candidates were swept into office on election day. Gould stood Tweed's bond of $1,000,000, and charges were dropped but were later reinstated largely through Tilden's efforts. He was finally convicted in 1873 of plundering the city and sentenced to 12 years in prison. That was reduced, and he served one year, only to be charged by New York in civil court and held in a debtors' prison. He escaped and fled to Cuba and from there to Spain. He was arrested by Spanish authorities at the request of the United States and returned to American custody. The Spanish authorities identified him by the use of Nast's cartoons as informal wanted posters. He died in prison in 1878.

Tweed's crony, James Fisk, was already dead, shot by a business partner in 1872. That same year Gould's hold on the Erie Railroad was finally broken. Sharpe's old commander and friend, Maj. Gen. "Immortal Dan" Sickles, had been appointed by Grant as ambassador to Spain and at the same time been retained by the outraged stockholders of the Erie Railroad to include Attorney General Barlow to find a way to wrest control of the company from Gould. In early 1872 Sickles had returned to New York on a leave of absence from his post in Madrid and called upon Sharpe for help. Barlow wanted help in preparing the vast amount of evidence necessary to prove a case against Gould. Sharpe agreed; he was only too glad to help out an old friend, drive out the notoriously corrupt Gould, and strike at one of Tweed's more important allies. He added the proviso that he would do it only if it did not take him from his duties as marshal. This proved to be no problem, and he accepted no remuneration, only a modest amount to cover his own expenses. At the same time, Sickles told Sharpe that he had a shorter way to his goal and asked if Sharpe could provide him with a number of men who were accustomed to serving papers. Sharpe would later testify, "I told him I knew of the right kind of men and suggested my deputies" in an off-duty capacity. Sharpe was, indeed, the man to ask. He had had the knack of finding the "right kind of men" for the most dangerous and rough work as scouts in the war.

In March Sickles had persuaded several of the trustees to trick Gould into calling a board meeting. Sickles marched into the company's headquarters in the white marble Grand Opera House in New York City. He was escorted by a half-dozen of Sharpe's deputies, led by one John E. Kennedy, and with most of the board of trustees in tow. The board officially met, declared all offices vacant, and elected a new and honest slate. Gould heard the cheer, immediately suspected what had happened, and locked his office door. Dan directed Sharpe's deputies to smash down the ornate door and swung through the debris on his crutches to corner Gould in his bathroom to "encourage" him to leave quietly.[28]

By the time of the 1872 national elections, Sharpe found that a much lighter hand was necessary to ensure a clean election. He instructed his marshals to "exercise a liberal discretion in all cases where a reasonable explanation is offered by a person arrested." The battle had been largely won. If the remnants of the Tweed Ring in Tammany Hall were still engaged in corruption, it was no longer through the ballot box.[29]

Shortly before he resigned as marshal, Sharpe was sued for wrongful arrest. Though the jury found against him, it signaled its overall approval of Sharpe's conduct by awarding the plaintiff six cents in damages.[30]

Marshal Sharpe and the Greek Church

Leading Grant's assault on the Tweed Ring did not constitute all of Sharpe's duties as marshal. Sharpe was also acting as Grant's agent in Republican politics. An example was the letter he wrote on Grant's behalf in his mid-October 1870 visit to the White House to Utah Congressman James B. McKean. "Being in Washington to-day, I am asked in an important quarter if you cannot immediately retire your brother from the Congressional Canvass in our state, where his running as a third candidate is endangering a district. It is suggested that you must be deeply interested in the matter. Please answer me in New York." It did not take a mind reader for McKean to figure out who Sharpe meant by "an important quarter."[31]

New York remained the focus of a large part of the Federal Government's business on a number of levels that required Sharpe's attention. One of those who employed Sharpe's talents of investigation and delicacy was Grant's distinguished Secretary of State, Hamilton Fish. On one occasion he asked Sharpe if he could clear up the nationality of Siam's commissioner to the U.S. Centennial who had been arrested in that country shortly before departing for the United States. Fish was especially concerned that the U.S. Government be able to offer the protection "of our citizens."[32]

In the summer of 1871, Fish had cause to ask Sharpe to investigate the purchase of property for a "Greek Church," meaning the Russian Orthodox Church, on behalf of the Emperor of Russia the previous year. The case had the interest of "high official circles"—an oblique reference to Grant himself—that the conveyance of the property to a Russian priest involved significant fraud. That high official had been piqued by the fact that the Russian ambassador himself, Constantine de Catacazy, had made the purchase and that the purchase price stated in the deed significantly exceeded the amount actually paid to the vendor. Furthermore the difference in the two figures had been made up with U.S. Revenue Stamps. Catacazy, a vulgar intriguer, had been an appalling choice as ambassador, but he was the protégée of the Russian foreign minister, Prince Gortchakoff, whose support for the Union in the Civil War had been diplomatically vital. To counter American claims for arms sold to Russia in the Crimean war, the ambassador made thinly veiled attacks in the press against the U.S. Government, Grant, and even the Grant family. He had thoroughly alienated the President and Fish, who refused to receive him. Their interest, then, in a matter of corruption involving the Russian ambassador was natural. Fish wanted Sharpe "to ascertain the accuracy" of this information "which will require skill and delicacy." Skill and delicacy were the very qualities which had become Sharpe's hallmark.[33]

Secretary of State Fish directed the American Ambassador in St. Petersburg to request the recall of the ambassador, but Gortchakoff declined, itself a diplomatic discourtesy. Yet, Grant was unwilling to dismiss the ambassador outright because the Civil War debt to Russia for its diplomatic assistance and advice was still strongly felt by the President. The arrival of Grand Duke Alexis, the Russian heir, at this time on a visit to the United States brought the matter to a head. Catacazy was unavoidably admitted to the White House for the last time to present the visiting Grand Duke. The government's distaste for Catacazy was laid out in detail to the Grand Duke's suite, including Sharpe's evidence of the ambassador's fraud. Catacazy was recalled almost immediately.[34]

Surveyor of the Port of New York

In 1872 Conkling asked Grant to fill the most important posts in the New York Custom House with his principal allies in the party. This was no small patronage request. The New York Custom House brought in $100,000,000 a year, making it the largest single source of Federal revenue and the most important office of the executive branch outside Washington. Grant acceded to the request and appointed Chester A. Arthur to be the collector of customs of the Port of New York and Alonzo B. Cornell as the chief naval officer of the port. The power patronage came from the ability to appoint the over one thousand employees of the Custom House and to expect them to make contributions to the Republican Party of New York, which Conkling, in turn, controlled. This "spoils" system had been the way official business had been done traditionally. It is difficult today to understand that at this time there was less a clear-cut divide between one's official position and political and personal interests. However, the growing sophistication and industrialization of the country were creating pressures for efficient change not only from reformers but from industry, commerce, and the general public. There was a growing demand for fundamental reform in the creation of a non-political Civil Service with appointment by merit. Conkling, however, had no intention of surrendering this patronage cornucopia of the Custom House as the price of change. Crucially, that meant he was not going to disturb the cozy level of corruption within the system.

The blurred line between public and political office, however, was about to begin to unravel. Some 10 years later, *The New York Times* would retrospectively review the situation at the time:

> The truth is that under the Presidents we have named [Grant, Hayes, Garfield, and Arthur] the leading Federal officers owed their appoints to their prominence in politics and after receiving them they continued without reproach save from a few reformers to whom in those days nobody paid much attention, to give a large part of their time and energy to their respective political machines. During President Grant's second term CHESTER A. ARTHUR, ALONZO B. CORNELL, and GEORGE H. SHARPE were three of the most active and influential Republican politicians in the State of New York. Mr. ARTHUR held the Republican machine in this city in the hollow of his hand. Mr. CORNELL was during a part of this time Chairman of the Republican State Committee, and Gen. SHARPE, then as now, was indefatigable in political activity.[35]

The third most important position was the surveyor of customs for which Conkling wanted Sharpe. This came open in 1873, and he took office on April 1 working for Arthur. Grant was all too glad to appoint Sharpe as a reward to his friend for breaking the Tweed Ring. Sharpe described himself in his new position as "the executive officer for all that part of the business of the Collector done outside of the general office. His office attended to the discharge of passengers and merchandize from vessels and the supervision of all goods which pass through the Custom-house in transit to Canada, South America, and Europe."[36]

The system was as large as it was antiquated. Sharpe's department was responsible for 24 miles of waterfront, divided into 40 districts. He had 282 inspectors as well as hundreds more of weighers, gaugers, clerks, watchmen, and laborers working for him in a system that had not been modernized in decades. The work of the Custom House was complicated by having to administer 17 different laws. These were the days of patronage and spoils writ large. At times there was no clear line between party and government office, but that was accepted practice in this period. In the Custom House as elsewhere, most appointees were faithful party men and politically organized. That organization assessed a percentage of their pay for the party. Sharpe did state emphatically that no one had been punished for refusing to pay what he considered a voluntary assessment. This was true, he maintained, not only of the surveyor's subordinates but of the entire Custom House as well. Both Sharpe and Arthur had the reputation of gentlemen who did not stoop to such methods. As a biographer of Arthur noted, "Under Collector Arthur, no employee was dismissed for failure to contribute, and compulsion to pay was felt principally by those who realized that other reasons might be discovered for removing them."[37] Nevertheless, the prudent employee paid up. Political connections were crucial. One man would testify that Arthur and Sharpe made it clear that his employment would depend on his naming "a political ally of their chairman of the inspectors of primary elections in his district."[38]

The surveyor was besieged with requests from powerful political figures to appoint friends, relatives, and cronies. And the surveyor had no standard of impartiality established by the law to shelter himself from this horde of office-seekers. Sharpe stated, "A member of Congress, or even a person higher in office, insists on having his friend appointed from Iowa or Pennsylvania, or the western portion of the State, and the Collector is compelled to comply. It is impossible to tell the man's qualifications before his appointment." It was not a system that he preferred; if the decision had been his he would have appointed "a very different class of men." He recounted how he had received a letter from a high official who had visited him a number of times for the same reason—the reappointment of a man who had been dismissed three times already, the last time for openly admitting that he had defrauded the government. Sharpe, however, did not comment on the requests from the White House such as the one in which President Grant's secretary, O. E. Babcock (with whom Sharpe had served on Grant's staff and on the Harris court-martial), wrote on October 27, 1875: "The President directs me to say that if you can give Genl Parker (E. S.) a position without injury to the service he would be pleased to have it done." Parker had been Grant's military secretary in the war and one of his family of generals, like Sharpe. Ultimately Grant found a job for him as a commissioner of the Police Department of New York City. Sharpe was not above using the spoils system himself by appointing his cousin Jansen Hasbrouck, Jr., to a clerkship at the Custom House.[39]

Despite these problems, the efficiency of the Surveyor's Department increased remarkably under Sharpe's direction. He appointed his cousin, a man he trusted, former Brig. Gen. Jacob Sharpe, to supervise the 115 inspectors in his department. That increase in efficiency was reflected in the sharp rise in the collection of duties of 40 percent on passenger baggage alone in 1875 over 1874. That was no small achievement when total imports in 1875 amounted to $368 million, with gold duties paid of $107 million or 34 percent. This was the single largest source of revenue for the federal government, and one of the choicest political plums in Grant's basket. That he would entrust it to Sharpe is indicative of his trust in his former intelligence chief.[40]

Despite Sharpe's improvements, the appointments of Arthur, Sharpe, and Cornell were only the beginning of trouble for Grant. He had supported efforts at Civil Service reform and had appointed a Civil Service Commission (CSC) headed by the militant reformer, George Curtis, who achieved almost complete control of the Civil Service and opposed Sharpe for the office. Grant was still supportive of reform, but he wanted flexibility in the appointment of senior officials. Although the office was technically within Civil Service control, it had always been filled by a prominent New York politician. After some hesitation, Grant was determined to have his way and appointed Sharpe on March 14, 1873 without notifying Curtis, who resigned in a huff.[41]

The issue of Civil Service reform raised its head again in the administration of Rutherford B. Hayes (1877–81) who determined to establish a professional Civil Service and eliminate patronage. Hayes had created numerous commissions to investigate the conditions in a number of custom houses. Where better to start than Conkling's patronage prize of the New York Custom House, no doubt reinforced by the senator's ill-graced failure to support him in the election? The commission for New York, which met in early May 1877, "found all sorts of petty inefficiency, petty bribe-taking (though it made no specific charge against anybody), playing of politics, carelessness, etc., etc., and calculated that one-fourth of the revenue was lost to the Government because of these conditions. It recommended a twenty percent reduction of the force."[42]

Sharpe had testified at length at the hearings and pointed out many inefficiencies, such as the patronage system, and out-of-date procedures and organization that was not within his competence to revise. He made a point of informing the commission that the Custom House had 17 laws to administer. He made a number of cogent recommendations for change. He testified that "The mode of appointing inspectors could be improved; politicians can be got rid of by indicating to them that there are no vacancies, but the Surveyor has no chance against the persistent pleadings of friends on personal grounds." He also pointed out that the system was so primitive that inspectors had no dockside facilities to competently organize their inspections of persons and goods. "Duties are assessed and receipts made out on the tops of whisky-barrels, and the passenger who put $200 to $300 in gold to a stranger, who slaps it into his pocket, believes half the time that he is being swindled."[43]

Throughout the commission hearings, Sharpe's defense of customs organization of the Port of New York was detailed and aggressive. In one hearing before the first witness could be called, Sharpe entered the room and boldly demanded to be able to cross-examine the witnesses. He refuted the claims of one surveyor who said the work force could be sharply reduced by citing the fact that large numbers of ships were waiting to land passengers because of a lack of inspectors. When the head of the commission declined to allow him to cross-examine, he stormed out. It was a typical Sharpe tactic to boldly try to seize the initiative in any matter. On this day, it did not work.[44] In the end, Arthur and Sharpe had to acquiesce to the findings of the commission and agree to a 20 percent reduction in the work force.

Assault on Broadway

Sharpe's earlier comment that he would have preferred "a different class of men" in the Custom House was subsequently brought home on July 20. Sharpe had just left the Historical Society and called in at the *Times*. He was loaded down with books and papers and carrying an umbrella when he passed William A. Grace, an inspector he had dismissed two years ago due to formal complaints of bribery and drunkenness, which Sharpe had documented. Grace was a large, powerful man, and without warning struck Sharpe a stunning blow that sent him into the street. Grace leaped on him, landing several more blows until citizens dragged him off and the police arrived to arrest him. Grace had worked Sharpe over badly, inflicting a badly cut right cheek, a black eye, a severe abrasion on the left check, bruised left arm, and damaged thumb.[45]

The reaction in the Customs House was almost universal outrage at Sharpe's treatment, and many threats of bodily violence were made by Grace's former co-workers. It was evident that the overwhelming majority of the Custom House employees had a healthy respect if not liking for the surveyor. It was believed that Sharpe's strong hand on his office brought on the animosity of a small clique, used to laxer conditions, who had egged Grace on.[46]

The subsequent trial attracted the cream of New York City's politicians, prose-cutors, and senior police officers. The testimony of the witnesses of the assault was damning as was that of a witness who stated that a disgruntled Grace had planned to do violence to Sharpe, whom he blamed for his dismissal which the prosecution attributed to drunkenness and blackmail. Grace himself would claim that he had been dismissed because Sharpe had "connived at the use of fraudulent scales for weighing sugar imported by a certain firm." He also said that Sharpe had provoked him by spitting at him, an act a gentleman such as Sharpe could not conceivably have committed. The jury convicted Grace after barely 35 minutes' deliberation, and the judge gave him four months in jail.[47]

Although he was not allowed to bring his charges up in court, Grace maintained that he had repeatedly brought to Sharpe's notice the wrongdoings of Donner & De Castro, a sugar importer, but that Sharpe took no action. Donner & De Castro had withdrawn the complaints after threats from Grace but maintained their charges were still valid. Sharpe was also convinced by his investigation that the charges were valid and his dismissal of Grace fully warranted. Two years later, the file of Sharpe's documentation would be reviewed by *The New York Times* and found credible. Grace accused the company and Sharpe of collusion in the bringing of these charges and that Sharpe used that complaint to dismiss him.[48]

Scapegoat Sharpe

To President Hayes there was a clear conflict of interest in the holding of federal office and office in political parties. The report of the Jay Commission prompted him to issue an executive order on June 22 forbidding office holders from taking an active role in politics, stating that "no officer should be required or permitted to take part in the management of political organizations, caucuses, conventions or election campaigns," and wrote to Secretary Sherman that "no assessments for political purposes on officers and subordinates should be allowed." He made it clear to Cornell that he was either to give up his position as chief naval officer of the port or his position as Republican state chairman. Cornell refused.[49]

The commission report also convinced him to replace the rest of the leadership of the Custom House. One critical recommendation read, "the success of every effort though the customs service to relive the national commerce and industry from the evils wrought by mismanagement and corruption, can be accomplished only by the emancipation of the service from partisan control." The report had painted a bull's-eye on Conkling's men in the Custom House. It was the weapon Hayes needed to move against Senator Conkling's patronage control of the Port of New York. On September 6 Hayes demanded the resignations of Arthur, Sharpe, and Cornell. Hayes named their replacements—which included Theodore Roosevelt, Sr. as collector of customs and Edwin A. Merritt as surveyor—in October. However, Arthur, Sharpe, and Cornell refused to resign. Arthur stated that he would not run "under fire" and that the abuses were inherent in the system and not due to any wrongdoing on his part.[50]

Sharpe had been so sure of his conduct that he had submitted his application for the surveyorship position. Interestingly, *The Sun* reported that Sharpe's term actually had expired in spring 1876, but with the failure of the confirmation of a replacement, he continued in office. Pointedly, *The Chicago Daily Tribune* observed that "the President has decided to select SOME OTHER GENTLEMAN."[51]

It appears at this point that the administration was willing to resort to extraordinary measures to drive Sharpe from office as a wedge to pry Conkling's hand off the Custom House. Governor Robertson pardoned William Grace on November 28 with only half his sentence served, giving his reason "that the sentence was excessive—that the requirements of justice have been fully satisfied," and that his family was suffering. Astoundingly, President Hayes and Secretary of the Treasury Sherman then had a "very pleasant interview with him" in Washington. It was reported that the Treasury had examined the issue and found Grace's accusations correct. His back pay was paid him. Conkling did not come to Sharpe's defense. Sharpe recognized the inevitable and withdrew his application for the surveyorship.[52]

Senator Roscoe Conkling was able to delay confirmation of Hayes's replacements by evoking "Senatorial Privilege," for Arthur but allowed the nomination of Merritt to go forward early in 1878. Conkling found he could not support Sharpe because of the Grace accusations and the fact that his term had actually expired. At that time the leading citizens of Kingston, to show their support in this crisis, made Sharpe the tender of a public dinner in his honor. He politely declined, saying that the calls upon public charity were especially severe at this time and that "I hesitate to be the means of diverting by a costly entertainment, any surplus expenditures which would otherwise relieve the necessities of the suffering."[53] Three months after Sharpe left office and during the summer Senate recess on July 11, Hayes removed Arthur and Cornell. Arthur, Cornell, and Sharpe had already been close, and this experience certainly deepened their friendship.

There was more than just being on the losing end of a policy battle; they felt they had been the targets of the presidential ambitions of Secretary of State Evarts and Secretary of the Treasury Sherman.

> There were some things that seemed to justify this view. General Arthur, shortly after he was removed, said to this friends that he could have been spared the humiliation of removal had he been willing to accept a bribe, and when asked what the bribe was replied that he had been offered a foreign mission if he would resign as Collector of the Port. To intimate friends he showed the letter in which that offer had been made.
>
> So too, Mr. Cornell and General Sharpe were confidentially informed that if they would resign their offices in the Custom House they would speedily be appointed to other posts.[54]

Living Well—Speaker Sharpe

The mud flung by the Grace issue did not stick among those in Kingston who thought well of Sharpe as the offered testimonial showed. After seven years of federal service, Sharpe leaped into the politics of Ulster County and Kingston and would demonstrate the old adage that the best revenge is living well. That city had been run by a corrupt Democrat ring for the last five years and was considered a stronghold of that party. The leaders of the ring found their muscle among the large Irish community that worked the local quarries. The ring had plundered the city shamelessly. Sharpe appeared like the white knight of the Republicans and other reformists in Kingston. Through their support and his powerful ability to speak and organize, he pulled off an upset in the 1878 election for his district in the state assembly. His demolition of the Democrat stronghold caused heads to turn in both Albany and New York City. Here was a man with an impressive future.

Sharpe was given the chairmanship of the insurance committee of the Assembly. Although an initial motion was defeated, *The New York Times* was impressed that it represented the first occurrence of "independent action" in the defense of the interests of policy holders against a committee stacked with those supportive of the interests of the insurance companies. *The Brooklyn Daily Eagle*, no friend of Sharpe's, crowed that after this defeat, "The Assembly has no further use for him, and he may be said to be upon the shelf." Sharpe was ultimately successful in preventing insurance company interests from abolishing the State Insurance Department which protected the interests of the stockholders.[55]

One of Sharpe's first acts was to help local reformers limit the ability of the ring to take control of polling places and deny the right to vote to their enemies, essentially the tax-paying citizens of Kingston of both parties whose rates had been sent through the roof in order to support the ring's largely indigent following. At Sharpe's behest the Assembly passed a bill to reduce the number of polling places to one instead of five in the expectation that the reformists could better ensure it was not taken over by the ring. Unfortunately, the law of unintended consequences trumped Sharpe's bill. The ring designated the single polling place in their own stronghold and at a local election on March 4 instigated a riot to prevent anyone they disliked form voting. One man was severely beaten and injured. The Assembly promptly sent an investigative committee, which reported back the outrages in detail. The Assembly passed a resolution encouraging the Grand Jury and the next circuit court to be held at Kingston to see that justice was done. That is exactly what happened next. The head of the ring was arrested and another man arrested and convicted for assault. This result had the effect of discouraging such election fraud throughout New York. Sharpe had set this process in motion with the introduction of his initial bill.[56]

In his first term in the Assembly Sharpe had made a most positive impression. His ability to make friends, his eloquence, and hard work on various reform measures had earned him the respect of the Republican majority as well as his own constituents. *The New York Times* judged that "His Legislative record was thoroughly honorable to himself and creditable to his constituents."[57]

That was confirmed by his victory in the November election for the Assembly where he increased his majority, being supported by a number of Democrats based on his record. After that it was quickly made known that both Conkling and *The New York Times* supported him for the speakership. In early January General Arthur arrived in Albany to also throw his weight behind Sharpe for speaker. His choice by the Republican caucus seemed assured.[58]

With the Republicans in a majority in the Assembly, his election followed on as a matter of course. The whole process had been so harmonious and inevitable that it prompted *The New York Times* to say, "There had not been so peaceful a struggle for the position for many years, and never before did a contest terminate with less disappointment apparent among the defeated candidates."[59]

Sharpe's performance as speaker was much praised. Sharpe did not let his party politics prevent fruitful cooperation with the Democrats who were then in the minority, and he remained personally popular across party lines. The normally hostile *Brooklyn Daily Eagle* wrote of Sharpe's conduct as he opened the Assembly: "General Sharpe made AN EXCELLENT IMPRESSION in the chair today and his speech, upon assuming the Speakership, was a model. If the execution be equal to the promise, if the policy laid down to be followed, all will be well." Then grudgingly it went on, "But will it? General Sharpe, in every respect socially a fine fellow, but always been known as a machine man, believing in Obedience to authority." As speaker, no man would prove to be his own man better than Sharpe.[60]

One of his first acts was to end the chaos on the Assembly floor. It had become a habit to allow a horde of lobbyists, office-seekers, visitors, and outright pests to wander the Assembly floor and even stroll into the speaker's own office, constantly interfering with official business. Sharpe immediately ordered a mahogany rail built to separate the seating and working floor of the Assembly from visitors. Only 23 reporters with special passes were allowed access and all other visitors had to request a pass from the speaker's office. The crowds shrank dramatically, with the business of the Assembly now much expedited.[61] His immediate embrace of farming interests earned him a resolution of appreciation from the farmers in the Assembly, thanking him for the "fair and satisfactory representations he has given to the agricultural interests of the States upon the committees of the House." He was making friends constantly as he strolled through this forum.[62] He did not neglect his own constituents. He worked to pass a bill that would allow Kingston to refinance its large debt incurred by the corrupt Democrat ring, and he had done so at the request of the Democrat senator representing Ulster.[63]

He also did not make an enemy of the press but won from them as much affection and respect as the breed is capable of. A correspondent reporting on the Assembly captured a glimpse of Sharpe at work as speaker.

> Sharpe was one of the queerest and most original speakers that the Assembly ever had. He did not seem to realize that there were other ears close at hand besides those of the clerk; and he kept up a constant fire of words not only as to the disposition, but even as to the merits of bills, as they came in. It was a very entertaining thing to the men in the newspaper row to listen to his comments, such as "What in the mischief does that man want to introduce that bill for now? Doesn't he know that we are not in that order of business?" "Here is that old bill again that we have seen so many years. Why doesn't Mr. _____ take some better time for introducing it than this, when we are so busy about other things?" "What does _____ mean by bringing in that bill at this time? I supposed that we had fixed him so that he wouldn't bring it here at

all." In spite of these odd tricks Speaker Sharpe was rather popular among the members, even with those who did not agree with him in politics.[64]

The legislative year ended with a sense of accomplishment under Sharpe's influence. In a highly unusual act, the Democrats were even moved to praise him:

> Mr. Rhodes spoke very heartily of the respect and esteem in which, every member, held the speaker, who had fulfilled all his promise of the fair treatment of the minority, and had only erred on the side of good nature. Mr. McCarthy ... spoke of the Speaker as being "brave, just, and king," and assured Gen. Sharpe that the best wishes of the minority would go with him." Speaking for the majority, Mr. Husted referred to Sharpe as "cordial, warm, and earnest."

Sharpe was clearly moved by the sentiment of the Assembly.[65] *The New York Times* editorialized:

> The tributes which have been paid to the ability and fairness with which Gen. Sharpe has discharged the duties of Speaker have been well deserved. The credible record of the Assembly is largely due to his judicious selection of committees, while the objectionable elements that entered into the composition of the Committee of Ways and Means were owing to causes which time honored precedent rendered it difficult, if not impossible, to neutralize. The exceptions which were taken by Gen. SHARPE's opponents at the beginning of the session to his ability as a presiding officer have been shown by actual to be baseless, and no Speaker of late years has been able to secure and retain so much of the respect and confidence of his fellow members, as well as of the approval of the people generally. Gen. SHARPE has conclusively disposed of the tradition that no member could make a satisfactory Speaker who did not bring to the office, years of familiarity with parliamentary forms, and how much of a benefit that service is likely to be to succeeding Legislatures.[66]

By any standard Sharpe's performance as speaker had been stellar and added luster to his reputation as well as to the number of his friends.

Kingmaker at the Convention

In fall 1880 he was chosen as a delegate to the Republican convention. The New York delegation was led by Senator Roscoe Conkling who, with Sharpe, was a leader of the so-called "Stalwarts," that part of the New York Republican Party that actively and loyally supported Grant for a third term. Their leaders represented old friends of Grant, such as Gen. John Logan of Illinois and Conkling of New York, "old school practitioners of patronage and machine politics who ruled the party in the states like princely fiefdoms" and younger members such as Sharpe. None of them had had any love for Hayes and his Civil Service reform measures, especially after his attempts to drive Arthur, Cornell, and Sharpe out of office. They got their revenge when they successfully froze Hayes out of any consideration for re-nomination and threw their support to Grant. Senator Blaine was the most prominent rival for the nomination and was an old enemy of Conkling's.

Sharpe was the convention floor leader of the fight for Grant, but his efforts could do no more than hold the Grant vote steady. Nevertheless, he led a vigorous and clever battle. Early in the convention he caused a sensation by offering a "resolution as a substitute for the majority report of the committee on rules [of whom he was a member], that the convention proceed to the nomination for president." It upset the Blaine faction and "looked as if the Grant men had made bargains somewhere." The object of the ploy may have been just that—to rush the nomination while the convention believed a deal making Grant the nominee had been made—making it a self-fulfilling prophecy. Sharpe and Gen. James Garfield made speeches pro and con, as "the most intense excitement prevailed" only to deflate as the measure was defeated with only 276 of the 399 votes needed.[67]

After 35 ballots, it was more than obvious that the opposition of the anti-Grant forces was too powerful an obstacle to overcome. Yet no other candidate could even get the 306 votes that Grant had secured but could not expand. Finally, the consensus among the non-Grant groups was that a dark horse was necessary.

John A. Garfield was nominated instead on the 36th ballot. John Logan took advantage of the obvious to support Garfield. Grant himself called on the Ohioan to pledge his support, and in the process the "306 stalwarts who stood by the general for thirty-six ballots [including Sharpe] were immortalized in Republican mythology."[68]

The next issue was the nomination of a vice-president, and here Sharpe's influence was crucial because Conkling essentially abandoned a constructive role so angry was he at the defeat of the Grant nomination. It especially galled him that Garfield was a close friend of his enemy Blaine. Conkling was proving to be a bad loser and predicted that Garfield would be handily beaten by the Democrats. He was not about to be cooperative with Garfield's supporters. They, in turn, came hat in hand to the Stalwarts begging, in the interest of party unity, for them to nominate a candidate for the vice-presidency. Conkling actively discouraged several prominent New Yorkers from accepting the nomination by stating, "the question is, whom shall we place upon the altar as a vicarious sacrifice?"

It was at this time that Sharpe seized control of the issue in defiance of Conkling's position. Garfield and he had known each other cordially for at least 15 years both in veterans affairs and politics. Sharpe was not about to cast this relationship away, especially when it offered a valuable opportunity for the New York party. He suggested Chester A. Arthur to an important group of Stalwarts who then sounded out Arthur. A New Yorker on the ticket was vital for carrying that state for Garfield. But Conkling, who could not have Grant and would not help Garfield, vehemently opposed it. In Sharpe's presence, Conkling "bitterly opposed placing a Stalwart upon the ticket and expressed in unmeasured terms his disapprobation of Arthur's acceptance." On their way back to the convention, Sharpe told former Brigadier General Woodford of the pungent flavor of Conkling's invective, and of Arthur's calm assertion of the propriety of his action. On the floor of the convention, Conkling "flatly refused Sharpe's request to put Arthur in nomination." Sharpe was not to be thwarted and persuaded another New York delegate, Woodford, to place Arthur's name in nomination. The ploy succeeded; Arthur was nominated much to his own gratified amazement. His ambitions had never looked beyond election to the U.S. Senate. Nevertheless, he was still much influenced by his friend Conkling. The two of them sat out much of the election and went fishing.[69]

The sure Democrat victory evaporated with their nomination of Maj. Gen. Winfield Scott Hancock. A political novice with little interest in active campaigning, he was beaten by Garfield with the help of the New York Republicans, especially Sharpe, who assumed the mantle of leadership in the absence of Conkling. As the campaign began in earnest, Sharpe helped organize a major political event at the Republican National Headquarters on 5th Avenue. Before a crowd of over 10,000 Sharpe delivered a memorable stem winder of a speech "in a clear, full voice that was heard distinctly almost to the limits of the extreme edge of the throng," laying out in powerful words the achievements and virtues of the party's nominee:

> He is associated with all the trials and triumphs of the party. He was associated with Ulysses S. Grant [cheers] in maintaining the honor of the flag, which, he says sweeps the ground and touches the stars. [cheers] He was associated with Abraham Lincoln in the grand measures which the boys in Blue were sustained. He has been associated with the Republican statesmen of every name and state in leading the country through the dark days which were the natural results of an exhausting war. Squatter sovereignty, human slavery, and secession and Rebellion and the rag baby of paper money fill the graves which mark the history of the Democratic Party, and not one of these corpses that does not give evidence of the blows of James A. Garfield. [cheers and applause]

The speech built on and on to a crescendo and ended mightily with, "Let us answer that bugle call with resolution and alacrity, so that on the morning following the great day in November, we may sing again as we used to sing in Virginia the battle hymn of the republic." *The New York Times* wrote:

> The closing remarks of Gen. Sharpe were drowned in a cheer that began in the centre of the throng and went rolling back and forth from one end of the vast body to the other. Men waved their hats frantically in the air, the ladies in the adjoining balconies shook their handkerchiefs, and the band played a spirited air, as Gen. Sharpe turned to Gen. Garfield to introduce him. Garfield bowed in acknowledgement, certainly impressed with a man who could whip a crowd into such enthusiasm. Garfield certainly marked him as a man of consequence and as an important ally.

His own speech reflected the party's support of black rights, a position of which Sharpe was an enthusiastic supporter, in the most dramatic terms. Before the crowed that Sharpe has so warmed up, he finished his speech with the following words:

> In all that period of terror and distress no Union soldier was ever betrayed by any black man anywhere and so long as we live we'll stand by those black allies of ours. We have seen white men betray the flag and fight to kill the union, but in all that long and dreary war you never saw a traitor under a black skin (cheers).

As the cheering subsided, "General Sharpe took Gen. Arthur by the arm, and leading him to the front of the balcony, introduced him as the 'Candidate for Vice-President,' as the crowd erupted in cheers." It was clear to everyone that it was Sharpe who had brought Arthur to that balcony.[70]

Sharpe was a tireless campaigner for the ticket, traveling up and down the state giving a speech a day, for example in Lockport, Rochester, Baldwinsville, and Lowville in western New York between October 11 and 14. On October 19 he himself was unanimously renominated for assemblyman by the county convention of Ulster County in Kingston.[71] So successful had Sharpe been in his position as speaker that the Democrat opposition did not have a chance. Large numbers of Democrats crossed party lines to attend the Republican convention and to vote for him in the general election.[72]

The national ticket also swept to victory, vindicating Sharpe's defiance of Conkling in meeting the Garfield supporters halfway by offering Arthur to balance the ticket. That vindication was reflected in the wire he sent to Garfield: "No congratulations can be warmer than mine."[73] The victory was doubly sweet for he had himself been reelected to the state assembly and his friend and ally, Cornell, elected governor.

Speaker Again

Sharpe must have thought he was secure in Garfield's good will, a thought that was quickly dispelled. Sharpe's record as speaker seemed to assure him an easy reelection. On January 3, 1881 the members of the New York legislature were stunned to read in the *New York Tribune* that President-Elect Garfield was supporting another candidate for speaker of the Assembly over Sharpe. Whitelaw Reid, editor of the *Tribune*, arrived to work the floor, in alliance with several senators and others, to encourage the candidacy of Assemblyman Skinner with hints of patronage from Garfield. That approach backfired badly. The effort collapsed, laughed out of consideration as the mischief of the Reid and Garfield so-called endorsement was dismissed as a falsehood. Yet the fact remains that Reid was considered Garfield's mouthpiece in the New York press. That should have served as a warning. The sentiment was for Sharpe. One member stormed out and went directly to Sharpe to tell him he had his support. Skinner finally realized he had been led by the nose by this cabal of senators and Reid. His truer friends urged him to withdraw. Seeing the game was up, Reid returned immediately to New York. Representatives of Skinner went to Sharpe to relate that Skinner had folded; they apologized for being part of the sordid proceedings.

Sharpe's name was now put in nomination by Colonel B. F. Baker, "as that of a man of commanding ability, heroic devotion to his country, of undisturbed courtesy to his opponents when Speaker, and at once frank, fair, and ready to right a wrong when it lay in his power to do it." Skinner himself seconded the nomination in a chastened tone of party unity. Former speaker Thomas Alvord put an end to all the speeches when he said, "I have known George H. Sharpe for a long time, and

I know him to be a very clever and a good Speaker. I move that his nomination be made unanimous." The nomination was then made unanimous by all 80 members.[74]

The New York Times described it in the following terms:

> [the] dullest and quietest canvas for the Speakership Albany has known in years … that there was no bitterness among General Sharpe's supporters toward those who for reasons good to themselves supported Mr. Skinner. It rarely happens that a canvass which is a real one closes with such general good feeling and with such an utter absence of the angry talk which often follows a defeat.

It praised Sharpe, saying that "there was not a man among those supporting Mr. Skinner who did not have the highest respect for General Sharpe, as well as for his personal qualities as his record as a soldier and in public life."[75]

Clearly, Sharpe's reputation stood high. The following character sketch illustrates why:

> Sharpe's credible service on Grant's staff, his cleverness as a Stalwart manager, and his acceptability as a speaker of the preceding assembly, brought him troops of friends. Although making no pretensions to the gift of oratory, he possessed qualities needed for oratorical success. He was forceful, remarkably clear, with impressive manners and a winning voice. As a campaign speaker few persons in the state excelled him. Men, too, generally found him easy of approach and ready to listen. At all events his tactful management won a majority of the Republican assemblymen before the opposition got a candidate into the field. Under these circumstances members did not fancy staking good committee appointments against the uncertainty of Presidential favors, and in the end Sharpe's election followed without dissent.[76]

After being sworn in the next day, Sharpe's address was gracious to his brief caucus opponents and to the Democrats with whom he had worked in the previous session and was met with their warm applause. He was ever the bridge-builder among factions. He made the sound recommendation to give the governor permission to appoint a commission to make recommendations on taxes. He also made a point of stressing the joint responsibility of the Assembly and Senate to choose a new senator in this session. There had already been rumors that the committee appointments would be made "to influence the results." The *Tribune* reported that "a majority of members refused to believe that General Sharpe would do such a thing or would manipulate the committees themselves to vote this way or that in the Senatorial contest. Certainly there is everything in General Sharpe's record to show that he would do none of these things." It was an ominous foretelling of events that would do much to damage his career.[77]

The Conkling Crisis

So far Sharpe had successfully ridden the coattails of Conkling's patronage by being his loyal and effective supporter. It was clear he was Conkling's man in the state assembly. The *Times* was particularly scathing. Shortly before the inauguration it stated that

Conkling "now seeks through Cornell and Sharpe to dragoon the legislature into the most abject submission. Cornell dictates the laws and Sharpe chastises the unruly members who dare to think and act for themselves" who were "ignored and insulted by his creature Sharpe." In the coming months the relationship between Conkling and Sharpe would undergo enormous strain to the breaking point.[78]

After the election, Conkling apparently sent Sharpe to see Garfield in February 1881 to mend fences. Asked by a reporter if New York would have a place in the cabinet, Sharpe replied confidently, "Yes, Sir, and a good one." Although he denied talking about cabinet appointees, it certainly was brought up. Ominously, Sharpe made no impression on Garfield. No New Yorker, much less a Conkling man, was appointed to the cabinet.[79]

One of Garfield's first acts was to appoint a new surveyor for the Port of New York, William H. Robertson, without extending the traditional courtesy of a nod from his home state senators. Garfield knew that nod would not be forthcoming because Robertson was a political opponent of Conkling. He had not forgotten Conkling's petulant refusal to support him at the convention. Conkling was surprised when the New York State Senate and Assembly both voted their support of the Robertson nomination. Up to that point the work of the Assembly had gone smoothly and Sharpe anticipated that it would complete its business in the first week of May and adjourn. He had a personal reason for looking forward to the adjournment, as the press was reporting, "for rumor with its thousand tongues comes up from Washington that he is to be chosen as Minister to Belgium... The appointment, if such shall be made, will be an excellent one for General Sharpe is a born diplomat, as well as an accomplished scholar and linguist."[80]

Conkling was about to kill that prospect as he decided to go to war with Garfield. At his bidding, Sharpe was able to force through a motion that the Assembly reconsider its vote. He was also able to get a majority of Republicans in the Assembly to sign a petition to Garfield protesting the nomination.[81]

Conkling, to his outrage, was not supported in this breach of custom by the rest of the Senate, and then took an enormous political gamble. He resigned and persuaded New York's newly elected other senator, Thomas C. Platt, to also resign, earning him the title, "Me too Platt." Conkling planned to demand vindication from the New York State legislature by obtaining reelection for both himself and Platt. Sharpe's support as the speaker would be vital if his ploy was to succeed.[82]

But that ploy was one act of arrogance too many. Conkling had ruled the party through a dictatorial style that brooked no discussion or opposition. Power cemented by fear is quickly dissolved when weakness is detected. Conkling had miscalculated badly. His resignation was seen as setting his private political interests against those of his party and state, an act of insufferable hubris. His imperious attempt to manage the process simply drove many former supporters into opposition. One of them was Sharpe, the one man he did not need to alienate. Sharpe saw Conkling's maneuver as an assault on the American system of government. In a subsequent statement he made to the press, he explained, "Mr. Conkling resigned for the purpose of being a candidate for reelection. He sought to introduce into American politics the English method of resigning and obtaining a reindorsement from his constituents in order that he might wage war upon the Administration untrammeled by party obligations."

Conkling added insult to this assault on American precedent by essentially ordering his friends in the Assembly to insure his reelection. This clearly set Sharpe off whose comments were later printed in *The New York Times*:

> So true was this that his friends in Albany were informed by the most expeditious methods. A special messenger was sent from Washington to Albany bearing the letters of resignation, and from the messenger it was ascertained that Mr. Conkling expected immediate steps to be taken by his friends to insure his reelection. I was myself informed from Washington that he was to be reelected. I was also asked to invite him by telegram to meet his friends in New York to consult about the steps to be taken. I refrained from sending any such telegram. Others were urged to send telegrams of like purport… It was notorious in Albany that the messenger who brought the resignations stated without reserve that a reelection was expected by the resigned senators.[83]

Sharpe also had practical political reasons for seeing Conkling's attempt at reelection as being badly timed. The Republicans no longer had a comfortable majority in the Assembly, and their own unity had been roiled by a series of disputes. It had been an exhausting five-month session, and the Assembly was ready to adjourn when the Conkling issue was dropped in its lap in late March. Sharpe called a meeting of the Stalwarts but all too few participated and many left before it adjourned. "I expressed myself as being in hope that we would not be called upon to meet such an issue," he stated. He then traveled to New York in the hope that the facts would convince Conkling's friends that "some other conclusion would be reached than the one which had been decided upon at Washington."

At this time Sharpe was sounding out Assemblymen on their views of the matter. One such was C. D. Chickering, a Stalwart Republican, and powerful chairman of the Ways and Means Committee, who made it clear that this issue would be ruinous to the party and throw his district to the Democrats. Sharpe then expressed his views forthrightly to Chickering. "Mr. Conkling's friends will not allow him to be a candidate. I shall go to New York to-morrow and shall advise him to decline to have anything to do with the matter. I do not believe he could be elected if he should be a candidate. I will not ask you to vote for him."[84]

On May 21, a Sunday, he called on Arthur and met other senior Republicans who had also called. They all agreed that "Mr. Conkling's resignation was a blunder, and his present candidacy for reelection a greater one; and from our intimate knowledge of the members and their views we came to the conclusion unanimously that Mr. Conkling's reelection was problematical." They also agreed to attempt to induce Conkling to change his mind though they were aware of the "difficulty of presenting any fact to Mr. Conkling that did not coincide with his wishes." He also observed that Conkling "desired that this reelection should come to him without solicitation… He wanted to be reelected without his appearing to have a hand in it."[85]

It was a triumph of hubris over practical politics. Sharpe, as speaker of the Assembly, must have inwardly flinched at the enormous political problem Conkling had thrown to him. Other callers, included Conkling and Platt, arrived, and a general discussion ensued. In no way was it a meeting called for the purpose of Conkling's friends to encourage Platt and him to seek reelection. Conkling and Platt, the latter in his autobiography, presented a different account of the meeting in which Platt noted that one of his supporters at this meeting, Louis Payn, "prognosticated that we would both be defeated. Speaker Sharpe angrily turned upon Payn and exclaimed, 'We shall win this battle without any trouble.' 'Huh, but you will be the first to desert us,' retorted Payn."[86]

Sharpe would flatly later deny making any speech "encouraging" Conkling to go to Albany. "I never made such a speech. It is a falsehood." His emphasis was entirely different. Sharpe told Conkling plainly that if he wanted to be reelected, he had to actively seek it in Albany, and that nothing but his presence and the active support of all his friends throughout the state could push through his reelection. "And I added, that with all this, the event was not certain." The group took an informal caucus of Republicans in the legislature based on a canvass of their views and discovered that the Senate was largely against him and that only half the Republicans in the Assembly would support him. It is an interesting comment upon the power that Conkling had as leader of the state Republican Party that even after this canvass, as Sharpe said, "The question of Mr. Conkling's candidacy was not discussed, but was taken for granted throughout the interview" by Conkling despite so many reservations. Sharpe was accurate when he said, "And I again assert there was at no time any conference, called or held, for the purpose of deciding upon Mr. Conkling's candidacy, at which I was present." It also says much of Conkling's personal power that he caused many other strong-minded men, such as Sharpe, to hold their tongues in making it emphatically clear, as Sharpe had promised Chickering, to plainly tell him not to run. Sharpe, in a much distressed state of mind, was the first to leave the meeting.[87]

Sharpe's account of his conduct at the meeting was thrown into question by the statements of Conkling loyalists. A major issue in subsequent party politics was the contention of other members of the meeting that he did, in fact, enthusiastically support Conkling's nomination, as Payn stated. Besides Platt and Payn, five other men at the meeting wrote Conkling stating that Sharpe had done so. These were all loyal Conkling men who helped their patron carry his heavy load of spite after his defeat. Whether their statements were a calculated act of political vindictiveness must be balanced against Sharpe's reputation for integrity. That Sharpe thought so was clear. The *Chicago Daily Tribune* reported that in June 1882 he was hunting up evidence in New York City "to sustain the statement made by him about Conkling.

He is very indignant at the issue of his veracity raided by the ex-senator's friends. He says he is prepared to stand by every assertion...",[88] as he did to a reporter of the *New York Tribune* the week before:

> Let Mr. Conkling vie the names of the men who advised him to go to Albany. I should like to know their names. I don't know who they were, and yet I think I would have known if any one knew them. Let Mr. Conkling disclose the names of these men and expose them to the shame of having given him such advice. Whom did he consult at Washington before resigning his place as United States Senator? Did he consult any of his friends there or in this State? He never consulted them. He went back on them, and now seeks to put the blame of his defeat for reelection on their shoulders. Yet, let us know who was responsible for that defeat.[89]

After the meeting and despite his misgivings, Sharpe was still willing to work for Conkling's nomination out of his ingrained sense of loyalty. *The Boston Advertiser* caught his dilemma: "General Sharpe acted on a rather unhappy compromise between events which drifted one way, and personal attachments, since severed, which drew him elsewhere."[90] Almost immediately he ran into his own prediction that the outcome would not be certain. In Albany on May 30, Sharpe, as chairman of the Republican caucus committee, attempted to convene a caucus of Republican members of the legislature to support Conkling's candidacy. There was a rush out the doors of the Assembly as a majority of members voted with their feet against the caucus. "The face of Speaker Sharpe ... wore an ominous blank look of disappointment, and Payn, Denison, and Johnson, standing by the door of the Speaker's room, looked as if they would like to bite something or somebody." It did not take a Cassandra to conclude that *The New York Times*' headline "Conkling's Cause Lost," was prescient.[91]

Conkling then sent Sharpe a message, asking him to "give notice from the Speaker's desk on the adjournment of the House that a majority of all the Republicans elected to both Houses having signified their willingness that a caucus be held, one would be held at a time and place decided." This clearly was not the case that a majority of party members had agreed to such a thing. Sharpe asked the meaning of this request and was told by Conkling's representative that besides those who had actually signed a request for a caucus, a number of others had expressed a "willingness" for such a meeting. It was hoped that Sharpe would devise such wording as to "not be subject to the charge of falsehood." Sharpe declined on the spot to be a party to such a ploy. That night he met Conkling, who coldly asked him, "What was the occasion for the failure this morning?" Sharpe described his reply: "I told him I was chairman of the Caucus Committee of the Assembly, and I did not intend, by making such a statement as I was desired to make, to be met by a challenge to produce my proof."[92]

It did not help that the next day the Democrats had some fun with Sharpe. Assemblyman Bradley put Sharpe's name in nomination. The Democrats applauded loudly while Sharpe blushed deeply. Normally Sharpe enjoyed a good-natured joke even at his own expense, but not this time. He was under a great deal of stress which tends to wear a sense of humor thin. He sternly rapped the gavel to quell the noise. He then sent Bradley to withdraw his name which the assemblyman did.[93]

Sharpe's serious assistance to Conkling appears to have ended when the former senator tried to pressure him to manufacture a caucus consensus. Now he would support the process that would lead to the election of other candidates. The Stalwart group, which had hung together as an unbroken phalanx for Grant and on so many issues, cracked wide open. Over 20 assemblymen and senators of the Stalwarts refused under any circumstances to vote for Conkling. Sharpe arranged for different groups of two assemblymen and one senator, who were Conkling supporters, to meet with Conkling to drive home just how hopeless his cause was. But as one senator stated, they were "talked out of court." With the formal caucus procedure non-functional, Sharpe now indicated that he would be guided by an informal caucus if it succeeded. He stated, "I made no secret of my proposed course." He supported the nomination of former President Grant and former Secretary of State Fish and sent to Conkling to suggest that he withdraw his nomination and support these new nominees. Conkling refused, arrogantly demanding that his opponents make the proposal.[94]

Then the tide began to run against Conkling. On the day (July 2) that Platt withdrew his nomination to give a boost to Conkling, Garfield was shot by an assassin, who was a public supporter of both Conkling and Platt. The public turned bitterly on Conkling, especially for his vituperative feud with the President. On the 6th, Sharpe, as speaker, was proposing a resolution of the Assembly on the attempted assassination. The Democrats had proposed it, and Sharpe "in fraternal recognition of the action of the minority" offered it in terms that could only drive more nails into Conklin's political coffin, "recognizing in James A. Garfield a chief magistrate sincerely desirous of fulfilling the responsible duties of his high office with loyal regard to the interest of the whole country."

The balloting and canvassing had gone on for seven weeks and 32 ballots for Platt's seat alone. Sharpe as leader of the Stalwarts had kept the group solid for Conkling through the first week in July, but after the attack on Garfield and the public reaction, he knew that he had to cut loose from Conkling for the sake of the Republican Party in New York and for the larger public interest. It was clear to him that the issue had become what *The New York Times* called "one of the bitterest and hardest fought in the political annals of the State." The means to this end were prepared by a majority of the Republicans in both houses, who now called for a caucus and nominated Elbridge Lapham for Conkling's seat and Warner Miller representing Herkimer County for Platt's seat. As chairman of the party caucus committee, Sharpe was in a position to fight this spontaneous caucus. He chose not to and spoke of acceding to the decision of that caucus. At a stormy meeting of the Stalwarts on July 16, Sharpe put his cards on the table, and, "In plain words he expressed anew the opinions he had rather hinted at than declared outright before, and told his comrades that he intended to abide absolutely by the majority as expressed by the caucus and to vote for both the caucus candidates." That simple statement provoked a flood of outrage, "that his desertion of Conkling was an act of treachery," and that his vote for the two nominees would brand him to the people of New York as an "ingrate and political scoundrel." Louis Payn, who allegedly had predicted Sharpe's defection, "gave him a piece of his mind," in direct and crude terms. Sharpe did not hesitate to defend himself and insisted that he would not turn back. He had come to the conclusion that Conkling's selfish obstinacy had reached a point where his continued support was no longer in the public interest. He had cut Conkling loose.

News of the attacks on Sharpe had spread to the Assembly and the hall buzzed with anticipation when Sharpe took his seat as members of the Senate entered for the joint session to fill Platt's seat. Before the clerk could read the roll, Sharpe stood. All eyes were upon him as he began to speak. He said that by courtesy his name was at the foot of the roll but that many were aware that he had something to say on the matter and it would be "manly to make the statement at the beginning of the roll." The chamber was pin-drop quiet.

He explained, "When the election of United States Senators was brought before the Legislature of the State of New York there was one course that was pursued to preserve harmony, and that was that a consultation named a 'caucus' should be called by persons authorized to call that caucus in the regular way." He had tried repeatedly as the caucus committee chairman to call such a caucus but to no avail, being unable to assemble a majority in favor. The hearers understood perfectly that a caucus called by Sharpe and the Stalwart-controlled committee would be directed toward the support of Conkling.

> I have always believed in the right of a majority of a body to control its action and if a caucus committee fails to perform its duty I know of no other way in the world than for the majority of that body to call themselves and those who choose to act with them for the performance of that duty.
>
> I am obliged, Mr. President, and have so stated from the time that caucus reached a result to accept its results [applause].

He begged not to be interrupted. For him there had been only one objection to the caucus—that it had gone outside the party rules—but he concluded that it was "not broad enough to affect the great question of the right of a majority to go into a caucus which was denied by its officers." He added a warning on the dangers of continued party strife over this matter. "Do not think, because the Democratic Party on the floor of this house have, by their course, demanded our admiration and respect, do not fail to remember they will be fertile in expedients to take advantage of this dangerous position." He concluded by saying, "Mr. President, when my name is called upon this ballot in place of the eloquent leader who in the darkest days has pointed us to the brilliant path of victory, I shall vote for Elbridge G. Lapham."

In the following debate, Sharpe was excoriated by his fellow Stalwarts for a "mistake that would not soon be forgotten." In the vote Lapham received 68 votes to Conkling's 29. Though it was not enough to win, it signaled a crushing defeat for Conkling. The next vote was to fill Platt's seat and was won by Miller. It would only be a matter of time before Lapham garnered the necessary majority to replace Conkling.

That followed quickly after Garfield died on September 19—and on the 56th ballot. Conkling would lament, "How can I speak into a grave? How can I battle with a shroud?"[95]

At the October convention preceding the state election that year, Sharpe was still working hard to help Conkling control the proceedings, but the former senator had been wounded mortally by his attempt at reelection. It was up to Sharpe to deliver the conciliatory speech to the anti-Conkling forces, and he did it with such grace that it was greeted by loud applause.[96]

Despite criticism that he had deserted Conkling, Sharpe's constituents supported his decision. He was nominated by a party's Ulster County convention 22 to 2, and handily reelected in the November general election later than year. *The New York Times* observed:

> It is a touching tribute to Gen. Sharpe that here in Kingston, where he is known intimately and respected highly, there was little disposition shown to misinterpret either his words or his actions. His word had always been good, his judgment promoted him to support Miller and Lapham, his utterances were accepted almost without question as the genuine expression of an honest conviction. If elsewhere in the State there may be a lurking hostility or coldness toward Gen. Sharpe for his course in the senatorial contest, his constituents do not, as a rule, share in it.[97]

Although reelected to the Assembly by a heavy majority in Kingston, the speakership was no longer within his grasp. He could see the price he paid, for his principled stand had earned him the eternal enmity of the Conkling wing of the Stalwarts. That enmity would dog him for the rest of his political life. His immediate prospects were not affected; his constituents in Kingston approved of his actions enough to reelect him that November with a "heavy majority," despite the state party ticket winning only by a slim margin.[98]

At the beginning of the 1882 session, Theodore Roosevelt, Jr., was a newly elected member of the New York Assembly. This was his first opportunity to see Sharpe, about whom Roosevelt's biographer, Edward P. Kohn, wrote, his "career seemed to have crossed paths with every prominent American since the Civil War."[99] Sharpe was the Stalwart favorite for speaker while Thomas Alvord was the choice of the Half-Breeds. Both groups were losing the favor of much of the Republican Party. Perhaps in light of his father's failed nomination to replace Sharpe as surveyor of the Port of New York, Roosevelt penned this appraisal of Sharpe:

> In the evening the Republicans held a caucus to nominate our candidate [for speaker]. The contest lay between Sharpe and [Thomas G.] Alvord; the former a 'stalwart', a man of ability and shrewd enough to recognize the advantage of being considered respectable, but unless I am mistaken decidedly tricky and unquestionably a machine man pure and simple; the latter a

rugged, white headed old assemblyman, a 'half breed' or [word unclear] dependent, but a bad old fellow. As a choice of evils I voted for Sharpe—but Alvord was chosen.[100]

The choice in the end was moot because the Democrats were in the majority. Nevertheless, Sharpe had been beaten by Alvord. The anger at Sharpe for turning against Conkling became venomous at the 1882 state Republican convention for the nomination of governor. The dispute over the direction of the meeting at Arthur's home had become all-too public. Accusations that could not be papered over were made by Conkling's men. *The New York Times* observed, "It was easy to see that the Conkling men had not got through with Gen. George H. Sharpe. The task set for him to demonstrate his repentance for having said something about an alleged conference Conkling declared to be false—had not been fully performed." Not only had Sharpe not repented; he had aggressively sought to disprove Conkling's allegation. Sharpe's speech nominating Secretary of the Treasury, Charles J. Folger, "was received for the greater part in grim silence."[101]

The *Brooklyn Daily Eagle* commented in later years that "Conkling never recovered either happiness or power and was a spite factory until he died," adding Sharpe among others, "to the number of those whom he decorated with his hate…" Platt, on the other hand, played a better game, learning that "implacable antipathies pay as poorly in politics as anywhere else," earning great influence in the party, though Sharpe and he remained wary of each other.[102]

Rewards of a Kingmaker

Overshadowing his reelection to the Assembly was Sharpe's role as a kingmaker, for Arthur was now president. Arthur had had himself immediately sworn in to office in New York but repeated the ceremony in the White House. Sharpe was conspicuous by his presence in a very select group that included the cabinet, General Sherman in full uniform, ex-Presidents Grant and Hayes, the Chief Justice and two associate justices, six senators, and one representative. Sharpe was the only private citizen attending the ceremony. When Arthur returned to the city on September 29, it was in the company of Sharpe.[103]

Sharpe's friendship with Arthur grew in the space once dominated by Conkling. The latter's attempt to dictate policy to his old friend and now President Arthur had roused the genial former sidekick into a lion of independence. With his friendship with Conkling shattered, that with Sharpe grew deeper. When Arthur vacationed in the Catskills it would be in company with Sharpe and his wife. Sharpe received a thank you note from Arthur's black servant, Alexander Powell, for the kindness shown him by General and Mrs. Sharpe. "Upon my word, I was never better treated in any place I have chanced to be with his Excellency."[104]

Sharpe also spent much time in Washington as a presidential advisor who added luster to the administration by his good council, which included the appointment of Frederick T. Frelinghuysen to be Secretary of State. Mark Twain would write, "[I]t would be hard indeed to better President Arthur's administration."[105]

Sharpe surely felt himself in an awkward position. He was close to both Grant and Arthur, but the two had gradually fallen out. Arthur had initially asked Grant's advice on appointments. Perhaps overly impressed with the prerogatives of the office, Arthur came to resent any further advice or requests for appointments. Within two years they were no longer speaking. It was a delicate situation for Sharpe, but he did not forget to help Grant when he could.[106]

One piece of advice from Sharpe that Arthur accepted only minutes before his term expired was the restoration of Grant's rank as full general in order to retire him at full pay. By 1884 Grant's affairs were in a shambles and his health ruined by untreatable cancer. He had been financially ruined by his investment firm partner. Already in 1881 former Confederate General Joseph E. Johnston, now a Democrat member of the Virginia congressional delegation, had moved to restore these honors to Grant, but the motion had fallen beneath bitter opposition. Now faced with Grant's rapidly failing health, the issue of his honors was revived. On May 27 Sharpe wrote Arthur from New York that the Democrats in Congress were planning to push the issue to reap the publicity benefits. He recommended that Arthur gather a group of Republican members of Congress to consult publicly on this matter and steal a march on the Democrats. Sharpe was wrapping in the guise of political necessity his own desire and that of Grant's many other friends to both honor their former general-in-chief and president and to ensure the well-being of his family. Arthur chose this moment to be jealous of his rights as president, refusing to sign a bill that named Grant because it infringed on his executive authority to appoint officers. Senator George Edmunds of Vermont pressed on with a bill nevertheless.[107]

As the new year crept toward inauguration on March 4, Grant's decline added new urgency to Edmund's bill which easily passed the Senate. In the House, the cause was taken up by Democrat Representative Samuel Randall of Pennsylvania, a Union veteran of Gettysburg and former Speaker of the House. With 20 minutes remaining in Arthur's term, Randall rose in the House to ask for unanimous consent to suspend the rules to bring the Grant matter to the floor. But a contested election in Iowa was still before the House, and the issue leader would not yield. Instead, the man whose seat was at stake jumped to his feet and personally yielded, thus sacrificing his seat in order "to do justice to the hero of Donelson and Appomattox." The measure passed by acclamation accompanied by Rebel yells. The bill was rushed to Arthur who signed it with less than 10 minutes left in his term. With six minutes before Grover Cleveland was to be sworn in, the president pro tempore of the Senate announced that the President had nominated Grant. All business was suspended in the thunderous applause. Cleveland's first act was to sign Grant's commission. Had Arthur been astute to follow Sharpe's advice of 10 months before, he would have been the one to have basked in the public approval in his last year in office and doing honor to Grant would not have been such a close run thing.

This was the last public service Sharpe could do for his hero Grant. While he had benefited from Grant's favor, he was sincerely devoted to the man. This final act of devotion was done long after Grant could no longer do anything for him. As Grant's condition worsened in April, the press was full of day-by-day reports. Sharpe quickly arrived and interviewed Grant's doctor three times and then accompanied him to Grant's home. There for over an hour he used all his powers of persuasion in an unsuccessful attempt to persuade the doctor to let him take the dying man to his country house in the Catskills where he thought the mountain air could only help. The general could only speak in a whisper by then, but he could still joke with Sharpe. To the chagrin of the press he refused to discuss Grant's health with anyone. The general would die on July 23. At the funeral Sharpe walked in the procession to the tomb. Sharpe would be a faithful attendant in the future at the annual dinner held on Grant's birthday.[108]

While Sharpe had been busy in Washington, his old Ulster County rival, Thomas Cornell, marshaled his forces against him. The conventions in the three districts of Ulster County were about to be held. Sharpe's long absences in Washington with Arthur had done nothing to dampen his feud with Cornell, which reached such a degree of animosity that the *Kingston Daily Freeman* stated in an editorial that the factions were so split "that it would be well to drop both contestants and select a delegate from one of the towns who will represent the whole party and not a part of it." It turned out to be wishful thinking. In early April Cornell bested Sharpe out of a delegate's seat to the state party convention in the first district in a vote of 14 to 10, "routed," in the words of *The New York Times*, "horse, foot, and dragoons." Sharpe was shortly again trounced in the second and third districts of Ulster County. His identification as a Stalwart and as an Arthur man worked against him. Defeats in other districts followed. His attachment to Arthur was dragging him down. Recognizing the inevitable, Sharpe announced he would not be a candidate for either the state or national party conventions.[109]

When the state convention met on April 23 to "vote for control of the organiza- tion," a slim, young Theodore Roosevelt was already a rising power whose presence was worthy of note. Sharpe, "sat constantly by the chairman's seat throughout the sessions, closely watching the proceedings." Though defeated for an official seat as a delegate, Sharpe, ever the master politician, had secured a seat at the center of the action weighing every word. He would have been familiar with Roosevelt from their service in the 1882 state assembly. One can imagine with what interest he listened to Roosevelt, whose star was rising as his own could well be setting.[110]

Sharpe would bide his time for political revenge. Cornell had served in Congress from 1881 to 1883 and was trying to secure the nomination to run again in 1884. Sharpe returned to Kingston for the September 18 county party nominating convention for congressional candidates. The reporter for *The New York Times* noted that Sharpe, "did not seem to be in happy mood." He called the convention to order and slipped a knife into Cornell's reputation by stating that the Congressman chosen must be one who, if elected, would attend to the duties of his office. He then proceeded to crush Cornell's slate of candidates and with them Cornell's ambitions to return to Congress. Those who predicted that all this feuding would cause many Republicans to bolt and thereby hand the 17th District of New York to a Democrat were proved wrong as the staunch, liberal Republican James G. Lindsley was elected in November.[111]

Sharpe's defeat as a delegate to the Chicago Convention held in early June did much to undercut his ability to push Arthur's nomination for a second term which he had been pushing strongly. Not being a delegate, however, did not prevent him from going to Chicago to exert what influence he could as an "Arthur leader." The press was titillated when it leaked out that Sharpe had visited the room of Warren, New York State Republican Party chairman, at 2 a.m. in the morning dressed only in his nightshirt and overcoat for a one-hour close consultation. Prophetically he told a reporter that Senator James G. Blaine (Maine) who was favored over Arthur could not carry New York but that Arthur could. It did not help that Arthur was lukewarm to the idea of a second term and not a dynamic candidate. The vice-presidency had fallen to him almost by accident four years before, and he had done nothing to seek it. He simply did not have the fire in the belly for the contest, especially since his health was not the best. Blaine of Maine won the nomination on the third ballot.[112]

In July Arthur had honored Sharpe with the appointment as chairman of the U.S. Commission to Central and South America, for the purpose of increasing commerce, and with the rank of Envoy Extraordinary and Minister Plenipotentiary and a yearly salary of $7,500. Sharpe actively chaired the commission, insisting in public hearings that merchants state clearly what obstacles they were experiencing in the South American trade so that the government could address them. It became clear that Britain had so engrossed trade with the Hispanic Americas that communication with them often had to go through Liverpool. American butter was sold to the British who then re-exported it to Central and South America.

In a bow to his former general-in-chief, Sharpe along with the other members of the commission called on Grant at his home to solicit his views. Grant's reputation has suffered from the scandals of his administration; even the Society of the Army of the Potomac at its 1883 reunion had defeated his nomination for president of the society, no doubt to Sharpe's intense chagrin. Now Grant's suggestions to the commission showed a wide-ranging understanding of the issues and made sound recommendations, such as a reform of the consular service to "act as drummers for manufacturers of the United States." Unfortunately, his suggestions were never to be transformed into legislation. Arthur was to be out of office in less than a year. A new administration, especially a Democratic one, would be unlikely to support Grant's and Sharpe's recommendations.[113]

Sharpe also led the commission on fact-finding trips to Mexico, Central, and South America. For Sharpe the job was no sinecure but the opportunity to perform a valuable public service. Arthur rather than simply rewarding friendship had chosen an extremely well-qualified man for the job—cosmopolitan, skilled in languages, astute, and from his time at the Custom House, familiar with American trade with Latin America. With the election of the Democrat Grover Cleveland in November, whose views opposed the commission, Sharpe resigned in order that the President might be served by someone more in harmony with his position.[114]

Sharpe and Arthur vacationed at Sharpe's summer place in the Catskills that August and on their way had some unexpected excitement. They travelled on a special train on the Ulster and Delaware Railroad at record-breaking speed along the numerous curves of the line. Rain was pounding through an open window, which were unusually large for this special train. Sharpe got up to close it when a sharp turn of the car along a curve nearly threw him out the window. He was barely saved by a reporter who instantly grabbed him by his coattails. Given how stout Sharpe had become by then, it must have taken a strong man.[115]

About that time in early September upon the resignation of the Secretary of the Treasury, a rumor spread quickly that Arthur would appoint Sharpe to fill that post for the rest of his term. The rumor had credence because Sharpe, it was noted in the press, was "one of the President's warmest personal friends, and was his constant companion during his extended visits to the White House and during the President's return visit to General Sharpe's residence in the Catskills." The rumor quickly collapsed as the White House denied it. It may have been a trial balloon, but there is no evidence of it. However, the *Chicago Daily Tribune* of September 18 stated that Sharpe had been offered and declined the appointment.[116] The friendship shared by these two men was so pronounced that it would lead to more than a few insinuations of cronyism in the press.

Frustrated to secure his friend the presidential nomination, Sharpe switched his efforts to push Arthur for senator of New York in November and December. However, he could not summon the support in the legislature in the face of Platt's opposition. Again, Arthur's interest was tepid. Sharpe may have had some satisfaction for having played Cassandra at the June Republican convention. Blaine lost the election to Grover Cleveland by losing New York by 1,149 votes or 0.10 percent, the margin of victory for the Democrat, just as Sharpe had predicted.[117]

The charges of cronyism arose again early in 1885 as Arthur's term was about to expire. The previous year the army's judge advocate general, Brig. Gen. David G. Swaim, had been court-martialed for financial improprieties and was suspended from his position. Arthur clearly wanted to reward Sharpe with appointment to the position and exerted his influence to have Swaim dismissed from the service. The army was opposed to Sharpe's appointment and the President's unseemly influence on his behalf and strung out the final court-martial proceedings until Arthur's term expired. It became a "contest between the court martial and President Arthur, the one desiring to preserve Swaim long enough to head off Sharpe, the other being credited with an intention to get Swaim out soon enough to get Sharpe in." The army's delaying tactics won out; Fabius Maximus would have been proud. The appointment was also doomed by the opposition of a number of Republican senators who opined that no nomination the President made for the office was "likely to be confirmed." President Cleveland reinstated Swaim who then resigned.[118]

Arthur's premonitions about the fragile state of health came true; he suffered a cerebral hemorrhage and died on November 17, 1886, at the age of 57. Sharpe served as a pall bearer along with General Sheridan, Robert Todd Lincoln, and Cornelius Vanderbilt. Conkling also attended the funeral and, seeing Sharpe, remarked to a friend, "Is that Gen. Sharpe over there?" When confirmed, he mused, "How much older he looks." Sedentary good living was taking its toll of Sharpe; he was described as "rotund" by this time.[119]

Sharpe's influence in Washington dried up with Cleveland in the White House. But his advancing age and increasing waistline did not drain his energy for New York state politics. He again was elected to the Republican state convention held in September and chaired the important Committee on Contested Seats enlivening its report with a dash of humor.

> General Sharpe, in closing the debate for the committee, supported its report. In his remarks he said that in the deliberations of the committee-room the principal evidence against the Republicanism of certain delegates seemed to be that they had Irish names. He thought it high time that the fact of a man being Irish should no longer be taken as prima facie evidence that he was a Democrat [laughter].[120]

Sharpe did not neglect oiling his Ulster County machine either. It ran so smoothly that in September 1886 for the first time he led a unified county delegation to the state convention as the undisputed leader. The next year the wheels went off the machine as Sharpe suffered a complete reversal of fortune. He was decisively defeated in the party election to select delegates for the state convention on September 10. *The New York Times* reported that the reason was the allegation that had been floating around since the 1884 presidential nomination contest that Sharpe had not supported John G. Blaine, the party's eventual candidate. "The General had again and again denounced the statement as a malicious lie," but apparently to no avail. The rumor may well have been the work of Cornell. If so, it was payback. The lingering animosity of the pro-Conkling Stalwarts also played a role. *The New York Times* commented, "Ulster County for years has been a capital school in which to study politics, but even the flouters never anticipated such a situation..." This reverse effectively ended his influence in Ulster County politics for the time being. Sharpe may have been down, but he was not out. He gave up his law practice and devoted his efforts for the time being to his duties as president of the National Bank of Roundout.[121] He would tilt no more with Cornell who died in March 1890.

Cornell's son-in-law, Coykendall, was all too happy to continue the animosity, viewing it almost as an inheritance.

Sharpe the Appraiser—Final Public Service

With Republican Benjamin Harrison in the White House in 1889, Sharpe once again had a friend in the President. New York Senator Frank Hiscock, in acknowledgment of Sharpe's services in his nomination, recommended him for appointment to the United States Board of General Appraisers, a body created to exercise judicial and administrative power in appeals made against customs duties. Members were chosen from those who had risen to the top of the legal profession. The appointment was considered to be of a semi-judicial nature and was permanent as with the tenure of federal judges and carried a salary of $7,000 a year, second only to that of justices of the Supreme Court.[122]

His enemies raised a hue and cry in the press. *The New York Times* wrote, "Everyone in New York State knows him as a tricky, unscrupulous politician who is true to his Hessian blood, enlists under the banner of the highest bidder." The *Kingston Daily Freeman* ran a vituperative editorial against Sharpe quoted in *The New York Times* that gushed all the bile of the allegations of his betrayal of Conkling and failure to support Blaine. Later that year *The New York Times* accused Sharpe of being responsible for the loss of the 17th Congressional District to a Democrat for the first time.[123]

Sharpe brushed off these partisan slings and arrows; he had no illusions as to the fickle and vituperative nature of politics. In July he resigned as President of the National Bank of Roundout in order to avoid any conflict of interest with the new judicial position as an appraiser, although he continued as a trustee of the Ulster County Savings Institute. The next year the bank shuddered under a major scandal. It came to light that the treasurer and his assistant had been systematically robbing the institute for 20 years, and they were promptly arrested. The trustees were stunned, but immediately took action to ascertain the true condition of the bank. Once they determined that the surplus on hand and other assets could not cover the theft, they called on the State Banking Superintendent to take over the bank. That unleashed a three-day run on the bank, which ended only when other Ulster banks came to the rescue, and the trustees publicly announced there was a surplus of funds. The amount withdrawn fortunately did not exceed the surplus. The passbook holders, now reassured, returned their deposits. The press accused the trustees of being guilty of criminal negligence for not having known what was going on. Rather than negligence, the trustees had been systematically deceived. Besides Sharpe, the trustees included two judges, the postmaster, and the editor of a local paper—the pillars of local society. It would be difficult to conclude that so many men had been simply negligent. The theft was described as "most ingenious, and for twenty years baffled the skill of expert examiners in the employ of the state."[124]

None of these problems seem to have put any nails in the coffin of Sharpe's influence. It took him barely a year to reestablish his position in Ulster and he was chosen as one of three delegates to the yearly state Republican convention in 1891. His feud with Coykendall continued a good deal due to sheer momentum. One old Ulster County Republican commented that they did not pull together simply because "They have been opposed to each other so long they would not feel natural if they did." The next year he controlled the county convention to select delegates to the Congressional District Convention through his son Severyn. Similarly, Sharpe, with the assistance of his "wide awake son" Severyn, dominated the 1892 county convention to select delegates to the national convention to be held in Minneapolis. That Sharpe found the need to use his son was a signal of his last hurrah in Ulster politics. There is no apparent future reference to his active role. It had been an active political life of over 30 years that now came to a gradual end as Sharpe's continued involvement in veterans' affairs and the duties as appraiser were enough to occupy his late in life energies.[125]

Hasbrouck wrote, "The duties of the office would intrigue any man having the quality of intelligence or the expert training which fitted him for a place on the board. Some of the hearings had the foundation of romance." Sharpe was able to call upon not only his considerable legal background and experience as surveyor of the Port of New York, in which he had run the customs collections, but also upon his fine education and cultured cosmopolitan nature. One hearing bore upon the duties to be levied on the plumes in women's hats and "brought out [the] most interesting fund of information respecting the habits of birds in other lands, the method of their capture and the quality of the plumage, which in some case were so rare and costly that they justified a duty much more than their weight in gold."[126] Another case involved the custom's determination to levy a duty of 40 percent on an oriental carpet for which the owner had paid 22,000 francs. Sharpe was able to identify the carpet as an antique over 400 years old and thus entitled to "free entry as an antiquity."[127]

Sharpe's cases were not limited to luxury goods and antiques. Cases ranged from those involving carpet wools (1891) to Cuban tobacco leaf (1898). His shrewd determinations had important consequences for importers of raw materials such as woolens in 1893, involving $1,000,000 in tied up products "and the future importation of $20,000,000 worth of woolen goods." The range of the board's decisions covered just about everything that the United States imported. For example, in September 1897 the board took up protests under the old tariff law on importations of oils, paints, chemical products, coal-tar preparations, medicinal preparations, and plants.[128]

There was occasionally a lighter side to the work of the appraisers. An importer was contesting the duty on kites imported from Japan. He demanded they be taxed at the lower rate for paper, as they were only decorative, than for toys. To prove they were kites the collector ordered several of his senior subordinates to fly them on the roof of the building. The article describing this incident concluded, "As this test may not suit the Board of General Appraisers in New York, the small boys and police may have amusement next week when they look up at the roof of 534 Canal street and see Appraisers Tichenor, Sharretts, and Sharpe flying the Japanese kites."[129]

A reorganization of the Board of Appraisers by the Treasury Department in October 1897 lessened Sharpe's workload. Sharpe had always intended to retire from public life at the age of 70, which he would reach in 1898. That intention unhappily coincided with the death of his wife on February 12, 1898. Her death hit him hard. On the last day of the month he announced his need for absolute rest and his intention to resign as he took 20 days' official leave. He went so far as to remove his private papers from his office. The Treasury Department almost eagerly announced his intention to resign. Perhaps the McKinley Administration saw his departure as a patronage opportunity. The rest, however, did him good and he returned to his duties at the end of his leave, "apparently improved in health and spirits." He repeated his desire to resign but left the when up in the air.

These comments encouraged some in "high official quarters" to express the opinion that his resignation "would lead to a more perfect harmony of action." The reference to "high official quarters" may have been a political euphemism for President William McKinley himself. The justification was a supposed friction on the board. McKinley essentially sought to replace four of its eight members (two Republicans and two Democrats). *The New York Times*, however, specifically refuted any claims of friction and stated that the work of the board had been harmonious and that Sharpe had "done much of an important character" since his appointment in 1890. Senator Platt, remembering old antipathies, was quick to recommend a replacement for Sharpe. However, Sharpe still had a large number of "strong political friends," who felt "that such an old and distinguished public servant" was "entitled to much consideration, and they object[ed] to his being forced out of office."[130]

The outbreak of the Spanish-American War at the end of April put a stop to any more official encouragement to resign. Neither did Sharpe speak further of resignation. However, the war was short-lived and over by August, and by the end of December "the controlling powers of the Treasury Department" renewed their desire to see him resign. He had already anticipated them in November by asking McKinley to accept his resignation, but this time the President asked him to postpone his departure by a few more months. On February 4, 1899, Sharpe finally submitted his resignation effective on the last day of the month. McKinley replied with a gracious note that acknowledged Sharpe's reason for putting aside his duties. "I regret that you find your advanced years inconsistent with a continuation in the public service."[131]

CHAPTER SEVENTEEN

The Bugle Echoes

Among the veterans of the Union army, Sharpe's reputation was not dimmed by the years. Like many veterans, the war had been the defining experience of his life and a central part of his identity. Despite the decades of political and social prominence that lay ahead, the war and its stamp marked him. He would evermore be General Sharpe, not Mr. Sharpe, Marshal Sharpe, or Speaker Sharpe. It was a lifelong badge of honor with which none of the tamer titles of civilian life could compare; it was also the sign that he had passed through the fire of his generation and had the dross in him burned away. A sentimental man, he was fond of songs of the Civil War. His favorite was the jaunty "Jordan Am a Hard Road to Trabble," a variation of "Richmond is a Hard Road to Travel." He requested it a number of times on Grant's visit to Kingston in 1873.[1]

For Sharpe the experience of soldiering had created a "band of brothers" bond with others who had worn blue. He was active for decades in the major veterans' organizations that grew up in the North, particularly the Society of the Army. He was one of those who founded the Society of the Army of the Potomac on July 5, 1869 at Steinway Hall in New York. Between 1869 and 1896 he would serve either as the society's recording or corresponding secretary 22 times, alternating most of the time with Maj. Gen. Horatio C. King. In those positions he was in correspondence with all the senior officers who had served in the war and would later go on to prominence and national leadership. It was the ideal position for a masterful networker like Sharpe.[2] In 1870, for example, he penned an invitation to former Maj. Gen. James A. Garfield to respond to the toast, "To the Armies of the West," at the society's annual meeting. Two years later he would again request his attendance as the guest speaker of the annual meeting after conferring with Grant on the choice.[3]

As the corresponding secretary he would have been the one to invite Mark Twain as a guest speaker at the 12th reunion in 1881. Twain brought down the house when he opened with, "I have always maintained, with great enthusiasm, that the only wise and true way is for the soldier to fight the battle and the unprejudiced civilian to tell him how to do it."[4]

Sharpe was a popular member of the society, not only for his dedication and oratorical skills but also because he knew how to have a good time, the very quality that Brig. Gen. Marsena Patrick had found so objectionable at St. Patrick's Day in 1863. At the close of the reunion banquets, the "Society of Bummers" would be convened. It was time for jokes, good-natured pranks, and "high carnival till 2 a.m.," in the euphemism of the time. Sharpe was in his element and was voted permanent president of the society. At the 1884 reunion he "mounted a table as [the] chairman put a motion which was carried, electing the Mayor an honorary member of the Society of Bummers, amid tremendous laughter… Then General McQuade was elected chairman, and as he was about to take the chair General Sharpe seated himself in it and turned the laugh on McQuade." Part of the fun was to press ridiculous court-martial charges against a member who then defended himself in a similar vein. At the 1878 reunion, Maj. Douglas MacArthur, Sr., was the object of a charge of "sheer cussedness" by Sharpe.

> GENERAL SHARPE: It is proposed that the charges against Major MacArthur be sustained. All in favor say, Aye.
> All: Aye
> GENERAL SHARPE: Opposed, No.
> All: No
> GENERAL SHARPE: The motion is unanimously carried that the charges against Major MacArthur be sustained and that his name be stricken from the rolls.
> Sing from page 11 of the hymn-book, "Mary had a little Lamb."
> All joined in singing to the tune of "The Battle Cry of Freedom." The closing verses created much amusement.
>
> The Lamb
> It swam across the Rapidan
> Our Pickets saw it too,
> Shouting the Battle Cry of Freedom?
> And speedily simmered down,
> Into a mutton stew,
> Shouting the Battle Cry of Freedom.
>
> Full Chorus
> Hurrah for Mary! Hurrah for the lamb
> Hurrah for the soldiers who didn't care (ahem)!
> For we'll rally round the flag, boys, we'll rally once again
>
> And Mary never more did see
> Her darling little lamb—Cho.
> For the boys in blue they "chawed" it up,
> And didn't care a _____ Cho.[5]

Sharpe was never one to leave a party early. On one occasion, as the meeting of "fun and regulated disorder ended," Sharpe led the "'revelers' with band playing," and "marched in procession to the trains."[6]

Sharpe would remain always a fierce defender of the Army of the Potomac. On one occasion he referred to the army as the "breastplate of the nation, which had stood through all the trials and struggles of the war, the Army which was often complained of for not moving enough, but never for not dying enough, and whose heroic labors were finally crowned by the surrender of the bravest and most successful of the Confederate forces—the Army of Northern Virginia."[7]

The men he rubbed shoulders with and shared podiums with in veterans' affairs were a "who's who" of the Union army in the Civil War—Grant, Sherman, Sheridan, Hancock, Hooker, Sickles, Humphreys, Pleasonton, Kilpatrick, to mention only a few. His powerful oratorical gifts, his profound dedication to the memory of the achievement of the "Boys in Blue," as well as his talent for being well liked, made him a favored and popular speaker at veterans' gatherings. Invitations to speak even came from the Boys in Gray, such as the Confederate Veterans Camp of New York in January 1893, who hosted him at their third annual banquet.[8] He genuinely took great pleasure in the company and service of old comrades, and the fact that it served him politically in New York politics did not make it any less genuine. That he did not rest on his laurels when he returned from the war but went on to a distinguished life in politics and public service added luster to his military reputation and currency to the influence with the society of veterans.

Sharpe was one of the founding officers of the Military Order of the Loyal Legion of the United States (MOLLUS). Formed in the immediate wake of the Lincoln assassination by veteran officers who were determined to thwart any threats to the government, it would come to include in its members almost every distinguished officer of the war. In 1875 and 1876 he was elected as the senior vice-commander of the New York Commandery of MOLLUS. In 1876 and 1877 he was made commander and led the legion in the funeral procession of Maj. Gen. George Armstrong Custer on October 10, 1877, at West Point. Sharpe was one of the "Companions" of the order. Membership was open to sons of the founding officers, and in early 1878, his older son, Severyn, would be elected while attending Yale. His cousin, Bvt. Brig. Gen. Jacob Sharpe, was also an active member, serving as chancellor in 1871 and on the organization's council from 1873 to 1874.[9]

Beginning in 1873 and for a number of years thereafter, Sharpe gave a favorite speech to a large number of venues, entitled, "The Last Days of the Confederacy," which was his only apparent public relation of his experiences in the war. His local Kingston newspaper described it in the most fulsome terms:

> The General handled his subject with an eloquence, elegance and animation that brought vividly to the eyes and minds of the audience the closing scene of the great drama of the century. Using no manuscript, the orator told the story of the Appomattox surrender and the eventful days immediately previous thereto in a ready, unhesitating manner portraying the events of the march and the battlefield, enlivening the story with occasional sketches of the comical incidents in which the irrepressible freedmen figured or the natural spirit of fun of the soldier boys cropped out; telling now some pathetic story and then of some thrilling episode, till at the last climax of

the war was painted in the scene of the surrender of Lee to Grant. In these events the General was a participant and spoke not as one who had read of them, but as one who had been a part thereof. The audience paid the closest attention and frequently applauded enthusiastically.[10]

Other reviews were as equally positive. Unfortunately, they seldom related any of Sharpe's specific information of events in the war.

Sharpe was never in doubt about the true meaning of the war, and in this he was reflecting the Republican Party's emphasis on freedom and opportunity. For Sharpe, the war had been a crusade for those concepts, whether it was crushing the rebellion against the constitutional order or the emancipation of millions of slaves. For Sharpe, the concept of American exceptionalism was never more clearly shown than by the effect that victory had on the rest of the world. In another speech he delivered in June 1878 to commemorate the Union war dead on Decoration Day he said:

> What would have been the consequence if those men had failed? Don't you remember that liberty-loving millions in Europe—in Germany, Ireland, and elsewhere—had their eyes on us; saw in the success of the struggle on our side, a triumph, also, against the despotism of the Old World! Don't you remember Garibaldi who said that if the danger become more imminent, his sword would be found on our side? The first embassy from Japan was in consequence attendant of it. The first great effort at Republicanism was made after our great victory had been won. And Spain, my friends, will try again; and there will be other trials in different parts of the world; and the time will come when they will not fail. It was after the close and success of our effort that Italy made her effort after the men who be here had given up their lives in the cause for which they fought. Germany asserted herself and became a united nation; and it was due to the influence of the success of the Union arms in America that John Bright [applause] became a Minister of the crown of England. He would never have become a Minister of the crown of England had these men not fallen.[11]

Despite his political career, Sharpe never lost touch with the men of the 120th and remained a vital part of their fraternity and close friends with many. Sharpe was at the bedside of Lieut. Col. J. Rudolph Tappen when he passed away on January 20, 1875 from an illness contracted in the war. Sharpe noted that his mind wandered over all the old battlefields. Then, "In his last hours he said to me, in a faint voice: 'There is not much left of me, but I mean to fight it out to the last minute.'"[12]

In the years immediately after the war the men of the regiment focused on reestablishing their lives in society. From time to time they had talked of forming an association, but it was not until December 26, 1868 that a meeting was called for that purpose with Sharpe as its chairman. It was resolved that "The One Hundred and Twentieth New York Regimental Union" be formed. Sharpe was promptly elected as president, and thereupon he chaired a committee to write its by-laws. The Regimental Union was to meet annually on Washington's birthday for many years. Guests of honor included Generals Hooker (1868), Kilpatrick (1871), and Stewart L. Woodford (1872). By far its most distinguished guest was Lt. Gen. William Tecumseh Sherman in 1888, now retired, living in New York, and much in demand as a speaker. Despite the competition for his appearance, Sherman eagerly accepted

Sharpe's invitation in the warmest manner. "Don't dwell so much on the pretty girls," he wrote. "I have had my day and must surrender them to the younger fellows, but count on me because of love for you and other comrades which grows in strength with the years."[13]

Although Sharpe had not served under Sherman, he had briefed him on more than one occasion at the close of the war and been impressed. After the war their relationship had deepened. They were both members of the Union League Club in New York City, and he drew the following character sketch in 1891 of Sherman, who had retired seven years before:

> We believe with a great many other people, that General Sherman is the most accomplished conversationalist in the country. When he sat down to talk the circle around him grew larger and larger until he would be surrounded by a regiment of friends. He liked to meet everybody here, and there is no one in the country the Union League club would miss more than he. He is the first citizen of America.
>
> What a man he is for engagements. He was so busy making calls once that I saw him take his engagement book and give a friend a night six weeks ahead. He is the most conspicuous figure wherever he goes. He is so ready with replies that he is never caught. We have never heard him repeat himself in conversations or in telling stories, and has entertained us for years.[14]

During the war, the Northern soldier had acquired a hard respect for the Southern man's martial qualities. By the mid-1880s that bond of comradeship of which Sherman spoke had been thrown over all men who had fought in the war, as the sections reconciled themselves. Sharpe gladly joined Sherman at a mass meeting held at the Cooper Union in New York in spring 1884 to speak in favor of the establishment of a home for former Confederate soldiers in Richmond. Eleven years later the Society of the Army of the Potomac invited the R. E. Lee Camp of Confederate Veterans of Richmond to its annual reunion. The 116 "gallant ex-Confederates were cheered at every step" as they moved through Baltimore.[15]

In May 1888 Sharpe and Gen. Horatio King, representing the veterans of the Army of the Potomac, traveled to Richmond to meet a committee of the Grand Camp of Confederate Veterans (the precursor of the United Confederate Veterans established in 1889) to extend an invitation to Southerners to join them in a reunion to be held in Gettysburg on the anniversary of the battle the following year. Sharpe spoke eloquently that "the sentiments of both societies seemed to be concentrated on Gettysburg," and looked forward to the "great good to grow out of it." He then reported that Congress had proposed to finance shelter and meals at the reunion and to subsidize transportation for veterans unable to afford the trip, and that the War Department would send artillery batteries to fire salutes and soldiers for guard duty. The veterans of the Grand Camp heartily accepted this open-handed invitation.[16]

Sharpe had every reason to be pleased with the results of his efforts. On the first day, "A party of Union Generals visited the camp of the Regular Troops where they had quite a pow-wow" where the regular officers "entertained the old Veterans quite royally." Among them was Sharpe, who was always a convivial guest not adverse to enjoying a good drink, as Brigadier General Patrick had noted on St. Patrick's Day in 1863.[17]

Among the honored Confederate guests were James Longstreet and John B. Gordon. *The National Tribune* observed that "Gens. Sharpe, Slocum, Sickles, and Butterfield were constantly with the rebel leaders." Major General Joshua Chamberlain called for three cheers for Longstreet.

The climax of that day was the dedication of the monuments of the regiments that had fought on Culp's Hill. Sharpe spoke as the orator at the dedication of the monument of the 145th New York Volunteers, raised in New York City in the same wave that gave birth to Sharpe's own 120th NY. Sharpe also gave a speech at a special reception that day during which Dixie was played.[18]

With the publicity of this event and as the regimental and state monuments began to proliferate over what was to become the Gettysburg National Military Park, the first of such battlefield parks in the country, the men of the 120th turned their thoughts to commemorating their own struggle and the memory of their fallen comrades. The 1888 Regimental Reunion meeting elected Sharpe to head a monuments committee. In December Sharpe presented a design at a special meeting of the Union; the design was adopted at a cost of $2,500; $1,500 was provided by the State of New York for any regiment that desired to set up a monument, and the other $1,000 was raised by the union itself. At the 1889 meeting Sharpe reported that the monument would be finished and installed in May and recommended that the members of the union attend its dedication shortly thereafter. A special train was chartered to bring the members to Gettysburg for the July 25 dedication. The men wandered the battlefield, reliving the glory point of their lives, and were to converge at the monument in the afternoon for its dedication and speech by Sharpe, as ever the regiment's chosen orator. Driven indoors by an afternoon rainstorm, the men gathered instead to hear their old colonel speak in their hotel's ample public rooms. According a press report, "The General was an impressive and eloquent public speaker. He had a commanding presence, powerful voice and was at his best in describing army scenes." The men had always chosen him whenever they wanted to hear the ghosts of memory and youth summoned. He began, "Comrades, you are here to discharge a final tribute to the gallantry and fame of an organization, which reached the very highest standing in the resplendent galaxy of the historic army of the Potomac—an army that was criticized for not moving fast enough but never for not having died enough." Sharpe drew their minds back across time to the great purpose of the battle—that the very fate of the Union hung in the balance.

> Here the greatest deeds have been wrought, and here the most eloquent words have been spoken; for here on these heights of Gettysburg, contemporaneously with Vicksburg, were the crucial hours of that stupendous conflict, when it was settled, not for a day, but for all time, that the government of the people, for the people and by the people should not perish from the earth.

He saluted their former enemies by recounting how 25 years after the battle two of Lee's most illustrious generals had led Confederate veterans in a meeting of reconciliation with the men in blue on this field. "On behalf of their comrades, who marched and fought under the Southern Cross, they came to accept the arbitrament and issues of the conflict; and if there was joy in heaven that day, it was in the heart of Abraham Lincoln as he looked down upon that field of Gettysburg."

Then he recounted the valor of the regiment, step by step, as tides of Southern valor crashed and broke upon Northern adamant, until III Corps gave way, leaving only the 120th as "the men who held the line" on that fateful day. Again and again the color guard fell to enemy fire, only to be instantly replaced even by the officers until another soldier could take it from his hands. The last color bearer continued to hold it aloft, even when shot had snapped the staff; he merely grasped the upper portion to hold it up. Confederate fire from an entire brigade scythed through the ranks, but they held, as even the wounded concealed their injuries to stay in the line. When the regiment was finally relieved and withdrawn, the roll was called, at which only three officers and 18 men answered. The rest were stricken on the field or searching for their comrades.

> I would that I could name them all; all of those 203, who out of a total of 356 armed men and 27 officers, make a proportionate loss nearly unequaled on this field.
>
> But since this cannot be, we dedicate this monument to-day to their everlasting memory. We dedicate it also to their comrades who joined them from other fields of victory and defeat; to the memory of Fredericksburg and Chancellorsville; of James City and Mine Run; of the Wilderness and Spotsylvania; of the North Anna and the Totopotomoy; of Cold Harbor and Petersburg; of Strawberry Plains and Deep Bottom; of Poplar Spring Church and the Boydton Plank Road; of Hatcher's Run and Tucker's House; of the White Oak Road and Amelia Springs; of Farmville and Appomattox Court House—to them and their glories forever.
>
> How rich are the treasures of the 120th in this clear upper sky! Oh! Brothers, whose valor is the occasion of this solemnity, bend an ear from the peaceful fields which are now your home and pardon the last efforts of a voice which was not unknown to you.[19]

He had been with them all the way, even though he had moved to the army staff after Fredericksburg. They were always close at hand in the army he served, and he never forgot them. He cared for their families throughout the war, stayed in close touch with their daily concerns, grieved at their losses, and tried unsuccessfully to get them closer to him by transfer to the provost guard. Other men would command them in battle and be loved and respected by them in turn, but Sharpe was always first in their hearts, and first to be asked to speak when they wanted their old wounds and the indefinable joy of comradeship to be remembered in golden words.

His meeting with Gordon at Gettysburg sparked a continuing friendship. In a series of lectures in the North, where, upon at least one occasion, Sharpe introduced the Georgian warrior, Gordon thanked his "distinguished friend, Maj. Gen. H. Sharpe ... for his too partial tribute to himself."[20]

Sharpe was responsible for one last military innovation two years after the dedication at Gettysburg. Late in his life, he commissioned and paid for a statue that summed up his deepest loyalty. On October 17, 1896, he dedicated that statue to the "rank and file" of his beloved 120th New York Volunteer Infantry Regiment in his hometown of Kingston. The 7-foot statue represents "Patriotism" and is the figure of a young and beautiful woman who stands in a graceful attitude on top of the pedestal holding a flag. The pedestal was of the same red granite as used for the base of the stature of the "Goddess of Liberty," as they then called the Statue of Liberty in New York Harbor. Its motto read, "Patriotism, Daughter of the Regiment." It was the only known moment erected by a Civil War commander at his own expense to honor his men. So that this honor to his men would remain unique and uncopied, Sharpe ordered the sculptor to break the molds.

The moment's inscription read:

> TO THE UNDYING RENOWN
> OF THE RANK AND FILE
> OF THE
> ONE HUNDRED AND TWENTIETH
> INFANTRY
> NEW YORK VOLUNTEERS
> ONE OF
> THREE HUNDRED FIGHTING REGIMENTS
> IN THE
> WAR FOR THE UNION
> BY THE COLONEL OF THE REGIMENT
> 1896

The reference to the "Three Hundred Fighting Regiments" is to the work of Colonel W. F. Fox, entitled, "Regimental Losses in the American Civil War," which identified the most distinguished 300 fighting regiments fighting for the Union. The 120th had earned its place on that roll, having suffered 587 killed and wounded and 51 dead in Confederate prisons, out of a total of 1,626 who served throughout the war.[21] The rear panel of the pedestal listed the battles in which the regiment fought. The two side panels held the coats of arms of the United States and New York.[22]

The monument had taken five months to build in the churchyard of the Old First Reformed Dutch Church, facing Main Street near the corner of Fair. On the day of dedication the veterans of the regiment began to arrive in the early morning, until, by the early afternoon, the crowd has swelled to thousands, not only of the people of Kingston and Ulster County but by train from elsewhere in New York. An especially large contingent were from chapters of the Daughters of the American Revolution and included the sister of President Cleveland and the daughter of former president Harrison. At 1 p.m. the veterans were fed lunch by the ladies of Kingston.

When all had assembled again for the dedication, Sharpe spoke. It was a speech where ghosts gathered around Sharpe as he summoned them, like Odysseus did the heroes of Troy from the mists of oblivion. He looked back on the roster of those who served and noted that the regimental association had but 350 names 31 years after the regiment had returned home from the war, and they were sure only that 280 were still "with us in this life. From some who went to the far west after the war we have not heard in years, and we may never see them until we are mustered on the other shore." He recounted their battles and glories, and the honors he had brought them in the postwar years.

> This was a regiment of extraordinary quality and it therefore accomplished extraordinary results. Your career was early remarked and continued to command the attention of those who had known you in the service. You have been permitted to take by the hand your great commander, General Grant, while he was President of the United States. Your reunions have been made memorable by the presence of some of the illustrious of the war. Kilpatrick has been with you to try to make amends for the blunder at James City. Glorious Joe Hooker has brought you the light of the flashing eye that penetrated the clouds at Lookout mountain. And surrounded by a great concourse of your fellow citizens you have stood up and sung "Marching Through Georgia": with the man [Sherman] who marched through Georgia.

He read the roll of the fallen officers and said, "These all passed in battle and in the storm with hundreds of the Rank and File to whom with you this monument is dedicated." Now the ghosts pressed in even closer, hungry for the drops of remembrance that gave the glimmer of life.

> How the old memories crowd upon us, as I make this recital:
> "Take, O boatman, thrice they fee, —
> Take, I give it willingly;
> For, invisible to thee,
> Spirits twain have crossed with me."[23]

One More War

War with Spain in 1898 quickly brought Sharpe to the support of the troops. He joined with other prominent Civil War veterans to plan for the victorious return of the young men marching off to war. He was elected as permanent secretary to the new Society of the Army of Santiago.[24]

Even in old age, he was still an impressive and powerful speaker. His last act fittingly was a military one. Among the many hundreds of speeches he had given, those of commemorating the War of the Rebellion and his own service were his dearest felt. Now there had been the new war with Spain that provided the occasion when "he presented medals to Company M, New York Volunteers, on behalf of the city, shortly after its return from Honolulu."[25]

He surely was proud of his son Henry's performance in the war. By now he was a major, and "[H]is good work at Camp Thomas, Georgia, then in Puerto Rico, finally the Philippines, contrasted sharply with the army's general dismal logistical performance." In this he followed in the footsteps of his father in eschewing the glories of the battlefield for the hard and unsung but vital work of the staff without which an army cannot peel a potato.[26]

The conclusion of the war gave him the opportunity to make an acerbic observation, an old soldier's harrumph.

> In speaking to the correspondent of the action of the war commission he showed little patience for those who complained of the hardships of the Cuban campaign. War is hardship, he says, and he believed it to be a fact that those who served in the War of the Rebellion on either side in their hearts felt contempt for those who complain of the lack of luxuries and comfort during the hundred days war of last Spring. As he spoke he seemed to recall an experience of his own, for he said: "I wonder what General Meade or General Hancock would have said if they had heard these complaints."[27]

The retired life Sharpe had intended to enjoy was to last barely 11 months. His wife, ill for over a year with rheumatic gout, had died two years before in February 1898, and the energy seemed to drain away from him as from a broken heart in the quiet days in Kingston. He promised his son, Henry, that he would come to Washington where the lieutenant colonel was stationed to begin writing his memoirs, but first he would spend the holidays with his daughter in New York City. He had been unwell for some time. By this time he is reputed to have weighed 300 pounds. His condition worsened as the year ended, and he had an operation on January 2, 1900. The operation was successful, but his body could not survive the shock. With his children, Severyn, Henry, and Katherine, about him, he passed away between 11 and midnight on Saturday, January 13, fully conscious to the end.[28]

The next day, Robert A. Snyder rose in the New York State Assembly to announce Sharpe's passing and offered resolutions in the memory of "a former member of the legislature and a distinguished ex-speaker of the assembly of the state" and "citizen, soldier, and statesman." Thereafter, as a mark of singular honor, the assembly immediately adjourned.[29]

Funeral services were held at his Kingston home on Tuesday, January 16, at 3:30 in the afternoon. The Kingston schools were let out of their afternoon classes to allow their teachers to attend. The house was thronged with his many friends in Kingston and by his associates in public and private life. His body lay in a black casket, draped with the "battle-scarred flag of the One Hundred and Twentieth Regiment." In his eulogy, the Rev. Dr. J. G. Van Slyke, said:

> Who is there who would hesitate to yield to his name the tribute of honor? Our recollections of his lifelong and illustrious career have lent a luster to this town and these recollections will do sentinel duty above his ashes. The homage which the world is waiting to pay is due in part to the superior compass of his intelligence, in part to the embellishments of culture which draped his native vigor and in part to the astounding generosity of his heart.

He was buried in the family plot in Kingston's Wiltwyck Cemetery.[30]

The eulogies poured in, all bearing the same themes that had so clearly stamped themselves on everyone's memory of Sharpe. *The Argus* wrote, "General Sharpe's prominent traits were sterling honesty, and fidelity to every trust. He was frank, manly, cordial, hearty, a good fighter and a most loyal friend." No ancient Roman hero could have wished for more.[31]

The directors of the National Bank of Roundout of whom Sharpe had been president, agreed that he was "one with whom association was a delight; for his cheerful good fellowship, his genial humor, his cultured mind and kindly heart were wont to lighten even the dreariness of irksome routine, and frequently made our business meetings a social pleasure."[32]

An unsourced eulogy in the Sharpe collection reads:

> No one who searches for the truth can fail to realize that General Sharpe was a modest man. He never told the country in any book, nor his countrymen on any platform what he did, what his work was. When his comrades met, he was praising them and their leaders ... never himself. He persisted in this generosity until ignorant people said Sharpe was no soldier, and the common run of people never credited him with having won his military titles in the stern calling of war.[33]

The *Kingston Daily Freeman* wrote that from Sharpe's appointment to create the BMI in March 1863, "until the close of the war the Bureau of Military Information, Army of the Potomac, had no other head. Gathering a staff of keen-witted men, chiefly from the ranks, Sharpe never let his commanding general suffer for lack of proper information as to the strength and movements of Lee's army." The article continued:

> He located armies, tracked generals and commanders, captured the spies and scouts and couriers and letters of the enemy. From Chancellorsville to Appomattox when there were no search lights though impenetrable forests, through Wildernesses, from streams and floods, from dreary marshes, from untrodden mountains, out a labyrinth of roads and paths he brought to the leaders of the Union Army the knowledge of the enemy. Is there anything more important in warfare, besides fighting the battle than to know from whence the enemy comes and whither he goes, and in what force? For this knowledge [they] looked not in vain to Sharpe.[34]

One of the enlisted men of the old 120th, George Barber, spoke of his respect and admiration for his former commander and gave him the finest accolade that any officer could hope to receive.

> Mr. Barber wanted to say that the General was as brave a soldier as ever wore the stars. His whole effort on the field seem[ed] to be to look after his men in their tents at night to assure himself that they were provided with sufficient food. He also made it a point to visit wounded men in the hospital. As for his gallantry on the field, Mr. Barber could not speak too highly.[35]

Fading Away

Thursday, August 22, 1912 was remembered as a golden late summer's day; it was 50 years since the 900 men of the 120th New York had marched out of Kingston with

Col. George H. Sharpe at their head. Gathered on that day were 71 survivors who had come from all over the country to blow on the embers of memory one last time. They posed around Sharpe's monument to them, one of them holding the national colors they had carried to war, below the bronze flag carried by the Daughter of the Regiment on her pedestal. "Their thoughts were turned backward at the sight of a life size picture of their old commander, General Sharpe, which graced the stage and seemed to smile upon them a warm welcome." Their former corps commander—tough old one-legged Dan Sickles, crippled at Gettysburg where so many of their friends had perished—spoke to them as Sharpe's picture looked over his shoulder. He was followed by Sharpe's son, Severyn, with a "touching and appropriate address." His brother, Henry, and sister, were there as well. Severyn's little 10-year-old daughter, Katharine, awarded to each of the veterans a medal of their old commander's image in bas-relief. This day was the last gleam in the public memory of George H. Sharpe. It would dim quickly as the veterans one by one now quickly went to their reward.[36]

With Sharpe's passing, the national public memory of his lifetime of accomplishments, especially his contributions to the preservation of the Union, were largely forgotten in all but Kingston, where the organization Sons of Veterans was organized as Camp George H. Sharpe. In 1920 at a meeting of the Ulster Society given in honor of now Major General Henry Sharpe, a committee was formed for the building of a "fitting monument … to be placed at the apex of the triangle of Kingston Academy Green." The reunion that August of his old regiment urged that a statue be chosen as the monument. Unfortunately, nothing came of it. Those who remembered him most intimately were passing away; only 26 veterans of his regiment were able to attend that reunion. Kingston eventually named a fire company (George H. Sharpe Hand Engine Company No. 6) after its most illustrious son.[37]

Sharpe's monument could have resided in the collection of his papers. He was a tireless correspondent, but all that has survived outside his official wartime correspondence in the National Archives are 19 Civil War letters and one from his hunt for John Surratt. They have been enormously informative, but they are only 20 letters. They are the only letters from him in the Senate House in Kingston. These letters have only survived by accident. Edwin Fishel had employed a research assistant in Kingston in the early 1950s. She came across a family member, Mrs. William Hasbrouck, who had the letters. This person was about to split them up among other members of the family when the research assistant persuaded her to donate them to the Senate House. A few minor letters survive in the Huntington Library in Pasadena.[38]

More documents may have gone the way of his library. After Severyn sold The Orchard in 1922, his father's entire library, over a half-ton of books, was sold "for a pittance" to the Salvation Army. Jerome Williams, who had led the orchestra at the wedding of Sharpe's daughter, shared an interest in the Civil War with the general and lamented the loss. He wrote:

… it is impossible to estimate the value of those books at the present day prices for such books as they were mainly of an historical interest, and many of them were no doubt presentation copies from the authors. Undoubtedly many would have been headliners in a New York auctioneer's catalogue, and to sell them for junk was a crime.[39]

Sharpe was not forgotten at Gettysburg either. During World War II, Camp George H. Sharpe was established in November 1943 on the site of an old Civilian Conservation Corps (CCC) camp on the battlefield to accommodate about 200 men. The camp was subsidiary to another larger nearby camp. Camp George H. Sharpe lasted barely eight months and was closed in July 1944. The flicker of memory had burned out.[40]

That was greatly due to his light footprint in the postwar literature of the Civil War. He was simply overlooked. Had he written a memoir of his experiences and accomplishments in the war, it would have taken its place as one of the primary records of the period and established his rightful place, but he did not. It was not for want of ability; he was a gifted public speaker and an able writer with a keen interest in history. He spoke often in public on the war, but those speeches were often limited to general themes centered on his beloved regiment. The exception was the one on the surrender at Appomattox. Another favorite of his was on Ulysses S. Grant of which no detail has survived; it would have aided immeasurably in the historical understanding of the man Sharpe would come to regard not only as a great general but as a close friend. He loved to tell war stories to reporters and a few of them ended up appearing in the press after his death, to include the supreme moment before Meade's council of war on the night of July 2, 1863, Grant's whittling at the Wilderness, and Meade's reception of British visitors at Petersburg.

Those who worked with him and had much to thank him for were noticeably reticent as well. Sharpe is invisible in Meade's wartime letters, *The Life and Letters of George Gordon Meade* (1913), prepared by his son. Meade's primary personal staff officer, Theodore Lyman in his *With Grant and Meade* (originally titled *Meade's Headquarters, 1863–1865*) barely mention Sharpe, who was a fixture at the headquarters of the Army of the Potomac. Meade's chief of staff, A. A. Humphreys, to whom hundreds of Sharpe's reports were addressed, also completely overlooks him in his *The Virginia Campaigns of 1864 and 1865* (1883). Grant never mentioned him in his *Personal Memoirs of U. S. Grant* (1885)—a noticeable lapse—although he appears here and there in *The Papers of U. S. Grant*, collected after his death, but these are wartime references. Giving Sharpe his due perhaps would have dimmed Grant's own star too much, but Grant would find other ways to thank Sharpe. Certainly Sharpe never held it against him as their continued friendship showed. Horace Porter, the authority on Grant's staff, makes only four references to him and never as an important player in his *Campaigning with Grant* (1897).

His deeds were not entirely lost, but were hidden in the diaries of those who served with him, such as Provost Marshal General Patrick (*Inside Lincoln's Armies*,

1964) and to a lesser extent in *The Civil War Diaries of Theodore B. Gates* (1991). But as the dates of publication of these diaries indicate, they were made public long after the pantheon of well-known heroes of the Civil War had been fixed in the eye of both the general public and of historians. Sharpe's accomplishments especially spring to life in the many volumes of the *Official Record of the Rebellion* which record hundreds of Sharpe's reports and analyses and those of his subordinates, particularly Babcock and McEntee. The neglect of historians to mine this gold has been regrettable.

To Edwin Fishel, author of the seminal *The Secret War for the Union* (1996), however, goes the honors of bringing Sharpe back to life. It was he who blew on the ashy embers of history and made them glow again. For Fishel had found in 1959 an even richer treasure trove hidden away in a room in the archives, along with miscellaneous records of the Army of the Potomac—the records of the Bureau of Military Information, neatly tied in red ribbons, retired right after the Civil War, and filed away to be forgotten. They had lain undisturbed for over 90 years.

Sharpe's own reticence to write his memoirs reflects the natural reserve of the intelligence professional to keep his mouth shut. There were still people who could be harmed by his strolling down memory lane, especially the Unionists in Virginia who did so much to help their country at Sharpe's direction. For others who had appealed to the government to compensate them for their sacrifices for the Union, such as Van Lew, Sharpe was a generous supporter, and his letter in support of her claim for compensation is the most extensive account of BMI operations in his hand.

The most likely factor was Sharpe's natural reluctance to engage in self-promotion. It was not that Sharpe was not an ambitious man, for he was that in great measure. Yet there was in some ways a great divide between Sharpe the soldier and Sharpe the politician. It may be found in Sharpe's wartime BMI correspondence in which he eschews "I" for "we." Sharpe's wartime loyalties were the essence of his life. Politics, was, however, politics. He had remained loyal to Conkling until the man's actions went against the public interest. In contrast, he never once betrayed Grant's trust in him. Therein lies another possible reason for his failure to write the story of the BMI. Perhaps he did not want to write anything that might have shown his hero in a less than perfect light. Grant wrote his own memoirs with no reference to the BMI, and Sharpe was not going to contradict him and violate their friendship even after Grant's passing. Sharpe treasured Grant's memory as he had his friendship.

Despite the lack of a memoir, it is clear that Sharpe remained the essence of the story of the BMI, the indispensable man. The mass of the BMI correspondence in the National Archives and the Huntington Library viewed in chronological sequence reveals an enormous amount of information. Only modern computer programs allow it to be gathered in one place and organized in a searchable form. Yet, the historical record is far the poorer for the lack of his memoirs, because Sharpe is not there to tie the whole story together, to clarify the reports and episodes that appear in the record with no background or conclusion. It was the newspaper he so detested, the *New York Herald*, that put it best. "The remarkable incidents connected with the operations of that bureau of secret military information would fill a volume of most intense interest."[41]

In replying to a letter from Babcock in 1904, Sharpe's son, Henry, recounted his efforts to get his father to write a history of the BMI. It stands as an epitaph for his father and the entire staff.

> For many years I endeavored to persuade my father to write an account of the "Bureau of Information": for the benefit of the War Dept., and when in 1899 I was assigned to duty in Washington he promised to come there and spend the winter with me and to occupy himself in preparing the account of his "Bureau of Information," but unfortunately he was called away in January. Col. McEntee has since died, and from your letter I infer that Capt. Oliver is also dead. I regret that my frequent absences from home [on duty in the Philippines] have prevented my keeping in touch with the different members of that Bureau.
>
> No more important work was done during the Civil War than that rendered by the Bureau of Information, and it is a great loss to the Govt. not to have a full report of its operations. It has amused me to see how an act, daily performed by all the members of that Bureau during the Civil War is regarded nowadays. If the recognition now accorded was rendered in the same degree during the Civil War, every member of the Bureau should have been entitled to the rank, honors and compensation awarded to a Marshal of France. Is not this a commentary on the difference between engaging in, and playing at, War?[42]

APPENDIX A

Sharpe's Report of the Conduct of the 120th NY Volunteers at the Battle of Fredericksburg

Numbers 160. Report of Colonel George H. Sharpe, One hundred and twentieth New York Infantry.

CAMP NEAR FALMOUTH, VA.
December 17, 1862

SIR: I respectfully beg leave to submit the following report of the movements of this regiment in connection with the late operations against Fredericksburg:

On the 4th instant, the regiment was ordered to report to Brigadier-General Woodbury for special duty, the details of which are set forth in a supplementary report, herewith forwarded to you for the information of the colonel commanding.*

The regiment returned to the camp near Falmouth on the 11th instant, and at 1 p.m. of the 13th instant, pursuant to orders, marched to join the brigade on the field of battle, on the other side of the river. I reached the field with full ranks at 4 p.m. in the midst of a heavy cannonading and was immediately on arrival placed in the front line of battle, within easy musket range of the enemy. Skirmishers were thrown out (to the number of 80), who found some cover in a ditch within a few rods of the opposing forces, and were from time to time relieved by other details.

Firing was brisk between our skirmishers and the enemy during the morning of the 14th, after which it was only occasional. On the night of the 14th, toward morning, the skirmishers were driven in by an advance, accompanied with rapid firing on the part of the enemy. The regiment immediately arose from where it was lying in line, and without noise or confusion prepared to receive any proposed attack; but our skirmishers soon, in their turn, drove back the enemy's skirmishers. I directed a small squad from each company to remain on the alert during the night, and ordered the men again to lie down on their arms.

On the 15th, there was little firing on the picket line occupied by this regiment, and in the evening we were relieved with the brigade to occupy the second line of battle.

---

* Supplementary report not included.

At 9 p.m. of the same day, I received an order to hold the men in readiness to march at a moment's notice, and about midnight we recrossed the river and went into camp with the brigade about half a mile on this side, returning to our former camping-grounds on Tuesday morning.

I shall also add that a small detachment of 60 men from the regiment, under Lieutenant-Colonel Westbrook, who had been left behind as a camp guard was with the brigade in its occupation of the heights opposite Fredericksburg and marched with the brigade across the river in advance of the regiment, on the arrival of which it rejoined this command.

To most of the men of this regiment this was the first opportunity they had had of finding themselves in the presence of the enemy and under fire both of musketry and artillery, and I take the liberty of respectfully adding, for the approval of the colonel commanding, under whose eye we were during the whole time, that, although the operations of this command were not of the most serious nature, the conduct of the officers and men under my command was marked with coolness and propriety in the discharge of their duties.

Yours, respectfully,
GEO. H. SHARPE,
Colonel, Commanding One Hundred and Twentieth
New York Vols.*

---

* *Source:* OR, Series 1, Vol. 21, Part 1, pp. 388–89.

Members of the Bureau of Military Information (BMI), Army of the Potomac, 1863–65, and The Armies Operating Against Richmond, 1864–65

The following is a list of 233 names of members of the Bureau of Military Information (BMI), the intelligence operation of the Army of the Potomac.[1] Except for the officers in the analytical staff, the list was derived from the payrolls of that organization and correspondence of the BMI. These men were paid for what was considered a unique service from a special War Department Secret Service Fund. Subsequently, they were paid through regular quartermaster channels.[2]

Under the heading below of "Scouts and Guides" are the names compiled from the overall payroll heading of "Guides." The heading causes some confusion, since guides were not considered to be scouts who were on the permanent rolls of the army as soldiers or contract civilians with wide-ranging reconnaissance and intelligence collection duties. Guides were local men who had a knowledge of the immediate area of operations. Often they were African-American slaves, most of whom were considered to have little knowledge outside of a 5-mile radius of the plantations or farms on which they lived.

Clearly, this category of Guides included both scouts and guides, though there are only a few indications of who was a scout and who was a guide. However, in those cases where the individual is named as a colored guide, his pay is at the lower rates of $1.00 to $2.00 a day. Some of the guides and most of the civilian staff were identified in the payroll as either white or colored. All soldier scouts were presumed to be white. The status of most of the scouts and guides remains unknown.

It should be noted that the date an individual first appears on the payrolls is sometimes preceded by mention as a scout in earlier correspondence of the BMI. There appears to be a lag in some cases between beginning work as a scout and appearance on the payroll.

The total of 233 men is broken down into the following categories:

Analytical Staff	6
Scouts & Guides	180
Civilian Support Staff	46
Military Mail Agent	1

This total represents all the personnel working for the BMI over the entire life of that organization. There were never at any one time more than 70 men in the BMI, with 40–50 being the usual number, depending on the mission requirements. Major General Meade was not supportive of any large increase in the size of the organization.

Analytical Staff		
Name	Unit/Status	Joined BMI
Analytical Staff[3]		
Sharpe, George H.	Col. 120th NY Infantry	02-13-63
McEntee, John C.	Capt., 20th NY State Militia[4]	03-22-63
Manning, Frederick L.	Lieut., 148th NY Infantry	03-08-63
Oliver, Paul A.	Lieut., 12th NY Infantry	01-65
Babcock, John C.	Civilian Analyst	02-13-63

Scouts & Guides			
Name	Unit/Status	On BMI Payroll[5]	Contract[6] Date
Scouts and Guides			
Anderson, Allen	Civilian White[7]	03-63	03-10-63
Ball, J. P.	Unknown	09-63	
Bates, Rueben	Unknown	10-63	
Battle, Lewis[8]	Unknown	06-63	
Bensen, John	Unknown	09-64	
Beverley	Unknown	07-63[9]	
Blake, William	Unknown	04-63[10]	
Botts, Thomas	Unknown	05-64	
Bremen, M. H.	Unknown	01-64	
Bromly?, John	Unknown	07-63	
Brooks, Isaac	Unknown	10-63	
Brown, R. J.	Unknown	06-63	
Brown, Carter	Unknown	10-63	
Bryant, Jerry	Unknown	09-63	
Cammack, James M.	Unknown	09-63	
Carney, Anson B.[11]	G/5th U.S. Cavalry	04-19-63	05-03-63
Carney, Edward A.	G/5th U.S. Cavalry	04-19-63	05-03-63
Carney, Philip	F/5th NY Cavalry	07-05-63	
Carter, Dick	Unknown	10-63	
Charles, Jack	Unknown	09-63	

	Scouts & Guides		
Name	*Unit/Status*	*On BMI Payroll*[5]	*Contract*[6] *Date*
Chase, William H.	B/20 NYSM	04-63	04-01-63
Cline, Milton W.	C/3rd IN Cavalry	04-63[12]	04-01-63
Cline, Walter[13]	Civilian White	10-63	
Coburn, H. M.	Unknown	04-63	
Cole, Daniel R.	D/3rd IN Cavalry	04-63[14]	04-16-63
Cole, Samuel R.	Unknown	06-64	
Danes, Robert	Unknown	01-65	
Davis, Robert	Unknown	01-65	
Dawson?, John	Unknown	01-64	
Dillard, Charles L.	Unknown	05-64	
Dodd, Henry Wood	H/1st OH Light Artillery	04-63[15]	04-14-63
Doughty, James R.	Unknown	10-63	
Doughty, John G.	Unknown	10-64	
Dushal, Clark	Unknown	12-63	
Dykes, Joel R	Unknown	10-64	
Edwards, Aaron	Civilian Colored	03-65	
Edwards, Eugene	Unknown	04-64	
Evans, Henry[16]	Civilian Colored	11-64	
Fay, William[17]	Civilian White	06-64	
Flomer, Henry	Unknown	09-64	
Flomer, Samuel	Unknown	09-64	
Ford, Ben	Unknown	08-64	
Forrestal, Charles	Unknown	04-64	
Foster, J. D.	Unknown	06-64	
Fox, James	Unknown	04-64	
Frazier, Cezar	Unknown	05-64	
Gaines, Benjamin F.	Unknown	05-64	
Gardener, Alfred	Unknown	04-64	
Gardener, Dan	Unknown	Unknown	
Goldman, William	Unknown	05-64	
Graham, Michael	Civilian White	11-63	
Green, Bushrod	Unknown	07-63	
Greenwood, Joseph W.	Unknown	06-63	
Gunn, John	A/1st NJ Cavalry	01-65	
Gutheridge, R.	Unknown	04-63	04-10-63

Scouts & Guides			
Name	Unit/Status	On BMI Payroll[5]	Contract[6] Date
Halleck, Ebenezer[18]	Unknown	02-65	
Harding, John	Civilian White	01-63	01-12-63
Harding, Phillip	Civilian White	03-63	03-10-63
Harris, Hiram	Unknown	08-64	
Harrison, Benjamin	Civilian Colored	12-64	
Harter, Thomas O.[19]	Civilian White	11-64	
Hart, Major	Unknown	05-64	
Hatch, J. M.	1st ME Cavalry	94-64	
Hatton, James	D/3rd IN Cavalry	04-64	
Hawkins, J. W.	Unknown	09-64	
Hill, Thomas	Unknown	09-64	
Hirth, Frederick	Unknown	06-64	
Hodges, Thomas	Unknown	05-63	05-01-63
Hogan, Martin E.[20]	I/1st IN Cavalry	06-64	
Holmes, Essex	Unknown	05-64	
Homer, Henry	Unknown	09-64	
Homer, Samuel	Unknown	09-64	
Hopkins, Edward P.	H/1st OH Light Artillery	04-63	04-14-63
Howard, Moses	Unknown	08-64	
Humphreys, Joseph M.	Civilian White	03-63[21]	03-11-63
Hunnicutt, Mordecai P.	I/73rd OH Infantry	04-63	04-14-63
Hyson, Fielding	Unknown	02-64	
Irby, James	Unknown	04-64	
Jack, Charles	Unknown	09-64	
James, Watkins	Unknown	07-63	
Johnson, Dick & Richard[22]	Civilian Colored	05/06-64	
Johnson, Oliver	Civilian Colored	12-64	
Johnson, William	Unknown	09-64	
Jones, John	D/3rd IN Cavalry?	01-65	
Jones, Ned	Unknown	07-64	
Jones, Stephen	Civilian Colored	03-65	
King, Samuel	Unknown	12-63	
Knight, Judson	Civilian White[23]	10-63	
Lee, William J.	Civilian White	11-63	

Scouts & Guides			
Name	Unit/Status	On BMI Payroll[5]	Contract[6] Date
Leitch, Benjamin	Unknown	12-63	
Lesh, James	Unknown	10-63	
Lewis, Philip	Unknown	10-63	
Lickland, George	Unknown	07-63	
Littral, William	Unknown	03-63	03-10-63
Llyod, Adolphus W.	Unknown	04-64	
Lymmerick, James	Unknown	12-63	
Lyon, Jack	Unknown	05-64[24]	
Mahoney, Frank	Unknown	05-64	
Major, Charles[25]	Civilian White	07-64	
Marcus, P. M.	Unknown	05-63	05-01-63
Maybee, Thomas	Unknown	06-63	
McCord, Benjamin Frank	H/1st OH Light Artillery	04-63	04-14-63
McCraken, Thomas	Unknown	05-64	
McEneany, Patrick	Unknown	04-64	
McFarlane, I. H.	Unknown	01-64	
McGee, Edward	Civilian White	04-63	04-01-63
McGee, Robert M.	Civilian White	12-63	
McGee, Sandford	Civilian White	12-63	
Menito?, E.	Unknown	11-63	
Merritt, Edward	Unknown	08-63	
Miller, James	Unknown	04-64	
Miller, William H.	Unknown	07-63	
Mitchell, James A.	Unknown	04-64	
Moore, Isaac E.	Unknown	06-63	
Morris, James F.	Unknown	04-64	
Myers, Alexander[26]	Civilian White	10-64	
Myers, John	Unknown	09-64	
O'Boyline, Joseph	Unknown	01-64	
O'Conner, Richard	Unknown	12-63	
Orrick, Robert	Civilian White	05-64	
Otto, D. G.[27]	NY Cavalry	Unknown	
P.?, John	Unknown	11-64	
Parum, Sidney	Unknown	02-65	

	Scouts & Guides		
Name	Unit/Status	On BMI Payroll[5]	Contract[6] Date
Patrick, B. B.	Unknown	12-64	
Payne, ? R.	Unknown	12-63	
Pelham, John	Unknown	07-63	
Pettis, Major	Unknown	11-63	
Phelps, Charles A.	5th NY Cavalry	04-64	
Plew, Daniel	C/3rd IN Cavalry	05-63[28]	
Poole, Albert	Unknown	02-64	
Powell, John M.	F/3rd IN Cavalry	05-64	
Price, Isaac	Unknown	01-64	
Price, James	Unknown	02-64	
Prince, George	Unknown	07-64	
Randall, Richard	Unknown	09-63	
Reed?, D. C.	Unknown	09-63	
Reese, William	Unknown	02-65	
Roach, Henry	Unknown	09-64	
Robison, John	Unknown	12-63	
Rose, William	Unknown	09-64	
Roses, Edmond	Unknown	02-64	
Rowen, M.	Unknown	05-64	
Russ, Lewis	Unknown	09-64	
Sanford, Henry	Unknown	04-64	
Scott, Alexander	Unknown	12-64	
Scott, S. F.	Unknown	07-63	
Scott, Thomas	Unknown	07-64	
Sheppard, Henry	Unknown	09-63	
Sherman, Thomas	Unknown	01-65	
Silver, Isaac	Civilian White	09-63	
Silver, John	Civilian White	08-64	
Simons, William	Unknown	04-65	
Simpson, John	Unknown	08-63	
Skinker, John Howard	Civilian White	03-63	03-08-63
Skinker, M. H.	Civilian White	01-64	
Skinner, W. H.	Unknown	02-64	
Smith, Charles W.	Unknown	11-64	

	Scouts & Guides		
Name	*Unit/Status*	*On BMI Payroll*[5]	*Contract*[6] *Date*
Smith, E. P.	Unknown	04-63	04-15-63
Smith, George S.	Civilian White	04-64	04-01-63
Smith, James H. B.	Unknown	11-64	
Staian, J. L.	Unknown	04-64	
Stevens, John F.	Unknown	05-64	
Stile, E. W.	Unknown	09-63	
Swicher, Jacob	I/1st IN Cav	06-63	
Thomas, Barrett	Unknown	08-64	
Toppin, William	Unknown	10-64	
Tuisley, Charles	Unknown	11-64	
Tyson, John "Jack"	Unknown	03-63	03-01-63
Vadden, John	Unknown	08-64	
Van Pelt, A. M.	Unknown	01-64	
Wagoner, I. S.	Unknown	07-63	
Walker, Dabney[29]	Civilian Colored	06-63	
Weams, William	Civilian White	02-63	02-02-83
Weaver, William	Unknown	11-02-63[30]	
Weekly, Benjamin	Unknown	10-63	
Weekly, Calhoun	Unknown	10-63	
White, Daniel	Unknown	11-64	
Williams, Joseph	Unknown	09-64	
Wilson, William[31]	White	09-63	
Wood, James R.	Unknown	02-64	
Yager, Ernest	Unknown	05-63	05-01-63

	Civilian Support Staff	
Name	**Unit/Status**	**On BMI Payroll**
Clerks		
Ransom, A. F.	Civilian clerk	06-63
Taylor, M. B.	Civilian clerk, Q.M.D.	03-64
Wagon Masters		
Algaien, Elias	Civilian	06-63
Fox, David E.	Civilian	09-64

Civilian Support Staff		
Name	Unit/Status	On BMI Payroll
Teamsters		
Averson, Henry	Civilian Colored	04-65
Brom, Armistead	Civilian Colored	02-65
Brown, Samuel	Civilian White	11-64
Bug, Henry	Civilian teamster	12-63
Coin, Abram[32]	Civilian White	12-63
Elmendorf, Edgar	Civilian White	03-64
Davis, Washington	Civilian Colored	09-64
Edwards, Aaron	Civilian Colored	03-65
Evans, Robert	Civilian White	04-64
Fingle, William	Civilian Colored	11-64
Franise, Hiram	Civilian White	12-64
Fry, Thorton	Civilian Colored	06-64
Green, Samuel	Civilian White	11-64
Harris, George	Civilian Colored	05-64
Hill, John	Civilian Colored	08-64
Hills, George	Civilian Colored	11-64
Jackson, Jerry	Civilian Colored	04-65
Johnson, William	Civilian Colored	02-65
Jones, Addison	Civilian Colored	12-64
Jones, Eugene	Civilian Colored	06-64
Jones, Stephen	Civilian Colored	03-65
Logan, Joseph	Civilian Colored	04-65
Low, George	Civilian White	12-64
Marshall, S.	Civilian Colored	04-65
Mason, Samuel	Civilian Colored	09-64
Maury?, E. S.	Civilian teamster	06-63
Merriweather, Israel	Civilian Colored	06-63
Miner, Robert	Civilian Colored	07-63
Oliver, Robert	Civilian Colored	07-63
Pendleton, Nathan	Civilian Colored	09-63
Quales, Henry J.	Civilian Colored	07-64
Scott, Lewis	Civilian Colored	06-64
Scott, Warren	Civilian Colored	12-64

Civilian Support Staff		
Name	**Unit/Status**	**On BMI Payroll**
Thomas, Jefferson	Civilian Colored	11-64
Watts, Oliver	Civilian White	06-64
Widey, Nelson	Civilian Colored	06-64
Young, Albert	Civilian Colored	04-65
Other		
Elmendorf, Edgar	Blacksmith White	01-65
Hawkins, George	Cook	09-64
Miner, Robert	Cook	09-64
Palmer, E. W.	Blacksmith	11-64
Quales, Henry J.	Blacksmith Colored	08-64
Also Paid on BMI Payroll		
Mail Agent		
Parker, David B.	Mail Agent, 72d NY Inf	07-64

Strength of the Bureau of Military Information February 1863–April 1865

	Analysis Group	Scouts Guides	Clerks	Mail Agent	Wagon Masters	Teamsters	Cooks	Black-Smiths	Carpenters	Total
1863										
Feb	2	2								4
Mar	2	8								8
Apr	3	19								22
May	4	24								28
Jun	4	33								37
July	4	33								37
Aug	4	30								34
Sep	4	36								40
Oct	4	42								46
Nov	4	36								40
Dec	4	57								61
1864										
Jan.	4	40				2				46
Feb	4	33	1			2				40
Mar	4	34	1			3				42
Apr	4	50	1			2				57
May	4	59	1			3				67
Jun	4	37	1	1		11				54
July	4	39	1	1		9				54
Aug	4	35	1	1	1	15	1	1		59
Sep	4	35	1	1		15	1	1		58
Oct	4	46	1	1	1	17	2	1		73
Nov	4	18	1	1	1	17	2	1		45
Dec	4	34	1	1	1	17	2	1		61

	Analysis Group	Scouts Guides	Clerks	Mail Agent	Wagon Masters	Teamsters	Cooks	Black-Smiths	Carpenters	Total
1865										
Jan	4	31	1	1	1	14	1		1	59
Feb	5	30	1	1	1	14	2		1	57
Mar	5	24	1	1	1	11			1	44
Apr	5	28	1	1	1	23	1		1	61
May	1	14	1	1	1	15				33

Expenditures of the BMI[33]

	Pay Due	Not Paid
1863		
Jan	40.00	none
Feb	108.00	40.00
Mar	522.00	148.00
Apr	1200.00	670.00
May	1670.00	1870.00
Jun	2048.99	none
Jul	2379.00	none
Aug	2011.00	none
Sep	2675.00	none
Oct	3519.00	none
Nov	2880.00	none
Dec	3637.00	none
1864		
Jan	3190.00	none
Feb	2609.00	2609.00
Mar	3107.16	none
Apr	3840.00	none
May	4022.50	none
Jun	3153.00	none
Jul	3302.00	none
Aug	2943.00	none
Sep	3025.00	none
Oct	3998.00	4754.56
Nov	3036.67	6097.00
Dec*	3665.98	3665.98

	Pay Due	*Not Paid*
1865		
Jan*	3307.83	948.33
Feb*	3490.68	210.00
Mar	3753.50	2993.00
Apr*	7319.00	8467.00
May	2743.00	2743.00

*Months for which special service payments were made above the normal pay rates.

The BMI's Intelligence Preparation of the Battlefield (IPB) For the Battle of Chancellorsville Roads, Railroads, Fords[34]

(Spelling and punctuation reproduce the originals)

Roads

Roads running from Fredericksburg

Old Stage Road from Fredericksburg to Richmond known as the Bowling Green or Baseline Road. This is the best wagon road leading from F[redericksburg] to R[ichmond].

Fredericksburg	[distance from Fredericksburg]
Hazel Run 60 ft wide Good ford	½
Deep Run 40 ft wide Good ford steep ascent and descent	2
Massaponax Great Bridge. Can be forded	6
Intersection of road from Bowling Green	7
Hicks Hill	9
Sycamore's	11
Villeboro	14
Bowling Green	22
Burkes Brides Crossing Mattapomy River	
Ready Swamp	
Pamunkey River	43
Hanover CH	45
Chickahominy Swamp	
Richmond	65
The Port Royal Road diverges from the above road 7 miles from Fredericksburg. From hence to Port Royal the distance is	15
From Fredericksburg to Port Royal	22
From Port Royal to Bowling Green	15

Telegraph Road from Fredericksburg to Richmond

Fredericksburg	0
Hazel Run 60 ft wide Good ford	1
Diverges from Spottsylvania CH road	5
This road is probably the shortest route leading to Richmond. It is a common earth road, good in dry weather but liable to become very bad in wet weather.	
Massaponax Creek two small bridges	6
Massaponax Church	9
Smith Millon Niy River. Bridge 20 ft long and 15 ft high—banks steep	11
It is 7 miles from this point to Spottysvlania CH. The Telegraph road turns to the left while the most direct road leads to the CH.	
Blacksmith Shop	12
Stannards Mill on Po River. Bridge is perhaps 60 ft long & 10 high. Can be Forded in law water. Bank bad	13
Mud Tavern	14
Gerrells Mill on Ta River known as Thornburg. Good fords. No bridges.	
Negro foot road here diverges to the right.	15
The Ny River is not deep but it would be very difficult to ascend this hill on the South side from the bed of the stream.	
Crossing of road leading to Bowling Green	17
N fork of Mat River—(fordable)	20
S fork of Mat River—(fordable)	21
Theses streams [two above] are easily crossed, the hills on each side are not steep	
North Anna River	32
Dry bridge crossing of RR	35
Hanover CH	43
Richmond	60

Orange and Fredericksburg Plank Road

Fredericksburg	0
Tabernackle Church Road diverges toward old Court House	7
Old Barharpin Road leads to the left	8
Chancellorsville	10
Dorndalls Tavern	12
Intersection of Plank Road from Culpeper CH	13½
Parkers Store	17
Verdierville	20
Orange CH	36

Distances on Roads from Fredericksburg via Falmouth to Bealton Station

	Intermediate Distances	Distances from Fredericksburg
Fredericksburg	0	0
Falmouth	2	2
Bora Church	4	6
Heartwood (take March road to left)	4	10
Road to Richards Ferry to left distances 5 miles		
Embury's Mill on Deep Run	5	15
Grove Church (Road to left 4 miles to Ellis Mill)	2	17
Embury's (Road to left as below)	1	18
Wycoff's Quartz Mill	1	19
Morrisville (Kellysville on right hand road 5½ miles)	2	21
Road crossing from Elk Run to Kellysville 5 m. to R	1	22
Wheatleys	22	24½
Morgansburg	1½	26
Bealton Station on Orange & Alex Raid-Road	1	37
4 miles north of Rappahannock Station		
By taking left h and road at Embury's 18 miles from Fredericksburg		18
Liberty Quartz Mill	1	19
Crittendens Mill & Tan yard	1	20
Intersection of Road to Ellis Mill	½	20½
Road which diverges to left at Boro Church comes in again	½	21
Road from Morrisville comes in from N.E.	2	24
Mt Holly Church (By keeping to left 1½ miles to Kellysville)	1	26½
Rappahannock Station	2½	29

Roads Running Near Orange & Alexandria RR

Rappahannock Station	0	0
To crossing of Rappahannock River at low ford	½	½
Stringfellows	3½	4
Brandy Station	2	6
Forks of road (left hand leads to Stevensburg 4 miles)	1	7
Culpeper C.H.	5	12
By taking the left hand Road toward Richard Ferry at Heartwood		
Heartwood	10	15
Richards Ferry	5½	15½
Richardsville, left hand road to Ellys Ford 5 miles	4	19
Shepherds Grove P.O.	4	23
Rod from S.E. ermanna Mills and		
Bridge 3 miles		
Road from Kellysville?	2	25
Stevensburg	5	30
Georgetown	5	35
Culpeper	2	37

Road from Fredericksburg to Culpeper Court House

Tabernacle Church Road toward Spottsylvania CH	7	7
Old Catparthin Road	1½	8½
Chancellorsville	1½	10
Elley's Ford on Rapidan River	5	15
Richardsville (Road comes on from Richards Ferry 4 miles easterly)	5	20
Shepards Grove	4	24
Culpeper CH	14	38
At Chancellorsville (see above)		
Chancellorsville	10	10
Dordalls Tavern	2	12
Take Stevensburg Plank Road leaving Gordonsville – Plank Road	1½	13½
Wilderness Tavern	2	15½
Flat Fun	3	18½
Germanna Bridge	1½	20
Shepards Grove	3	23
Culpeper CH	14	37

Railroads

Richmond Fredericksburg and Potomac Rail Road [RF&P]

Distances from Fredericksburg	
Fredericksburg	0
Hazel Run	½
Massaponax Creek	6
Summit	8
Guinea's Sta	12
Milford Sta	21
Massapony River	22½
Pole Cat River & Sta	25
Reedy Swamp	26
Chesterfield	30
North Anna River	36
Junction	38
Taylorsville	40
Little River	41
South Anna River	43
Ashland	45
Hungary Station	53
Chicahominy Swamp	55
Richmond	61½

Bridges on the Richmond Fredericksburg & Potomac RR

Hazel Run (½ mile) Wooden Deck bridge 54 ft long and about 40 ft high
Deep Run (1 ½ m) Stringers 12 ft +
Massaponax Creek (6 m) about 120 ft long and 40 ft high. Timber bents & 3 pans
Massapony or Buck Hole Bride (2 ½ m) Two bridges 1t 40 ft long, 2d 110 ft long—each 30 ft high
Pole Cat Creek (25 m) Long bridge on piles nearly 1000 ft long. 3 short Spans crossing channels. Height 8 feet.
North Anna River (36 m) about 400 ft long and 25 feet high. Trestlework
Little River (41 m) about 200 feet long. Trestlework with timber bents.
South Anna River (43 m) 600 ft long 73 ft high. Stone piers and abutments. Same character as the bridge across the Rappahannock at Fredericksburg, though 3 ft or 5 ft shorter.
Chickahominy Swamp () Stone culverts or Small bridges.

The Central Railroad

The Central Rail Road from Richmond to Gordonsville crosses the RF&P RR at the junction between North Anna and Little River which is 24 miles from R[ichmond] by the RF&P RR and 28 miles by the Central Road. Both roads are of the same grade and gauge at the junction.

The bridges across Little River and the South Anna on the Central Road are shorter, lower and less substantial than those on the road being supported by timber bents.

Distances on the Virginia Central RR

From Richmond	
Atlees	9
Hanover CH	18
Hanover Junction	28
North Tavern	33
Beaver Dam	40
Bumpas Turn out	50
Frederick Hall	56
Louisa C.H.	62
Travellian Sta	64
Milton Sta	73
Gordonsville	76

Fords

Fords on the Rapidan River

Blind Ford	
Elly's Ford	Tolerably good (much used)
Ford near Vancluse mine	Crossed by cavalry
Germanna Bridge Ford	
Mitchell's Ford	
Tobaccostick Ford	
Stringfellows	River is fordable in many places above here
Norton's Ford	
Racoon Ford	
Somerville Ford	
Downs Ford	
Willis Ford at Holladays near Rapidan Sta	
Burnetts Ford	
Walkers Ford	

Fords on the Rappahannock River

Opposite Falmouth crossing a mill race and winding up diagonally across	Rocky & Crooked
Scotts Ford near Scotts Mill	Just above the mill not very good for Cavalry & is not crossed by teams
Banks Old Ford	Is crossed at low stages of water and is Tolerably good
Barrow's Old Ford	Obstructions by a dam—disused
U.S. Ford	Obstructed by a canal on S. side of R. The ford is good one.
Richard's Ferry	Formerly a ferry. Now forded at low water navigation having changed the character
Embury's Old Ford	
Skinker's Ford	Rocky can be crossed by cavalry
Ellis Ferry or Barnett's Ford & Ferry	
Kemper's Ford	Good but steep approaches
Field's Ford	
Kelly's Ford	
Wheatley's Ford	
Cowford just below the O&A RR.	Good, used in Aug. by Genl Pope
Beverely Ford above RR crossing 2 miles	Is good crossed by roads from Liberty and Rappahannock Sta in Berryville
Freeman's Ford	Best on the river
Col. Fants Mill Ford	Good
Foxville Ford	Good
Sulpher Springs Ford	

Bank's Ford

Bank's Ford proper is accessible in either side by a road passable for Artillery and Conveyances; but no teams can cross the river, as the water is too deep at the point where the road reaches it, being from three to four feet deep. Rifle pits, protected by abattis, have been constructed so as to guard the passage of the ford.

Opposite these works the depth of the water is from two to four feet. If the water were sufficiently low, infantry might cross at the ford with a front of about two hundred men. The banks at the crossing on this side, are steep and difficult to descend, and have been made more so by an abattis of trees felled from the outer bank of the canal; on the enemy's side, the bank is low and easy to ascend.

United States Ford

At the United States ford, the river is fordable as to depth and bottom nearly everywhere, the water being no where over three feet deep, except just abreast a perpendicular ledge a short distance above the ford.

The banks along the front are mostly very steep and high. There are two approaches on the rebel side—only one on this. This practicable for Cavalry and Artillery—could be easily obstructed by felling trees. Forces cold cross here with any front, but could not land wider than four men abreast. On our side the only roads practicable for Artillery or Cavalry are now effectually blocked. The banks are high and precipitous, and leave a margin of a few rods wide at the water's edge, upon which rifle pits have been constructed, about 20 yards from the river.

Rifle pits have also been made on the crest of the bluff above, some three hundred yards from the river.

Scott's Dam

Scott's Dam is 1 ½ miles distant from US Ford. Here are no fordable places, except ½ of a mile above the dam, and perhaps immediately below the dam.

Infantry and Cavalry would cross in single file above, Artillery not at all. The banks very steep every where. All approaches can be easily obstructed; quite a number of rebel works near the dam.

Hersepen Run 1 ½ miles from Scotts Dam, not fordable; water deep and bottom soft; banks steep and precipitous.

Richard's Ford

At Richard's ford, there are roads and paths to all points on the river; three practicable for Cavalry and Infantry – one for Artillery. The banks are steep and rocky with ravines up which there are paths.

Cavalry, Infantry, and Artillery can pass at some points, Infantry division front. Rifle pits protected by abattis have been constructed to guard the crossing, both at the bottom and the top of the banks. All the roads and paths can be obstructed by felling trees.

Powell's Dam

[no entry]

Lye Island

Lye Island, which is about 300 yards long is covered with rocks and a dense undergrowth. The main stream runs on the south side of the island and appears to be fordable both above and below it.

There are no roads for the access of any considerable body of troops. The banks of the river are high and covered with timber.

It is impracticable for Cavalry and Artillery, and difficult for infantry.

It may be easily obstructed.

The water is over three feet deep.

Crowley's or Deep Run Dam

There are no roads at this dam, or access for any considerable force.

The banks on the south side are high and steep; they are high also on the north side, but not so steep. Both sides are thickly covered with timber and underbrush, near the river scattered pines—further back oak and other hard wood.

It is impracticable for Artillery and Cavalry and difficult for Infantry.

The ford and its approaches may be obstructed easily so as to be nearly useless.

The water is above three feet deep.

Skenker's Ford and Mill

Approaches not good.

Banks on both sides high, steep, and wooded, and the bottom rocky.

Not practicable for Cavalry or Artillery and difficult for Infantry.

Ford can be made less practicable, but can hardly be destroyed.

Difficult to ascertain depth of water, as the river is divided into many little streams by large rocks and small islands covered with dense undergrowth. There is an old mill race running from above Skenker's Dam to below the mill one this side say half mile. It is now a good deep ditch.

The ford is just below the Mill and could never have been much used; single men can doubtless pick their way across here and any where above for half a mile, but it would be very difficult. The river from this point runs in nearly a straight line through clay banks not high in the immediate vicinity of the stream, but rising further back.

The hills on this side commanding those opposite. The water here must be from five to eight feet deep.

Skenker's Dam

There is a road to Grove Church practicable for Infantry and Cavalry, no indication of road on the opposite side.

Banks south side high and steep—not practicable for Artillery and Cavalry, north side not so high but steep—south side wooded.

Impracticable for Cavalry and Artillery, difficult for Infantry.

Little means of obstructing this crossing.

Water varies from two to three & one half feet in depth. The bottom is general covered with large rocks in many of which there are soil and undergrowth. The river appears to be of the same nature for about half a mile below.

Ellis Ford

The roads are good and access easy. North bank of river sloping—south bank steep with winding road from ford. Cavalry, Artillery and Infantry can pass the ford. The ford or the access to it cannot be obstructed so as to make it less practicable or wholly useless by an ordinary means, or means known to me. The water is two feet deep at this date as determined by personal observation and information from Mr. Ellis who lives at the ford.

There are no other places in the immediate vicinity of Ellis' Ford, that can be forded except between Ellis' Dam one mile up river and the ford, and which can only be forded by footmen with considerable difficulty.

Kemper's Ford

There is but one road to the ford for nearly a mile, but many horse paths through the woods.

Banks generally rocky and abrupt, thickly wooded.

Artillery & Infantry cannot cross except at Ford.

May be obstructed to some extent.

Water supposed to be from 2 to 3 feet in depth; the bottom being rocky.

No other mode of crossing except by swimming horses.

Mountain Run Ford

Roads not very difficult on the opposite side.

Low and easy of access. On this side the banks low but rocky and rough

Cavalry and Infantry can cross.

Not easily obstructed. Water from three to five feet deep.

Kelly's Ford

Good road and easy of access.

The banks are low on both sides.

Cavalry, Artillery and Infantry can cross.

The ford may be made less practicable by obstructions and an abattis, and defended by a line of rifle pits.

The water is about two feet deep known from personal observation.

Between Wheatley's Ford on the right, and Mountain Ford on the left, there are two places may be crossed by Infantry only.

Wheatley's Ford

The roads are easy of access.

On this side the banks are rough and rocky, on the opposite side, low and easily approached.

Cavalry, Artillery and Infantry could cross by removing slight obstructions.

The road can be made less practicable by obstructions.

The water about three feet deep, judging from the appearance.

Fords Across the Rappahannock & Rapidan Rivers

Rappahannock River Fords	Rapidan River Fords
Opposite Falmouth	Blind Ford
Scott's Ford	Elly's Ford
Banks Old Ford	Ford near Vanduse Mine
Barrow's Old Ford	Germanna Bridge Ford
U.S. Ford	Mitchell's Ford
Richard's Ferry	Tobaccostick Ford
Embury's Old Ford	Stringfellows Ford
Skinker's Ford	Norton's Ford
Kemper's Ford	Racoon Ford
Field's Ford	Gomerville Ford
Kelly's Ford	Dowrie's Ford
Wheatley's Ford	Willis Ford
Cowford just below the O&A RR	Burnett's Ford
Beverely Ford	Walker's Ford
Freeman's Ford	
Col. Tant's Mill Ford	
Foxville Ford	
Sulpher Springs Ford	

Abstracts from Field Returns of the Army of Northern Virginia*

	Present for Duty	Effectives Present	Aggregate Present	Aggregate Present & Absent	Pieces Artillery
Month of Jan 1863	78,074	72,226	93,300	144,614	93
Month of Feb 1863	62,067	58,559	74,436	114,186	37[35]
Month of Mar 1863	64,799[36]	60,298	77,379	109,859	96
Month of May 1863	74,459	68,352	86,735	133,652	208
Jul 20 1863	41,692		50,178	109,915	
Month of Jul 1863	45,396	41,135	53,286	117,277	229
Aug 10, 1863	58,671		68,104	130,317	
Month of Aug 1863	61,202	56,326	71,954	133,254	246
Sep 10, 1863	46,184		54,009	97,776	
Sep 30, 1863	48,067	44,362	55,221	95,164	174
Month of Sep 1863	48,067	44,362	55,221	95,164	174
Oct 20, 1863	47,052		53,031	96,706	
Month of Oct 1863	49,502	45,614	57,251	97,912	174
Nov 20, 1863	48,613		56,088	96,576	
Dec 10, 1863	49,490		57,418	97,033	
Jan 10, 1864	46,313		54,735	92,085	
Jan 31, 1864	38,604	35,849	45,127	79,672	190
February 10, 1864	33,991		39,551	68,421	
February 20, 1864	41,395		47,871	85,480	
March 10, 1864	39,634		46,141	79,190	
March 20, 1864	47.045		55,000	98,572	
April 10, 1864	52,952		61,206	97,564	
April 20, 1864	54,344		62,913	98,174	

* *Source:* War of the Rebellion: The Official Records of the Union and Confederate Armies

Field Returns of the Provost Marshal Battalion and Battalion of Scouts, Guides, & Couriers Army of Northern Virginia, January–April 1864

Present for Duty	PM Bn	Bn, Scouts etc.
January 10	296	100
January 31	295	120
February 10	245	130
February 20	256	199
March 10	256	198
March 20	257	212
April 10	308	235
April 20	320	230

Regiments/Battalions from which Deserters and Prisoners Were Interrogated by the BMI, Feb–Apr 1863

Regiments from which prisoners and deserters [previous two words added in Sharpe's hand] have been taken since Feb 1863.

	Feb		*March*
1st	Latham's Battery, Pickett's Division	3rd	11th Virginia Infantry
1st	6th Georgia Regt	16th	11th Mississippi Infantry
1st	4th Virginia Battery	16th	3d North Carolina Infantry
1st	13th Virginia Regt	26th	19th Mississippi Infantry
1st	41st Virginia Regt	26th	23d North Carolina
1st	Coopers [sic] Battery	26th	15th Louisiana
1st	6th Virginia Cavalry	26th	10th Louisiana
1st	9th Virginia Cavalry	28th	4th Virginia Infantry
10th	30th Virginia Infantry	30th	1st North Carolina Infantry
13th	49th Virginia Infantry	30th	1st North Carolina Cavalry
13th	8th Alabama	31st	1st South Carolina Cavalry
15th	15th Virginia Cavalry	31st	2d South Carolina Cavalry
15th	55th Virginia Infantry		*April*
15th	40th Virginia Infantry	2d	9th Louisiana Infantry
18th	10th Virginia Cavalry	10th	8th Louisiana Infantry
18th	4th Louisiana Infantry	10th	48th Mississippi Infantry
18th	Pegrams [sic] Battery	12th	5th Louisiana Infantry
20th	47th Virginia Infantry	13th	22d Virginia Battalion
20th	21st Mississippi Infantry	18th	2d North Carolina Cavalry
21st	4th Virginia Cavalry	18th	8th Virginia Infantry
21st	9th Alabama Infantry	18th	51st Georgia Infantry
21st	12th Mississippi Infantry	18th	26th Georgia Infantry
21st	6th Virginia Infantry	21st	1st Louisiana Volunteers
25th	1st Virginia Cavalry	22d	Cobbs Legion Cavalry
		28th	5th Alabama Infantry
		28th	46th Virginia Infantry

These regiments comprise all from which prisoners of war have been taken or from which we have had deserters to date. From many of these regiments we have had but one, from others 10 or twelve, but frequently deserters have been able to furnish us with complete organizations of their Brigades Divisions & Co.*

---

* *Source:* Report written in Lieut. Frederick Manning's hand and signed by Col. George H. Sharpe, April 30, 1863, NARA, Microcopy 2096, Box 45.

Order-of-Battle of Jackson's Corps at Chancellorsville Comparison of Babcock's Estimates

	Known OB	Babcock April 28th	Babcock May 1st
Hill's Light Division			
Heth' Bde	40th VA	40th VA	40th VA
	47th VA	47th VA	27th VA
	55th VA	55th VA	55th VA
	22nd VA Bn	22nd VA Bn	22nd VA Bn
Pender's Bde	13th NC		13th NC
	16th NC	16th NC	16th NC
	22nd NC	22nd NC	22nd NC
	34th NC	34th NC	34th NC
	38th NC	38th NC	38th NC
McGowan's Bde	1st SC	1st SC	1st SC
	1st SC Rifles	11th SC	11th SC
	12th SC	12th SC	12th SC
	13th SC	13th SC	13th SC
	14th SC	14th SC	14th SC
Lane's Bde	7th NC	7th NC	7th NC
	18th NC	18th NC	18th NC
	28th NC		28th NC
	33rd NC	33rd NC	33rd NC
	37th NC	37th NC	37th NC
Archer's Bde	1st TN	1st TN	1st TN
	7th TN	7th TN	7th TN
	14th TN	14th TN	14th TN
	13th AL	19th GA	19th TN
	5th AL Bn	5th AL Bn	5th AL BN

	Known OB	Babcock April 28th	Babcock May 1st
Thomas' Bde	14th GA	14th GA	14th GA
	35th GA	35th GA	35th GA
			16th GA
	45th GA		45th GA
	49th GA	49th GA	49th GA
Rodes' Division			
Dole's Bde	4th GA	4th GA	4th GA
	12th GA		12th GA
	21st GA		
	44th GA	44th GA	44th GA
		1st NC	
		3rd NC	
			10th NC
Iverson's Bde			3rd NC
	5th NC	5th NC	5th NC
	12th NC	12th NC	12th NC
		13th NC	13th NC
			14th NC
	20th NC	20th NC	
	23rd NC	23rd NC	
Colquitt's Bde	6th GA	6th GA	6th GA
		13th GA	
	19th GA		
	23rd GA	23rd GA	23rd GA
	27th GA	27th GA	27th GA
	28th GA	28th GA	28th GA
			13th AL
Ramseur's Bde	2nd NC	2nd NC	2nd NC
(Anderson's)	4th NC	4th NC	4th NC
	14th NC	14th NC	14th NC
		15th NC	15th NC
	30th NC	30th NC	30th NC
O'Neal's Bde	3rd AL		
	5th AL		

	Known OB	Babcock April 28th	Babcock May 1st
	6th AL		
	12th AL		
	26th AL		
Early's Division			
Gordon's Bde	13th GA	13th GA	13th GA
	26th GA	26th GA	26th GA
	31st GA	31st GA	31st GA
	38th GA	38th GA	38th GA
	60th GA	60th GA	60th GA
	61st GA	61st GA	61st GA
Hoke's Bde	6th NC	6th NC	6th NC
	21st NC	21st NC	21st NC
	54th NC	54th NC	54th NC
	55th NC		55th NC
		57th NC	
	1st NC Sharpshooters		1st NC Bn
Smith's Bde (Walker's old)	13th VA	13th VA	13th VA
		26th VA	
		44th VA	44th VA
	49th VA	49th VA	49th VA
	52nd VA	52nd VA	
			57th VA
	58th VA		58th VA
Haye's Bde	5th LA	5th LA	5th LA
	6th LA	6th LA	6th LA
	7th LA	7th LA	7th LA
	8th LA	8th LA	8th LA
	9th LA	9th LA	9th LA
Colston's Division (Trimble's old)			
Paxton's Bde	2nd VA	2nd VA	2nd VA
	4th VA	4th VA	4th VA
	5th VA	5th VA	5th VA
		23rd VA	
	27th VA	27th VA	27th VA
	33rd VA		33rd VA

	Known OB	*Babcock April 28th*	*Babcock May 1st*
Jones' Bde		1st VA	1st VA
	21st VA	21st VA	21st VA
	42nd VA	42nd VA	42nd VA
	44th VA		
	48th VA	48th VA	48th VA
	50th VA		50th VA
Warren's Bde	1st NC	1st NC	1st NC
	3rd NC	3rd NC	3rd NC
	10th VA	10th VA	10th VA
	23rd VA	23rd VA	23rd VA
	37th VA	37th VA	37th VA
Nicholl's Bde	1st LA	1st LA	1st LA
	2nd LA		2nd LA
		7th LA	
	10th LA	10th LA	10th LA
	14th LA	14th LA	14th LA
	15th LA	15th LA	15th LA
Number of Regts/Bns	91	84	91

Order-of-Battle of Longstreet's Corps at Chancellorsville Comparison of Babcock's April 28th Estimate

Anderson's Division		
Mahone's Bde	6th VA	6th VA
	12th VA	12th VA
	16th VA	16th VA
	41st VA	41st VA
	61st VA	61st VA
Posey's Bde	12th MS	12th MS
	16th MS	16th MS
	19th MS	19th MS
	48th MS	48th MS
Perry's Bde	2nd FL	
	5th FL	
	8th FL	
Wilcox's Bde	8th AL	8th AL
	9th AL	9th AL
	10th AL	10th AL

	Known OB	Babcock April 28th	Babcock May 1st
	11th AL	11th AL	
	14th AL	14th AL	
Wright's Bde	3rd GA	3rd GA	
	11th GA		
		22nd GA	
	48th GA	48th GA	
	2nd GA Bn		
		28th AL	
		44th AL	
McLaws' Division			
Kershaw's Bde	2nd SC		
	3rd SC		
	7th SC		
	8th SC		
	15th SC		
	3rd SC Bn		
Semme's Bde (Bennings' old)	10th GA	10th GA	
	50th GA	50th GA	
	51st GA	51st GA	
		58th GA	
Woford's Bde	16th GA	16th GA	
	18th GA	18th GA	
	24th GA	24th GA	
	Cobb's GA Legion		
	Phillips's GA Legion	Phillip's GA Legion	
Barksdale's Bde	13th MS	13th MS	
	17th MS	17th MS	
	18th MS	18th MS	
	21st MS	21st MS	
Number of Regts/Bns	39	31	
Total Regts/Bns	130	115	

Sharpe's Report Alerting Hooker of Lee's Imminent Invasion of the North that Led to the Gettysburg Campaign

PROVOST-MARSHAL-GENERAL'S OFFICE, ARMY OF THE POTOMAC
May 27, 1863.

Brigadier General S. WILLIAMS, Assistant Adjutant-General:

SIR: By direction of the general commanding, I furnish the following memoranda of the position of the enemy and other data obtained within the last few days:

1. The enemy's line in front of us is much more contracted than during the winter. It extends from Banks' Ford, on a line parallel with the river, to near Moss Neck. Anderson's division is on their left. McLaws' is next, and in rear of Fredericksburg. Early is massed about Hamilton's Crossing, and Trimble's is directly in the rear of Early. Rodes' (D. H. Hill's old division) is farther to the right, and back from the river, and A. P. Hill is the right of their line, resting nearly on Moss Neck. Each of these six divisions have five brigades.

2. Pickett's division, of six brigades, has come up from Suffolk, and is at Taylorsville, near Hanover Junction.

3. Hood's division, of four brigades, has also left from the front of Suffolk, and is between Louisa Court-House and Gordonsville.

4. Ten days ago there was in Richmond only the City Battalion, 2,700 strong, commanded by General Elzey.

5. There are three brigades of cavalry 3 miles from Culpeper Court-House, toward Kelly's Ford. They can at present turn out only 4,700 men for duty, but have many dismounted men, and the horses are being constantly and rapidly recruited by the spring growth of grass. These are Fitz. Lee's, William H. Fitzhugh Lee's, and Wade Hampton's brigades.

6. General Jones is still in the Valley, near New Market, with about 1,400 cavalry and twelve pieces of light artillery.

7. Mosby is above Warrenton, with 200 men.

8. The Confederate army is under marching orders, and an order from General Lee was very lately read to the troops, announcing a campaign of long marches and hard fighting, in a part of the country where they would have no railroad transportation.

9. All the deserters say that the idea is very prevalent in the ranks that they are about to move forward upon or above our right flank.

GEO. H. SHARPE,
Colonel.

[Indorsement.]
HDQRS. ARMY OF THE POTOMAC, May 27, 1863.
Respectfully forwarded for the information of the General-in-Chief. Colonel Sharpe is in charge of the bureau of information at these headquarters.

JOSEPH HOOKER, Major-General, Commanding.
(Received, Headquarters of the Army, June 8, 1863.)*

---

* *Source:* OR, Series 1, Vol. 25, Part 2, p. 528.

Sharpe's Recommendations on Psychological Warfare Policy to Encourage Confederate Desertions

HEADQUARTERS, ARMY OF THE POTOMAC PROVOST MARSHAL GENERAL'S DEPARTMENT

December 12, 1863

General MARTINDALE,
Military Governor Washington:

GENERAL: By the direction of General Patrick, Provost Marshal General, Army of the Potomac I respectfully ask leave to call your attention to the deserters and prisoners of war, held by the government, referring more particularly to those which have been forwarded from the Army of the Potomac, but including also in some of the remarks hereinafter made, such as have come in any way from any of the rebel forces in Virginia and North Carolina.

As the officer under General Patrick, in charge of the Bureau of Information since the month of January last, all such persons (with refugees and prisoners of State) have passed through my hands and have been the subjects of examinations more or less extended, as our operations permitted. These examinations have on manifold occasions, and sometimes by request been extended into long and repeated interviews in which the mind and heart of the plain people of the South have developed.

I have had the occasion in laying the foundation for the department assigned me, and after its successful organization, upon special exigencies in the field to hold out to numbers of these prisoners a hope of their speedy liberations, upon their making full discovery of their knowledge of the enemy. These pledges have been given for the purpose of obtaining valuable information for the use of the Commanding General, and they were to the effect, that the Government only desired the insurgents to lay down their arms, and return to their allegiance. The men were at the same time told that they could not expect to return to their homes during the war, except as these might be found within our advancing lines. Large numbers have gladly embraced such assurances, and although often in the field a separate examination (which can only be a full test) has not been within reach, and often large bodies had to be forwarded with the examination of but a few, I am led to express the opinion, carefully formed, that more than a majority of the prisoners of war now held would gladly accept such conditions to their release. Some of them were found to be persons raised and educated in, and sympathizing with the North, but forced into the Rebel Army, and others were Union men from North Carolina and Tennessee, whom, it cannot be the purpose of this Government to return to the rebel ranks.

We are now continually in the receipt of letters from these men in confinement, asking for a consideration of their cases, and in these instances with scarce exceptions, our after experience has shown that their stories were true, and their disclosures honestly given. Indeed for some time past the state of our information has been such as to form a standard of credibility by which these men were gauged, while each was adding to the general sum.

It is respectfully suggested that a discrimination should be made among the persons now held. The rebel officers have always among other falsehoods, told their troops that all soldiers were not exchanged, were forced by us into our army; so that the rebel soldier sees only the alternative fighting with, or against his relatives and friends.

This should be corrected, and soldiers in the rebel army should be disabused of the idea that no distinction is made between those coming voluntarily to us, or preferring to remain with us when taken, and those who demand to be exchanged and returned to the ranks of the enemy. We have great reason to believe that such a policy of discrimination toward our prisoners would have the most beneficial results—that it would create a disorganizing influence within the rebel army, particularly at this juncture, when their conscription is about to be made extreme—that it would create a healthy Union sentiment among the families of those who are set at liberty and permitted to go to work in the North—that it would prepare those men to be better citizens when they return south with some of the rewards of labor in their hands—and that it would in a considerable measure replenish the field of labor in the North.

The spirit of the rank and file of the rebel army is much changed within the past year; their air of confidence and defiance which met us last winter among the prisoners at Falmouth, is abated; rebel officers have lately deserted to us and the President's proclamation would seem to be the fitting opportunity for the action proposed.

It is respectfully suggested that after an examination by a discreet officer or officers, and upon a recommendation made in cases of reasonable assurances [last 's' crossed out in pencil] of good faith, the oath pre-scribed by the President may be given, and those taking it be permitted to go and remain during the war north of such point, or within such States as may be indicated, to report to the provost marshal of the district with the privilege of making application from time to time to such officer as may be named, supported by recommendations and affidavits of employers and trustworthy citizens, for permission to return to their homes when the public interest may permit the same. As these men have been taken with arms in their hands, some addition may be made to the obligation, with a clear statement of an extreme penalty expressed therein; and full descriptive lists may be made of the persons for future reference and proof; and refugees, and other persons forwarded from the front for prudential motives might also be included in the indulgences proffered. Many of these latter persons have been sent in at times which admitted of none, or only brief explanation and the reasons for their detention may have passed.

You will permit me to remark General, not I hope with too much confidence, but what is thoroughly understood by General Patrick and such distinguished officers as have noted our work within the past year, that we are able to give considerable means to assist in determining the good faith of the men who shall decide not to return to the ranks of the rebel army.

We are entirely familiar with the organization of the rebel forces in Virginia and North Carolina, with each regiment, brigade, and division, with the changes therein, and in their officers and locations. These and many other data which have been carefully collected will throw light upon the credit to be given to professions of considering—

The truth of the general story told by the prisoners or deserters;—The circumstances of their capture;—the locations in which their commands were raised;—The corroborative statements of other prisoners from the same commands, sometimes made before and sometimes after capture; Their conduct and declarations at the time of coming in or capture compared with their present frame of mind.

It is known that there are difficulties; that among these men are largely intermingled deserters from our own army, who have found it a simple method to escape service, to come in reporting themselves as deserters from some rebel regiment of which they have heard. During the past season such desertions by way of the Valley have been very numerous. But our knowledge of the rebel army is so complete that it is not believed that we could be successfully deceived in many instances, and these cases could be weeded out, and the men returned to the army.

I cannot close without expressing the opinion, formed from the opportunities hereinbefore set forth, that were the permission afforded a considerable number of the persons referred to herein would embrace the military service of this Government, and that carefully selected they are to be trusted. Indeed were I to raise another regiment I should want no better field; and for certain services such as scouts and partizan companies, which the enemy have made so useful for information they present material which could be rendered highly effective.

These considerations are respectfully submitted in the hope that being molded by a wise hand they may be productive of the happiness to many misguided men now held by us; to many suffering families over the border; and to the general advancement of our cause.

I am General with respect your obedient servant

GEORGE H. SHARPE
Colonel & Deputy Provost Marshal General, Army of the Potomac*

GENERAL ORDERS WAR DEPT., ADJT. GENERAL'S OFFICE,
NO. 64. *Washington, February 18, 1864.*

REFUGEES AND REBEL DESERTERS

Whenever refugees from within the rebel lines, or deserters from the rebel armies, present themselves at U. S. camps or military posts they will be immediately examined by the provost-marshal with a view to determine their character and their motive in giving themselves up. If it appear that they are honest in their intention of forever deserting the rebel cause, care will be taken to explain to them that they will not be forced to serve in the U. S. Army against the rebels, nor be kept in confinement. The President's proclamation of December 8, 1863, will be read to them, and if they so desire the oath therein prescribed will be administered to them. They will then be questioned as to whether they desire employment from the United States; and if so, such arrangements as may be expedient will be made by the several army commanders for employing them on Government works within their commands. Those who come to the Army of the Potomac will be forwarded to the Military Governor of the District of Columbia, at Washington, with reports in their cases, that employment may be given them if desired; or, if not, that they may be sent as far north as Philadelphia.

By order of the Secretary of War:

E. D. TOWNSEND,
Assistant Adjutant-General.†

---

* *Source:* NARA, Microcopy 2096, Box 45, Report to Martindale written in the hand of John McEntee, signed by Sharpe.

† *Source:* OR, Serial 3, Vol. IV, p. 118.

Sharpe's Report on the Raising of Negro Troops for the Confederacy

Private & Confidential

OFFICE OF THE PROVOST MARSHAL GENERAL
ARMIES OPERATING AGAINST RICHMOND
City Point, Feb. 23. 1865

Lieut Col Bowers,
Asst. Adjt. General &c.

Colonel,

With reference to the several communications from persons in the north, that have been referred to me, calling attention to the fact, that it is believed, by various people who have communication with or have left Richmond, that the city is undermined for the purpose of blowing up our troops when they shall take possession, I have to say;

Inquiry has been directed to the point, and we cannot learn from our friends in Richmond that there is any foundation for the same, within their knowledge, except that it has been known for a long time that Libby Prison was in a condition to be blown up if necessary, and that the York River Rail Road, about half a mile from Rockett's old field and near the powder magazine below Blakey's Mill, has been tunneled or undermined. The object of this tunnel is not understood by our informants, but we are told that these are the only facts to which they can point as a foundation for the opinion referred to. The inquiry will be prosecuted, and we except other messages on the subject.

Since Mr. Ruth, superintendent of the Fredericksburg R.R., has removed the suspicion leading to his late arrest, and been returned to duty, he has been asked to direct his attention to what might be said by persons in the employ of the Danville R.R. Co., in reference to preparations for the evacuation of Richmond. He says the opinion of the clerks and employees of the Danville R.R. is that we [the enemy] are about to evacuate. They say "we seem to be drawing in; getting everything ready."

At one time there were numerous facts pointing to the evacuation of Richmond, but I am bound to say that the best informed of our friends in Richmond do not believe that such is the plan of the Confederate authorities. They think that whatever removals of machinery and workshops have taken place from Richmond and the Bellona Arsenal have simply been steps of prudence and not of preparation. They say that the Confederate authorities believe, that by holding four or five points, one of which would be Danville, another Lynchburg, another some point on the north of Richmond—perhaps Gordonsville, another Richmond itself, that such a sweep of country can be controlled as will enable General Lee, for a long time to come, to support his army. Richmond will not be evacuated because it is the capital of the Confederacy, and so long as they retain their capital, they are as much of a country as they have ever been. Richmond is also the means of communication between Lynchburg and Danville—as circuitous as it may be— because the country between Danville and Lynchburg is crossed by no railroad or other great line of communication, and from its character is not susceptible of such. The country about Lynchburg, and between it and Danville, is a great grain bearing section. Every pound of forage that now reaches Richmond comes from Lynchburg. General Lee's army is mainly composed of Virginians and North Carolinians, who are expected to fight better in those states than in any other; and it is believed that by holding the points named, the enemy will be able to move their troops upon the lines of Railway connecting them, with such rapidity as always to meet us in strong force at the most greatly threatened points.

That negro regiments are to be raised is now settled. Two hundred thousand will be the number attempted to be raised, and it is for us to consider whether, if some steps are not taken toward their disorganization, as fast as they are prepared to be put in the field, they will not be able by this accession to prolong the war to an indefinite extent. Out of this number, by taking fifty thousand negro troops and placing them in the intrenchments south of Richmond and Petersburg, with the assistance of white officers, and a few white troops in their rear to control and embolden them, cannot the present line of the enemy be held, and will <u>not</u> General Lee then have at his disposal all or nearly all of the white forces left under his command for a movable column to throw upon any threatened point, or for unexpected and diverting attacks? If the same policy be followed out and the other points named, Danville, Lynchburg, Gordonsville, etc., be intrenched, will not negro troops, under like government, be able to hold those points; and will not the white forces still under the control of the Confederacy be substantially free, for supporting and aggressive movements?

If there be anything of this, is it not well for us to consider whether we have not the means of disintegrating and disorganizing negro regiments before, by habit, discipline and experience with arms, they shall have grown to that aptitude of a soldier's which will bring them to obey orders under any circumstances? We must have among our negro troops, colored men from most parts of Virginia, and many parts of North Carolina, and other states. They know the character of like men who will be put into the ranks of the enemy; they will recognize many of them as their former associates, friends and relatives; and can we not select some good field officers, who can now get together a carefully selected number of negroes from the different regiments in our command and elsewhere, who by preparation would be able, at the earliest moment, to go into the negro ranks of the enemy and bring them over in bodies to us? I believe that a reasonable body of colored men could not be put to any better use, and that if officers with the faculty of organization, and at the same time of secretiveness, can be set at this work, we shall have the material ready to our hands, in the spring, to be sent into the enemy's lines, and here and there to raise perhaps our own flag, and with it march in bodies into our lines. The publication of an order of like nature with the one issued by the Lieut. General for the benefit of deserters and refugees, comprehending the purchase of arms and other property brought by the negroes, with other rewards, is suggested. Perhaps it might not be well that this order should be made public, but that being printed it should be put into the hands of the negroes, selected as hereinbefore suggested, who of course should be able to read, and who could then expound it, as negroes are fond of doing, to their compatriots on the other side. The negroes are an eminently secretive people; they have a system of mutual understanding amounting almost to free masonry among them; they will trust each other when they will not trust white men; and I believe that some plan, marked out by a wise hand, could be made to produce great results.

It is understood, of course, that the forgoing suggestions are crude. I have as yet been able to give them little consideration; but believing it to be the duty of a staff officer to submit such observations as his specialty may bring before him, I have the honor to forward them.

Very respectfully
Your obedient servant
George H. Sharpe [signature]
Col &c

Sharpe's Eye-Witness Account of the Surrender at Appomattox

APPOMATTOX – INCIDENTS OF LEE'S SURRENDER

The story as told by a Union officer who was there. The meeting of the two Generals – A Painful Scene in which the Victor was as much Embarrassed as the Vanquished.

An interesting contribution to the current discussion about the circumstances of General Lee's surrender was made by General George H. Sharpe, formerly of the Army of the Potomac, in a Decoration Day [May 31] address at Mount Kisco, New York. We give the story as General Sharpe related it.

I remember – and it was recalled to me tonight in conversation, when the name of General Grant came up in the course of conversation – the wonderful scene that transpired in the little place in Virginia on 6th [sic 9th] April, 1865. It was late in the afternoon when it became known that General Lee had sent for General Grant to surrender to him. It was between 2 and 3 o'clock when we met in the little room in the house where the surrender of Lee's army took place. I know there is a belief that the surrender took place under an apple tree, where Grant and Lee met and exchanged a few words. The surrender took place in the left-hand room of that old-fashioned double house. The house had a large piazza which ran along the full length of it. It was one of those ordinary Virginia houses with a passageway running through the center of it. In that little room where the meeting took place sat two young men—one a great-grandson of Chief Justice Marshall, of the Supreme Court, reduced to writing the terms of the surrender on behalf of Robert E. Lee, the other, a man with dusky countenance—a great nephew of that celebrated chief, Red Jacket—acting under General Grant. The two were reduced to writing the terms of the surrender of the Army of Northern Virginia to the Army of the Potomac. Gathered around the room were several officers, of whom I was one.

A Hesitating Talk

At some distance apart sat two men, one the most remarkable man of his day and generation. The larger and older of the two was the most striking in his appearance.

His hair was white as the driven snow. There was not a speck upon his coat, not a spot upon those gauntlets that he wore, which were as bright and fair as a lady's glove. That was Robert E. Lee. The other was Ulysses S. Grant, whose appearance contrasted strangely with that of Lee, his boots were nearly covered with mud, one button of his coat—that is the buttonhole was not where it should have been—it had clearly gone astray, and he wore no sword, while Lee was fully and faultlessly equipped. The conversation was not rapid by any means. Everybody felt the overpowering influence of the scene. Everyone present felt they were witnessing the proceedings between the two chief actors in one of the most remarkable transactions of this nineteenth century. The words that passed between Grant and Lee were few. General Grant—endeavoring to apologize for not being fully prepared and noticing the faultless appearance of Lee—while the secretaries were busy said—"General Lee, I have no sword. I have been riding all night." And Lee with that coldness of manner and all the pride—almost haughtiness—which after all became him wonderfully well, never made any reply, but in a cold, formal manner bowed. And General Grant, in an endeavor to take away the great awkwardness of the scene, said: "I don't always wear a sword because a sword is a very inconvenient thing." That was a remarkable thing for him to say, considering that he was in the presence one who was about to surrender his sword. Lee only bowed again. Another, trying to relieve the awkwardness of the occasion, inquired, "General Lee, what became of that white horse you rode in Mexico? He might not be dead yet, he was not so old?" General Lee bowed coldly, and replied, "I left him at the White House in Pamunky river, and I have not seen him since." There was one moment when there was a whispered conversation between Grant and Lee, which nobody in the room heard.

The Surrender Made

The surrender took the form of correspondence; these letters were then signed in due form, by the chief actors, in the presence of each other. Finally when the terms of the surrender had all been arranged, and the surrender made, Lee arose, cold and proud and bowed to every person in the room on our side. I remember each one of us thought he had been specially bowed to. And then he went out and passed down the little square in front of the house, and bestrode that gray horse that carried him all over Virginia, and when he had gone away, we learned what the whispered conversation had been about. General Grant called his officers about and said: "You go to the 24th and you to the 5th," and so on, naming the corps, "and ask every man who had three rations to turn over two of them. Go to the commissaries and go to the quartermasters, etc." General Lee's army is on the point of starvation! And 25,000 rations were carried to the Army of Northern Virginia.*

---

* Source: *Philadelphia Times*, June 30, 1877

Sharpe's Report of the of Northern Paroling of the Army Virginia

SPECIAL ORDERS,
HDQRS. ARMIES OF THE UNITED STATES,In the Field, April 9, 1865.

Major General John Gibbon, Bvt. Major General Charles Griffin, and Bvt. Major General Wesley Marritt are hereby designated to carry into effect the stipulations this day entered into between General R. E. lee, commanding C. S. Armies, and Lieutenant-General Grant, commanding Armies of the United States, in which General Lee surrenders to General Grant the Army of Northern Virginia.

Bvt. Brigadier General George H. Sharpe, assistant provost-marshal-general, will receive and take charge of the rolls called for by the above-mentioned stipulations.

By command of Lieutenant-General Grant:

E. S. PARKER,
Lieutenant-Colonel and Acting Assistant Adjutant-General.

SPECIAL ORDERS, HDQRS. ARMIES OF THE CONFED. STATES, Numbers—.April 9, 1865.

Lieutenant General J. Longstreet, Major General J. B. Gordon, and Brigadier General W. N. Pendleton are hereby designated to carry into effect the stipulations this day entered into between Lieutenant General U. S. Grant, commanding Armies of the United States, and General R. E. Lee, commanding Armies of the Confederate States, in which General Lee surrendered to General Grant the Army of Northern Virginia.

By command of General R. E. Lee:

W. H. TAYLOR,
Lieutenant-Colonel and Assistant Adjutant-General.
[Parole of General Robert E. Lee and Staff.]

We, the undersigned prisoners of war belonging to the Army of Northern Virginia, having been this day surrendered by General Robert E. Lee, C. S. Army, commanding said army, to Lieutenant General U. S. Grant, commanding Armies of the United States, do hereby give our solemn parole of honor that we will not hereafter serve in the armies of the Confederate States of America, or render aid to the enemies of the latter, approved by the respective authorities.

Done at Appomattox Court-House, Va., this 9th day of April, 1865.

R. E. LEE,
General.

W. H. TAYLOR,
Lieutenant-Colonel and Assistant Adjutant-General.

CHARLES S. VENABLE,
Lieutenant-Colonel and Assistant Adjutant-General.

CHARLES MARSHALL,
Lieutenant-Colonel and Assistant Adjutant-General.

H. E. PEYTON,
Lieutenant-Colonel and Assistant Adjutant-General.

GILES B. COOKE,
Major and Assistant Adjutant and Inspector General.

H. E. YOUNG,
Major, Assistant Adjutant-General, and Judge-Advocate-General.

[Indorsement.]
The within named officers will not be disturbed by the United States authorities so long as they observe their parole and the laws in force where they may reside.

GEORGE H. SHARPE,
Assistant Provost-Marshal-General.*

---

* *Source:* OR, Series 1, Vol. 46, Series 3, pp. 851–53.

HEADQUARTERS ARMIES OF THE UNITED STATES,Washington, D. C.,
April 20, 1865.

Bvt. Colonel T. S. BOWERS,
Assistant Adjutant-General, Armies of the United States:

COLONEL: I have the honor to report that, according to instructions received from
headquarters Armies of the United States, I remained at Appomattox Court-House,
Va., after the surrender of General R. E. Lee and the Army of Northern Virginia, to
receive from the officers thereof their paroles and those of the men forming their late
commands. The work was commenced as soon as a single roll was received from the
officers of late rebel army, and was followed with all possible dispatch from daylight
to a late hour each night until the 15th instant, when I was enabled to leave with
the papers, and reported to you personally yesterday. The language of the parole, as
submitted by me to the chief of staff and approved by him, was held; and inclosure
A is the from signed by the officers, while inclosure B is a copy of a slip which was
firmly attached to the several rolls of the men as furnished by the officers. The addition
thereto, marked C, certifying that "the within-named men will not be disturbed by
the U. S. authorities so long as they observe their parole and the laws in force where
they may reside," was appended by the officers composing the commission, and by
their direction was signed by me as assistant provost-marshal-general. Inclosure D
is a copy of the certificate of parole given by each rebel commissioned officer to his
men, the senior office of each brigade, division, and corps, giving the same to his
officers, and General Lee at his own request receiving one from the undersigned"
by command of Lieutenant-General Grant." In order that these certificates of
parole might be respected by officers and men of our army, Major-General Gibbon
issued the inclosed order, marked E; but as many of those bearing such certificates
have already passed and are still passing within the limits of other commands, it is
respectfully suggested that an order from the lieutenant-general is desirable to insure
full efficacy thereto thought the United States.

The slip or addition marked C was also added to the rolls of the officers. On
account of the very considerable disorganization of General Lee's army, the work was
difficult and laborious, and infinite pains were required to reduce the same to some
system, with what success will be observed from an examination of the duplicate
rolls herewith respectfully forwarded. After the dark of Lieutenant General A. P. Hill
his corps was placed under the command of Lieutenant-General Longstreet, while
at the time of the surrender General Gordon's corps comprised his own (late that of
Lieutenant-General Early) and also the corps or command of Lieutenant-General
Ewell, previously captured, the highest officer in which was a lieutenant-colonel.

Thus many of the rebel officers did not clearly understand their own organization, and to add to the difficulties many officers and men came in after the

paroling of their command, when they had heard the terms offered by General, preferring to receive the benefits thereof to a successful escape. Some of the rebel commanding officers also left at an early hour after perfecting their own papers, leaving their men and subordinate officers without advice or assistance, and toward the end I was obligated to apply to Major General Fitzhugh Lee to detail an officer to remain with me for the purpose of taking up men of various commands, which he did by directing his assistant adjutant-general, Captain Cove to report for that purpose.

Officers and men of the rebel army were found most willing to obey directions for the faithful carrying out of the terms of the surrender, under the expectation that the same would result in personal benefit to them, and many of them while expressing thankfulness to our officers animadverted strongly upon their abandonment by their own officers, but, as the latter could not be heard in explanation, I have not considered it proper to include any names officially. Wherever the same could be done an attempt was made to parole officers and men by brigades, and it will be seen that this method was substantially followed with accuracy throughout General Longstreet's command. In General Gordon's, however, only a proportion could be done in that way, and future reference thereon will have to be made by regiments and will be found difficult at that. The paroling of the artillery and the cavalry command of General William H. F. Lee was personally superintended by the commanding officers thereof, and the papers are methodical to a considerable extent. Great care was taken on our part as to the exactitude of the duplicates, and, where commanding officers had left prior to the completion of the patrols of their men, the papers belonging to the other side were taken by Captain Oliver for delivery to General R. E. Lee at Richmond. Summaries have been made by actual count of each command, and will be found to accompany the papers, the whole number paroled of officers and men being a little over 26,000.

I should also add that at the request of General Lee and other officers of rank of the rebel army, and by the advice of the officers commanding the commission on our side, a few of the certificates of parole were countersigned by me, where the bearers were about to proceed immediately to distant points. Such were given to officers commanding detachments, and in a few cases, which were specially represented, to individuals who were not able to proceed to their homes in the company of any organized bodies. The kindest co-operation was received from the officers of the commission on our side, and from the provost-marshals of the Fifth and Twenty-fourth Army Corps, and the assistance rendered throughout by Captain Paul A. Oliver was invaluable and highly meritorious.

Very respectfully, your obedient servant,
GEORGE H. SHARPE,
Brevet Brigadier-General and Assistant Provost-Marshal-General.

[Indorsement.]
HEADQUARTERS ARMIES OF THE UNITED STATES, June 17, 1865.
Respectfully forwarded to the Secretary of War together with the rolls of officers and men of Lee's army.

U. S. GRANT,
Lieutenant-General.

[Inclosure.*]

B.
I, the undersigned commanding officers of —, do for the within-named prisoners of war belonging to the Army of Northern Virginia, who have been this day surrender by General Robert E, Lee, C. S. Army, commanding said army, to Lieutenant General U. S. Grant, commanding Armies of the United States, hereby give my solemn parole of honor that the within named shall not hereafter serve in the armies of the Confederate States, or in any military capacity whatever, against the United States of America, or render aid to the enemies of the latter until properly exchanged, in such manner as shall be manually approved by the respective authorities. Done at Appomattox Court-House, Va., this 9th day of April, 1865.

C.
The within-named men will not be disturbed by U. S. authorities so long as they observe their parole and the laws in force where they may reside.

D.
APPOMATTOX COURT-HOUSE, VA.,
April 10, 1865.
The bearer,—, of Company—,—Regiment of—, a paroled prisoner of the Army of Northern Virginia, has permission to go to his home and there remain undisturbed.*

---

* *Source:* OR, Series 1, Vol. 46, Part 3, pp. 666–67.

Sharpe's Letter in Support of the Financial Claims of Elizabeth Van Lew

Kingston, Ulster County, N.Y.
January 1867

General C. B. Comstock
Head Quarters, Armies of the U.S.

My dear General

When I last saw you in Washington, we conferred upon a matter, heretofore spoken of, and for sundry reasons delayed, which was understood between us was to be put on paper by myself, and would then be presented by you to the consideration of General Grant.

I refer to the case of the Van Lews of Richmond. During my visit to that city in the past summer, I became possessed of the facts of many of which I had some knowledge before which tend to show that they have a very strong claim upon the assistance of the Government. The family consists of Mrs. Van Lew, a widow, her daughter, Miss Elizabeth Van Lew, and a son, Mr. John C. [sic] Van Lew, with his little children. They reside on Church Hill in Richmond, and before the war were accounted among the most substantial people of that city, having been left by Mr. Van Lew, the father, many years since deceased, in the enjoyment of a handsome patrimony.

The son, Mr. J. C. [sic] Van Lew, was a well known hardware merchant of high character.

From the beginning, the family, with all its influences, took a strong position against the rebel movement, and never ceased fighting it until our armies entered Richmond. Their position, character and charities gave them a commanding influence over many families of plain people, who were decided and encouraged by them to remain true to the flag and were subsequently able during the war to receive our agents – assist our prisoners – to conceal those who escaped and to convey information to our armies.

By her talents and enthusiasm Miss Elizabeth L. Van Lew became the leader of the little union party in Richmond, and indeed in Virginia. By her attractive manners and free use of money she soon gained control of the rebel prisons, and our officers and men felt the effects of her care. Regular reports were taken to her of the conditions of our prisoners, and for all and each according to his necessities, she obtained indulgences; for one additional food, for others raiment and bedding, for some a few hours a week more in the fresh air, and for others escape and protection to our lines.

She influenced rebel surgeons to send our men to the hospitals, and when she got them in the hospitals, she alone went from cot to cot where lay a sufferer in blue, while all the other women of Richmond attended the men in gray. In these visits she was attended by her colored servants having beautifully laden baskets, whose contents have been the means of returning many a man to his northern home.

For a long, long time, she represented all that was left of the power of the U.S. Government in the city of Richmond. John Minor Botts wrote from prison for her advice and protection and Franklin Sterns took her orders.

Not only clothing and bedding but even furniture was sent in to prisoners, and I was informed in Richmond by the plain union people that the Van Lews marketed as regularly for Libby Prison, as they did for their own house. They put their hands on whatever of their patrimony they could realize and expended it in what was substantially the service of the U.S. Government. When their convertible property, or a good portion of it, was gone, they used in the same way the receipts of the brother's hardware store, until he (having steadily refused to bear arms even for local defense) was seized and put in the ranks, when he immediately made his way to our lines near Cold Harbor in 1864 with valuable information. This of course closed his store and nearly took away the means of subsistence of this family. But still the charities went on. The mother and daughter raised money in one way or another. They sent emissaries to our lines; when no one else could for the moment be found, they sent their own servants. They employed counsel for union people on trial – they had clerks in the rebel war and navy departments in their confidences; and soon after our arrival at City Point, Miss Van Lew mastered a system of correspondence in cipher by which specific information asked for by the General was obtained.

A near as I can learn without going to the family, reference can be made to the following persons to sustain my statements. Col. S. M. Bowman of Wilkesbarre [sic], Penn., and Captain Chase, who was there with him, know of the care of the prisoners early in the war. So also do Col. Cogswell of the N. Y. Tammany regiment, Capt. R. T. Shillinglaw of the 79th (Highlanders) N.Y.S.M., Captain H. McQuade, 38th N.Y. Vols., and Hon. Alfred Ely, form N.Y. who ought, I am told, to know all about this.

Major General [J.R.] Ricketts and wife can perhaps furnish considerable testimony, and I think there is a clerk in the Treasury Department, or in a branch of it in Winder's building named Edward Taylor, who is conversant with many of the facts.

I enclose a letter from General [William Raymond] Lee of Massachusetts, who is known to General E.D. Townsend, prepared some time since with a view of a public claim being made for the benefit of the Van Lews. Such a claim before Congress, would perhaps, necessitate the removal of the family from Richmond, and the virtual abandonment of their remaining property there, which they now hope to save.

I have understood and believe that Col. Streight and party owed their escape to the Van Lews, and I think that Captain Boutwell formerly of the U.S. Navy, was kept in their house several months after his discharge from prison; while in defiance of the rebel government Mr. Calvin Huson was taken from prison to their home, died there, and his funeral was from their house. Col. J. Harris Hooper of Massachusetts is, I think, well known in Washington and can give evidence on many points referred to herein.

For the military information readily conveyed by Miss Van Lew to our officers, I refer to Major General Butler, who ought to be able to speak largely concerning it; while General Grant, General [John Aaron] Rawlins, General [Marsena Rudolph] Patrick (the last named particularly) and other officers serving at Headquarters during the winter of 1864 & 5 are more or less acquainted with the regular information obtained by our Bureau from the City of Richmond, the greater portion of which [is] in its collection, and in a good measure in its transmission we owed to the intelligence and devotion of Miss. E.L. Van Lew.

In addition to what is said above, I have sufficient evidence to show that a valuable library belonging to the Van Lews was strewn broadcast through Libby prison, and that the cash amounts furnished to Union prisoners in place of other assistance would amount to a large sum.

The expenditures of the family during the war have greatly reduced their means; the balance of which do not now, I am told, produce any income of importance. The brother is endeavoring to reestablish his hardware business, but this of course must come gradually.

After the occupation of Richmond, General Grant directed the sum of two thousand dollars to be paid to Miss Van Lew on presentation of the case by Colonel [Theodore] Bowers and myself, "as a partial reimbursement to her or her brother from whose store the funds came." This language I find in my letter to General Prick of May 31st, 1865, covering the order given me by Colonel Bowers, and which was made on General Patrick's formal recommendation.

If it be not inappropriate, I respectfully recommend that an enquiry be made into the facts herein stated, some of which are on my own knowledge, and all of which I believe to be true.

A reference to General Butler may open up more information on many of the points, while Mr. [Charles S.] Palmer, Mr. [Robert] Dudley, Mr. [Horace] Kent and other union gentlemen of like standing in Richmond ought to be able to ensure accurate relies to any enquiries made.

In our last interview, you told me that I ought to name some sum, and altho' I am afraid of doing injustice in complying therewith, and hope that thro' the representation of other parties the sum may be made much larger, I feel bound to recommend from a very considerable knowledge of the matter that the sum of fifteen thousand dollars be paid to Miss Elizabeth Van Lew for valuable information and services rendered to the U.S. Government during the war.

I do this now without waiting for a future reference, because I am just leaving home to be absent some little time; and now, General, leaving with you, what I believe to be the most meritorious case I have known during the war.

I am with respect & esteem your obedient servant,
George H. Sharpe

P.S. I ought to state that the order referred to was carried out by Captain H.P. Clinton, acting Post Q.M. in Richmond after I left, who, if I am correctly informed, is in business in Richmond as a member of the tobacco firm of D.C. Mayo & Co.*

---

* *Source:* This letter was found among the papers of Elizabeth Van Lew.

Sharpe's Report to Sec. State Seward on his Overseas Investigation of Involvement of Any American Citizen in the Assassination of President Lincoln

July [no day given], 1867

40TH CONGRESS	HOUSE OF REPRESENTATIVES	Ex. Doc
2d Session		No. 68

ASSASSINATION OF PRESIDENT LINCOLN

MESSAGE
FROM THE
PRESIDENT OF THE UNITES STATES
TRANSMITTING
A report of George H. Sharpe relative the assassination of President Lincoln

---

DECEMBER 19, 1867.—Referred to the Committee on the Judiciary and ordered to be printed.

To the House of Representatives:
I transmit, for the information of the House of Representatives, a report from the Secretary of State, with an accompanying paper.
ANDREW JOHNSON
WASHINGTON, December 17, 1867.

DEPARTMENT OF STATE,
Washington, December 17, 1867
I have the honor to lay before you, with a view to its communication to the House of Representatives, a transcript of the report made to this department by Mr. George

H. Sharpe, who, under its instructions, visited Europe in the early part of the present year to ascertain, if possible, whether any citizens of the United States in that quarter, other than those who have heretofore been suspected and charged with the offense, were instigators of, or concerned in, the assassination of the late President Lincoln, and the attempted assassination of the Secretary of States.

Respectfully submitted:
WILLIAM H. SEWARD
THE PRESIDENT

╖╖╖╖╖╖╖╖╖╖

Mr. Sharpe to Mr. Seward
KINGSTON, NEW YORK, July, 1867

SIR: In the month of January last I left for Europe pursuant to instructions from the State Department, in which I was told that there might be reason to apprehend that "citizens of the United States in Europe, other than those who have theretofore been suspected or charged with the offense, were instigators of, or concerned in, the assassination of the late President Lincoln, and the attempted assassination of the Secretary of State." It was deemed proper, in connection with the anticipated trial of John H. Surratt, to make an effort to identify those persons, and it was made my duty to examine any evidence existing abroad, so that government might judge whether or not it ought to demand the surrender of any persons in Europe.

My attention was drawn to the circumstances, already developed, that the conspirators had made use of considerable sums of money in travelling [sic] to and from Canada and elsewhere, in the pay of the confederates, in providing means for retreat and refuge, in the hire of horses and boats, and in liberal expenditures through the long preparations and execution of the plot.

These moneys, which must have amounted, in the aggregate, to large sums, were furnished to them in gold, at a time when it was very difficult for private individuals to obtain it, and when even official personages omitted its employment unless imperatively demanded for the uses of government.

It was further hoped that upon the indictment of Surratt, such papers and evidence might be brought forward as would tend to direct inquiries in Europe.

On my arrival in England, I thought best to make an effort to learn if Surrat had communicated with leading rebels there or on the continent on his way to the Papal States.

Surratt reached Liverpool on September 27, 1865, and on Saturday morning, September 30, he left for London in the nine o'clock train, arriving at the Euston Square station about two o'clock p.m.

After following out the working of a municipal regulation which controls a portion of the London cabs, it was thought that a clue was obtained to the particular cab which took Surratt as a passenger on the arrival of the train.

The driver of the cab referred to was found, but he was an old man, prostrated with a serious and lingering disease, from which he did not recover during my stay in London, and incapacitated from recalling incidents to promote the inquiries.

A patient investigation was given to all circumstances tending to throw light on Surratt's connection with revels known to be in London at that time, and through letters from Mr. Adams I was brought into communication with our consuls at London and Liverpool, from whom, as well as from Mr. Moran, secretary of legation, and some American gentlemen, long resident abroad, every assistance was received, so that, it is believed, every fact was inquired into which had any significance under my instructions.

This examination failing to disclose any state of facts deemed sufficiently well established or of sufficient importance to bring to the knowledge of the department, attention was turned to the manner in which Surratt entered the Papal States, in order to learn whether his flight there was through the procurement of any persons, citizens of the United States.

An inquiry having been made at the British foreign office, it was learned that on October 12, 1865, application was made for a passport for John Watson, of Edinburgh, over the signature of the country manager of a banking institution in London, and on the following day, October 13, 1865, the passport was issued.

There were several circumstances about this which led me to inquire into it.

The date was soon after Surratt's arrival in London; the name was the one under which he had enlisted in the Papal Zouaves; and the direction of the bank under whose auspices the application was made, included some of the most notorious rebel sympathizers in England.

It was fair to suppose that, although Surratt had gone under other names, he would have less facility for changing one chosen for a passport, and that he probably enlisted under the one by which he entered the Stats of the church.

With such probabilities that Surratt's passport was obtained at the British foreign office, and that the influences which procured it could be traced, an examination was made at Edinburgh, where five John Watsons were found, one of whom proved to be the person who received the passport of October 13, 1865, which was seen and verified.

This incident is briefly detailed in order to show proper reasons for the time occupied, as in each instance care had to be taken that no wrong should be done, and no suspicions raised unless justified by the result.

On the 15th of April I left London and proceeded direct to Rome, bearing a note of introduction from Mr. Adams to General King, with whom, and with Mr. Hooker, I consulted.

General King introduced me, informally, to General Kansler, the Papal minister of war, with whom I had three interviews, and during them I requested that I might be permitted to see any papers or effects left by Surratt.

General Kansler caused a search to be made, and informed me that Surratt left no papers, having, in all probability, destroyed such as he had at the time of his discovery of General King's letter to Ste. Marie.

Surratt also left no effects. He was obliged, by military regulation, to dispose of citizen's apparel on entering the service, to prevent facilities for desertion, a regulation which, in the end, contributed to his identification and arrest.

General Kansler also caused a search to be made for the original passport by which Surratt entered the Roman States, and upon its production, and my request to be permitted to take a copy, he offered to deliver the original to me, his office retaining a copy.

This offer was accepted, and the passport subsequently forwarded to the State Department.

It may not be improper for me to add, that my interviews with General Kansler were at the war office, and that his instructions to his Italian subordinates, and the reports from them, were made in my presence, with the strongest evidence of the good will and good faith of himself and of his government.

Surratt's passport showed that it was obtained by some influences from the provincial government of Canada, and had received the vise of the United States consul-general there.

It had been approved for entry into the States of the Church at the office of the nuncio, in Paris, but bore no evidence that Surratt had received assistance in any other quarter in Europe.

The nuncio's vise had been given gratis, which was unusual, and inquiries were made at his office to ascertain under what circumstances the same had been procured.

These steps, although taken with great care, and after permission for the interview had been asked, were met with rudeness and discourtesy on the part of the nuncio himself and his secretary; but I was subsequently informed, through our legation in Paris, that the nuncio stated his vise had been obtained, not through any letter or special recommendation, but upon the personal presentation of the passport by Surratt, whom that official remembers to have seen, and upon the former's statement that he was going to Rome for the purpose of enlistment.

There being nothing to throw doubt on the statement, other than the discreditable conduct of the official, by whom better treatment must have been accorded to Surratt than myself, no further inquiry was made in regard to the passport.

I subsequently saw Mr. Sanford, our minister in Brussels; the United States consul at Paris, and other Americans of distinguished loyalty long resident there, and had full conversations with them concerning all matters which had come to their knowledge, and which were within my instructions. These interviews did not lead to an extension of my stay, but believing that every inquiry which I had been directed to make was completed, so far as there were means to do it, I returned home in July.

Conscious that earnestness was brought to the attempt at identifying the loathsome instigators of the great crime, and that every possible assistance was received, I have to report that, in my opinion, no such legal or reasonable proof exists in Europe of the participation of any persons there, formerly citizens of the United States, as to call for the action of the government.

Very respectfully, your obedient servant,
GEORGE H. SHARPE
Hon. WILLIAM H. SEWARD,
Secretary of State*

---

* *Source:* NARA, Doc. No 68, 40th Congress, 2nd Session.

Sharpe's Family

Twenty years after Sharpe's death, the city of Kingston and a major hotel chain sought to buy the Sharpe family estate of The Orchard. Sharpe's children resisted because of its sentimental value to them but eventually sold The Orchard in 192?.[37]

Sharpe's older son, Severyn after a successful career as a lawyer, died in New York in 1929 of arterial sclerosis at the age of 73.[38] Severyn left only one child, Katharine S. Sharpe, who married Aldo Newton Dana, a graduate of Yale and World War I veteran, in 1921, in her Aunt Katherine's apartment. She bore two sons, Severyn Sharpe Dana in 1924 and Arnold G. Dana in 1926, the latter of whom died in 2004. Severyn and Arnold are the only known descendants of George H. Sharpe. Severyn served in the U.S. Army Air Corps in World War II in the rank of corporal, serving in the China-India-Burma Theater and thus maintaining the family tradition begun by his great grandfather to serve his country in wartime.[39]

Sharpe's younger son, Henry, had a successful military career that would certainly have made his father proud. He was a military scholar who translated a number of books on supplying armies in wartime from French, an act reminiscent of his father's translation of a book in French on the establishment of a secret service for Major General Hooker. His original work on the subsistence of the Union army in the Civil War won the first prize of the Military Service Institute of the United States. The most important of the several books he was to author—*The Provisioning of the Modern Army in the Field*—achieved international recognition and was used by the British Army and taught at the military school of instruction at Aldershot. Even as a lieutenant colonel it was said of him:

> Colonel Sharpe enjoys the reputation of being one of the most accomplished and best equipped officers who ever belonged to the commissary corps; He possessed a thorough knowledge of the history, scope and details of the subsistence department; has analyzed all the multifarious articles of food that are purchased or procured for the army, and which go from the supply depots of the government to the stomach of the soldier.[40]

He was promoted to brigadier general in 1905, and two years later he traveled to Europe at his own expense to study the supply systems of the British, French, and

German armies. At the 1913 Gettysburg reunion he was charged with feeding all 40,000 attendants. Sharpe was promoted to major general and became the quartermaster general of the army in 1916. National unpreparedness at the time of the United States' entry into World War I resulted in a disjointed supply effort despite Sharpe's talents. "When the United States declared war, Sharpe faced the formidable challenge of housing, feeding, clothing, and equipping a massively expanded army. He made great progress, but not fast enough to meet political demands. In December 1917, he was replaced by George Goethals (Class of 1880)."[41]

> On December 15, 1917, a War Council was formed consisting of the Secretary of War, the Assistant Secretary of War, the Quartermaster General, the Chief of Artillery, the Chief of Ordnance, the Judge Advocate General, and the Chief of Staff. The War Council was to oversee and coordinate all matters of supply and to plan for the more effective use of the military power of the nation. While serving on the Council, General Sharpe was required to delegate all his administrative duties to an acting chief Quartermaster designated by the Secretary of War. In June 1918, General Sharpe was relieved from duty with the War Council and assigned to the command of the Southeastern Department. The following month he was appointed a Major General in the line of the Army, with rank from July 12 and officially ceased to be Quartermaster General.[42]

He then was transferred to command the Southeastern Department and served in France the summer of 1919. He retired in 1920 and would come to be known as the father of the modern Quartermaster Corps. Sharpe settled in Providence, Rhode Island, where his sister lived. Sharpe and his wife, Kate Morgan Sharpe, were childless, and she died in 1941. Sharpe passed away after a brief illness in 1947 while visiting New York City.[43]

The death of her husband, Ira Davenport, in 1904 left Sharpe's daughter Katherine a wealthy woman. There does not appear to have been any children. Katherine was a supporter of the arts and in 1930 donated to the Senate House Association in Kingston a celebrated engraving of Daniel Huntington's painting of the reception of Mrs. George Washington which had hung in her father's library. Katherine died in 1946. The estate sale of her property included many remaining items from the estate of her father.[44]

Notes

Foreword

1   US War Department, *The War of the Rebellion: The Official Records of the Union and Confederate Armies*, 128 vols. (Washington, DC: GPO, 1880–1911), vol. 46, pt. 1, p. 481.

2   George H. Sharpe to "General Martindale," Dec. 12, 1863, RG 393, entry 3980, National Archives and Records Administration, Washington, DC.; Grant to Henry W. Halleck, July 26, 1864, John Y. Simon, ed., *The Papers of Ulysses S. Grant,* 31 vols (Carbondale: Southern Illinois University Press, 1967–2012), vol. 11, p. 317.

3   Edwin C. Fishel, "The Mythology of Civil War Intelligence," *Civil War History* 10 (December 1964): 352; Peter Maslowski, "Military Intelligence Sources During the Civil War: A Case Study," in Lt. Col. Walter T. Hitchcock, ed., *The Intelligence Revolution: A Historical Perspective* (Washington, DC: GPO, 1991), p. 42.

Introduction

1   Horace Porter, *Campaigning with Grant* (The Blue and Gray Press, December 1984), p. 232.

2   Headquarters, Department of the Army, *Intelligence, FM 2-0* (Washington, DC: May 17, 2004) pp. 1–30.

3   Paraphrased in Correlli Barnett, *The Swordbearers: Studies in Supreme Command in the First World War* (Bloomington, IL: Indiana University Press 1963), p. 35.

4   Peter G. Tsouras, *Scouting for Grant and Meade, The Reminiscences of Judson Knight, Chief of Scouts, Army of the Potomac* (New York: Skyhorse Publications, 2014), p. 110, found originally in Judson Knight, "Fighting Them Over: How Scouts Worked," *The National Tribune*, March 30, 1893.

5   Promotion by brevet was a former type of military commission conferred especially for outstanding service, by which an officer was promoted to a higher rank without the corresponding pay and place in the regular establishment. Sharpe, as a volunteer officer, had no postwar military ambitions and received no regular army appointment. Regular army officers often had a permanent rank in the army and a higher brevet rank earned by distinction. At the end of the war they would revert to their permanent rank, often far below their brevet rank. Former Maj. Gen. John Gibbon was talking to Grant on one occasion when he brought up the subject of the most important change of rank in their careers. Grant believed for him it was from brevet second lieutenant to second lieutenant. Gibbon remarked that for him it was after the war, "when one drops from a Major General to a Captain." *John Gibbon, Personal Reminiscences of the Civil War*, 1928.

6   Edmond P. Kohn, *Heir to the Empire City: New York and the Making of Theodore Roosevelt* (New York: Basic Books, 2013), pp. 65–66.

7   Cornelius Van Buren, *Kingston Daily Freeman*, March 25, 1925.

8   DeAlva Stanwood Alexander, *A Political History of the State of New York*, Vol. III (BiblioBazaar, 2008), pp. 402–403.

9   Military Order of the Loyal Legion of the United States, Headquarters Commandary of the State of New York, "In Memoriam: George Henry Sharpe" (New York, September 15, 1900), p. 3.

10 Sir Basil Liddell Hart, *The Sword and the Pen: Selections from the World's Greatest Military Writing* (New York: Thomas Y. Crowell Company, 1976), p. 12.

11 Stephen Sears, forward to Edwin C. Fishel, *The Secret War for the Union: The Untold Story of Military Intelligence in the Civil War* (Boston: Houghton Mifflin Company, 1996), p. xiii. Even historians were unable to keep the achievements of the BMI's all-source operation alive because its records disappeared into the National Archives to be lost among miscellaneous records of the Army of the Potomac. They were only rediscovered by Fishel in 1959, still tied in bundles with red ribbons. They were the foundation of Fishel's seminal work on Civil War intelligence and a priceless addition to the history of the war.

12 Finely, James P Finely, *U.S. Army Military Intelligence History: A Sourcebook* (Fort Huachuca, AZ: U.S. Army Intelligence Center & Fort Huachuca, 1995); John Patrick Finnegan, *Military Intelligence* (U.S. Army Lineage Series) (Washington, DC: Center of Military History, United States Army, 1998) pp. 183–84.

Chapter One: Enter Sharpe

1   "General Sharpe at the Unveiling," *Olde Ulster Journal*, Vol. VIII, November, 1912, No. 11, p. 330.

2   Edwin C. Fishel, *The Secret War for the Union* (Boston: Houghton Mifflin, 1996) pp. 647–48ff.; "Notes on the Ancestry of Gen. George H. Sharpe, of Kingston," extracted from a series of articles entitled, "Our Palatine Settlers," *Rhinebeck Gazette*, September 5, 1896, Senate House State Historical Site, Kingston, NY, Sharpe Collection; Mary Isabella Forsyth, "Old Kingston: New York's First Capital," *New England Magazine*, Vol. 15, issue 3, November, 1893.

3   "Lived a Hundred and Ten Years," *Harrisburg Daily Independent* (Harrisburg, PA), July 17, 1897.

4   George H. Sharpe, "The Old House of Kingston," *The Journal* of Kingston, December 29, 1875; and "Old Times and Customs: The Old Houses of Kingston," *New York Times*, December 31, 1875.

5   Louise Heron to Edwin Fishel, April 21, 1963, The Papers of Edwin C. Fishel, Box 2, Folder 15, Georgetown University Library. Heron was the able researcher employed by Fishel to scour the Kingston area for information on Sharpe. Much of what she found was related by the elderly residents of Kingston who had known Sharpe when they were young.

6   Sharpe to Bruyn, February 20, 1849, Sharpe Collection, Senate House State Historical Site, Kingston, New York; *History of Ulster County New York* (New York: Overlook Press, 1977, reprint of 1880 edition).

7   Sharpe to Bruyn, May 1850, The Sharpe Collection, ibid.

8   G. D. B. Hasbrouck, "Address on Major General George H. Sharpe," *Proceedings of the Ulster County Historical Society 1936–1937*, p. 26; Fishel, *The Secret War for the Union*, p. 288; John Riddle, R-MC 028, *Guide to the Augustus Hasbrouck Bruyn Letters, 1832–1848*, May 1, 1995, Special Collections and University Archives, Rutgers University Libraries.

9   Sharpe to Severyn Bruyn, October 3, 4, and 13, 1848, Sharpe Collection.

10 Sharpe to Severyn Bruyn, January 24 and February 3, 1849, Sharpe Collection.

11 Sharpe to Severyn Bruyn, February 20, 1849, Sharpe Collection.

12 Statement of Power of Attorney of Helen Sharp, Sharpe Collection.

13 Heron to Fishel.

14 Sharpe to Severyn Bruyn, February 3, 1849, Sharpe Collection.

15 Sharpe to Severyn Bruyn, October 7, 1849, Sharpe Collection.

16 Sharpe to Severyn Bruyn, March 21, 1850, Sharpe Collection.

17 Sharpe to Severyn Bruyn, August 16, 1854, Sharpe Collection.

18 Hasbrouck, p. 27; Sharpe family lineage, The Sharpe Collection.

19 Seward would recommend to Governor Edwin Morgan of New York in the summer of 1862 that Sharpe be asked to raise a regiment, and in January 1867 Seward would ask Sharpe to conduct a delicate overseas mission in connection to the Lincoln assassination. Postwar correspondence indicates that they were well known to each other.

20 Sharpe to Severyn Bruyn, August 16, 1854, Sharpe Collection.

21 Phyllis F. Field, "Republicans and Black Suffrage in New York State: The Grass Roots Respond," *Civil War History: A Journal of the Middle Period* (published quarterly by Kent State University Press), Vol XXI, March 1975, pp. 136–43; Forsyth, "Old Kingston."

22 Sophie Miller, "Do you remember," *The Kingston Daily Freeman*, August 26, 1954, p. 6. Miller quotes extensively from a *Freeman* article of October 23, 1878.

23 At the time, the building that Sharpe refers to as a church was actually the Uptown Armory. It did not become a church until after the Civil War; information courtesy of Seward Osborne.

24 Information on Colonel Pratt's role was provided courtesy of Seward Osborne.

25 George H. Sharpe, "Memorial Address of General George H. Sharpe," *Seventh Annual Reunion of the 120th N. Y. V. Regimental Union—Lieut.-Col. J. Rudolph Tappen* (Kingston, NY, The Daily Freeman Steam Printing House, 1875), p. 5; "Death of General George H. Sharpe," *Kingston Weekly Freeman and Journal*, January 18, 1900; Hasbrouck, ibid, p. 28; The Departure of the Twentieth Regiment," *Olde Ulster Journal*, Vol. VII, June, 1911, No. 6, pp. 169–70.

26 Seward R. Osborne, *The Three-Month Service of the 20th New York State Militia, April 28–August 2 1861* (Hightstown, NJ: Longstreet House, 1998) p. 9.

27 Theodore B. Gates, *The Ulster Guard and the War of the Rebellion* (New York, 1884), pp. 206–07.

28 Osborne, *Three-Month Service*, pp. 27–28.

29 Hasbrouck, p. 28; Seward R. Osborne, *The Civil War Diaries of Col. Theodore B. Gates, 20th New York State Militia* (Hightstown, NJ: Longstreet House, 1991) pp. xi, 146 (hereafter, Gates Diary).

30 "Memorial Address of General George H. Sharpe," p. 7; Organization of the Army of the Potomac, Maj. Gen. George G. Meade, U.S. Army commanding, July 31, 1863, *War of the Rebellion: Official Records of the Union and Confederate Armies* (Hereafter OR) (Washington, DC: Government Printing Office) Volume 27, Part 3, p. 794.

31 Hasbrouck, pp. 28–9.

32 Fishel, pp. 288–89; Hasbrouck, p. 29.

33 Edwin Ford (Historian of the City of Kingston, NY), "The Genie," January 2000; C. Van Santvoord, *The One Hundred and Twentieth Regiment of New York State Volunteers* (Rondout, NY: Press of the Kingston Freeman, 1894) pp. 10–11, 326; "Death of General George H. Sharpe," *Kingston Weekly Freeman and Journal,* January 18, 1900; Fishel, p. 289.

34 Sharpe to Jansen Hasbrouck, October 29, 1862, Sharpe Collection, Senate State Historical Site, Kingston, NY.

35 "Military Movements in the City: Recruiting for the Fire Zouaves," *New York Times*, August 5, 1862.

36 Camp Sampson was named in honor of Gen. Henry A. Samson, commander of New York 3rd Brigade, and resident of Roundout; information courtesy of Seward Osborne.

37 "Memorial Address of General George H. Sharpe," p. 7.

38 *Regimental Letter and Consolidated Morning Report Book* (120th NY Infantry), RG 94, Vol. 4 of 8, National Archives and Records Administration (NARA).

39 Van Santvoord, pp. 14–16.

40 "General Sharpe at the Unveiling," *Olde Ulster Journal*, Vol. VIII, November 1912, No. 11, p. 324; Van Santvoord, p. 17. Sharpe's memory may have been faulty about the timing of the selection of the regiment's number. Special Order No. 43, General Headquarters, State of New York, Adjutant General's Office, August 11, 1862, already states that of that date, "the 120th commanded by Col. Sharp [sic] had already received its number." Additionally, the regiment's correspondence began using the unit designation as early as August 14; in fact, the designation was changed in the middle of the day, *Regimental Letter and Order Book, 120th NY Infantry*, RG 94, Vol. 3 of 8, NARA.

41 "General Sharpe at the Unveiling," *Olde Ulster Journal*, Vol. VIII, November 1912, No. 11, p. 324; Roger D. Hunt and Jack R. Brown, *Brevet Brigadier Generals in Blue* (Gaithersburg, MD: Olde Soldier Books, 1991), p. 548. Jacob Sharpe was six years younger than his cousin, George H. Sharpe, born on July 31, 1834, in Red Hook, Dutchess County, NY. He attended the US Military Academy at West Point but finished his education at Dartmouth. After the war he was a real estate agent and customs official. He died on April 27, 1882 in Detroit, MI.

42 Van Santvoord, pp. 19–20.

43 Van Santvoord, pp. 20–21.

44 C. A. Winchell, "Old Timer's Civil War Notes," *The Kingston Daily Freeman*, July 1, 1961, p. 28.

45 Letter of Capt. Daniel Gillette, September 15, 1862; *Regimental Letter and Order Book, 120th NY Infantry*, ibid.

46 Special Order No. 6, August 27, 1862; Special Order No. 10, September 24, 1862, *Regimental Letter and Order Book, 120th NY Infantry*, ibid.

47 Special Order No. 9, October 8, 1862; General Order No. 10, September 24, 1862; Special Order No. 8, October 1, 1862; Special Order No. 10, October 15, 1862, Special Order No. 18, October 28, 1862, *Regimental Letter and Order Book, 120th NY Infantry*, ibid.

48 Special Order No. 12, October 30, 1862, *Regimental Letter and Order Book, 120th NY Infantry*, ibid.

49 Sharpe to Hasbrouck, October 29, 1862.

50 Sharpe to Hasbrouck, October 29, 1862.

51 Sharpe to O. J. Hunt, telegram, October (no specific date), 1862, Microcopy 504, Roll 88, NARA.

52 Van Santvood, pp. 25–27; "The Horse of General Sharpe and His Tombstone," *Olde Ulster Journal*, Vol. IX, February 1913, No. 2, p. 43.

53 General Order No. 15, *Regimental Letter and Order Book, 120th NY Infantry*, ibid.

54 Sharpe to Mysenbergh, letter, November 4, 1862, Microcopy 504, Roll 88, NARA.

55 Van Santvoord, p. 35.

56 "Memorial Address of General George H. Sharpe," pp. 7–8; Report of Col. George H. Sharpe, December 17, 1862, OR, Vol. 21, Part 1, pp. 388–89.

57 Van Santvoord, pp. 36–37.

58 Report of Col. George H. Sharpe, December 17, 1862, OR, Vol. 21, Part 1, pp. 388–89.

59 Report of Brig. Gen. Daniel E. Sickles, U.S. Army, commanding Second Division, December 18, 1862, OR, 21:380.

60 Sharpe to Hasbrouck, January 26, 1863.

61 Sharpe to Hasbrouck, January 26, 1863, Sharpe Collection; Van Santvoord, p. 40.

62 Patrick Diary, diary entry for January 24, 1863, pp. 207; Sharpe to Hasbrouck, January 26, 1863.

63 General Order No. 3, January 28, 1863, *Letter and Order Book, 120th NY Infantry*.

64 Memorandum by James Van Hoevenburgh, regimental surgeon, *Regimental Letter and Order Book, 120th NY Infantry*, ibid.

65 Westbrook to Dickerson, December 21, 1862, *Regimental Letter and Order Book, 120th NY Infantry*, ibid; lest the two enlisted men who died that same day be forgotten, their names were Isaac Shultis of Co. A and Matthew Stokes of Co. C.

66 Westbrook letter, December 28, 1862, *Letter and Order Book, 120th NY Infantry*; Van Santvoord, p. 39.

67 Van Santvoord, p. 38; Gates Diary, ibid., diary entries for January 7 and February 6 and 14, 1863, pp. 58, 66.

Chapter Two: Joe Hooker: The Transformational Man

1 Charles Francis Adams, *An Autobiography* (Boston, 1916), p. 161.

2 C. Van Santvoord, *The One Hundred and Twentieth Regiment of New York State Volunteers* (Rondout, NY: Press of the Kingston Freeman, 1894), p. 41.

3 OR, Vol. 5, p. 63.

4 "History of Military Intelligence" (training course), U.S. Army Intelligence Center; John Patrick Finnegan, *Military Intelligence* (Army Lineage Series) (Washington, DC: Center of Military History, 1998), foreword.

5 Edwin C. Fishel, *The Secret War for the Union: The Untold Story of Military Intelligence in the Civil War* (Boston: Houghton Mifflin Company, 1996), pp. 278–79.

6 F. Stansbury Haydon, *Military Ballooning during the Early Civil War* (Baltimore: The John Hopkins University Press, 2000), p. 356.

7 Fishel, pp. 278–79.

8 Fishel, pp. 102–03.

9 Stephen W. Sears, editor, *The Civil War Papers of George B. McClellan: Selected Correspondence 1860–1865* (New York: Da Capo Press, 1992), pp. 91, 96, 116, 203. See also Sears, *Chancellorsville* (Boston: Houghton Mifflin Company, 1996), p. 69; Fishel, pp. 102–13.

10 Joseph T. Glatthaar, *Partners in Command: The Relationship Between Leaders in the Civil War* (New York: The Free Press, 1994), pp. 237–42.

11 William B. Feis, "That Great Essential of Success: Espionage, Covert Action, and Military Intelligence," Aaron Sheehan-Dean, editor, *Struggle for a Vast Future: The American Civil War* (Oxford: Osprey Publishing, 2006) p. 157.

12 Fishel, p. 541.

13 *Reports of the Congressional Joint Committee on the Conduct of the War* (JCCW), 1865, Vol. 1, p. 174.

14 Walter H. Hebert, *Fighting Joe Hooker* (Indianapolis: The Bobbs-Merrill Company Publishers), p. 180.

15 David S. Sparks, ed., *Inside Lincoln's Army: The Diary of Marsena Rudolph Patrick* (New York: Thomas Yoseloff, 1964), pp. 11–12. (hereafter Patrick Diary)

16 Theodore B. Gates, *The War of the Rebellion* (New York: 1884), pp. 191–92.

17 Gates, *War of the Rebellion*, pp. 192–93, 526.

18 Gates, *War of the Rebellion*, pp. 194–95.

19 Patrick Diary, pp. 202–04.

20 Bureau of Pensions Form 3–389 dated January 13, 1905; Form 3–447, dated January 20, 1905; and Declaration of Invalid Pension Form 3–002, dated January 3, 1905, Military Pension File of John C. Babcock (NARA).

21 Babcock to Grace Black, December 26, 1861, John C. Babcock Collection, Library of Congress.

22 Babcock to Black, ibid.; Record of Service of John C. Babcock during Civil War of 1861–1865, Babcock Collection, Library of Congress.

23 Babcock to unidentified uncle March 4, 1862; Babcock to Grace Black, June 6, 1862, Babcock Collection.

24 Babcock to Grace Black, June 6, 1862, Babcock Collection.

25 Ibid.

26 Babcock to William A. Pinkerton, April 9, 1908, Babcock Collection.

27 Babcock to Grace Black, December 7, 1862, Babcock Collection.

28 Babcock to William A. Pinkerton, April 9, 1908, Babcock Collection.

29 Babcock Record of Service and Babcock to Grace Black, December 7, 1862, Babcock Collection; Fishel, ibid., pp. 153–54, 258–59, 262.

30 NARA, Microcopy 2096, Roll 45. Babcock's order-of-battle went down to regiment.

31 Babcock Record of Service, Babcock Collection, ibid.

32 "Eloquent Tribute to General Sharpe," *Kingston Freeman*, date unknown, Folder 2609/4864, Senate House Museum, Kingston, NY.

33 Dickinson to Patrick, February 4, 1863, in AP records, bk. 24, p. 143, cited in Fishel, p. 287, n. 646; Patrick Diary, entry for February 5, 1863, p. 211.

34 It was not a political connection, however; Patrick was a war Democrat, while Sharpe and Gates were very much Republicans.

35 Van Santvoord, p. 38; Gates Diary, p. 15, diary entries for February 6 and 14, 1863, pp. 61, 66.

36 G. D. B. Hasbrouck, "Address on Major General George H. Sharpe," *Proceedings of the Ulster County Historical Society 1936–1937*, pp. 30–31. "The New United States Marshal," *New York Herald*, April 8, 1870, p. 3.

37 Sharpe to Jansen Hasbrouck, February 3, 1863, Sharpe Collection, Senate House State Historical Site, Kingston, NY.

38 Patrick Diary, diary entry for February 8, 1863, ibid., p. 212.

39 John Bigelow, Jr., *The Campaign of Chancellorsville* (New Haven, CT: University of Yale Press, 1910), p. 47.

40 General Order No. 8, February 11, 1863, Headquarters 120th Regt. NY Vol., *Regimental Letters and Orders Book, 120th NY Infantry*, NARA, RG 94, Vol. 3 of 8.

41 "Eloquent Tribute to General Sharpe," *Kingston Freeman.*

42 Fishel, p. 288. Butterfield and Sharpe may have known each other in the New York militia before the war; OR, 25.2:167; "The Horse of General Sharpe and His Tombstone," *Olde Ulster Journal*, Vol. IX, February 1913, No. 2, p. 43; General Orders No. 50, Head Quarters, Army of the Potomac, February 19, 1863, Military Service Record of George H. Sharpe, NARA.

43 Fishel, p. 290.

44 Fishel, p. 290; Sharpe letter to commander, Centre Grand Division, January 27, 1863, Military Personnel File of George H. Sharpe (NARA); Van Santvoord, p. 41.

45 George H. Sharpe, "Memorial Address of General George H. Sharpe," *Seventh Annual Reunion of the 120th N. Y. V. Regimental Union—Lieut.-Col. J. Rudolph Tappen* (Kingston, NY: The Daily Freeman Steam Printing House, 1875), p. 8.

46 Patrick Diary, entry for March 17, 1863, p. 225.

Chapter Three: The Bureau of Military Information: Stands Up

1 Revere to Dickinson, March 14, 1863, Military Service Record (MSR) of George H. Sharpe, NARA.

2 Hooker to Dix, March 17, 1863; and undated returns summary, Military Service Record of Frederick L. Manning, NARA.

3 Louise Heron to Fishel, February 18, 1863, Fishel Collection, Georgetown University Library.

4   Report of Brig. Gen. Daniel Butterfield, July 2, 1862, OR, Vol. 11, Part 2, p. 321; H. C. Bradsby, "O Surnames, History of Luzerne County, Pa," 1893, http: www.rootsweb/~paluzern/bios/obios.htm.

5   OR, Vol. 25, Part 2, p. 39.

6   Fishel, pp 292–93. OR, Vol. 25, Part 2, pp. 99, 137. For some reason, Yager used the first initial "A" in his reports.

7   Military Pension File of Anson B. Carney, Archives and Records Administration (NARA).

8   Military Service Record and Pension File for Martin E. Hogan, NARA; for an example of Hogan and Carney on the same expedition, see Sharpe to Humphreys, NARA, September 11, 1863, RG 393, Part 1, Entry 3988.

9   Declaration for Pension by William J. Lee, November 8, 1910. Lee to the Commissioner of Pensions, March 24, 1913, Pension File of William J. Lee, NARA.

10   Declaration for Pension (Form 3-014a), February 27, 1907, Military Pension Files of Milton W. Cline, NARA. http://www.newbedford-ma.gov/library/whaling-archives, retrieved October 2, 2015.

11   Military Service Record of Milton W. Cline, NARA. There is an incomplete reference in this file to the horses Cline lost in service, apparently which the Army replaced; OR, Vol. 25, Part 2, pp. 99, 137.

12   Certificate of Disability for Discharge, December 18, 1862; letter from Dr. J. H. Knight [Sgt. Knight's brother] to Maj. Gen. George Meade, January 1, 1867; H Company, 2nd NJ Infantry, muster rolls, July 1861 to February 1863, Military Service Record of Judson H. Knight, NARA. Hough to Baker, March 25, 1863, NARA, Microcopy 794, RG 94, Roll 0051. Report No. 467, March 6, 1888 (U.S. Senate) and Report No. 1839, April 22, 1888 (U.S. House of Representatives), both to accompany bill S. 1192, 50th Congress, 1st Session; Military Pension File of Judson H. Knight

13   Peter G. Tsouras, *Scouting for Grant and Meade: The Reminiscences of Judson Knight, Chief of Scouts, Army of the Potomac* (New York: Skyhorse Publications, 2014), pp. xxvi–xxx.

14   L. P. Roe, "Union Scouts and Rebel Guerillas," *The New York Herald*, October 26, 1869.

15   General Orders, No. 32, Headquarters Army of the Potomac, March 30, 1863, OR, Vol. 25, Part 2, p. 167. John Dahlgren, Memoir of Ulric Dahlgren (Philadelphia: J. B. Lippincott & Co., 1862). Dahlgren reported for duty on March 21, having served as an aide-de-camp on Maj. Gen. Franz Sigel's corps staff.

16   NARA, RG 92, Entry 238, Files 0447 for 1864 and 0447 for 1865 (BMI Payrolls); http://www.civilwarhome.com/Pay.htm, accessed February 13, 2013.

17   Scott to Inspector General, December 14, 1865, NARA, M619, RG94, Roll 0420.

18   Stephen Budiansky, "America's Unknown Intelligence Czar," *American Heritage Magazine* (AmericanHeritage.com), October 2004; Fishel, ibid., pp. 294–95; Sharpe to Butterfield, NARA, March 15, 1863, Microcopy 2096, Roll 45.

19   Edward J. Stackpole, *Chancellorsville: Lee's Greatest Battle* (Harrisburg, PA: Stackpole Books, 1958), p. 16.

20   Fishel, p. 286.

21   John Esten Cooke, *Wearing of the Gray: Being Personal Narratives and Adventures of the War* (Baton Rouge, LA: Louisiana State University Press, 1997), p. 467.

22   Cooke, p. 468.

23   Feis, "The Great Essential of Success," pp. 160–66.

24   Fishel, pp. 315, 363; Certificate of Parole of D. G. Otto, signed by Capt. Robert Randolph, 4th Virginia Cavalry, Papers of Edwin Fishel, Box 17, Folder 1, Georgetown University Library.

25   Judson Knight, "How Scouts Worked: Sergt. Knight Tells How They Went About Getting Information," *The National Tribune*, March 9, 1893.

26 "Last Hours of the Confederacy," *The New York Times*, January 21, 1876.

27 Knight, March 2, 1893.

28 "Last Hours of the Confederacy," *New York Times*.

29 Fishel, p. 272; Knight, March 2, 1893.

30 Knight, March 2, 1843.

31 Fishel, pp. 314–15.

32 Sharpe to Martindale, December 12, 1863, NARA, RG 393, Entry 3980.

33 Feis, *Grant's Secret Service*, p. 200.

34 Sharpe to Martindale, December 12, 1863, NARA, RG 393, Entry 3980.

35 General Orders No. 64, February 18, 1864, OR, Serial 3, Vol. 4, p. 118.

36 Circular, Headquarters, Army of Northern Virginia, April 7, 1864, Clifford Dowdey and Louis H. Manarin, *The Wartime Papers of Robert E. Lee* (Boston: 1961), p. 693.

37 Donald E. Markle, *Spies and Spymasters of the Civil War* (New York: Hippocrene Books, 1995), pp. 64–65.

38 Lee to Critcher, May 22, 1863, OR, Vol. 25, Part 2, p. 826.

39 Hayden, p.317, n. 47.

40 Headquarters, Department of the Army, *Intelligence*, FM 2-0 (Washington, DC: May 17, 2004), pp. 1–30.

41 Feis, "Struggle for a Vast Future," p. 162.

42 Fishel, pp. 347–49. Colonel Albert Meyers had invented the first reliable tactical flag signaling system before the Civil War, but it received little official attention. His assistants at the time were Southern officers who immediately after the war began were able to set up the very system Myers had invented but which languished on the Union side for lack of interest.

43 William A. Tidwell, *Come Retribution: The Confederate Secret Service and the Assassination of Lincoln* (Jackson: University Press of Mississippi, 1998), p. 108. Venable saved hundreds of pieces of intelligence correspondence which have come down to the Southern Historical Society Papers at the University of North Carolina at Chapel Hill.

44 Thomas Nelson Conrad, *The Rebel Scout: A Thrilling History of Scouting Life in the Southern Army* (Westminster, MD: Heritage Books, 2009), p. 10.

45 Ibid.

46 Thomas J. Ryan, "A Battle of Wits: Intelligence Operations During the Gettysburg Campaign. Part 1: Clandestine Preparations for Invasion vs. Quest for Information," *The Gettysburg Magazine*, Issue No. 29, pp. 11–12.

47 Thomas N. Conrad, *A Confederate Spy: A Story of the Civil War* (New York: J. S. Ogilvie Publishing Company, 1892, reprinted Lynchburg, VA: Artcraft Print Com., 1961), pp. 31–32.

48 Thomas J. Ryan, "A Battle of Wits: Intelligence Operations During the Gettysburg Campaign. Part 2: Strategy, Tactics, and Lee's March," *The Gettysburg Magazine*, Issue No. 30, p. 14.

49 David Winfred Gaddy, "Confederate Signal Corps at Gettysburg," *The Gettysburg Magazine*, Issue No. 4, pp. 110–11.

50 Gaddy, pp. 110–11.

51 Fishel, pp. 347–49; David S. Sparks, ed., *Inside Lincoln's Army: The Diary of Marsena Rudolph Patrick, Provost Marshal General of the Army of the Potomac* (New York: Thomas Yoseloff, 1964), pp. 211–12.

52 Peter G. Tsouras, ed., *The Book of Military Quotations* (St. Paul, MN: Zenith Press, 2006), p. 168.

53 James Morice, "Organizational learning in a military environment: George H. Sharpe and the Army of the Potomac," Vitae Scholasticae, Caddo Press, 2009. http://www.freepatentsonline.com/article/Vitae-Scholasticae/277602573.html.

54 Geoffrey Perret, *Old Soldiers Never Die: The Life of Douglas MacArthur* (New York: Random House, 996), p. 362.

55 "NIEs are the Intelligence Community's (IC) most authoritative written judgments on national security issues and are designed to help U.S. civilian and military leaders develop polices to protect U.S. national security interests. Several IC analysts from different agencies produce the initial text of the estimate. The NIC then meets to critique the draft before it is circulated to the broader IC. Representatives from the relevant IC agencies meet to hone and coordinate line-by-line the full text of the NIE. Working with their agencies, representatives also assign the confidence levels to each key judgment. IC representatives discuss the quality of sources with intelligence collectors to ensure the draft does not contain erroneous information." Rosenbach, Eric and Aki. J. Peritz, *Confrontation or Collaboration? Congress and the Intelligence Community* (Harvard: Belfer Center for Science and International Affairs, 2009).

Chapter Four: First Test: The Chancellorsville Campaign

1   J. E. Hammond to S. L. M. Barlow, April 22, 1863, Barlow Papers, Huntington Papers.
2   *Intelligence Preparation of the Battlefield*, Field Manuel 34–130 (Washington: Headquarters of the Army, July 8, 1994), chapter 1, p. 1.
3   Edwin C. Fisher, *The Secret War for the Union: The Untold Story of Military Intelligence in the Civil War* (Boston: Houghton-Mifflin Company, 1996), pp. 310–12.
4   Fishel, pp. 306–08.
5   Ibid., pp. 308–09.
6   Patrick Diary, entry for March 5, 1863, p. 219.
7   Request of Sharpe to Taylor, March 5, 1863, NARA, Military Service Record of Scout Daniel R. Cole.
8   Babcock Memorandum on Expedition of scout Daniel R. Cole, March 22, 1863, NARA, Microcopy 2096, Roll 34.
9   Skinker to Sharpe, March 13, 1863, NARA, RG 2096, Box 45.
10   Sharpe to Butterfield, 15 March 1863, NARA, RG 2096, Box 45.
11   Abstract from return of the Army of Northern Virginia (March 1863), OR, Vol. 25, Part 2, p. 696.
12   Babcock Memorandum, NARA, Microcopy 2096, Box 45.
13   Memorandum by Col. Sharpe, March 15, 1863, NARA, Microcopy 2096, Box 45.
14   Sharpe to Hasbrouck, April 22, 1863, Sharpe Collection, Senate House State Historical Site, Kingston, NY.
15   Sharpe to Butterfield, March 21, 1863, NARA, Microcopy 2096, Box 45.
16   Sharpe to Butterfield, March 22, 1863, NARA, Microcopy 2096, Box 45.
17   Sharpe to Butterfield, March 22, 1863, NARA, Microcopy 2096, Roll 34.
18   General Order No. 48, Army of the Potomac, April 30, 1863, OR, Vol. 25, Part 2, p. 316; "From Fredericksburgh," *The New York Times*, February 24, 1963, p. 2.
19   Babcock to Butterfield, "Report of John Skinker," NARA, March 11, 1863. Fishel Papers, Box 8, Folder 27.
20   Babcock to Butterfield, March 11, 1863, NARA, RG 108, Entry 112 and RG 393, Entry 3980; Babcock's obituary (Mount Vernon, NY) *Argus*, November 20, 1908; OR, Vol. 25, Part 2, pp. 135–36.
21   Sharpe to D. F. Van Buren, March 10, 1863, NARA, Microcopy 504, Roll 198
22   "Distances on Roads running Westerly from Fredericksburg," Hooker Papers, Huntington Library; Sears, pp. 367–68.
23   Sharpe to Butterfield, May 13, 1863, NARA Microcopy 2096, Roll 45. Reference for the Falmouth fords is Capt. Ulrich Dahlgren, aide-de-camp to Hooker.

24 Stephen W. Sears, *Chancellorsville* (Boston: Houghton-Mifflin Company, 1996), p. 368 and p. 554 n. 2.

25 Report written by Manning and signed by Sharpe, April 30, 1863, NARA, Microcopy 2096, Box 45.

26 Report written by Manning and signed by Sharpe, April 30, 1863, NARA, Microcopy 2096, Box 45.

27 Fishel, pp. 335–39.

28 The Record of Benjamin F. Butler: Compiled from the Original Sources (Boston: 1888, Bibliobalzar Reproduction Series), pp. 24–25.

29 Sharpe to Butterfield, April 10, 1863, NARA, RG 393. "The Bread Riot," *National Republican*, April 9, 1863, p. 2. "Affairs in Richmond and Lee's Army: Statement of a Refugee," *National Republican*, April 14, 1863, p. 2. The April 9 article cited the *Richmond Sentinel* for the information that "all the papers had after consultation, concluded at the time not to mention the matter."

30 Butterfield to Pleasonton, April 28, OR, Vol. 25, Part 2, p. 273.

31 "Fords of the Rappahannock," Hooker Papers, Huntington Library.

32 Williams to Stoneman, April 12, 1863, OR, Vol. 25, Part 2, pp. 1066–67.

33 Sears, *Chancellorsville*, p. 218; John Bigelow, Jr., *The Campaign of Chancellorsville* (New Haven, CT: Yale University Press, 1910), p. 145.

34 Carl Smith, *Chancellorsville 1863: Jackson's Lightning Strikes* (Osprey, 1998), pp. 33–34.

35 Sharpe to Hasbrouck, April 28, 1863, Sharpe Papers, Senate House State Historical Site, Kingston, NY.

36 Hooker to Stanton, April 21, 1863, OR, Vol. 25, Part 2, p. 239.

37 Papers related to Civilians, Union Provost Marshal's File of Paper Relating to Individual Civilians, NARA, M345, RG109.

38 Henry C. Jenckes, April 16, 1863, OR, Vol. 25, Part 2, pp. 217–18.

39 Patrick to Williams, April 22, 1863, OR, Vol. 25, Part 1, pp. 218–19.

40 "A Submarine Telegraph to Confederate Headquarters—Traitors in Gen. Hooker's Army," *The Times-Picayune* (New Orleans), May 14, 1863, p. 2, reprinted from the *Philadelphia Enquirer*, April 26, 1863.

41 "Important Arrest—A Telegraph Working across the Rappahannock—Rebel Soldier Tries to Desert," *The New York Times*, April 28, 1863, p. 1; Fishel, p. 355.

42 Fitzhugh Lee to Stuart, March 16, 1863, OR, Vol. 25, Part 1, p. 60; Averell to Butterfield, March 20, 1863, OR, Vol. 25, Part 1, p. 47; Browne to Trowbridge, March 19, 1863, OR, Vol. 25, Part 1, p. 56.

43 Lee to Stuart, March 12, 1863, OR, Vol. 25, Part 2, p. 664; Fishel, p. 354.

44 Butterfield to Hooker, Oliver to Lowe, Butterfield to Hooker, April 28, 1863, OR, Vol. 25, Part 2, pp. 276–78.

45 Babcock, "Organization and estimated strength of Lt. Gen. Jackson's Corps, Bureau of Information, May 1, 1863," NARA, Microcopy 2096, Box 45; Bigelow. *Chancellorsville*, pp. 132–34.

46 BMI, "Organization of the Rebel Army of Northern Virginia," May 10, 1863, Southern Historical Society; Bigelow, *Chancellorsville*, p. 134.

47 "Correspondence and Orders Concerning the Army of the Potomac from January 25 to May 26, 1863," Hooker Papers, Huntington Library, p. 901.

48 Sears, *Chancellorsville*, p. 35.

49 Almira Hancock, *Reminiscences of Winfield Scott Hancock* (New York: Charles L. Webster, 1887). Major General Winfield Scott Hancock noted the effect of this statement on the army when he said, "Pray, could we expect a victory after that? ... Success cannot come to us through such profanity."

50 Noah Brooks, "Personal reminiscences of Lincoln," *Scribner's Monthly*, XV (March 1878), p. 673.

51 Sharpe to Hasbrouck, April 28, 1863, Senate House State Historical Site, Kingston, NY.

52 Hayden, pp. 325–26; Charles M. Evans, *War of the Aeronauts: A History of Ballooning in the Civil War* (Mechanicsburg, PA: Stackpole Books, 2002), p. 283; Butterfield to Sedgwick, May 3, 1863, Papers of Edwin C. Fishel, Box 17, Folder 1, Georgetown University Library.

53 Butterfield to Kelton, May 1, 1863, 10:05 p.m., OR, Vol 25, Part 2, p.332.

54 Bigelow, *Chancellorsville*, n. 2, pp. 477–78. This was in response to the question by Maj. Gen. Doubleday, "Hooker, what was the matter with you at Chancellorsville?"

55 Butterfield to Hooker, May 1, 1863, 2:05 p.m., Huntington Library, Hooker Papers, Correspondence and Orders Concerning the Army of the Potomac from January 25 to May 26, 1863, p. 899; OR, Vol. 25, Part 2, p. 3227.

56 Butterfield to Hooker, May 1, 1863, 5:30 a.m., OR, Vol. 25, Part 2, p. 322.

57 Peck to Butterfield, May 1, 1863, 7:30 p.m., Huntington Library, Hooker Papers, Correspondence and Orders Concerning the Army of the Potomac from January 25 to May 26, 1863, p. 902.

58 Cooper to Longstreet, April 29 & 30, 1863, OR, Vol. 18, pp. 1029, 1032.

59 Butterfield to Sedgwick, May 1, 1863, Huntington Library, Hooker Papers, Correspondence and Orders Concerning the Army of the Potomac from January 25 to May 26, 1863, p. 906.

60 Butterfield to Hooker, May 1, 1863, 10:30 p.m., OR, Vol. 25, Part 2, pp. 332–33; Fishel, p. 393.

61 Sharpe to Babcock, May 2, 1863, NARA, Microcopy 504, Roll 198.

62 Sharpe to Babcock, May 2, 1863, NARA, Microcopy 504, Roll 198.

63 Peck to Butterfield, May 2, 1863, 11:10 a.m., OR, Vol. 25, Part 2, p. 370.

64 Butterfield to Peck, May 2, 1863, 11:10 a.m., OR, Vol. 25, Part 2, p. 370.

65 Lee to Davis, May 2, 1863, OR, Vol. 25, p. 765.

66 Fishel, p. 402.

67 Patrick, diary entry for May 6, 1863, covering the preceding five days, pp. 240–41.

68 Walter H. Hebert, *Fighting Joe Hooker* (New York: The Bobbs-Merrill Company, 1944), p. 225. The author claims that the source is "an unidentified clipping from the Huntington collection." A diligent search of the Hooker Papers at the Huntington Library did not reveal this document.

69 Elzey to Lee, May 3, 1863; Bigelow, *Chancellorsville*, p. 447.

70 Sears, pp. 367–70.

71 Butterfield to Sedgwick, May 3, 1963, 8:42 a.m., OR, Vol. 25, Part 2, p. 387.

72 Babcock to Butterfield, May 3, 1863, 9:00 a.m., Hooker Papers, Huntington Library.

73 Babcock to Butterfield, May 3, 1863, 3:00 p.m., Hooker Papers, Huntington Library.

74 Butterfield to Hooker, May 3, 1863, 5:30 p.m., Huntington Library, Hooker Papers, Correspondence and Orders Concerning the Army of the Potomac from January 25 to May 26, 1863, p. 948.

75 Jeffry D. Wert, *General James Longstreet: The Confederacy's Most Controversial Soldier* (New York: Simon & Schuster, 1993), p. 238.

76 Babcock to Butterfield, May 3, 1863, Huntington Library, Hooker Papers.

77 Butterfield to Hooker, May 3, 1863, 5:30 p.m., OR, Vol. 25, Part 2, p. 394.

78 Babcock to Sharpe, May 5, 1863, OR, Vol. 25, Part 2, p. 417.

79 Butterfield to Peck and Peck to Butterfield, May 4, 1863, Huntington Library, Hooker Papers, Correspondence and Orders Concerning the Army of the Potomac from January 25 to May 26, 1863, p. 949.

80 Babcock to Sharpe, May 5, 1863, 10:10 a.m., OR, Vol. 25, Part 2, p. 421

81 Babcock to Sharpe, May 5, 1863, 10:00 a.m., OR, Vol. 25, Part 2, p. 421.

82 See extensive correspondence between Hooker and Lee about the Union wounded in OR, Vol. 25, Part 2, pp. 42, 47–48.

83 Patrick Diary, entry for May 8, 1863; General Orders Number 49, May 6, 1863, OR, Vol. 25, Part 1, p. 171.

84 "Southern News," *The Pittsburgh Gazette*, May 13, 1863, p. 3.

85 Babcock to Sharpe, May 30, 1863, "Estimated loss of the Army of Northern Virginia in the late battle at Chancellorsville Va"; Papers of Edwin C. Fishel (Box 17, Folder 6), BMI, Georgetown University Library.

86 McEntee & Sharpe, "Summary of the Fords," May 13, 1863, NARA, Microcopy 2096, Roll 45.

87 Sharpe to Steele, May 10, 1863, OR, Vol. 25, Part 2, p. 47.

88 Patrick Diary, entry for May 14, 1863, p. 249.

89 Patrick Diary, entry for May 14, 1863, pp. 248–49; Peter G. Tsouras, *Scouting for Grant and Meade: The Reminiscences of Judson Knight, Chief of Scouts, Army of the Potomac* (New York: Skyhorse Publications, 2014), p. 94.

90 Wert, *Longstreet*, p. 243.

91 Sharpe to Yager, May 10, 1863, NARA, Microcopy 504, Roll 198.

92 Hooker to Lincoln, May 13, 1863, OR, Vol. 25, Part 2, p. 473.

93 Hooker to Lincoln, May 13, 1863, 10:30 p.m., OR, Vol. 25, Part 2, p. 477.

94 Butterfield to Hooker, May 14, 1863, OR, Vol. 25, Part 2, p. 479.

95 Fishel, p. 415.

96 Sharpe to Hasbrouck, May 12, 1863, Sharpe Papers, Senate House State Historical Site, Kingston, NY.

97 "'I was in the Secret Service of the Army of the Potomac'—Isaac Silver of Spotsylvania County, Part 1. https://npsfrsp.wordpress.com/2010/10/07/%E2%80%9Ci-was-in-the-secret-service-of-the-army-of-the-potomac%E2%80%A6%E2%80%9D-%E2%80%93-isaac-silver-of-spotsylva-nia-county-part-1/; accessed October 25, 2015.

98 "Death of General George H. Sharpe," *Kingston Weekly Freeman and Journal*, January 18, 1900.

99 Williams to Sharpe, May 13, 1863, OR, Vol. 25, Part 2, p. 476.

100 Sharpe to Butterfield, May 13, 1863, Hooker Papers, Huntington Library.

101 Sharpe to Butterfield, May 14, 1863, Hooker Papers, Huntington Library.

102 Sharpe to Butterfield, May 14, 1863, 3:30 p.m., Hooker Papers, Huntington Library.

103 Butterfield to Pleasonton, May 15, 1863, OR, Vol. 25, Part 2, p. 483.

104 "Death of General George H. Sharpe," *Kingston Weekly Freeman and Journal*; Edwin Ford (City of Kingston Historian), *The Genie*, January 2000, as cited by Cathy Hoyt, Green Mountain Civil War Round Table, Woodstock, VT, http://www.gmcwrt.org/william_ellsworth.htm; OR, Vol. 25. Part 2, p.853, Patrick Diary, entry for May 14, 1863, p. 249; G. B. D. Hasbrouck, "Address on Major-General George H. Sharpe," *Proceedings of the Ulster County Historical Society 1936–1937*.

Chapter Five: The Gettysburg Campaign: Movement to Contact

1 Dahlgren to Hooker, May 23, 1863, OR, Vol. 27, Part 2, pp. 518–19.

2 Marsena R. Patrick, *Inside Lincoln's Army: The Diary of Marsena Rudolph Patrick*, editor David Sparks, Diary entry for May 23, 1863 (New York: Thomas Yoseloff, 1964), p. 251.

3 OR, Vol. 25, Part 2, p. 528.

4 Edwin C. Fishel, *The Secret War for the Union: The Untold Story of Military Intelligence in the Civil War* (Boston: Houghton Mifflin Company, 1996), p. 424.

5 "Nearly Prevented Gettysburg Fight: Union Scout's Message to Gen. Meade, if Heeded, Might Have Halted Battle," June 26, 1913, newspaper clipping of interview with former scout William J. Lee (possibly the *Washington Star*) found in the John C. Babcock Collection, Library of Congress.

6   Seward B. Osborne, ed., The *Civil War Diaries of Col. Theodore B. Gates, 20th New York State Militia* (Hightstown, NJ: Longstreet House, 1991), p. 84.

7   Sharpe to Butterfield, June 7, 1863, Abraham Lincoln Papers, Library of Congress, Series 1, Reel 53, Item 23919. McEntee to Sharpe, June 6, 1863, NARA, Microcopy 2096, Roll 34. "Stuart's Projected Raid," *The Pittsburgh Gazette*, June 12, 1863, p. 2.

8   Report of Brig. Gen. Alfred Pleasonton, U.S. Army, commanding Cavalry Corps, Army of the Potomac, June 15, 1863, OR, Vol. 27, Part 1, p. 1046.

9   John Dahlgren, *Memoir of Ulric Dahlgren* (Philadelphia: J. B. Lippincott & Co., 1872) pp. 147–48.

10 Patrick, *Inside Lincoln's Army*, Diary entry for June 10, 1863, p. 256.

11 McEntee to Sharpe, June 11, 1863, OR, Vol. 27, Part 3, p. 80.

12 McEntee to Sharpe, June 12, 1863, NARA, Microcopy 473, Roll 264, p. 549, NARA; McEntee to Sharpe, June 12, 1863, RG 393, Entry 3980. On June 13 Butterfield sent a message to Pleasonton asking him if his references to a contraband (Charlie Wright) are of the same person in McEntee's telegram to Sharpe. This highlights the lack of real cooperation between the cavalry and the BMI, if both are reporting the same but uncoordinated information up the chain of command.

13 Fishel, pp. 440–41.

14 Lincoln to Hooker, 9:30 a.m., June 17, 1863, OR, Vol. 27, Part 1, p. 48.

15 Evans, pp. 294–95. Brigadier General Edwin Porter Alexander, Longstreet's chief of artillery, commented after the war, "I have never understood why the enemy abandoned the use of military balloons early in 1863 after using them extensively up to that time. Even if the observers never saw anything they would have been worth all they cost for the annoyance and delays they caused us in trying to keep our movements out of sight."

16 Tyler to Hooker, June 17–25, 1863, OR, Vol. 27, Part 2, pp. 19–33.

17 Edwin B. Coddington, *The Gettysburg Campaign: A Study in Command* (New York: Charles Scribner's Sons, 1968), pp. 456–57; Fishel, pp. 456–57.

18 Glen Tucker, *High Tide at Gettysburg* (New York: Bobs Merrill, 1958), p. 43.

19 Norton to Butterfield, September 18, 1863, OR, Vol. 27, Part 1, p. 200.

20 Williams to Pleasonton, June 17, 1863, OR, Vol. 27, Part 3, pp. 171–72.

21 "The Colored Washerwoman's Signal Below Fredericksburg," *Lincoln Progress* (Lincolnton, IL), August 6, 1881.

22 Patrick Diary, entry for June 17, 1863, p. 261.

23 Fishel, pp. 461–64; Hunnicutt to Butterfield, June 18, 1863, OR, Vol. 27, Part 3, p. 207.

24 Sharpe to Jansen Hasbrouck, June 20, 1863, Sharpe Collection.

25 Patrick Diary, entry for June 19, 1863, p. 261.

26 Sharpe to Jansen Hasbrouck, June 20, 1863, Sharpe Collection.

27 Norton to Williams, OR, Vol. 27, Part 1, p. 198, from the Gettysburg after-action report of the signal officer of the Army of the Potomac, Capt. Lemuel B. Norton.

28 Pleasonton to Williams, June 20, 1863, 7 a.m., OR, Vol. 27, Part 3, pp. 223–24.

29 Pleasonton to Hooker, June 21, 1863, 5:30 p.m., OR, Vol. 27, Part 1, pp. 911–12; Stuart to Lee, August 20, 1863, OR, Vol. 27, Part 2, p. 690.

30 Pleasonton to Hooker, June 20, 1863, 12.30 a.m., and Pleasonton to Hooker, June 21, 1863, 5:30 p.m., OR, Vol. 27, Part 1, pp. 911–12.

31 Lee to Ewell, OR, Vol. 27, Part 3, pp. 914–15.

32 John C. Babcock, informal notes on his military service, John C. Babcock Collection, Library of Congress; Sharpe to Jansen Hasbrouck, August 15, 1864, Sharpe Collection; Hooker to Babcock, June 20, 1863, 10:10 a.m., OR, Vol. 27, Part 3, p. 225.

33 Babcock to Hooker, June 20, 1863, 3:10 p.m, and Babcock to Sharpe, June 20, 1863, 5:30 p.m., OR, Vol. 27, Part 3, pp. 227–28.

34 Babcock to Sharpe, June 21, 1863, OR, Vol. 27, Part 3, p. 248.

35 Sharpe to Butterfield, June 23, 1863, OR, Vol. 27, Part 3, p. 266. "The Situation in Maryland," *National Republican* (Washington, DC), June 24, 1863, p. 2.

36 Fisher to Slocum, 10:40 a.m., June 24, 1863, OR, Vol. 27, Part 1, p. 201.

37 John Bell Hood, *Advance and Retreat* (Edison, NJ: The Blue and Gray Press, 1985), p. 54.

38 Fishel, p. 415; Stephen W. Sears, *Gettysburg* (Boston: Houghton Mifflin Co., 2003), pp. 47–48, 95; Tucker, p. 39.

39 For two opposing treatments of Stuart's conduct in the Gettysburg Campaign, see Mark Nesbitt, *Saber and Scapegoat: J. E. B. Stuart in the Gettysburg Controversy* (Mechanicsville, PA: Stackpole Books, 1994) and Scott Bowden and Bill Ward, *Last Chance for Victory: Robert E. Lee and the Gettysburg Campaign* (New York: Da Capo Press, 2001).

40 Stuart to Robertson, June 24, 1863, OR, Vol. 27, Part 3, p. 927.

41 Ryan, "A Battle of Wits: Intelligence Operations During the Gettysburg Campaign. Part 1: Clandestine Preparations for Invasion vs. Quest for Information," *The Gettysburg Magazine*, Issue No. 31, pp. 17–18.

42 OR, Vol. 27, Part 3, p. 151, returns of the Army of the Potomac for June 30, 1863.

43 Tucker, p. 73.

44 John C. Babcock, Record of Service of John C. Babcock during the Civil War 1861–65, John C. Babcock Collection, Library of Congress.

45 "Reports of Scouts," *National Republican*, June 30, 1863, p. 1.

46 Reynolds to Butterfield, June 29, 1863, 3:15 p.m., OR, Vol. 27, Part 3, p. 397 & Butterfield to Sharpe, June 29, 1863, p. 399; Fishel, p. 503.

47 OR, Vol. 27, Part 3, p. 459.

48 Sharpe's letter is in the McConaughy Collection in the Civil War Institute of Gettysburg College. "Headquarters Army of the Potomac," *The Adams Sentinel* (Gettysburg, PA), October 3, 1863, p. 4.

49 Hood, p. 55.

50 Buford to Smith, June 27, 1863 & Buford to Smith, June 30, 1863, OR, Vol. 27, Part 3, pp. 926, 414.

51 Order, Army of the Potomac (Williams), June 30, 1863, OR, Vol. 27, Part 3, p. 416.

52 "Regimental Histories: 3rd Indiana Cavalry," http://www.bufordsboys.com/3rd INHistory.htm; Buford to Pleasonton, June 30, 1863, OR, Vol. 27, Part 2, p. 923.

53 Buford to Pleasonton, 10:30 p.m., June 30, 1863, OR, Vol. 2, Part 2, pp. 923–24.

54 Fishel, p. 510.

55 Ryan, "A Battle of Wits," p. 27.

Chapter Six: Gettysburg and Sharpe's Three Golden Gifts: To Meade

1 A. B. Jerome to W. S. Hancock, October 1865, Bachelder Papers, New Hampshire Historical Society, cited in Bill Cameron, "The Signal Corps at Gettysburg," *The Gettysburg Magazine*, Issue No. 3.

2 OR, Vol. 27, Part 3, p. 488. The *Official Records* dates this message as sent on July 2 but apparently is an error as pointed out by Cameron, "The Signal Corps at Gettysburg."

3 OR, Vol. 27, Part 1, pp. 201–02; Cameron, "The Signal Corps at Gettysburg."

4 C. Van Santvoord, *The One Hundred and Twentieth Regiment New York State Volunteers: A Narrative of its Services in the War for the Union* (Rondout, NY: Press of the Kingston Freeman, 1894), p. 221.

5   OR, Vol. 27, Part 3, p. 202.

6   OR, Vol. 27, Part 3, pp. 201–02, 458–59.

7   Santvoord, p. 223.

8   Marsena R. Patrick, *Inside Lincoln's Army: The Diary of Marsena Rudolph Patrick*, editor David Sparks, diary entry for July 1, 1863 (New York: Thomas Yoseloff, 1964), p. 267.

9   Lee to Cooper, January 30, 1863, OR, Vol. 27, Part 2, pp. 317–18, Lee's official report of the Gettysburg Campaign, dated January 20, 1863.

10   Lee to Cooper, January 30, 1863, OR, Vol. 27, Part 2, p. 318.

11   Longstreet to Chilton, "Report of Lieut. Gen. James Longstreet, C. S Army, commanding First Army Corps, July 27, 1863," OR, Vol. 27, Part 2, pp. 357–58; Ewell to Chilton, "Report of Lieut. Gen. Richard S. Ewell, C. S. Army, commanding Second Army Corps (no month and day), 1863," OR, Vol. 27, Part 2, pp. 444–48; Hill to Chilton, "Report of Lieut. Gen. Ambrose P. Hill, C. S. Army, commanding Third Army Corps, November, 1863," OR, Vol. 27, Part 2, pp. 606–07.

12   "Sharpe: a Great Man," *The Inter Ocean Courier* (Chicago), January 21, 1900.

13   Edwin C. Fishel, *The Secret War for the Union: The Untold Story of Military Intelligence in the Civil War* (Boston: Houghton Mifflin Company, 1996), p. 526.

14   Patrick, ibid.; Thomas J. Ryan, "A Battle of Wits: Intelligence Operations During the Gettysburg Campaign. Part 4: The Intelligence Factor at Gettysburg," *The Gettysburg Magazine*, Issue No. 32, p. 30.

15   Hall to Meade, July 2, 1863, OR, Vol. 27, Part 3, pp. 486–87.

16   Norton to Williams, September 18, 1863, OR, Vol. 27, Part 2, p. 202.

17   Stephen W. Sears, *Gettysburg* (Boston: Houghton Mifflin Company, 2004), pp. 253–55.

18   Lee's Official Report, January 30, 1863, OR, Vol. 27, Part 2, pp. 321–22.

19   Ewell to Chilton, 1863, OR, Vol. 27, Part 2, p. 447.

20   Cameron, "The Signal Corps at Gettysburg," *The Gettysburg Magazine*, Issue No. 3. OR 27, Part 2, p. 358. Longstreet was clear in laying blame on Lee for the difficulties with the route in his official report, an indication of how severely he had disagreed with his orders.

21   Peter G. Tsouras, ed., *The Greenhill Dictionary of Military Quotations* (London: Greenhill Books, 2000), p. 346.

22   Hall to Butterfield, July 2, 1863, 2:10 p.m., OR, Vol. 27, Part 3, p. 488.

23   W. Pfanz, *Gettysburg: The Second Day* (Chapel Hill: University of North Carolina Press, 1987), p. 142.

24   Norton to Williams, September 18, 1863, OR, Vol. 27, Part 1, p. 202.

25   Pfanz, pp. 201, 505 n. 1. In 1877 Warren recounted that he suggested to Meade that he be sent to Little Round Top. His aide, Lt. Washington A. Roebling (the builder of the Brooklyn Bridge), claimed to remember Meade's statement verbatim. The two statements are not inconsistent, as Pfanz concludes.

26   Willard J. Brown, *Signal Corps, U.S.A. in the War of the Rebellion* (New York: Arno Press, 1974), pp. 188–89.

27   Oliver Wilcox Norton, *The Attack and Defense of Little Round Top* (New York: The Neale Publishing Company, 1913), p. 264.

28   Patrick Diary, entry for July 2, 1863.

29   "The Fight at Gettysburg," *The Times-Picayune* (New Orleans), July 14, 1863, p. 1.

30   Haupt to Halleck, July 2, 1863, OR, Vol. 27, Part 3, p. 512; T. B., "From the Army of the Potomac," *National Republican* (Washington, DC), July 6, 1863, p. 1; "The Battle of Gettysburg," *The Pittsburgh Gazette*, July 7, 1863, p. 2.

31   John Dahlgren, *Memoir of Ulric Dahlgren* (Philadelphia: J. B. Lippincott & Co., 1872), p. 159.

32 Dahlgren, pp. 92–115.

33 Edward G. Longacre, *The Cavalry at Gettysburg* (Lincoln: University of Nebraska Press, 1993), p. 208.

34 Butterfield to Sharpe, June 29, 1863, OR, Vol. 27, Part 3, p. 399. An undated newspaper article, currently in the Kingston Senate House State Historical Site and written shortly after Sharpe's death in January 1900, quoting this telegram, was found among Sharpe's effects. Apparently, Sharpe kept a copy of the telegram as a treasured souvenir of his contribution in the war.

35 Dahlgren, p. 160. See also Longacre, *The Cavalry at Gettysburg*, p. 208, in which he cites the *Louis Fortescue Memoirs* (Philadelphia: War Library, Military Order of the Loyal Legion of the United States (MOLLUS)), p. 93, for Cline's story of discovering the information about the couriers. This is the only source for this vital connection. Fortescue was an acting signal officer who was also at the army headquarters at Taneytown on June 30, the day Dahlgren learned of the dispatches. That same day, he was sent to operate a signal station at Emmitsburg, MD, and was there when Dahlgren galloped back with the dispatches on the night of July 2. See OR, Vol. 27, Part 1, pp. 199–207. Fortescue was captured by Stuart's cavalry on July 5 during the Confederate retreat.

36 F. A. Bushey, "That Historic Dispatch," *The National Tribune*, May 14, 1896. Bushey relates the story of the raid as told by Daniel A. Carl, Co. K, 6th US Cavalry, a participant in the raid and a subsequent resident of Hancock, MD.

37 Jacob Hoke, *The Great Invasion of 1863* (Gettysburg: Stan Clark Military Books, 1992; originally published in Dayton, OH, 1887), pp. 180–82.

38 Bushey, "That Historic Dispatch," *The National Tribune*, May 14, 1896.

39 Longacre, p. 209.

40 Bushey, "That Historic Dispatch," *The National Tribune*, May 14, 1896.

41 "Our Special Correspondent," *The New York Times*, July 2, 1863. "A Provost Guard at Winchester," *National Republican* (Washington, DC), July 6, 1863, p. 2.

42 E. J. Edwards, "Unselfishness of Meade," *Daily Press* (Sheboygan, WI), June 21, 1910. Edwards was a prominent journalist at the time and wrote several articles such as this one (which he copyrighted) in which he states the story was told him by Sharpe. In that case it is not known how much embellishment Edwards employed in writing them for publication, but the prose and style are reminiscent of Sharpe. Sharpe was known to tell war stories to journalists, and this appears to be one of them.

43 Sears, p. 343.

44 Abner Doubleday, *Chancellorsville and Gettysburg* (New York: Charles Scribner's Sons, 1886), p. 157.

45 Meade to Halleck, July 3, 1863, OR, Vol. 27, Part 1, p. 72.

46 G. B. D. Hasbrouck, "Address on Major General George H. Sharpe," *Proceedings of the Ulster Country Historical Society 1936–1937* (Kingston, NY: Ulster County Historical Society, 1937), p. 24. This same article was also published in its entirety in the *Kingston Daily Freeman*, June 5, 1937.

47 Fishel, p. 527.

48 This famous report exists only in a photocopy in the Papers of Edwin C. Fishel at Georgetown University Library. It is not found in the National Archives records of the BMI. It probably was among the 150 BMI documents stolen from NARA subsequent to Fishel's discovery of those records. However, it is clearly written in the neat hand of John C. Babcock, which attests to its authenticity.

49 "A Story of Gettysburg," *The Kane Republican* (Kane, PA), January 7, 1899. The corps that Meade inquired about was probably VI Corps, though it is unlikely that he would not have known about its arrival in the late afternoon of that same day since he used part of it to turn back the

last gasp of Longstreet's attack; see Sedgwick to Meade, August 8, 1863, and Meade to Halleck, October 1, 1863, OR, Vol. 25, Part I, pp. 114, 663. It is difficult to know what Sharpe meant by this reference. He admitted he did not remember which corps. Perhaps he was referring to an interaction of earlier in the day since Meade had him rushing about the battlefield on various missions. Ascertaining the whereabouts of VI Corps earlier in the day might have been one. Nevertheless, his memory was faultless in his description of the Confederate situation. His comments as reported in January 1889 were almost exactly what was in the report that Babcock prepared that evening 25 years before.

50 The same statements by Meade and Sharpe are cited in the *Kingston Daily Freeman*, January 18, 1899, from an interview by Sharpe. The verb "to nick" has largely gone out of American English usage in its meaning "to catch at the right time," although it retains that meaning in the phrase, "in the nick of time." In British usage it has the connotation of catching a thief.

51 John C. Babcock, untitled summary of military service, John C. Babcock Collection, Library of Congress. "Service at Gettysburg—locating from ex[amination] of prisoners the disposition of Lee's forces, and the result of Examination & moving of [word illegible]—in determining Meades [sic] judgment in holding the position he was in."

52 "Abstract from returns of the Army of the Potomac, June 10–July 31, 1863," OR, Vol. 27, Part 1, p. 151; "List of divisions, brigades, and regiments, with names of commanding officers, in the First and Second Army Corps, June 22, 1863,", OR, Vol. 27, Part 3, p. 919. Ryan, *The Gettysburg Magazine*, Issue No. 32, p. 32, n. 145.

53 "Minutes of Council," July 2, 1863, OR, Vol. 27. Part 1, p. 73.

54 Richard A. Sauers, *Gettysburg: The Meade-Sickles Controversy* (Washington, DC: Brassey's, 2001), p. 150. Doubleday quotes from a letter he received from Slocum on February 19, 1883 in which he states that Meade ended the council by angrily stating, "Well, gentlemen, the question is settled. We will remain here, but I wish to say that I consider this no place to fight a battle" (Doubleday, pp. 184–85). Maj. Gen. John Gibbon, who was at the council, gives a different impression, writing that Meade stated, "quietly but decidedly, 'Such then is the decision.' He said nothing which produced a doubt in my mind as to his being perfectly in accord with the members of the council" (John Gibbon, "The Council of War on the Second Day," Robert Johnson and Clarence Buell, *Battles and Leaders of the Civil War*, Vol. 3, New York: 1884–1888), pp. 313–14. Given that both Doubleday and Slocum had deep grievances against Meade and Gibbon had none, interpretation of the former two is doubtful.

55 Cooper to Lee, June 29, 1863, OR, Vol. 27, Part 1, pp. 75–76.

56 Davis to Lee, June 28, 1863, OR, Vol. 27, Part 1, pp. 76–77.

57 John Dahlgren, *Memoir of Ulrich Dahlgren* (Phildelphia, PA: J. B. Lippincott & Co., 1872), p. 163.

58 William Lawrence Royall, *Some Reminiscences* (New York: Neal Publishing Company, 1909), p. 23; Glenn Tucker, *High Tide at Gettysburg* (New York: Bobbs-Merrill Company, 1958), p. 314.

59 Stanton to Thomas, July 3, 1863, 4:40 p.m., OR, Vol. 27, Part 3, p. 526; Samuel P. Heintzelman diary, entry for July 4, 1863, Samuel P. Heintzelman Papers, Manuscripts Division, Library of Congress, Washington, DC; "Those Intercepted Dispatches," *The New York Times*, July 30, 1863, p. 2.

60 Van Santvoord, p. 227; George H. Sharpe, "Memorial Address of General George H. Sharpe," Seventh Annual Reunion of the 120th NYV Regimental Union—Lieut.-Col. J. Rudolph Tappen (Kingston, NY: The Daily Freeman Steam Printing House, 1875), pp. 9–10.

61 Van Santvoord, pp. 227–28.

62 Gibbon, pp. 313–14.

63 George Gordon Meade, Jr., *The Battle of Gettysburg* (Ambler, PA: 1924), p. 89.

64 Meade, pp. 92–93; Coddington, pp. 530–32.

65 Peter G. Tsouras, *Gettysburg: An Alternate History* (London: Greenhill Books, 1997). This book examines just such a scenario.

66 Fishel, pp. 527, 530.

67 Butterfield to Sharpe, July 3, 1863, NARA, BMI records, RG 393.

68 "Return of casualties in the Army of Northern Virginia, at the battle of Gettysburg, July 1–3," OR, Vol. 27, Part 2, pp. 341–42; Carl Smith, *Gettysburg 1863: High Tide of the Confederacy* (London: Osprey, 1998), pp. 35–36.

69 Sharpe to Butterfield, 8:00 a.m., July 2, 1863, BMI, RG 393; Fishel, p. 685 n. 26, 27. A minor controversy exists about the date of the two notes exchanged between Sharpe and Butterfield on the issue of Ewell's strength. Butterfield initiated the exchange with his note dated July 3. Sharpe replied on the back of Butterfield's note and dated it July 2. Sharpe's note is probably misdated because Babcock's report cites prisoner interrogation, identifying Longstreet's Corps in action with heavy casualties. Longstreet's Corps did not go into combat until the late afternoon of July 2. Babcock was too good to have misidentified I Corps in battle on July 1. Sharpe's note also states that Ewell's Corps was attacking at the time the note was written, shortly after 8:00 a.m. which, indeed, it was. On July 2, Ewell only began his attack at 6:30 p.m.

70 Norton to Williams, September 18, 1863, OR, Vol. 27, Part 1, pp. 202–03; Bill Cameron, "The Signal Corps at Gettysburg," *The Gettysburg Magazine*, Issue No. 3.

71 "The Three Days," *National Tribune*, July 12, 1888.

72 Gates to Doubleday, January 30, 1864, OR, Vol. 27, Part 1, pp. 319–21.

73 Sharpe to Romeyn, July 8, 1863, Sharpe Collection, Kingston Senate House.

74 "Pursuit of the Enemy," *The New York Times*, July 7, 1863.

75 Dahlgren, pp. 175–77.

76 Coddington, p. 565.

77 Sharpe to Williams, 12.30 p.m., no date but probably July 8, 1863, Microcopy 2096, Roll 35, NARA.

78 Sharpe to Williams, 9 a.m., July 9, 1863, Microcopy 2096, Roll 34 and Babcock and/or Cline to Williams, 9 a.m., July 9, 1863, Microcopy 2096, Roll 34, NARA.

79 Sharpe to Williams, July 10, 1863, RG 18, Entry 112, NARA.

80 Coddington, p. 570.

81 Justus Scheibert, *Seven Months in the Rebel States during the North American War 1863* (Tuscaloosa, AL: 1958), pp. 121–22, cited in Coddington, p. 570.

82 Longacre, p. 210.

83 Babcock, untitled summary of military service, John C. Babcock Collection, Library of Congress; Fishel, p. 529.

84 "History of Military Intelligence."

85 Fishel, p. 571.

Chapter Seven: "This Period of Inaction"

1 Sharpe to Jansen Hasbrouck, July 18, 1863, Sharpe Collection, Senate House State Historical Site, Kingston, NY.

2 Homer, *The Iliad*, tr. Robert Fagles, Book 13, pp. 908–12; Field Marshal Viscount Montgomery of Alamein, *Memoirs of Field Marshal Montgomery*, 1958.

3 Seward B. Osborne, ed., *The Civil War Diaries of Col. Theodore B. Gates, 20th New York State Militia* (Hightstown, NJ: Longstreet House, 1991), diary entries for 17, 21, 28, 29–31 July 1863,

pp. 97–100. Hereafter, Gates Diary. Patrick makes no mention of this situation in his diary. The day after Gettysburg (July 5) Gates gave Sharpe several letters to be forwarded to Kingston.

4   Gates Diary, diary entries for December 18–19, 25, 1863, pp. 118–19.

5   Theodore B. Gates, *The War of the Rebellion* (New York, 1884), p. 534. On February 13, 1864, Gates, eight officers, and 161 enlisted men left on a 30-day veterans' furlough to be greeted with great enthusiasm by the people of Kingston; in Albany they were seated in the State Assembly and honored with a resolution admitting them to "the privileges of the floor of the house."

6   Kendig to Manning, August 15, 1863; Manning to Williams, August 15, 1863; endorsement by Sharpe, August 15, 1863, Military Personnel File of Frederick L. Manning, NARA.

7   Sharpe to Jansen Hasbrouck, July 28, 1863, Sharpe Collection.

8   C. Van Santvoord, *The One Hundred and Twentieth Regiment, New York State Volunteers: A Narrative of its Services in the War for the Union* (Rondout, NY: Press of the Kingston Freeman, 1894), p. 82.

9   New York State Military Museum and Veterans Research Center, undated newspaper clipping, "120th Regiment Infantry New York Volunteers," https://dmna.ny.gov/historic/reghist/civil/infantry/120thInf/120thInfCWN.htm

10 Sharpe to Jansen Hasbrouck, September 18, 1863, Sharpe Collection.

11 Edwin C. Fishel, *The Secret War for the Union* (Boston: Houghton Mifflin Company, 1996), pp. 540–43.

12 Sharpe to Humphreys, October 28 & December 11, 1863, Microcopy 2096, Box 45, NARA.

13 Ross to Kilpatrick, August 28, 1863, OR, Vol. 29, p. 105.

14 Grant, p. 770.

15 Fishel, p. 541.

16 William B. Feis, *Grant's Secret War for the Union: The Intelligence War from Belmont to Appomattox* (Lincoln: University of Nebraska Press, 2002), p. 198; John C. Babcock, Record of Military Service, John C. Babcock Collection, Library of Congress.

17 Custer to Pleasonton, August 13, 1863, OR, Vol. 29, Part 2, pp. 38–39.

18 Kilpatrick to Cohen, August 17, 1863, OR, Vol. 29, Part 2, p. 61; Pleasonton to Humphreys, August 18, 1863, OR, Vol. 29, Part 2, pp. 67–68; Smith to Kilpatrick, August 28, 1863, OR, Vol. 29, Part 2, p. 106.

19 Marsena R. Patrick, *Inside Lincoln's Army: The Diary of General Marsena R. Patrick, Provost Marshal General, Army of the Potomac* (New York: Thomas Yoseloff, 1964), p. 279, diary entry for August 10, 1863; Sharpe to Jansen Hasbrouck, August 21, 1863, Sharpe Collection.

20 "From Meade's Army," *Sunbury American*, August 8, 1863 (Sunbury, PA), p. 3.

21 Beckwith to Sharpe, August 13, 1863, OR, Vol. 29, Part 2, pp. 40–41& NARA, RG 393, Part 1, Entry 4033, pp. 400–02; Sharpe to Williams, August 13, 1863, NARA, RG 393, Part 1, Entry 4033, p. 102.

22 Memorandum by Sharpe, August 22, 1863, NARA, RG 393, Part 1, Entry 4028–4049.

23 Sharpe to Warren, August 23, 1863, NARA, Microcopy 504, Roll 198.

24 Statement of Lieut. Charles H. Shepherd, February 2, 1863 & Statement of Anne Jones, March 14, 1864, NARA, RG 94, Entry 286, Special File No. 19, Box 1 of 2. Jones would spend three months in the Capitol Prison where the warden would state that she received more privileges than any other female prisoner had ever had. Due to the intervention of Rep. (D) Fernando Wood on her behalf, Lincoln gave her a pardon since no evidence of spying was ever brought to light. She eventually did serve as a nurse at Vicksburg in 1864.

25 "Confiscation of Immoral Material," *The Semi-Wisconsin* (Milwaukee, WI), December 30, 1863, p. 1. "Application for Miss Annie E. Jones to remain with the Army," August 18, 1863 & Sharpe's negative endorsement, August 20, 1863, NARA, RG 393, Part 1, Entry 4036, p. 23.

26 "120th Regiment Infantry New York Volunteers, Civil War Newspaper Clippings," Unit History Project, https://dmna.ny.gov/historic/reghist/civil/infantry/120thInf/120thInfCWN.htm.

27 Babcock's Journal, RG 393, Part 1, Entry 3988, pp. 1–133.

28 "Rebel News—General Lee's Army," undated *New York Herald* article, probably early September 1863, Babcock's Journal, RG 393, Part 1, Entry 3988, pp. 146–47.

29 Sharpe to Humphreys, August 4, 1864, OR, Vol. 29, Part 2, p. 4; Lee to Davis, August 17, 1863, Robert E. Lee, *Lee's Dispatches: Unpublished Letters of Robert E. Lee, C. S. A., to Jefferson Davis and the War Department of the Confederate States of America 1862–1865*, Douglas Southhall Freeman, ed. (Baton Rouge: Louisiana State University Press, 1957), pp. 122–24.

30 Sharpe to Humphreys, August 4, 1864, OR, Vol. 29, Part 2, p. 4.

31 Sharpe to Humphreys, August 4, 1864, OR, Vol. 29, Part 2, p. 4; Walter H. Taylor, *General Lee: His Campaigns in Virginia, 1861–1865* (Lincoln: University of Nebraska, 1994) pp. 219–20.

32 Sharpe to Humphreys, August 4, 1863, NARA, Microcopy 2096, Roll 34; OR, Vol. 29, Part 2, pp. 3–4

33 "From Gen. Meade's Army," *Sunbury American* (Sunbury, PA), August 22, 1863, p. 3; Humphreys to 1st Corps Commander, August 15, 1863, OR, Vol. 29, Part 2, p. 49; George Gordon Meade, *The Life and Letters of George Gordon Meade*, Vol. 2 (New York: Charles Scribner's Sons, 1913), p. 143.

34 McPhail to Sharpe, August 17, 1863, NARA, M2096, Roll 34.

35 Sharpe to Humphreys, August 23, 1963, NARA, Entry 112 and RG 393, Entry 3980.

36 Sharpe to Humphreys, August 20, 1863, NARA, Microcopy 2096, Boxes 34 & 45; August 24 & 29, 1863, NARA, Microcopy 2096, Roll 45; September 1, 1863; NARA, Entry 112 and RG 393, Entry 3980.

37 Sharpe & Babcock to Humphreys, September 12, 1863, NARA, Entry 112 and RG 393, Entry 3980.

38 James Longstreet, *From Manassas to Appomattox: Memoirs of the Civil War in America* (New York: Mallard Press, 1991), p. 435.

39 Babcock's Journal, entry for September 9, 1863, NARA, RG 393, Entry 3988, p. 27.

40 Sharpe to Humphreys, September 9, 1863, NARA, Microcopy 2096, Roll 45.

41 Babcock's Journal, entry for September 9, 1863, NARA, RG 393, Entry 3988, p. 29.

42 Sharpe to Humphreys, September 14 and 15, 1863, NARA, Microcopy 2096, Rolls 34 & 45; Meade to Halleck, September 14, 1863, OR, Vol. 29, Part 2, pp. 177–78; Sharpe to Humphreys, September 18, NARA, Microcopy 2096, Roll 45.

43 Meade to Halleck 10:30 p.m., September 14, 1863, OR, Vol. 29, Part 2, pp. 179–189.

44 Sharpe to Jansen Hasbrouck, September 18, 1863, Sharpe Collection.

45 Sharpe to Humphreys, September 14, 1863, Entry 112 and RG 393, Entry 3980; Sharpe to Humphreys, October 15, 1863, NARA, Microcopy 2096, Box 45; Garfield to Granger, September 16, 1863, OR, Vol. 30, Part 3, p. 687; Fishel, pp. 541–42; Rosecrans to Meade, October 18, 1863, OR, Vol. 30, Part 4, p. 456.

46 Sharpe to Humphreys, October 1, 1863; OR, Vol. 29, Part 2, pp. 28, 118, & 126.

47 Sharpe to Humphreys, October 4, 1863, Entry 112 and RG 393, Entry 3980.

48 McPhail to Sharpe, October 4, 1864, NARA, Microcopy 2906, Roll 35.

49 Meade to Halleck, October 7, 1863, OR, Vol. 29, Part 2, p. 262; Halleck to Meade, October 7, 1863; OR, Series 1, Vol. 29, Part 2, p. 262; Sharpe to Humphreys, October 8, 1863, NARA, Microcopy 2096, Roll 45; Sharpe to Humphreys, October 8, 1863, NARA, Microcopy 2096, Roll 45.

50 Sharpe to Humphreys, October 10, 1863, NARA, Microcopy 2096, Box 45; Meade to Halleck, October 10, 1863, OR, Vol. 29, Part 2, p. 279.

51 Graham to Sharpe, October 19, 1863, OR, Vol. 29, Part 2, p. 358; NARA, Microcopy 2096, Roll 35.

52 Sharpe to Graham, October 16, 1863, NARA, Microcopy 504, Roll 198.

53 Meade to Halleck and Sharpe to Humphreys, October 23, 1863, Vol. 29, Part 2, pp. 370–71, Microcopy 504, Roll 198.

54 Lincoln to Halleck, October 24, 1863, Vol. 29, Part 2, pp. 375–76.

55 Lee to Longstreet, October 26, 1863, cited in Longstreet, p. 470.

56 Sharpe to Humphreys endorsed by Meade to Halleck, October 23, 1863, OR, Vol. 29, Part 2, p. 592. Sharpe to Jansen Hasbrouck, February 24, 1864, Sharpe Collection.

57 Sharpe to Humphreys, November 29, 1863, OR, Vol. 29, Part 2, p. 512.

58 Marsena Patrick, *Inside Lincoln's Army: The Diary of Marsena Rudolph Patrick, Provost Marshal General, Army of the Potomac*, diary entry for October 5, 1863 (New York: Thomas Yoseloff, 1964), p. 292.

59 "Reunions of the Blue and Gray," *The Atlanta Constitution*, May 27, 1894; "Story by General Sharpe," *Weekly Leader*, Kingston, NY, June 14, 1902; "Tales Worth Telling," *The Times* (Philadelphia), June 3, 1902. Sometime between the first article in 1891 relating his incident and those of 1902, the 137th RI became the 147th RI.

60 "Army of the Potomac—Interesting Items," *National Republican*, August 28, 1863, p. 2.

61 Report of Capt. Abram L. Lockwood, October 12, 1863, OR, Vol. 29, pp. 328–29.

62 Van Santvoord, p. 90.

63 Report of Captain Lockwood.

64 Sharpe to Jansen Hasbrouck, October 18, 1863, Sharpe Collection.

65 Van Santvoord, p. 168.

66 Sharpe to Jansen Hasbrouck, October 18, 1863, Sharpe Collection.

67 Humphreys to Sharpe, November 1, 1863, NARA, Microcopy 2096, Box 45.

68 Meade to Halleck, November 2, 1863, OR, Vol. 29, Part 2, pp. 409–10.

69 Meade to Halleck, November 4, 1863, OR, Vol. 29, Part 2, p. 415.

70 Sharpe to Patrick, November 10, 1863, NARA, RG 504, Entry 303; Sharpe to Humphreys, November 11, 1863, NARA, Microcopy 2096, Box 45.

71 Lee to Davis, November 12, 1863, OR, Vol. 29, Part 2, p. 832.

72 Lee to Davis & Lee to Seddon, November 12, 1863, OR, Vol. 29, pp. 832–33.

73 Pleasonton to Humphreys, November 15, 1863, OR, Vol. 29, p. 927.

74 Sharpe to Humphreys, November 14, 1863, NARA, Microcopy 2096, Box 45.

75 Humphreys to Meade, November 14, 1863, OR, Vol. 29, Part 2, p. 454.

76 Sharpe to Humphreys, November 16, 1863, NARA, Microcopy 2096, Box 45. "Uproar in Fredericksburg 150 years later, Part 2: the end of Union, March 11, 1861," Fredericksburg Remembered; https://fredericksburghistory.wordpress.com/2011/03/10/uproar-in-fredericksburg-150-years-later-part-2-the-end-of-union-march-11-1861/, accessed November 9, 2015. Roger Pickenpaugh, *Captives in Gray: The Civil War Prisons of the Union* (Tuscaloosa, AL: University of Alabama Press, 2009), p. 7.

77 Sharpe to Humphreys, November 19, 1863, NARA, Microcopy 2096, Box 45.

78 Lawton to Lee, November 12, 1863, OR, Vol. 29, Part 2, pp. 784–85.

79 Sharpe to Humphreys, November 19, 1863, NARA, Microcopy 2096, Box 45.

80 Sharpe to Humphreys, November 20 & 22, 1863, NARA Microcopy 2096, Box 45.

81 Sharpe to Humphreys, November 21, 1863, NARA Microcopy 2096, Box 45.

82 Patrick, diary entry for November 26, 1863, which covered the period through December 2, 1863, pp. 313–19.

83 Patrick Diary, entry for December 12, 1863, p. 323.

84 Clifford Dowdey and Louis H. Manarin, eds, *The Wartime Papers of Robert E. Lee* (New York: Da Capo Press, 1987), p. 693; Ryan, "Questioning Rebels pays off at Gettysburg," ibid.

85 Thomas J. Ryan, "Questioning Rebels pays off at Gettysburg"; OR, Serial 3, Vol. 4, p. 118; Sharpe to Martindale, December 12, 1863, NARA, Microcopy 2096, Box 45; NARA, Military Service Record of Brevet Maj. Gen. George H. Sharpe.

86 Sharpe to Humphreys, December 9 & 14, 1863, NARA, Microcopy 2096, Box 45.

87 Babcock Report, December 12, 1863, NARA, Microcopy 2096, Box 45; Sharpe to Humphreys, December 11 & 12, 1863, NARA, Microcopy 2096, Box 45.

88 McEntee to Sharpe, May 31, 1863, NARA, Microcopy 2096, Roll 34.

89 Sharpe to Humphreys, September 30, 1863; NARA, Microcopy 2096, Roll 45; Peter G. Tsouras, ed., *Scouting for Grant and Meade: The Reminiscences of Judson Knight, Chief of Scouts, Army of the Potomac* (New York: Skyhorse Publishing, 2013), pp. 50–53, contains Carney's own account of his capture. That capture is also referenced in Humphreys to Warren, August 21, 1863, OR, Vol. 29, Part 2, p. 84.

90 Kilpatrick to Cohen (Pleasonton), August 21, 1863, OR, Vol. 33, p. 84; Taylor to King, August 4, 1863, OR, Vol. 33, p. 63. Sharpe's interrogation of Curtis Merritt, undated but apparently in the winter, on the flyleaf of Babcock's Journal.

91 Special Order No. 127, Office of the Provost Marshal General, December 23, 1863, NARA, RG 393, Part 1, Entry 4052.

92 Meade to Halleck, December 2, 1863, OR, Vol. 29, Part 2, p. 571.

93 McEntee to Williams, December 28, 1863 and McEntee to Patrick, January 9, 1864, NARA, Military Service Record of John M. McEntee (NARA); Sharpe to Williams, January 5, 1864, Military Personnel File of George H. Sharpe; Special Order No. 31, January 21, 1864, War Department, Military Service Record of George H. Sharpe; Gates Diary, entry for February 15, 1864, pp. 126–27. Gates had returned to Kingston with the men who had reenlisted and were thus awarded furloughs.

94 Fishel, pp. 195, 427–28, 455.

95 McPhail to Sharpe, December 31, 1863, NARA, Microcopy 2096, Box 34.

96 Sharpe, December 18, 1863, NARA, Microcopy 345, RG 106.

97 Sharpe, January 9, 1864, NARA, Microcopy 345, RG 109, Roll 0282.

98 Sharpe to Comstock, January 1867, Van Lew Papers, Rare Books and Manuscripts Division, New York Public Library.

99 *New York Herald*, August 14, 1862, as quoted in Varon, *Southern Lady*, p. 88; "The Prisoners from Richmond," *The New York Times*, August 17, 1862, p. 5.

100 Varon, *Southern Lady*, p. 111.

Chapter Eight: Enter Grant

1 Sharpe to Williams, January 5, 1864, Military Service Record of George H. Sharpe (NARA); Special Order No. 31, January 21, 1864, War Department; Gates Diary, entry for February 15, 1864, pp. 126–27. Gates had returned to Kingston with the men who had reenlisted and were thus awarded furloughs; NARA, Microcopy 473, Roll 269, p. 445, also Microcopy 504, Roll 303; C. Van Santvoord, *One Hundred and Twentieth Regiment New York State Volunteers, A Narrative of its Services in the War for the Union* (Cornwallville, NY: Hope Farm Press, 1983), p. 264.

2 *The National Tribune*, April 29, 1886.

3 "The Knickerbocker Kitchen," *The New York Times*, May 1, 1864; C. A. Winchell, "Old Timer's Civil War Notes," *The Kingston Daily Freeman*, December 29, 1961, p. 2.

4   Sharpe to Jansen Hasbrouck, March 16, 1864, Sharpe Collection; Special Orders No. 84, War Department; Adjutant General's Office, Washington, February 20, 1864, Military Service Record of C. D. Westbrook (NARA); Van Santvoord, p. 235.
5   Sharpe to Humphreys, January 1, 1964, NARA, Microcopy 2096, Box 45.
6   Patrick, Special Order No. 1, January 7, 1864, Provost Marshal Department, NARA, RG 393, Part 1, Entry 4052.
7   Sharpe to Humphreys, NARA, January 5, 1864, NARA, Microcopy 2096, Roll 34; January 1, 3, 4, 5 (2), 8, 10, 1864, RG 2096, Rolls 34 & 45.
8   McPhail to Sharpe, January 4, 16 (2), 1863, and McEntee to Patrick, February 2, 1863, NARA, Microcopy 2096, Box 34.
9   McPhail to Sharpe, March 25, 1863, NARA, Microcopy 2096, Roll 34.
10 McPhail to Sharpe, February 14 & March 24, 1864, NARA, Microcopy 2096, Roll 34.
11 Sharpe to Humphreys, January 10, 1864, NARA, Entry 112 and RG 393, Entry 3980; Lee to Davis, January 11, 1864, OR, Vol. 33, pp. 1076–77.
12 Sharpe to Humphreys, March 1, 1864, NARA, Microcopy 2096, Roll 34.
13 Abstracts from the field return of the Army of Northern Virginia, January–April 1864, OR, Vol. XXXIII; "The 1st Virginia (Irish) Battalion at Kernstown, 1862," http://irishamericancivilwar.com/2012/07/22/the-1st-virginia-irish-battalion-at-kernstown-1862/, accessed April 6, 2014.
14 Patrick McEneany, "Gettysburg: Snapshot Impressions of a Great Battle as Told by the Chief of Orderlies," *The National Tribune*, March 22, 1900, p. 7. McEneany was assigned to the headquarters, Army of the Potomac, from December 1862 to March 1864 when he transferred to the scouts of the BMI.
15 Sharpe to Humphreys, February 26, 1864, NARA, Microcopy 2096, Box 45.
16 Sharpe to Humphreys, March 3, 1864, NARA, Microcopy 2096, Box 45.
17 McPhail to Sharpe, February 14, 1863, OR, Vol. 33, p. 559; Library of Congress, Papers of U. S. Grant, Series 5, Reel 28, Vol. 94, p. 280; OR, Vol. 33, pp. 1075 & 1135.
18 "Last Days of the Confederacy," *New York Times*, January 21, 1876.
19 Elizabeth R. Varon, *Southern Lady, Yankee Spy: The True Story of Elizabeth Van Lew, A Union Agent in the Heart of the Confederacy* (New York: Oxford University Press, 2003), pp. 111–12.
20 Van Lew to Butler, January 30, 1863, OR, Vol. 33, pp. 519–21.
21 Theodore Lyman, entry for February 5, 1864, *Meade's Headquarters: From the Wilderness to Appomattox* (Boston: The Atlantic Monthly Press, 1922), p. 68.
22 Sedgwick to Butler, February 4, 1863, OR, Vol. 33, pp. 512–13. Van Lew to Butler, January 30, 1863, OR, Vol. 33, pp. 519–21. Halleck to Sedgwick, February 4, 1863, OR, Vol. 33, p. 514.
23 Van Lew to Butler, January 30; Butler to Stanton, February 5, 1863, OR, Vol. 33, pp. 519–51.
24 Statement of George H. Sharpe in U.S. Senate, Report No. 821, 48th Congress, 1st Session, Report to accompany bill S. 1192, July 1, 1884, Pension File of William J. Lee; Statement of George H. Sharpe in U.S. Senate, Report No. 467, 50th Congress, 1st Session, Report to accompany bill S. 1192, March 6 1889, Pension File of Judson Knight (NARA); Sharpe to Hancock, May 2, 1864, OR, Vol. 34, Part 2, p. 3.4
25 Judson Knight, "How Scouts Worked: Serg't Knight Tells How They Went About Getting Information," *The National Tribune*, March 2, 1892; Sharpe to Butler, March 3, 1864, NARA, Microcopy 504, Roll 303.
26 Knight, March 2, 1892.
27 John Dahlgren, *Memoir of Ulric Dahlgren* (Philadelphia: J. B. Lippincott & Co., 1872), pp. 198–200.
28 Undated extract of unidentified document, in the hand of George H. Sharpe, BMI.
29 Conversation with William Feis, September 27, 2006.

30 William Gilmore Beymer, *Scouts and Spies of the Civil War* (Lincoln: University of Nebraska Press, 2003), pp. 71–72.

31 Williams to Pleasonton, February 11, 1864, OR, Vol. 33, pp. 52–55; Samuel J. Martin, *Kill-Cavalry: The Life of Union General Hugh Judson Kilpatrick* (Mechanicsburg, PA: Stackpole Books, 2000), pp. 148–49.

32 Martin, pp. 150–51.

33 Feis, p. 304 n. 38. McEntee and Cline accompanied Kilpatrick's column and were not with Dahlgren on the expedition; Babcock, untitled record of military service, Babcock Collection; Patrick Diary, entry for February 27, 1864, pp. 338–41; Babcock to Dahlgren, undated, but probably February 26, 1864, OR, Vol. 33, Part 1, p. 221; Aylett to Winder, March 15, 1864, OR, Series 2, Vol. 6, Part 1, p. 1053.

34 Sharpe to Dahlgren, February 28, 1864, NARA, Microcopy 504, Roll 303.

35 Sharpe to Dahlgren, February 28, 1864, NARA, Microcopy 504, Roll 303.

36 Judson Knight, "Scouting Adventures," *The National Tribune*, July 21, 1892.

37 Sharpe to Pleasonton, February 29, 1864, OR, Vol. 33, Part 1, p. 66; Mitchell to Whitaker, March 15, 1864, OR, Vol. 33, Part 1, pp. 194–97; Duane Shultz, *The Dahlgren Affair: Terror and Conspiracy in the Civil War* (New York: W. W. Norton & Company, 1999), p. 109.

38 Sharpe to Jansen Hasbrouck, March 16, 1864, Sharpe Collection; Sharpe to Humphreys, March 2, 1864, NARA, Microcopy 2096, Box 45.

39 Fishel, p. 543; Aylett to Winder, March 15, 1864, OR, Series 2, Vol. 6, Part 1, pp. 1053–54; Schultz, p. 149; deposition of John McEntee, March 19, 1887, Military Pension File of Anson B. Carney (NARA).

40 Patrick Diary, entry for March 12, 1864, pp. 347–48; Babcock, untitled record of military service, Babcock Collection.

41 Edward C. Garrigan, "One of the Five Hundred: Col. Ulric Dahlgren's Command, and What Became of It," *The National Tribune*, October 25, 1894. Garrigan was a trooper in the Harris Light Cavalry and a participant in the raid. He is the only one to suggest that Martin became so drunk that he accidently misled Dahlgren. He also states that the event that led to Martin's hanging by Dahlgren was their arrival in front of a Confederate fort instead of the rain-swollen James River where a ford had been expected. Other eyewitnesses provided their testimony closer in time than Garrigan. A. B. Carney, "In Tight Places: Adventures of One of Our Scouts on the Kilpatrick Raid," *The National Tribune*, April 5, 1894; J. W. Landegon, "He Was There: And Proceeds to Tell How Richmond Was Not Entered," *The National Tribune*, May 31, 1894. "The Dahlgren Papers Revisited," *Columbiad for America's Civil War* http://www.historynet.com/acw/bldahlgrenpapersrevisited. In his essay, Sears states that the black man hanged by Dahlgren was the guide provided by Babcock.

42 General Orders No. 100, April 24, 1863, Paragraph 97, OR, Series 3, Vol. 3, p. 158.

43 Sears, "The Dahlgren Papers Revisited," Sears, in this comprehensive analysis, presents a convincing case that the orders found on Dahlgren were original and not forged.

44 Report of Capt. F. B. Mitchell, March 15, 1864, OR, Vol. 33, p. 197.

45 Dahlgren, p. 235. Bartley's letter was published on December 29, 1864.

46 Sears, "The Dahlgren Papers Revisited," ibid.

47 Schultz, p. 260.

48 Meade to Mrs. Meade, March 6, 1864, George Meade, *The Life and Letters of George Gordon Meade* (New York: Charles Scribner's Sons, 1913), Vol. 2, p. 170.

49 Meade to Mrs. Meade, April 18, 1864, *Life and Letters of Meade*, pp. 190–91.

50 Sharpe to McEntee, March 11, 1864, OR, Vol. 33, p. 666.

51 Aylett to Winder, March 15, 1864, OR, Series 2, Vol. 6. Part 1, pp. 1053–54.

52 Grant, pp. 408–10.

53 John C. Babcock, untitled record of military service, John C. Babcock Collection, Library of Congress.

54 General Order No. 155, April 8, 1864, Washington, D. C., War Department, Adjutant General's Office, OR, Vol. 33, p. 802.

55 Bruce Catton, *Grant Takes Command* (Boston: Little, Brown and Company, 1968), p. 135.

56 Merlin E. Summer, ed., *The Diaries of Cryus B. Comstock* (Dayton, OH: Morningside House, Inc., 1987), p. v; Catton, *Grant Takes Command*, pp. 125 & 134.

57 Lloyd Lewis, *Captain Sam Grant* (Boston: Little, Brown and Company, 1950), pp. 408–09.

58 "Sold Abraham Lincoln Appoints Leet to Ulysses S. Grant's Staff and Gives Him a Promotion As Grant Arrives in Washington to Take Control of All Union Forces in 1864," http://www.raabcollection.com/abraham-lincoln-autograph/abraham-lincoln-signed-sold-abraham-lincoln-appoints-leet-ulysses-s-grant, accessed November 10, 2015.

59 Meade to Mrs. Meade, March 8 & 22, 1864, *Life and Letters of Meade*, pp. 176, 182; U. S. Grant, *Grant: Personal Memoirs of U. S. Grant, Selected Letters 1839–1865* (New York: The Library of America, 1990), p. 508.

60 Meade to Henry A. Cramm, November 24, 1864, *Life and Letters of Meade*, p. 246.

61 Sharpe to Jansen Hasbrouck, March 16, 1864, Sharpe Collection.

62 Theodore B. Gates, *The War of the Rebellion* (New York: 1884), p. 477; Fishel, p. 543; "Gen. Grant Returned to the Army," *Pittsburgh Daily Commercial*, May 29, 1864, p. 3; Leet to Adjutant General, May 3, 1864, NARA, Microcopy 1064, RG 94.

63 Patrick to Canby, March 16, 1864, Entry 112 and RG 393, Entry 3980.

64 War Department orders, April 13, 1864, Military Service Record of John McEntee, NARA.

65 Sharpe to Jansen Hasbrouck, March 16, 1864, Sharpe Collection, Senate House State Historical Site, Kingston, NY.

66 Sharpe to Jansen Hasbrouck, March 16, 1864, Sharpe Collection.

Chapter Nine: The Overland Campaign

1 Sharpe to Humphreys, April 2, 1864, NARA, RG 108, Entry 112; OR, Vol. 33, p. 1234.

2 Lee to Davis, April 5, 1864, and Lee to Bragg, April 13, 1864, OR, Vol. 33, pp. 1260–61, 1278–79; Abstracts from the return of the Army of the Potomac for the months of January and March,1864, and abstract from tri-monthly return of the Army of the Potomac for April 30, 1864, OR, Vol. 33, pp. 462, 777, 1036; Sharpe to Humphreys, April 22, 1864, NARA, RG 108, Entry 112.

3 Abstract from the return of the Ninth Army Corps, for the month of April 1864, OR, Vol. 33, p. 1046; Ulysses S. Grant, "Preparing for the Campaign of '64," *Battles and Leaders of the Civil War*, Vol. 4 (New York: Castle Books, 1956), p. 103.

4 Sharpe to Humphreys, April 21, 1864, NARA, RG 108, Entry 112; Lee to Davis, March 12, 1864, in Clifford Dowdey and Louis H. Manarin, *The Wartime Papers of Robert E. Lee* (Boston: Little, Brown, 1961), p. 698.

5 Sharpe to Humphreys, April 18 and 19, 1864, NARA, RG 108, Entry 112.

6 Judson Knight, "How Scouts Worked: Serg't Knight Tells How They Went About Getting Information," *The National Tribune*, March 2, 1893.

7 No orders have been found on Manning's assignment, but his regimental field and muster roll for March and April 1864 show him on detached service to Fortress Monroe. Also in early April all intelligence reports he had often written in his own hand for Sharpe's signature ceased; Special Order No. 39, Patrick to McEntee, April 7, 1864, RG 393, Part 1, Entry 4052; Brig. Gen. E. R. S. Canby to McEntee, April 13, 1864, NARA, Military Service Record of Lieut. Col. John M. McEntee.

8   Theodore Lyman, *Meade's Army: The Private Notebooks of Lt. Col. Theodore Lyman*, edited by David W. Lowe (Kent, OH: Kent State University Press, 2007), p. 128.

9   George H. Sharpe, "Scouts," March 15, 1864, NARA, RG 393 and Microcopy 2096, Box 45; Meade to Halleck, March 16, 1864, OR, Vol. 33, pp. 681–82; Douglas Southall Freeman, *R. E. Lee: A Biography*, Vol. 2 (New York: Charles Scribner's Sons, 1945), pp. 259–61.

10 Williams to Pleasonton, March 16, 1863, OR, Vol. 33, pp. 682–83; Kilpatrick to Smith, March 21, 1864, OR, Vol. 33, p. 708. Since one quarter of Stuart's artillery horses had died in the winter, it is unlikely that his cavalry mounts would have been in good enough shape for a raid at the end of a hard winter.

11 James Longstreet, *From Manassas to Appomattox: Memoirs of the Civil War in America* (New York: Mallard Press, n.d), p. 547; Sharpe to Humphreys, April 1 and 3, 1864, NARA, RG 108, Entry 112; Lee to Davis, April 5, 1864, OR, Vol. 33, p. 1261.

12 Lee to Bragg, April 16, 1864, OR, Vol. 33, p. 1286; Sharpe to Humphreys, April 17, 1864, RG 108, Entry 112; Longstreet, p. 548; Sharpe to Humphreys, NARA, April 22, 1864, RG 108, Entry 112.

13 Lee to Davis, March 30, 1864, OR, Vol. 33, p. 1244; Sharpe to Humphreys, April 25, 1864, NARA, RG 108, Entry 112.

14 Bragg to Lee, April 16, 1864, OR, Vol. 33, p. 1286; Lee to Davis, April 23, 1864, OR, Vol. 33, pp. 1306–07; Sharpe to Humphreys, April 26, 1864, NARA, RG 108, Entry 112; "April 28, 1864—Reconnaissance to Madison County Court House, Va.," OR, Vol. 33, p. 314; McEntee to Sharpe, April 28 and 29, 1864, OR, Vol. 33, pp. 1003, 1014; James Longstreet, *From Manassas to Appomattox* (Philadelphia: J. B. Lippincott and Co., 1896), p. 553. Longstreet cites the location of Mechanicsville, but that location is in the Shenandoah Valley. The *West Point Atlas of the Civil War*, Vol. 1, plate 120, shows his concentration at Mechanicsburg immediately south of Gordonsville. The confusion was apparently Longstreet's.

15 "Miss Elizabeth Van Lew," *Chicago Daily Tribune*, April 14, 1887, p. 10. Butler's troops attacked on May 2 and overran Fort Darling's outworks, but command difficulties threw away the advantage. Beauregard gathered his forces and threw the Army of the James back.

16 "Brave Women—Shall They Be Rewarded?" *National Republican*, April 12, 1864, p. 2.

17 "Miss Elizabeth Van Lew."

18 "Miss Elizabeth Van Lew"; Maddox to Sharpe, April 1864, NARA, Microcopy 2096, Roll 34; Sharpe to Humphreys, April 21, 1864, NARA, RG 108, Entry 112.

19 Lee to Bragg, April 7, 1864, OR, Vol. 33, p. 1266.

20 Lee to Davis, April 8, 1864, OR, Vol. 33, p. 1268.

21 Thomas Nelson Conrad, *The Rebel Scout: A Thrilling History of Scouting Life in the Southern Army* (Westminster, MD: Heritage Books, 2009), pp. 44–45.

22 Lee to Davis, April 9, 1864, OR, Vol. 33, p. 1269.

23 Lee to Davis, April 12, 1864, OR, Vol. 33, p. 1276.

24 Lee to Breckinridge, April 19, 1864, OR, Vol. 33, p. 1295; Lee to Davis, April 29, 1864, OR, Vol. 33, p. 1326; William Tidwell, *Come Retribution: The Confederate Secret Service and the Assassination of Lincoln* (Jackson: University of Mississippi, 1988), p. 109.

25 Lee to Davis, April 30, 1864, OR, Vol. 33, pp. 1331–32.

26 Theodore Lyman, entry for March 1, 1864, *Meade's Headquarters: From the Wilderness to Appomattox* (Boston: The Atlantic Monthly Press, 1922), p. 77.

27 Lee to Seddon, April 30, 1864, OR, Vol. 33, pp. 1330–31.

28 Lee to Davis, April 18, 1864, OR, Vol. 33, pp. 1290–91.

29 U. S. Grant to Halleck, April 29, 1864, *The Papers of Ulysses S. Grant* (Carbondale: Southern Illinois University Press, 1967), Vol. 10, p. 371.

30　Sharpe to Humphreys, May 1, 1864, NARA, RG 108, Entry 112; Sharpe to Humphreys, May 4, 1864, OR, Vol. 36, Part 2, p. 72.

31　Sharpe to Humphreys, Feis, p. 206; Sharpe to Hancock, May 2, 1864, OR, Vol. 36, p. 34.

32　OR, Vol. 36, Part 2, pp. 371–72; Porter, *Campaigning With Grant* (New York: The Century Co., 1887), p. 44.

33　Judson Knight, "How Scouts Worked: Serg't Knight Tells How They went About Getting Information," *The National Tribune*, March 9, 1893.

34　John Michael Priest, *Nowhere to Run: The Wilderness, May 4th & 5th, 1864* (Shippensburg, PA: The White Mane Publishing Company, Inc., 1995), p. 23.

35　Meade to Grant, May 5, 1864, OR, Vol. 36, Part 2, pp. 404–05.

36　Edwin C. Fishel, *The Secret War for the Union: The Untold Story of Military Intelligence in the Civil War* (Boston: Houghton-Mifflin Co., 1996), p. 544; Knight, "How Scouts Worked: Serg't Knight Tells How They Went About Getting Information," *The National Tribune*, March 23, 1893.

37　E. J. Edwards, "Grant Whittled During Battle," *Cook County Herald* (Arlington Heights, IL), October 28, 1910.

38　J. H. C. Brewer, "A Story About Grant," *The National Tribune*, June 29, 1890.

39　Grant to Halleck, May 7, 1864, OR, Vol. 36, Part 1, p. 2; Edwin Stanton, "Washington, May 9," *The Jeffersonian* (Stroudsburg, PA), May 12, 1864, p. 1; James H. Wilson, *The Life of John A. Rawlins: Lawyer, Assistant Adjutant-General, Chief of Staff, Major General of Volunteers, and Secretary of War*, letter of May 9, 1864 (New York: The Neale Publishing Co., 1916), p. 218.

40　Knight, *The National Tribune*, May 23, 1893; William D. Matter, "The Federal High Command at Spotsylvania," in Gary Gallagher, ed., *The Spotsylvania Campaign* (Chapel Hill: University of North Carolina Press, 1998) p. 33.

41　"'I Was in the Secret Service of the Army of the Potomac'—Isaac Silver of Spotsylvania County. Part 2." https://npsfrsp.wordpress.com/2010/10/08/i-was-in-the-secret-service-of-the-army-of-the-potomac-%E2%80%93-isaac-silver-of-spotsylvania-county-part-2/.

42　Knight, *The National Tribune*, March 23, 1893.

43　Bruce Catton, *Grant Takes Command* (Boston: Little, Brown and Company, 1969), p. 208.

44　Feis, p. 209; Warren to Meade with endorsement by Meade, May 6, 1864, OR, Vol. 36, Part 2, p. 540; Matter, p. 33.

45　James H. Wilson, *The Life of John A. Rawlins*, p. 218.

46　Matter, pp. 33, 36.

47　Meade to Grant, May 10, 1864, OR, Vol. 36, Part 2, p. 596.

48　Humphreys, pp. 84–85.

49　Knight, *The National Tribune*, April 20, 1983.

50　Anson B. Carney, cited in *Our Boys in Blue: Heroic Deeds, Sketches and Reminiscences of Bradford Country Soldiers in the Civil War*, Vol. 1, 1899, by C. F. Heverely.

51　George H. Sharpe, "The Virginia Campaign: Casualties in the 120th Regt," *Kingston Journal Extra*, May 18, 1864, The Sharpe Collection.

52　Knight, *The National Tribune*, May 30, 1893.

53　Edwin Stanton, "May 19. 9 A. M.," *The Soldier's Journal* (Alexandria, VA), p. 6; Torbert to Williams, May 18, 1863, OR, Vol. 36, Part 1, p. 803.

54　Knight, *The National Tribune*, May 30, 1893.

55　"The Potomac Army," *The Pittsburgh Gazette*, April 22, 1864, p. 3.

56　Knight, *The National Tribune*, May 30, 1893.

57　Knight, *The National Tribune*, April 20, 1893.

58　Sharpe to Humphreys, May 13, 1864, OR, Vol. 36, Part 2, p. 699.

59　Grant to Meade, May 13, 1864, OR, Vol. 36, Part 2, p. 698.

60   Cline to Sharpe, May 13, 1864, OR, Vol. 36, Part 2, p. 699.

61   Cline to Sharpe, May 13, 1864, OR, Vol. 36, Part 2, pp. 699–700.

62   U. S. Grant, *Personal Memoirs of U. S. Grant, Selected Letters (1839–1865)* (The Library of America, 1990), pp. 556–57.

63   Knight, *The National Tribune,* April 20, 1893.

64   Berry Benson, *Civil War Book: Memoirs of a Confederate Scout and Sharpshooter* (Athens: University of Georgia Press, 1992), pp. 84–88.

65   George Meade, *The Life and Letters of George Meade* (New York: Charles Scribner's Sons, 1913), Vol. 2, p. 201.

66   Sharpe to Humphreys, 9 a.m., May 17, 1864, OR, Vol. 36, Part 2, p. 842.

67   Grant to Halleck, May 26, 1864, *The Papers of Ulysses S. Grant*, 10:491.

68   Sharpe to Humphreys, May 22, 1864, OR, Vol. 36, Part 3, p. 80; Sharpe to Humphreys, May 25, 1864, OR, Vol. 36, Part 3, p. 184; Abstract from field return of troops in Hoke's Division, Maj. Gen. Robert F. Hoke commanding, for May 21, 1864, OR, Vol. 36, Part 3, p. 617; Hancock to Williams, May 21, 1864, OR, Vol. 36, Part 3, p. 47; Grant to Halleck, May 25, 1864, OR, Vol. 36, Part 3, p. 184.

69   Patrick to Williams, NARA, RG 393, Part 1, Entry 3032, p. 266. Patrick's report showed the following captures:

From May 1st to May 12th	7, 078
May 12th to July 31st	6,506
July 31st to Aug 31st	573
Aug. 31st to Sept. 30th	78
Sept. 31st to Oct. 31st	1,138
Total	15,373

70   Sharpe to Humphreys, May 26, 1864, OR, Vol. 36, Part 3, pp. 208–09.

71   Lee to Anderson, May 31, 1864, OR, Vol. 36, Part 3, p. 858.

72   Knight, *The National Tribune*, April 20, 1983.

73   Knight, *The National Tribune*, January 12, 1893.

74   Knight, *The National Tribune*, January 19 & 26, 1893.

75   "Last Hours of the Confederacy," *New York Times*, January 21, 1876.

76   Sharpe to Humphreys, June 3, 1864, OR, Vol. 36, Part 3, pp. 527–28.

77   Lyman, entries for June 4 and 7, *Meade's Headquarters*, pp. 153–54.

78   Knight, *The National Tribune*, January 26, 1893.

79   Sharpe to Jansen Hasbrouck, June 7, 1864, Sharpe Collection.

80   Sharpe to Humphreys, June 8, 1864, OR, Vol. 36, Part 3, pp. 696–97.

81   Extract of letter by Patrick, June 10, 1864; NARA, RG, 393, Part 1, Entry 4040.

82   Dana to Stanton, June 9, 1864, OR, Vol. 36, Part 1, p. 93.

83   Wilson, *The Life of John A. Rawlins*, p. 227.

84   Grant to Halleck, May 25, 1864, OR, Vol. 36, p. 183; Ulysses S. Grant, *Personal Memoirs of U.S. Grant, Selected Letters, 1839–1865* (New York: The Library of America, 1990), p. 595. Wilson, *The Life of John A. Rawlins*, pp. 230, 232, 236.

85   Knight, *The National Tribune*, April 20, 1863.

86   Knight, *The National Tribune*, April 27, 1863.

Chapter Ten: Petersburg and Intelligence Overhaul

1   Sharpe to Humphreys, June 11, 1864, OR, Vol. 36, Part 3, p. 747.

2   Grant to Halleck, June 5, 1864, U. S. Grant, *Grant: Personal Memoirs of U. S. Grant, Selected Letters 1839–1865* (New York: The Library of America, 1990), pp. 590–91.

3   Theodore Lyman, *With Grant and Meade From the Wilderness to Appomattox* (Lincoln: University of Nebraska Press, 1994), p. 159.

4   Brig. Gen. Vincent J. Esposito, *The West Point Atlas of American Wars, Vol. I, 1689–1900* (New York: Frederick A. Praeger, Publishers, 1959), Map 137.

5   The Editors of Time-Life Books, *Death in the Trenches: Grant at Petersburg* (Alexandria, VA: Time-Life Books, 1987), p. 35.

6   Earl J. Hess, *In the Trenches of Petersburg: Field Fortifications & Confederate Defeat* (Chapel Hill: University of North Carolina Press, 2009), p. 16; Sharpe to Humphreys, June 14, 1864, OR, Vol. 40, Part 2, p. 19.

7   Judson Knight, *The National Tribune*, "How Scouts Worked: Sergt. Knight Tells How They Went About Getting Information," April 27, 1893.

8   Sharpe to Williams, June 8, 1864, NARA, Microcopy 2096, Roll 34; Williams to Sharpe, June 9, 1864, NARA, RG 108, Entry 112.

9   Marsena R. Patrick, *Inside Lincoln's Army: The Diary of Marsena Rudolph Patrick, Provost Marshal General, Army of the Potomac*, diary entries for June 18–19, 1864 (New York: Thomas Yoseloff, 1964), p. 385.

10   Sharpe to Humphreys, June 17, 1864, OR, Vol. 40, Part 2, p. 119.

11   Sharpe to Humphreys (six reports), June 18, 1864, OR, Vol. 40, Part 2, pp. 158–60.

12   Douglas Southall Freeman, ed., *Lee's Dispatches: Unpublished Letters of General Robert E. Lee, C. S. A., to Jefferson Davis and the War Department of the Confederate States of America 1862–65* (Baton Rouge: Louisiana State University Press, 1994), p. 249.

13   Peter G. Tsouras, *Scouting for Grant and Meade: The Reminiscences of Judson Knight, Chief of Scouts, Army of the Potomac* (New York: Skyhorse Publications, 2014), pp. 192–93.

14   Sharpe to Humphreys, June 19, 1964, OR, Vol. 40, Part 2, p. 212; Meade to Grant, June 20, 1864, OR, Vol. 40, Part 2, p. 233; Sharpe to Humphreys, June 20, 1864, OR, Vol. 40, Part 2, p. 235; Humphreys to Warren, June 21, 1864, OR, Vol. 40, Part 2, pp. 243–44.

15   Peter G. Tsouras, ed., *Scouting for Grant and Meade: The Reminiscences of Judson Knight, Chief of Scouts, Army of the Potomac* (New York: Skyhorse Publications, 2014), pp. 193–94; originally published in the *National Tribune*, May 4, 1893, as a separate article.

16   Sharpe to Humphreys, June 20, 21, 23 and 24, 1864, OR, Vol. 40, Part 2, pp. 235, 271, 306, 336, 337, 375–76; McEntee to Sharpe, June 28, 1864, RG 393, entry 3980; Hancock to Williams, July 1, 1864, OR, Vol. 40, Part 2, p. 566.

17   McEntee to Sharpe, June 28, 1864, OR, Series I, Vol. 37, Part 1, p. 684; William B. Feis, *Grant's Secret Service: The Intelligence War from Belmont to Appomattox* (Lincoln: University of Nebraska Press, 2002), p. 229.

18   McEntee to Sharpe, July 1, 1864, NARA, Microcopy 2096, Roll 34.

19   Grant to Meade, July 3, 1864, Grant Papers, Vol. 11, p. 167; Meade to Grant, July 3, 1864, OR, Vol. 40, Part 2, p. 600; Grant to Halleck, July 3, 1864, Grant Papers, Vol. 11, p. 167.

20   Sharpe to Patrick, July 3, 1864, OR, Vol. 40, Part 2, pp. 600–01; Seward R. Osborne, *The Civil War Diaries of Col. Theodore B. Gates, 20th New York State Militia* (Hightown, NJ: Longstreet House, 1991), diary entries for July 3 and 4, 1864, p. 148; Patrick Diary, entries for July 2 and 3, p. 392.

21   Sharpe to Humphreys, July 4, 1863, OR, Vol. 40, Part 2, p. 620; Grant to Halleck, July 4, 1864, OR, Vol. 40, Part 2, p. 618.

22   James Harrison Wilson, *The Life of John A. Rawlins: Lawyer, Assistant Adjutant-General, Chief of Staff, Major General of Volunteers, and Secretary of War*, letter of July 4, 1864 (Sagwan Press, 2015), p. 241.

23   Grant to Halleck and Halleck to Grant, July 5, 1864, OR, Vol. 40, Part 3, p. 3.

24 Halleck to Grant, July 5, 1864, OR, Vol. 40, Part 3, p. 4.

25 Sharpe to Humphreys, July 5, 1864, OR, Vol. 40, Part 3, pp. 6–7; Meade to Grant, July 5, 1864, OR, Vol. 40, Part 3, p. 5.

26 Grant to Halleck, July 5, 1864, OR, Vol. 40, Part 3, p. 4.

27 Sharpe to Humphreys, July 6, 1864 (two reports), OR, Vol. 40, Part 3, pp. 37–39.

28 Grant to Halleck, July 6, 1864 (two messages), OR, Vol. 40, Part 3, p. 31.

29 Halleck to Grant, July 6, 1864, OR, Vol. 40, Part 3, pp. 31–32.

30 Sheridan to Humphreys, July 6, 1864, OR, Vol. 40, Part 3, p. 50; Halleck to Grant, July 8, 1864, OR, Vol. 40, Part 3, p. 72.

31 McEntee to Sharpe, July 13, 1864, NARA, Microcopy 2096, Roll 34; Sharpe to McEntee, July 10, 1864, NARA, Microcopy 504, Roll 303; *Jubal Early, Jubal Early's Memoirs: Autobiographical Sketch and Narrative of the War Between the States* (Baltimore: The Nautical & Aviation Publishing Company of America, 1989), p. 381; Charles C. Osborne, *Jubal: The Life and Times of General Jubal A. Early*, CSA (Chapel Hill: Algonquin Books of Chapel Hill, 1992), p. 263.

32 Sharpe to Humphreys and Meade to Grant, July 9, 1864, OR, Vol. 40, Part 3, p. 96.

33 Fishel, p. 546; Meade to Grant, July 9, 1864, OR, Vol. 40, Part 3, p. 95.

34 Gates, *Civil War Diaries*, diary entry for July 11, 1863, p. 149; Sharpe to Jansen Hasbrouck, July 14, 1864, Sharpe Collection.

35 Sharpe to Jansen Hasbrouck, July 14, 1864, Sharpe Collection. Emphasis is in the original.

36 Theodore Lyman, Meade's Army: *The Private Notebooks of Lt. Col. Theodore Lyman*, edited by David W. Lowe (Kent, OH: Kent State University Press, 2007), p. 235.

37 Lincoln to Grant and Halleck to Grant, July 12, 1864, OR, Vol. 40, Part 3, p. 175.

38 Meade to Grant, July 12, 1864, OR, Vol. 40, Part 3, p. 179.

39 Babcock to Humphreys, July 12, 1864, NARA, RG 108, Entry 112; *Wilson, The Life of John A. Rawlins*, p. 244; Meade to Grant, July 15, 1864, OR, Vol. 40, Part 3, p. 254.

40 Lee to Davis, July 10, 1864, Robert E. Lee, *The Wartime Papers of Robert E. Lee*, eds. Clifford Dowdey and Louis H. Manarin (Boston, 1961), pp. 817–18.

41 Babcock to Humphreys, July 11, OR, Vol. 40, Part 3, p. 146.

42 Meade to Grant, July 11, 1864, OR, Vol. 40, Part 3, p. 147.

43 Grant to Meade and Meade to Grant, July 11, 1864, OR, Vol. 40, Part 3, pp. 147–48.

44 Babcock to Humphreys, July 12, 1864, OR, Vol. 40, Part 3, pp.177–78.

45 Hdqrs, Armies of the United States, Special Orders No. 48, City Point, VA, July 4, 1864, OR, Series 1, Vol. 40, Part 2, p. 622.

46 "Some Hit and Miss Chat," *The New York Times*, April 12, 1885, p. 14.

47 Gates, *Civil War Diaries*, entry for July 5, 1864, p. 148.

48 Patrick Diary, *Inside Lincoln's Army*, entries June 7–8 and July 6, 1864, pp. 381, 394–95. Getting on the bad side of the press has become a constant in the modern world, as the late Russian general Pavel Lebed remarked that it is impossible to win an argument with a woman or the press.

49 Patrick Diary, *Inside Lincoln's Army*, diary entries June 7–8 and July 6, 1864, pp. 381, 394–95.

50 Patrick Diary, entries for July 7 and 9, 1864, pp. 394–96; Gates, diary entries for July 7 and 9, 1864, pp. 148–49.

51 Edwin Fishel, *The Secret War for the Union: The Untold Story of Military Intelligence in the Civil War* (Boston: Houghton Mifflin, 1996), p. 547.

52 Sharpe to Jansen Hasbrouck, August 15, 1864, Sharpe Collection.

53 Fishel, p. 548.

54 John C. Babcock, "Record of Service of John C. Babcock during the civil war of 1861–65," John C. Babcock Collection, Library of Congress.

55 Fishel, pp. 546–47; Feis, p. 235; Gates, diary entry for July 8, 1864, p. 148.

56 Knight, *The National Tribune*, May 4, 1893.

57 Sharpe to Jansen Hasbrouck, August 15, 1864, Sharpe Collection.

58 Simpson D. Brooks, *Ulysses S. Grant: Triumph over Adversity, 1822–1865* (New York: Houghton Mifflin, 2000), p. 458.

59 Patrick, *Inside Lincoln's Army*, diary entry for July 21, 1864, pp. 400–01.

60 Feis, pp. 236–37; Knight, *The National Tribune*, June 8, 1893.

61 Knight, *The National Tribune*, May 4 and 11, 1893.

62 Knight, *The National Tribune*, May 11 and 25, 1893.

63 Knight, *The National Tribune*, May 25, June 1 and 8, 1893; Elizabeth R. Varon, *Southern Lady, Yankee Spy: The True Story of Elizabeth Van Lew, A Union Agent in the Heart of the Confederacy* (Oxford: Oxford University Press, 2003), pp. 157–56.

64 Patrick, *Inside Lincoln's Army*, diary entry for July 22, 1864, p. 401.

65 William J. Lee to Ulysses S. Grant, February 23, 1874, *Papers of U. S. Grant*, Vol. 30, p. 92; Feis, p. 237.

66 Beymer, *Scouts and Spies of the Civil War*, pp. 56, 59–60. The Van Lews were a prominent and wealthy family."

67 Beymer, "Miss Van Lew," *Harpers Monthly*, June 1911, pp. 86–99.

68 Sharpe to Bowers, OR, Vol. 46, Part 2, p. 191; RG 108, Entry 112; Feis, p. 327.

69 McEntee to Bowers, November 10, 1864, OR, NARA, RG 108, Entry 112; Sharpe to Meade, January 10, 1865, OR, Vol. 46, Part 2, p. 171.

70 Beymer, *Scouts and Spies of the Civil War*, p. 54; Harnett T. Kane, *Spies for the Blue and Gray* (New York: Doubleday, 1954); "Death of Noted Union Spy," *The National Republican*, October 4, 1900, p. 8; "Miss Elizabeth Van Lew," *Chicago Daily Tribune*, April 14, 1887, p. 10.

71 Patrick, *Inside Lincoln's Army*, diary entries for July 24 and August 19, pp. 402, 415, 442, 445.

Chapter Eleven: The Siege of Petersburg

1 William B Feis, *Grant's Secret Service: The Intelligence War from Belmont to Appomattox* (Lincoln: University of Nebraska Press, 2002), p. 253.

2 McEntee to Humphreys, September 3 and 5, 1864, OR, Vol. 42, Part 2, pp. 657–58, 698.

3 "From Grant's Army," *The Brooklyn Daily Eagle*, August 24, 1864, p. 3. This article appears to be an official release from the Army of the Potomac.

4 Fishel, pp. 550–51.

5 Sharpe to Humphreys, 8:30 a.m, June 18, 1864, OR, Vol. 40, Part 2, p. 158.

6 Sharpe to Humphreys, June 18, 1864, OR, Vol. 40, Part 2, pp. 158–59.

7 Sharpe to Humphreys, 10:30 a.m., June 18, 1864, OR, Vol. 40, Part 2, p. 159.

8 Judson Knight, *The National Tribune*, April 27, 1893.

9 Lee to Seddon, June 21, 1864, OR, Vol. 40, Part 2, pp. 671–72.

10 Noah Andre Trudeau, *The Last Citadel: Petersburg, Virginia June 1864–April 1865* (Baton Rouge: Louisiana State University Press, 1991), p. 72.

11 Knight, "How Scouts Worked: Sergt. Knight Tells How They Went About Getting Information," *The National Tribune*, May 4, 1893; Trudeau, pp. 78–9. Lee's victory was due to not only Mahone's and Wilcox's fighting abilities but to the cumulative losses of II Corps. John Gibbon cited the losses in his own division to make the point. He began the Overland Campaign at the beginning of May with 6,799 men; his losses up to June 30 were 6,183, and he had received only 4,263 replacements. "These facts serve to demonstrate the wear and tear on the division, and to show why it is that troops, which at the commencement of the campaign were equal to almost any undertaking, became toward the end of it unfit for almost any."

12 Sharpe to Humphreys, 4 p.m., June 22, 1864, OR, Vol. 40, Part 2, p. 307.

13 Sharpe to Humphreys, 6 a.m. and 1 p.m., June 23, 1864, OR, Vol. 40, Part 2, p. 337.

14 Sharpe to Humphreys, 8 a.m., June 29, 1864, OR, Vol. 40, Part 2, p. 496; Robert E. Lee, *The Wartime Papers of Robert E. Lee*, Clifford Dowdey and Louis H. Manarin, eds. (New York: Da Capo Press, 1987), p. 811.

15 Sharpe to Humphreys, June 30, 1864, OR, Vol. 40, Part 2, p. 517.

16 Trudeau, p. 90.

17 Sharpe to Jansen Hasbrouck, June 25, 1864, Sharpe Collection.

18 Sharpe to Jansen Hasbrouck, June 25, 1864, Sharpe Collection.

19 "Confederate Military Hospitals in Richmond," by Robert W. Wait, Jr., Official Publication #22 Richmond Civil War Centennial committee, Richmond, Virginia 1964. Also called: The General Hospital, City Home Hospital, Alms House Hospital. Built shortly before the outbreak of the Civil War by the City of Richmond as a poor house. Rented by the City Council to the Confederate authorities in June 1861 as a military hospital. Continued in use as such until December 1864 when it was reclaimed by the City for rental to the Virginia Military Institute as their temporary location. Suffered heavy exterior damage when the nearby powder magazine was exploded on evacuation night. Taken over by Federal authorities and again used by them as a poor house. Returned to the City in December 1865. It was used for many years as the City Alms House. Still in use and owned by the City of Richmond. Earliest use by the Confederacy was for wounded Union prisoners. Soon became the first of the large General Hospitals. Capacity about 500 patients. Dr. Charles Bell Gibson, surgeon-in-charge. Location: northside of Hospital Street, between 2nd and 4th Streets, opposite Shockoe Cemetery.

20 Sharpe to Humphreys, June 25, 1864, OR, Vol. 40, Part 2, p. 403.

21 McEntee to Humphreys, July 31, 1864, OR, Vol. 40, Part 2, p. 692.

22 Babcock to Humphreys, July 8, 1864, OR, Vol. 40, Part 3, p. 75; Lee to Davis, July 6, 1864, Robert E. Lee, *Lee's Dispatches, Unpublished Letters of General Robert E. Lee, C. S. A., to Jefferson Davis and the War Department of the Confederate States of America, 1862–65*, ed. Douglas Southall Freeman (Baton Rouge: Louisiana State University Press, 1957), p. 277.

23 Babcock to Humphreys, July 17, 1864 (five reports), OR, Vol. 40, Part 3, pp. 291–294; Babcock to Humphreys, July 17, 1864, RG 108, Entry 112.

24 Meade to Grant, July 17, 1864, OR, Vol. 40, Part 3, p. 291.

25 Babcock to Humphreys, July 18, 1864, OR, Vol. 40, Part 3, p. 313; Grant to Butler, July 18, 1864, *The Papers of U. S. Grant*, Vol. 11, p. 275; Sharpe to Humphreys, July 18, 1864, OR, Vol. 40, Part 3, p. 315.

26 Feis, p. 254.

27 Babcock to Humphreys, July 26, 1864, OR, Vol. 40, Part 3, p. 459; Andrew A. Humphreys, *The Virginia Campaign of 1864 and 1865* (New York: Charles Scribner's Sons, 1883), p. 251.

28 Babcock to Humphreys, July 28, 1864, OR, Vol. 40, Part 3, p. 556.

29 Humphreys to Warren, July 29, 1864, OR, Vol. 40, Part 3, p.605.

30 W. Gordon McCabe, address before the Association of the Army of Northern Virginia, November 2, 1876, quoted in Robert E. Lee, Jr., *Recollections and Letters of Robert E. Lee* (New York, 1904), p. 135.

31 Bruce Catton, *The Army of the Potomac: A Stillness at Appomattox* (New York: Doubleday & Company, 1953), pp. 238–40; Catton, *Grant Takes Command*, p. 321; Humphreys, p. 252.

32 Catton, *Grant Takes Command*, pp. 321–22; Stephen R. Taafe, Commanding the Army of the Potomac (Lawrence: University of Kansas Press, 2006), p. 188. Ledlie's division had an inordinate number of former artillerymen who had been taken out of the comfortable defenses of Washington and elsewhere and now found themselves as infantry. They were known to have little fight in them and had performed poorly recently.

33 Meade to Mrs. Meade, July 31, 1864, George Meade, *The Life and Letters of George Gordon Meade* (New York: Charles Scribner's Sons, 1913), Vol. 2, p. 217.

34 Horace Porter, *Campaigning With Grant* (New York: The Century Company, 189), p. 267. Porter appears to have combined the statements made by Grant in his message to Halleck of August 1, 1864, in the *U. S. Grant Papers*, Huntington Library; and Grant's testimony before Congress in *CCW Report*, Vol. I, p. 111, into a single observation made to his staff at the time. Burnside went on a leave of absence two weeks after the debacle at the Crater and never returned to active service. Ledlie was quietly released from the service at the same time.

35 Letter of Captain George K. Leet to Colonel W. R. Rowley dated August 23, 1864, quoting a letter from Bowers; microfilm in the U.S. Grant Association, from original in the Illinois State Historical Library, cited in Catton, *Grant Takes Command*, ibid., pp. 365–66.

36 Theodore Lyman, *With Grant & Meade: From the Wilderness to Appomattox* (Lincoln: University of Nebraska Press, 1994), p. 208.

37 Allan Nevins, *The War for the Union: The Organized War 1863–1864* (New York: Charles Scribner's Sons, 1971), pp. 219–20; Philip Shaw Paludan, "A People's Contest," *The Union and the Civil War 1861–1865* (New York: Harper & Row Publishers, 1998), pp. 281, 284. In 1860 almost 20 percent of the population of the North was foreign-born. As much as 25 percent of the men who served in the army and navy in the war were foreign-born. Between 1861 and 1865, 800,000 immigrants arrived in the United States; nearly 631,000 were adults of whom two-thirds were males. Of that number, 183,440 or almost 44 percent were recruited by the Union army. The *New York Tribune* reported that in the first five months of 1864 one-tenth of the immigrants who landed in New York joined the army and navy. Great Britain sent the largest number of immigrants in 1863, Ireland in 1864, and Germany in 1865. The newest immigrants enlisted in the army could not be expected to have the same enthusiasm for the Union cause as those who had been acculturated and already set down roots.

38 Humphreys to Meade, August 8, 1864, OR, Vol. 42, Part 2, p. 84.

39 Porter, pp. 273–74; Catton, *Grant Takes Command*, pp. 349–50; Theodore P. Gates, *The War of the Rebellion* (New York: 1885), p. 547; OR, Vol. 40, Part 3, p. 1250; OR, Series 3, Vol. 5, Part 1, p. 383; Feis, p. 258.

40 OR, Series 3, Vol. V, Part 1, p. 383.

41 Trudeau, pp. 148–49.

42 Fitzhugh Lee, *General Lee* (Philadelphia: D. Appleton & Company, 1894), p. 352.

43 Babcock to Humphreys, OR, 42, Part 2, p. 85.

44 Babcock to Humphreys, OR, Vol. 42, Part 2, p. 86.

45 Grant to Meade, August 11, 1864, OR, Vol. 42, Part 2, pp. 114–15.

46 Trudeau, p. 148; Dowdey and Manarin, *Lee's Wartime Papers*, pp. 834, 836–37.

47 Trudeau, p. 151.

48 Lee to Hampton, August 14, 1863, Lee, *The Wartime Papers of Robert E. Lee*, Ibid., p. 835; Trudeau, p. 152; Humphreys, pp. 270–73.

49 Lee to Fields, August 15, 1863, Lee, *Wartime Papers of Robert E. Lee*, pp. 837–38. Lee telegraphed fields at 12:36 a.m. that the infantry had been dispatched by rail at 7:30 and 9:30 p.m. on August 14.

50 Sharpe to Babcock, August 16, 1864, OR, Vol. 42, Part 2, p. 213.

51 Babcock to Sharpe, August 16, 1864, OR, Vol. 42, Part 2, p. 213.

52 Shape to Babcock, August 16, 1864, OR, Vol. 42, Part 2, p. 213.

53 Babcock to Sharpe, August 16, 1864, OR, Vol. 42, Part 2, p. 213

54 Fisher to Humphreys, August 17, 1864, OR, Vol. 42, Part 2, p. 245.

55 Grant to Meade, August 17, 1864, OR, Vol. 42, Part 2, p. 244.

56 Grant to Seward, March 19, 1865, OR, Vol. 40, Part 3, p. 48.

57 Grant to Meade, 10:00 p.m. and 10:30 p.m., August 17, 1864, Meade to Grant, OR, Vol. 42, Part 2, p. 245.

58 Lyman, p. 217.

59 Lee to Davis, August 21, 1863, Lee, *Wartime Papers of Robert E. Lee*, pp. 842–43.

60 Trudeau, p. 173; OR, Vol. 42, Part 2, p. 359. "I understand the following to be the disposition of troops in our front from the enemy's left to right: Bushrod Johnson' s division, Martin's and Hagood's brigades, of Hoke's division, and Kirkland's and MacRae's brigades, of Heth's division; Mahone's division, and Fry's and Davis' brigades, of Heth's division; Colquitt's and Clingman's, of Hoke's division. We learn of no troops having arrived from the north side of the James River, except these three brigades of Heth's division."

61 Sharpe to Humphreys, August 25, 1864, OR, Vol. 42, Part 2, pp. 473–74.

62 Trudeau, p. 189.

63 McEntee to Humphreys, OR, Vol. 42, Part 2, pp. 274–75; Humphreys, pp. 280–83. Humphreys points out that the new recruits sent to the army were without training.

64 Lyman, p. 226.

65 Sharpe to Bowers, August 26, 1864, NARA, RG 108, RG 112.

66 Lee to Davis, September 2, 1864, Lee, *Wartime Papers of Robert E. Lee*, p. 848.

67 Knight, "New Rebel Torpedo," *Scientific American*, 1011, No. 15 (Oct. 8, 1864), p. 288.

68 Knight, "How Scouts Worked: Sergt. Knight Tells How They Went About Getting Information," *The National Tribune*, June 8, 1893.

69 Sharpe, September 13, 1864, OR Navies, Vol. 10, pp. 466–67.

70 Babcock to Humphreys, September 11, 1864, OR, Vol. 42, Part 2, p. 785.

71 "Counterfeiting in the Army," *Daily National Republican*, September 30, 1864.

72 Babcock to Humphreys, October 9, 1864, OR, Volume 42, Part 3, pp. 144–45; Meade to Humphreys and Meade to Parke, October 13, 1864, OR, Vol. 42, Part 3, pp. 209–10; Babcock to Humphreys, October 13, 1864, OR, Vol. 42, Part 3, p. 198.

73 Marsena Patrick, *Inside Lincoln's Army: The Diary of Marsena Rudolph Patrick, Provost Marshal General, Army of the Potomac*, diary entry for September 8, 1864 (New York: Thomas Yoseloff, 1964), p. 420; OR, Series 1, Vol. 27, Part 3, p. 794; "Army and Navy Personnel," *The Times-Picayune* (New Orleans), October 2, 1864, p. 4.

74 Gates, *Civil War Diaries*, diary entry for September 28, 1864; Patrick, *Inside Lincoln's Army*, diary entries for September 20 & 26, 1864, pp. 422, 425. Although the two diary dates do not match, they are obviously talking about the same visit by Gates to Patrick.

75 Gates, *Civil War Diaries*, diary entry for December 7, 1864, p. 162.

76 Patrick, *Inside Lincoln's Army*, diary entries for 16, 18, and 21 November 1864, pp. 442–43.

77 Sharpe to Williams, October 12, 1864, NARA, Military Service Record of George H. Sharpe.

78 Patrick, *Inside Lincoln's Army*, diary entry for November 16 & 28, 1864; Dick Nolan, *Benjamin Franklin Butler: The Damnedest Yankees* (New York: Presidio Press, 1991), pp. 311–12. Butler would later say that failing to declare Grant the rightful candidate was a fatal mistake which turned Grant against him.

Chapter Twelve: Settling with Early in the Valley

1 Grant to Sheridan, September 6, 1864, OR, Vol. 42, Part 2, p. 717; William B. Feis, *Grant's Secret Service: The Intelligence War from Belmont to Appomattox* (Lincoln: University of Nebraska Press, 2002), p. 244.

2 Phillip H. Sheridan, *Personal Memoirs of P. H. Sheridan* (New York: Charles L. Webster, 1888), vol. 2, pp. 499–500; Feis, p. 244; Sharpe to Humphreys, September 15, 1864, OR, Vol. 42, Part 2, p. 833; Sheridan to Leet, September 15, 1864, OR, Vol. 42, Part 2, p. 89.

3 Sheridan, Vol. 2, p. 1; Allan L. Tischler, "America's Civil War: Union General Phil Sheridan's Scouts," The HistoryNet.com, http://historynet.com/acw/blshseridanscouts/index.html; David L. Phillips, "The Jesse Scouts," West Virginia in the Civil War, http://www.wvcivilwar.com/jessie.shtml.

4 Sheridan, Vol. 2, pp. 2–3, 5n, 6n; Jeffry Wert, *From Winchester to Cedar Creek: The Shenandoah Campaign of 1864* (Mechanicsburg, PA: Stackpole Books, 1997), p. 42; OR, Vol. 43, Part 2, p. 90.

5 Sharpe to Humphreys, September 17, 1864, OR, Vol. 42, Part 2, pp. 881–82; Babcock to Sharpe, September 17, 1864, NARA, Microcopy 2096, Roll 35.

6 Meade to Grant, September 17, 1864, OR, Vol. 42, Part 2, p. 879.

7 Lee to Early, September 17, 1864, OR, Vol. 42, Part 2, pp. 1258–59.

8 Grant to Meade, September 22, 1864, OR, Vol. 42, Part 2, pp. 963–64; Sheridan to Grant, and Grant to Sheridan, September 23, 1864, OR, Vol. 42, Part 2, p. 152.

9 Lee to Anderson, September 23, 1864, Clifford Dowdy and Louis H. Manarin, eds., *The Wartime Papers of Robert E. Lee* (New York: Da Capo Press, 1987), pp. 856–57.

10 Sharpe to Humphreys, September 24, 1864, OR, Vol. 42, Part 2, p. 988; Sharpe to Davenport, September 25, 1864, p. 1025; Sharpe to Humphreys, September 25, 1864, p. 1010; Grant to Halleck, September 27, 1864, p. 186; Babcock to Humphreys, September 27, 1864, pp. 1048–49; Babcock to Sharpe, September 27, 1864, p. 1051; Babcock to Humphreys, September 28, 1864, pp. 1065–66.

11 Ulysses S. Grant, *Grant: Personal Memoirs of U.S. Grant, Selected Letters 1839–1865* (New York: The Library of America, 1984), pp. 625–27.

12 Grant, p. 625; Babcock to Humphreys, September 27, 1864, OR, Vol. 42, Part 2, pp. 1048–49.

13 Babcock to Humphreys and Babcock to Sharpe, September 28, 1864, OR, Vol. 42, Part 2, p. 1066; Sharpe to Davenport, September 28, 1864, OR, Vol. 42, Part 2, p. 1079; Babcock to Humphreys, September 30, 1864, OR, Vol. 42, Part 2, p. 1123; Sharpe to Davenport, October 1, 1864, OR, Vol. 42, Part 3, p. 32.

14 Babcock to Humphreys, September 30, 1864, OR, Vol. 42, Part 2, p. 1123.

15 Babcock to Humphreys, September 30, 1864, OR, Vol. 42, Part 2, p. 1123; Douglas Southall Freeman, *Lee's Lieutenants: Gettysburg to Appomattox* (New York: Charles Scribner's Sons, 1944), p. 595.

16 Babcock to Humphreys and Butler to Grant, September 30, 1864, OR, Vol. 42, Part 2, pp. 1122–23, 1144.

17 Jubal Early, *An Autobiographical Sketch and Narrative of the War Between the States* (Philadelphia, 1912), p. 435; Grant to Halleck, October 5, 1864, OR, Vol. 43, Part 2, p. 288.

18 Lee to Early, OR, Vol. 43, Part 2, p. 892.

19 Wright to Sheridan, October 16, 1864, OR, Vol. 43, Part 1, p. 52.

20 Phillip H. Sheridan, *Civil War Memoirs* (New York: Bantam, 1991), pp. 270–71.

21 Sheridan, p. 274.

22 Sheridan, pp. 279–80.

23 Sheridan to Halleck, November 24, 1864, OR, Vol. 43, Part 1, pp. 37–38.

Chapter Thirteen: Winter Hiatus

1 Babcock to Meade, December 10, 1864, OR, Vol. 42, Part 3, pp. 924–25.

2 "Yankee Deserters," *Richmond Dispatch*, January 24, 1864, p. 4.

3   McEntee to Terry, November 12, 1864, OR, Vol. 42, Part 3, pp. 608–09.

4   McEntee to Meade, December 11, 1864, OR, Vol. 42, Part 3, pp. 954–55.

5   Peter G. Tsouras, ed., *Scouting for Meade and Grant: The Reminiscences of Judson Knight, Chief of Scouts, Army of the Potomac* (New York: Skyhorse Publications, 2014), pp. 202–03.

6   Sheridan to Leet, November 17, 1864, and Leet to Sheridan, November 18, 1864, Sheridan to Leet, November 23, 1864, OR, Vol. 43, Part 2, pp. 637, 641, 662.

7   Leet to Sheridan, November 18, 1864, Sheridan to Leet, November 23, 1864, OR, Vol. 43, Part 2, pp. 641, 662; Rawlins to Grant, McEntee to Humphreys, and Butler to Grant, November 20, 1864, OR, Vol. 43, Part 2, pp. 666–67, 669; Marsena Rudolph Patrick, *Inside Lincoln's Army: The Diary of Marsena Rudolph Patrick*, ed. David S. Sparks (New York: A. S. Barnes & Company, Inc., 1964), diary entry for December 3, 1864, p. 447.

8   Lee to Davis, December 6, 1865, OR, Vol. 43, Part 2, p. 936; Abstract from the return of the Middle Military Division, Maj. Gen. Philip H. Sheridan, U.S. Army, commanding, for the month of November, 1864, OR, Volume 43, Part 2, p. 716; Abstract from return of the Army of the Potomac, Maj. Gen. George G. Meade, U.S. Army, commanding, for the month of December, 1864, OR, Vol. 43, Part 2, p. 1114 (figures for both abstracts are under the headings, "Aggregate present").

9   Sheridan to Grant and Leet to Sheridan, December 8, 1864, OR, Vol. 43, Part 2, pp. 756–57.

10 Babcock to Meade, December 9, 1865, OR, Vol. 43, Part 2, p. 898; Abstract from monthly return of the Army of Northern Virginia, General Robert E. Lee commanding, November 30, 1864, OR, Vol. 43, Part 3, p. 1237.

11 Babcock to Meade, December 9–11, 1864, OR, Vol. 43, Part 3, pp. 893–94, 924, 954–56.

12 Lee to Davis, December 14, 1864, OR, Vol. 43, Part 3, p. 1272.

13 Babcock to Meade, December 19, 1864, OR, Vol. 43, Part 3, p. 1039; McEntee to Babcock, December 22, 1864, OR, Vol. 43, Part 3, p. 1056; Theodore B. Gates, *The War of the Rebellion* (New York, 1884), p. 562; Field and Muster Report, 80th NY, November & December, 1864, Military Service Record of John McEntee, NARA.

14 Lee to Davis, December 14, 1864, in Robert E. Lee, *The Wartime Papers of Robert E. Lee*, eds. Clifford Dowdey and Louis H. Manarin (New York: Da Capo Press, 1987), p. 877; Lee to Davis, December 19, 1864, OR, Vol. 43, Part 3, p. 1280; Latrobe to Hoke, December 20, 1864, OR, Vol. 43, Part 3, p. 1282.

15 McEntee to Babcock, December 22, 1864, OR, Vol. 43, Part 3, p. 1056; Ord to Grant, December 22, 1864, OR, Vol. 43, Part 3, p. 1060; Terry to Turner, December 23, 1864, OR, Vol. 43, Part 3, p. 1067.

16 "Southern News," *Cleveland Daily Reader*, December 7, 1864, p. 1; "Grant's Army," *Pittsburgh Daily Post*, December 21, 1864, p. 2; James Harrison Wilson, *The Life of John A. Rawlins: Lawyer, Assistant Adjutant-General, Chief of Staff, Major General of Volunteers, and Secretary of War* (Sagwan Press, 2015), p. 296.

17 Wilson, *The Life of John A. Rawlins*, p. 296.

18 Babcock to Meade, December 23, 1863, OR, Vol. 42, Part 3, pp. 1062–63; Babcock to Meade, December 25, 1863, OR, Vol. 42, Part 3, p. 1073; Sharpe to Babcock, December 25, 1865, OR, Vol. 42, Part 3, p. 1073; NARA, Microcopy 504, Roll 303; Babcock to Sharpe, December 25, 1863, OR, Vol. 42, Part 3, pp. 1073–74; "Sherman—Savannah Evacuated," *Richmond Dispatch*, December 27, 1863, p. 3; Sharpe to Bowers, December 27, 1863, NARA, RG 108, Entry 112.

19 Patrick, *Inside Lincoln's Army*, diary entries for October 25 and November 23, 1864, pp. 433, 444; Patrick bizarrely prefaces his mention of the turkeys with a comment about his investigation of the army's embalmers. The Editors of Time-Life, *Death in the Trenches: Grant at Petersburg* (Alexandria, VA: Time-Life Books, 1986), pp. 160–71; this source cites 123,000 bread rations a day baked by the Bake House.

20 "Roger A. Pryor Captured," *The Nashville Daily Union* (Nashville, TN), November 30, 1864; "Roger A. Pryor Captured," *The Daily Milwaukee News*," December 4, 1864; *The Wilmington Messenger* (Wilmington, NC), May 18, 1889.

21 Patrick, *Inside Lincoln's Army*, diary entries for November 16, 18, and 21, 1864, pp. 442, 443; Military Service Record for George H. Sharpe, NARA; Patrick to Williams, November 29, 1864, NARA, M2906, Roll 37.

22 Meade to Warren, OR, Vol. 42, Part 3, p. 611; E. J. Edwards, "Gen. Mead's [sic Meade's] Real Character," *Dakota County Herald* (Dakota City, NE), August 5, 1910.

23 Cyrus B. Comstock, *The Diary of Cyrus B. Comstock* (Dayton, OH: Morningside Press, 1987), p. 279.

24 Hdqrs, Armies of the United States, Special Orders Number 141, City Point, Va., December 2, 1864, OR, Vol. 43, Part 3, p. 779.

25 Special Orders Number 10, Office of the Provost Marshal General, City Point, Va., December 2, 1864, Military Service Record of George H. Sharpe, NARA.

26 Ulysses S. Grant, *The Papers of Ulysses S. Grant*, Vol. 13, November 16, 1864–February 20, 1865 (Carbondale, IL: Southern Illinois University Press, 1985), pp. 487–88.

27 Adam Badeau, *Reminiscences of Ulysses S. Grant* (Portland, OR: Wetware Media LLC, 2012), p. 154.

28 Theodore Lyman, *With Grant and Meade from the Wilderness to Appomattox*, letter of November 13, 1864 (CreateSpace Independent Publishing Platform, 2014). Amazingly, this edition has no page numbers; Grant to Stanton, March 19, 1865, OR, Vol. 46, Part 3, p. 38

29 Sharpe to Bowers and Sharpe to Meade, January 21, 1864, OR, Vol. 46, Part 2, p. 191 (RG 108, Entry 11) and OR, Series 1, Vol. 46, Part 2, pp. 191–92.

30 Rawlins to Parker, January 21, 1865, OR Navies, Vol. 11, p. 632.

31 Gibbon to Parker, Parker to Porter, Parker to Gibbon, OR Navies, Vol. 11, pp. 632–33.

32 Grant to Fox (2), Grant to Welles, Grant to Parker, OR Navies, Vol. 11, pp. 634–36.

33 Military Service Record of John McEntee, NARA; Theodore B. Gates, *The War of the Rebellion* (New York: 1884), p. 562; Patrick, *Inside Lincoln's Army*, diary entry for November 26, 1864, p. 444.

34 Military Personnel Record of Frederick L. Manning, NARA, letter from Sharpe to Bowers, requesting the transfer of Capt. Paul Oliver.

35 Casualty Sheet, January 1, 1878, Pension File of Paul A. Oliver, NARA; Horatio Seymour to Meade, Pension File of Paul A. Oliver, April 11, 1864, NARA; Hooker to Stanton, February 7, 1865, NARA, M 1064, O 025 CB 1865.

36 Roger D. Hunt and Jack R. Brown, *Brevet Brigadier Generals in Blue* (Gaithersburg, MD: Olde Golden Books, 1990); Meade to Mrs. Meade, February 27, 1865, *George Gordon Meade, The Life and Letters of George Gordon Meade: Major-General United States Army*, Vol. 2 (Nabu Press, 2009), p. 264.

37 Sharpe to Jansen Hasbrouck, February 24, 1864, Sharpe Collection; General Order 94, May 26, 1865, NARA, Military Service Record of George H. Sharpe.

38 "From Grant's Army," *Richmond Dispatch*, January 24, 1865; Babcock to Webb, January 17, 1865, NARA, Microcopy 2096, Roll 38.

39 Sharpe to Jansen Hasbrouck, February 24, 1864, Sharpe Collection; Geoffrey Perret, *Old Soldiers Never Die: The Life of Douglas MacArthur* (New York: Random House 1996), p. 362.

40 Shape to Patrick, November 28, 1864, NARA, Microcopy 345, RG 109, Roll 0180.

41 Sharpe to Jansen Hasbrouck, February 24, 1864, Sharpe Collection.

42 Babcock to Sharpe, November 19, 1864, NARA, RG 108, Entry 112.

43 Leet to Bowers, November 20, 1864, NARA, RG 108, Entry 112.

44 Sharpe to Patrick, December 15, 1864, NARA, Microcopy 504, Roll 303.

45 Peter G. Tsouras, ed., *Scouting for Grant and Meade: The Reminiscences of Judson Knight, Chief of Scouts, Army of the Potomac* (Skyhorse Publications, 2014), pp. xxxiii–xxxiv.

46 Theodore Lyman (ed. David W. Lowe), *Meade's Army: The Private Notebooks of Lt. Col. Theodore Lyman* (Kent, OH: The Kent State University Press, 2007), p. 338.

47 Sharpe to Meade, January 9, 1865, OR, Vol. 43, Part 3, pp. 75–76.

48 Sharpe to Meade, January 13, 1863, OR, Vol. 43, Part 2, pp. 114–15; Lee to Seddon, January 11, 1863, OR, Vol. 43, Part 2, p. 1035.

49 Sharpe to Meade, January 13, 1863, OR, Vol. 43, Part 2, pp. 114–15; Seddon to Lee, January 11, 1863, OR, Vol. Part 2, p. 1034. Lee was uncharacteristically blunt with Seddon because the Secretary had suggested that he impress supplies from southwestern Virginia "without limit" and that a "call by you on the people would be more influential in inducing acquiescence, perhaps voluntary contributions, than from any other source." Then he had the temerity to suggest that Lee also provide the wagons for such an expedition. Lee's deference to civilian authority was being severely tried. The impressments of supplies at that distance and scale was a responsibility of the Quartermaster Department, not the sorely pressed field army. Yet, Seddon and so many of the rest of the senior members of the Confederate Government realized that the only remaining public figure with unquestioned moral authority throughout the dwindling south was Robert E. Lee. They were all too eager to dump their civic responsibilities on him, a prospect that appalled him.

50 Sharpe to Meade, January 13, 1863, OR, Vol. 43, Part 2, pp. 114–15; Sharpe to Meade, January 18, 1865, OR, Vol. 43, Part 2, p. 171.

51 Sharpe to Meade, January 18, 1865, OR, Vol. 43, Part 2, p. 171.

52 Sharpe to Meade, January 21, 1865, OR, Vol. 43, Part 2, p. 192.

53 Grant to Stanton, February 4, 1865, OR, Vol. 43, Part 2, p. 366.

54 *Papers of U.S. Grant*, Vol. 13, p. 262; Elizabeth Varon, *Southern Lady, Yankee Spy: The True Story of Elizabeth Van Lew, A Union Agent in the Heart of the Confederacy* (New York: Oxford University Press, 2003), pp. 186–87; "Samuel Ruth," *The Daily Confederate* (Raleigh, NC), February 4, 1865, p. 2.

55 "Miss Elizabeth Van Lew: The Full Story of Her Work as a Union Spy," *Chicago Daily Tribune*, April 14, 1887, p. 10. The article refers to John Slidell as the one who sent Pole to New York; however, Slidell was the Confederate agent in Paris. Mason was the London representative of the Confederacy. Biographical letter of Benjamin C. Pole, probably May 19, 1865, NARA, M619, RG 94, Roll 0397.

56 Pole to Seward, July 29, 1864; Murray to Seward, July 30, 1864; Seward to Wilding, August 6, 1864, NARA, M619, RG 94, Roll 0397.

57 Dudley to Seward, September 22, 1864, NARA, M619, RG 94, Roll 0397.

58 "Protest and Demand found in the City of Richmond Va July 9th, 1866 by Benjamin Pole, a British Subject and in the name of his government," NARA, M619, RG 94, Roll 0397; Pole to Seward, July 10, 1866, NARA, M619, RG 894, Roll 0397.

59 Statement of 1st Lieut. Henry Wagner, July 15, 1866, NARA, M619, RG 94, Roll 0397.

60 Pole to Sharpe, January 31, 1865, NARA, M619, RG 94, Roll 0397.

61 Special Order No. 32, Headquarters Post City Point, VA, February 18, 1865, NARA, M619, RG 94, Roll 0397.

62 Diary of Elizabeth Van Lew for early 1865, in David D. Ryan, ed., *A Yankee Spy in Richmond: The Civil War Diary of "Crazy Bett" Van Lew* (Mechanicsburg, PA: Stackpole Books, 1996), p. 101.

63 *A Yankee Spy in Richmond*, p. 102.

64 Babcock to Schoumaker, August 14, 1865 (Office of Special Agent, District of Henrico, Richmond, VA), NARA, M619, RG 94, Roll 0397.

65 "Local Matters, *Richmond Dispatch*, February 27, 1865, p. 4. Strangely, the article refers to a Gen. Carr as Pole's director instead of Sharpe. The only general officer named Carr with the army at Petersburg was Brig. Gen. Joseph Carr, commanding the 4th Division of II Corps. He was an infantry officer with no known connection to intelligence operations. By coincidence, it seems, Carr would, after the war, run on the same ticket for state office in New York as Sharpe's future son-in-law, Ira Davenport.

66 "Local Matters," *Richmond Dispatch*, February 27, 1865, p. 4. The spy's name is variously shown as Pole and Pool. *A Yankee Spy in Richmond*, pp. 102–03.

67 *War Diary of "Crazy Bet" Van Lew*, p. 103.

68 Peter G. Tsouras, *Scouting for Grant and Meade: The Reminiscences of Judson Knight, Chief of Scouts, Army of the Potomac* (New York: Skyhorse Publications, 2014), pp. xxxiii–xxxiv, derived from NARA, RG 92, Entry 238, Files 0447 for 1864 and 0447 for 1865 (BMI Payrolls); http://www.civilwarhome.com/Pay.htm, accessed February 13, 2013.

69 Patrick, *Inside Lincoln's Army*, diary entries for February 13 and March 6, 1865, pp. 470, 476.

70 Patrick, *Inside Lincoln's Army*, diary entry for March 15, 1865, p. 479.

71 Theodore Lyman, entry for March 2, 1865, *Meade's Headquarters: From the Wilderness to Appomattox* (Boston: The Atlantic Monthly Press, 1922), p. 305.

72 Lee to Breckinridge, February 28, 1865, OR, Vol. 46, Part 2, p. 1265; *Inside Lincoln's Army*, p. 1964; Patrick Diary, entry for February 22, 1865, p. 473; Breckinridge to Lee, March 8, 1865, OR, Series 46, Part 2, pp. 1292–93.

73 General Orders, No. 8, Headquarters, Army of Northern Virginia, March 27, 1865; Lee, *Wartime Papers*, p. 970.

74 Babcock to Webb, February 9, 1865, NARA, Microcopy 2096, Roll 38.

75 W. G. McGregor, "Headquarters Army of the Potomac," *Burlington Weekly Hawk-Eye* (Burlington, IA), February 18, 1865, p. 5.

76 Adam Badeau, *Military History of Ulysses S. Grant*, Vol. III (New York: D. Appleton and Company, 1882), p. 135.

77 John B. Gordon, *Reminiscences of the Civil War* (New York: Charles Scribner's Sons, 1903), pp. 424–25.

78 Patrick, *Inside Lincoln's Army*, diary entry for December 15, 1864, p. 450.

79 Special Orders No. 82, August 28, 1864, *Grant Papers*, Vol. 13, p. 435; Patrick to McEntee, February 27, 1865, Military Service Record of John McEntee, NARA.

80 Sharpe to Bowers, February 27, 1865, NARA, RG 393, entry 3980.

81 Patrick to the Adjutant General of the U.S. Army, April 29, 1865 with attachment, "Names, etc. of officers serving on the staff of Brig. Gen. W. R. Patrick, United States Volunteers," NARA, Microcopy 619, RG 94, Roll 0397.

82 Ulysses S. Grant, *Personal Memoirs of U.S. Grant* (New York: 1886), Vol. 2, pp. 167, 345.

83 Howell and Elizabeth Purdue, *Pat Cleburne: Confederate General* (Hillsboro, TX: Hill Jr. College Press, 1973), pp. 268–74. Cleburne's proposal had the effect of destroying his career. He had been slated to command a corps but was passed over by a far less capable officer. It was another self-inflicted wound by the Confederacy's commander-in-chief, who had recognized Cleburne's high military talents when he had given him the ultimate epithet, Stonewall of the West, after the debacle at Chattanooga when he had saved the army by his rearguard action. He was arguably the most capable division commander of either army in the Western theater. He was killed in action at the battle of Franklin, leading what was a suicide charge ordered by the army commander, Lt. Gen. John Bell Hood.

84 Grant to Halleck, February 8, 1864, OR, Vol. 46, Part 2, p. 475.

85 *Richmond Mercury*, February 9, 1865.

86   Grant to Canby, February 27, 1865, OR, Vol. 49, Part.1, pp. 780–81.

87   Sharpe to Jansen Hasbrouck, February 24, 1864, Sharpe Collection.

88   Gordon to Taylor, February 18, 1865, OR, Vol. 51, Part 2, p. 1063.

89   Gordon to Dear, February 26, 1863, John Brown Gordon Collection, University of Georgia.

90   Sharpe to Bowers, February 23, 1865, RG 108, entry 112, box 1, cited in William B. Feis, *Grant's Secret Service: The Intelligence War from Belmont to Appomattox* (Lincoln: University of Nebraska Press, 2002), pp. 260–61.

91   Ord to Rawlins, March 15, 1865, OR, Vol. 46, Part 2, p. 991; Sharpe to Ord, March 22, 1863, OR, Vol. 46, Part 3, pp. 78–79.

92   Homepage of the U.S. Senate, http:///www.senate.gov/artandhistory/history/common/generic/VP_Andrew_Johnson.thm.

93   Sharpe to Jansen Hasbrouck, March 7, 1864, Sharpe Collection.

Chapter Fourteen: The End

1   John B. Gordon, *Reminiscences of the Civil War* (New York: Charles Scribner's Sons, 1903), pp. 391–92.

2   Manning to Sharpe, March 15, 1865, NARA, M2096, Roll 37; Manning to Sharpe, March 15, OR, Series 1, Vol. 46, Part 2, p. 991.

3   Sharpe to Bowers, March 24, 1865, NARA, RG 108, Entry 112.

4   U.S. Congress, House of Representatives, 43rd Congress (June 22, 1874), 1st Session, Report No. 792 ("Samuel Ruth, W. F. E. Lohman, and Charles Carter").

5   Babcock to Meade, March 25, 1865, OR, Vol. 46, Part 3, p. 116.

6   Noah Andre Trudeau. *The Last Citadel: Petersburg, Virginia, June 1864–April 1865* (Baton Rouge: Louisiana State University Press, 1991), pp. 351–52.

7   Sharpe to Bowers, March 26, 1865, NARA, RG 108, Entry 112.

8   David D. Ryan, ed., *A Yankee Spy in Richmond: The Civil War of "Crazy Bet" Van Lee* (Mechanicsburg, PA: Stackpole Books, 1996), p. 49.

9   Oliver to Bowers, March 27, 1865, OR, Vol. 46, Part 3, p. 237; Oliver to Bowers, March 29, 1865, NARA, RG 108, Entry 112; Oliver to Bowers, March 31, 1865, RG 108, Entry 112.

10   Sparks, David S., ed., *Inside Lincoln's Army: The Diary of Marsena Rudolf Patrick, Provost Marshal General, Army of the Potomac* (New York: Thomas Yoseloff, 1964), diary entry for March 28, 1865, p. 484.

11   *The Kansas City Daily Gazette*, July 10, 1889. The article states that "He has letters on file from Generals Grant, Meade, Hancock, Sheridan and many others."

12   Harnett T. Kane, *Spies of the Blue and Gray* (Garden City, NY: Hanover House, 1954), pp. 248–49; "Personal Effects of the Late Miss Van Lew Disposed of at Auction," *Alton Evening Telegraph* (Alton, IL), November 24, 1900. After Van Lew's death in 1900 the flag was auctioned off for $75.

13   "Latest by Telegraph from Washington," *The Cincinnati Enquirer*, April 5, 1864, p. 3.

14   Noah Trudeau, *The Last Citadel: Petersburg, Virginia—June 1864–April 1865* (Baton Rouge, LA: University of Louisiana Press, 1991), pp. 411–12; Horace Porter, *Campaigning with Grant* (Secaucus, NJ: The Blue & Gray Press, 1984), pp. 450–51.

15   Grant to Sheridan, April 3, 1865, OR, Vol. 46, Part 3, p. 529.

16   Sharpe to Rawlings, April 6, 1865, NARA, RG 108, Entry 112.

17   L. E. Babcock to Patrick, April 23, 1865, NARA M345, RG 109, Roll 0012; "Charges and Specifications against B. C. Pole, Private, F Company, 1st Battalion, 11th U.S. Infantry," NARA, M619, RG 94, Roll 0397; "Military Prisoners in Richmond," *Norfolk Post*, August 29, 1865, p. 1.

18   Grant to Sheridan, April 3, 1865, OR, Vol. 46, Part 3, p. 529.

19 Gordon, pp. 426–27.

20 Gordon, pp. 427–28.

21 Sheridan to Grant, 9:20 p.m., April 8, 1865, OR, Vol. 46, Part 3, p. 653.

22 Horace Porter, *Campaigning with Grant* (New York: Charles Scribner's Sons, 1887), p. 473.

23 "At the Surrender of Lee," sketch by Alfred Waud, Library of Congress DRWG/US—Waud, no. 634 verso; Elizabeth R. Varon, *Appomattox: Victory, Defeat, and Freedom at the End of the Civil War* (New York: Oxford University Press, 2013), p. 57.

24 Sharpe, "At Appomattox," *The Philadelphia Weekly Times*, June 30, 1877; Sharpe, "The Last Day of the Lost Cause," *The National Tribune* (Wash., DC), October 10, 1879, p. 6.

25 Sharpe, "Appomattox: Incidents of Lee's Surrender," *Philadelphia Inquirer*, June 30, 1877.

26 Burke Davis, *To Appomattox: Nine April Days, 1865* (Short Hills, NJ: Buford Books, n.d., originally published in 1959), p. 386,

27 Porter, p. 483.

28 Porter, p. 487.

29 "Grant and Lee at Appomattox," *The Shippensburg News* (PA), March 11, 1876, p. 1.

30 "Organization of the Late Rebel Army of Northern Virginia," *The Wilmington Herald* (Wilmington, NC), April 25, 1865.

31 The original of Lee's note was retained by Sharpe and is now part of the Sharpe Collection in the Senate House State Historical Site, Kingston, NY.

32 Sharpe to Bowers, April 20, 1865, OR, Vol. 46, Part 3, pp. 851–53.

33 "Organization of the Late Rebel Army of Northern Virginia," *The Wilmington Herald*, April 25, 1865, p. 4.

34 Sharpe to Bowers, April 20, 1865, OR, Vol. 46, Part 3, pp. 851–53; Sharpe, "At Appomattox."

35 "Military Prisoners in Richmond," *Norfolk Post* (Norfolk, VA), August 29, 1865, p. 1, reprinted from the *Chicago Republican*; Ordway to Oliver, May 9, 1865, NARA, M619, RG 94.

36 G. B. D. Hasbrouck, "Address on Major General George H. Sharpe," *Proceedings of the Ulster Historical Society 1936–1937*, p. 39.

37 Catalog Number 961, Object: Sword of General George Henry Sharpe, Sharpe Collection, Senate House State Historical Site, Kingston, New York. The sword was donated to the museum by Sharpe's son, Henry, and his daughter and is described as: "Dress Sword; hilt of brass with crepe attached; silver colored scabbard; Engraved on scabbard "Brev. Maj. Gen. Geo. H. Sharpe with dates and list of battle he fought in."

38 William J. Seabrook, "Maryland's Part in Saving the Union," Emmitsburg Area Historical Society; Special Orders No. 196, War Department, Military Service Record of George H. Sharpe, NARA; Biographical History of the U.S. Congress, http://www.bioguide. Congress.gov; Record of the Court Martial of Benjamin G. Harris, File MM1957, NARA; "Treason at Home: Trial of Hon. Benj. G. Harris," *New York Times*, May 12, 1865.

39 Ordway to Oliver, May 9, 1865, NARA, M619, RG 94; Oliver to Patrick, May 9, 1865, NARA, M619, RG 94.

40 Sharpe to Rawlins, May 16, 1865, OR, Vol. 46, Part 3, p. 1158; and also at NARA, Microcopy 504, Roll 415.

41 John S. Mosby, *Mosby's Memoirs* (Nashville, TN: J. S. Sanders & Company, 1995), p. 388.

42 Special Orders No. 276, Headquarters of the Army, Washington, June 3, 1865, OR, Vol. 46, Part 3, p. 1250.

43 G. B. D. Hasbrouck, "Address on Major General George H. Sharpe," *Proceedings of the Ulster County Historical Society 1936–1937*, p. 37; "The Army," *New York Times*, July 29, 1866.

44 C. Van Santvoord, *The One Hundred and Twentieth Regiment, New York State Volunteers, A Narrative of its Services in the War for the Union* (Rondout, NY: Press of the Kingston Freeman, 1894), pp. 192–98.

45 Sharpe to Dix, telegram June 10, 1865, Military Service Record of George H. Sharpe, NARA.

46 Dix to Dodge, June 11, 1863, and Dodge to Dix, June 12, 1865, Military Service Record of George H. Sharpe, NARA.

47 Ulysses S. Grant, *Personal Memoirs of U. S. Grant* (New York: The Library of America, 1990), p. 771.

48 Marsena R. Patrick, *Inside Lincoln's Army: The Diary of Marsena Rudolph Patrick*, editor David Sparks, editor's comments (New York: Thomas Yoseloff, 1964), p. 19.

49 J. W. Schaffer, "Patrick," *The Times Picayune* (New Orleans), September 27, 1865.

50 "The President's Reply to the Colored Delegation," *The Times Picayune* (New Orleans), June 26, 1865,

51 Patrick, *Inside Lincoln's Army*, p 19; Virtual Museum—National Military Home Dayton Ohio: http://www.dayton.med.va.gov/museum/headquar.html; http://www.forgottenoh.com/Counties/Montgomery/dayton.html.

52 John Dahlgren, *Memoir of Ulric Dahlgren* (Philadelphia, PA: J. B. Lippincott & Co., 1872), pp. 263–85; Duane Schultz, *The Dahlgren Affair: Terror and Conspiracy in the Civil War* (New York: W. W. Norton & Co., 1998), pp. 259–61.

53 "The Richmond Post Office," *The Times* (Richmond, VA), July 25, 1891. At the time of Van Lew's appointment, the current postmaster was Alexander Sharpe, Grant's brother-in-law, who had been appointed by Lincoln. To make room for Van Lew, Grant appointed him U.S. Marshal of the District of Columbia. "Woman as Postmasters," *Newport Daily News* (Newport, RI), March 10, 1869; *Virginia Pilot*, October 12, 1890; *Harrisburg Daily Independent* (Harrisburg, PA), March 22, 1881; *The Daily Review* (Wilmington, NC), June 10, 1877.

54 William Gilmore Beymer, *Scouts and Spies of the Civil War* (Lincoln: University of Nebraska Press, 2003), p. 79.

55 Beymer, p. 54.

56 Beymer, p. 80; "Miss Van Lew's Debts," *The Times* (Richmond, VA), April 27, 1902.

57 Declaration for Pension (Form 3-014a) February 27, 1907, Pension Files of Milton W. Cline (NARA); Historic Cimarron—Curecanti National Recreation Area (U.S. Park Service) http://www.nps.gov/cure/learn/historyculture/cimarron.htm

58 "Rescued: The White Captives Released," *Ouray Times* (CO), October 25, 1879. http://www.coloradohistoricnewspapers.org/Repository/OTM/1879/10/25/009-OTM-1879-10-25-001-SINGLE. PDF#OLV0_Entity_0003_0003

59 Bureau of Pensions Statement, July 14, 1904 and State of Colorado. Town of Cimarron, death certificate dated October 30, 1911, Military Pension File of Milton W. Cline; "Milton W Cline." FindAGrave.com., retrieved October 2, 2015.

60 J. H. Knight [Sgt. Knight's brother] to Meade, January 1, 1867; Sharpe to Headquarters, Department of the East, January 25, 1867, Military Service Record of Judson H. Knight, NARA.

61 50th Congress, 1st Session, House of Representatives, Report No. 1839 entitled, "Judson Knight."

62 Private—No. 428, "An Act granting a pension to Judson Knight,"; Report No. 467, March 6, 1888 (U.S. Senate) and Report No. 1839, April 22, 1888 (U.S. House of Representatives), both to accompany bill S. 1192, 50th Congress, 1st Session, Military Pension File of Judson H. Knight

63 50th Congress, 1st Session, Senate, Report No. 467, and House of Representatives, Report No. 1839.

64 50th Congress, 1st Session, S. 1192 [Report No. 1839] entitled "An Act Granting a pension to Judson Knight."

65 Military Pension File of Judson Knight, Appeal of John Hunter (Knight's Attorney), Certificate Nos. 409 and 319, February 17, 1902, NARA.

66 Pension File of Judson Knight, document, Department of the Interior, Board of Review Division, "Decision to Appellant, June 38, 1902," NARA. One cannot but draw the parallel between the

treatment of Civil War veterans by the Pension Bureau and of our current veterans of Vietnam, Afghanistan, and Iraq by the Veterans Administration.

67 Declaration for Original Invalid Pension, dated April 14, 1879, Pension File of William J. Lee, NARA; General Affidavit of John Landegon, April 22, 1879 and General Affidavit of George H. Sharpe, December 13, 1879, Pension of William J. Lee, NARA; Grant to Lee, *Papers of U.S. Grant*, Vol. 30, p. 92. Report No. 821, U.S. Senate, 49th Congress, July 1, 1884; An Act granting a pension to William J. Lee (July 5, 1884) true copy of Department of State, July 17, 1884.

68 "Nearly Prevented Gettysburg Fight: Union Scout's Message to Gen. Meade, if Heeded, Might Have Halted Battle," June 26, 1913, newspaper clipping (possibly *The Washington Star*) found in the John C. Babcock Collection, Library of Congress; Letter from Harry Lee to the Commissioner of Pensions, November 28, 1917, Pension File of William J. Lee, NARA.

69 "Scout Carney Visits Kingston," *The Kingston Daily Freeman*, September 3, 1915.

70 A. B. Carney, "Carney Protests: Thinks Comrade Landegon Not Warranted in His Reflections," *The National Tribune*, July 5, 1894; deposition of John McEntee, March 19, 1887, Military Pension File of Anson B. Carney, NARA.

71 Babcock to Schoumaker, August 14, 1865, NARA, M619, RG 94, Roll 397.

72 Seward to Kelton, December 19, 1865, NARA, M619, RG 94, Roll 397.

73 Seward to Kelton, December 25, 1865, NARA, M619, RG 94, Roll 397.

74 Pole to Seward, July 10, 1866, NARA, M619, RG 94, Roll 397.

75 Registers of Enlistment in the United States Army Compiled 1798–1914, NARA, M233, RG 15; *Annual Report of the Secretary of the Navy for the Year 1888* (Washington: Government Printing Office, 1888), p. 241; Pension Application for service in the U.S. Army between 1861 and 1900, NARA, T289, RG 15. Benjamin C. Pole, findagrave.com, accessed November 14, 2015.

76 "Boiler Tested," *Kingston Daily Freeman*," January 21, 1874; "Complimentary," *Kingston Daily Freeman*, June 4, 1874.

77 Seward R. Osborne, "Officer Biographical Information, 20th New York State Militia (80th NYV)."

78 Bvt Maj. Gen. John Turner to Col. Warren, Notification of appointment, Headquarters, District of Henrico, June 27, 1865; Field and Staff Muster-out Roll, 80th NY, Jan. 29, 1866; and Special Orders No. 197, War Department, Adjutant General's Office, Washington, April 28, 1863 (Discharge), Military Service Record of John McEntee, NARA; Declaration for Invalid Pension, dated May 1, 1903; Military Pension File of John McEntee, NARA.

79 "Death of Col. John McEntee," undated article found in the Military Pension File of John McEntee, NARA.

80 Patrick to Babcock, May 5 and 15, 1865 and S. F. Adams to Babcock, January 12, 1903, John C. Babcock Collection, Library of Congress. Stanton was the determined and controlling figure in the hunt for Lincoln's assassins.

81 John A. Cockerill, "A Pair of Pistols," *Wichita Daily Eagle*, August 27, 1892.

82 "Military Prisoners in Richmond," *Norfolk Post* (Norfolk, VA), August 29, 1865, p. 1, reprinted from the *Chicago Republican*.

83 US Census 1870.

84 Henry G. Sharpe to Babcock, November 14, 1905; Theodore Lyman to Babcock, March 4, 1876, Babcock Collection.

85 Cockerill, "A Pair of Pistols."

86 Bureau of Pensions Declaration for Pension Form 3-014, dated February 1907; Declaration for Increase of Pension Form 3-004, dated January 2, 1907; Military Pension File for John C. Babcock, NARA.

87 Henry G. Sharpe to Babcock, July 7, 1904, Babcock Collection.

88 Henry G. Sharpe to Babcock, January 11, 1905, Babcock Collection.

89 Henry G. Sharpe to Babcock, November 11, 1905, Babcock Collection.

90 Babcock to William A. Pinkerton, April 9, 1908, Babcock Collection.

91 Military Service Record of Frederick L. Manning, NARA; Journal of the Executive Proceedings of the Senate 1871–1877; *Democrat & Chronicle*, July 19, 1895; "Regimental Reunion," *Geneva Gazette*, September 8, 1899; "Prize Speaking," *Democrat & Chronicle*, March 18, 1905; "Obituary," *The Brooklyn Daily Eagle*, August 14, 1908, p. 2.

92 "Brevet Brigadier General Paul A. Oliver, U.S. V.," http://www.all-biographies.com/soldiers/paul_a_oliver.htm.

93 H. C. Bradsby, "O Surnames, History of Luzerne County, Pa," 1893, www.pagenweb.org/~luzerne/bios/obios.htm, accessed October 29, 2015; "Nobody Was Hurt," *Altoona Tribune* (Altoona, PA), March 22, 1892; "Several Workmen Injured," *The Sun and Erie County Independent* (Hamburg, NY), December 16, 1892, p. 1.

94 "Preventing Forest Fires," *Altoona Tribune* (Altoona, PA), July 31, 1901, p. 2; "Penn Treaty Tree," *Indian Chieftain* (Vinita, OK), March 21, 1895, p. 2.

95 "To the Unknown Dead," *The Olean Democrat* (Olean, NY), July 4, 1893, p. 6; "Subscribing for Mrs. Hancock," *The Wilkes-Barre Record*, March 12, 1886, p. 4; "Honoring Grant's Memory," *Wilkes-Barre Times Leader* (Wilkes-Barre, PA), August 1, 1885, p. 1; John C. Babcock Papers, Library of Congress.

Chapter Fifteen: A Full Life: Sharpe's Progress

1 "The Horse of General Sharpe and His Tombstone," *Olde Ulster Journal*, Vol. 9, February 1913, No. 2, p. 43–45; "Gen. Sharpe's War Horse is Dead," *The Courier Journal* (Louisville, KY) (from the *Kingston Freeman*), November 12, 1882.

2 Sharpe to Stanton, March 21, 1866, The Papers of William H. Seward, LC.

3 David D. Ryan, *A Yankee Spy in Richmond: The Civil War Diary of "Crazy Bet" Van Lew* (Mechanicsburg, PA: Stackpole Books, 1996), pp. 114–19. Sharpe's letter is reproduced in the appendix.

4 "The New United States Marshal," *New York Herald*, April 8, 1870.

5 Papers of Benjamin Moran, Manuscripts Division, LC, Vol. 18, February 11, 1867.

6 Moran, Vol. 18, February 18, 1867.

7 Moran, Vol. 18, March 14, 1867.

8 Moran, Vol. 18, March 16, 1867.

9 Moran, Vol. 18, March 21, 1867.

10 "Message from the President of the United States Transmitting a Report of George H. Sharpe Relative to the Assassination of President Lincoln," December 17, 1867, *Executive Documents Printed by Order of the House of Representatives During the Second Session of the Fortieth Congress 1867–'68* (Washington: Government Printing Office, 1868), Document 68; Seward to Sharpe, December 18, 1866, The Papers of William H. Seward, Manuscript Division, LC.

11 Sharpe to Jansen Hasbrouck, May 15, 1867, letter from London, Sharpe Collection.

12 Sharpe to Jansen Hasbrouck, May 15, 1867. Emphasis in the original.

13 "Our Victory in the War," *New York Times*, June 8, 1877.

14 U.S. Census for 1860 and 1870.

15 Hasbrouck, p. 45; "Wake the Echoes," *Kingston Times,* July 6, 2006; "The Ulster Family Feud," *New York Times*, September 4, 1891.

16 Cornelius Van Buren, *Kingston Daily Freeman*, March 25, 1925.

17 "Death of General George H. Sharpe," *Kingston Weekly Freeman and Journal*, January 18, 1900; Sandra Lanman, "Rutgers Hall of Distinguished Alumni to Induct Eight," *Rutgers FOCUS*, May 30, 2006.

18   "This City and Vicinity," *The Kingston Daily Freeman*, January 8, 1889.

19   "Kingston Knights of Pythias," *The Kingston Daily Freeman*, February 20, 1889, p. 4.

20   "Told by Old Soldiers," *The Kingston Daily Freeman*, February 23, 1889, p. 2.

21   "Soldier and Sailors' Monument," *The Kingston Daily Freeman*, April 22, 1889, p. 4.

22   "Old Soldiers and Their Friends," *The Kingston Daily Freeman*, May 15, 1889, p. 4.

23   "Old Soldiers and Their Interests," *The Kingston Daily Freeman*, May 17, 1889, p. 4.

24   "Meeting Held at the Court House," *The Kingston Daily Freeman*, June 7, 1889, p. 4.

25   "The 120th Regiment Monument," *The Kingston Daily Freeman*, June 25, 1889, p. 4.

26   "No. of Bank—1,120," *The Kingston Daily Freeman*, July 20, 1889, p. 2.

27   "Pertaining to Friendly Societies," *The Kingston Daily Freeman*, September 15, 1889, p. 4.

28   "The Local Mortuary Records," *The Kingston Daily Freeman*, September 19, 1889, p. 4.

29   "A New Bank Superintendent," *The Kingston Daily Freeman*, December 24, 1889, p. 4.

30   Genealogical record, Saint Nicholas society of the city of New York, organized February 28, 1835. Severyn "served as Associate Member of a Legal Advisory Board, Selective Service, in New York City, 1917–1918. He was also Chairman of Local Board No. 136, New York City, 1917–1918." Sharpe family lineage, The Sharpe Collection, Senate House State Historical Site, Kingston, New York.

31   "Henry G. Sharpe, 89, Retired General," *The New York Times*, July 14, 1947; Sharpe family lineage, The Sharpe Collection, Senate House State Historical Site, Kingston, New York; Jean Edward Smith, *Grant* (New York: Simon & Schuster, 2001), p. 618; *Kingston Daily Freeman*, March 25, 1941.

32   "Married Amid Flowers," *The New York Times*, April 28, 1887.

33   "Sharpe-Patnyr," *The New York Times*, February 18, 1897.

34   Hasbrouck, p. 41.

35   *Kingston Daily Freeman*, July 28 and July 31, 1873; Hasbrouck, pp. 45–46.

36   Sharpe to Grant, July 1, 1873, *The Papers of Ulysses S. Grant*, Volume 24 (Carbondale, IL: Southern Illinois University Press), p. 95.

37   *Kingston Daily Freeman*, August 7, 1873.

38   Sharpe to McKean, October 6, 1870, Ulysses S. Grant Papers, Series 2, Vol. 5, p. 26, Manuscript Division, Library of Congress.

39   *Bangor Daily Whig and Courier*, October 18, 1874.

40   "Personal," *Kingston Daily Freeman*, May 23, 1874

41   "Why G. W. Childs, A. M., Hates Gen. Sharpe," *The Indianapolis News*, September 11, 1875. Unfortunately, the young Grant Sartorious (b. July 11, 1875 d. May 21, 1876) would not survive the coming year.

42   *The National Republican*, January 3, 1876; "Grant," *The National Republican*, June 14, 1876.

43   George H. Sharpe, "The Old House of Kingston," *The Journal* of Kingston, December 29, 1875; and "Old Times and Customs: The Old Houses of Kingston," *New York McKeank Times*, December 31, 1875.

Chapter Sixteen: A Public Life

1   "Political: Republican State Convention at Syracuse," *The New York Times*, September 30, 1869; *Kingston Daily Freeman*, October 4, 1873.

2   David Stuttard, *A History of Greece in Fifty Lives* (London: Thames & Hudson, Ltd, 2014), p. 250.

3   Gerald M. Best, *The Ulster and Delaware Railroad Through the Catskills* (San Marino, C: Golden West Books, 1972), p. 28. At its founding *The Kingston Daily Freeman* was named the *Rondout Daily Freeman*.

4   Best, pp. 38–30; "Appointment of Trustee of the NY, K. & S. RR," *Kingston Daily Freeman*, November 27, 1873; "A Railroad War," *The New York Times*, November 29, 1873.

5   Best, p. 29.

6   "That Ulster County Feud," *The New York Times*, September 4, 1891; Best, p. 30. Coykendall and Cornell had become associates in 1859.

7   Hasbrouck, p. 41; Jean Edward Smith, *Grant* (New York: Simon & Schuster, 2001), p. 618.

8   "Grand Army," *The Brooklyn Daily Eagle*, April 7, 1891, p. 1.

9   "An Enthusiastic Meeting at West Bright—Speeches of Gen. Davis and Gen. Sharpe," *The New York Times*, September 6, 1872.

10 *The Kingston Daily Freeman*, November 17, 1873.

11 "Grant and Colfax," *The New York Times*, September 18, 1872.

12 The appointment and its salary may have been welcome to Sharpe at this time because the 1870 census shows the value of his real estate at $15,000 and his personal estate at $4,000.

13 "The New United States Marshal," *The New York Herald*, April 8, 1870.

14 *New York Herald*, April 15, 1870.

15 "The Ninth Census," *The New York Times*, June 4, 1870; "Refutation of Census Complaints," *The New York Times*, September 16, 1870.

16 "Local Politics: Colored Mass Meeting at Cooper Institute," *The New York Times*, October 13, 1870.

17 "Politics and the Census," *The New York Times*, September 13, 1870; "Refutation of Census Complaints, *The New York Times*, September 16, 1870; "The City Census," *The New York Times*, October 24, 1870.

18 "An Unusually Large Vote Registration Yesterday," *The New York Times*, October 19, 1870.

19 "Constitutionality of the Election Law," *The New York Times*, November 3, 1870.

20 Fish to Grant, November 2, 1870, *Papers of U.S. Grant* (Carbondale, IL: Southern Illinois University Press), Vol. 21, pp. 5–6; Col. James Fisk, Jr., "On His High Horse," *The New York Daily Tribune*, November 8, 1870.

21 Fish to Grant, November 7, 1870, *Papers of Ulysses S. Grant*, Vol. 21 (Carbondale, IL: Southern Illinois University Press,), p. 5; "The Election Today," *The New York Times*, November 8, 1870.

22 Fish to Grant, November 7, 1870, *Papers of Ulysses S. Grant*, p. 5; "The Election Today," *The New York Times*, November 8, 1870.

23 Grant to Shaler, November 7, 1870, *Papers of Ulysses S. Grant*, p. 4.

24 Belknapp to McDowell, Papers *of Ulysses S. Grant*, p. 5.

25 "The Election Today," *The New York Times*, November 8, 1870.

26 "The United States Officials—Measures for the Enforcement of the Congressional Law—Troops Held in Readiness—Conferences of national and Local Authorities—Protection Extended to the Deputy Marshals," *The New York Times*, November 9, 1870; "The Tammany Ticket Elected," *New York Daily Tribune*, November 9, 1870.

27 *New York Herald*, October 26, 1870.

28 Thomas Kneally, *American Scoundrel: The Life of the Notorious Civil War General Daniel Sickles* (New York: Doubleday, 2002), pp. 334, 336–37; "Erie: Testimony of Gen. Sharpe on the Sickles Coup-de-Main—Senator O'Brien's Story," *The New York Times*, April 17, 1872.

29 "Night Before Election," *The New York Times*, November 5, 1872.

30 *Kingston Daily Freeman*, June 22, 1874.

31 Sharpe to McKean, February 6, 1870, Library of Congress, Papers of Ulysses S. Grant; OR, Series 2, Vol. 5, p. 26.

32 Fish to Sharpe, February 12, 1871, Library of Congress, Papers of Hamilton Fish.

33 Fish to Sharpe, June 17 and July 28, 1871, Library of Congress, Papers of Hamilton Fish; Adam Badeau, *Grant in Peace: From Appomattox to Mt. McGregor, a Personal Memoir* (Freeport, NY: Books for Libraries Press, 1971 (reprint of 1887 first edition)), pp. 375–78.

34 Badeau, p. 378.

35 "An Encouraging Comparison," *The New York Times*, August 8, 1887, p. 4.

36 "The Custom House Inquiry," *New York Tribune*, May 1, 1877.

37 "The Custom House System," *The New York Times*, May 1, 1877; George Frederick Howe, *Chester A. Arthur: A Quarter-Century of Machine Politics* (New York: Dodd, Meade & Company, 1934), p. 53. "Arthur's only aid to the collection of these percentages must have been in permitting a list of the officials and their salaries to be taken for the party treasurers."

38 Thomas C. Reeves, *Gentleman Boss: The Life and Times of Chester Alan Arthur* (Newton, CT: American Political Biography Press, 1975), p. 116.

39 "The Custom House System," *The New York Times*, May 2, 1877; O. E. Babcock to Sharpe, October 27, 1877, Grant Papers at the Library of Congress. Eli S. Parker, a full-blooded Iroquois, had been Grant's secretary for much of the war and had been in the room at the McLean House when Lee surrendered at Appomattox. *The Kingston Daily Freeman*, March 10, 1874.

40 "The Surveyor's Department," *The New York Times*, January 11, 1876.

41 Hasbrouck, p. 41; Murray N. Rothbard, "Bureaucracy and the Civil Service in the United States," *Journal of Libertarian Studies*, Summer 1995; "New York and Suburban News, *The New York Times*, April 2, 1873.

42 Donald Barr Chidsey, *The Gentleman from New York: A Life of Roscoe Conkling* (New Haven, CT: Yale University Press, 1935), p. 245.

43 "Custom-House Methods," *New York Tribune*, May 2, 1877; "The Custom House System," *The New York Times*, May 1, 1877.

44 "The Custom House Inquiry," *The New York Times*, May 17, 1877.

45 "Law Reports, Trial of ex-Inspector Grace," *The New York Times*, September 22, 1877.

46 "Custom House Matters, *The New York Times*, July 22, 1877.

47 "Four Months in Jail," *The New York Times*, September 25, 1877; Treasury Department, Exec. Files, Letters of William H. Grace; pamphlet published in NY, 1879, *Grace's Exposure, or Unsweetened Sugars*, cited in Howe, p. 68.

48 "Our New York Letter—Notes on Miscellaneous Metropolitan Topics: The Case of William H. Grace," *The Hartford Weekly Times* (Hartford, CT), October 4, 1977, p. 7; "Is This Civil Service Reform?", *The New York Times*, July 2, 1879, p. 5.

49 Donald Barr Chidsey, *Gentleman from New York: A Life of Roscoe Conkling* (New Haven: Yale University Press, 1935), p. 245; Reeves, *Gentleman Boss*, pp. 119, 121.

50 Chidsey, *Gentleman from New York*, pp. 245, 251.

51 "Is Gen. Sharpe Surveyor?" *The Sun* (NYC), December 4, 1877, p. 4; "Notes and News: The New York Custom House," *Chicago Daily Tribune*, August 2, 1877; "The Surveyorship of New York," *The New York Times*, August 2, 1877; Hasbrouck, p. 41; NNDB Tracking the World, entries on Rutherford B. Hayes and Chester A. Arthur, http: www.nndb.com. These latter sources and others state that Sharpe was also dismissed from his office, but they are not contemporaneous. Hasbrouck, who is also not contemporaneous, states that he left the office when his term expired as does the *Brooklyn Union-Argus* of July 21, 1879 which lists all the collectors of customs and surveyors of the Port of New York and lists Sharpe's term as having expired. Numerous other holders of these offices were listed as dismissed or removed, including Chester A. Arthur; "Testimonial to Gen. Sharpe," *The New York Times*, January 28, 1878.

52 "An Extra Ordinary Proceedings," *The New York Times*, December 18, 1877, p. 1; "Grace's Vindication," *The Brooklyn Daily Eagle*, December 18, 1877, p. 2. Two years later Grace appeared

at the Custom House and presented official documents that said he had been given his job back. His presence was met with disgust by the staff and no one would comply since he had not taken the required Civil Service examinations. The *Times* speculated that some underling in the Treasury had issued the appointment in the Secretary's absence, for "he is said to have declared that under no circumstances would Mr. Grace be renominated." If this is true, it indicates that Sherman knew that Grace was disreputable but used him as a tool to rid the Custom House of Sharpe. "Is This Civil Service," *The New York Times*, July 2, 1879, p. 5.

53   "Testimonial to Gen. Sharpe," *The New York Times*, January 28, 1878; Hasbrouck, p. 41.

54   "Sharpe Resigns as Appraiser," March 5, 1899, unidentified New York newspaper, Sharpe Collection, Senate House State Historical Site, Kingston, NY.

55   "A Good Beginning," *The New York Times*, January 23, 1879. p. 4; "Albany: The End of the Preliminaries Reached," *The Brooklyn Daily Eagle*, January 26, 1879. p. 4; "In the Committee Rooms," *The New York Times*, March 14, 1879, p. 5; "New York Legislature," *The Sun* (NYC), March 15, 1879, p. 3.

56   "City and Town Elections: Democratic Ruffiansim in Kingston," *The New York Times*, p. 5; "Imitation of the Southern Plan in New York," *The New York Times*, March 24, 1879, p. 1; "The Kingston Election Inquiry," *The New York Times*, March 25, 1879, p. 1; "The Kingston Rascality," *The New York Times*, April 2, 1879, p. 1; "Election Rioters at Kingston," *The Daily Gazette* (Port Jervis, NY), May 6, 1879, p. 2; "The Ulster Election Frauds," *The Brooklyn Daily Eagle*, June 22, 1879, p. 4; "Results of Democratic Misrule," *The New York Times*, September 15, 1879, p. 1.

57   "The Next Legislature," *The New York Times*, October 24, 1879.

58   "Cornell-Conkling Candidate for Speaker," *Chicago Daily Tribune*, November 24, 1879, p. 2; "The Speakership Contest," *The New York Times*, January 4, 1879, p. 1

59   "End of the Speakership Fight," *The New York Times*, January 6, 1880, p. 1.

60   "The Legislature Getting to Work," *The Brooklyn Daily Eagle*, January 8, 1880, p. 2.

61   "Legislators at Albany," *The New York Times*, January 20, 1880, p. 1.

62   "New York Legislators," *The New York Times*, January 17, 1880.

63   "State Legislature Work," *The New York Times*, January 21, 1880, p. 1.

64   "About General Sharpe," undated and unidentified newspaper article, Sharpe Collection.

65   "Legislative Work Ended," *The New York Times*, May 28, 1880, p. 5.

66   *The New York Times*, May 29, 1880, p. 4.

67   "Saturday's Proceedings," *The Daily Gazette* (Port Jarvis, NY), June 8, 1880, p. 1.

68   Smith, pp. 614–17.

69   Hasbrouck, p. 42; James D. Sullivan, ed., *The History of New York State* (Lewis Publishing Co., Inc. 1927), Book XII, Chapter 9, Part 3, online edition by Holice, Deb & Pam, http://www.usgennet.org/usa/ny/his/bk12/ch9/pt3.html; Chidsey, *Gentleman from New York*, p. 293; DeAlva Stanwood Alexander, *A Political History of the State of New York*, Vol. III (BiblioBazaar, 2008), p. 384.

70   "The Candidates Honored," *The New York Times*, August 7, 1880.

71   "Garfield and Arthur," *The New York Times*, October 11, 1880; "Ulster County's Complete Ticket," *The New York Times*, October 20, 1880.

72   "Candidates for the Assembly," *The New York Times*, October 17, 1880.

73   Sharpe to Garfield, November 4, 1884, James A. Garfield Papers, LOC.

74   "Gen. Sharpe the Speaker," *The New York Times*, January 4, 1881, p. 1.

75   "Party Caucus Held," *The New York Times*, January 4, 1881, p. 1.

76   Alexander, pp. 402–03.

77   "Opening Day at Albany," *The New York Times*, January 5, 1881, p. 5; *The Brooklyn Daily Eagle*, no heading, January 5, 1881; "Activity at Albany," *New York Tribune*, January 5, 1881, p. 1; "The Senatorial Contest, *New York Tribune*, 1st edition, p. 1.

78   "Executive Interference," *The New York Times*, March 1, 1881.

79   "Visiting Gen. Garfield," *The New York Times*, February 26, 1881, p. 1.

80   "The State Legislature," *The Olean Democrat* (Olean, NY), March 24, 1881.

81   Thomas C. Reeves, *Gentleman Boss: The Life and Times of Chester Alan Arthur* (Newtown, CT: American Political Biography Press, 1975), pp. 224–26.

82   In the days before the 17th Amendment, Senators were elected by their state legislatures.

83   "Sharpe and Conkling," *The New York Tribune*, June 10, 1882. This article consists of a lengthy statement by Sharpe during the reporter's interview.

84   C. D. Chickering to Sharpe, May 31, 1882, cited in "Sharpe and Conkling," *New York Tribune*, June 19, 1882.

85   "Sharpe and Conkling," *The New York Tribune*, June 19, 1882.

86   Thomas Collier Platt, *The Autobiography of Thomas Collier Platt* (New York: B. W. Dodge & Company, 1910), p. 160.

87   "Sharpe and Conkling," *The New York Tribune*, June 19, 1882; "General Sharpe's Side of It," *Chicago Daily Tribune*, June 9, 1982.

88   "Gen. Sharpe in Search of Documentary Evidence to Sustain His Assertions," *Chicago Daily Tribune*, June 16, 1882.

89   "Between Mr. Conkling and Gen. Sharpe," *Chicago Tribune*, June 9, 1882.

90   "Adding to his Humiliation," *New York Tribune* (reprinted from the *Boston Advertiser*), June 14, 1882.

91   "Conkling's Cause Lost," *The New York Times*, May 31, 1881.

92   "The Coming Conflict; Marshalling the Force For and Against Conkling," *The New York Times*, May 24, 1881; "Sharpe and Conkling," *The New York Tribune*, June 19, 1882.

93   "Naming the Candidates," *The New York Times*, June 1, 1881, p. 1.

94   "Sharpe and Conkling" and "Conkling's Ranks Broken," *The New York Times*, July 17, 1881.

95   "Voice of New York Legislators," *The New York Times*, July 7, 1881; "Conkling's Ranks Broken," Senate Historical Office, http://www.senate.gov/artandhistory/hitory/common/generic/VP_Chester_Arthur.htm.

96   "The Conkling Men Routed: An Orderly and Short Convention," *The New York Times*, October 5, 1881, p. 1.

97   "Outlining the Campaign: Recognized Need of Harmony in Ulster County," *The New York Times*, p. 7.

98   Hasbrouck; Sullivan; "Nominations in the State," *The New York Times*, October 27, 1881. p. 1; "Republican Majority," *The New York Times*, November 9, 1881, p. 1.

99   Edward P. Kohn, *Heir to the Empire City: New York and the Making of Theodore Roosevelt* (New York: Basic Books, 2014), p. 65.

100 *Diary kept by Theodore Roosevelt during the New York Assembly*, pp. 1–2, Theodore Roosevelt Birthplace Historic Site, http://www.theodorerooseveltcenter.orgt/Research/Digital-Library/Record-aspx! libID=o283076.

101 "Candidates Put in Nomination, *The New York Times*, September 21, 1882.

102 "More Facts About It," *Brooklyn Daily Eagle*, December 30, 1893.

103 Ben Perley Poor, "Chester Alan Arthur," *The Bay State Monthly: A Massachusetts Magazine*, Vol. 1, No. V, May 1884; "The President in the City," *The New York Times*, September 30, 1881.

104 Hasbrouck, p. 48; "The President's Summer Trip," *The New York Times*, August 19, 1884; "Alek had a good time," *The National Republican*, September 11, 1884.

105 Hasbrouck, p. 48; "The President's Summer Trip," *The New York Times*, August 19, 1884; Ruth Tenzer Feldman, *Chester A. Arthur* (Twenty-First Century Books, 2006), p. 95.

106 Badeau, pp. 334–41.

107 Sharpe to Arthur, May 26, 1884, James A. Garfield Papers, LOC; Jean Edward Smith, *Grant* (New York: Simon & Schuster, 2001), p. 622,

108 "Gen. Grant Disappointed," *The New York Times*, April 18, 1885; "Getting Stronger," *The Inter-Ocean* (Chicago), p. 5; "U.S. Grant's Memory," *The Brooklyn Daily Eagle*, April 28, 1893, p. 7; Smith, p. 625; "At Rest in the Tomb," *Chicago Tribune*, August 10, 1885; "Will Dine on Grant's Birthday," *The New York Times*, February 26, 1890.

109 "Kingston, NY," *The New York Times*, April 6, 1884, p. 1; "The Preliminary Conventions," *The New York Times*, April 10, 1884, first edition; "Ulster's Three Districts Anti-Arthur," *The New York Times*, April 13, 1884, p. 1; "The Recent Skirmishes," *The New York Times*, April 14, 1884; "Gen. Sharpe, 'Done for'," *Chicago Tribune*, April 15, 1884.

110 "The Temporary Organization," *The New York Times*, April 24, 1884, p. 1.

111 "Gen. Sharpe's Revenge," *The Sun* (NYC), 1st ed., September 19, 1884; "Gen. Sharpe Wins His Point," *The New York Times*, September 19, 1884.

112 "Gen. Sharpe," *Chicago Daily Tribune*, May 30, 1884; "All the Whooping if for Blaine," *The Sun* (NYC), June 5, 1884.

113 "Trade with Central America," *The New York Times*, October 10, 1884, p. 8; "Central and South America: General Grant Suggests that Commercial Agents be Appointed for Manufacturers of the United States," *Dunkirk Evening Observer* (Dunkirk, NY), p. 1; "A Great Stir Over Grant," *The Times* (Philadelphia), May 17, 1883, p. 1.

114 Hasbrouck, pp. 41–45; U.S. Department of State, Despatches Received by the Department of State from the U.S. Commission to Central and South America, July 14, 1884–December 26, 1885, Washington: National Archives, 1964 (microfilm); "Trade With Southern Nations," *The New York Times*, September 17, 1884; "South American Trade," *The New York Times*, 1884.

115 "Gen. Sharpe's Narrow Escape," *The New York Times*, August 10, 1884.

116 "Who Will Succeed Folger," *The Critic* (Washington, DC), September 12, 1884; "The Treasury Portfolio," *The New York Times*, September 13, 1884; *The Chicago Daily Tribune*, September 18, 1884.

117 1884 Presidential General Election Data—National, http://uselectionatlas.org/RESULTS/data.php?year=1884&datatype=national&def=1&f=0&off=0&elect=0, retrieved December 21, 2014.

118 "A Danger to be Removed," *Brooklyn Daily Eagle*, February 25, 1885; "For Gen. Swaim's Place," *The New York Times*, March 2, 1885.

119 "Chester A. Arthur Sudden Death from Apoplexy of the ex-Pres," *National Tribune*, November 28, 1886; *The New York Times*, November 28, 1886.

120 "New York Politics," *The Decatur Herald*, September 24, 1885, p. 1.

121 "Gen. Sharpe's Defeat," *The New York Times*, September 11, 1887; *The Times* (Philadelphia), July 21, 1889.

122 Hasbrouck, p. 44.

123 "New General Appraisers," *The New York Times*, July 3, 1890; "Another Estimate of Sharpe," *The New York Times*, July 6, 1890; "Gen. Sharpe a Judas as Usual," *The New York Times*, November 6, 1890.

124 "Wrecked by its Officers: Ulster County Savings Institute Closes its Doors," *The New York Times*, p. 1.

125 "That Ulster Country Feud," *The New York Times*, September 4, 1891; "Bossed by Gen. Sharpe," *The New York Times*, April 20, 1892; "Sharpe Ran the Convention," *The New York Times*, April 27, 1892.

126 Hasbrouck, p. 44.

127 "Custom House," *The Times-Picayune* (New Orleans), February 12, 1891.

128 "The Duty on Carpet Wool," *Chicago Daily Tribune*, July 19, 1891; "The Board of Customs," *The New York Times*, April 19, 1898; "Woolen Imports," *The Saint Paul Globe*, October 28, 1893; "Work of the General Appraisers," *The New York Times*, September 4, 1897.

129 "Proved to be Kites," *The Sun* (NYC), March 8, 1891.

130 Hasbrouck, p. 44; "Reorganization of the Board of Appraisers," *The Times* (Philadelphia), October 24, 1897; "Gen. Sharpe No Longer an Appraiser," *The New York Times*, March 1, 1998; "Walter S. Chance to Succeed Gen. George B. Sharpe," *The New York Times*, March 3, 1898; "Gen. Sharpe's Record," *The New York Times*, March 8, 1898; "Requested to Resign," *The Morning Times* (Washington, DC), January 26, 1899; "Sharpe Returns to Duty," *The New York Times*, April 1, 1898; "The Board of Customs," *The New York Times*, March 8, 1898.

131 "Appraisers Asked to Resign," *The New York Times*, January 24, 1899; Hasbrouck, pp. 44–45.

Chapter Seventeen: The Bugle Echoes

1 "Jerome Williams Talks of General G. H. Sharpe," *Kingston Daily Freeman*, July 1, 1937.

2 Society of the Army of the Potomac, *Report of the 13th Annual Re-Union at Detroit, Michigan, June 14 & 15, 1882* (New York: Macgowan & Slipper, Printers, 1882), pp. 99–110; "Army of the Potomac," *Vermont Phoenix* (Brattleboro, VT), May 15, 1896.

	Recording Secretary	Corresponding Secretary
1869	George H. Sharpe	Horatio C. King
1870	George H. Sharpe	Horatio C. King
1871	George H. Sharpe	W. C. Church
1872	George H. Sharpe	W. C. Church
1873	George H. Sharpe	W. C. Church
1874	George H. Sharpe	W. C. Church
1875	No meeting held that year	
1876	George H. Sharpe	W. C. Church
1877	Horatio C. King	T. R. Rondenbough
1878	Horatio C. King	T. R. Rondenbough
1879	Horatio C. King	George H. Sharpe
1880	Horatio C. King	George H. Sharpe
1881	Horatio C. King	George H. Sharpe
1882	Horatio C. King	George H. Sharpe
1883	Horatio C. King	George H. Sharpe
1884	Horatio C. King	George H. Sharpe
1885	Horatio C. King	George H. Sharpe
1886	George H. Sharpe	Horatio C. King
1887	Horatio C. King	George H. Sharpe
1888	Horatio C. King	George H. Sharpe
1889	Horatio C. King	George H. Sharpe
1890	Horatio C. King	George H. Sharpe
1891	Horatio C. King	George H. Sharpe
1892	Horatio C. King	George H. Sharpe
1893	Horatio C. King	George H. Sharpe
1894	Horatio C. King	George H. Shape
1895	Horatio C. King	Horatio C. King
1896	Horatio C. King	George H. Sharpe

3 "Gallant Boys in Blue," *Erie County Independent*, July 3, 1891, p. 1; Sharpe to Garfield, March 19, 1870 and March 5, 1872, James A. Garfield Papers, LC.

4 *Report of the 12th Annual Re-Union of the Society of the Army of the Potomac at Hartford, Connecticut, June 8, 1881* (New York: MacGowan & Slipper, 1881), pp. 61–62.

5   "The Bummers' Meeting," *The Brooklyn Daily Eagle*, June 13, 1884, p. 2; *Vermont Watchman*, June 23; *Report of the Ninth Annual Re-Union of the Army of the Potomac at Springfield, Mass., June 5, 1878* (New York: MacGowan & Slipper, 1878), pp. 86–87.

6   *Report of the 15th Annual Re-Union of the Army of the Potomac at Brooklyn, New York, June 11 and 12, 1884* (New York: MacGowan & Slipper, 1884), p. 63.

7   "Last Hours of the Confederacy," *The New York Times*, January 21, 1876, p. 5.

8   "News of the Day," *Alexandria Gazette* (Alexandria, VA), January 3, 1893, p. 2.

9   G. B. D. Hasbrouck, "Address on Major General George H. Sharpe," *Proceedings of the Ulster County Historical Society 1936–1937*, p. 47; *Military Order of the Loyal Legion of the United States, Roster of the Commandery of the State of New York from January 17th, 1866, to January 1st, 1895* (no publication citation); *Brooklyn Daily Eagle*, "Custer's Funeral," October 11, 1877; Military Order of the Loyal Legion of the United States website: http://suvew.org/mollus.htm, and information kindly provided by Keith G. Harrison, National Junior Vice Commander-in-Chief and National Webmaster & Membership List Coordinator, Military Order of the Loyal Legion of the United States; "Military Gossip," *New York Times*, January 13, 1878.

10 "Gen. Sharpe's Lecture," *Kingston Daily Freeman*, December 17, 1873, p. 3.

11 George H. Sharpe, "Our Victory in the War," *The New York Times*, June 8, 1877, p. 5.

12 George H. Sharpe and, "Memorial Address of General George H. Sharpe," *Seventh Annual Reunion of the 120th N. Y. V. Regimental Union—Lieut.-Col. J. Rudolph Tappen* (Kingston, NY: The Daily Freeman Steam Printing House, 1875), p. 19.

13 Van Santvoord, pp. 199–210.

14 "Sherman Socially," *The Galveston Daily News*, February 13, 1891, p. 6.

15 "Home for Ex-Confederate Soldiers," *Harrisburg Daily Independent*, April 9, 1884, p. 1. Confederate generals John B. Gordon and Mathew W. Ransom also spoke at the meeting. "Army of the Potomac," *Dunkirk Evening Observer* (Dunkirk, NY), p. 1.

16 "The Battlefield Reunion," *The New York Times*, May 13, 1888, p. 2.

17 "Gettysburg: Preparations for the Great Quarter Centennial," *The National Tribune*, July 5, 1888, p. 8.

18 "The Three Days," *The National Tribune*, July 12, 1888, p. 8; "Gettysburg Heroes: Events of their Celebration on the Battlefield," *Weekly News and Democrat* (Auburn, NY), July 5, 1888, p. 1.

19 Hasbrouck, p. 47; "Death of General George H. Sharpe," *Kingston Weekly Freeman and Journal*, January 18, 1900; Van Santvoord, pp. 211–29.

20 "Old Timer's Civil War Notes," *Kingston Daily Freeman*, April 11, 1961.

21 "Gen. Sharpe's Gift," *Kingston Daily Freeman and Journal*, October 17, 1896; "General Sharpe at the Unveiling," *Olde Ulster Journal*, Vol. VIII, November 1912, no. 11, p. 327.

22 "A Statue of Patriotism," *The New York Times*, p. 4. The battles are the official list provided by the War Department and read:
    Fredericksburg, Chancellorsville,
    Gettysburg, James City, Mine Run,
    Wilderness, Spotsylvania, North Anna,
    Totopotomy, Cold Harbor, Petersburgh,
    Strawberry Plains, Deep Bottom,
    Poplar Spring Church,
    Boydton Plank Road, (Oct. 27–28, 1864)
    Dabney's Mills (or Hatcher's Run)
    Petersburgh (or Tucker's House, March 25, 1865),
    Boydton Plank Road, (March 31, 1865),
    White Oak Road. Aemelia Springs,
    Farmsville, Appomattox Court House.

23 "Gen. Sharpe's Gift," p. 328. The verse is from *The German of Johann Ludwig Uhland*, "The Passage," anonymous translator.

24 "To Welcome the Troops," *New York Times*, August 4, 1898, p. 3; "The Seventy-First Sails," *The Morning Times* (Washington, DC), August 9, 1898, p. 1.

25 "The Death of George H. Sharpe," *The Argus* (NY), January 17, 1900.

26 West Point in the Making of America, http://americanhistory.si.edu/westpoint/history_5b2.html, accessed December 13, 2014.

27 "A Story of Gettysburg," *The Kane Republican* (Kane, PA), January 7, 1899, p. 2.

28 "Death of General George H. Sharpe," *Kingston Weekly Freeman and Journal*, January 18, 1900; "Obituary," *New Paltz Independent* (New Paltz, NY), February 18, 1898, Sharpe Collection.

29 "Gen. Sharpe's Death: How It Was Announced to the Assembly," *Kingston Weekly Freeman and Journal*, January 18, 1900.

30 "Funeral of Gen. Sharpe," *Kingston Daily Freeman*, January 16, 1900.

31 "Death of George A. Sharpe," *Argus*, January 17, 1900, Sharpe Collection.

32 "Tribute to Gen. Sharpe," *Kingston Daily Freeman*, February 12, 1900.

33 Unsourced newspaper report of Sharpe's death, Sharpe Collection.

34 "Eloquent Tribute to General Sharpe," *Kingston Daily Freeman*, no date given, Sharpe Collection.

35 "The Late Gen. Sharpe," *Weekly Leader* (Kingston, NY), January 20, 1900.

36 Charles T. Coutant, "General Sharpe and Lee's Surrender," *Olde Ulster Journal*, Vol. VIII, September 1912, No. 9, pp. 2274–79.

37 "The General George H. Sharpe Memorial Committee Organized," *Kingston Daily Freeman*, April 29, 1920; "120th Regiment Reunion Held," *Kingston Daily Freeman*, August 24, 1920; *Kingston Daily Freeman*, February 13, 1953.

38 Mary Black Terwilliger to Fishel, August 21, 1962, Fishel Collection, Georgetown University Library. Mrs. Terwilliger was the Historic Site Superintendent, Senate House Museum.

39 "Jerome Williams Talks of General G. H. Sharpe," *Kingston Daily Freeman*, July 1, 1937.

40 "Temporary Camp on Field," *Gettysburg Times*, November 11, 1943; "Camp George H. Sharpe Closed at Gettysburg," *Morning Sun* (Baltimore), July 27, 1944; "Camp Sharpe Moved to Nearby Area," *Gettysburg Times*, July 28, 1944.

41 "The New Unites States Marshal," *New York Herald*, April 8, 1870.

42 Henry G. Sharpe to Babcock, July 7, 1904, Babcock Collection.

Appendices

1 This list is not comprehensive but has pieced together from various sources to include BMI reports, military personnel records, and pension records held by NARA.

2 Edwin Fishel, *The Secret War for the Union: The Untold Story of Military Intelligence in the Civil War* (Boston: Houghton-Mifflin, 1996), p. 295.

3 These officers' ranks are those held when they joined the BMI. Sharpe was brevetted to brigadier general in January 1865 and to major general after the war; McEntee, Manning, and Oliver were all promoted to lieutenant colonel before the end of the war. They were brevetted to full colonel after the war.

4 Also known as the 80th New York Infantry.

5 NARA, RG92, Entries 0910 (1863), 0447 (1964), 0447 (1865).

6 NARA, RG92, Entry 0910 (1863). Scout contract dates were only listed for payrolls Jan–May 1863.

7 Allen's father, Thomas, was a resident of Fauquier County and considered to be "off color," a quarter black, and was denied the right to vote. The entire family was strongly Unionist.

8 Fishel, *The Secret War for the Union*, p. 295. Fishel states that Louis Battail (Lewis Battle) and Dabney Walker "went on the payroll as cooks," although they are listed as guides on the June 1863 payroll.

9 NARA, Microcopy 2096, Roll 34, Sharpe to Williams, July 9, 1863. Although Beverely is not listed in the payrolls, Sharpe definitely writes of him as "one of our scouts" in this report.

10 Blake was not listed on the BMI payrolls but was identified as a scout in the company of Judson Knight in NARA, RG 110, Entry e31, Box 2, File 80, by a letter dated April 13, 1863.

11 Anson Carney earlier served in B Co., 20th NY State Militia.

12 Cline's Military Service Record at NARA states he was on detached duty at Army of the Potomac headquarters since February 25, 1863.

13 Walter Cline was the teenage son of Chief of Scouts Milton Cline.

14 Cole's Military Service Record at NARA contains a letter from Col. Sharpe attesting to Cole's presence in the BMI as of March 5, 1863.

15 First mention of Dodd with the BMI was in March 1863.

16 NARA, RG92, Entries 410 (1864) and 410 (1865). A Henry Evans is listed in the November 1864 payroll, and a Henry Evans described as colored is listed in the March 1865 payroll.

17 William Fay, shipbuilder, was one of the runners for the Richmond Unionist spy ring run by Elizabeth Van Lew.

18 Ebenezer Halleck, grocer on Main St., was one of the runners for the Richmond Unionist spy ring run by Elizabeth Van Lew.

19 Harter had been a member of the Co. I, 1st IN Cavalry until his discharge on October 9, 1863, after which he was employed by the BMI.

20 NARA, Military Service Record of Martin E. Hogan. Hogan was a 22-year-old Irish immigrant and member of Co. A., 1st Indiana Cavalry where he served as a scout. He had already been captured once on August 5, 1862 and paroled and exchanged. Sharpe had requested his transfer to the BMI on June 6, 1863. He was to be captured again on this expedition and escape in January 1865.

21 First mention of Humphreys in the BMI was February 13, 1863.

22 John C. Babcock Collection, Library of Congress. This may well be the colored guide, Richard Johnson. In 1902 a lawyer for Johnson's widow inquired of Babcock if he could confirm Johnson's service, and cited May 1864 as the date he joined the BMI.

23 NARA, Military Service Record for Judson Knight. Knight had been in H Co., 2nd New Jersey Infantry before being medically discharged on Dec 31, 1862. He then joined the BMI as a civilian.

24 Jack Lyon is referred to as a scout in a BMI report of April 5, 1863.

25 Charles Major was one of the runners for the Richmond Unionist spy ring run by Elizabeth Van Lew.

26 Alexander Myers was one of the runners for the Richmond Unionist spy ring run by Elizabeth Van Lew.

27 Edwin Fishel, *The Secret War for the Union*, p. 292. Fishel identifies D. G. Otto as an early scout for Sharpe who had proven himself scouting for Pleasonton; however, there is no D. G. Otto in the Military Personnel Records at NARA.

28 Daniel Plew's Military Service Record at NARA states he was on detached duty as a scout with the Secret Service at the headquarters of the Army of the Potomac as of June 14, 1863.

29 Fishel, *The Secret War for the Union*, p. 295. Fishel states that Dabney Walker and Louis Battail (Lewis Battle) "went on the payroll as cooks," although they are listed as guides on the June 1863 payroll.

30 Weaver is identified by Sharpe in a message dated August 11, 1863 (NARA, BMI files) as employed by the BMI although his name does not appear on the payrolls.

31 William Wilson appears in Library of Congress photos, LC-USZ62-108336, by James Gardner, and is identified by name as a scout with the Headquarters, Army of the Potomac. Wilson's name does not appear in the BMI payroll records.

32 Abram Coin had been a wagoner in the 20th NYSM, which was part of the Provost Brigade, and was wounded in the explosion of the ammunition ship at City Point in August 9, 1864. He was mustered out at City Point on September 18. He appeared on the BMI payroll only once, in December 1864, as a teamster. He's an example of how fluid was the personnel make-up of the BMI.

33 Figures were obtained from NARA, RG 92, Entry 238, Files 191 (1863), 447 (1864), 447 (1865).

34 The originals of these tables are found in the Hooker Papers at the Huntington Library in Pasadena, CA. There are four copies in different hands of most of these tables. This author has not been able to find copies in the National Archives.

35 Incomplete returns

36 Does not include detachments absent from the battle of Chancellorsville

37 "Oscar Talks of His Plans for the New Kingston Hotel," *Kingston Daily Freeman*, July 23, 1922, p. 1.

38 "Severyn B. Sharpe, Lawyer, Dies at 73," *The New York Times*, November 26, 1929.

39 Application for Membership, National No. 94105, The Rhode Island Society of the National Society, Sons of the American Revolution, March 29, 1966.

40 "Colonel Henry G. Sharpe," *The Minneapolis Journal*, February 23, 1901; "Gen. Sharpe Promoted," *The Washington Post*, September 17, 1916.

41 West Point in the Making of America, http://americanhistory.si.edu/westpoint/history_5b2.html, accessed December 13, 2014; "Meade's Men Meet Lee's at Gettysburg," *The New York Times*, June 22, 1913.

42 U.S. Army Quartermaster Foundation, http://www.qmfound.com/MG_Henry_Sharpe.htm, accessed December 13, 2014; "General Sharpe promoted."

43 "Henry G. Sharpe, 89, Retired General," *The New York Times*, July 14, 1947.

44 "Ira Davenport," *Brooklyn Daily Eagle*, October 7, 1904; "Mrs. Davenport Presents Copy to Senate House, *Kingston Daily Freeman*, December 3, 1930; "Auction Sale," *Daily Messenger* (Canandaigua, NY), October 1, 1946.

Bibliography

Primary Sources

The John C. Babcock Collection, Library of Congress, Washington, DC.

Badeau, Adam. *Military History of Ulysses S. Grant*, 3 vols. New York: D. Appleton & Company, 1882.

Benson, Berry. *Civil War Book: Memoirs of a Confederate Scout and Sharpshooter*. Athens: University of Georgia Press, 1992.

Beymer, William Gilmore. *Scouts and Spies of the Civil War*. Lincoln: University of Nebraska Press, 2003.

Conrad, Thomas Nelson. *The Rebel Scout: A Thrilling History of Scouting Life in the Southern Army*. Westminster, MD: Heritage Books, 2009.

Cooke, John Esten. *Wearing of the Gray: Being Personal Portraits, Scenes, and Adventures of the War*. Baton Rouge, LA: University of Louisiana Press, 1997.

Dahlgren, John. *Memoir of Ulric Dahlgren*. Philadelphia: J. B. Lippincott & Co., 1872.

Dowdey, Clifford and Manarin, Louis H., eds. *The Wartime Papers of Robert E. Lee*. Boston, 1961.

Early, Jubal. *Jubal Early's Memoirs: Autobiographical Sketch and Narrative of the War Between the States*. Baltimore, MD: The Nautical & Aviation Publishing Company, 1989.

Freeman, Douglas Southall, ed. *Lee's Dispatches: Unpublished Letters of General Robert E. Lee, C. S. A. to Jefferson Davis and the War Department of the Confederate States of America 1862–65*. Baton Rouge: University of Louisiana Press, 1994.

Gates, Theodore B. *The War of the Rebellion*. New York, 1884.

Gibbon, John. "The Council of War on the Second Day," Robert Johnson and Clarence Buell, *Battles and Leaders of the Civil War*, volume 3, New York, 1884–88.

Gordon, John B. *Reminiscences of the Civil War*. New York: Charles Scribner's Sons, 1903.

Grant, Ulysses S. *Ulysses S. Grant: Personal Memoirs of U. S. Grant, Selected Letters 1839–1865*. New York: The Library of America, 1990.

Heverly, C. F. *Our Boys in Blue: Heroic Deeds, Sketches and Reminiscences of Bradford County Soldiers in the Civil War*. Towanda, PA: The Bradford Star Print, 1898.

Hood, J. B. *Advance and Retreat*. Edison, NJ: Blue and Gray Press, 1985.

The Hooker Papers, Huntington Library, Pasadena, CA.

Humphreys, Andrew A. *The Virginia Campaign of 1864 and 1865*. New York: Charles Scribner's Sons, 1883.

Lee, Fitzhugh. *General Lee*. New York: D. Appleton and Company, 1894.

Lee, Robert Edward, Jr. *The Recollections & Letters of Robert E. Lee*. New York: Konecky & Konecky, n.d. (originally published in 1904 by Doubleday, Page & Co., New York).

Longstreet, James. *From Manassas to Appomattox: Memoir of the Civil War in America*. New York: Mallard Press, 1991.

Lyman, Theodore. *Meade's Headquarters 1863–1865, Letters of Colonel Theodore Lyman from the Wilderness to Appomattox*. Boston: Atlantic Monthly Press, 1922.

Meade, George, ed. *The Life and Letters of George Gordon Meade*, 2 vols. New York: Charles Scribner's Sons, 1913.

Meade, George Gordon, Jr. *The Battle of Gettysburg*. Ambler, PA: 1924.

Osborne, Seward R., ed. *The Civil War Diaries of Col. Theodore B. Gates, 20th New York State Militia*. Hightstown, NJ: Longstreet House, 1991.

Porter, Horace. *Campaigning With Grant*. New York: The Century Company, 1897.

Regimental Letter and Order Book, 120th NY Infantry, RG 94, Vol. 3 of 8, National Archives and Record Administration (NARA).

Ryan, David D., ed. *A Yankee Spy in Richmond: The Civil War Diary of "Crazy Bet" Van Lew*. Mechanicsburg, PA: Stackpole Books, 1996.

Sheridan, Phillip. *Civil War Memoirs*. New York: Bantam Books, 1991.

Society of the Army of the Potomac Eleventh Annual Re-Union Held in the City of Burlington, June 16, 1880. New York: MacGowan & Slipper, 1880.

Society of the Army of the Potomac Twelfth Annual Re-Union at Hartford, Connecticut, June 8, 1881. New York: MacGowan & Slipper, 1881.

Society of the Army of the Potomac Fourteenth Annual Re-Union at Washington, D.C., May 16 and 17, 1883. New York: MacGowan & Slipper, 1883.

Society of the Army of the Potomac Fifteenth Annual Re-Union of the Army of the Potomac at Brooklyn, New York, June 11 and 12, 1884. New York: MacGowan & Slipper, 1884.

Sparks, David S., ed. *Inside Lincoln's Army: The Diary of Marsena Rudolf Patrick, Provost Marshal General, Army of the Potomac*. New York: Thomas Yoseloff, 1964.

Summer, Merlin E., ed. *The Diary of Cyrus B. Comstock*. Dayton, OH: Morningside House, Inc., 1987.

Tappen, Lieut.-Colonel J. Rudolph. *Addresses Delivered at the Music Hall of Kingston at the Seventh Annual Meeting of the 120th Regimental Union by General George H. Sharpe and General Theodore B. Gates*. Kingston, NY: The Daily Freeman Steam Printing House, 1975.

Taylor, Walter H. *General Lee: His Campaigns in Virginia, 1861–1865, With Personal Reminiscences*. Lincoln: University of Nebraska Press, 1994.

Tsouras, Peter G., ed. *Scouting for Grant and Meade: The Memoirs of Judson Knight, Chief of Scouts, Army of the Potomac*. New York: Skyhorse Publications, 2014.

U.S. War Department. *The War of the Rebellion: Official Records of the Union and Confederate Armies*, 128 vols (*OR* henceforth). Washington, DC: U.S. Government Printing Office, 1880–1901.

Van Santvoord, C. *The One Hundred and Twentieth Regiment New York State Volunteers: A Narrative of its Services in the War for the Union*. Rondout, NY: Press of the Kingston Freeman, 1894.

Wilson, James Harrison. *The Life of John Rawlins: Lawyer, Assistant Adjutant-General, Chief of Staff, Major General of Volunteers, and Secretary of War*. New York: The Neale Publishing Co., 1916.

Articles

"Addressing the Boys in Blue." *The New York Times*, August 7, 1880.

"A Lonely Life: Miss Elizabeth L. Van Lew, the Noted Federal Spy." *Virginia Pilot* (Norfolk, VA), October 12, 1900.

"A Pair of Pistols." *The Wichita Daily Eagle* (Wichita, KS), August 27, 1892.

"A Paper by Gen. George H. Sharpe—the Characteristics of the Old Citizens—Their Habits of Life and Methods of Trade—a Sincerely Religious Community." *The New York Times*, December 31, 1875.

"A Startling Scene in the New York Legislature." *The National Republican*, June 10, 1881.

"A Statue of Patriotism." *The New York Times*, October 18, 1896.

"A Story of Gettysburg." *The Kane Daily Republican* (Kane, PA), January 7, 1899.

"A Submarine Cable to Confederate Headquarters." *The Times-Picayune*, May 14, 1863.

"An Enthusiastic Meeting at West Brighton—Speeches of Gen. Davis and Gen. Sharpe." *The New York Times*, September 6, 1872.

"Army of the Potomac." *Dunkirk Evening Observer* (Dunkirk, NY), May 7, 1885.

"Between Mr. Conkling and Gen. Sharpe." *Chicago Daily Tribune*, June 9, 1882.

"Canine Reasoning." *The Alexander County Journal* (Taylorsville, NC), October 27, 1887.

"Capitol Notes." *Kansas City Daily Gazette* (Kansas City, KS), July 10, 1889.

Carney, Anson. "Carney Protests: Thinks Comrade Landegon Not Warranted in His Reflections." *The National Tribune*, July 5, 1894

———. "One of Carney's Stories: The Close Call a Scout Experienced in the hands of Bloodless Secessionists." *The National Republican*, January 4, 1994.

———. "In Tight Places: Adventures of One of Our Scouts on the Kilpatrick Raid," Fighting Them Over series. *The National Republican*, March 20, 1894.

"Conkling's Cause Lost," *The New York Times*, May 31, 1881.

"Conkling's Ranks Broken." *The New York Times*, July 17, 1881.

"Conkling's Servile Band." *The New York Times*, July 14, 1881.

"Domestic News: The Great Senatorial Fight in New York—A Remarkable Editorial." *The Record Union* (Sacramento, CA), May 22, 1882.

Edwards, E. J. "Gen. Mead's [sic] Real Character." *Dakota County Herald* (Dakota City, NE), April 5, 1910.

Edwards, E. J. "Grant Whittled During Battle." *Cook County Herald* (Arlington Heights, IL), October 28, 1910.

Edwards, E. J. "Unselfishness of Meade." *Daily Press* (Sheboygan, WI), June 21, 1912.

"Gen. G. H. Sharpe Dead." *New York Tribune*, January 15, 1900.

"Gen. G. H. Sharpe Dead." *The New York Times*, January 15, 1900.

"Gen. Grant as a Tobacco User." *Lane County Journal* (Dighton, KS), February 24, 1911.

"Gen. Grant Disappointed." *The New York Times*, April 18, 1885.

"Gen. Grant vs. Greeley." *The New York Times*, October 1, 1872.

"Gen. Sharpe's Lecture." *The Kingston Daily Freeman*, December 17, 1873.

"Gen. Sharpe's Narrow Escape." *The New York Times*, August 10, 1884.

"Gen. Sharpe's War Horse Dead." *The New York Times*, October 28, 1882.

"Gen. Sharpe the Speaker." *The New York Times*, January 4, 1981.

"Getting Stronger: General Grant Resting Better." *The Inter-Ocean* (Chicago), April 18, 1885.

"Grand Army: The Twenty-fifth Anniversary of the Organization." *The Brooklyn Daily Eagle*, April 7, 1891.

Holland. "Sharpe and the War Commission." *The Inter-Ocean*, January 1, 1899.

"Home for Ex-Confederate Soldiers." *Harrisburg Daily Independent*, April 9, 1884.

"Jerome Williams Talks of General G. H. Sharpe." *The Kingston Daily Freeman*, July 1, 1937.

Knight, Judson D. "A Scout's Adventures," Fighting them Over series. *The National Tribune*, April 9, 1891.

———. "A Shooting Experience." *The National Tribune*, April 10, 1890.

———. "How Scouts Worked: Serg't Knight tells How They Went About Gathering Information." *The National Tribune*, March 2, 9, 23, 30, April 6, 20, 27, May 4, 18, 25 & June 8, 1893.

———. "Scout's Adventures." *The National Tribune*, February 26, 1891.

———. "Scouting Adventures," *The National Tribune*, July 21, 1892.

———. "With the Scouts: Serg't Knight's Adventures in the Swamps of the Pamunkey," Fighting Them Over series. *The National Republican,* January 19, 26 and July 12, 1893.

Landegon, J. W. "He Was There: And Proceeds to Tell How Richmond Was not Entered," Fighting Them Over series. *The National Republican*, May 31, 1894.

_____. "Scouting Experiences: Sheridan's Chief of Scouts is Wounded, but Escapes Capture" Fighting Them Over series. *The National Republican*, July 17, 1893.

"Legislative Work Ended." *New York Times*, May 28, 1880.

"Lived a Hundred and Ten Years." *Harrisburg Daily Independent*, July 17, 1897.

"Married Amid Flowers." *The New York Times*, April 28, 1887.

McEneany, Patrick. "Some Scouting Experiences: With Guerillas, Gunboats, and 100-Days Men at the James," Fighting them Over series. *The National Tribune*, August 17, 1899.

"Memorial Exercise at Steinway Hall." *The New York Times*, May 3, 1974.

Miller, Sophie. "Do You Remember." *The Kingston Daily Freeman*, August 26, 1954.

"Mr. Sharpe, Mr. Conkling and the President." *New York Tribune*, June 10, 1882.

"Naming the Candidates." *The New York Times*, June 1, 1881.

"Organization of the Late Army of Northern Virginia." *The Wilmington Herald*, April 24, 1865.

"Our Special Army Correspondent." *The New York Times*, July 2, 1863.

"Outlining the Campaign." *The New York Times*, September 28, 1881.

Plank, Will. "Mark 100th Anniversary." *The Kingston Daily Freeman*, April 9, 1965.

"Reunions of the Blue and Gray." *The Altoona Constitution* (Altoona, PA), May 27, 1894.

"Sharpe A Great Man." *The Inter-Ocean* (Chicago), January 21, 1900.

Sharpe, George H. "Assassination of President Lincoln: Message from the President of the United States Transmitting a report of George H. Sharpe relative to the assassination of President Lincoln." House of Representatives, 40th Congress, 2d Session, Ex. Doc. No. 86.

Sharpe, George H. "At Appomattox." *The Philadelphia Weekly Times*, June 30, 1877.

———. "Casualties of the 120th Regt." *Kingston Journal Extra*, May 18, 1864.

———. "Grant and Lee at Appomattox." The Shippensburg News (Shippensburg, PA), March 11, 1876.

———. "Last Hours of the Confederacy." *The New York Times*, January 21, 1876.

———. "Our Victory in the War." *The New York Times*, June 8, 1877.

———. "Speech of Gen. Sharpe." *The New York Times*, September 18, 1868.

———. "Speech of Gen. Sharpe." *The New York Times*, October 26, 1871.

———. "Speech of Gen. Sharpe." *New York Tribune*, November 4, 1870.

———. "The Last Day of the Lost Cause." *The National Tribune*, October 1, 1879.

———. "The Old Houses of Kingston." *The Journal* (Kingston, NY), December 29, 1875.

"Sherman Socially." *The Galveston Daily News*, February 13, 1891.

"Some Hit and Miss Chat." *The New York Times*, April 21, 1885.

"Tales Worth Telling." *The Times* (Philadelphia), June 3, 1902.

"The Battlefield Reunion." *The New York Times*, May 13, 1887.

"The Bummers' Meeting." *The Brooklyn Daily Eagle*, June 12, 1884.

"The Colored Washerwoman's Signal Below Fredericksburg." *Richmond Dispatch*, July 28, 1881.

"The Conkling Controversy: Gen. Sharpe's Reply." *The Bangor Daily Whip and Courier* (Bangor, ME), June 15, 1882.

"The Last Days of the Confederacy." *The New York Times*, December 5, 1873.

"The New United States Marshal." *New York Herald*, April 8, 1870.

"The Sharpe-Conkling Controversy." *The Record Union* (Sacramento, CA), May 26, 1882.

"The tributes which have been paid to the ability and fairness with which Gen. Sharpe discharged his duties..." *The New York Times*, May 29, 1880.

"The Ulster County Feud." *The New York Times*, September 4, 1891.

"Union Scouts and Rebel Guerillas." *New York Herald*, October 26, 1869.

"U. S. Grant's Memory." *The Brooklyn Daily Eagle*, April 28, 1893.

Winchell, C. A. "Old Timer's Civil War Notes." *The Kingston Daily Freeman*, July 1, November 1 & December 29, 1961.

Secondary Sources

Civil War Military Intelligence-Related Sources

Articles

"Black Dispatches: Black American Contributions to Union Intelligence During the Civil War." Central Intelligence Agency. https://www.cia.gov/library/center-for-the-study-of-intelligence/csi-publications/books-and-monographs/black-dispatches/

Budiansky, Stephan. "America's Unknown Intelligence Czar." *American Heritage Magazine*.

Butler, Shannon. "Far From Dull: It's a sharpe Sword! Gen. George H. Sharpe and the Artifacts he Left Behind." http://www.academia.edu/7509449/Far_from_Dull._Its_a_sharpe_Sword_Gen._George_H._Sharpe_and_the_Artifacts_he_Left_Behind

Fishel, Edwin C. "The Gray Fox Swallowed the Bait," National Security Agency (NSA).

———. "Military Intelligence 1861–1863 (Part I: From Manassas to Fredericksburg," Vol. 10, No. 3, pp. 81–86. Studies in Intelligence (CIA).

———. "Military Intelligence 1861–1863 (Part I: Chancellorsville & Gettysburg," Vol. 10, No. 4, pp. 69–93. Studies in Intelligence (CIA).

———. "The Mythology of Civil War Intelligence." *Civil War History* 10, no. 4 (Dec. 1964): 344–67.

———. "Myths That Never Die." *International Journal of Intelligence and Counterintelligence* 2, no. 1 (Spring 1988): 27–58.

———. "Pinkerton and McClellan: Who Deceived Whom?" *Civil War History* 34, no. 2 (1988): 115–42.

"General Sharpe and Lee's Surrender." *Olde Ulster Journal*, Vol. VIII, September 1912, No. 9.

"General Sharpe at the Unveiling." *Olde Ulster Journal*, Vol. VIII, November 1912, No. 11.

Morice, James. *Organizational learning in a military environment: George H. Sharpe and the Army of the Potomac*. Vitae Scholasticae, Caddo Gap Press, 2009.

Phillips, David L. "The Jessie Scouts." West Virginia in the Civil War. http://www.wvcivilwar.com/Jessie/shtml.

Rose, P. K. "The Civil War: Black American Contributions to Union Intelligence." Central Intelligence Agency. https://www.cia.gov/library/center-for-the-study-of-intelligence/kent-csi/vol42no5/html/v42i5a06p.htm

Taylor, Charles E. "The signal and Secret Services of the Confederate State." *North Carolina Booklet*, Vol. II, March 1903, No. 11. Capital Printing Company, 1903.

"The Colors of the One Hundred and Twentieth." *Olde Ulster Journal*, Vol. VII, May 1911.

"The Departure of the One Hundred and Twentieth." *Olde Ulster Journal*, Vol. VII, July 1911, No. 7.

"The Departure of the Twentieth Regiment." *Olde Ulster Journal*, Vol. VII, June 1911, No. 6.

"The Horse of General Sharpe and His Tombstone." *Olde Ulster Journal*, Vol. IX, February 1913, No. 2.

Tischler, Allan L. "America's Civil War: Union General Phil Sheridan's Scouts." The HistoryNet.com, July 9, 2006. http://historynet.com/acw/blshsheridanscouts/index.html.

Tyler, Rashida. "The Men Who Held the Line." The Hudson River Valley Institute. http://hudsonrivervaley.net/themes/CivilWar/120th/.

Books

Allen, Thomas. *Intelligence in the Civil War*. Washington, DC: Central Intelligence Agency, n.d.

Bigelow, John Jr. *The Campaign of Chancellorsville*. New Haven, CT: Yale University Press, 1910.

Evans, Charles M. *War of the Aeronauts: A History of Ballooning in the Civil War*. Mechanicsburg, PA: Stackpole Books, 2002.

Feis, William B. *Grant's Secret Service: The Intelligence War from Belmont to Appomattox*. Lincoln: University of Nebraska Press, 2005.

Finely, James P. *U.S. Army Military Intelligence History: A Sourcebook*. Fort Huachuca, AZ: U.S. Army Intelligence Center & Fort Huachuca, 1995.

Finnegan, John Patrick. *Military Intelligence* (Army Lineage Series). Washington, DC: Center of Military History, United States Army, 1998.

Fishel, Edwin C. *The Secret War for the Union: The Untold Story of Military Intelligence in the Civil War*. Boston: Houghton Mifflin Company, 1996.

Haydon, F. Stansbury. *Military Ballooning during the Early Civil War*. Baltimore: The John Hopkins University Press, 2000.

Hoke, Jacob. *The Great Invasion of 1863*. Gettysburg: Stan Clark Military Books, 1992.

Intelligence in the Civil War (Central Intelligence Agency). https://www.cia.gov/library/publications/ intelligence-history/civil-war/Intel_in_the_CW1.pdf

Lonn, Ella. *Desertion During the Civil War*. Lincoln: University of Nebraska Press, 1998.

Markle, Donald E. *Spies and Spymasters of the Civil War*. New York: Hippocrene Books, 1995.

Tidwell, William A. *Come Retribution: The Confederate Secret Service and the Assassination of Lincoln*. Jackson: University Press of Mississippi, 1998.

Varon, Elizabeth R. *Southern Lady: Yankee Spy*. Oxford: Oxford University Press, 2003.

General Sources

Alexander, DeAlva Stanwood. *A Political History of the State of New York, Vol. III, 1862–1882*. Charleston, SC: BiblioBazar, 2008.

Best, Gerald M. *The Ulster and Delaware Railroad Through the Catskills*. San Marino, CA: Gold West Books, 1972.

Bowden, Scott and Bill Ward. *Last Chance for Victory: Robert E. Lee and the Gettysburg Campaign*. New York: Da Capo Press, 2001

Cauble, Frank P. *The Proceedings Connected With the Surrender of the Army of Northern Virginia, April 1865*. Appomattox, VA: Appomattox Court House National Historical Park, revised edition 1975.

Chidsey, Donald Barr. *The Gentleman from New York: A Life of Roscoe Conkling*. New Haven, CT: Yale University Press, 1935.

Cleaves, Freeman. *Meade of Gettysburg*. Norman: University of Oklahoma Press, 1960.

Coddington, Edwin B. *The Gettysburg Campaign: A Study in Command*. New York: Charles Scribner's Sons, 1968.

Davis, Burke. *To Appomattox: Nine April Days, 1865*. Short Hills, NJ: Buford Books, n.d. (originally published in 1959).

The Editors of Time-Life. *Death in the Trenches: Grant at Petersburg*. Alexandria, VA: Time-Life Books, 1986.

Esposito, Vincent J., gen. ed. *The West Point Atlas of American Wars, 1689–1900*, vol. 1. New York: Frederick A. Praeger, Publishers, 1959.

Flood, Charles Bracelen. *Grant's Final Victory: Ulysses S. Grant's Heroic Last Year*. New York: Da Capo Press, 2011.

Furgurson, Ernest B. *Ashes of Glory: Richmond at War*. New York: Alfred A. Knopf, 1996.

Hasbrouck, G. B. D. "Address on Major General George H. Sharpe," *Proceedings of the Ulster County Historical Society 1936–1937*.

Howe, George Frederick. *Chester A. Arthur: A Quarter-Century in Machine Politics*. New York: Dodd, Mead & Company, 1934.

Kenealy, Thomas. *American Scoundrel: The Life of the Notorious Civil War General Dan Sickles.* New York: Doubleday, 2002.

Kohn, Edward P. *Heir to the Empire City: New York and the Making of Theodore Roosevelt.* New York: Basic Books, 2014.

Long, E. B. with Barbara Long. *The Civil War Day by Day: An Almanac 1861–1865.* New York: Doubleday, 1971.

Longacre, Edward. *The Cavalry at Gettysburg.* Lincoln: University of Nebraska Press, 1986.

Martin, Samuel J. *Kill-Cavalry: The Life of Union General Hugh Judson Kilpatrick.* Mechanicsburg, PA: Stackpole Books, 2000.

Nesbitt, Mark. *Saber and Scapegoat: J. E. B. Stuart in the Gettysburg Controversy.* Mechanicsville, PA: Stackpole Books, 1994.

Nolan, Dick. *Benjamin Franklin Butler: The Damnedest Yankee.* New York: Presidio Press, 1991.

Osborne, Seward R. *The Three-Month Service of the 20th New York State Militia, April 28–August 2, 1861.* Hightstown, NJ: Longstreet House, 1998.

Paludan, Phillip Shaw. *A People's Contest: The Union and Civil War 1861–1865.* New York: Harper & Row Publishers, 1988.

Reeves, Thomas C. *Gentleman Boss: The life of Chester Alan Arthur.* New York: Alfred A. Knopf, 1975.

Sears, Stephen W. *Chancellorsville.* Boston: Houghton Mifflin Co.,1996.

Sears, Stephen W. *Gettysburg.* Boston: Houghton Mifflin Co., 2003.

Smith, Jean Edward. *Grant.* New York: Simon & Schuster, 2001.

Swanberg, W. A. *Sickles the Incredible.* Gettysburg: PA: Stan Clark Military Books, 1956.

Trudeau, Noah Andre. *The Last Citadel: Petersburg, Virginia, June 1864–April 1865.* Baton Rouge: Louisiana State University, 1991.

Tsouras, Peter G. *Gettysburg: An Alternate History.* London: Greenhill Books, 1997.

Tucker, Glenn. *High Tide at Gettysburg.* New York: Bobbs-Merrill Co., 1958.

Journals

Cameron, Bill. "The Signal Corps at Gettysburg." *The Gettysburg Magazine,* Issue No. 3, July 1990.

———. "The Signal Corps at Gettysburg: Support of Meade's Pursuit." *The Gettysburg Magazine,* Issue No. 4, January 1991.

Gaddy, David Winfred. "The Confederate Signal Corps at Gettysburg." *The Gettysburg Magazine,* Issue No. 4, January 1991.

Ryan, Thomas J. "A Battle of Wits: Intelligence Operations During the Gettysburg Campaign. Part 1: Clandestine Preparations for Invasion vs. Quest for Information," *The Gettysburg Magazine,* Issue No. 29.

———. "A Battle of Wits: Intelligence Operations During the Gettysburg Campaign. Part 2: Strategy, Tactics, and Lee's March." *The Gettysburg Magazine,* Issue No. 30.

———. "A Battle of Wits: Intelligence Operations During the Gettysburg Campaign. Part 3. Searching for Lee." *The Gettysburg Magazine,* Issue No. 31.

———. "A Battle of Wits: Intelligence Operations During the Gettysburg Campaign. Part 4. The Intelligence Factor at Gettysburg." *The Gettysburg Magazine,* Issue No. 32.

Index